Modern World Affairs

Made Simple

The Made Simple series
has been created
especially for self-education
but can equally well
be used as
an aid to group study.
However complex the
subject, the reader is
taken step by step,
clearly and methodically,
through the course. Each
volume has been prepared
by experts, taking
account of modern
educational requirements,
to ensure the most
effective way of
acquiring knowledge.

Accounting
Acting and Stagecraft
Additional Mathematics
Administration In Business
Advertising
Anthropology
Applied Economics
Applied Mathematics
Applied Mechanics
Art Appreciation
Art of Speaking
Art of Writing
Biology
Book-keeping
Britain and the European
  Community
British Constitution
Business and Administrative
  Organisation
Business Calculations
Business Economics
Business Law
Business Statistics and Accounting
Calculus
Chemistry
Childcare
Child Development
Commerce
Company Law
Company Practice
Computer Programming
Computers and Microprocessors
Cookery
Cost and Management Accounting
Data Processing
Economic History
Economic and Social Geography
Economics
Effective Communication
Electricity
Electronic Computers
Electronics
English
English Literature
Financial Management
French
Geology
German

Housing, Tenancy and Planning
  Law
Human Anatomy
Human Biology
Italian
Journalism
Latin
Law
Management
Marketing
Mathematics
Metalwork
Modern Biology
Modern Electronics
Modern European History
Modern Mathematics
Modern World Affairs
Money and Banking
Music
New Mathematics
Office Administration
Office Practice
Organic Chemistry
Personnel Management
Philosophy
Photography
Physical Geography
Physics
Practical Typewriting
Psychiatry
Psychology
Public Relations
Rapid Reading
Religious Studies
Russian
Salesmanship
Secretarial Practice
Social Services
Sociology
Spanish
Statistics
Technology
Teeline Shorthand
Twentieth-Century British
  History
Typing
Woodwork

Modern World Affairs

Made Simple

Peter King, BA, MLitt

Made Simple Books
HEINEMANN : London

Printed and bound in Great Britain
by Richard Clay (The Chaucer Press) Ltd, Bungay, Suffolk,
for the publishers William Heinemann Ltd,
10 Upper Grosvenor Street, London W1X 9PA

British Library Cataloguing in Publication Data

King, P.
    Modern world affairs made simple.—
    Made simple books ISSN 0464–2902
    1. History, Modern—SS—1945–
    I. Title
    909.82'5   D840

ISBN 0 434 98582 1 Pbk

Editorial: Robert Postema, Martin Corteel
Production: Martin Corteel, Mary Gibson
Cover Illustration: David Hazeldine Associates
Text Diagrams: Reproduction Drawings Ltd

Foreword

Modern World Affairs Made Simple is designed to explain the origins and development of the political world as it is to be found in the last quarter of the twentieth century. The modern world in many respects stems from the events and upheaval caused by the Second World War which is, therefore, the starting point of the book, but where earlier history is perhaps unfamiliar, particularly to Western readers, or where concepts like apartheid or communism stem from events earlier in the century full attention is given to their origins.

The book is arranged as follows. Chapter 1 provides an introduction to the study of Modern World Affairs. Chapter 2 gives an outline of the campaigns of the Second World War going on to explain how every part of the world was influenced by what amounted to a world revolution between 1939 and 1945. Chapters 3 and 13 provide a survey of international relations: the first chapter dealing with the post-war and Cold War period, and the second with the super power, and detente era of more recent times. The three major world powers—Russia, America and China each have a chapter devoted to their internal history and leading statesmen (chapters 4, 5, 6). Other areas of the world are then dealt with: Europe in chapter 7, the Middle East in chapter 10 and Latin America in chapter 12 while the new nations of Asia and Africa are to be found in chapters 8, 9 and 11. The last chapter surveys the major issues in world politics of a political, geo-political and economic nature.

Several aids are provided for students, but I should like to stress that a good atlas is essential to study a subject which visits every corner of the globe and deals with many countries which are not well known. Each chapter is divided into sections, and cross references (i.e. 12G4) refer the reader to other aspects of a particular topic. The contents and index should be used to locate topics. A list of frequently used abbreviations is given at the start, and others will be found in the index where alternative names, i.e. Iran/Persia, Siam/Thailand, Salisbury/Harare are used. Diagrams draw attention to some of the causes and effects of major world events besides tabulating some useful information. Revision questions and guides to further reading follow each chapter.

I should like to thank Mrs Bridget Sayers who valiantly typed the manuscript in six months, Mr Robert Postema and Mr Martin Corteel of William Heinemann for their ever thoughtful advice and Robert J. Ebdon who drew the diagrams with such care. I should like to dedicate this book to my colleagues and friends at Hurstpierpoint College, Sussex, and particularly to those involved in studying or teaching history there.

Peter King

Contents

List of Figures

Abbreviations

These abbreviations occur frequently in the text. Those which occur only a few times will be found in the index.

ABM	Anti Ballistic Missile System
ACC	Allied Control Commission (in Germany)
ANC	African National Council (in Rhodesia) also African National Congress (in South Africa)
ANZUS	Australia, New Zealand and the United States of America Pact
ASEAN	Association of South East Asian Nations
CAP	Common Agricultural Policy (of the EEC)
CCP	Chinese Communist Party
CGT	Confederation Generale du Travail (French Communist trade union organisation)
CIA	Central Intelligence Agency
CORE	Commission for Racial Equality
ECSC	European Coal and Steel Community
EEC	European Economic Community
EFTA	European Free Trade Association
EPU	European Payments Union
ERP	European Recovery Programme (of the EEC)
FBI	Federal Bureau of Investigation
FNLC	French National Liberation Committee
GATT	General Agreement on Tariffs and Trade
ICBM	Inter Continental Ballistic Missile
IMF	International Monetary Fund
IRA	Irish Republican Army
IRBM	Intermediate Range Ballistic Missile
KMT	Kuomintang
MBFR	Mutual Balanced Force Reduction Talks
MEDO	Middle East Defence Organisation (abortive)
MIRV	Multi Independent Re-entry Vehicle
MLF	Multi Lateral (Nuclear) Force
MRBM	Medium Range Ballistic Missile
NAACP	National Association for the Advancement of Coloured People
NATO	North Atlantic Treaty Organisation

NKVD (later MVD/KGB)	Ministry of the Interior in Russia which included CHEKA (OGPU)—the secret police
NVA	North Vietnamese Army
OAS	Organisation of American States (also in French context right wing political group in Algeria)
OAU	Organisation of African Unity
OCAS	Organisation of Central American States
OECD	Organisation for Economic Co-operation and Development
OEEC	Organisation for European Economic Co-operation
OPEC	Organisation of Petroleum Exporting Countries
PAC	Pan African Congress
PLO	Palestine Liberation Organisation
PFLP	Popular Front for the Liberation of Palestine
RDF	Rapid Deployment Force
SALT	Strategic Arms Limitation Talks
SAS	Special Air Service (British anti-terrorist group)
SEATO	South Eastern Asia Treaty Organisation
SHAPE	Supreme Headquarters Allied Powers Europe
SLBM	Sea Launched Ballistic Missile
SVA	South Vietnamese Army
SWAPO	South West African Peoples' Organisation
UNO	United Nations Organisation
UNRRA	United Nations Relief and Rehabilitation Administration
WEU	Western European Union
WHO	World Health Organisation

1
Introduction to World Affairs

The world is divided into nearly 200 different political units and to write an account of each of their separate histories would be both tedious and of little historical value. World affairs is essentially concerned with a study of the modern world in the light of the main factors affecting and main trends emerging from the events now being enacted in the world. Some of these events have their origins deep in the past while others stem from recent emergencies and personalities. There is therefore no arbitrary date which can be fixed for the start of modern times. The Second World War was so catastrophic an event, involving virtually every country on the globe, that it can serve as a convenient point to start the study of modern power relationships, economic infrastructure and social concepts, but it itself was the product of causes stretching back years into the nineteenth century. World history must also be somewhat arbitrary in its ending because as this book is written events change with startling rapidity and analysis can become quickly dated.

However, in spite of a certain lack of chronological precision world history is a meaningful concept and its content can be fairly clearly defined. The world at present has three major powers—America, Russia and China—in terms of their resources and military might. Both they and the other countries of the world live in a post-colonial era following a period of world history almost solely dominated by the nations of Western Europe; their political ideas, economic concepts and territorial conquests. It is thus a world in which historical studies are undergoing major changes. Patterns of development in regions like Latin America or Africa are seen in a different light and with closer reference to the indigenous sources of their historical evolution. World history must seek to take a world view. Easier communications and major inter-mixtures of population have broken down the mono-cultural societies into which most of the world was still divided in the middle of the century. Every problem has become, as Thomson has suggested, a world problem. Issues such as the national ownership of territory, or the fate of political institutions are still important, but to them historical studies, with the aid of ancillary sciences, has added new concerns—ecological and geographical issues concerning resources and sociological concepts about the distribution of income, class and race throughout the world are now a part of the historian's business. Professor Barraclough has rightly observed that 'one of the distinctive facts about contemporary history is that it is world history', which he has defined as 'the global system of international relations in which we live today'.

Before beginning with a study of the scope and impact of the Second World War and moving on to consider the three great global powers in turn—as is done in the early chapters—perhaps it would be as well to outline some of the outstanding issues to which students should relate the events of each chapter and around which they should make, some although not all, their judgements about where they stand as citizens of the world and voters in a particular country. Since the previous epoch was essentially dominated by European countries it is almost inevitable that the new world epoch has first to consider the altered position of the European powers and the consequences of this changed position. The First World War, followed by the fascist era, the Great Slump and then the Second World War constituted a period called by some, Europe's Civil War. After 90 million people had perished in two world wars the economies and political power of the nations created at the end of the Middle Ages were permanently changed and severely weakened.

Germany lost her overseas empire in 1918 and Hitler's rule left her defeated and exhausted in 1945. Italy was impoverished by Mussolini and her empire lost in 1945. But in the struggle to defeat fascism France had been divided internally and her empire also split apart, while Britain had used up many of her commercial and economic assets and faced the necessity of obtaining an immediate loan from America. Under these circumstances neither Holland nor Belgium was likely to retain the will to preserve their empires, which they lost in 1950 and 1960 respectively. Finally, by 1976 Portugal and Spain had lost their empires. Although the European powers still retain a few minor possessions and a residue of imperial problems they have ceased in military and political terms to be world powers. Yet if one consequence of this was the rise of new nations to world status it is important to see that the recovery of Western Europe at least has been secured since 1945. NATO and the Common Market have secured a period of 30 years' peace and economic progress in spite of the nuclear threat and the oil crisis which precipitated a Western economic depression. Further, as Thomson points out, however much the rest of the world has rejected Western political control, the world still remains dominated by Western concepts. Democracy, the rule of law, marxism, capitalism, organised Christianity, technology, science and education, the welfare state, and the United Nations, to name but some key influences on the world, are Western creations. In the wake of imperial decline pessimism was fashionable in the 1960s, but there is little need to despair of Europe's future or influence as yet.

The new power balance resulting from Europe's decline led to the use of the term super power. The destructive power of nuclear weapons, the fundamental nature of the economic and moral struggle between capitalism and communism since 1945 and the sheer size of America, Russia and China somehow dwarfed the previous term—great powers. America had long been a world economic force, but only in 1941 did she emerge from isolation to make treaties, dominate diplomacy, command massive armed forces, establish bases world-wide and, with the initial monopoly of the atom bomb and the all powerful dollar, become the leader of the Western world. Similarly Communist Russia had been primarily concerned with internal development and strategic safety until the war opened up the world to her influence as an ally and through her military strength. By 1945 Russia had made vast territorial gains and secured a monopoly of power in the East of Europe. Communist parties were flourishing in many countries in Europe and Asia and the Cold War was already starting to freeze the minds of statesmen on both sides of what was to shortly become the Iron Curtain. It was one world, but a divided one, and this issue has remained politically the most dangerous and far reaching of our time. China became communist in 1949 and within 20 years had become a third power with a billion people, a bounding economy and a nuclear military machine. If Russia menaced Europe first, China clearly threatened America with the fear of some new Pearl Harbor.

Relations between the super powers dominate world politics and although other issues such as the fate of the Third World are important in their own right, they too have become entangled in this conflict. These relations have passed through several stages—wartime allies, Cold War, actual wars and threats of wars in Berlin, Cuba, Korea, Vietnam, Afghanistan and elsewhere, containment and peaceful coexistence, detente and the recent renewal of the arms race and tension. In this struggle each side has drawn to it mighty alliances—NATO, CENTO, SEATO, the Warsaw Pact—involving all parts of the world; and the relations between the three powers have changed. In particular China, though ideologically committed to Communism, is a military threat to Russia. Yet the realities of power—the intentions of the statesmen in Moscow as well as in the West—tend sometimes to be forgotten and strategic issues to be obscured by the human consequences of the nuclear arms race that this new situation has created. There are five nuclear powers four of which are modernising and expanding their nuclear forces at the moment. Seventeen other countries have nuclear potential and there are constant scares that countries like Iraq, South Africa or Argentina possess these fearsome weapons. The issue of nuclear deterrence, or disarmament remains fundamental to the whole course of world history.

Since mutual destruction is so certain the great powers have not gone to war directly for 38 years, but they have fought wars by proxy and come close to outright war in 1962 and 1973. It is one of the tragic paradoxes of modern history that a period in which attention has been focused on the evils of war as never before has been one of almost unceasing world conflict. Since 1945 there have been over 140 wars, or civil wars in the world, and if one adds to this total the growth of international terrorism and its victims, the international espionage systems and their victims and the wide-spread existence of brutal dictatorships with active firing squads and prison camps, the new world summoned into existence by the breakdown of European supremacy has not been a 'tropical paradise'. The delicate nature of super power relations has forced them often to assist, or stand aside, from conflicts in smaller countries. The United Nations has only rarely proved effective as a substitute for such forces as the British Navy in keeping world peace and the existence of world terror organisations and arms traffic made starting a war all too easy. When discussing issues like world poverty it is important to recall that these political matters too need attention if the world is to prosper for peace is as ever the first requirement before prosperity; and little enough of the world's population knows it. Near at home, Britain has seen only one year, 1968, when her troops were not in action in the world, and since 1969 has in Northern Ireland fought the longest war against internal terrorism, so far without success.

A second fundamental political shift brought about by the decline of Europe's world role has been, of course, the establishment, or in some cases, the re-establishment, of a large number of countries loosely known as the Underdeveloped, Developing, or Third World. According to Thomson this was 'the most far reaching historical outcome of the Second World War' which has changed the face of the globe more than any other events since the Voyages of Discovery in the sixteenth century, and the consequences have still to be worked out. Imperialism was, in Barraclough's words, a paradox releasing pressures 'which made its own tenets unworkable'. It spread concepts like nationalism, capitalism and literacy which could only lead to demands for independence. In one sense the great colonial revolt was negative: against white rule and philosophies. On the other hand the absorption of European ideals and the survival or revival of national characteristics had its more positive side. After freedom there came stages of rejection and imitation. Many of the wars mentioned in the paragraph above were either colonial revolts, or subsequent strife between ex-colonies, or tribes within them. This phase has passed in some countries and many like Malaysia, Sri Lanka and Kenya are thriving. Others, indeed a majority, have succumbed to dictatorship and guided economies, but it is early days yet: Europe too went through similar phases and there are many international pressures from organisations like the Commonwealth, or the United Nations working for a more democratic Third World.

Although the European powers have given up their power and bases the Third World has not escaped the cut and thrust of the Cold War. At first under the leadership of India and other countries the concept of non-aligned countries was popular. Given the serious economic and social problems of the new lands it was hoped they might stand aside from strife over capitalism or communism and resist arms expenditure they could ill afford. As late as 1970 the Lusaka Conference was attended by 54 countries claiming to be non-aligned. Unhappily this stance has proved hard to maintain. In Asia the presence of Russia and China as adversaries has polarised the Indian Continent. India is allied to Russia and Pakistan has a treaty with China. The two countries have been to war. In South East Asia North Vietnam imposed Communist regimes on South Vietnam, Laos and Cambodia. In Africa, Angola and Ethiopia have been seized by Cuban (i.e. Russian) controlled governments In Latin America Castro's aggressions have led to similar regimes in places like Guyana and Nicaragua. To match Western bases a chain of Soviet bases has appeared in the last ten years. Comecon has several Third World members. In the Middle East America supplies Israel with arms and Russia supplies Syria and Iraq. In this struggle for world hegemony between West and East the Third World has often been a helpless, and sometimes a willing, pawn. It is easy to forget in our concern for the great human problems facing the Third World that their most important problem is to create free governments, to sustain them against outside pressures and to arm themselves for defence without being forced into great power conflicts of little basic concern to them.

During the heyday of European empires there was racial discrimination in every part of the globe and yet paradoxically it was scarcely referred to and very rarely enforced by discriminatory laws, like those in South Africa or the Southern States of America. It was only when the non-white races secured independence, and yet at the same time through aid, trade and inherited factors like language were dependent on the West, that racialism became a world political issue. Neo-colonialism, involving the retention of power by Western commercial or defence agreements, has been vigorously resisted and the Third World has turned, as a matter of priority, to political issues in which race is involved: apartheid, the Rhodesian Rebellion and the struggle for Civil Rights in America.

In the ex-colonial powers too there are now racial minorities creating difficulties for them in Europe: Britain's New Commonwealth immigrants, the French colons and the Moluccans in Holland, for example. Segal has gone so far as to say that the racial question is 'the major pre-occupation of mankind'. This is not, furthermore, only a black versus white issue. Clashes between Israel and the Arabs, Pakistanis and Indians, Malays and Chinese, Guyanese blacks and Indians show that racial division is widespread in the world.

Equally widespread in the Third World is poverty. The industrial nations of Western Europe, Northern America, Eastern Asia and the Antipodes are being slowly joined by others. South Korea, Taiwan and Singapore, Egypt, Mexico, Brazil and Saudi Arabia, for example cannot, in terms of per capita income, amount of industrial investment, educational facilities and other statistics be regarded as poverty stricken in the sense that some others are. Communism has brought some wealth to the peasants of China, and other places. Oil has enhanced the wealth of many Middle Eastern Countries. Overall the per capita incomes, social facilities and available aid for the Third World has increased immensely. As early as 1964 the first UN Conference on Trade and Development was attended by 120 nations and was followed by others in 1968 and 1972. The Brandt Report of 1980 has highlighted the needs once more. But at the same time, in Barraclough's words, 'the gap between the rich nations and the poor nations was becoming a central issue of international politics'. Third World dictators with lavish military expenditure and incompetent economic growth plans are partly to blame for their own misfortune; the West might claim with justice that 100 years of colonial rule gave much of the world nearly every aspect of 'civilisation' it now possesses. But the presence of two rival economic systems in the world, and the legacy of colonial oppression makes this issue acute. The shrinking world brought about by television and satellite makes the plight of others in remote places an everyday concern.

In contradiction to the massive problems of underdevelopment the world is also faced by major crises stemming from overdevelopment. According to Barraclough 'the great question mark which overhangs the future' is the pollution of the biosphere and the squandering of finite resources. Looking at the world in 1973 James Joll commented: 'If the forebodings of the most pessimistic demographers, geographers and ecologists are correct, the historian will have to face not just the end of European history but the end of world history as we have known it.' In the developed parts of the world too there are disappointed expectations. The Communist system has nowhere delivered a high standard of living. Khrushchev's boastful prediction that

Russia would equal America in ten years has proved hollow. The siege economies of Eastern Europe, South East Asia and Cuba are no advertisement for marxism. The Western world with millions of unemployed is not at the moment a successful example of capitalist prosperity. The quality of life, the degree of civilisation and law and order in the Western world are under threat; and nowhere more than in the great cities and conurbations where unhealthily and noisily most of the Western world chooses to live. Affluence and the welfare state, the endless emphasis on growth and rapid technological change has upset traditional moral and religious patterns, brought authority at all levels into question and encouraged a ceaseless search for material gain and notional equality. In 1975 the Rambouillet Conference was the first of an annual series by developed nations to discuss the issues of oil prices, industrial stagnation, trade barriers and currency difficulties that have retarded growth in recent years. Since the late 1970s the post-Keynesians have altered the whole shape of Western thinking on the role of government in the economy and it is too early to say whether this new initiative will work. Keynes and Beveridge provided an answer to Marx and Lenin, but it was essentially a compromise: the failure of capitalism may yet be followed by success for marxism, which itself has little to recommend it. Both capitalism and marxism have placed emphasis on raising living standards, exploiting natural resources, state planning and growth targets. There are shortages of raw materials and energy supplies on both sides of the Iron Curtain making the wheat and oil lands of the world the focus of possible future conflict. A world of rising expectations and population facing a contracting residuum of energy and food resources is a world in which aggressive war is all the more likely. Some hope, as yet slight, rests with the international organisations and agencies, the breakdown of trade, culture and race barriers and the mutual help of developed and developing nations. The Ancient World of Rome faced with similar difficulties lacked either the will or skill to meet them; time alone will tell if our generations act any differently.

Further Reading

Barraclough, G., *An Introduction to Contemporary History*, Penguin, Harmondsworth, 1967.

Barraclough, G., ed., *The Times Atlas of World History*, Times Books Ltd, London 1978.

Brandt, W., *et al.*, *North–South: A Programme for Survival*, Pan Books, London, 1980.

Joll, J., *Europe Since 1870*, Weidenfeld and Nicolson, London, 1973.

Laqueur, W., *Europe Since Hitler*, New edition, Penguin, Harmondsworth, 1982.

Roberts, C. M., *The Nuclear Years 1945–70: The Arms Race and Arms Control*, Praeger, New York, 1970.

2
The Revolution of War 1939–45

A The Course and Extent of the Second World War

A1 Introduction

The Second World War lasted six years from September 1st, 1939 to September 2nd, 1945 and during that time the struggle between the Axis and the Allies brought in every part of the world directly or indirectly. It is, therefore, an appropriate point to start any study of modern world affairs. The war was between three fascist-militarist powers (Germany, Italy and Japan), and the Big Three (America, Britain and Russia). But of course each side sought allies, bases and supplies thus bringing in more countries. Among those supporting the fascists were Hungary, Rumania and Bulgaria. The Big Three were backed by the Free French and China and eventually by most other countries in the world. Those parts of the European powers' empires that were not controlled by the enemy were, of course, also involved on the Allies' side. Russia occupied a position on both sides supporting Hitler until June 1941 and thereafter opposing him. This chapter does not attempt to give an account of the campaigns of the war, but to trace the way in which the whole world was drawn in by the campaigns creating in the process a revolution in the world power structure. It provides the basis for considering the state of the world at the start of modern times.

A2 European War 1939–41

Between 1938 and 1939 Hitler without war occupied Austria, Czechoslovakia and Memel. Britain and France offered guarantees to Poland, Rumania and Greece and war began with the German invasion of Poland. But the conquest of Western Poland by Germany was accompanied by the seizure of Eastern Poland by Russia, as the result of an alliance between Hitler and Stalin made in 1939. Stalin was able under this agreement to recover Russian territorial losses suffered in 1918 and to start the preparation of a security zone in Eastern Europe, reversing the position between the wars when a bloc of states protected Europe from Communism. Finland was attacked and deprived of Karelia (1940). Three small Baltic countries, Estonia, Latvia and Lithuania, were annexed and Hitler persuaded Rumania to cede Bessarabia to the

Russians. These gains were a prelude to further Russian gains once their advance against Germany began after 1944 (see section A4).

In Western Europe Hitler was able to conquer Denmark, Norway, Belgium and Holland and by June 1940 France also had fallen. The smaller countries were subjected to varying degrees of occupation with the help of pro-fascist governments where possible. France was at first divided into a northern military zone and a 'puppet' government at Vichy, but in November 1942 all France was directly occupied by the Germans. A resistance movement sprang up and De Gaulle was recognised by Churchill as head of the Free French (see section A6). The French Empire divided between the two sides, weakening French authority permanently. Britain occupied Syria and Madagascar to prevent their falling to Vichy, which aroused great French bitterness. In the Far East the Japanese took the opportunity to seize French Indo–China (1941).

The Germans occupied the Channel Isles, but were unable to effect a landing on mainland Britain as a result of the Battle of Britain (July–September 1940). This was of the greatest significance. A base was left for the future reconquest of Hitler's Europe. There was a refuge for governments in exile. Poland, for example, had such a government under Sikorski, and after 1943, Mikolajczyk: and there were half a dozen others. Resistance within Europe could be organised first in the West and after 1943 in Eastern Europe. Since left wing parties played key roles in resistance movements, political problems were created because Churchill backed monarchist and right wing forces. Thus, a Greek government in exile with its king was in Cairo. Peter II, the exiled king of Yugoslavia, was in London, but the royalist resistance led by Mihailovitch was unable to establish itself in the country and Churchill was compelled to transfer support to Tito's Partisans in 1944. Britain's pre-war guarantees and wartime involvement with exiled governments and resistance involved her in an ever widening responsibility for areas where she lacked effective power while arousing Soviet suspicions about her intentions.

Hitler was pressed by his naval advisers to strike at Britain indirectly by a full Mediterranean campaign, but his failure to get support from the fascist dictator of Spain, Franco, the uncertain role of Vichy and his contempt for his ally, Mussolini, convinced the Fuehrer such involvement was unwise. He turned his attention to the planned destruction of Soviet Russia only to be diverted by Mussolini's involvement in South East Europe. Hitler wanted the resources of this area and was able to attract support from the reactionary governments of the region who feared Bolshevism. Hungary had already profited from the partition of Czechoslovakia and joined the Anti-Comintern Pact (1939). Later when the government showed signs of resistance Hitler occupied the country and installed a fascist government. Rumania (1940) and Bulgaria (1941) joined the Tripartite Pact with Germany, Italy and Japan. This collaboration with fascism was to finally discredit right wing government in Eastern Europe and pave the way for Russian occupation.

Mussolini was annoyed by Hitler's gains and he desired the prestige of more territory for Italy. In 1940 he attacked Greece but was easily defeated. When Yugoslavia repudiated the Tripartite Pact and Allied troops landed in Greece Hitler was forced to rescue his partner, in April 1941 invading the Balkans. Yugoslavia was partitioned between Hitler's lackeys while Greece was defeated by German, Italian and Bulgarian troops. Although this secured the resources of a vast area it was a serious mistake. In Occupied Western Europe 60 divisions were already tied down and to these were now added 21 divisions in South Eastern Europe. Moreover, by agreeing later to help Mussolini in Africa scarce air resources were frittered away; and when Italy fell another 26 divisions were committed to preserving Italian fascism. This division of resources prevented Hitler from defeating Russia and paved the way for sweeping Russian advances into Eastern and central Europe in 1944–5.

A3 From European War to World War

Barnett in *The Collapse of British Power* has argued that the British Empire was strategically indefensible and an economic liability by 1939, but the support given to Britain during the war was very great. Ireland chose to remain neutral and in South Africa the nationalist (Afrikaans) Party under Hertzog had to be replaced by another government under Smuts, but elsewhere the dominions rallied to Britain. In 1940, for example, they provided 256 vital pilots for the Battle of Britain. India, Canada, Australia, New Zealand and South Africa lost 125,749 killed, and the British colonies, 21,085. The Eighth Army in Africa and the Fourteenth in Burma were imperial armies, and the Empire, of course, made a significant contribution in resources. Similarly the Belgian Congo, and those parts of the French Empire under the Free French were available to the Allies. This brought fighting to Africa when De Gaulle tried to seize Dakar and the Free French controlled Duala and Chad; and it later presented problems when the Allies decided to land in French North Africa which was largely loyal to Vichy and not De Gaulle.

Although Hitler toyed with grandiose schemes for a pincer movement in the Middle East his main concern was always with Europe, and it was Mussolini that presented the first threat to the British Empire. In 1940 he seized British possessions in East Africa where he had already annexed Abyssinia (Ethiopia), and then invaded Egypt. The war that followed in Africa was no small affair for it eventually accounted for one million Axis casualties and prisoners, but it was seen by the Russians and the Americans as old-fashioned Imperialism. If it diverted some of Hitler's resources it strained those of the Allies. Britain was able to reconquer the whole of the Italian Empire in East Africa (1941), but German aid, and scarce resources made victory in the Northern deserts harder to attain. Concern with this area led Churchill to launch diversions to Greece, Syria (see section A2) and Iraq during 1941, and to depose (with Russian support) the Shah of Persia (Iran) later that year. When the King of Egypt threatened to desert that year he was coerced by British tanks (see section 10C2). The Arab world was stirred by these events, and even more so by the influx of Jews into Palestine and the start of a guerilla war there directed against the British. War thus stirred national feelings among the peoples of Africa and the Middle East with momentous consequences for the imperial powers.

Before 1939 America had been isolationist as far as events in Europe were concerned, even if in Central America and the Pacific she had a more active policy. Neutrality Acts, a devastating depression and run down defences meant that America was in no position to enter a European war. But from the start America began to provide economic aid on a massive scale culminating in the Lend Lease Act (1941), which provided aid for Britain, Russia and China, and was a prelude to dollar diplomacy and American involvement in reorganising the world's economy after 1945. During 1940 Roosevelt began the creation of a vast American war machine with a two ocean navy, selective military service and the building of 50,000 planes. During the same year an agreement on defence was signed with Canada, bases obtained from Britain in her colonies and the Act of Havana sought to rally the South American states (see section 12C5). America occupied Greenland, Iceland (see section A2) and even Dutch Guiana. But American involvement was in self-defence and for economic gain, and did not mark a change in isolationist attitudes to the European war. It was two mistakes by the Axis powers that converted the war into a global conflict.

With her large population subjected to immigration restrictions by America and Australia, Japan was determined to pursue an expansionist policy. Wars with China (1894–5) and Russia (1904–5), which she won with gains of territory like Formosa (Taiwan), had been the start of a process which involved Japan in imperialist activity. In 1910 she annexed Korea, and after the First World War obtained several Pacific islands. Taking advantage of divisions between Chiang Kai Shek, Mao Tse Tung and Chinese warlords, Japan had invaded and occupied Manchuria (1931–2) and mainland China (1937) forcing Chiang's government to the inland city of Chungking. Chiang himself had forced Mao north in 1934, but the two co-operated to fight the Japanese, and the Western powers sent supplies. This northwards thrust against China had brought the Japanese into conflict with Russia, and in 1939 they were defeated by the Russians at Nomonhan. This led to an alteration in policy, strongly backed by Germany who at that time was Russia's ally. In April 1941 Japan and Russia concluded a non-aggression pact with momentous consequences.

Japan's ambitions swung southwards against the colonial powers whose possessions were cut off from European aid, and whose appeasement policies had convinced the Japanese they could obtain a swift victory. But of course this move later enabled Stalin to move 25 vital divisions from the Far East to Europe in December 1941 and halt Hitler's victorious advance, and from that move Hitler's ultimate defeat followed. At first the southwards thrust of the Japanese seemed only to involve the existing colonial powers. A blockade of the Western concession at Tientsin was followed by the closing of the Burma Road. Japanese occupation of French Indo-China became effective in July 1941. The Tripartite Pact (September 1940) which strengthened the old Anti-Comintern Pact between the three dictators seemed to menace Britain's survival by posing threats over so wide an area of the globe. Japanese success stirred the Indian Nationalist movement, and the Japanese helped to train an army (the Jiffs) to fight the British.

Roosevelt could not stand idly by while one power obtained such predominance in East Asia, and he was under strong economic, strategic and missionary pressure to take action. American aid was given to Chiang, and eventually Roosevelt began steps to curb Japanese aggression including the

ending of a 1911 trade treaty and an economic embargo in July 1941. Manila
was activated as a base and the Japanese were convinced America would
have to be excluded from East Asia if they were to succeed. When in August
1941 Churchill backed Roosevelt this became a certainty for Japanese
military planners. The result was the attack on Pearl Harbor (December
7th, 1941). The Burma Road was reopened and later an American air force
went to Chiang's aid, but at first America was unable to do anything, and
the Axis powers sensed victory. Hitler and Mussolini therefore declared war
on America thus linking the two conflicts. At the Washington Conference
between America and Britain early in 1942, a Combined Chief of Staffs
structure was established and Roosevelt accepted the defeat of Germany
as the first priority of the war. The result was American participation in
North Africa by the summer of that year when many American strategists
wanted to defeat Japan first. The war had become a single strategic conflict
of unprecedented global proportions.

A4 The Soviet War with Nazi Germany 1941–5

Hitler had made clear in *Mein Kampf* his determination to create 'lebens-
raum' in Eastern Europe by destroying the 'inferior' Slavs. His hatred of
Communism and its Jewish leaders, his desire for the vast resources of the
Soviet Union and his treatment of German Communists left no doubt that
Hitler saw Russia as a prime enemy. Hitler's Anti-Comintern Pact (1936)
with several countries was directed at the international organisation set up
in 1919 to spread Communism, and when he invaded Russia Hitler took
with him Spanish, Italian, Finnish and other national contingents. In
Western Europe Waffen SS Legions were recruited from countries like
France, Holland and Norway to fight Bolshevism. Yet Stalin cynically
made a pact (see section A2), claiming later he was only buying time. This
is difficult to reconcile with a further economic agreement made in 1940 and
the refusal of Stalin to listen to numerous warnings that Hitler would attack
him.

Hitler's attack on Russia in June 1941 made it easy to forget some events
that had occurred before in Russia in the 1930s. Stalin soon became 'Uncle
Joe' to the West. Twice—in 1941 when they reached the very gates of Moscow
and Leningrad, and in 1942 when they took Rostov and besieged Stalingrad—the Germans came close to victory in a war of titanic proportions,
but by November 1942 they had reached their limits. Beyond them Stalin
reorganised Soviet industry in the interior, and by measures of extreme
severity created a great military machine which by 1944 was pouring out
aircraft and tanks on a scale matched only by America (see section 4B1).
Although the German invasion and Stalin's own 'scorched earth' policy
cut production particularly in agriculture, Russia ended the war as a modern
industrial and military power. After relieving Leningrad and Stalingrad early
in 1943 the Russians launched their first major offensive in the summer,
and after great battles at Kursk and Kharkov entered Kiev in November.
In 1944 a second offensive was launched, and by August the Soviet Union
was cleared and the Russian army poised to enter Europe. German bestiality
had been met with partisan fury, and the civilian losses of Russia were
incalculable. A figure as high as 20 million is given for military and civilian

losses and none can deny Soviet Russia made the greatest military sacrifices of any ally in the war against fascism.

But the nature of Stalin's rule did not change. The people of Russia suffered appallingly for his previous mistakes and his scorched earth policy, and such was the discontent that when Leningrad was relieved the first to enter the city were the NKVD to liquidate dissidents. During the war regions seized by Stalin were subjected to racialist policies. Seven nationalities containing about 1.7 million people were killed or deported. Germans from the Ukraine and elsewhere naturally suffered, but it is hard to explain the slaughter of the middle class in the Baltic provinces and the deportation of over 100,000 from this region. As Stalin advanced westwards the Germans in eastern Europe were also forced to flee, and nearly two million died. Stalin was determined to establish Soviet power in Eastern Europe, and ended the war with 20 million new subjects. Of these the most unwilling were the Poles, but already Stalin had liquidated 15,000 officers of the Polish army at Katyn in April 1943. When the Poles under Bor-Komorovski rose in August 1944 Stalin allowed 300,000 of them to be destroyed by the Germans and refused to allow Allied planes to land with supplies. In spite of these grim events the West could only see Stalin as an ally, and at Yalta in 1945 agreed to return to Russia all their citizens in Western Europe. The deportation, murder and sufferings of two million people that followed have been detailed in N. Tolstoy's *Victims of Yalta* (1977).

From the first Britain and America hastened to end the isolation of Soviet Russia and extend the hand of friendship. An Anglo-Russian Agreement was signed as early as July 1941, and in May 1942 a 20 year treaty of mutual assistance. In spite of the Battle of the Atlantic which reached its peak in 1942–3, Britain sent convoys to Russia (with two small interruptions) from August 1941 to September 1943, and delivered 22,000 aircraft and 13,000 tanks. America signed agreements in October 1941 and June 1942 under which the Soviet Union received credits of a billion dollars, 6,500 planes and 1.5 million tons of food mainly from convoys through Persia (Iran). Yet from the start Stalin urged a second front in Europe. He ignored the several fronts that existed, and the half of the German forces tied down in Europe. He rejected any offers of joint military planning, and he sent no aid to any other front. Although he said he would enter the war against Japan as early as October 1943 Stalin constantly increased the demands he made as a condition for this, and in fact only entered the war in that sphere two days after the first atom bomb. In Europe and Asia Stalin used the war to extend Russia's borders and defend her interests, at the expense of the capitalist powers.

But it made useful propaganda to advocate a Second Front. It was a means of recovering Communist influence outside Europe. Although Stalin dissolved the Comintern in 1943 this was only to give Communism a more human face. The reality was that Communist involvement in resistance movements placed them in a position to enter governments in nearly every European state in 1945 including France and Italy. In Moscow those who had been members of the old Comintern waited—Bierut, Rakosi, Dimitrov, Togliatti and Ulbricht—for the time when they might supplant socialist moderates. At a deeper level Stalin used the new spirit of comradeship to establish a spy network among his allies. Directly a Soviet mission opened in Canada it became the centre of spying on the atom plant at Chalk River. In September 1945 the defection of Gouzenko from that mission revealed the situation, and was followed in early 1946 by the arrest of Nunn May the first of a string of traitors which was to include Burgess, Maclean, Philby and Blunt in Britain, Gold, Greenglass and the Rosenbergs in America, and the most notorious of all, Klaus Fuchs, who also in September 1945 motored from Los Alamos to Santa Fe with the secrets of the atom bomb thus making sure Russia would manufacture the weapon. The Cold War was in being before the Second World War ended (see section 3A–F).

It was clear that when the Red Army entered Eastern Europe the political future of that area would be in question. In 1943 Stalin bluntly stated the Balkans would be liberated by his armies, and complained about the Polish government in exile. Instead, he set up a rival Polish government at Lublin. Churchill became increasingly worried. He saw Stalin and Roosevelt reject any attempt to extend the Italian campaign into Central Europe, and agree instead to divert troops to Southern France delaying Allied advance still further. He was forced to accept demarcation lines between the Allied forces in Central Europe that gave Berlin, Prague and Vienna to the Russians. Churchill tried to bargain, and at Moscow in October 1944 got Stalin to accept some measure of Allied participation in events in Eastern Europe. His hope was that free elections would prevent Communist regimes taking over, and in this he had Roosevelt's support. Roosevelt produced the Declaration on Liberated Europe in which the three powers agreed to support free elections. But Churchill had to intervene militarily in Greece (December 1944), and at Yalta, Stalin demanded a fusion of the two Polish governments under Russian control instead of free elections. Since Warsaw had fallen to Russia in January 1945 there was nothing the Western powers could do.

The rest of Eastern Europe fell to Stalin's advancing forces. In August 1944 Rumania surrendered. King Michael kept his throne by accepting territorial losses to Russia and a Communist government to which, after Allied protests, representatives of the National Peasant Party were added. Bulgaria surrendered the next month, and a pro-Communist government began purges. In Yugoslavia Tito entered Belgrade in October, but he did not need Russian troops who left after a brief occupation. In Albania, Hoxha, a Communist came to power, and from there and Yugoslavia partisans helped the Greek Communists. Hungary put up stiff resistance, but Budapest fell in February 1945. For a time a Smallholders Party took office under Tildy and the Communists kept in the background. The Russian armies entered Vienna in April 1945, and a Socialist government under Renner was appointed. In May came the fall of Berlin, and soon after the fall of Prague. That month writing to Truman, the new President of America, Churchill said: 'I am profoundly concerned about the European situation . . . An iron curtain is drawn down upon their front. We do not know what is going on behind.' But Truman warned him not to 'gang up' on the Russians, and on July 1st, 1945 Allied forces withdrew to the agreed zones placing Berlin deep inside Russian controlled territory. In Europe at least the true victor of the war was Stalin.

A5 The Great Pacific War with Japan 1941–45

Because of American unpreparedness and Western commitments elsewhere, swift Japanese victory over a wide area was to be expected after Pearl Harbor (section 2A3). The Japanese succeeded in seizing the whole of South East Asia, the East Indies and a large number of Pacific islands, and inflicting humiliations on the colonial powers including the easy capture of Singapore, the loss of Malaya and Burma by the British, naval defeat for the British and Dutch in the Java Sea and the expulsion of the Americans from the Philippines. The Japanese bombed Colombo in Ceylon and Darwin in Australia, and their submarines penetrated Sydney Harbour. This led to considerable panic. Curtin of Australia recalled troops from North Africa, and the dependence of his country on America rather than Britain became apparent with long lasting effects on her defence policy. Quarrels broke out within the American high command and between the Allies over apportioning resources. Roosevelt desperately urged Churchill to launch a major offensive in Burma to help Chiang Kai Shek when he met Churchill in January 1943, because Chiang's armies held down 50 Japanese divisions which might move elsewhere.

Early in 1942 Chiang Kai Shek obtained aid including £50 million from Britain and 500 million dollars from America, and he received more Lend Lease than any other ally. He was given Stilwell as adviser, and American troops in Northern Burma helped to reopen the Burma Road in 1945. Before that aid was flown in and was followed in 1942 by the Fourteenth Air Force which raided Japan from its bases near Chungking. 60,000 Chinese were sent to India for training in an attempt to modernise their army, but little progress was made in fighting the Japanese. Indeed in April 1944 the Japanese launched a successful offensive which nearly doubled their territorial holdings in the country. In January 1943 Chiang was given the European concessions extracted from China ever since 1842, and Roosevelt urged Churchill to give up Hong Kong. Chiang was summoned to summit meetings, and promised the return of territory including Manchuria and Formosa.

The Japanese Co-Prosperity Sphere covered a sixth of the world, and was nearly 3,000 miles in circumference. Centralised for the benefit of Japan through the Ministry for Greater Asia it helped her to survive while by its extent making her ultimate victory impossible. There was little attempt to govern this vast empire systematically. Only in South East Asia were there territorial changes when King Mahidol of Siam (Thailand) secured parts of Indo-China, Burma and Malaya. The Japanese encouraged nationalist movements, and this forced the colonial powers to make counter-concessions. Even left wing guerilla leaders became useful in the fight against fascism. Thus, in Burma after the Japanese proclaimed its independence in 1943, Aung San was accepted by the British, his guerillas armed in 1945, and a promise of dominion status was given. In Indo-China the Vietminh was formed in 1941, and by 1943 was under the control of Ho Chi Minh whose guerillas were then backed by the West. On the last day of war Ho Chi Minh proclaimed independence for the new country of Vietnam. The Japanese proclaimed the independence of the Dutch East Indies in 1943, and Soekarno the guerilla leader followed this with his own declaration on being liberated. In 1945 the colonial powers' position had been permanently undermined in the area of Japanese pre-eminence.

By June 1942 the Americans and Australians were holding the Japanese advance, and by July 1943 a Pacific offensive had been launched. By mid 1944 the South Pacific was cleared, and Japan was being directly bombed from island air fields, but to save face the Japanese defended every island with appalling losses, and the rate of progress was slow. War in Europe (see section 2A6) was taking the full resources of the Allies, and Chiang was proving less effective as the years passed. At Cairo in 1943 the Allies had agreed to force unconditional surrender on Japan and to deprive her of all gains made since 1895, and these stringent terms made her surrender less likely unless she was crushed. Roosevelt was determined to secure Russian help in order to save American lives. Stalin had promised (see section 2A4) to intervene, but made no moves. In October 1944 he agreed again to intervene, but only in return for territorial compensation. Roosevelt accepted these terms at Yalta behind Chiang's back, and as a result in August 1945 a treaty between Chiang and Stalin ceded Outer Mongolia to Russia together with Port Arthur.

Roosevelt's conciliation of Stalin proved superfluous. The intensity of attack on Japan led the Chiefs of Staff to say in April 1945 that Russian intervention was now unnecessary. They did not even want British assistance as they prepared plans for direct landings in Japan in November 1945 using men redeployed from Europe. Although war had ceased in Europe there was still no sign of Russian help. Truman decided to use the new atom bombs because attempts at mediation seemed to have failed and casualties from direct assault would be great. There were only three bombs. One was tested on July 16th. One was dropped on Hiroshima (August 6th) and the other on Nagasaki (August 9th). The deaths caused were lower than those in Allied bombing of either Germany or Japan, but the horrific nature of the weapon proved enough to encourage the Japanese to negotiate. The existence of the bomb was enough also to ensure Russian intervention on August 8th. In ten days against Japanese troops who hardly resisted the Russians occupied Manchuria and Korea.

By agreements made in September 1945 the whole of Japan's vast possessions were placed in the hands of the three future super powers—China, Russia and America—who were in truth the new imperial powers. Britain's weakness and the close co-operation of Australia and America helped to re-orientate Pacific defences. Above all colonial power had been brought into question and left wing movements in Asia had been given fresh strength. By 1947 an Advisory Commission for the South Pacific had been set up including Britain, France, America, Holland, Australia and New Zealand to improve the lot of indigenous peoples in the area. Japan's contribution to the making of the modern world like that of Germany was unintended, but decisive.

A6 The War of the Grand Alliance 1941–5

Britain was the only power to fight Germany from start to finish in the war, and from June 1940 to June 1941 she fought alone against Germany which was receiving economic aid from Russia. Britain did not have the

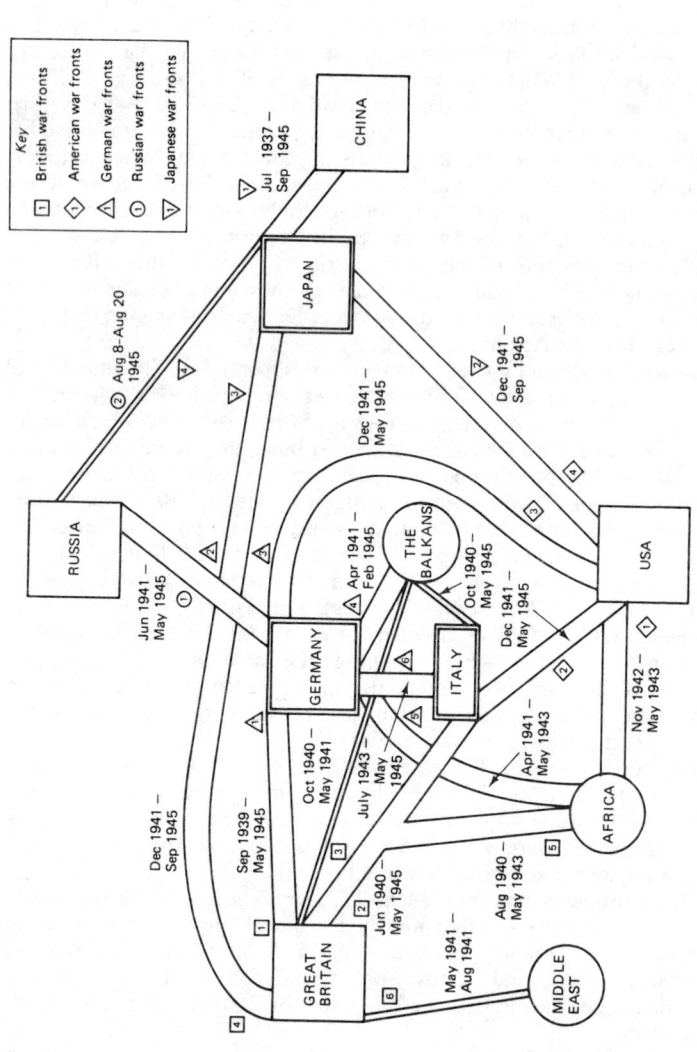

Fig. 1. The scope of the Second World War

Key
☐ British war fronts
◇ American war fronts
△ German war fronts
⊙ Russian war fronts
▽ Japanese war fronts

resources to take on the German army, and her war had to be at long range achieved by a careful use of limited men and materials. Her land war was chosen for her by Italy (see section 2A3), and the involvement of the Germans in North Africa after April 1941 gave this front strategic importance in the wider war as well as to Britain's imperial interests. Britain sustained air attack by conventional bombing, and later by rockets, contained the blockade by U boats in the Battle of the Atlantic and mounted bomber offensives on Germany. She had to fight the German, Italian and Japanese navies, protect her world interests against Axis attacks such as Reschid Ali's in Iraq and sustain the exiled governments and resistance movements.

Churchill's leadership and speeches invested this struggle with glamour and significance beyond its strategic importance. Britain's gold reserves were virtually exhausted before Lend Lease came to her aid, and without the resources of the Empire she could not have survived. Britain's industrial production peaked during 1943, and thereafter she became increasingly dependent on American supplies. In spite of mobilising a higher proportion of her population than any other power, the total available for the services was only five million. To fill the gaps in industry caused by withdrawing vital manpower, women were employed and 200,000 prisoners of war set to work. From the start Churchill urged America to become involved in Europe's war because its support was vital, and became more so after world war began, but this involvement had its awkward side. As American resources overtook British, American strategy took precedence over British. As Britain was committed on every front, whilst America had a much simpler strategy this produced conflicts between Churchill and Roosevelt of far reaching importance. They impeded clear thinking on the issues the campaigns raised in Eastern Europe and the Far East, and many future difficulties were to flow from the wartime decisions.

North Africa was Britain's major campaign, and Churchill wished to invade Europe from the South and not the West so he put every effort into winning this part of the war recklessly urging generals to offensives that failed, and then dismissing them. During 1941 the Axis drove the British back, and were then driven back in turn at the end of the year. In 1942 the Axis again attacked, Tobruk fell, and the Axis was only held at the first Battle of El Alamein in the summer. By this time America had been won over to involvement in North Africa. However, Churchill was determined to win before they arrived. The main British offensive opened with victory at the second Battle of El Alamein, and ended with Libya and Tunisia in British hands. It was the last purely British campaign of the war.

Before America entered the war co-operation with Britain had become considerable. America took over defence of the Western Atlantic in April 1941. Britain's scientific war research secrets were given to America so that she could implement their findings more effectively and in October 1941 efforts to produce an atom bomb were combined. Joint staff conversations began in secret, and as soon as America was directly involved the Washington Conference (December 1941—January 1942) created the Joint Chiefs of Staff whose 200 meetings were to determine broad strategy and allocation of resources. It was a remarkable example of world co-operation rendered possible by the speed of communication, and essential by the vastness of the war effort. It was agreed that Germany had to be defeated first, and this produced the first rift. Churchill was committed to Africa, but Roosevelt wanted to help Russia, and open a 'second front' in Western Europe. The American Chiefs put forward a whole series of proposals which Churchill would not endorse, his view being confirmed by a catastrophe at Dieppe when an amphibious landing was attempted.

Unfortunately the Russians had long been pressing for a second front (see section 2A4), and Molotov, their Foreign Minister, visited the West where he received an impression that such a front would be launched in 1942. Churchill visited Roosevelt to stress Britain could not agree, and to persuade Roosevelt to an 'Africa First' strategy. Since the main bulk of the forces were British, Roosevelt agreed, and plans for an offensive in North Africa by the Allies were put in hand. This left Churchill with the disagreeable task of visiting Moscow to tell Stalin there would be no second front. It is possible he may have hinted at one for 1943. To the Russians it seemed like deceit and putting imperialist interests first. In November 1942 Allied landings occurred in Morocco and Algeria, and by May 1943 Axis forces in Africa had been defeated. The Mediterranean was cleared for passage of ships to the Far East, and the Allies at once faced with their next problem.

Churchill and Roosevelt met at Casablanca in January 1943. The Americans wanted direct western invasion of Europe, and Churchill one from the south through Italy. Churchill's view prevailed, but with two provisos. Plans were to be laid for invasion in the west in 1944, and landing craft were to be diverted to the Pacific front. This decision meant that throughout 1943–4 there was constant tension between planning for the western attack (Overlord), war in Italy and war in the Far East as a result of which all three were delayed, and the Russians complained they were doing all the fighting. As the tide had turned in the Allies' favour on all fronts the statesmen issued their 'unconditional surrender' of the Axis powers statement at Casablanca. As far as Germany went this was sensible for at the end of the First World War the Germans had argued they were not defeated in the field, but the decision did not help elsewhere. When Mussolini was overthrown (July 1943) Churchill wanted to make a quick agreement with the new government, but Roosevelt insisted on unconditional surrender. The result was valuable time given to the Germans to enter Italy, and the loss of the Italian air force to them. Japan's determination to fight on was strengthened by the demand for unconditional surrender.

At Casablanca there was another difficulty. France had returned to the war with a force trained in Chad. But the North African French colonies were pro-Vichy, and at first the Allied troops were attacked. A ceasefire was arranged with the help of Darlan from the Vichy government, but the British did not trust Darlan. Their candidate for French leadership was De Gaulle, equally distrusted by Roosevelt. Late in 1942 Darlan was murdered and the Allies compromised by appointing General Giraud as Chief of State to the fury of De Gaulle. The National Resistance Council formed in May 1943 urged the two leaders to agree, and they formed the French National Liberation Committee together. By the end of the year Giraud stood down for De Gaulle, and in May 1944 the FNLC proclaimed itself the provisional government of France, being recognised by the Allies in October. Owing to Roosevelt's objections, De Gaulle did not participate in planning Overlord, and France was only included in the four power occupation of Germany as a result of British requests. These insults were later to have important political consequences. (See section 7B4.)

Sicily was conquered (July—August 1943), and the effect was to bring about the fall of Mussolini, but Hitler was aware of his fellow dictator's failing nerves and had decided to support him. Mussolini was rescued and eventually 26 German divisions entered Italy greatly prolonging the campaign. Churchill was still convinced the main Allied thrust should be in Italy where it was harder for the Germans to fight than in Western Europe. He saw Italy as a second front capable of extension into Central Europe to Vienna and Prague. Roosevelt would not agree to this because he was increasingly convinced of Stalin's sincerity, and suspicious of Churchill's intentions in urging such a front. When the two leaders met at Quebec (August 1943) Roosevelt insisted on diverting landing craft to the Far East and providing a greater build up for Overlord. This substantially weakened the Italian offensive, and when mainland Italy was invaded in September 1943 the campaign that followed was dogged with difficulty. But at Quebec a further American shock was in store for Churchill. In order to forestall any attempt by him to launch a Balkan campaign Roosevelt supported an additional Allied operation in Southern France and eventually 13 divisions were drawn into this campaign. This enabled the French to join in the liberation of their country, but in military terms the troops were wasted as the D–Day advance would have forced a German withdrawal from the area. The same troops either in Italy or Northern Europe would have hastened Allied advance, and left less of Europe in Stalin's hands. Meanwhile the Italian campaign ground on, and Rome was not entered until June 1944. A provisional Italian government was set up, but Italy was governed by the Allied Control Commission and Advisory Council. The campaign continued to hold down German divisions, and cost them 556,000 casualties before it ended in May 1945, but it lacked strategic sense after the start of Overlord.

In November and December 1943 there took place a series of three meetings: Cairo I (Roosevelt, Churchill and Chiang Kai Shek), Teheran (Stalin, Roosevelt and Churchill), Cairo II (Roosevelt and Churchill). At the time desire to defeat the Axis powers and act as allies was uppermost at least in the Western leaders' minds, and their decisions were taken on military rather than political grounds. Unfortunately it was not possible to divorce the two. Stalin was determined to guarantee Soviet security, and secure reward for his immense sacrifices. Churchill wished to preserve the British Empire intact, and prevent Russian hegemony in Eastern Europe. Roosevelt was determined to conciliate Stalin because he disliked Churchill's mixing of political and military decisions. He was convinced of the need to conciliate Stalin so that he would enter the war against Japan and back the scheme for a United Nations.

To please Roosevelt at Cairo Churchill agreed to an operation against the Japanese in the Bay of Bengal, but when he reached Teheran the atmosphere changed. Stalin said he had discovered a plot to kill Roosevelt, and secured his removal into the Russian Embassy which was wired by the KGB. Roosevelt met Stalin privately three times, calling him 'Uncle Joe', and joking about Churchill's cigars, while he declined to meet Churchill privately. Roosevelt was convinced all Stalin wanted was security for his own country, and that in return he would work for 'democracy and peace'. Churchill's advocacy of advance in Southern Europe was repudiated by Stalin who insisted his armies would liberate that area. Asked point blank if he supported 'Overlord' Churchill had to say he did and May 1944 was accepted with pleasure by Stalin as the invasion date. Although no definite political decisions were made the discussions which took place (see section 2B2) indicated to Stalin that Roosevelt did not share Churchill's worries about the political future of the Balkans, and of course as bait Stalin repeated his pledge to intervene against Japan. When the two Western leaders returned to Cairo Roosevelt completed Churchill's discomfiture by announcing Eisenhower must be Supreme Commander for Overlord as America was now providing the majority of the resources.

Overlord was the largest amphibious undertaking in world history involving three million men, 13,000 planes and 5,000 ships landing on a fortified coast to oppose 60 German divisions. The invasion took place in June 1944, and within a few weeks two million men had landed in Northern France. Paris was liberated in August, and De Gaulle was allowed to enter the city. It might have been thought that this great success would have pleased all parties, but there was no decline in friction between the Allies. At Quebec (September 1944) Roosevelt declared he backed a broad advance into Germany. Churchill wanted concentration on Northern Europe partly to destroy rocket sites, and more to drive to Berlin while the Russians had halted in the east and swung into the Balkans. But as the bulk of British forces lay in the north and an election was due in America Roosevelt could hardly let victory be secured by his smaller ally. He was determined, and so were the American generals, to share in the victorious march across the Rhine. Thus, the weight of the advance shifted south, and the armies fanned out creating vast transport problems, and slowing down the advance. When Hitler counter-attacked for the last time in the Ardennes (December 1944—February 1945) this was sufficient to seriously delay the Allies. Meanwhile the Russians began to advance again, and this was the position when the Big Three met at Yalta (February 1945) for their last important conference directly affecting strategy. Roosevelt was desperate for Stalin's aid in the Far East, and Stalin's agreement to this was enough to secure Roosevelt's backing for decisions that with hindsight appear grave errors. Churchill was convinced by now of a Russian threat, but in no position to do anything since the Red Army advanced swiftly eastwards while the Allies only crossed the Rhine in strength in March 1945. Eisenhower insisted first on linking up with the forces from Southern France, and then with the Allies in Italy. Since at Yalta he was given the right to communicate directly with Zhukov, the Russian commander, Eisenhower felt bound to observe only military reasons for acting, and he stressed his belief that Hitler's last stand would be in a 'Redoubt' in Southern Germany. Yet even in this southwards thrust Eisenhower would not advance into Prague, or Vienna and accepted a Russian message that it was their intention to enter those capitals.

Eisenhower thought it was militarily unsound to advance on Berlin when Soviet forces were nearer. The result was that Allied troops were halted on the Elbe, and Berlin fell to the Russians on May 2nd. Hitler had of course planned his last stand there, and not in a mythical redoubt and he had perished in his bunker by his own hand on April 30th. All that followed

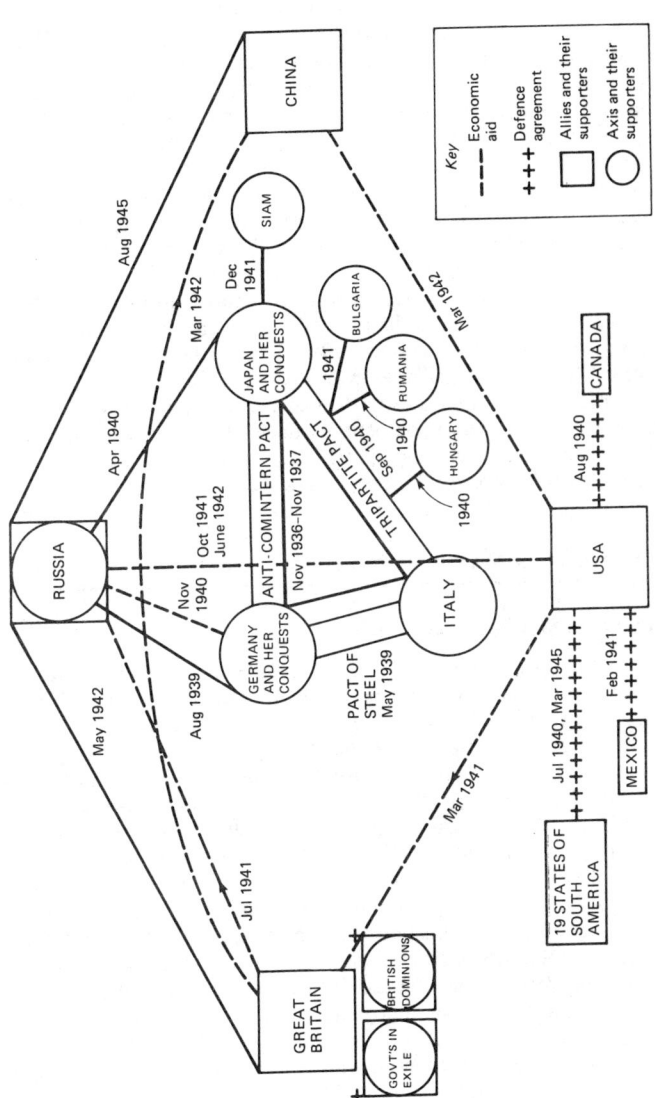

Fig. 2. The wartime alliances

was in direct conformity with the decisions already made by the Allies and Russia (see section 2B3). Formal surrender was made by Germany on May 7th, and celebrated next day. On June 5th Eisenhower, Montgomery and Zhukov formed an Allied Control Commission. On July 1st the Western powers withdrew to the agreed zonal boundaries accompanied by numerous German refugees, but the Russians showed little gratitude. They disputed access rights to Berlin, and on July 3rd the British and Americans had more or less to force themselves in followed by the French. It was only now that some politicians at least began to appreciate what Michel has called 'the most spectacular event of the war' in its full significance. This was the meeting at Torgau in the middle of Europe of units of the Soviet and American armies. Six years before such an event would have been deemed incredible. Now Europe lay prostrate before these two mighty powers, and down the middle gaped an ugly and widening wound. Apart from Stalin the leaders who had created this situation had already passed from the political scene. Hitler and Mussolini died in April 1945, and in the same month so did Roosevelt. Churchill was defeated in an election in July 1945. An American Secretary of State said that during the war every meeting of the Big Three had given the impression of complete harmony, but 'that was a war diet of soothing syrup'. Quite suddenly in 1945 the whole world was in a post-war situation full of the gravest difficulties (see section 2B5).

B The Effects of the War on the World

B1 'The Abyss of a New Dark Age'

The decline of European civilisation as it had been in the era of European world dominance was in evidence before 1939. Even in the nineteenth century the German writer, Nietzsche, had said European ideology was bankrupt, and at the turn of the century 'decadence' was a word variously used to describe the plays of Ibsen, Impressionists' paintings, Stravinsky's music or the Diaghilev ballet. All the word meant in critical terms then was that the new works offended against the traditional cultural norms; they seemed to threaten great changes. The First World War was held by many to have destroyed 'the old Europe', and reaction to it varied between a frantic desire to return to pre-1914, or an even more frantic desire to break with the past. It was the age of the Bloomsbury Group in England, Weimar culture in Germany and Futurists in Italy. In 1918 Spengler wrote *The Decline of the West*, and the years of democratic failure and economic depression that followed seemed to confirm this picture. Fascism protested against this decline by burning decadent art and banning modern philosophy, music and even science. It sought to exalt pride in country and in race. It preached the certainty of economic recovery, and the possibility of a new heaven on earth. 'I am building for all eternity', said Hitler. Mussolini saw himself as the direct descendant of the Roman emperors, who would again dominate the Mediterranean world.

Yet in 1945, in Michel's words, 'what was certain was that the decline of western and central Europe, impoverished and drained of its life blood, was becoming more marked,' and 'no one could be sure when and to what extent the tremendous material and moral havoc would be put right'. Fascism had dragged much of Europe and Asia into an era of political terror, genocide and torture, slaughtering millions and devastating the economies and lives of their own peoples. The achievements were virtually nil because every ideal was subordinated in the end to the drive to power and the war economy, and this made the disillusion of most of fascism's followers certain. Fascism, in the words of Bracher, 'reversed all former concepts of order and value', and in so doing it helped to destroy its own right wing values. The legacy of military civilisation was a hatred of war. The legacy of fascist corporatism was acceptance of socialist collectivism. By preaching white racial superiority they had raised the hopes of other races that racialism, too, would pass.

It was an era based on the concentration camps of the Third Reich and Japan's Co-Prosperity Sphere. There were 20 major, and 165 affiliated camps in Europe alone in April 1944. In them millions died and every known Christian and humane principle was violated. Torture, mutilation and immoral medical experiments were carried on across the length and breadth of Europe and Eastern Asia. The First World War had been regarded with horror because it killed 20 million, but the Second World War killed 60 million, and no one has ever calculated the injured. Half of these victims were civilians. Russia is said to have lost 20 million, China and Germany about 8 million each and Japan 3 million. In Poland 22 per cent of its people were annihilated. Nearly 6 million Jews were slaughtered once the 'Final Solution' was fully adopted by Nazi Germany in January 1942. The Western powers escaped comparatively lightly. Britain lost 326,000 military and 62,000 civilian casualties while the United States lost only 300,000 dead. Nor was frightfulness confined to one side after a time. The Japanese, said Churchill, would be 'ground to powder', and 600,000 were killed in air raids. Two million Germans perished in Allied air raids. Lord Russell's books *The Scourge of the Swastikas* and *The Knights of Bushido* describe in graphic detail why the Second World War was necessary, and why at its end the dropping of atom bombs was received with relief, for the suffering they inflicted was small indeed compared with what had happened in the previous six years. At the war's end 30 million refugees wandered the world, and 12 million people were in prisoner of war camps.

B2 Reconstruction

Yet this awful abyss of horror did not dampen human endeavour to reconstruct a better world, even if there was determination at first to seek revenge. Collaboration was more widespread than many since have admitted. By 1943 of 38 Waffen SS regiments only 15 were German, and the rest came from places as far apart as Palestine, India and Norway. At the end of the war Norway imprisoned 50,000 collaborators from a population of only three million. In a country like Vichy France which attempted to create a Catholic corporate state and work with Hitler it took time for the resistance to gather strength. But the work of guerillas, partisans and secret armies was the first symbol of hope. However there were clearly negative aspects to resistance—the black market, killing and vengeance played a large part in politics for some years after the war. The Nuremberg War Trials (1945), and the Japanese Trials (1947) accounted for many of the leaders, and were followed by some 2,000 executions. A number of countries reintroduced the death penalty to deal with fascism. In France the execution of three leading Vichy men was followed by 767 other executions, and there were plenty of unofficial reprisals. But the death and flight of hundreds of discredited right wing politicians cleansed the political stables and opened the way for new governments dedicated to social reform, political democracy and just economic recovery. In 1946 every European country involved in the war had a government containing socialists or communists.

Throughout the war the Allied leaders had been conscious of the importance of promising economic and social reform to counteract Axis propaganda, and with the civilian population under attack and more heavily mobilised than before, to ensure their support. Stalin was quite willing to talk the language of social change. Roosevelt was celebrated for his 'New Deal' reforms in America. Churchill's early political career had been as a reforming Liberal, and his wartime coalition contained sufficient members of the Labour Party to ensure that it carried out major social reforms. The first indication of this object of wartime politics was the Atlantic Charter (August 1941) in which Churchill and Roosevelt said, 'they desire to bring about the fullest collaboration between all nations in the economic field, with the object of securing for all improved labour standards, economic advancement and social security'. They also forecast 'the establishment of a wider and permanent system of general security' to ensure peace. The work of Leith-Ross (Britain), and Acheson (U.S.A) brought about the United Nations Relief and Rehabilitation Administration (1943–8) to provide aid for liberated countries. In the end this affected 17 countries playing an important role, for example, in saving Italy. Also in 1943 a United Nations Food and Agriculture Organisation was established at Warm Springs, Virginia, and next year the International Labour Organisation was reorganised. At Bretton Woods in 1944 steps were taken to create the International Monetary Fund with a credit of 8,800 million dollars and a World Bank with a capital of 10,000 million dollars.

To this determination by the Allies to seek a new world order another factor has to be added. The war helped to make the United States the richest country in the world and to impoverish all her nearest competitors. America was thus in the position Britain had been after the Napoleonic Wars—her currency dominated world markets, her goods needed free trade and therefore expediency and morality coincided. During the war Lend Lease disbursed 43 billion dollars. At the end of the war Lend Lease to Europe and China was cut off by Congress, and it was not until 1947 that the Truman Doctrine marked a full resumption of the flow of American aid. However, from the start American aid was a vital ingredient of recovery. During the war South America had been cut off from European trade and America had taken every opportunity under the guise of 'Good Neighbour' policies (see section 2B4) to increase her power. At Chapultepec in 1945 an economic charter and social reform in Hispanic America were put forward to help this region. In the French Empire similar proposals were in the Brazzaville Declaration (1944) which 'worked out a vast programme of social and economic reforms to ensure gradual advancement for the natives'. The British Colonial Development Acts (1940, 1945, 1955) led to the quadrupling of expenditure on a declining empire. Within individual countries there had to be parties willing to implement the changes. Belgium, Holland and Luxemburg had already formed the Benelux Union (1944), although it took some years to complete, and Gutt and Spaak were able to carry out reconstruction against that background. The French Resistance Charter (March 1944) enabled Monnet's plans to be launched. In Britain, Attlee (1945–50) nationalised 20 per cent of industry and created a welfare state. Meanwhile what Thomson calls 'the first phases of an economic revolution' affected the Communist states of Eastern Europe with the ending of the power of the landed aristocracy.

It would be oversimplifying matters to suggest that the reforms were all simply a socialist reaction to fascism. Much will for change came from wartime experience itself. Marwick has argued wars create a triple effect on society. They test the existing structure, they dissolve parts of it and they create new parts. During the 1920s Roosevelt's New Deal, Chile's Popular Front government, Hansson's Swedish government and others indicated the way reforming democratic governments were already tending. Welfare states already existed in countries as far apart as New Zealand and Uruguay. Now state regulation of the economy and an active social role for the state became generally acceptable. The two main intellectual protagonists of social capitalism were both British Liberals—Keynes (1883–1946) and Beveridge (1879–1963)—and their followers like Harry Hopkins or Paul Hoffman in America were not socialists but people convinced that the appalling pre-war unemployment followed by the direct suffering of the war years had induced what Thomson has called 'the collectivisation of wartime expediency and post war necessity'. Soviet actions halted the trend to the left in 1947, but the governments of the 1950s Conservative, Christian Democrat or Republican, did not reverse the changes made in these years. Welfare states and affluent societies seemed to be the answer to peoples' democracies and the demands of the new states outside Euro-America.

In January 1942 a United Nations Declaration was issued stating the Allies would fight for the principles in the Atlantic Charter. It was signed by the Big Three and 23 other countries, and subsequently joined by 19 others. In October 1943 at Moscow Stalin agreed to support a new international organisation. In some ways Roosevelt in 1944 resembled Wilson in 1919. He was convinced the new scheme to replace the League of Nations would be the answer to the world's problems, and tended to ignore old-fashioned diplomacy in areas like Eastern Europe or the Middle East for what he saw as the greater gain. In October 1944 the Dumbarton Oaks Conference began the planning of the new United Nations, and although Russia insisted on 16 (later reduced to three) delegations for the Soviet Union, and created difficulties about the right of veto and membership, Roosevelt was convinced that the creation of this body alone could save the world. From April to June 1945 fifty Nations met at San Francisco to work out the charter. The original plans for such an organisation had been drawn up by Jebb of Britain as early as 1942, but the final draft was an American document presented by Stettinius, the Secretary of State. Agreement was reached, and United Nations Organisation (UNO) came into existence in October 1945. Its first meeting was in London in 1946 when

Spaak of Belgium became President and Trygve Lye of Norway the first Secretary–General, while the headquarters building was being constructed in New York (see section 3B6)

B3 Teheran, Yalta and Potsdam

The well-known pictures of Roosevelt, Stalin and Churchill taken during the war showed three leaders united in common purpose. Yet their relationship was a flawed amalgamation of three irreconcilables brought together by their common interest in destroying fascism (see section 2A6). Stalin's Russia had been isolated behind a wall of suspicion for years, and through the Comintern had sought to spread world revolution covertly or overtly. America pursued an imperialist policy of her own, but had recently taken to a 'Good Neighbour' policy in her own hemisphere, and was eager to criticise British Imperialism. Churchill had once been a leading anti-Communist, and shared few of Roosevelt's political and economic beliefs. He stated in 1942 he had not become Prime Minister to preside over the destruction of the British Empire, and he had been an opponent of the semi-dominion status given to India in 1935. Behind the difficult journeys made by Churchill and Roosevelt to meet Stalin lay a host of difficulties far greater than the military ones that brought them together.

In the past traditional diplomats had discouraged such meetings. After the First World War Wilson, Clemenceau and Lloyd George had been the Big Three, and their settlement at Versailles was now in question as an underlying cause of the Second World War. The 'Big Three' had even more individual power than their predecessors and could well misuse it. Roosevelt was in office from 1933 to 1945, Stalin held power from 1924 to 1953, and Churchill headed a coalition which had been in office since 1931. They tended to ride roughshod over military and political advisers. Much was made of their friendly personal relations, but their sharp differences particularly those between Churchill and Stalin were also to be reckoned with as a negative factor in negotiations. All three were under immense strain, and at Yalta both Roosevelt and his closest adviser, Hopkins, were seriously ill. Since they had gone to so much trouble to meet, face-saving formulae had to be devised at each meeting which themselves led to more disputes; while those discussed like the French, Poles or Chinese might well have felt summits served only to divide allies. Yet the conferences were significant. In the long term they set a precedent. 'Summitry' became part of world diplomacy practised by some like Macmillan and Khrushchev, while opposed by others like Eisenhower and De Gaulle, and future summits suffered from the same disadvantages, and created the same difficulties.

The meetings of the Allied leaders, were concerned with three matters. They were primarily about fighting the war (see sections 2A4–6). They acted as spokesmen and organisers for rehabilitation measures, and the creation of new international organisations (see section 2B2). They had to decide the fate of the Axis powers, and the territorial reorganisation of the post-war world. It must be frankly stated they left as much unsolved as resolved at the end of their deliberations in 1945, but it is too easy to blame the conferences for some decisions taken under the stress of war, or for accepting the inevitable. The Big Three were primarily concerned with their own national interests, and their meetings were not conscious attempts to create some new kind of international order. Stalin sought security in Europe and Asia, and the establishment of Communism as a political force throughout the world. Roosevelt sought to extend American influence in Hispanic America and Eastern Asia for the same reason of security, and to forward American economic interests. Both super powers seized territory and sent their forces into countries round the world. Churchill sought the preservation of the British Empire, the maintenance of conservative regimes and the rolling back of Soviet power in Eastern Europe because he believed American troops would leave Europe and Russia would menace Britain's Middle Eastern and African power.

Even before the 'alliance' began to operate Stalin had obtained the first of his territorial gains, and when Eden arrived in Moscow in 1941 to make soundings for an alliance Molotov (Foreign Minister of Russia 1939–49, 1953–56) demanded recognition for Russia's gains (see section 2A2). During 1942 each side was locked in decisive battle, the British in North Africa, the Americans in the Pacific and the Russians in the Ukraine, and disputes centred on the second front, but even in March 1942 Roosevelt was telling Churchill: 'I think I can handle Stalin better than either your Foreign Office or my State Department', and he was anxious for a meeting. This enthusiasm prompted his backing for a second front which created immense bitterness. In 1942 Churchill had to go to Moscow to tell Stalin there would be none that year, and the decision at Quebec in 1943 that there would be none in the West that year either was, in Knapp's view, the event which 'more than any other single factor' infuriated Stalin. Russian ambassadors were actually withdrawn from London and Washington as a result. During 1943 a second stumbling block appeared. The Katyn Massacre of Polish officers was made public, and the Poles blamed the Russians. This led to a breach in relations and the creation of a rival Polish government by the Russians. The Russians also set up a 'Free Germany Committee' with the intention of creating a left wing government there as well. The fate of Eastern Europe thus became an issue between the Big Three.

Once each side had secured decisive victories, the Russians at Stalingrad, the British at El Alamein and the Americans at the Coral Sea and Midway, matters concerning the future became more complex. In October 1943 a Foreign Ministers' meeting was held at Moscow between Molotov, Eden (British Foreign Secretary 1935–38, 1940–45), and Hull (American Secretary of State 1937–44) which was a turning point in wartime diplomacy. An Advisory Council for Europe was set up to deal with Germany. The Allies accepted Russia's wish to include Austria among the defeated powers. General accord flourished on setting up the United Nations and the trial of war criminals. At the end Hull was told Russia would enter the war against Japan. Roosevelt was so pleased he suggested a personal meeting in Alaska with Stalin, and then accepted a Big Three gathering at Teheran.

Clearly by the time of the Teheran summit the various positions were being defined. Churchill was cautious, and concerned about Eastern Europe, Roosevelt was building a brave new world and knew he had to do it with a new super power not the declining British Empire. Above all, Stalin continued to press for practical gains. Stalin out-manoeuvred Roosevelt (see section 2A6) promising intervention against Japan, and praising American aid saying, 'without American supplies we should have lost the war'. Overlord was sufficient to divert Churchill away from Eastern Europe (see section 2A6) where he proposed a Danubian Confederation, and action in the Balkans to bring Turkey into the war. These proposals were militarily difficult to defend, and the principle of unconditional surrender clearly would apply to Rumania, or Hungary as much as to any country on Hitler's side. No specific decisions of a political nature were taken, but the Western powers accepted the movement of Poland's borders and Stalin must have realised he could continue to press his demands with Roosevelt's approval.

During 1944 Stalin took full advantage of his advancing armies. In Poland he stood aside during the Warsaw Rising, and in December recognised his Lublin Committee as the Polish government. Churchill went to Moscow in October and arrived at an agreement for Eastern Europe accepting virtual Russian control of Rumania and Bulgaria, common action in Hungary and Yugoslavia and Western influence only in Greece. It was noticeable that Poland was not discussed. Churchill had swung support behind Tito after meeting him, but this did not prevent Tito sending help to the Communist partisans (ELAS) in Greece. Churchill arranged a truce between them and the right wing guerillas (EDES) and when this broke down British troops entered Greece, set up a puppet government (December 1944), and fought a six week campaign to drive back left wing forces. Roosevelt privately supported him, but the new Secretary of State (Stettinius 1944–5) criticised him; words which America would later regret. Various strategic decisions (see section 2A6) had ensured Western advance was slowing down in France and the Pacific while the renewed Russian offensive that year meant that Bucharest, Sofia and Warsaw were in Russian hands by January 1945. Churchill's worries increased, but Roosevelt was determined to secure Russia's long promised participation against Japan, and the resolution of disputes about the new United Nations. By the time of Yalta in February 1945 the Big Three were no longer really united.

The Yalta Conference has become the centre of a major historical argument (see section 3A2). Knapp's view that it 'laid a firm basis for subsequent conflict' can be interpreted either by arguing that Stalin got the better of Roosevelt and Western interests were damaged, or that the West misinterpreted subsequent Russian actions, and a valuable settlement was overturned as a result of policy decisions in the West. At the time Yalta was regarded by nearly everyone as a success. Roosevelt made a speech full of wordy idealism, and he was backed by Hopkins who argued the balance of concessions went against Russia. Churchill praised the agreement in Cabinet saying he trusted Stalin and commended it to Parliament where only 17 voted against. This euphoria was due partly to the impending end of war, and to the secrecy of much that was decided. It later turned to great bitterness. Eisenhower in his *Crusade for Europe* defended cooperation with the Russians over withdrawal from Central Europe, and said the decisions over Berlin were sensible because the city was to be an 'experimental laboratory for the development of international accord'. By the time he was in office Eisenhower's party was calling for the repudiation of the Yalta agreement.

Roosevelt's motives were complicated. It is true he was ill and strained, but Stettinius said American proposals were prepared well in advance.

Name	Date	Strategic matters	Political matters
Havana	Jul 1940	Defence of Latin America.	
Placentia	Aug 1941		Issued the 'Atlantic Charter'.
Washington	Dec 1941 – Jan 1942	Established Joint Chiefs of Staff. Made defeat of Germany the first priority.	
Hyde Park, USA	Jun 1942	Africa to be invaded before Europe.	Issued Declaration of the United Nations.
Casablanca	Jan – Feb 1943	Italy to be invaded after Africa and then Western Europe. No A-Bomb secrets to be given to Russia.	Unconditional surrender of the three Axis powers to be demanded.
Hyde Park, USA	May 1943	Sicily to be invaded; then mainland Italy.	
Quebec	Aug 1943	Proposal of front in Southern France as well.	Disagreement over Italian peace terms.
Moscow	Oct – Nov 1943	Russia promised to join war against Japan.	Advisory Committee to deal with terms to be imposed on Germany. Austria to be treated as a defeated power. Chiang's China recognised as legitimate representative of that country in UNO.
Cairo/Teheran/Cairo	Nov – Dec 1943	Front in Southern France confirmed. Russia to liberate Balkans. Russia again promised to join war against Japan. Eisenhower to be Allied Supreme Commander.	Discussion about Poland. Stalin to keep 1940 gains in Eastern Europe. Trial of war criminals to be carried out.
Bretton Woods	Jul 1944		To set up IMF, World Bank and plan GATT.
Dumbarton Oaks	Aug – Sep 1944		To plan organisation of UNO
Quebec	Sep 1944	Overlord to be in May and have its main thrust in Northern Germany.	Occupation zones for GB/USA/USSR in Germany agreed. Germany to be pastoralised.
Moscow	Oct 1944		Spheres of influence in Eastern Europe roughed out.
Yalta	Feb 1945	Eisenhower to communicate directly with Zhukov. Russia yet again promised to enter war against Japan.	France included in zonal division of Germany; Austria to be divided into zones. Berlin and Vienna to be divided into zones. Russia to obtain Far Eastern territory from China and Japan. Declaration on Liberated Europe; Allied Commissions to supervise free elections in E. Europe. Polish borders to be changed in west *de facto*. Two Polish govt's to be united and free elections to be held. Russia accepted distribution of seats in UNO.
Chapultepec	Feb – Mar 1945	Joint action for Latin American defence.	Economic Charter for Latin America.
San Francisco	Apr – Jun 1945		To complete terms of the United Nations Charter.
Potsdam	Jul – Aug 1945	Russia agreed to enter the war against Japan on August 8th. Stalin told of Atomic Bomb.	Council of Foreign Ministers to draft peace treaties. Rows over Italian Advisory Commission from which Russia had been excluded; reparations and Poland discussions. West accepted Oder–Neisse line *de facto*. Stalin demanded trusteeship in Libya and territory from Turkey and Syria. Stalin promised free elections in Poland. Agreement on form of the Nuremberg Trials.

Fig. 3. The wartime conferences of the Big Four

Roosevelt had increasingly grown to dislike British Imperialism. In September 1944 Hull actually proposed Britain, France and Holland set dates for their Asian colonies to get self-government. Since America occupied Italy and Japan, established bases world-wide and seized Pacific islands this seemed hypocritical, but it was part of American mentality to dislike British colonialism. Thus, when Churchill offered Bomber Command and the main fleet to help defeat Japan the American Chiefs of Staff resisted, and Britain was allocated a token part only in the planned offensives thus making Russian help even more necessary at Yalta.

In Europe Roosevelt had a fanciful view that republicanism formed a common bond with Soviet Russia, whereas Churchill represented outmoded power politics. Hull condemned Churchill's agreement on Eastern Europe, and Stettinius attacked British interference in Italy and Greece. The British, some Americans thought, were seeking a return in Eastern Europe to the 'unsavoury status quo' of monarchies and landowning governments. The 'Declaration on Liberated Europe' urged co-operation on relief in the region and in setting up democratic governments, but any attempt to formalise this was rejected. Within a month of the conference the overthrow of the government in Rumania, and Russian contempt for Allied protests revealed Stalin had no intention of yielding democratic control in his part of Europe.

Lastly, Roosevelt's actions were dominated by Japan. Marshall had spoken of a million casualties and war into 1947, and Roosevelt chose to believe him rather than others who said Russian aid was not necessary. Even with the knowledge of the atom bomb Roosevelt chose to press for Soviet intervention in spite of Soviet refusal in December to allow the use of Russian territory for American bombers and naval forces. Stalin's list of territorial requests and the actual nature of his intervention showed he was primarily concerned about the strategic advantage to be gained. Roosevelt conceded much, and at the expense of his ally, Chiang Kai Shek, who was to be kept in the dark until later about the concessions at Yalta.

If Stalin gave in on four occupation zones for Germany he did not bend on the frontiers of Poland where he insisted on the Oder–Neisse western boundary at Yalta. This infuriated Churchill, but he had to accept it just as he had to accept the fusion of London and Lublin Poles against their wishes. A Polish Commission was to meet in Moscow to supervise the transition to democracy, but this proved ineffective. On July 5th the Soviet dominated government was recognised by the Allies. On reparations Stalin demanded 20 billion dollars, half going to Russia. Churchill knew from experience this would not work, but to please Russia the principle was conceded and a Reparations Commission established. The decision to give Eisenhower the right to communicate direct with the Soviet commander was perhaps the most surprising of all. He was not a politician, and refused to take political decisions. From this followed the southward swing, decided on March 28th without consulting the Combined Chiefs of Staff, the halting of troops before Prague, and Berlin, and the withdrawal from Central Europe giving Berlin, Vienna and Prague to the Russians. So to some Yalta was a wartime Munich, and to others the last chance of world power co-operation.

After the conference Roosevelt maintained the need for co-operation with the Russians whatever he might complain about in individual cases such as Poland. 'I would minimise the general Soviet problem as much as possible' he wrote on the day he died, by which time Churchill's letters were becoming more and more extreme. In March he spoke of 'a great failure and an utter breakdown of what was settled at Yalta', and in May he wrote to Truman: 'I am profoundly concerned about the European situation.' He felt that with the withdrawal of half the American Air Force and many troops Europe was being left defenceless. Truman had no alternative but to follow Roosevelt's line although a new Secretary of State, Byrnes, was more cautious, and in individual matters Truman was prepared to be firmer with Russia. Churchill wanted another summit before the impending British election, but Truman stalled. A mission came to London headed by Davies (American Ambassador to Russia 1937–9) who ran into hot water by saying Truman was going to meet Stalin alone in Alaska. At the same time Hopkins was in Moscow, and proposed a three power meeting at Potsdam to which Stalin agreed.

Potsdam was more in the nature of a postscript to events than a conference. It lacked Roosevelt, and after a few days, Churchill as well. Truman, Byrnes, Attlee and Bevin were faced with the skilful Stalin–Molotov combination. A Council of Ministers was set up to decide the detailed peace treaties later, and as far as reparations went Stalin was promised goods from the Western zones of Germany as well as his own. The West would not recognise the new Oder–Neisse line, but Poland was to 'administer' the area behind it. There was agreement on the trial of war criminals and on Russian entry into the war. But in spite of the atmosphere of goodwill the underlying drive for Soviet expansion continued unabated. At this time demands for Tripoli and territory from Turkey were made, and the Russians were setting up a border puppet state in Northern Iran. Yergin's work *Shattered Peace* (1978) makes it clear that soon after Potsdam a revaluation of Russian policy was started by America, but by then Soviet gains from the wartime period were sufficient to excite fear in many quarters and in that fear a Cold War was growing fast.

B4 New Worlds for Old

As the guns fell silent in September 1945 there were two predominant emotions in the world—proud thankfulness for victory over the evils of aggression, and mute despair at the state of much of the civilised world. In Europe destruction, destitution and starvation faced a large part of the continent. Displaced slave labourers, refugees, the injured, the released concentration camp victims, the stateless, the hungry and the homeless numbered millions. Germany had suffered more than any other country. Bismarck's Reich created in 1871 was at an end after nearly a century of warmongering and militarism, subject to Allied Military Occupation, divided into four zones, and with its Eastern territories seized by Poland and Russia. In towns like Hamburg and Dresden over 50 per cent of the houses were destroyed, and to feed the people only 40 per cent of what was needed was available. Yet in 15 years West Germany was a prosperous country, and in 20 years German foreign policy was to dominate the creation of a peace settlement in Central Europe and the search for detente with Russia (see section 13D3). The new state of West Germany, although smaller than the Germany of 1939, soon added some seven million to its population—

partly due to forced German emigration from East European countries, particularly Poland and Czechoslovakia, and partly to flight from East Germany at the rate of 1,000 a day for twenty years. With Allied help the task of reconstruction soon began. As German industry had suffered little direct damage from Allied bombing its recovery was swift.

The other defeated power in Europe was Italy which seemed even nearer to total collapse in 1945. The whole of her empire was taken away, but this, of course, proved a blessing since it had always been an unprofitable burden on the Italian economy. The Provisional government of De Gasperi set up under the authority of the Allies received massive aid. America gave the dollar equivalent of £478 million between 1943 and 1948, and thereafter Marshall Aid started. In the chaos the Communist Party under Togliatti became the largest outside the Soviet Union, and in 1948 polled 30 per cent of the votes, but by then Allied aid had established De Gasperi's Christian Democrats in power, and Italy experienced her only period of stable democratic government followed by her entry into the Common Market.

France proved more unstable in the post-war period than either of the defeated powers. The effect of the collapse in 1940 was long lasting. The Third Republic had gone, and in 1946 the Fourth Republic began, but without De Gaulle. The war period gave rise to a left wing revival in France through the resistance, local liberation committees and CGT union with its five million members. Although at first coalition government was tried between radical, socialist and communist parties this was to collapse during 1947. Unfortunately, unlike West Germany or Italy where there was a new strong Christian Democratic Party, France had only a discredited right wing unable to govern without thinking of the past. In retrospect the French decision to try and restore herself fully as a world power was a political and economic error which prevented her full recovery, and helped to increase instability (see section 7B1).

During the resistance years the Brazzaville Declaration (see section 2B1) and the creation of the French Union in 1946 among the colonies seemed to indicate a more liberal policy, but the temptation to recover lost prestige was too great. The humiliations of military defeat, and being rescued by the British could only be eliminated by a return to former imperial glories. During the war independence for Syria had been conceded, but in May 1945 the French tried to retake the former colony (see section 10C1). Bad relations between France and the Arab world intensified as a result of events in North Africa where a revolt in Algeria (May 1945) was put down with over 1000 deaths (see section 8D1). In South East Asia, although prepared to make changes, the French rejected the new state of Vietnam, and in November 1946 bombarded Haiphong with the loss of 6,000 lives. It was the beginning of a new long war, and a period of gravely mistaken French policy (see section 3E4).

The British position in 1945 was superficially still that of a great power. The role she had played in the war as protector of many small nations, the rallying point of a world-wide imperial effort, the only power to fight the Nazis from start to finish, and the instigator of the Grand Alliance with America had given the British an inflated view of their power which had been shaken to its very core. With less than half her pre-war trade and gold reserves, with substantially reduced overseas investments, a massive trade deficit, run down national assets and no Lend Lease the country was in deep waters. The Treaty of Washington (December 1945) which gave her £4,400 million, followed by Marshall Aid (of which she took the largest slice) and devaluation (1949) enabled a spectacular recovery to take place with exports back to the 1939 figure by 1950, and a favourable trade balance. This was achieved at the same time as the costs of nationalisation and a welfare state were added. But it was illusory. Britain's success was built on a lack of competitors and did not embrace the start from scratch virtues of German, French, and later, Japanese industry.

Yet, after 1945 Britain's world role continued to increase. The Labour government introduced conscription, decided to build the atom bomb and entered the Korean War. Britain became linked in a permanent military alliance, with her troops in Europe as a result of NATO while her own island became a base for foreign troops in 1948. Britain undertook the role of occupying power in Germany, Austria, Trieste and French and Dutch Asia for a time. She took over the running of the former Italian empire. She created the Baghdad Pact (later CENTO) in the Middle East and SEATO in South East Asia. Britain therefore saw herself as a European power, having a 'Special Relationship' with America, as an Atlantic power, and still very much a world power—a massive, triple commitment. This position could not last. India became independent taking the heart out of the empire. Britain could not carry on helping the Greeks and transferred responsibility to America, nor could she carry on the Palestine mandate responsibility for which she handed to the United Nations. But in spite of this Britain continued to pursue an active world policy which involved her in massive defence spending, and a series of colonial wars which did not end until 1967. At a time when she needed to recover economically Britain became for 20 years a vigorous world power combating Communism and seeking to contain the Colonial Revolution. As a result she lost her chance in Europe, her empire and her special relationship with America (see section 13D1).

In Britain's place there stood in 1945 not one but two world powers, and if neither was quite ready for an active world role each had the military might and economic power to sustain such a role far beyond that to which former European powers could aspire. Russia had emerged from isolation, taking 20 million new subjects and sending troops into ten countries. She had a vast military machine with 10.8 million in her forces, and nearly half her budget went on this military conglomerate. Her massive war effort and her gains had overstretched her resources. She drew back from Finland, Czechoslovakia, Persia and Mongolia during 1945–6, but there could be no doubting her continued intention to press for greater world influence. Modern communications and the elimination of other powers had left America face to face with this new force to which she was ideologically hostile. Russia was about to launch a new Five Year Plan (1946) for internal recovery (aided by massive seizure of reparations, and the forced labourers of her vast prison camps), but the secrecy of her policy and the statements of her Communist ideology gave every indication that further advances were intended by Stalin.

America had taken her place as a great power as a result of the war. Of her 12 million servicemen America lost only 300,000 and she had no civilian casualties. Her economy was little distorted by war industries which affected only 40 per cent of the workforce, and therefore the war years had seen a rapid rise in the standard of living for Americans. The National Income had doubled. She controlled two thirds of the world's shipping, and 60 per cent of the world's gold supplies. She had taken advantage of the sea war to enter new fields in trade, and had 4,000 million dollars invested overseas ousting Britain, for example, from traditional South American markets. Her wealth sustained new relief programmes and international agencies, and her policies inevitably protected her dollars. Initially America alone possessed the capacity to make atom bombs. She alone had 15,000 aircraft capable of crossing the world's oceans in commercial flight. Involvement in the war had broken down American isolationism. Her troops occupied Italy, Germany, Austria, South Korea and Japan. Under these circumstances it was inevitable she would oppose the extension of communism, and the next 20 years were to be dominated by the relations of Russia and America.

In the Far East in 1945 the third Axis power, Japan, lay prostrate. Her output was only 30 per cent of the pre-war total and 40 per cent of her urban areas lay in ruins. Like the European countries she was ruled by an Allied Commission, but in fact was occupied by the Americans. Yet defeat was a blessing. Her empire was of little use to her and had become an economic burden. The Americans were soon forced by the Communist threat in Asia to rebuild the Japanese economy and reform Japanese society, and by the 1960s Japan emerged once more as a successful captialist power. This was an ironic reversal of the situation in 1945 when America pinned her hopes on a revived China. The Americans sent Marshall to China to mediate, but he gave up, and the Civil War was renewed (see section 6B6). The Americans had signed a treaty with Chiang Kai Shek and felt they must support him. From this resulted the two Chinas of 1949, when Mao won the Chinese Civil War, and it was many years before the Americans could free themselves from Chiang, and enter into relations with Red China.

It is easy to forget Fascism like Communism aimed at world domination; indeed was a response to the 1917 Revolution in Russia. Just as the Russians established the Comintern to spread world revolution, so did the fascist powers seek to overturn the established order. Mussolini proclaimed himself Protector of the Arabs to stir them up against British power in the Middle East. The Germans sheltered the Grand Mufti of Jerusalem who opposed Britain in Palestine, and created Arab SS units. The Japanese plan for an Asian New Order (September 1940) was directed against Western imperialists, and encouraged support for national movements in Burma, the Philippines and the Dutch East Indies. Franco's Falange party in Spain wished to restore the Spanish Empire and set up an Hispanidad Council (1940) which had some influence in Latin America. In Germany the complicated structure of foreign policy planning included the Foreign Countries Organisation (1937) whose aim was to organise ethnic Germans abroad and stimulate support for fascism. There was an SS School for Diplomats, and by using German commercial and diplomatic contacts the cause of Fascism was encouraged wherever possible. There were small attempted coups in Brazil, Chile and Uruguay. Nazi agents were widespread like those of the KGB. In 1941 Leibbrandt landed in South Africa to make contact with extremists in the Nationalist Party. In June 1942 eight landed in America only to be caught and executed.

These moves had several implications. They stimulated the Allies to counter measures. The British SOE and the American OSS encouraged subversion and partisans. The colonial powers were forced to make counter concessions. The threat of totalitarianism from the right encouraged moves to social reform and paved the way for the spread of left wing politics. Divisions among the Western powers shed new light on their power among the subject peoples of their empires. In order to forestall fascist influence economic aid, bases and military agreements were secured by America, and to a lesser extent Britain, with a range of countries. Aid was withheld from regimes that supported fascism so that by 1945 Spain and Portugal were the only fascist states. In South America fascist dictators found themselves under pressure from America and their own left wing parties. Vargas's Estado Novo dictatorship was overthrown in Brazil. The American envoy tried to bring down the Peron dictatorship in Argentina. Spain was excluded from UNO and Russia tried to get Argentina excluded. Throughout the world new forces were set in motion and old nationalist feelings revived. Fascism made the right wing answers unpopular and the world was ready to try those of the left.

It would be wrong (see section 1B3) to claim that the colonial revolution was directly caused by the war, but the campaigns and the political involvement of so much of the world made change inevitable. When this change began it is hard to say. Men like Bolivar and San Martin who freed South America from colonialism in the early 1820s might be regarded by some as the first non-European nationalists. Revolutions in Japan (1867), Mexico and China (1911) had heralded change before the First World War, and that was followed by others in Egypt, Turkey and Persia (Iran). As early as 1920 Lenin summoned 34 Communist parties to a meeting at Baku, and during the 1930s Burma, Indonesia and India witnessed Communist subversion. But in spite of these anticipations, and the formation of early nationalist groups like the Congress Party in India or Boedi Octomo in Indonesia, the great empires were intact in 1945. Indeed the vast military forces of Britain and America and the defeat of Japan seemed to presage easier Western domination of the world.

The reality was different (see section 1B3). Within 20 years the biggest political change in world history since the collapse of the Roman Empire had occurred. It began in Asia where Britain gave up India in 1947 and the Dutch were forced out of Indonesia by 1950. French rearguard action was beaten by 1954. In the Middle East Anthony Eden had backed the Arabs to deflect Axis influence, and the Arab League was formed in 1945. That July Egypt requested Britain to end her occupation (see section 10D2). Already American influence was increasing in the region. Meeting Ibn Saud of Arabia in 1945 Roosevelt told him, 'the colonial era is at an end'. The plight of the European Jews had added a new perspective to the Middle East. In 1942 the Biltmore Programme for a Jewish state was announced by Ben Gurion, and soon backed by Roosevelt whereas the Arabs were demanding all of Palestine once the British withdrew.

Africa, where the most changes were to come, was still regarded as the least likely place for them, and an African expert like Perham could write in 1951 that independence might come for the British colonies by the end of the century. The first African National Congress had met in 1919, and its meeting in Manchester in 1945 was little noticed, but already the combination of West Indian nationalism, and a war economy in West Africa had stimulated nationalism in the Gold Coast and Nigeria. In French Africa negritude was being developed as a cultural base for opposition to the pervasive French culture. In France's North African territories parties like Destour and Istiq Lal were already fomenting opposition. In South Africa an opposite trend was in motion. The backing of South Africa for the war had been due to General Smuts, while the opposition Nationalist Party wanted a republic based on white supremacy. Through organisations like the Broederbund Nazi ideas had obtained considerable currency in South Africa, and in 1941 Von Rensburg's 'Stormjaers' had caused riots. With an economy stimulated by the war, and the world's second largest gold reserves South Africa was ready for a different course of action (see section 11B2).

In South America the picture was more confused. American power had been increased in the region in a variety of ways. Economic agreements like that for the exclusive use of Brazil's minerals in June 1941, and the blacklisting of 1,800 Axis firms had enabled the Americans to step into the gap left by the decline of European trade. In 1940 an agreement with Britain had left America bases in seven West Indian islands, and she had others in Nicaragua and Cuba. She still occupied Puerto Rico where an American reporter in 1941 saw: 'Misery, disease, squalor, and filth' after 43 years of American rule. The Americans continued to back a string of unsavoury dictators like Somoza of Nicaragua and Batista of Cuba, while American business organisations like the United Fruit Company held colonial power in the poverty stricken republics.

On the other hand America had embraced a 'Good Neighbour' policy, and at Chapultepec in 1945 backed economic reform. She had established good relations with Mexico which was the main socialist state in the hemisphere. Here economic aid was stimulating demands for further reforms, and she could not be seen to stand in the way of democratic change. Thus, in Chile Communists entered the government in 1946, and there was a left wing rising in Bolivia against the military dictator. South America would clearly witness a double challenge: to American imperialism, and to internal conservatism, or as Morinigo of Paraguay said in 1940: 'The inertia of the liberal state should give way to the dynamics of the protecting and directing state in the interests of social justice' (see section 12D1). In every part of the world a new dynamic of politics to replace capitalism and imperialism was being created even if it was largely in the mould of European socialism and nationalism. The world war had produced a world revolution.

Revision Questions

1. A large number of places are mentioned in this chapter. Are you clear where they are? If not, consult an historical atlas as this will help your study of the subject.

2. Explain what is meant by the terms 'Axis' and 'Allies'. How did a European war become a world war by 1941?

3. How did the military campaigns of the Second World War affect the peoples of the main countries involved?

4. What was 'The Grand Alliance'? How did it work, what were its main achievements, and why did it fail by early 1945?

5. In what ways did the Second World War stimulate new thinking on
   (a) economic and social matters
   (b) international organisation?

6. How did America and Russia emerge as super powers during the war? Explain what their respective power was based on.

7. Explain why fascism and imperialism were discredited ideas by the end of the war, and why socialism and nationalism had greatly increased support throughout the world.

Further Reading

Arnold Forster M., *The World at War*, Collins, London, 1973 (also in paperback).

Knapp, W., *A History of War and Peace*, OUP, London, 1967, chapters 1 and 2.

Michel, H., *The Second World War*, Andre Deutsch, London, 1975 (particularly part VI).

Taylor, A. J. P., *The Second World War*, Hamish Hamilton, 1975. Penguin, 1976.

Wilmot, C., *The Struggle for Europe*, Collins, 1952, parts 1 and 3 (available in paperback).

Yergin, D., *Shattered Peace*, Andre Deutsch, London, 1978. Penguin, 1980, pages 1–122.

3
The World Divided:
The Cold War 1945–62

A The Origins of the Cold War

A1 Communism: Origins and Meaning

The idea that possessions should be held in common found in the New Testament, or in the Middle Ages with the common fields, was not really the basis of communism. Communism is a doctrine specifically created to meet the needs of the worker in modern industrial society after the Industrial Revolution. It aims to overthrow capitalism where workers (wages) and owners (capital) have in theory separate and opposing interests, and replace it with a system in which the producers are also the owners of wealth in a classless society. The theory of communism was a nineteenth-century economic doctrine set forth in *Das Kapital* by Karl Marx (1818–83). The theory had certain attractions from the start. It aimed at social justice for the masses (proletariat) in a time of grinding poverty for many. It was a comprehensive theory that seemed to give a dynamic to men's lives at a time when some of the driving forces of Western civilisation seemed to be dying. It was in a sense a substitute religion, based on materialism. It offered a practical answer to life on earth in terms of enhanced wealth for its supporters, and therefore power in the state. Marx, said Engels, 'discovered the law of evolution in human history', which was that 'history is nothing but the activity of man in pursuit of his ends'. In his *Critique of Political Economy* Marx argued the economic structure of society was the base for all the 'social, political and spiritual processes of life'. The dynamic of history was thus 'the history of the class struggle', and everything must be subordinated to the one goal of completing that struggle successfully. To destroy capitalist society all methods were permissible. 'Morality', said Lenin, 'is what serves to destroy the old exploiting society.'

A2 Communism: Evolution and Divisions

As with all theories no one could agree how marxism should be put into practice, and as a result numerous divisions exist in communism over the methods of securing and keeping political power, and achieving Marx's goals. Essentially there are three main groups. The first are parliamentary socialists who believe in using the ballot box to achieve their aims. They are gradualist parties like the Labour Party (1900), and the French Socialist

Party (1905). The second are anarchists who believe in direct revolutionary activity in the state or in industry (syndicalism). This concept originated with Michael Bakunin, and was particularly strong in Italy and Spain, and for a time in Russia (Nihilists). The third group are revolutionary parties that work with the political system, only to overthrow it such as the Social Democratic Party (1898) in Russia, or the Minority Social Democrats in Germany in 1919. In only one country (Chile) has marxism secured power through the ballot box. Anarchist revolts like those in Spain (1909), or Italy (1914), and general strikes like that in Russia (1905) failed. Success has come through organised revolutionary marxist parties, and therefore a set of new ideas had to be grafted on to Marx's original concepts since he had little to say about the idea of an organised party.

A3 Modern Marxism

A modern marxist is no closer to Marx than a modern capitalist is to Adam Smith for their ideas have been substantially modified, particularly by Vladimir Ilich Lenin (1870–1924) who took control of the Social Democrats in Russia in 1903, and brought about the Bolshevik Revolution from which Communism's success in the present century has stemmed. He worked out a strategy of internal revolution, and devised the concept of the 'dictatorship of the proletariat' as an intermediary stage before full Communism. He extended Marx's theory to one of permanent world revolution thus making marxism applicable to underdeveloped societies as well as advanced industrial countries.

It is noticeable that Communism has spread most rapidly where the workers least share the benefits of capitalism particularly in countries like Russia and China. Lenin's views were put forward in *The State and Revolution* (1918), and his concept of world revolution found fulfilment in an organisation called the Comintern. Marxist–Leninism has become the theoretical basis of Marxist activity, and it was subsequently modified further by Joseph Stalin in his *Foundations of Leninism* (1924). Here the central issues of the party, and the state were grasped, and it became clear that Marxism was no longer merely a socio-economic theory; it was a new form of totalitarian one party state. Stalin also argued for 'socialism in one country' (1925) to secure its base in Russia, and this led to bitter differences with Leon Trotsky (1879–1940), Lenin's closest supporter, who wanted to pursue world revolution. Trotskyites therefore are more extreme marxists willing to resort to force to overthrow the existing state. It must be stressed, as Carew Hunt does, that Stalin did not abandon world-wide revolution as events during the Second World War showed, but only subordinated it for a time to domestic considerations. This remains the present position. World revolution only stops because of internal necessity not because marxists think the other side might be right after all, or have resorted to democratic means of forwarding their aims.

A4 The World Importance of Marxism

Marxism by drawing attention to the structure of society had profound effects. It moved away from the contemplation of the individual, central to religion and liberal democracy, and towards the masses. It therefore had increasing success in an age of mass democracy in the industrial nations and emancipation for the coloured masses of the Third World. It proved the most successful new force in twentieth-century politics not only because it controls one third of mankind, but because it has forced its opponents to alter their views as well. Capitalism was at war with marxism from the start as the bloody Paris Commune of 1871 showed, but the capitalist state was forced to concede many workers' demands, to raise their living standards, to permit trade unions and to pay for welfare states in order to draw the teeth of its main challenger. Marxism has moulded modern history because it helped to stimulate fascist opposition; one extreme created another, and the Fascist era (1922–45) was one result. Fascism's collapse marked, as we have already seen, a substantial gain for marxism in the world. In 1939 Communism controlled one country (Russia), and through Popular Fronts had brief influence on three others (Spain, France and Chile). By 1980 Communism controlled 20 countries. What has become known as the Cold War is one aspect of a much greater conflict of principle similar to that of the Christians and the Muslims in the Middle Ages. It is the most fundamental division, and therefore the most important development, in modern political history.

A5 The Growing Rift 1917–41

The seizure of power by the Bolsheviks in 1917 initiated the world divide. The new government made peace with the Germans at Brest–Litovsk in 1918, breaking an agreement not to do so, and threatening the Allied position on the Western Front. No sooner was Germany defeated than Russia tried to recapture her lost territory invading Finland and Poland. The Soviet government repudiated its foreign debts and set up the Comintern to spread world revolution. An attempt to bring Russia to the peace conference at Versailles failed, and she was effectively isolated from the rest of the world. The Allies intervened in Russia and this widened into backing for the various 'White' armies fighting the 'Reds' or Bolsheviks in a bloody civil war. The Allies accepted Brest–Litovosk, and gave Poland, Finland, Estonia, Latvia and Lithuania their independence. When Poland was threatened by Bolshevik armies the West sent military aid to help repel them at the Battle of Vistula (1920). The Poles then forced the Russians to sign the Treaty of Riga which effectively moved the agreed frontier with Russia 300 miles eastwards.

The Comintern had begun work at once. Russian agents had been sent to Berlin and Munich to encourage Revolution in Germany. Communists led by Bela Kun seized control briefly in Hungary. The Western powers experienced severe industrial unrest, and in America Woodrow Wilson, so often regarded as a liberal idealist, imprisoned and deported thousands of left-wingers during 1919. Communist parties were often banned in reactionary countries, particularly South American and East European ones, and diplomatic contacts were broken and trade stopped. It is arguable that the West had some justification for the line that they took. Subversion, and the establishment of front organisations was fully endorsed as a foreign policy technique in 1921, and it is well known that in Britain in the 1930s, for example, future agents were recruited by an active world-wide organisation. Internal opponents of Russia were struck down by the NKVD (later KGB), and even Trotsky (murdered in Mexico in 1940) was no exception. Moreover, Russia was an Asiatic power, and in 1920 at Baku a conference of over 20 Asiatic Communist parties was held. Subversion spread in Asia particularly in China where Communism played on Chinese dislike of Western power in their country (see section 6B1), and there were Communist troubles in Indonesia (1926) and India (1929). In South America early Marxists like de la Torre (Peru) and Prestes (Brazil) attempted to stir the peons to revolt (see section 12C2).

The Russians tried to break the isolation of their country, and were drawn to those opposing the world settlement created in 1919. In 1921 Lenin signed a treaty with Mustafa Kemal, the creator of modern Turkey, and this was followed by other treaties with Persia (Iran) and Afghanistan the same year. In 1922 Lenin signed a treaty with Germany, and provided secret factories for making planes and submarines, and allowed training for German troops. This treaty was renewed by Hitler immediately on coming to power in 1933, in spite of Hitler's slaughter of German Communists that year. It was a treaty the West had to consider when deciding if Russia could be brought to their side in opposing Hitler, and the 1939 Nazi–Soviet Pact indicated Stalin's main aim was to break the cordon sanitaire by destroying Poland, and recapturing the lost territory of 1918. This confusion between the aim of spreading world Communism and strategic Russian expansion from her land-locked mass gave the West every opportunity to see world revolution in Russian moves after 1939.

The 1930s saw some improvement in Russia's political standing due to two developments. One was the role of Litvinov (Foreign Minister, 1930–9) who involved Russia in talks about disarmament, and secured Russian admission to the League of Nations (1934). The other was the adoption of socialism in one country by Stalin which led to the abandonment of Mao, for example, in China, and his failure to give more than token military support to Marxists in Spain. Stalin switched to the concept of 'the popular front' which became official policy in 1935. The aim was to obtain electoral success by alliance with parliamentary socialists, and forward Communist aims. This led to the formation of such governments in Spain (1936), France (1936) and Chile (1938). This method was to be extensively used after 1945 by entering coalition parties, and it proved a most effective way of obtaining power in Eastern Europe. But in spite of these moves the left remained unsuccessful in the 1930s. In Spain Franco suppressed the Popular Front in a bloody civil war (1936–9), and attempts by Communists to foster revolution under the cloak of industrial discontent caused by the Great Depression were defeated in countries as far apart as Austria (1933) and the United States (1934, 1937). The end result of the depression was to install right wing dictatorships in many countries including Japan, Brazil and many East European states. In 1939 only one country—Mexico—had a genuine socialist government outside Europe, and only one—Sweden—inside.

A6 Papering Over the Cracks 1941–5

The need to defeat fascism appeared after 1941 to create a common purpose between Russia and the West, and on the surface the meetings of the Big

Three, admiration for the Red Army, and praise for 'Uncle Joe' seemed to indicate genuine improvement. Countries in the West hastened to recognise Russia, and for her part Russia abolished the Comintern. This had the effect of making Communism a respectable political force. It was strong in resistance movements in Asia and Europe, thus inevitably came to mould aspects of policy, and at the end participate in 'popular front' governments. Communist political representation reached its peak in countries like Britain and Denmark. They were admitted to government in France, Italy and further away in Chile, while socialist governments were returned democratically in some countries like Britain and Norway, continued in office in Sweden, and installed under Russian pressure in Finland and Austria during 1945. It was a temporary tide as Communists had been removed from Western governments by 1947, and their vote soon plunged in Finland (1948) and Austria (1949). But at the time it seemed irresistible, and coupled with events in Eastern Europe and the seizure of Asian territories like Korea seemed to presage the onset of a new world conflict. There is considerable evidence (see section 2A4) that Russia was continuing subversion and preparation for new Communist regimes throughout the war period.

The conduct of the war created bitter differences between the Allies. Russia would not participate in joint military planning, but confused Anglo-American plans by insisting on a second front. She would not pool military expertise, or espionage methods, nor would she allow the Allies to use her territory. Britain and America were refused access to Russian territory to help Poland and Russia refused America territorial facilities against Japan. Although Russia profited from Lend Lease and other aid she constantly criticised Western efforts. Her advances in Europe were made with the specific intention of creating her own *cordon sanitaire*, and the Western Allies had to swallow the Russian gains of 1939–40 obtained with Hitler's aid, the destruction of Poland as a free state for which Britain at least was specifically fighting and the establishment by force of Communist governments. The Russians obtained an occupation zone in Germany and insisted on obtaining one in Austria. As a sweetener for entering the war against Japan at the very last minute Russia obtained territories in the Far East she had not held since 1905.

Many in the West began to see a Communist conspiracy in all these gains. Some have argued they were simply for Russian security, or a just reward for her sacrifices during the war, but this seems hard to support when their full extent is realised. Stalin may have abided by his promises not to help partisans in Greece (1944), or Mao in China (1945) and to have withdrawn from some places. He did not annex every country like Finland which he could have obtained. But on the other hand he demanded a base in Tripoli, territory from Turkey, set up a puppet regime in Iran, and as late as March 1947 demanded a base in Spitzbergen from Norway. When the swing against Communism resulted in the removal of Russian supporters from government each country concerned experienced severe industrial unrest. In Chile this led to the breaking of diplomatic relations with Russia and the banning of the Communist Party (1948). In France the removal of five Communist ministers was followed by strikes in 1947 and 1948, while in Italy the failure of the Communists in the 1948 elections was followed by an attempted general strike. The fate of every non-Communist including dedicated socialists in eastern European governments was well known (see section 4A).

Russia saw matters differently. They saw Western support for reactionary regimes in Europe like Greece and Portugal, in Asia like Chiang's China, and in Hispanic America for any number of oppressive dictators. The attempt to re-create Poland seemed to be a re-run of 1919, and the Polish government in exile included right wing elements from the previous reactionary government of the country. Demands by the West to be involved in free elections in Eastern Europe after they had ignored fascist and military regimes that denied them from 1919 to 1939 seemed to be unwarranted interference. The West had tried to exclude Russia from the Italian settlement, and Churchill had systematically urged military campaigns directed against Eastern and Central Europe with limited strategic advantages in order to reduce Soviet power. The colonial powers were resuming their former empires using force in some cases to do so. They partitioned the Italian and Japanese empires in 'good' old imperialist style. America occupied Japan, and had troops in Italy. She had obtained a range of bases in Hispanic America, Europe and the Far East, and deployed 11 million troops. She was economically all powerful while Russia was weakened by her war efforts. If at first by holding off from Prague and Berlin the Americans had appeared reasonable this mood soon passed as the Allies vigorously opposed Tito in Trieste, and American troops entered South Korea. If Russia had not been co-operative over military planning neither had the West, which decided to deny knowledge of the atom bomb to Russia and gave the news in the most casual fashion at Potsdam to Stalin, who no doubt regarded this as another example of Western duplicity. The world-wide nature of the war had created a situation in which both sides regarded the other with suspicion, and left a whole range of world problems which could only make matters worse.

B The Peace Settlement Years 1945–47

B1 The Foreign Ministers Conferences

Yalta and Potsdam (see section 2B3) had revealed major differences on many aspects of the post-war settlement like the composition and role of UNO, the future of Poland and other territories, the fate of Germany and the payment of reparations, and it had been decided to call Foreign Ministers Conferences to settle matters before making the final settlement. The statesmen clearly had 1919 in mind when an attempt at one large conference within six months had produced major errors of judgement. The result was that final peace treaties were long delayed. In Europe, for example, the settlement between Russia, Poland and Germany was not finalised until 1972. In Asia peace between Japan and America (1951), Nationalist China (1954), and Russia (1956) was achieved a little more quickly. The Foreign Ministers in old-fashioned style were able to finalise treaties with the smaller powers so that in 1947 treaties affecting Italy and Eastern Europe were concluded at Paris. But the conferences that were held between Bevin (Britain), Molotov (Russia) and Byrnes (from January 1947 Marshall) for

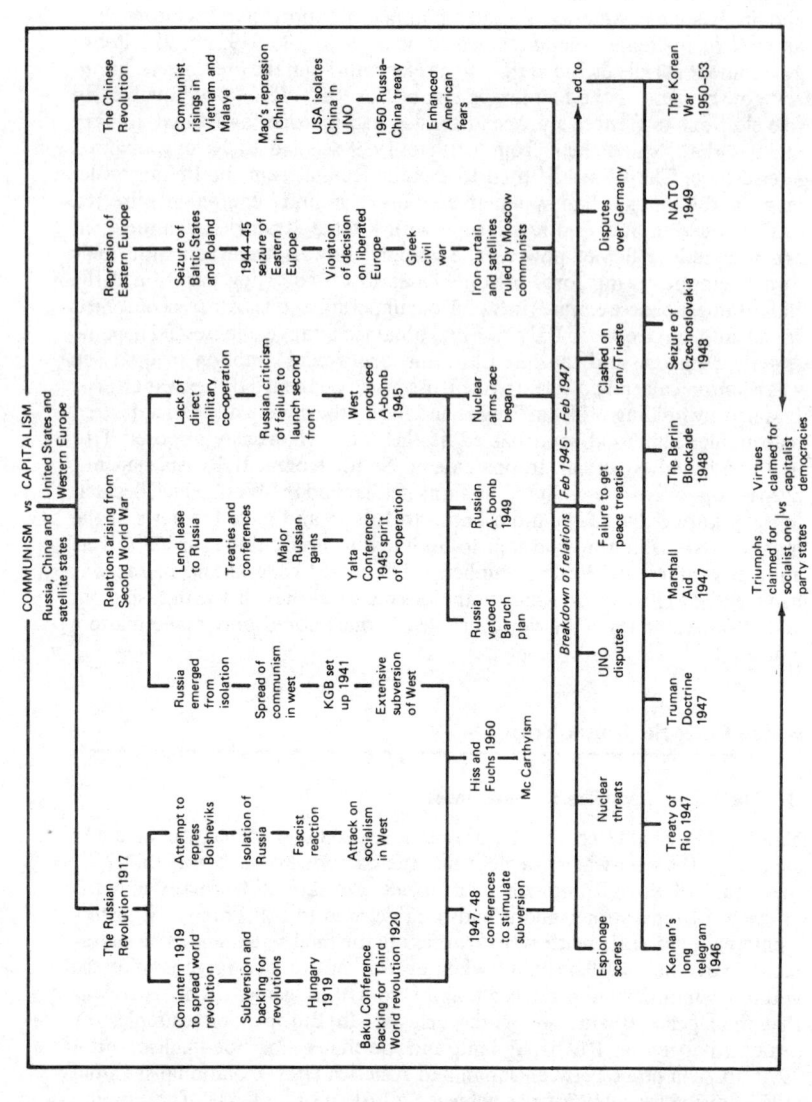

COMMUNISM vs CAPITALISM

Russia, China and satellite states — United States and Western Europe

The Russian Revolution 1917

Comintern 1919 to spread world revolution
— Attempt to repress Bolsheviks
— Isolation of Russia
— Fascist reaction
— Attack on socialism in West

Subversion and backing for revolutions
— Hungary 1919
— Baku Conference backing for Third World revolution 1920

1947–48 conferences to stimulate subversion

Hiss and Fuchs 1950
McCarthyism

Relations arising from Second World War

Russia emerged from isolation
— Spread of communism in west
— KGB set up 1941
— Extensive subversion of West

Lend lease to Russia
— Treaties and conferences
— Major Russian gains
— Yalta Conference 1945 spirit of co-operation

Lack of direct military co-operation
— Russian criticism of failure to launch second front
— West produced A-bomb 1945

Russian A-bomb 1949

Russia vetoed Baruch plan

Nuclear arms race began

Repression of Eastern Europe

Seizure of Baltic States and Poland
— 1944–45 seizure of Eastern Europe
— Violation of decision on liberated Europe
— Greek civil war

Iron curtain and satellites ruled by Moscow communists

The Chinese Revolution

Communist risings in Vietnam and Malaya
— Mao's repression in China
— USA isolates China in UNO
— 1950 Russia–China treaty
— Enhanced American fears

Led to

Breakdown of relations   Feb 1945 – Feb 1947

Espionage scares | Nuclear threats | UNO disputes | Failure to get peace treaties | Clashed on Iran/Trieste | Disputes over Germany

Kennan's long telegram 1946 | Treaty of Rio 1947 | Truman Doctrine 1947 | Marshall Aid 1947 | The Berlin Blockade 1948 | Seizure of Czechoslovakia 1948 | NATO 1949 | The Korean War 1950–53

Triumphs claimed for socialist one | vs | Virtues claimed for capitalist democracies
party states

America produced a steady break down in relations between the powers. The main conferences were London in 1945, Paris in 1946 and a further meeting in New York later that year. During 1947 first at Moscow and then at London further conferences on the German problem were held. Thereafter there were no more until 1954.

B2 The German Problem

Germany was treated far more severely at the end of the Second than the First World War. She was confined to her borders in 1936 losing all gains since that time except the Saar returned in 1957. Germany was to disarm, her munitions industry was to be destroyed and her government was put on trial at Nuremberg. She lost territory to Poland and Russia east of the Oder–Neisse Line including the heartland of Prussia from which Germany had grown, and this involved the movement of some 8 million refugees. The Four Powers occupied Germany militarily in their zones: British in the North West, French in the South West, America in the Centre and Russia in the East, and the government of Germany was entrusted to the Allied Control Council. Berlin was divided between the four powers, and placed under a 'kommandatura'. A programme of re-education and the creation of new political parties was to ensure Nazism was destroyed, and reparations were to be taken particularly by the Russians who secured industrial equipment from the eastern zone and food from the western ones. The intention when a final peace treaty was drawn up was for the powers to jointly restore democratic government to the country.

But such did not prove to be the case. The sufferings of Germany were intense, and the British found the burden of feeding their own sector too much to bear. They approached the Americans for help, and in May 1946 General Clay stopped reparation shipments to the Russians. Although as late as this decisions were still being made to destroy German industry this became impracticable, and in January 1947 the British and Americans combined their zones economically (Bizonia), and later set up an Economic Council to aid reconstruction. With Bevin's help, for example, German trade unions were reorganised on an efficient modern basis and made a substantial contribution to the future German miracle. In August German industry was required to return to production levels of 1936. Former industrialists and even ex-Nazis began to work for the Allies in their zone, and denazification and trials rapidly declined.

The Russians viewed all this as a deliberate violation of Potsdam, and dreaded the revival of Germany. In April 1946 they created a single party in their zone under Grotewohl and Ulbricht which proceeded to collectivise agriculture and industry, and in 1948 the Russians conceded economic authority to a commission. The West retaliated by establishing a Christian Democratic Party led by Konrad Adenauer, and a Social Democratic Party led by Karl Schumacher in their zones. Local elections were permitted in order to prevent Communists winning in the Allied zones of Berlin late in 1946. In September 1946, the same month as the Nuremberg Trials ended, Byrnes announced that American troops would stay in their sector. The division of Germany already looked like deadlock by the end of 1947 (see section 3C6).

B3 Central and Eastern Europe

In Austria the Russians had established a Socialist government under Karl Renner (1870–1950), but it was not until October that the Allies accepted him after the Russians had agreed to free elections. Austria, like Germany, was divided into four zones (as was Vienna) under another Allied Control Council. The elections resulted in a Socialist–Peoples Party coalition which ruled until 1966. In July 1955 Austria became a free (though neutral) country once again. In Finland the pro-Axis government had resigned in 1944, and the Russians had tried to create a Communist government, but this failed and the country emerged with a Social Democratic government in 1948. However, they lost Petsamo in the north, Karelia in the south and the naval base of Porkkala which Russia later returned. Italy was forced to give small pieces of territory to France, Albania and rather more to Yugoslavia. Greece obtained the Dodecanese Islands from her. Two serious problems remained. In the Tyrol she was reluctant to give considerable autonomy to the Germans, and they began a campaign of agitation. Trieste had been occupied by the Allies and Tito, but as relations with the Communists worsened it was decided to ask for a return of the whole city to Italy (March 1948). This led to a bitter dispute with riots in 1952, until in 1954 it was decided to accept partition of the city instead.

All the other changes in Eastern Europe were imposed by Russia, and accepted by the Allies in the 1947 treaties. Russia obtained in addition to territory from Finland and Poland, part of East Prussia from Germany, Ruthenia from Czechoslovakia (which was compensated with small gains from Hungary) and Bessarabia from Rumania. Bulgaria was allowed to retain the Dobrudja. The changes were less spectacular than in 1919, but they enabled the Russians to achieve three ends: to create a security zone in depth, to extend Communism westwards and to send the Red Army into any country in the area soon to be locked behind the Iron Curtain.

B4 The Middle East and Africa

The main problem in this area was the fate of the former Italian Empire. Abyssinia (Ethiopia) was restored to its emperor, and Eritrea was added to it in 1950. Italian Somaliland was administered by UNO, and in 1960 incorporated in the new country of Somalia with British Somaliland. Libya became a kingdom closely linked to Britain by treaty in 1951. The difficulty in the Middle East arose from Russian claims to Kars and Ardahan in Turkey, and for the revision of the 1936 convention on the Straits. In early 1946 the USS *Missouri* arrived off Istanbul as the first American gesture of support. The claims were dropped. The Russians also laid claim to Azerbaijan in Northern Iran, and in 1946 this became the first major issue to come before the new United Nations. By June 1946 Russian troops had left the country, but as in the case of Turkey American aid was soon forthcoming when in 1947 an American military mission arrived in Iran.

B5 Eastern Asia

It was here that the greatest post-war changes took place. Japan was occupied by America, and the arrangements not completed until the Treaty of San Francisco in 1951, but as in the case of Germany, an external threat led to a reversal of policy from destruction to construction in May 1949 with the end of reparations, and the return of some 10,000 dismissed officials the following year. As well as the treaty Japan agreed to a mutual security pact and rearmament on a modest scale. But the vast Japanese Empire was not returned. Manchuria, Formosa, Hainan, the Pescadores and Tientsin were restored to China. South Sakhalin and the Kuriles were left in Russian hands. North Korea (1948) and South Korea (1949) freed of occupying troops declared separate independence. All the Pacific islands given to Japan in 1919 were taken by the United States who also occupied until 1972 some of the home islands like Okinawa. In agreement with China Russia left Mongolia and Manchuria, but kept a lease on Dairen and Port Arthur surrendered in 1954. The mutual territorial grab by Russia and America indicated the likelihood of serious conflict between them in the area.

B6 The Founding of the United Nations

The United Nations was similar to the old League of Nations in many ways. Its principal organs were a general assembly, a security council, a Secretariat, a host of social and economic organisations grouped now under the Economic and Social Council, a Trusteeship Council to replace the Mandates Commission, a reorganised Court of Justice at The Hague and International Labour Organisation at Geneva together with a number of new organisations like WHO, FAO and UNESCO. Roosevelt had been convinced this new organisation held the key to world peace, but from the start this seemed very doubtful. There were bitter disputes about membership starting with a Russian demand for 15 seats as she would be heavily outvoted in the General Assembly by the West, and although this was later reduced Russia would not accept new members so that between 1945 and 1950 of 31 applications only 9 were accepted, and this log jam on membership was not broken until 1955. The Security Council consisted of the Big Five (Britain, USA, USSR, China, and France) with six non-permanent members of which only one was from Eastern Europe, and this seat was often denied to them by the West. The result was that Russia often used the veto, and it looked as if the United Nations might go the way of its predecessor. The Cold War was fought by the West as well since America would not recognise Communist China in order to keep Russia isolated on the Security Council. The Security Council was later broadened by the addition of four more members. Even if a majority of seven (later nine) was required for small matters the veto remained in large ones used by Britain at the time of Suez, or Russia at the time of the Afghanistan invasion. Action in Korea in 1950 was only made possible because Russia was boycotting meetings in protest over the decision not to recognise China.

During its early years the United Nations had a mixed effect on world relations. It was able to bring pressure to bear on Russia to leave Iran, but not the British in Greece in 1946. When handed the Palestine problem

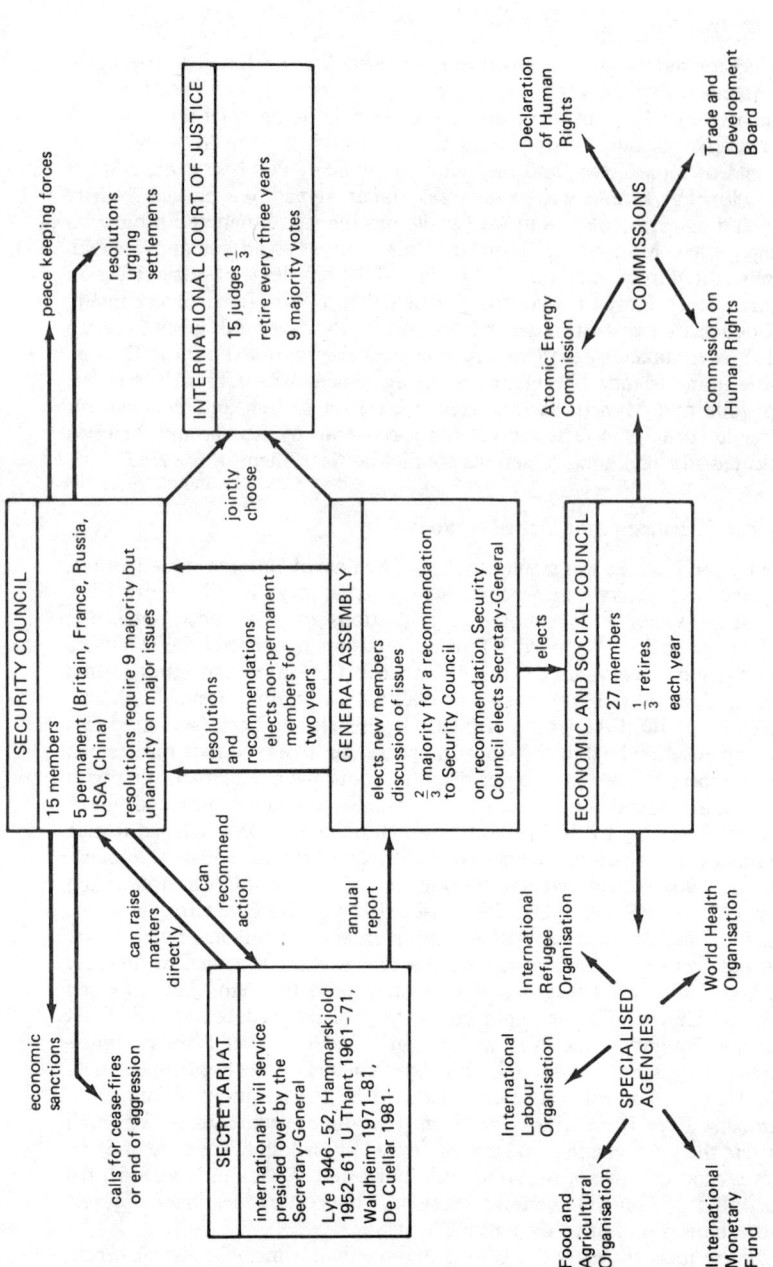

Fig. 5. The structure and functions of the United Nations

it recommended partition, but had no means of enforcing its decision. When war broke out between Arabs and Jews it attempted to enforce a cease fire, but its mediator, Count Bernadotte, was killed and the war went on. When handed Korea in 1947 it recommended independence and unification, but the UN Mission was denied admission to the Soviet zone in early 1948 thus making the division of the country certain. In Southern Africa demands for South West Africa (Namibia) to be made a trust territory were rejected in 1947, and although the International Court ruled against annexation by South Africa in 1950, full integration of the territory was carried out. Thus, although Article 43 of the charter provided for military action none was taken until Korea, and that, it could be argued, was simply a cloak for American intervention. The involvement of the United Nations in Cold War politics, and its domination by the Western powers meant that in this early period it contributed little to preserving the peace, or containing the rift between the West and Russia. It was indeed the provision in the charter (Articles 52 to 54) for creating regional pacts that was to prove more to the liking of the powers. It was not until the admission of Third World countries, and the creation of a series of UN Forces starting in 1956 that UNO came to play a more effective international role.

C The Iron Curtain Era in Europe 1945–49

C1 The Satellite States

The Declaration on Liberated Europe (see section 2B5) had supported the restoration of democracy by agreement between the great powers, but between 1945 and 1949 changes occurred in East Europe that created eight Communist states of which only one (Yugoslavia) was free from direct occupation by the Red Army, and rule by an appointee from Moscow. This development is detailed elsewhere (see section 4E), and it was the most vivid illustration of the great divide. As early as March 1946 Churchill had publicly used his phrase about an Iron Curtain arousing considerable criticism of himself, but there could be no doubt about its reality. The West protested at rigged elections and trials, the execution of party leaders, the imprisonment of religious leaders and in some cases, such as incidents off Albania in 1946, direct attacks on the West, but to no avail. Yugoslavia, Albania, Bulgaria, Poland, Rumania, Czechoslovakia, Hungary and East Germany became one party dictatorships. In 1947 the Cominform was re-established to co-ordinate their policies, and the Treaty of Paris brought the Allied missions in Eastern Europe to an end. Since none of these states threatened Russia's security her policy could only be regarded as expansionist, and the time approached when the West felt the need to curb this expansion.

C2 America Turns

Roosevelt had said American troops would leave Europe after the war, and massive demobilisation took place so that by early 1947 their numbers were down to 1½ million which was less than half the Russian total. From February 1945 to February 1947 America tried co-operation with Russia, but over the peace treaties, the occupation of Germany, proposals for nuclear arms control, the United Nations and the treatment of Eastern Europe found themselves driven to the view that Roosevelt had been wrong, and that a new policy was needed to meet America's position as a world power. Gradually America began to abandon her isolationist role. In December 1945 the Senate accepted membership of UNO. In September 1946 Byrnes announced American troops would stay in Europe. In February 1947 the agreement with Canada on defence was continued with the start of the first early warning system. In March came the announcement of the Truman Doctrine (see section 3C4), and in June the Vandenberg Amendment in Congress allowed the President to enter into defensive alliances. In September the Rio de Janeiro Treaty created a defence zone covering the whole American hemisphere.

This shift in policy was due partly to a change at the top. Truman was a firm and powerful personality, deeply imbued with traditional American values and little versed in world politics who saw Communism as a serious threat. Advisers like Hopkins, Hiss and Davies were replaced by new names. The most important of these was George Kennan who in *The Long Telegram* (1946) outlined the policy which came to be known as containment—curbing Communism by alliances, bases, economic aid and subversion. In a way it was matching the Communists at their own game. It carried with it the need for rapid rearmament, nuclear superiority, extensive state security, a re-organised CIA to operate abroad and war if necessary. Some Americans indeed favoured the roll back doctrine by which the Iron Curtain would gradually be rolled back. Events in Europe, and even more those in China (see section 6B6) acted as backdrop to a fundamental change in policy called by Yergin—the creation of the national security state. But it should be re-membered the change was brought about reluctantly, and in response to an existing challenge made more acute by the serious weakness of Britain who by 1947 had to inform America she could not continue her European role.

To put these new ideas into practice new men were required. General Marshall (1880–1959) was Secretary of State (1947–9), and later of Defence (1950–1). In the State Department was Dean Acheson (1893–1971) who was mainly responsible for drafting the Marshall Plan (see section 3C5), and was Secretary of State (1949–52). James Forrestal (1892–1949) became the First Secretary of Defence, and Allen Dulles (1893–1969) reorganised the CIA, and was its director from 1953 to 1961. His brother, John Foster Dulles (1888–1959) was Secretary of State from 1953 until his death. General MacArthur (1880–1964) as Governor of Japan backed the policy in the Far East, and even General Eisenhower (1890–1969) Governor of the American zone in Germany, began to change his tune in 1947, and was to follow Truman as the second Cold War president (1952–60). The presence of generals in positions of high authority in a democracy, though not un-precedented in America, was in itself an interesting illustration of the prevail-ing mood.

C3 The Policy of Containment

American policy developed along six major lines. At home there was intense concern with security and espionage which was to lead to McCarthyism (see section 5B3). The MacMahon Act (1946) forbade the sharing of nuclear secrets even with allies, and the National Security Act (1950) seriously curbed the liberty of the subject. At home the FBI, and abroad the CIA were concerned to combat the KGB. Defence had to be reorganised. The decision was made to produce a hydrogen bomb. Draft laws were followed by universal conscription. A National Security Council was created in 1947, and amalgamation of the services carried out under the umbrella of the Pentagon which was opened in August 1949. Military agreements were sought with other countries for bases, and by 1959 America had 1,400 bases including 275 major ones in 31 countries. The Mutual Defence Assistance Act and the Mutual Security Act provided for the sale of arms to allies. A series of regional and bilateral security pacts were made so that by 1959 America had treaties with 40 countries including Spain, Turkey, Pakistan, Iran, Saudi Arabia, Taiwan, the Philippines, South Korea, Thailand and Japan. She was the key member of NATO and SEATO, and backed CENTO. She was the key member of OAS (1948) and ANZUS (1951), flanking her own hemisphere. These treaties had the effect of throwing a containing ring round Russia and China, and directly protecting America from attack on either side. Economic and military aid was to be given under the Truman Doctrine and the Marshall Plan to any country which opposed Communism. Finally America was prepared for direct war in Korea and Formosa. Within a few years America's isolation had been reversed and direct confrontation between two massive world powers was in full swing.

C4 Greece and the Truman Doctrine

After the British intervention in Greece (see section 2A4) a truce had been arranged, and a regency installed with the backing of 20,000 British troops. An election resulted in victory for the right wing, and it was followed by a plebiscite leading to the return of George II in 1946. But Markos, the leader of the left, was unwilling to give up the struggle since Albania and Bulgaria could supply him with arms, and civil war resumed with Markos proclaiming his own government. The British economy could not bear the strain of the continuing war, and the Labour Party was little inclined to support the reactionary forces of General Zervas. In February the British appealed to Truman for help, and this was the moment the Cold War warriors in Washington had been waiting for to reverse Roosevelt's policy of keeping clear of the Balkans. Truman announced in March 1947:

I believe that it must the policy of the United States to support free people who are resisting attempted subjugation by armed minorities or by outside pressures. I believe that our help should be primarily through economic and financial aid which is essential to economic stability and orderly political processes ... The free peoples of the world look to us for support in maintaining their freedom.

Thus was launched a world-wide American commitment. It was a strange statement because it presumably did not apply to non-Communist dictators like Somoza or Franco who were friends of the USA. It had presumably also been inapplicable to Poland or Greece in 1944, and it is still inapplicable to Puerto Rico or Samoa. However, by May 1947 Congress had agreed to a programme starting with the dollar equivalents of £75 million for Greece and £25 million for Turkey. The American effort in the Aegean was co-ordinated by Henry F. Grady, the Ambassador, and in October 1949 the Civil War ended with the defeat of the Communists. Intervention certainly worked. Greece and Turkey joined NATO in 1952, and Greece, Turkey and Yugoslavia signed a defensive alliance in 1954 (see section 4E2)

C5 Czechoslovakia and the Marshall Plan

Czechoslovakia was Nazi occupied from 1938 to 1945 and had suffered terribly. At the end of the war the Sudeten Germans were expelled from the country and the Slovaks subjected to persecution. The country lost Ruthenia. Russian troops left in December 1945, and in the ensuing elections (May 1946) the Communists were the largest party. Benes became President, and Gottwald Prime Minister, with Communists in the Interior, Defence and Information Ministries, but others like Masaryk as Foreign Minister made it a genuine coalition. An agreed programme of economic reform was started, but the Communists were determined on sole control, and the matter was brought to a crisis by the government's acceptance of an invitation to attend a Marshall Plan conference. Dean Acheson had worked out a more thorough and effective plan for economic aid, and this had been launched by Marshall in a speech in June 1947 when he said:

> It is logical that the United States should do whatever it is able to do to assist
> in the return of normal economic health in the world, without which there can be
> no political stability and no assured peace ... Its purpose should be the revival
> of a working economy in the world so as to permit the emergence of political and
> social conditions in which free institutions can exist.

Although it is true that America gave generously in aid between 1941 and 1952 it is also true this aid enabled American business to thrive, and softened governments in their left wing stance. The Russians were right to suspect it, but once more they appeared as heavy handed when they forced East European countries like Czechoslovakia to turn down aid they badly needed while they were still paying heavy reparations to Russia.

In Czechoslovakia the Communists feared they would lose their majority position in the coming elections because of this decision. A series of measures including greater control over the police by the left angered the moderates who unwisely resigned leaving the President no alternative to a fully Communist government under Gottwald. During the winter of 1947–8 political parties were purged, and in the elections of May 1948 there was a Communist victory. Masaryk was found dead in March, and Benes resigned in June, to die soon after. (See section 4E5.) Elsewhere in Europe Communists tried their best to stir up opposition to dollar imperialism as Russia called the Marshall Plan. In France and Italy there were strikes, but the governments of both countries accepted aid, and only countries in Eastern Europe like Poland and Hungary were forced to refuse it. Marshall Aid passed Congress in May 1948. Between then and 1952 13,150 million dollars poured into Europe, and by 1950 European production was back to 1938 levels. The plan stimulated European co-operation since the European Recovery Committee became the Organisation for European Co-operation and Development (OECD). (See section 7A6.)

C6 The Treaty of Brussels and the Berlin Air Lift

Each of the Western countries was ruled by an effective and stable government by 1948. In France Schumann and Monnet influenced foreign policy; in Germany, Adenauer; in Italy, De Gasperi; and in Britain, Bevin. The Labour Foreign Secretary had come to politics from the Transport Workers Union where he had gained much experience of opposing Communists, and his anger at Molotov's behaviour had been apparent even at Potsdam. It was Bevin who urged Truman to act in Greece, and he was the first to back Marshall Aid seeing these moves as means of drawing America closer to Europe. In 1947 a treaty was signed between Britain and France, and in March 1948 this was expanded to include the Benelux countries. It was to last for 50 years and embrace all forms of co-operation, and it was noticeable that a defence committee was part of the immediate follow up. The disappearance of Czechoslovakia behind the Iron Curtain seemed to make matters more urgent, and the Western powers decided to proceed with their plans for modernising their German zones (see section 3B2) in the face of strong Russian protests.

Tension began to build up. General Clay on the American side began to think in terms of a possible war. The Russians demanded to know what the West were proposing for Germany, and when this was refused they left the Allied Control Commission. In June 1948 the Western powers agreed to include their zones in Marshall Aid and draft a constitution. The Russians thereupon announced a draft constitution for their zone. As part of the economic recovery programme a new currency was issued in the Western zones. The problem in Berlin was that Western currency was more popular than the existing one favoured by the Russians. When the Russians failed to stop the Western currency circulating, they were forced to introduce their own, and this deepened the split in the City. The same day as this happened—June 23rd—communications with the West were severed.

From June 1948 to May 1949 the Allies supplied the two million Berliners by air. Over two million tons of goods were flown in mainly by the Americans and British with the loss of 36 planes and 79 men. Clay was determined to stand firm saying: 'if we believe that we are to hold Europe against Communism we must not budge'. Stalin had to admit defeat. But it was 'the great divide', as Yergin calls it, in post-war politics. It committed America to the front line defence of Europe for in July 1948 B–29s returned to their bases in England, and the same month discussions began that were to lead to the creation of NATO next year. In the Western zones an Occupation Statute replaced military occupation and in May 1949 the Federal Republic of West Germany was created. Military occupation formally ended in September, and the new state joined the Marshall Plan in December. The Russians replied by creating the German Democratic Republic in October 1949. The Soviet Control Commission left in 1953, and in 1956 the Russian zone of Berlin was fully incorporated in East Germany. West Berlin became a state of the Federal Republic. The two Germanies served to highlight even more dramatically the differences of east and west, and nowhere more so than in the contrasting zones of Berlin. Both sides remained pledged to German reunification which remained an unsolved issue, and a source of continued Cold War tension (see section 3E3).

C7 The North Atlantic Treaty Organisation 1949

It was Bevin who urged Marshall to act sensing that with a dramatic blockade in progress American opinion would be favourable to a drastic commitment to Europe. The passing of the Vandenberg Amendment put forward by the Republicans who were the most isolationist party indicated this was the way American opinion was going since it allowed the President to join a defence pact. During the year Truman's election victory strengthened the government's hand as did Stalin's decision to end the Berlin Blockade. NATO was formed in April 1949 by the United States, Britain, Canada, France, Holland, Belgium, Luxemburg, Italy, Portugal, Iceland, Denmark and Norway. The treaty was to last for 20 years, and cover all the countries named, Algeria, the occupation forces including Berlin, and islands, vessels or aircraft north of the Tropic of Cancer. It was a mutual defence pact providing that an armed attack against one or more of them in Europe or North America would be considered an attack against them all.

America had pledged itself to defend Europe although Europe would also act as a shield while America prepared the sword that would defeat Russia. At the time NATO was formed Iron Curtain divisions in Europe outnumbered the West by 125 to 14. The treaty envisaged an army of 50 divisions, and after the early 1950s this rose to 175, but the Soviets deployed 263 by then. The effect of the treaty was to make Europe dependent on American manpower, and later nuclear power for its defence. This more than anything else reflected the change from 1939 when Britain, Germany, Italy and France could all be involved in war without American military aid, while now combined together they would be ineffective without it.

Knapp points out that NATO was 'a totally new form of international organisation'. It provided for mutual defence aid on an unprecedented scale, and it was followed by Acts of Congress which enabled America to provide military aid to Western Europe. One billion dollars was allocated in the first year. From 1950 to 1952 Eisenhower became NATO Supreme Commander, and headquarters (SHAPE) were set up near Paris. The treaty also created a North Atlantic Council, a Committee of Foreign Ministers, a Council of War (later Defence) Ministers and a Chiefs of Staff Committee. Later in 1952 the Council was made a permanent body holding three ministerial meetings a year, with permanent representatives and a Secretary-General. It was noticeable that the Chiefs of Staff met in Washington and that all subsequent Supreme Commanders were Americans, and there was a certain amount of resentment in France and Britain at the new realities of power. The French particularly felt that 'the special relationship' of the British and Americans created in the wartime Chiefs of Staff duplicated itself in SHAPE to their disadvantage. On the other hand for the first time in her history Britain was definitely pledged to defend her continental allies, and America was involved directly in war on Europe's behalf once her army and bases were established there.

The scheme was thus remarkable, if incomplete, and changes were made when the Korean War encouraged greater co-operation. Later (see section 3E1) it was enlarged territorially. It did not fulfil directly its military intention of raising a massive European army, and came to depend on a nuclear umbrella held on the other side of the Atlantic. Its consequences were considerable. With failure in Berlin and Greece Communist direct aggression came to an end in Europe, and the Eastern bloc had to start building up their own defences which their great poverty made difficult. The resulting hardship led in 1953 to the first signs of dissent in East Berlin and Poland. NATO led therefore eventually to the Warsaw Pact in 1955. It encouraged moves towards European unity in the West, and even if in defence matters these did not always succeed the double impetus of Marshall Aid and American defence aid helped to cement together a more prosperous Europe. It was thus the beginning of the acrimonious relations of France and the Anglo-Saxons, the rapprochement of France and Germany, the direct involvement of Britain in European defence, and the direct involvement of America in European politics. At one and the same time it helped to unite and divide Europe.

D Red China and the Korean War

D1 America and Chiang Kai Shek

In 1945 the situation in China was that Chiang was recognised by both Russia and America as the legitimate ruler of the country, and with a well equipped army and the end of the Japanese war his ultimate victory seemed certain (see section 3B4). The Americans sent Marshall to mediate, but he failed and withdrew. However, under a friendship treaty signed in November 1946 Chiang received 2,400 million dollars of aid, and it was his own incompetence and corruption that brought his defeat. In August 1949 America stopped its aid, and in October Mao proclaimed the People's Republic of China (see section 3A7 and 3B6). In December Chiang fled to Formosa (Taiwan). This sudden collapse alarmed the Americans and aroused great bitterness among the 'China Lobby' in Washington backed by missionary and commercial interests. In April 1950 Mao seized Hainan, and in September invaded Tibet. An attack on Formosa was clearly coming if Chiang did not receive American backing. The Americans refused to recognise the new Communist government, and during the Korean War the 7th Fleet took station in the Formosa Strait to protect Chiang. Other countries did not share this view, and it was noticeable that India was the first to recognise a new Asian power which had thrown off Western control. Although tempers in Britain had been aroused by an attack on HMS *Amethyst* while evacuating civilians, Attlee's government recognised Communist China in 1950.

D2 Communism in Asia

Mao's triumph was only part of a widespread Communist offensive in Asia which dated from a Cominform Conference in September 1947 which urged colonial peoples to expel their oppressors, and the Calcutta Asian Youth Conference of February 1948 which discussed guerilla warfare. In the Philippines, Communist 'Huk' rebels waged guerilla war from 1950 to 1954. In Indonesia Muso returned from Moscow, and there were revolts in 1948 and 1951. In 1948 there was a Communist rising in Burma which played on a separatist movement by the Karens, and there was warfare until the fall of the Communist stronghold of Prome in 1950. In Malaya Chen Ping, leader of the local Communist Party, had visited Mao and decided to adopt his revolutionary methods of guerilla warfare. Trouble began in April 1948, and was to continue for many years with ultimate British success (see section 3E4). In Vietnam Ho Chi Minh had been a Comintern agent since 1925, and had started war with the French in 1946. His army, the Vietminh, had been formed in 1941, and was commanded by Vo Giap who had received training in guerilla war in Yenan from Mao. By 1949 the French had been forced to recognise Vietnam, but refused to accept Ho as ruler. China, of course, recognised Ho Chi Minh 1950.

D3 The 'Red Menace'

The success of the Communists in China and the existence of endemic revolt in parts of South East Asia provided the background for rapidly rising American fear that full scale war with either Russia or China or both was approaching, and air raid precautions for major cities were put in hand. In September 1949 Russia's possession of the atom bomb was announced, and in January 1950 Truman sanctioned the start of a hydrogen bomb. American leaders including Truman, Eisenhower and Dulles considered the use of atomic weapons in China and Indo-China in the next few years such was their paranoia. In January 1950 the Hiss Case raised fears of direct Communist penetration of the State Department, and in July McCarthy made such a charge at the start of his campaign (see section 5B3). In February Stalin and Mao buried the hatchet, and signed a 30 year treaty. Russia was pursuing a policy of backing Kim Il Sung in North Korea who was receiving tanks and fighters. 125,000 North Korean troops, in June 1950, crossed the 38th Parallel at eleven points in an attempt to seize South Korea. Truman was not particularly happy with Syngman Rhee as ruler of South Korea, and had denied him arms in order to encourage more moderate policies. To America this invasion seemed like another Pearl Harbor, and it came after a period of sustained tension in Europe, Asia and at home. Truman at once announced his Doctrine applied to Asia, despatched the 7th Fleet to Formosa, sent bombers from Japan and ordered MacArthur to prepare for war. On June 27th in the absence of the Russians the Security Council agreed to help Korea, and on June 30th American forces in Japan went on a war footing.

D4 The Korean War 1950–3

The war may be divided into five main periods. Since the North Korean attack was premeditated, and neither South Korea nor America ready to act the first stage of the war was (a) the successful advance of North Korea. The South Koreans were forced to withdraw from their capital, Seoul, and driven back to an area in the south-east of the country surrounding Pusan. Although American troops arrived they did so only slowly, and were hampered by lack of airfields and the existence of only one railway line to the front. After defeats at Taejon and Chinju it looked as if the Americans would be driven out. MacArthur decided to counter-attack half way up

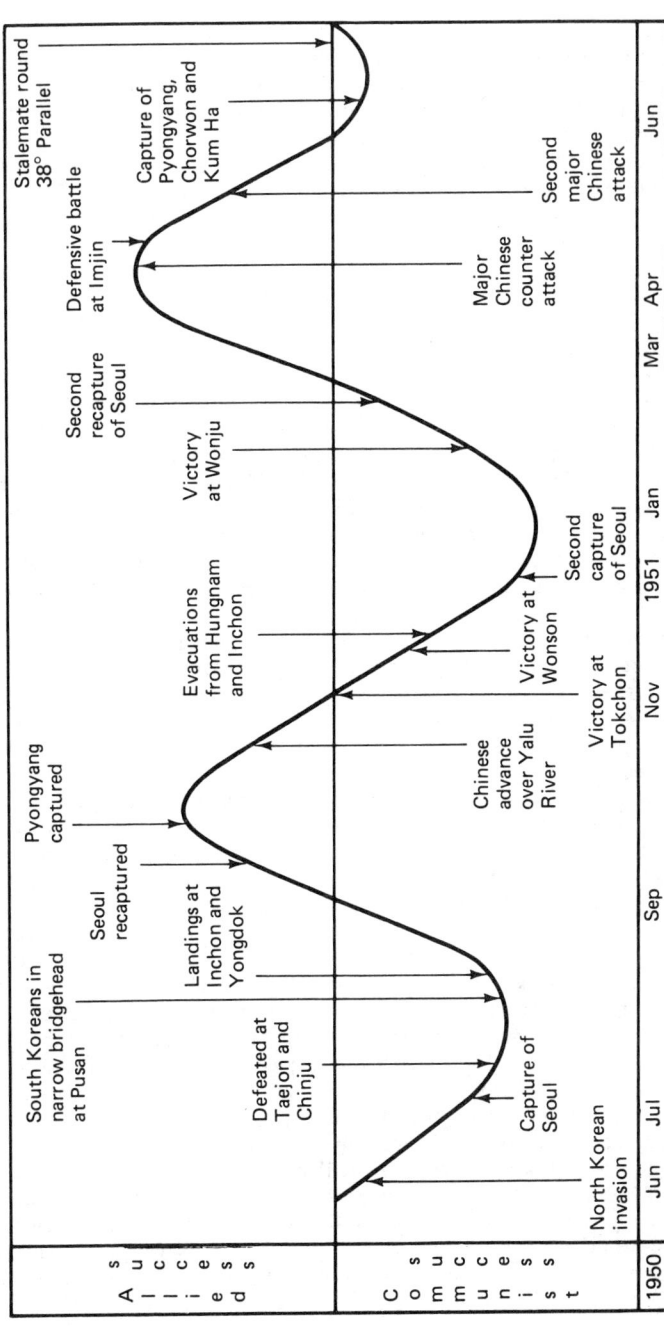

Fig. 6. The main stages in the Korean War

the peninsula, and on September 15th landings were made, with the aid of a British naval bombardment, at Inchon on the west coast, and Yongdok on the east coast. This led to the (b) first Allied successful advance. Seoul was besieged. The Communists killed 20,000 anti-Communists inside the city before withdrawing leaving 20,000 military and 30,000 civilian dead. With massive fire power the two Allied forces joined up and advanced to the 38th Parallel. This startling success led all concerned to back MacArthur and Syngman Rhee in an advance north. On October 9th this advance began, and Pyongyang the capital of North Korea fell to be followed by a Rhee massacre in the city. By this time the North Korean army of 350,000 had largely ceased to exist, and it seemed possible to achieve quick victory.

But China was now taking a hand, and on October 10th stated her armies would enter the conflict. They did so on October 27th, and in north-east Korea resistance stiffened early in November. MacArthur assured Truman that he could achieve a swift victory on the Yalu River even though the British and other forces on the north-west front were also experiencing stronger resistance caused by Chinese tanks. MacArthur bombed the bridges across the Yalu, but it was too late. 500,000 Chinese were massed in North Korea, and when he launched what he hoped would be his final offensive in appalling winter conditions on November 24th, the outcome was (c) the victorious advance of the Chinese. A wedge was driven into the Allied lines at Tokchon, and a retreat was forced on them throughout the winter by five Chinese divisions euphemistically called 'volunteers'. After defeat at Wonson forces in the north-east had to be evacuated, and Chinese troops reached the 38th Parallel in a month. The American field commander died, and was replaced by General Ridgeway late in December, but his first taste of battle was of defeat. On January 1st the Chinese crossed the Imjin, capturing Seoul three days later and a hasty evacuation from Inchon followed.

Truman nearly panicked. He considered the use of nuclear weapons and made an agreement with Chiang to provide troops. A state of national emergency was declared on December 16th, and a massive rearmament programme started. But it was clear the war would have to be fought over again. On January 25th (d) the second Allied advance began. This proved much more difficult than the first, and fighting raged to and fro across the 38th Parallel along a hundred mile front. Using napalm and massive bombing the Allies slowly advanced, and on February 5th, 1951 five armoured columns led the advance towards Seoul which fell on March 14th. MacArthur was involved in a dispute with Truman, and sacked in April, and few noticed that Ridgeway had recrossed the Parallel at last on April 3rd. They were met by the (e) second Chinese attack which was suicidal in its intensity since they pitted the weight of numbers against the weight of armament, and lost 12,000 in the first day's fighting alone. By May 22nd the Chinese had been driven over the Parallel for the last time, and by the end of June the Allies were back in Pyongyang. Although truce negotiations began in July 1951 they did not succeed, and the Chinese created a defensive perimeter in the country which was to cost the Allies 60,000 more casualties before the war ended. The continuation of the war meant a steadily increasing number of air strikes by the Americans, and in July and August 1952 Pyongyang was devastated by napalm and ordinary bombs.

D5 The Significance of the Korean War

All the major powers were involved in Korea, and it was therefore world war by proxy between America, China and Russia. America was helped by 15 other countries that sent military aid, and 13 with economic support, but the brunt of the war was borne by her. Half the ground troops, and 90 per cent of the naval and air forces were American, and her casualties (30,000) were a tenth of those in the Second World War. The Allies lost 4,000 of which 800 were British. Eventually 768,000 Allied troops faced a million Chinese. In America it gave impetus to the internal 'Red Scare', and led to the Acts that banned the Communist Party. It led also to a massive defence programme involving conscription, and in September 1950 Acheson urged that more American troops should be sent to Europe. Four divisions were sent in 1951, and in addition Britain and France embarked on major rearmament. Impetus was given to enlarge NATO, and bring in West Germany (see section 3E1). On the other hand the war indicated that Britain and America were not in complete accord. In December 1950 and April 1951 British policy differed from that of America, and even Churchill insisted there must be no extension of the war in 1952. The British accepted Communist China, and would not be drawn into support for Chiang. Dulles, the new Secretary of State, was angered by this with fatal consequences in the 1950s when the rift widened over the Offshore Islands and Vietnam.

Truman tried to recoup American losses by backing Chiang Kai Shek, but he was reluctant to use Nationalist troops for an invasion of the mainland. However early in 1951 military aid was extended to him, and in March this was made explicit. Thus, America was committed to aid Chiang, and to a series of dangerous disputes during the 1950s. Aid was given to the French in Vietnam thus bringing America directly into that area of the globe, and by 1954 three quarters of French effort was sustained by American cash. Treaties with Japan (1952), Formosa and South Korea (1954) were designed to form a defensive perimeter of benefit to the United States. During 1954 meetings with Churchill and Eden produced the Potomac Charter emphasising agreement on opposing Communists in Eastern Asia, and from this stemmed SEATO as a new element in containment (see section 3E4). The Russians sent 5,000 technicians into North Korea which later joined Comecon. The Chinese had left by 1958, but it remained a fiercely Communist state thus compelling the Americans to keep troops in the South. America backed Syngman Rhee (1949–1960) and Park (1961–1979), and the country remained a source of tension.

The question of how much support Chiang Kai Shek should receive split the Americans. Truman's earlier truculent statements about the use of atom bombs led MacArthur to believe a full scale invasion of China was possible destroying China's industry before it became effective, and using Chiang's forces. Privately Truman did not flinch from this alternative, and as late as May 1952 his diary contained comments about 'all out war' in which Moscow, Peking and 'every manufacturing plant in China and the Soviet Union will be eliminated', but publicly he knew he could not carry America's allies with him and that direct war would bring the Russian nuclear threat into matters. When MacArthur started to make his views public he was sacked in April 1951, but this did not mean the Americans had abandoned either the use of nuclear weapons, or war with China. It was done because Truman was outraged by MacArthur's insubordination. When under the next Eisenhower government truce talks seemed to be breaking down Dulles made warning threats in January 1953, and in May moved atom bombs to Okinawa.

D6 The Korean Settlement

Truce talks had first opened (see section 3D4) in July 1951 after Malik and Jebb, the Soviet and British representatives at UNO, had met in New York. The talks broke down, but were resumed in October at Panmunjon. Many issues arose to prevent the truce talks being successful. The Koreans accused the American of resorting to germ warfare, and then refused a UNO investigation of their charges. They accused the Americans of brainwashing prisoners as only 6,000 of the North Koreans captured wished to return, and the Americans rejected forcible repatriation of the others. On their part the Americans accused the Koreans of secretly building airfields, and ill-treatment of South Korean prisoners. The talks broke down again in October 1952. Eisenhower pledged an end to the war, and won an election on that platform. He received strong backing from Churchill in January 1953, and the death of Stalin in March weakened Russian support for Korea. China was already in grave economic difficulty. In April talks resumed, and in July a cease-fire along the 38th Parallel was achieved, but attempts to make a full scale peace failed during 1954. The North Koreans made difficulties about returning prisoners, and 50,000 South Koreans were never returned. For their part the Americans allowed 27,000 to 'escape', and shipped 21,000 to Formosa (Taiwan). During the war 1.5 million Chinese, 500,000 North Koreans and 70,000 South Koreans had perished in battle, and on both sides famine, air raids and purges accounted for nearly three million civilian casualties. But as in Berlin in 1948–9, Korea in 1950–1 indicated that containment worked. During the next decade America and her allies continued to pursue this policy with a fair measure of success.

E NATO, CENTO, SEATO: The Era of Containment

E1 The Strengthening of NATO

The Korean War helped European rearmament and the strengthening of NATO. A UNO resolution against Franco's Spain was revoked, and the Americans wanted her admitted to NATO. In 1953 a direct Spanish–American Treaty gave the United States five bases in the country, and Spain was admitted to UNO in 1955. In 1951 an agreement with Portugal brought the Azores within NATO. In 1952 Greece and Turkey joined NATO. Plans were put forward to create fully integrated European forces (the Pleven Plan, October 1950) called the European Defence Community. In spite of strong Russian opposition the Community was created by 1952, but depended on ratification by each of its members. Annoyed by American pressure the French failed to do so in August 1954. Eden proposed a Western European Union to replace it including Italy and West Germany. Britain

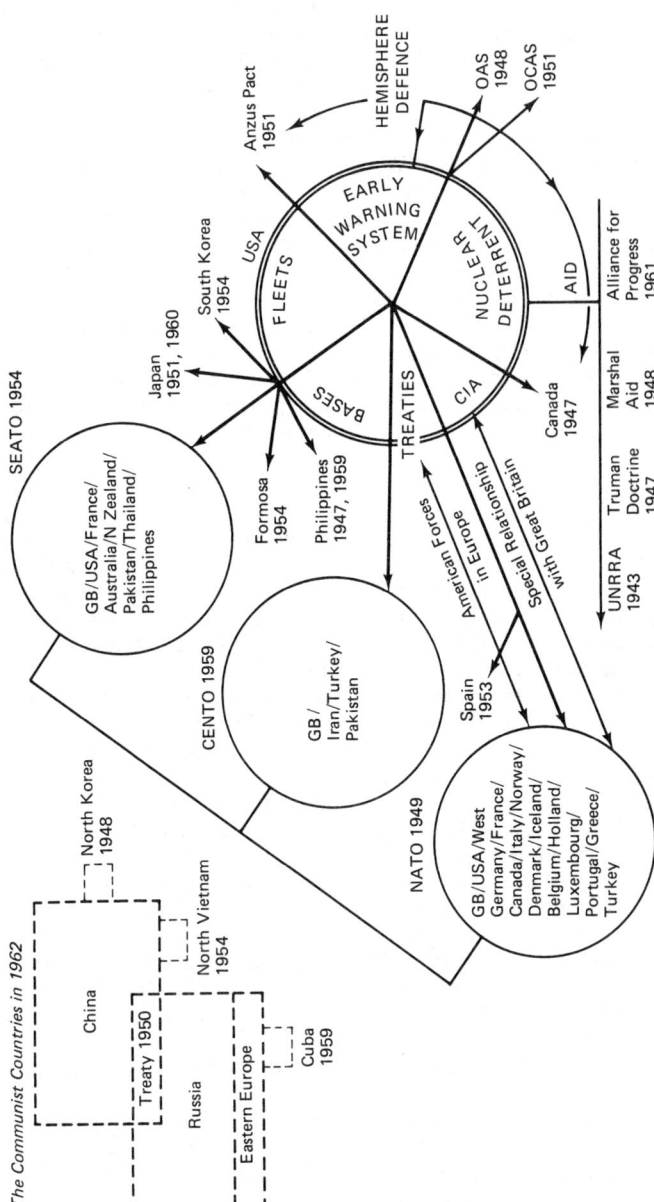

Fig. 7. The extent of Containment to 1962

The Communist Countries in 1962

China

North Korea 1948

North Vietnam 1954

Treaty 1950

Russia

Eastern Europe

Cuba 1959

SEATO 1954

GB/USA/France/ Australia/N Zealand/ Pakistan/Thailand/ Philippines

CENTO 1959

GB/ Iran/Turkey/ Pakistan

NATO 1949

GB/USA/West Germany/France/ Canada/Italy/Norway/ Denmark/Iceland/ Belgium/Holland/ Luxembourg/ Portugal/Greece/ Turkey

EARLY WARNING SYSTEM

FLEETS

BASES

TREATIES

CIA

NUCLEAR DETERRENT

USA

Anzus Pact 1951

South Korea 1954

Japan 1951, 1960

Formosa 1954

Philippines 1947, 1959

HEMISPHERE DEFENCE

OAS 1948

OCAS 1951

AID

Alliance for Progress 1961

Marshal Aid 1948

Truman Doctrine 1947

UNRRA 1943

Canada 1947

Spain 1953

American Forces in Europe

Special Relationship with Great Britain

agreed to station four divisions and a strategic air force in Europe, and the French, satisfied with the denial of nuclear weapons to West Germany, accepted. Agreement was reached in October 1954 at the Treaty of Paris.

The other way in which NATO was strengthened was by admitting West Germany in 1955. This created serious difficulties because of French opposition to a restored Germany, and Russian opposition. As West Germany moved towards full independence the Russians strongly objected demanding a united Germany, but the West rejected this demand since free elections were impossible, and a foreign ministers' meeting of the West and Russia in early 1954 failed to produce agreement. For their part the Russians allowed East Germany to form its own army and in March 1954 announced full sovereignty for their zone. West Germany joined NATO, and East Germany joined the newly formed Warsaw Pact making the division of Germany even more certain. The Warsaw Pact of May 1955 was a belated Russian response to NATO, but also provided a fresh reason for retaining Soviet troops in Eastern Europe where they were increasingly resented. As with NATO the new treaty contained a political consultative committee, and this enabled Russia to abolish the Cominform in 1956.

E2 The Geneva Spirit

The return of Churchill (1951) to office and the victory of Eisenhower (1952) was soon followed by the death of Stalin (1953) who was succeeded by Malenkov, and subsequently by Bulganin and Khrushchev. The new generation of leaders began to explore the restoration of relations which had collapsed in 1947–8. Churchill and Eisenhower met at Bermuda in the first of a new generation of summit meetings. This was followed by Foreign Ministers Meetings on German reunification and Austrian independence, and in July 1955 at Geneva the Big Four (Britain, France, America and Russia) met for the first time. They achieved nothing concrete; nor did a second foreign ministers meeting later in the year, but the fact of their meeting seemed to bring to an end the first stage of the Cold War, and the new atmosphere was hailed as 'the Geneva Spirit'. This enabled a range of post-war disputes and problems to be resolved. The Trieste Dispute was ended (1954), Austria given independence (1955) and Porkkala restored to Finland (1955). The Russians recognised West Germany although the West could not bring itself to accept East Germany. Outside Europe a truce was made in Korea (1953), in Vietnam (1954) a general settlement was arrived at by the powers and Port Arthur was restored to China (1954). Khrushchev visited Yugoslavia early in 1955 to restore good relations following the dispute that had started in 1948. In December 1955 Russia at last lifted her veto on new countries joining UNO, and 16 new members including Italy and Japan were admitted.

This thaw did not in fact mark the end of the Cold War as was thought at the time, but only a change in approach. Khrushchev himself was involved in a lengthy struggle to obtain power from February 1955 to March 1958, and his foreign policy initiatives strengthened his internal position. Moreover, continued reparations, and the military occupation of Eastern Europe were causing dissent in the Soviet satellites as revolts in East Berlin and Czechoslovakia in 1953 indicated. In February 1956 in secret session of the Supreme Soviet Khrushchev denounced Stalin for his repression, and for the purge of 'national' Communists (see section 4C2). The formalisation of Russian occupation armies by treaty, and the scrapping of the Cominform were part of a process of maintaining Communist authority in Eastern Europe which came just in time. During 1956 there were revolts in Poland and Hungary, and concessions had to be made. In another way too Russian policy emphasis was changing. By denouncing Stalin Khrushchev was left free to project a new and more humane face of Communism, and he sought to do this in the Third World. The Chinese had already given a lead in this respect at the Bandung Conference in 1955, and Chou En Lai, their Foreign Minister, had begun a series of visits. Khrushchev followed in his footsteps visiting such countries as India and Afghanistan in 1955. More ominously perhaps during 1955–6 Czechoslovakia and Poland agreed to supply Egypt with arms thus indicating that the Cold War had found a new focus in the Middle East.

E3 The Berlin Crisis

Outwardly accord between the two sides in the Cold War seemed to be developing. Khrushchev visited Britain in 1956, and Macmillan became the first Western leader to reach Moscow in 1959; Khrushchev's visit to the United States followed in September that year. Kennedy met Khrushchev at Vienna in 1961. But this preoccupation with summit meetings did not lead to any practical achievements, and indeed produced a serious break in relations. The whole period was one of steadily escalating nuclear arsenals, and spectacular spy cases which indicated the underlying tensions remained, and it was not surprising that Germany became the focus for these.

Since 1949 two million Germans had fled westwards from East Germany, and West Germany already contained several million people deprived of their homelands in 1945. Adenauer's government adopted a pro-Western stance enabling Western agents to operate from West Berlin, and allowing radio stations to attack Russian policy in Eastern Europe. The economic growth of the country was a standing reproach to the East; nowhere more so than in Berlin. In November 1958 Khrushchev announced that all Berlin should be part of East Germany, and Western access denied next year. A Foreign Ministers meeting (May—July 1959) seemed to avert this threat, but Macmillan was determined to settle the matter at a summit, and pressed a reluctant Eisenhower to agree. Eleven days before the summit Khrushchev announced the capture of a US pilot whose plane had been brought down near Sverdlovsk. Since 1956 the Americans had sent these 'spy' planes into Russian air space from bases in Turkey and Norway, and it was in fact a minor case of spying typical of both sides. But Khrushchev used it to get himself out of an impasse over Berlin demanding an apology which was not given. The Paris Summit collapsed as it began in May 1960.

In June 1961 when he met Kennedy at Vienna Khrushchev described Berlin as 'a bone that must come out of the Soviet throat', and renewed his threat to sign a separate peace treaty. On August 13th, 1961 a wall was built between the two zones in order to stop flight from the East, and perhaps bring pressure on the West to withdraw reminiscent of 1948. General Clay sent American troops into the Eastern sector to demonstrate Allied rights, and reinforcements arrived. On August 28th tanks of both sides drew back, and the immediate crisis was past for although the Wall stopped the flood of refugees it advertised the failings of Communism. A series of escapes began, and since it was built 81 people have been killed crossing the wall. The Western powers remained in Berlin, and so did the Wall. Containment in Europe had reached stalemate. (See section 13DE.)

E4 The Geneva Conference and SEATO

In South East Asia Communist insurgents were under control in Burma, Indonesia and the Philippines by 1954, and in Malaya the British had succeeded in defeating the guerillas. For this there were several reasons. The Communists were not able to get outside aid, and they had little appeal to the local Malays. The British military response was flexible springing from long years of unconventional colonial warfare. They utilised the new SAS Regiment, the Gurkhas and colonial troops skilled in jungle warfare. The British forces were able to kill some 6,700 of the 10,000 terrorists for the loss of 1,865 men. 2,473 civilians were killed, but the majority of the population was won over in two ways. The first was the Briggs Plan of settlement bringing the Malaysian villagers into 'kampongs' where they could be supervised, and thus denying the guerillas supplies. To this was added a policy to win 'the hearts and minds' of the people by social reform and political development. The British backed the Alliance Party of Tenku Abdul Rahman, and in 1955 elections were held. Independence for Malaya came in 1957, and in July 1960 the emergency ended.

For the French, however, no such success was possible. From 1946 to 1954 they were engaged in a full scale war with the Vietminh. (See section 3D2.) In 1949 France recognised Bao Dai as the ruler of Vietnam, but Russia and China recognised Ho Chi Minh and began to supply arms. The Chinese built railways to the border and provided equipment like anti-aircraft guns. The Russians supplied transport and weapons, and the existence of China meant that the Vietminh would have space to regroup. The war was largely fought in Northern Tonkin close to the Chinese border. In the early stages of the war the French were successful because they established strong points and defensive perimeters and the Vietminh tried to storm them with heavy losses. However, the Vietminh soon adopted Mao's guerila tactics withdrawing from major towns, and so dispersing the French that they could be slowly destroyed piecemeal. The French tried to bring the Vietminh to battle, and this was to prove their undoing. When in February 1954 it became apparent that the Vietminh were helping the Pathet Lao guerillas in Laos the French decided to cut their supply lines at Dien Bien Phu. They underestimated the fire power of the guerillas, and after being besieged from January to May 1954 losing 7,000 killed surrendered with 11,000 men.

The French suffered a shattering blow in Indo-China equivalent to the loss of Singapore by the British in 1942. It was clear to the indigenous peoples that European forces could be defeated. The French lost 21,000 dead besides 11,620 Legionaires, and 30,000 colonial troops during the war. The Vietminh had lost many more—150,000, but their numbers had been vastly increased by a People's Militia which did much transport work, and they had secured their area by political education. The Americans had been the main financial support of French efforts, and on March 24th, 1954 France appealed to America for military aid. Dulles wanted air strikes including atom bombs on the hills round Dien Bien Phu, but there was strong opposition from Congress and Eden, the British Foreign Secretary, so that Eisenhower refused to support Dulles. The French were forced to seek terms, and a conference met at Geneva (April–July 1954) to arrange them.

Geneva was the last of the imperial conferences at which the Western powers imposed a settlement. Vietnam was divided at the 17th Parallel. In the North Ho Chi Minh's government was recognised, and in the South, after some difficulty caused by Vietminh infiltrating with refugees from the north, a republic was set up in 1955. Free elections were to be held, and both parts of the country were to be neutral and demilitarised. Outwardly it seemed as if containment had worked, but in reality the Vietminh had already established themselves in South Vietnam, and the Pathet Lao in Laos, and it was likely that a Korean partition solution would lead eventually to a conflict like that of the Korean War. In December 1960 Ho's government announced the Vietminh would extend their operations southwards to conquer South Vietnam, and in April 1961 Kennedy responded to this by sending 686 military advisers to organise the South Vietnamese army which was to be increased by 20,000 with American assistance (see section 13B1).

America did not sign the Geneva Treaty as Dulles felt let down once again by the British. Eden was keen to secure an alliance covering South East Asia in order to restrain American involvement. Dulles feared the spread of Communism after the failure of the French, and in September 1954 the Manila Pact created the South East Asia Treaty Organisation (SEATO) consisting of America, Britain, France, Australia, New Zealand, Pakistan, Thailand and the Philippines. Its purpose was to provide for the defence of Asia up to 21°30′ north which excluded Formosa (Taiwan). Conscious they were linking themselves to imperial powers the Americans issued a Pacific Charter stressing the need for economic development in the area. SEATO had a permanent organisation, and at first enjoyed some success as the British bases in the area made it an effective force, but British withdrawal from Hong Kong and Singapore weakened it considerably, and the French left in 1966. SEATO provided forces to deal with trouble caused by Indonesia (1963–6) and sent 72,000 troops to Vietnam.

E5 Brinkmanship: The Offshore Islands and Laos.

Russia and China had both sent aid to Ho Chi Minh, and their relationship was strengthened by agreements in 1953 and 1954. Mao was determined to reconquer territories occupied by Chiang, and his forces were clearly powerful enough to destroy the former ruler of mainland China. America concluded a defence treaty with Chiang, and the 7th Fleet remained in the Formosa Strait. This led to a series of international incidents in which Dulles blustered and threatened on the brink of war. In 1955 he had to evacuate Chiang's forces from the Tachens, but in 1958 when the Chinese began to shell Quemoy and Matsu (the Offshore Islands) the fleet was strengthened and Dulles was determined to use force. The fleet was deliberately used to escort Chiang's ships in September, and the Chinese fortunately did not open fire. The British once more disassociated themselves from these actions.

The Chinese turned their attention inland, and in 1959 attacked Tibet (see section 6E4). In September Tibet appealed to UNO, and a report in June 1960 accused China of genocide. The Chinese fully occupied the country bringing them to the borders of India (see section 6E3).

In South East Asia the first challenge to the Geneva Settlement came in Laos as soon as the Control Commission, set up in 1954, dissolved in 1958. The Pathet Lao demanded places in the government, and when this was rejected started a guerilla campaign aided by North Vietnam. In 1959 Laos secured American aid, and in 1961 this was followed by military advisers. The British and Russians who were co-chairmen of the Geneva Conference issued an appeal for a cease-fire and reconvened the conference next month. The Pathet Lao continued to advance, and a year later in 1962 Kennedy began moving troops and fleet units to Thailand. The British and Russians pressed for a settlement, and in July 1962 one was achieved. The Pathet Lao were given seats in a coalition government, and Laotian status under the 1954 agreement was reaffirmed. The Americans then withdrew their military advisers and an uneasy peace descended.

Containment in Asia had variable fortunes. The overwhelming power of China, and in the early 1950s the limited support of Russia, extended Communist power into North Korea and North Vietnam in each case preceded by a war in which the Western powers suffered defeats and were only able to impose compromises. China had secured Tibet and most of her Offshore Islands, and confined Chiang to Taiwan. America was left committed to the reactionary governments of South Korea and Taiwan, and to a rejection of Red China's existence in the United Nations. Communist revolution had been put down in Burma, Malaya and the Philippines, but the existence of the Vietcong and the Pathet Lao meant peace was not secure in South East Asia. There the Americans had rendered aid to reactionary rulers in South Vietnam and Laos. SEATO in theory protected the area from further attack, but the French were a broken reed and the British shedding imperial responsibilities, so that trouble would have to be met by America alone (see section 13B).

E6   The Eisenhower Doctrine and CENTO

Between 1945 and 1971 Britain's power in the Middle East disappeared and was partly replaced by America's, although by then Arab economic and political power was too strong to be controlled by the West. The region was from the first vital in the Cold War. It provided the link between Europe and the Far East. The Suez Base, for example, was valuable during the Korean War. Oil was becoming increasingly important to Western economies. Britain negotiated new oil treaties with Iraq and Iran, and America had an agreement with Saudi Arabia. Russia had made threatening noises about Turkey, Iran and Libya in 1945, and it was seen as vital therefore to maintain a chain of bases in Morocco, Gibraltar, Tunisia, Libya, Malta, Cyprus, the Canal Zone and Aden in order to warn off the Russians and provide aid for friendly regimes. After a short sharp war with neighbouring Arabs (1948–9) Israel had become independent, and in 1950 a joint American–British–French guarantee was given to a democratic pro-Western state thus complicating the Western position in the area.

The Western difficulty was that, unlike Asia or Africa where they still acted as colonial powers, their colonial role in the Middle East was in process of dissolution. France had already left Syria and Lebanon, and although she seemed determined to keep North Africa she had left there also by 1962. Britain surrendered full independence to Jordan in 1946, and in March 1957 King Hussein renounced his defence treaty with Britain. Egypt refused to ratify a new treaty with Britain, and in 1954 Britain agreed to evacuate her forces. The last British troops left Egypt in June 1956. In Iraq the pro-British ruler, Feisal II, was murdered in 1958, and the British had withdrawn by March 1959. Britain's Middle East base moved from Egypt to Cyprus to Aden during the period indicating her increasing weakness (see section 10D).

Arab nationalism proved to be too strong for the West, particularly since a Muslim revival and hatred of the pro-Western Jews were added to demands for national independence and social reform by the town-based Arabs who had little time for pro-Western kings and sheiks. Thus, in 1954 in Egypt the monarchy was replaced by a republic led by Gamal Nasser, and he proved to be the focus for Arab nationalism. The American position in the Middle East was difficult. During the war they had opposed British involvement in the region, and were eager to profit from investment there. Apart from Saudi Arabià where their treaty was renewed in 1957 the American had also been involved in Iran since 1947. When Iranian opposition to Western oil interests forced the Shah to flee, the American CIA staged a coup and restored him in 1953. Favourable oil agreements followed. The Americans offered aid to Nasser to construct a dam on the Nile. Thus, they were unwilling to give direct backing to the British. This led in 1956 to a serious division between Britain and France anxious to topple Nasser, and the Americans who wished to keep the peace in election year for Eisenhower. During the Suez War (October–November 1956) the Western powers were divided, and this gave the Arabs (and the Russians) their opportunity (see section 10D4). From the British point of view the annoying feature of American foreign policy was that Dulles already conceded there was a Communist threat, and readily responded to it while rejecting British and French arguments concerning Nasser. Yet Shepilov, the Russian Foreign Minister, visited Egypt in 1955, and arms agreements were soon followed by Russian finance for the very dam the Americans would not finance themselves, having got cold feet about Egyptian stability during 1956.

The British had first proposed the Middle East Defence Organisation (MEDO)—Britain, France and Turkey—but this was stillborn. Instead Eden was able to take advantage of concern among Middle East states about Communist subversion. In 1954 Turkey and Pakistan signed a treaty, and in 1955 Iraq joined them. In April 1955 Britain and Iran joined as well thus creating the Baghdad Pact. Dulles described this as 'a solid band of resistance to Communism', but would not join. Instead America concluded bilateral treaties with Turkey and Pakistan, creating what they called 'a northern tier' of defence. However, Russian threats of nuclear action at the time of Suez, clear evidence of Russian arms in Egypt and the backing given by Communist leaders to Nasser forced Dulles to switch his policy. In March 1957 the Eisenhower Doctrine was announced extending the Truman Doctrine specifically to the Middle East, and the Americans soon

showed they meant business. Once Hussein had denounced his treaty with
Britain Egypt became a threat to him, so in April 1957 the American 6th
Fleet moved into the Eastern Mediterranean, and next month America joined
the military planning side of the Baghdad Pact. Nasser formed a union
of Egypt and Syria, and Russian advisers arrived in both countries. In the
summer of 1957 Syria threatened Turkey, and was backed by Russia. Dulles
issued stern warnings, and in October the threat was lifted. 'You've done
a Suez on us', was Macmillan's comment. Lebanon had accepted American
aid, and Syria fomented trouble inside the country. When Faisal II was
killed in Iraq the new ruler, Kassem, looked as if he would join forces with
Syria to destroy Lebanon and Jordan. In May 1958 America landed forces
in the Lebanon, and Britain airlifted troops to Jordan. A demand by Russia
for a five power conference was rejected by the West who clearly still saw
the region as their preserve despite the proximity of the USSR. In 1959
with the departure of Iraq from the Baghdad Pact it was renamed the Central
Treaty Organisation (CENTO) and its headquarters fixed at Ankara. Turkey
agreed to allow missiles on her territory. Somewhat late in the day the
Americans were containing Communism in the Middle East. The Middle
East remained tense, but the sources of tension were changing, and with
Arab independence and radical governments increasingly adjusting their
focus towards the Arab–Israeli issue this would soon become of equal
importance (see section 10E)

E7 Hemisphere Defence

America's commitment to dollar imperialism and the defence of the 'free
world' against Communism was often portrayed as a moral crusade. It was
primarily concerned with an American fear that its traditional isolation was
vulnerable to Communist influence, and nowhere was this attitude more
apparent than in its own hemisphere. America criticised colonial powers
like Britain and France, but surrendered none of her colonies apart from
the Philippines in 1946. In 1951 the Office of Territories was set up to organise
them. Alaska and Hawaii were made the 49th and 50th States in 1959.
Australia and New Zealand were linked in the Australia, New Zealand and
United States (ANZUS) Pact in 1951 to provide protection in the south-
west, and in 1963 base facilities in Australia were obtained. The chain of
bases secured during the war was retained, and hemisphere defence became
of crucial importance. In 1947 the Treaty of Rio de Janeiro set up a mutual
defence system from Greenland to Antarctica (see section 12D1).
America's policy was to back her economic interests, and encourage
economic development through supporting the dictators of authoritarian
regimes rather than risking radical revolution to secure those interests,
possibly leading to Communist states. In order to secure aid most South
American countries agreed to ban the Communist Party even those like
Chile where it had recently entered the government. The Organisation of
American States (1948), eventually joined by 14 countries, and the Organisation of Central American States (1951), joined by five independent republics,
were the basis for American action. In 1952 states agreed to exclude Communism from the hemisphere, and in 1960 and 1963 this was reaffirmed.
At Bogota in 1960 America agreed to supply aid to 19 countries, and in

1961 Kennedy's Alliance for Progress created a ten year programme. Where there was risk this policy might fail America was prepared to use covert force. In 1954 American business interests organised the overthrow of a ten year old socialist government in Guatemala which had confiscated the companies' assets. When Castro took over Cuba (1959) the Americans did all they could to topple him. Aid was stopped (1961) following seizure of American companies, an invasion was covertly organised by the CIA, an economic boycott introduced and by 1964 America had persuaded the OAS powers to apply sanctions and break-off diplomatic contacts.

But this policy could not go on for ever. The American view of Hispanic America was sharply challenged as demands for political and economic reform accelerated with the spread of independence movements elsewhere in the world, and the pressure on resources caused by a rapid population rise. As early as 1958 Vice President Nixon was stoned in Venezuela, and Chile restored the legality of the Communist Party. Castro simply allied with Russia and joined Comecon to provide the aid he needed. In November 1960 the dictators of Honduras and Guatemala asked for American naval protection from Cuba, and during the 1960s guerilla movements began to spread. Latin American nationalism rejected American control. In 1964 Panama, which had been controlled by America since 1903, was the scene of riots and Bolivia withdrew from OAS because of frontier quarrels with Chile. At the United Nations Hispanic countries turned more to the Third World bloc than America's embrace as the 1960s developed a new pattern of world relations.

F The Cold War: Reflection

Barraclough says 'the Cold War dominated 25 years of history'. Yet some would argue the Cold War is still continuing. This is to confuse at least three separate issues. The first is the ideological struggle between capitalism and communism, and democracy and dictatorship. This has been at issue since 1848, and will remain so. The second is the struggle of the West against Russian Communism which began in 1917, and continues also to the present time. Russia could be argued to have pursued expansionist policies since her foundation, for her geography and strategic requirements dictate this. The third is the conflict between Russia and America (each surrounded by their satellites) which grew during the war years, and flowered after 1947. This struggle is no longer a straightforward American–Russian confrontation because 'a more pluralistic international order' has changed matters. The Communist bloc is divided between Russia and China, and their satellites are subject to increasing modification from within. The West is divided with the European powers led by France and Germany seeking closer detente than America would wish. In each of the areas of the former Cold War new countries have arisen, and new alignments formed which make the attitudes and events of even 20 years ago seem remote. Contrast, for example, the almost total silence concerning the French colonial campaign in Vietnam from 1946 to 1954 with the obsessive television coverage of the American one in the same region in the 1960s, and the different reactions of the powers involved to both struggles.

In 1945 only Russia was a Communist country. In 1962 there were seven in Europe (Poland, East Germany, Yugoslavia, Albania, Bulgaria, Rumania and Hungary), three in Asia (China, North Korea, North Vietnam), and one in the Americas (Cuba). In one sense containment clearly failed, therefore, but in another it succeeded for during the same period Communism was limited in Europe by the creation of NATO, and action over the Berlin Blockade and the Berlin Wall. It was limited in Asia by the Korean War, and the Geneva Agreement backed by the weaker SEATO treaty, and it made no progress in the Middle East where CENTO existed. Throughout most of the period the West had nuclear superiority over the Soviet Union. Taylor has said that by the 1970s it was agreed 'the Cold War had been a false alarm, a mistaken enterprise from the start'. Yergin argues that the breakdown of relations after Yalta was partly caused by American inexperience and wrong reactions. Others have disagreed. Donnelly in 'Struggle for the World' clearly sees the Cold War as vital to 'Western civilisation'. It was a period he says in which: 'The frontal challenge of Soviet Communism had been halted frontally', accepting there was a challenge, and that it was met successfully, Brian Crozier has gone further to say that the Cold War was not merely a matter of diplomacy and direct warfare, but covert subversion, economic infiltration, aid to guerillas and a host of actions not normally regarded as 'war' in the past, and that this war is still going on, and is being lost by the West. When Kennedy became President in 1961 he said: 'Let every nation know whether it wishes us well or ill, that we shall pay any price, bear any burden, meet any hardship, support any friend, oppose any foe to assure the survival and success of liberty.' This was one image of the West fighting for freedom against Soviet and Chinese expansionism. Another was of the West backing dictators, opposing colonial liberation movements founded on genuine nationalism, fostering its own economic interests at the expense of the Third World and covering this *realpolitik* with the words of Cold War jargon about liberty. The questions must always remain unanswered as long as Russian and Chinese archives remain closed, and we simply do not know why they acted as they did in Eastern Europe or South East Asia. But the questions still remain interesting ones. Was Russia determined on aggression or reacting to American policies? Were America and the West over-reacting to a nonexistent threat, or does the evidence of the last chapter suggest there was such a threat, and that it was successfully contained?

Revision Questions

1. What do you understand by the phrase the 'Cold War'?
2. Describe the long and short term reasons why the wartime Allies were almost immediately involved in the Cold War. (Refer back also to Chapter 2.)
3. What were the main characteristics of the 'Cold War', and what were the main regions of the world where it was fought out?
4. Describe what is meant by containment, and how NATO, CENTO, SEATO and OAS played key roles in it.
5. What is meant by: (a) the German problem (b) satellite states (c) the

Truman Doctrine (d) brinkmanship (e) the Eisenhower Doctrine (f) Marshall Aid (g) the Northern Tier (h) the Geneva Spirit?

6. Describe who was involved in the Korean War (1950–3), and Indo-Chinese War (1946–54). In what ways were the settlements at the end of the two wars similar and dissimilar?

7. In what ways was the world divided into two military 'blocs' in 1960? What weapons and defence systems were involved on each side, and what military alliances and bases did each side possess? Did this preserve the peace or contribute to the tension of the Cold War period?

Further Reading

Bown, C., and Mooney, P., *Cold War to Detente*, Heinemann, London, 1976.
Donnelly, D., *Struggle for the World*, Collins, London, 1965, pp. 145–428.
Hastings, D., *The Cold War*, Ernest Benn, London, 1969.
Howarth, P., *Twentieth Century History*, Longmans, Harlow, 1979.
Knapp, W., *A History of War and Peace*, OUP, London, 1967, chapters 3, 4, 7, 8, 10.
O'Ballance, E., *The Indo-China War 1945–1954*, Faber and Faber, London, 1964.
Rees, D., *Korea, the Limited War*, Macmillan, London, 1964.
Rees, D., *The Age of Containment: The Cold War*, Macmillan, London.
Windsor, P., *City on Leave: A History of Berlin, 1945–62*, 1963.
Yergin, D., *Shattered Peace*, Andre Deutsch, London 1978. Penguin, 1980.

4
The Communist World of Russia and her Satellites

A. Introduction: Russia 1917–41

A1 The Coming of Revolution

Karl Marx had thought Russia an unlikely place for Communist revolution because it was affected very little by industrialization. As late as 1914 Russia's population of 110 million had only about three million industrial workers, and although there were industrial troubles in the country culminating in strikes affecting a million workers in July 1914 the autocratic government of the Tsar was actually strengthened after the failure of revolution in 1905. The secret police effectively crushed radical parties forcing Lenin into exile, and arresting Stalin. Small concessions had resulted in a mock parliament or duma, and limited social reforms like primary education which had won over some moderates. When a combination of defeat in war and economic dislocation led to revolt in 1905 Bolsheviks like Lenin and Trotsky who hastened to Russia had little effect on the course of events, the risings were scattered and easily suppressed, and were followed by martial law, deportations and executions. When war came in 1914 the majority of Russians remained faithful to Tsar Nicholas II.

A2 The Bolshevik Party

Opposition to the tsars had originated with demands that the peasants be freed and used as the basis for change. The Social Revolutionary Party believed this to be the most effective way of changing the system. They based this view on the increasing number of serfs who were able to consolidate their farms, and become small landowners once they had been freed. One sixth of the peasants were 'kulaks' or small landowners by 1914. This class had some representation in a system of local government set up with zemstvo local councils. A Council of Zemstvos existed which was a focus for reforming demands, and for middle class Liberals (Octobrists) led by Miliukov. Others saw little hope except to overthrow the state by anarchy or Nihilism as it was known in Russia. Although not able to form a party their tradition of revolutionary violence remained powerful in the country, and during the 1900s over 4,000 government officials were killed. The marxist Social Democratic Party was organised in 1898, and for years was divided by doctrinal debates. Inside the country it confined activities to bank robberies, or distributing the party newspaper *Iskra*, and had only a small number of deputies in the duma. In these doctrinal debates Lenin became the most prominent intellectual and skilful politician until in 1903 he was able to secure control over part of the party known as the Bolsheviks or 'Majority' as opposed to their rivals, the Mensheviks or 'Minority'. By 1917 the Bolshevik Party had about 240,000 members, and some voting strength in St Petersburg and Moscow. Its chances of spear-heading a revolution, however, seemed remote.

A3 'War is the Locomotive of History'

From 1914 to 1917 Russia was engaged in the First World War. The Tsar's reasons were to protect fellow Slavs in the Balkans and to repel Austrian aggression, but many in the Tsar's Council saw the war as an opportunity to restore Russian prestige following humiliations in the Far East and the Balkans. The effect of the war was to inflict great suffering on the Russian people who lost some five million dead; to cripple the economy so that with massive inflation the peasants were threatened with starvation; and to destroy faith in autocratic government. The Tsar took personal command of his armies which were then overwhelmed. The government fell into the hands of inadequate ministers appointed at the whim of the Tsarina, and suspected of siding with the Germans. Twenty-one ministers were dismissed, but the government remained devoid of leaders capable of winning the war. Thus, the war weakened the Tsar, the army and the Duma politicians. In March 1917 the Tsar was deposed and a Provisional Government set up under Prince Lvov, and from July under Alexander Kerensky.

A4 The Bolshevik Revolution 1917

Kerensky's government proved inadequate. The war continued leading to further disaster, and Russian provinces like Poland and Finland declared their independence. The government was menaced by right wing extremists who attempted a coup, and by left wing extremists who also attempted a rising. In April and May Lenin and Trotsky returned, and taking advantage of press freedom and an amnesty organised 'soviets' (councils of workers) in Petrograd and Moscow. By September the Bolsheviks emerged as the largest single party in the Petrograd Soviet although they were still a small minority of the socialists involved. Lenin evolved a new doctrine of revolution, and Trotsky supplied the organising skill. On November 6th, 1917 the Bolsheviks during bread riots formed a Congress of the Soviets in Petrograd, and forced Kerensky to resign. On November 13th they seized control in Moscow and moved the capital there. Kerensky had already promised elections, and these took place on November 25th. They were the only democratic elections in Russian history and returned (with 41 millions voters) 225 Bolsheviks and 420 Social Revolutionaries and others.

    Lenin was not prepared to accept a democratic election. He believed in the dictatorship of the proletariat, and from the first had roused the masses knowing that in the ensuing chaos a small minority might triumph. In November decrees confiscated royal and noble land, and in December that of the church. Peasants seized land all over the country as a result. A peace decree ended the war, and returning troops were organised into the Red Guards. Police agents were hunted down, but in December Lenin ordered Dzerzhinsky to form the Cheka which was to be the first of the new secret police forces. In January 1918 parliament was dissolved by Red Guards, and the next month land nationalisation and a Red Army were formally started. By July 1918 a new constitution was devised, and the same month the Tsar was murdered. Using an attempt to kill Lenin in August 1918 as an excuse the Cheka launched a wave of terror dissolving all other political parties, and executing 500 people in reprisal. The dictatorship of the proletariat and one party rule by the Communists was thus established.

A5 The Great Civil War 1917–21

Lenin had promised peace, and in 1918 accepted the Treaty of Brest–Litovsk which took away vast parts of Russia and gave them to Germany. The Germans broke the treaty by invading Russia, and set up puppet governments in countries like Finland and Poland. When the war ended the Germans were required to renounce Brest–Litovsk in the armistice, but their army remained on the Baltic coast. The Allies intervened in Russia on the pretext of protecting their wartime supplies, and soon the British were in the north at Murmansk and Archangel, and in the south round the Black Sea and at Baku, while the French were at Odessa, the Czechs in Siberia, and the Japanese and Americans in the Far Eastern Provinces. The countries that had broken away in 1917–18 refused to return to Russia, and were seen by the Allies as a useful 'length of barbed wire' against Bolshevism. Inside Russia various 'White' Armies under a colourful and contemptible band of ex-tsarist military men began to advance on Moscow and Petrograd.

Lenin and Trotsky chose to counter-attack on 12 fronts. They had interior lines of communication, and Trotsky organised a war train that enabled him to co-ordinate the small Bolshevik armies. The opposition was hopelessly divided, and gradually lost support from the Allies during 1919 as it became clear that white terror was only a substitute for red terror. Lenin's attempts to spread Bolshevism by war outside Russia failed, and he accepted the independence of Finland, Estonia, Latvia and Lithuania. He was forced to accept Poland's movement of her frontiers east in 1921, and to concede land to Turkey in return for friendship. However, the Whites were defeated, the Allies withdrew, and the creation of the constitution of the Union of Soviet Socialist Republics (1922) embraced regions like the Ukraine and Transcaucasia.

A6 Lenin's Work for Russia

Lenin's principal achievements were to create an effective Communist Party with a new ideology, and through revolution to establish Soviet Russia as the world's first Communist state. He did not start the revolution, nor did he defeat its enemies unaided, but he was certainly the principal architect of success. At first he tried to introduce full Communism into Russia using the emergency of the civil war to justify stern measures. All land was nationalised by February, and all industry by June 1918 thus setting back the trend towards small kulak farms, and reducing industrial production because of the flight of foreign capital from the country. By early 1921 it was clear this was not working. There was a famine of Asiatic proportions, and discontent in the armed forces surfaced at Kronstadt naval base. Lenin therefore altered course and introduced his New Economic Policy which allowed the return of small holdings, small businesses for a profit and the banking system. With the new federal constitution, and the end of the civil war Lenin's work was completed with the vital exception of providing for a successor. This he failed to do because he was a semi-invalid from 1922, and also because he was unable to decide between his old comrades, feeling that Trotsky was over-ambitious and Stalin not to be trusted.

A7 Stalin obtains Power

The rule of Josif Stalin (1879–1953) was arguably the most appalling example of personal dictatorship the modern world has seen. Born near Tiblisi, the son of a Georgian shoemaker, he worked for the Social Democratic Party as a bank robber, and was deported to Siberia in 1913. By 1917 he was editor of *Pravda*, and joined the Politburo (the executive that ran Russia) as Commissar (minister) for Nationalities. He drafted the federal constitution and became Party Secretary in 1922, but Lenin disliked him, warning of a clash if he became leader. Stalin was a good party man building his support among the rank and file so that he was able to outflank the central revolutionary figures who might have been expected to take over when Lenin died. Zinoviev, Kamenev and Stalin took over, and began the process of easing out Trotsky. He was removed from the Politburo (1926), the party (1927) and lastly the country (1929). Stalin then felt strong enough to oust those he had used, and in 1927 Zinoviev and Kamenev were removed and a new group including Bukharin, Rykov, Tomsky and Voroshilov formed. Then in 1930 they were removed from the Politburo. In later trials in 1936 and 1938 they were purged so that eventually of the 15 members of the original Bolshevik government 10 had been executed, and four were dead leaving only Stalin. Between 1932 and 1938 half of his colleagues in the Politburo were removed. Although he held no official office until 1941 Stalin held absolute power through the Politburo and the police state he created.

A8 Socialism in One Country

Both Lenin and Stalin believed in international Communism, but they differed in their approach. Lenin had founded the Comintern (1919), and those in it like Trotsky and Bukharin advocated immediate world revolution. This failed, and Stalin sought to create an atmosphere of co-operation—backing the League of Nations and Popular Front governments (see section 3A5). Behind the scenes Moscow continued to be the centre of world-wide subversion, and many leaders both of post-war Communist governments like Dimitrov or Tito, and of colonial liberation movements like Ho Chi Minh or Jomo Kenyatta were to be found in Moscow in the 1930s. Abroad, the Russian secret service launched a recruiting campaign which in Britain, for example, was successful in securing the services of men like Philby. It was a change of emphasis not of direction. At home Stalin was determined to create a one party state, and to subordinate the whole country to the will of one man. This was contrary to the collective leadership implicit in the partnership of government and party set up by Lenin, but by the end of the 1930s the party was completely identified with the leader. Of the Central Committee of 139 only 41 remained in 1939 while ordinary members were purged, and the party cut by a third in size between 1936 and 1938. The new hierarchy of half a million officials were all of Stalin's creation. With such absolute power Stalin was able to apply full-blooded Communism to agriculture (collectivisation), and industry (the five year plans). The first was carried out with ruthless slaughter and caused an appalling famine, but in the end Russian agriculture was reformed and yields increased. The industrial revolution was carried through with the use of forced labour and the exploitation of workers, but it did provide the basis for the heavy industries necessary for a modern state. In spite of the shock of Hitler's invasion the industrial development of Russia continued during the war years, and was a key reason for its emergence as a world power in 1945.

A9 The Purges of the 1930s

Russian history is in many ways the most obscure branch of modern history because there has been no change of government since 1917. Communist propaganda has spread, and such facts as production figures, or war dead have been deliberately exaggerated. Conversely, defectors who escape are often biased against the regime. Since few government records are available, and the lives of the leaders are shrouded in secrecy the reasons for decisions remain conjectures, and if their records are ever opened they will contain as many surprises as the German documents after the war revealed about another dictatorship. During the 1930s Stalin was regarded by many in the west as a great leader who got to grips with the economic problems of Russia. Sidney and Beatrice Webb travelled to Russia, and subsequently wrote *Soviet Communism: A New Civilisation*. Since then views have changed not least because in 1956 Khrushchev denounced Stalin openly. There can be no doubt that the 1930s and 1940s were a period of continuous barbarity and tyranny made explicit in works like those of Alexander Solzhenitsyn in his *Gulag Archipelago*. During the five year plans at least 10 million workers were forced labourers. One in five of these died because the camps were deliberately kept short of food, heating and clothing. Robert Conquest in *The Great Terror* tried to arrive at numerical totals concluding that 20 million dead was a conservative estimate. Others have gone further. In November 1978 Pierre Dujardin claimed that between 1917 and 1957, including wars, famines and purges, 66 million died. He based this claim on study of the published population figures. Clearly it is stretching a point to blame Stalin for the war deaths but it is also true that even during the war purges continued unabated since Stalin feared an uprising. Whatever the exact figure it casts doubt on the claim that Communism is for the benefit of the ordinary working man.

A10 Men and Methods in the Purges

Explaining such horrors is not an easy task. Clearly Stalin's reversals of policy meant that Trotskyites and others would be likely to oppose him, and once Stalin started liquidating party members a chain reaction set in until he could trust no one. The basic motive was therefore to retain power. Some of his policies like collectivisation of agriculture created opposition, while industrial workers suffered harsh conditions. Collaboration with Germany added many more victims during and after the war. Stalin's own character which drove his wife to suicide in 1932, and his daughter Svetlana to denounce him, was clearly a root cause of the purges. He lived in a twilight world of fear within the Kremlin rarely visiting his people, and as the years passed he relied on a police state to keep him in power. In July 1934 the OGPU, which itself had replaced the Cheka, was fully incorporated within the NKVD or the Ministry of the Interior. Its leaders (Yagoda, Yezhov and Beria) were the most powerful men in Russia after Stalin, and like the SS Police State in Germany the system developed its own momentum. The activities of the terror state fell into several categories. There was the purging of the party and the politburo which involved the famous show trials which began in 1934. After warnings from abroad Stalin became convinced of a military plot and from 1937 there was a purge of the armed services. In the army three out of four generals, three out of four marshals, 12 lieutenant-generals, 60 out of 67 commanders, and 136 out of 199 divisional commanders were killed. In the navy only one senior officer was left alive. In the air force one third of all officers were purged. This fatal weakening of Russian forces in 1938–9 encouraged Hitler to fresh aggressions and Stalin to consider the need for a compromise with Germany. Lastly, there were the ordinary people affected by economic policies, the kulaks killed during 1928–30, and in the subsequent famine estimated at five and a half million, or the twelve million in camps or prison. Stalin's concentration camps numbered 200 grouped in 35 vast areas of Russia.

A11 A Modern Economic Base for Russia

Between 1928 and 1932 agriculture was collectivised; that is brought out of individual ownership into large state farms (kolkhoz and sovkhoz) where production would be according to state quotas, levies being taken, and the rest left for the peasants. Twenty-five million small holdings were eventually grouped into 250,000 larger ones, and surplus peasants (25 million) driven from the land to the cities. This enabled agriculture to become more efficient in certain aspects like wheat growing, and provided the towns with industrial workers and a minimum of food. The five year plans—1928, 1933, 1937, and 1946—were designed to create a heavy industrial base. Thus between 1928 and 1940 iron output rose from 3.3 to 14.9 million tons, steel from 4.3 to 18.3, and coal from 35.5 to 166 million tons. Although the targets were not met the growth was staggering, and could only have been achieved by low wages and long hours unthinkable in the west. Power industries and transport industries were also given attention, and there were a number of spectacular projects like the Baltic–White Sea Canal, and the

Moscow Underground. Small consumer industries like cars were also allowed, but the percentage of GNP going to the workers was small, and got smaller after a rearmament programme was launched to stimulate industry and equal German production figures. Workers did however benefit from some social reforms including universal secondary education and a health service.

B Stalin's last years 1941–53

B1 The Impact of the Great Patriotic War

The early years of the war passed with Stalin and Hitler as allies (see section 2A2). It is probable that Stalin chose this course because he feared Hitler's increasing strength in relation to his own forces, and because territorial gains were likely. Stalin's purges weakened his forces as the Finnish War showed, and he had to embark on modernisation. The political commissars were subordinated to the unit commanders, and ranks and other officer privileges were restored. Timoshenko (Defence Commissar), and Zhukov (Chief of Staff) were responsible for the reforms, but there was no intention of provoking Hitler. Stalin knew of Hitler's intentions, but disregarded the warnings because he feared an uprising by the Russian people after the horrors of the purges if the country was invaded. The war with Hitler may well have saved Stalin because it brought him and the people together against a common enemy. The war was not fought on ideological grounds, but on a simple patriotic appeal. Even the Orthodox Church was treated leniently for a time to rally its support. The Great Patriotic War had several decisive effects on Russia internally. Just as agriculture and industry were recovering they were prostrated by German attack. By 1942 63 per cent of coal, 58 per cent of steel and 38 per cent of wheat production lay in German hands. This compelled a major change in policy. Ten million workers were eventually moved to industrial sites further inland, and from early 1942 production began to recover. The workers again suffered, and personal consumption fell 40 per cent during the war, but the result was a spectacular advance in the Russian economy and technology. Production did not regain pre-war levels, but by any standards it was a remarkable achievement.

The war continued Russia's seemingly endless sufferings. Six million military casualties and 14 million civilian casualties were about one in ten of the population, and the labour force actually fell during the war. Many Russians deserted and joined an army led by Vlasov to fight against Stalin, and the NKVD carried out its usual purges behind the lines. Military law regarded prisoners of the Germans as traitors, and the partisan movement added to the toll of dead on both sides. Labour shortage dictated Stalin's demand at Yalta for all Russians in the west to be returned, and the Allies returned some two million whilst about three million emerged from captivity. These people were relegated to labour camps to help the reconstruction of the economy after the war. Hitler's devastations and cruelties were of course the major burden the Russians had to bear, but the 'scorched earth policy' of the Russian army added to their sufferings. By the end of the war 20 million were homeless and 17,000 towns had been destroyed. The fourth Five Year Plan (1946) set as its target a 50 per cent increase on 1939 figures, and by 1951 it was said these totals had been passed. Reparations, and trading agreements with the satellites helped this remarkable recovery. In agriculture matters were more difficult, and a famine in 1947 brought rioting. Here the trend was to enlarge the collectives which were reduced in number to about 100,000.

B2 Stalin and the Politburo

Until 1941 Stalin had held no official position except secretary of the party; the war enabled him to enhance his position. He became a Marshal of the army, and Chairman of the State Defence Committee. These changes suspended the existing constitution, enhanced Stalin's own role and enabled him to draw on a wider field of expertise. The Soviet government itself began to ossify. The Politburo was more or less the same for ten years with Malenkov, Zhdanov and Stalin forming its centre supported by Molotov, Voroshilov and Khrushchev. These men, distinguished generals like Zhukov and Rokossovsky and Admiral Kuznetsov were responsible for winning the war, and indicated that the government were not merely a set of puppets manipulated by Stalin. But inevitably the purges began again. In 1948 Zhdanov died, and a purge occurred to eliminate his supporters although one at least, Kosygin, was spared. By 1952 when the first party congress since 1939 met Malenkov and Khrushchev were the leading figures. Rumours began of a new purge signalled in January 1953 by the Doctors' Plot. Nine doctors were accused of killing Soviet leaders they had treated, and of being in a Jewish plot. Khrushchev later said a purge to include Molotov, Bulganin and himself was intended, but in March 1953 Stalin died apparently of a heart attack. One of the first tasks of the new government was to execute the head of the secret police, Beria, in order to forestall any revelations or counter-purges.

B3 Stalin's Russia at the end

Stalin's achievements from a Communist point of view were considerable. Abroad, Russia had become the world's second great power. Her efforts in the war had led to the creation of a stupendous military machine, and a massive extension of her borders while her common front with the west had ended her diplomatic isolation, enabling her to extend her influence far beyond her borders. The age old problem of military security was solved by the creation of the satellites. At home Russia was a major industrial power, her agriculture was modernised and her technical progress in some spheres enormous. Yet these achievements were secured at a cost. The country had been largely ruled either by Stalin himself and a few henchmen, or by the succession of secret police organisations. The party had been purged and ruthless economic policies pursued leading to the deaths of millions. The people's standard of living had been kept low. Intellectual absurdities were perpetrated in fields like history and biology at the whim of a tyrant. Events like the enforcement of Lysenko's views in biology, or the attack on composers like Shostakovitch in 1948 revealed in Westwood's

	V. I. Lenin 1917–24 Chairman	
A. I. Rykov 1924–30 (shot 1938) Chairman V. M. Molotov 1930–41 Chairman	J. V. D. Stalin Secretary 1922–41 (full power by 1929) Chairman of the Council of Commissars 1941–53	
	1953	
L. Beria (executed – 1953)	G. Malenkov Chairman Secretary for 10 days	V. M. Molotov Deputy Chairman (until 1957)
N. S. Khrushchev Secretary 1953–58	Chairman 1953–55 N. Bulganin 1955–58 Chairman N. S. Khrushchev Chairman and Secretary 1958–64	
L. I. Brezhnev Secretary 1964–82	Y. Andropov 1982–84 K. V. Chernenko 1984–	A. N. Kosygin Chairman 1964–80

Foreign Ministers

G. Y. Chicherin	1918–30	
M. M. Litvinov	1930–39	
V. M. Molotov	1939–49	
A. Vyshinsky	1949–53	
V. M. Molotov	1953–56	
D. Shepilov	1956–57	
A. Gromyko	1957–present day	

Fig. 8. The rulers of modern Russia

words 'censorship more intolerant and more rigorously applied than in tsarist times'. Moreover, if ordinary Russians had suffered much racial minorities had suffered more. Groups like the Baltic Germans, the Ukrainians and various nomadic peoples of Central Asia had been subjected to severe persecution and over 4 million Jews had been deported within the Soviet Union. Such crimes continued throughout the period even during the war, and in October 1952 Stalin was still stressing the need to toughen policy.

C Nikita Khrushchev (1894–1971)

C1 The Road to Power

The son of a miner, born at Kalinovka near Kursk, Khrushchev started life as a worker, but soon entered the party, and rose to be a member of the Politburo by 1939. During the war he was party chief in the Ukraine, and present at the siege of Stalingrad. At this time he had no doubt that it was 'our beloved leader and teacher Comrade Stalin' who had won the war, and after 1945 he was responsible for purging the Ukraine. In 1948 he came to Moscow after the fall of Zdhanov. While Khrushchev presented a contrasting image to Stalin, and denounced him, it is important to remember his early career as a close supporter of Stalin's. He did not denounce the collectivisation of agriculture or the five year plans, and remained convinced that socialisation of the world would take place during the life of his grandchildren. His policies were never designed to weaken Communism, but to present it in a new light, and to sustain himself in power. Strangely the man who was to be famous for denouncing Stalin's personality cult was to be notorious for his extrovert and world renowned personality. Although Stalin was succeeded by an attempt at collective leadership the period 1953 to 1958 strongly resembles that from 1924 to 1929 since it was a time when by successive stages Khrushchev removed all his opponents.

In February 1955 the Prime Minister, Malenkov, resigned accepting that he was partly to blame for the purge of 1948, and was replaced by Nikolai Bulganin who had worked for the secret police, and risen to be Defence Minister. Molotov sought to save himself by admitting his errors, but in 1956 he was replaced as Foreign Minister by the colourless Shepilov. The denunciation of Stalin that year naturally exposed many politburo members to the charge of being involved in his activities, and strengthened Khrushchev's hand within the party because he stressed the way its Central Committee had been neglected by Stalin. During 1957 in three stages the remaining challengers to Khrushchev's position went. In February Shepilov was replaced by Gromyko as Foreign Minister. While on a visit to Finland Khrushchev heard there was a proposal to restore Molotov and Shepilov. The politburo secured a majority for this change but the Central Committee refused to accept it, and Malenkov, Molotov and Shepilov were retired. To achieve this Khrushchev relied to some extent on Zhukov, but in October he too was removed. In March 1958 Bulganin retired, and Khrushchev became the effective ruler of Russia.

C2 The Party Congress of 1956

Khrushchev made two speeches at the Party Congress of 1956. One concerned the direction of policy. He argued peaceful co-existence was a better way of spreading Communism than direct war, and he accepted there were different roads to socialism in different countries. He denounced past events like the attack on Tito in 1948. He stressed that a process of rehabilitation was taking place for those national Communists who had been purged after 1947, and already some 7,679 had been so treated. This new direction in policy was not weakening Communist enthusiasm, but something made necessary by the failure of Stalin's policies, and growing discontent in Eastern Europe oppressed by defence and reparations burdens for the benefit of Russia. His attack enabled Khrushchev to present Communism with a human face to newly independent countries, and this had to be accompanied by some freedom for Eastern Europe. His visits to India (1955) and Indonesia (1960) indicated the way the world was moving; to a battle, not for European security, but for the hearts and minds of the Third World. Khrushchev was prepared to risk being criticised for not being forceful in pursuit of world revolution in return for the gains of peaceful co-existence.

His second speech was a systematic attack on Stalin which lasted six hours overnight on February 24th–25th. There is evidence the speech was written quickly, but the policy line had been there from the start. As the labour camps declined, and greater numbers of Soviet citizens secured higher education evidence of past misdemeanours and criticism were bound to accumulate. The speech distanced the government from past developments. Khrushchev had been a Stalinist, but his denunciation severed his links with this former period. By speaking to the Central Committee in a frank way, going over the heads of the politburo, Khrushchev appealed to the whole party, and secured backing for policy changes like his economic reforms. Since 1929 Stalin had been like a god to the Russians, and it was necessary to destroy this image. Stalinism was marked down as an error, and Leninism upheld as the true way forward. That party considerations played an important part is shown by the secrecy of the speech (it was smuggled out from Poland and published in June 1956 in the West), and the repeated use made of this line of attack in 1957 and 1961. The politburo was altered so that by 1962 only three were pre-1957 members.

The speeches were perhaps the most important documents ever to come from the Communist Movement. At first they were wrongly regarded as indicating some softening in Soviet attitudes. Clearly there was room for relaxation in censorship, reduction in labour camp inmates, less police power and similar moves. But what remained was no democracy, and Khrushchev showed by his actions in Hungary and Cuba that he was no soft alternative to Stalin. The speech singled out certain aspects of Stalin's rule, in particular his neglect and purging of the party. Stalin's personality cult was attacked, and in 1957 the process of naming places after politicians was ended (e.g. Stalingrad is now called Volgograd). In 1961 Stalin was removed from his place of honour next to Lenin, and buried beside the founder of Cheka in the wall of the Kremlin. Stalin was attacked as an incompetent war leader faced with Hitler's invasion who 'thought this was the end'. The victory, said Khrushchev, was due to the whole Soviet nation—a remark followed by 'tempestuous and prolonged applause'. Lastly, Stalin's increasing isolation from the people was condemned.

C3 De-Stalinisation in Russia

At the top of government de-Stalinisation involved the removal of many leaders appointed in his day. The Politburo was replaced from 1952 to 1965 by a larger body called the Praesidium which had the effect of making Khrushchev's power greater as he was able to bring in new faces. For example, a woman, Yekaterina Furtseva (1957–61) joined, and among the newcomers were Leonid Brezhnev and Alexei Kosygin. Denouncing Stalin naturally brought into question the police state he had created. The NKVD had become a ministry in 1946 (MVD), but in 1960 this was abolished. In its place came the KGB. This was originally part of the NKVD formed in February 1941 for interior security duties. It was separated from the MVD in 1953. This change coincided with more lenient treatment of dissidents, reduction of the labour camp population to two million by 1959 and less power for the military courts, but the moves also reduced the police as a force capable of opposing the government. Many decrees were repealed and trials became more open, but the first signs of dissent brought an extension of the death penalty, and the 'Law Against Parasites' in 1961.

In some ways the most enduring image of the de-Stalinisation era is that of Khrushchev himself. His cheery personality, his heavy drinking and liking for the good life, his jokes and antics were in utter contrast to Stalin. Moreover, he was accessible, and made frequent tours within Russia and abroad. In 1954 he was in China, in 1955 in Yugoslavia, in 1956 in Britain, in 1959 in America and in 1960 in Paris. This again was in direct contrast to Stalin, and made it appear as if a new policy was operating. He even brought his wife, Nina, and his surviving son, Sergei, with him to New York in 1959. Russia became more accessible with the establishment of Intourist, direct flights, cultural agreements with the West and visits to the West by the Bolshoi Ballet and the Red Army Dancers. For a time it looked as if even cultural and intellectual life was to become freer. The head of the Stalinist Writers Union committed suicide in 1956 and novels critical of Stalin began to appear including Solzhenitsyn's *A Day in the Life of Ivan Denisovitch* (1962), and later *Cancer Ward* (1968). Among the poets Yevtushkenko was the most well known abroad, and in 1962 his poems appeared in *Pravda*. An underground press circulating samizdat or photocopied literature began. But this change should not be exaggerated. Pasternak's *Dr Zhivago* had to be published abroad, and he was not allowed to receive the Nobel Prize in 1958. Absolute control was retained over the press with *Pravda* and *Isvestia*, the main papers, having a circulation of only about ten million copies, and over radio and television, education and the arts. Soon there was condemnation of Western decadence, and the revival of the practice of sentencing dissidents as mental patients. The gains were real and indicated an improvement over the days of Stalin, but they were a long way from conceding either democratic government or full human rights.

C4 Khrushchev's New Economic Policy

Khrushchev replaced Stalin's rigid, centralist policies with a period of radical change. His main interest was in agriculture for which he took personal responsibility from 1953 to 1964. The Ministry of Agriculture gradually lost its overall control, and the collectives (36,187) and state farms (12,773) were able to plan on a more individual basis. The centralised control of farm machinery through tractor stations was abolished in 1958. Khrushchev admitted that Soviet agriculture had produced less than in Tsarist times, and set about raising the output of wheat on the Virgin Lands. This undoubtedly increased overall yield, but since some of the development was on unproductive soil there were serious shortages in 1963 and 1965 which forced Russia to import wheat from the West, and this was one factor in discontent with his policies. The income of farmers doubled, and many peasants were able to acquire a small patch to cultivate crops for a local market.

In industry there were too many changes of direction, and overlapping plans to make for complete success. The sixth five year plan (1956–60), the seven year plan (1959–65), and the seventh five year plan (1961–65) overlapped, and caused confusion. There was greater emphasis on consumer goods with wage increases for poorer workers, the end of compulsory levies, better pensions and education and the slow introduction of the seven hour day and the five day week. An attempt was made from 1957 to decentralise planning by abolishing central control and setting up 105 'sovnarkhoz' or local economic councils. Emphasis began to move towards more modern industries like chemicals and plastics. The continued growth of heavy industry still dominated economic plans however. Oil, natural gas and hydro-electric power resources were developed, and industrialisation spread into Central Russia. Kazakhstan became the fastest growing region of the Soviet Union. But the targets were not met, and armaments reduced the overall growth rate. Khrushchev's boast that per capita income would pass America in 1970 was never fulfilled. On the other hand the world was aware of a new industrial power which was very much up to date. In the exploration of space the Russians sent up the first satellite (Sputnik I, 1957), and secured a series of spectacular triumphs with Vostok I (1961), Polyot I (1963) and Voskhod II (1965). In other fields like weaponry and the use of nuclear power the Russians were often in the lead. Khrushchev's period of office was the one in which the rapidly growing Russian population concentrated into towns and Russia ceased to be a predominantly agricultural country, which represented a major achievement.

C5 Khrushchev's Fall from Power

The reasons for the fall of Khrushchev are to some extent guesswork. He was called before the Central Committee in secret session in October 1964, resigned, and was allowed to live quietly in the country until his death. His successors were both men who had joined the Praesidium in 1957 as his supporters. Several deductions can be made. In foreign affairs Russia had suffered serious reverses in Cuba and Berlin where strong statements by Khrushchev had been defied by the West. His policy of separate socialist development had led to the events of 1956, and pressure for reform within the satellite states. It had produced clashes with China which advocated the Stalinist line in some respects, and in 1961 Albania had left the Warsaw Pact. That this most loyal of Stalinist states did so while Krhushchev was courting Tito of Yugoslavia was not pleasing to those in the Praesidium who thought their leader too outspoken, and too prone to changes in policy. Loosening censorship had produced a reaction inside Russia which any dictator would fear, and his economic policies seemed decadently Western. Moreover, the failures to reach the targets combined with the loosening of central control, and the harvest failure of 1963 could be cited as evidence the policies were unsound. Khrushchev had already indicated in March 1963 that there was to be no retreat from socialist realism in art, but this in itself indicated how far matters had gone, and Khrushchev's personal intervention on behalf of Solzhenitsyn identified him clearly with the changes. The return of a more restricted Politburo in 1965, the dour image of the new rulers, the curbing of several policies, escalating armaments particularly in rocketry and the navy and the lengthening terms of office of an aged band of Soviet leaders in the 1970s all suggest that 1964 marked a reaction against Khrushchev's policies in relation to freedom, better living standards and peaceful co-existence.

D Leonid Brezhnev (1906–82) and the Renewal of Cold War

D1 Leonid Brezhnev and the Politburo

The overthrow of Khrushchev showed that in spite of his personality cult he did not wield the absolute power of his predecessor. His successors preserved the appearance of collective leadership. Leonid Brezhnev was Party Secretary, Alexei Kosygin, Prime Minister, and in 1965 the aged Mikoyan was replaced by Podgorny as President. In fact the period saw the steady rise to power of Brezhnev who by the late 1970s was hailed in terms similar to those used of Stalin and Khrushchev, being made a marshal (1976) and given the Lenin Peace and Literature Prizes. In 1965 the unwieldy Praesidium was replaced by a smaller Politburo once more, and during 1967 Brezhnev consolidated his hold. The hard line Stalinist, Shelepin, who was his only rival was placed in charge of the trade union movement until 1975 when he was removed from the Politburo. Suslov on the other hand remained, and until his death in 1981 was loyal to Brezhnev. Three men were his closest supporters: Yuri Andropov, Head of the KGB in 1967, Marshal Grechko, Defence Minister until his death in 1976, and the long serving Andrei Gromyko, the Foreign Minister. All three entered the Politburo in 1973 when Brezhnev finally overcame opposition to detente policies. Kosygin was moved slowly into the background prior to his death in 1980, and when Podgorny died in 1977 Brezhnev took the presidency as well. By 1979 the average age of the Politburo was 70, and few changes were made in Brezhnev's last years.

It is too early to make a final judgement on Brezhnev's years, and as always in Soviet history much assessment is more in the nature of guess-work. Born in 1906 he spent his early years as an engineer and surveyor, and for a time was director of a technical college. He joined the party in 1931, and during the war served as a political/technical officer. In the Stalin era he was a harsh party boss first of Moldavia (1950), and then of Kazakhstan (1954) where he later implemented Khrushchev's disastrous Virgin Lands programme. He was Chairman of the Praesidium by 1960, and Party Secretary from 1964. Brezhnev began by reversing many of Khrushchev's acts quite apart from removing the chosen successor, Koslov. The Virgin Lands and sovnarkhoz policies were ended. Religious persecution in 1964 was followed by renewed persecution of dissidents from 1966, and of Jews when the Jewish department of the KGB was set up in 1971. The prison population rose again after the comparative leniency of the Khrushchev era. Severe laws were passed to curb juvenile delinquency and alcoholism, and the death penalty and internment in mental hospitals played a considerable part in maintaining an increasingly severe regime. Brezhnev went out of his way to praise Andropov and the KGB in December 1977, and celebration of Stalin's birth was allowed in 1979. The Brezhnev Doctrine (1968) reasserted firm control over the satellite nations of Eastern Europe, and the Brezhnev Constitution (1977) preserved virtually unchanged the Stalinist system of 1936 in spite of the usual statements about freedom and democracy. Russian foreign policy will be discussed below, but in outline it combined detente and initiatives on disarmament and ostpolitik with a massive nuclear rearmament programme, major internal military re-organisation and the creation of a world-wide naval presence. Containment was destroyed, and with the aid of subsidised and controlled Cuba, Russia staked out a major presence in South East Asia, the Indian Ocean, Africa and Central America. The invasion of Afghanistan and the influence on Poland are among the most recent examples of the Cold War activities of Russia under Brezhnev. That his successor should be the Head of the KGB, a successor of Yagoda and Beria, indicates there is no change of policy as yet.

D2 The Changing Face of Communism

During the 1960s it appeared as if the monolithic Communism of the Iron Curtain days was breaking down. In foreign policy 'detente' and 'convergence' seemed to suggest a meeting of minds in a spirit of compromise. The settlement of many outstanding European issues by ostpolitik (admittedly in a direction favourable to Russia) was followed by the Treaty of Helsinki (1975), and this in turn by increased action by various groups of dissidents inside the Soviet bloc. Whereas the Communist Congress of 1960 stressed total unity that of 1969 spoke differently saying 'there is no leading centre'. As the number of Communist countries substantially increased in the 1970s complete control from Moscow was physically impossible anyway. In Western Europe the majority of Communist Parties came to accept what was known as Eurocommunism: Communism paying regard to national interests, and not toeing the Moscow line. This was put forward most effectively by Berlinguer in Italy and Marchais in France, and Communists now share in the government of France for the first time since 1948. These parties condemned Russian intervention in Czechoslovakia in 1968 and Poland in 1981. Moreover, in the satellite states Rumania has pursued a successful policy of resisting Russian pressure firstly removing troops, and then refusing to help in Czechoslovakia, or rearm. In Poland the concessions to Roman Catholics and unions went too far, but the response of a people who have known no real democracy since 1926 indicated how little Communism means to many in the Soviet empire. After attempts to bring China round military clashes in 1969 marked a definite break, and during the 1970s in places like Angola the two Communist powers competed with each other. All these changes affected Brezhnev's regime: emphasis on consumer industries and welfare, some relaxation of the police state, lip service to human rights and national movements occurred. But the unanimous support of Communist states for Russia at UNO, the spreading of Comecon worldwide, the ubiquity of Cuban and KGB influence and Soviet forces do not point to a weakening of Russian world power. Fifteen per cent of the budget still goes on military spending, and Russian opportunism continues unabated.

D3 Opposition to the Soviet Regime

Russia so far has proved to be the most successful dictatorship the world has yet seen; it holds the record for exterminating its enemies and own people as a result. Yet opposition exists in many forms. Under Khrushchev a determined effort was made to crush the churches (30 million Orthodox Christians are claimed in Russia). A law in 1962 forbade all private worship, and the number of churches was cut from 17,500 to 10,000, but the campaign failed. In 1965 an amnesty was granted to imprisoned Baptists combined with a new law against spreading Bibles and other religious literature. There are now about 11,000 churches in the country. Stalin had proposed to move all Russia's Jews to Kazakhstan, and banned all Jewish works. In fact, during the 1970s up to 10 per cent of Russian Jews were allowed to leave, and their plight aroused world-wide opposition. In 1980 the ban on Jewish writing was lifted, but many Jews have become involved with dissident movements.

Under Stalin the most ruthless policy was pursued against national minorities within the USSR. Massacres of German, Poles and Ukrainians, and mass deportations occurred, but this policy was condemned by Khrushchev in 1956, and by 1967 those that were still alive were allowed to return. Russia is in theory a federal country with 15 republics, 20 autonomous republics, 8 autonomous regions and 10 national areas. In 1979 of 262 million Soviet citizens, 157 million (52 per cent) were Russians, while the rest consisted of nearly 130 racial and linguistic groups. These include, for example, 40 million Ukrainians with a long tradition of independence. But it is in Central Asia that Russia faces her most serious difficulty. Poverty has led to birth control policies, but these have been largely ignored by the Kazakhs, Kirghiz and Uzbeks of Central Asia. By the year 2000 Muslim peoples will make up 25 per cent of the population of the USSR. There have been revolts—one in Kazakhstan in 1945, for example—and the subject peoples can show their teeth against the central government. An attempt in 1978 to phase out the Georgian language had to be rescinded after passive resistance. Kazakhstan has become the centre of massive industrial development while the Chinese threat has substantially increased Russian troop concentrations there: it was made a separate military command in 1969. Training camps for overseas national groups have been sited there as brown-skinned Asian Russians have been frequently used in the Third World. But the attempt to suppress the Muslim faith in the 1960s which closed all but 400 mosques for a time, and the passions unleashed in the Middle East by Muslim revival present a threat to Russia. Some have suggested that the campaign in Afghanistan is as much for home consumption as anything else.

The dissidents whose names the West has become familiar with in recent years are of three kinds: those demanding a return to 'pure' Marxism attacking the bureaucratic Russian state, Christian and Jewish groups demanding freedom to worship, and liberal groups demanding human rights. In spite of Helsinki Brezhnev's regime pursued dissidents relentlessly, and at the time of writing only Medvedev is at all active. Trouble began with the arrest of Daniel and Sinyavsky in 1966, and Ginzberg in 1967. Solzhenitsyn launched a protest against this in 1967 but by 1974 was forced into exile. In 1968 Sakharov took up the struggle advocating 'convergence', but in 1980 he was exiled to Gorky. In 1972 Krasin and Yakir were arrested with 200 others in an attempt to curb the underground press or samizdat. In 1976, the year after Helsinki, Amalrik was expelled, and Bukovsky exchanged for a Chilean Communist. The monitoring group set up that year was soon suppressed when in 1977 Andropov denounced them, and Orlov, Ginzberg and Scharansky were arrested and exiled.

D4 The Slackening Economy

During the 1960s the Soviet economy began to show some signs of weakening brought about primarily by the failure of Soviet economic policies. The endless plans announced targets which were not attained because of the top heavy bureaucracy, regimented and ill-educated labour force, and inefficient party management. This was criticised internally by such writers as Nemchinov in the 1960s, but at first Brezhnev was interested only in reversing Khrushchev's changes, and the 1965–70 Plan did not go well ending with serious harvest failure in 1969. The riots in Poland that year convinced Brezhnev that concessions must be made to consumer demands and practical economics, and the 1971–6 plan placed strong emphasis on consumer goods for the first time. Khrushchev's plant committees were extended in the form of industrial associations to try to get decisions at a local level. Lack of technical advance (there are only 17 million telephones in Russia), shortage of skilled labour and heavy defence costs continued to stifle progress. The 1980 targets were the lowest since 1945 and they were not attained. This situation was one reason for Russian support for detente. Her world trading interests expanded, Western credits and trade deals were made, and above all technical agreements were of real benefit particularly those with France (1965), Britain (1970) and America (1973). In agriculture too the Soviet economy seemed to be faltering. Harvests in 1974–5 and 1979 were particularly bad providing 20 per cent less than Russia needed; hence the grain agreements with countries like America and Argentina. Even Lenin's New Economic Policy was revived to some extent. The peasants were included in the state security system in 1964, and allowed to take on small allotments. Although these make up only one per cent of the cultivable area they produced 25 per cent of agricultural output. Russia is of course immensely powerful, but like all military dictatorships guns before butter will have its limits. Her Western contacts have also produced a foreign debt of 17.2 million dollars. Gross National Product (GNP) growth fell from 3 per cent to 2 per cent per annum in the early 1980s. The outlook for the Russian economy is therefore to say the least, uncertain.

E The Fall of the Iron Curtain 1944–9

E1 The Pattern of Development

In 1939 Russia was the only Communist state in Europe but by 1949 there were nine others. Two were occupation zones where the Russians entered as Allies in 1945. Already their German zone had been turned into the German Democratic Republic although the Austrian zone, milked dry by reparations, was to become part of neutral Austria in 1955. As the Red Army advanced into Europe it brought liberation from years of right wing government, fascist collaboration and unstable democracy. To many people in Eastern Europe 1944–5 were truly 'liberation' years, and it should not be forgotten that the choice was not between former democracy and dictatorship, but between reaction and reform. Poland, Czechoslovakia, Hungary, Rumania, Bulgaria and Albania constituted the main bloc of Soviet satellites occupied by a Russian army, for which they paid through subordination to Moscow, politically and economically. Only Finland in the far north, compelled to adopt neutrality, and Greece, rescued by the British army and American aid, remained outside the Iron Curtain until in 1948 Tito's Yugoslavia was expelled from the Cominform.

A common pattern of development affected all these states. The course of the Soviet armies was directed by the nature of German resistance, but the intention of Stalin was to retain control over as much land as possible— to guard against another 1918 or 1941, to reap a just reward for Russian sacrifices and to spread socialism in countries where for many years Communist sabotage and union activities had come to nothing. At first Stalin made two concessions: he promised free elections, and he allowed coalitions to take office. But in the new governments, defence and interior ministries went to Communists, and before long the peasant parties and the socialists were eliminated. At first Stalin relied on nationals of the countries concerned trained in Moscow. Men like Bierut in Poland or Dimitrov in Bulgaria were Communists first and nationalists second, and once in power they adopted the whole apparatus of Stalin's Russia as well as the reforms in land and industry that the people wanted. Monarchies were abolished, church leaders forced into exile, elections rigged and exclusively Communist governments formed. Trials of fascist collaborators were widened to include all manner of politicians who were either shot or deported to Russia. Censorship and a secret police completed the subjugation of the countries concerned. But even this did not satisfy Stalin. Tito showed that a nationally minded Communist might well defy the Moscow line. Therefore purges of the kind the Nazis had specialised in began once more: show trials, torture, mass executions of the very people who had

Country	Russian occupation	Fully communist	Leaders of take overs	Fate	Later resistance to Russia
Estonia, Latvia and Lithuania	1940	1941			1980 strike in Estonia reported
Poland	1944	1947	Boleslaw Bierut Josef Cyrankiewicz	(Retired 1954) (Replaced by Gomulka 1956)	1953, 1956, 1970, 1976, 1980, 1982
East Germany (GDR)	1945	1949	Wilhelm Pieck Otto Grotewohl	(Replaced by Ulbricht, 1954)	1953 flight to West of two million Germans 80 died at Berlin wall
Czechoslovakia	1945 (temporarily)	1948	Klement Gottwald Zdenek Fierlinger Rudolf Slansky	(d. 1953) Executed 1952	1968 Charter 77 dissidents
Hungary	1944	1948	Erno Gero Matyas Rakosi Laslo Rajk	Replaced in 1956 Executed 1949	1956 revolution
Rumania	1944	1948	Anna Pauker Gheorghiu Dej	Removed 1952 (d. 1965)	1968 no military co-operation with Russia
Yugoslavia	1945	1945	Josif Tito Milovan Djilas	(d. 1980) Removed 1954	1948 expelled from Cominform
Bulgaria	1945	1947	Georgi Dimitrov Traicho Kostov	Died in Moscow 1950 Executed 1949	
Albania	—	1946	Erva Hoxha Koki Xoxe	Executed 1949	Left Comecon and Warsaw Pact 1961–78

Fig. 9. The communist states of Eastern Europe.

brought about the revolutions led to their replacement by men solely devoted to Stalin, like Ulbricht in East Germany, or Rakosi in Hungary. During the 1950s this monolithic structure was to be challenged, but not essentially altered, and for over 20 years East Europe became a forbidden land, penetrated by spies, and revealed by defectors and refugees.

E2 The Three Exceptions: Austria, Finland and Greece

Russia made great difficulties about the Allies asserting their rights, but by October occupation of Austria on lines similar to Germany had begun. Austria was useful to the Russians as a lucrative source of reparations, as a staging post for the return of prisoners of war and as a military wedge between Czechoslovakia and Yugoslavia. The government established under Karl Renner was a socialist one, but Russia was unwilling to concede independence. It was not until the rule of his successor, Julius Raab (1953–61) that Russia accepted an independent neutral Austria since by that time East Germany secured her control of Czechoslovakia, and Yugoslavia was no longer of concern.

Finland had lost considerable territory to Russia, and in 1946 Mannerheim the President who had co-operated with Germany resigned. A left wing government containing Communists was elected, and Russia was prepared to accept neutrality in a treaty in 1948. Refusal to allow Finland to apply for Marshall Aid led to considerable Communist losses in the election of 1948, but attempts by Communists to foment industrial trouble failed, and the government settled down as a coalition of Social Democrats and Agrarians.

Greece (see section 3C4) was a different matter. The Greek Communist Party (EAM) led by Veloukhiotis, a veteran of the Spanish Civil War, formed an army (ELAS) in April 1942. Moderates like Colonel Zervas formed a second resistance army (EDES) a few months later. In March 1944 the Communists set up a rival government to that of George II, and as the Germans withdrew sought to seize power. When they were ordered to disband riots broke out, and British troops were despatched to Greece (see section 2B3). Churchill installed Archbishop Damaskinos as Regent, and urged the return of the King after a plebiscite. The Communists made peace at Varkiza in February 1945.

Peace did not last since Communists in Yugoslavia, Albania and Bulgaria supplied the guerillas. Elections in 1946 which returned a pro-monarchist government under Tsaldaris, and a plebiscite followed by the return of George II convinced them they must act. Fighting broke out, and in August Markos Vaphiadis took command of a renewed campaign. The British could no longer sustain the military effort, and handed over to America although retaining troops there until 1948. ELAS launched a full scale civil war before the arrival of the Americans in August 1947, but a joint American–Greek General Staff was set up under General Van Fleet. The Americans began the economic reorganisation of the country, and by mid 1948 about £200 million had been spent in Greece. Tito cut off aid, and the guerillas found themselves in difficulties. In November 1948 Markos was replaced by Nikos Zakhariadis, but within a year the Communists had been defeated.

E3 The Two Hardliners: Albania and Bulgaria

Enva Hoxha was the guerilla leader in Albania against the Italians and Germans, and not surprisingly emerged as the ruler in November 1945. The shock of Tito's defection in 1948 led to a purge in 1949 involving the execution of Koki Xoxe, the Deputy Prime Minister, and numerous other party members. Albanian political history simply became a record of the Communist Party's activities until 1961. Then Khrushchev's liberalising moves proved too much for the hardline Stalinists of Albania, and a diplomatic break occurred followed by the opening of relations with China in 1964. Albania left Comecon in 1961, and the Warsaw Pact in 1968.

Bulgaria had been a notoriously reactionary country under Boris III (1918–43), and sided openly with Hitler to obtain territory from Yugoslavia and Greece. An attempted Communist rising in 1923 had been put down with at least 10,000 killed, and Georgi Dimitrov, the leader, fled to Moscow. He was arrested in 1933 in connection with the Reichstag Fire, was acquitted, and returned to Moscow where he was Secretary of the Comintern. King Boris died suddenly after a visit to Hitler, and was succeeded by Simeon II, and a Regency under Prince Cyril. As soon as Russia occupied the country a government was set up under Georgiev, and elections held in November 1945 for a Fatherland Front made up of the major parties, but under the control of Dimitrov who arrived that month. A purge of right-wingers accounted for several thousand lives, and forced Prince Cyril to flee. In September 1946 92 per cent voted against the monarchy, and Bulgaria became a republic. More elections were held, and the Communists emerged as victors with Dimitrov as Prime Minister. During 1947 Petkov and his Peasant Party were eliminated, and the country became Communist. Titoism produced the inevitable purge and the execution of Kostov, the deputy prime minister in 1949. A few months later Dimitrov died in Moscow, and was succeeded by Kolarov, the first of several hardline Communist rulers.

E4 The Fate of Poland

The war had begun with a partition of Poland (see section 2A2), and Stalin was determined to keep his gains, and add to them. Russian security demanded Poland no longer exercise the independent role it had played between the wars with its vigorous anti-Bolshevik line. The war had created two Polish governments (see section 2B3); one based in London the other set up in Moscow and installed at Lublin. The Poles had plenty of grievances against Russia—the Katyn Massacre, the failure of Stalin to help the Warsaw Rising, and the decision to give Poland land full of Germans in the West as compensation for the loss of territory to Russia. Throughout the war the borders of Poland had been an issue between the Big Three (see section 2B3), but at Yalta the West agreed to their being moved and interest focused on the future Polish government. The Allies secured agreement from Stalin that if the two governments were united free elections would be held, and supervised by a Three Power Commission. A new joint government was formed in July 1945 with 14 out of 21 posts in Communist hands, and during 1946 a programme of nationalisation was carried out.

Mikolajczyk's party was subjected to intimidation before the election held in January 1947 which was a massive Communist victory.

Bierut became President and Cyrankiewicz Prime Minister, and in October 1947 Mikolajczyk fled to London. The government pressed forward the reconstruction of the country with three and six year plans which were carried out by Hilary Minc, Ministry of Industry and Trade. The government denounced the Concordat with the Catholic Church, and began an era of persecution culminating in the confiscation of church lands in 1950, and the imprisonment of Cardinal Wyshinski. There were still non-Communists in the government, but they were slowly removed. By December 1948 the Socialist Party, for example, was merged with the Communist Party. Using the charge of Titoism, Stalin forced the resignation of the secretary of the party, Wladislaw Gomulka, and purged the party. Poland signed a trade agreement with Russia, joined Comecon and allowed Marshal Rokossovsky to reorganise the Polish army along Soviet lines. By 1950 it was clear that an independent Poland was no more.

E5 An Interlude of Freedom: Czechoslovakia

Czechoslovakia was ruled by the Nazis from 1938 to 1945, and ruthlessly exploited for economic purposes. The death of Heydrich at the hands of Czech resistance fighters, and the awful fate of Lidice (1942) were but two episodes in a catalogue of horror. As in the case of Poland the advance of the Russians stimulated a rising; this time among the Slovaks who had been ruled by Tiso, a puppet of Hitler. As in the case of Poland Russia rendered no help to this rising. Similarly the Allies advancing from the West knew of a rising in Prague, but halted on the agreed lines to allow Russia to occupy the country. Dr Benes had fled to London but angry with the British for not repudiating Munich, he had made agreements with Russia. He entered with the Russian forces and set up a government in April 1945. Benes appointed Fierlinger, Prime Minister of a 'National Front' government, and the Russians were willing to withdraw which they did by December 1945. The new government had shown itself a willing friend of Russia in ceding Ruthenia, expelling the Sudeten Germans and carrying out a purge of collaborators. Land reform and nationalisation were initiated.

In the election of May 1946, which was free, the Communists won 114 seats out of 300, and so a new government with more Communist members under Klement Gottwald was formed. It was a broadly based government including Masaryk as Foreign Minister, but the Interior and Information Ministries were in Communist hands. In July 1947 Czechoslovakia was forced by Russia to refuse Marshall Aid, and this caused the moderate elements in the government to rally. Fearing loss of power the Communist Minister of the Interior dismissed eight non-Communist police chiefs. The ministers of Benes's party then resigned. Communists seized other party headquarters in Prague, and a predominantly Communist government was set up in February 1948. In March Masaryk was killed or committed suicide, and the non-Communist ministers were removed. When Benes resigned Gottwald became President, and a Communist regime came into being. During 1949 Church resistance led by Cardinal Beran was overcome, and in 1950 trials purged the party while the army was reorganised with widespread dismissals. The trials continued under the guise of purging 'Titoists' until 1952 when Rudolf Slansky and ten others were executed.

E6 By the Blue Danube: Hungary and Rumania

Hungary had been a supporter of Hitler (see section 2A2), until February 1945. A provisional government was established under General Miklos containing only two Communists (one of which was the Minister of Agriculture, Imre Nagy). Western supervision of elections was easier, and when they were held in November 1945 the Smallholders Party secured a majority. In early 1946 Tildy became President, and Ferenc Nagy, Prime Minister, both members of the Smallholders Party. The government contained the Communist leader, Matyas Rakosi as Vice Prime Minister, and a Communist became Minister of the Interior. The Russians sent Marshal Voroshilov to represent them on the Allied Commission, and he clearly helped the Communists to increase their power. During 1947 the Secretary of the Smallholders, Kovacs, and the Prime Minister, Nagy, were accused of conspiracy against the state. Nagy was out of the country, and was advised not to return. A fresh election in August 1947 about which the Allies protested resulted in the Communists becoming the largest party although in a cabinet of 15 only 5 were Communists. But the Moscow Communists like Gero and Rakosi were well organised, and Laslo Rajk, the Interior Minister, suppressed the opposition parties setting up AVH as the secret police. By late 1948 the Communists completely controlled the government, although it was not until June 1950 that the last non-Communist ministers left it. During 1949 came the inevitable Titoist purge which led to the execution of Rajk and many others. The Catholic Church opposed these moves, but was forced to give in. Cardinal Mindszenty fled to the American embassy (1949) and Archbishop Groesz was imprisoned.

King Michael of Rumania had changed sides in August 1944 in an effort to survive, and Rumania had fought on the Russian side losing 150,000 men. But collaboration with Hitler had taken place, and it was only a matter of time before Russia (having seized territory) proceeded to install itself in power by the usual means. The National Democratic Front government of Petru Groza formed in March 1945 contained only three Communists including, however, the inevitable Interior Ministry. Allied observers complained about Communist tactics, and in January 1946 the government was broadened, but to little avail. Communists like Anna Pauker, and Gheorghiu-Dej, returned from Moscow, and during 1947 they decided to act. Michael was planning his marriage, and any demonstration of support could not be allowed. The Communists accused Maniu, the Peasant Party leader of treason, and purges began which led to the collapse of the party. In December Michael abdicated, and during 1948 a full Communist government came into being followed by the predictable purges. Maniu and Patrascanu were tried, and the latter executed much later in 1954. In 1952 Anna Pauker was removed. Gheorghiu-Dej's government was firmly in the Russian camp.

F Josif Tito 1892–1980

F1 Comintern Agent and Partisan Leader

Born in the old Austro–Hungarian empire Tito spent his early life in various jobs until he joined the army in 1914. Captured by the Russians, he experienced the Bolshevik Revolution first-hand and by the time he was repatriated in 1920 was a Communist. Working in the shipyards he became an active party worker later moving to Zagreb where he joined the Metal Workers Union. Imprisoned from 1924 to 1929 he became a prominent party member—adopting 'Tito' as his name in 1934—and in 1937 became the leader of the party. When Yugoslavia was seized by Germany, and partitioned it was Tito who organised the only truly national resistance movement. He fought against the reactionary Chetnik partisans, the Ustase wanting Croatian independence, and the armed forces of the three occupying powers tying down 28 divisions. As early as May 1943 Britain began to send him aid, and Churchill agreed that he should represent the country after the war. At Moscow in December 1944 Yugoslavia was to be 50–50 Western and Russian influenced, but Tito was always conscious that it was he, not the Russians, who liberated Belgrade in October 1944. In the war 1.7 million were killed, making Yugoslavia second only to Poland in her sufferings, and it was unlikely that Tito would tamely surrender since he had an army of 300,000, and was on good terms with Western as well as Soviet leaders.

F2 The Seizure of Power

In 1943 Tito set up his Committee of National Liberation which was to form the basis of a government. Agreement was reached with the exiled government in London, but Tito was determined to share power with no one. Under Rancovic a secret police (UDBA) was formed to destroy the remnants of the Chetnik and Ustase parties. Mihailovic was executed in July 1946. The leaders of the Peasant Party—Archbishop Stepinac and Dr Jovanovic—were imprisoned. The Croatian Separatist movement still operates abroad as a terrorist group after its expulsion from the country. King Peter II was forced to remain in exile, elections with little that was free about them were held in November 1945, and a republic proclaimed the same month.

At this juncture Tito was still a loyal Stalinist. He sent aid to the Communist guerillas in Greece, and refused to leave Trieste which became a flashpoint in the Cold War. During 1946 he sought aid from Moscow, and in 1947 joined the Cominform. Communist economic policies were adopted including nationalisation of industry, land and banks, and joint companies were set up with Russia for aircraft and shipping. In April 1947 a Five Year Plan was announced by Velebit and Zutjovic. The men round Tito were all Moscow trained Communists. Djilas, chief of party affairs and deputy prime minister, had fought in the Spanish Civil War, and headed Montenegrin resistance after 1941. General Rankovic, had gone to Moscow in 1939, and was Minister of the Interior from 1946. Outwardly Yugoslavia seemed no different from any other satellite country.

F3 The Break with the Cominform 1948

In March 1948 Russia withdrew her military and technical advisers from the country, and it became clear that things were not as they should be between Belgrade and Moscow. For this there were a series of reasons, domestic and international. Russian aid to Yugoslavia had been small in quantity, and Velebit had long complained of this (Stalin denounced him later as an English spy). The joint companies like Juspad seemed increasingly to be for the benefit of Moscow. Tito decided to slow down collectivisation, and in May 1948 to remove Zutjovic as economics minister. This brought accusations of deviationism from Moscow while in Yugoslavia itself attacks were made on the conduct of the Soviet forces and advisers. Tito felt Stalin no longer supported him in either Greece or Trieste, and he turned to his fellow Balkan Communists. Dimitrov of Bulgaria visited Belgrade in 1947, and there was talk about a Balkan Alliance. When Russia denounced this Dimitrov retreated, but Tito was furious. While a series of letters passed between the two leaders Stalin continued to heap insults on Tito. A Cominform meeting was shifted from Belgrade to Prague, and Tito was informed his country was actually freed by the Soviet Union. In May 1948 Tito was expelled from the Cominform, and it was clear Stalin was using pressure to bring him down. Tito acted swiftly. Jovanovic, the Army Chief of Staff, was shot after returning from Moscow. Zutjovic died in prison, and was the only key minister opposed to Tito. During 1948 over 14,000 people were arrested to forestall any Stalinist take-over. Stalin tried economic coercion cutting off his quarter of Yugoslavia's trade, and causing the abandonment of the Five Year Plan. In other satellite countries accusations of 'Titoism' followed by show trials and purges were designed to bring pressure to bear on those countries to take action, and hundreds of border provocations were offered to Yugoslavia. 'I will shake my little finger, and there will be no more Tito,' said Stalin, but Tito remained in power. To denounce him as a Trotskyite, a British agent, and 'Turkish and terroristic' was absurd, and Tito had substantial armed forces, and contacts with the West. Occupied in Czechoslovakia and with the Berlin Blockade Stalin could not risk armed intervention, and without it Tito was bound to triumph.

F4 Fifty–Fifty Communism

Tito was probably always more of a nationalist and pragmatic Serbian politician than a dedicated Communist, and after 1948 Yugoslavia developed along lines which were essentially those of a mixed economy. Profit sharing in industry, and small private firms were permitted. Some land was returned to the peasants. Wage differentials, and some emphasis on consumer industries for the benefit of workers were allowed. Yugoslavia was the first Communist country to develop a tourist industry. Centralisation was broken down, and when Rankovic opposed this trend he was removed from power. In political matters Tito was less liberal. His own position was that of a dictator, fond of good living and fine uniforms, and with five residences. There was only one party, and no deviations were allowed therein. Djilas was removed for criticising the leader, and advocating a party system, although by 1969 rejection of official party candidates by local parties were allowed. Tito's main problem lay with the separatist tendencies in the country. In 1963 an essentially federal constitution was introduced with six local republics, and this was further developed in 1968. Tito's death in 1980 proved that the system he created was durable, and apart from the Croat separatists little opposition to the present system now exists.

F5 A Non-Aligned State

After 1948 Yugoslavia was not behind the Iron Curtain. Tito gave up supporting the Greek terrorists, and in 1954 settled for the partition of Trieste. He was prepared to look to both West and East. In 1951 came the first agreement for American aid followed by others. Ties with Britain were particularly close, and in 1953 Tito visited Churchill, and received assurances of support. In 1954 a 20 year pact with Turkey and Greece was signed for mutual co-operation. Russia had to respond to this situation, and as early as June 1953 was asking for normal relations to be restored. In May 1955 Khrushchev visited the country, and early in 1956 came an economic agreement. In June Tito went to Moscow. In 1957 came a full economic agreement. Tito thus succeeded in obtaining aid from both sides in the Cold War. Moreover, this enabled him to support the new nations urging them to be non-aligned. He established good relations with Nasser of Egypt, and encouraged him to adopt socialist policies. Tito's example encouraged other satellites to seek modifications of the Moscow dictatorship, by opening up limited relations with the West.

G Development and Dissent in Eastern Europe

G1 Pattern of Change

Control of Eastern Europe by Russia was based on the Soviet army, and the creation of pro-Moscow regimes and it was co-ordinated through three bodies. In September 1947 Cominform was created to replace the old Comintern co-ordinating policies, and propaganda. Its meetings provided the means for forcing 'Titoists' or other dissidents into line. From the first Russia had insisted on linking the economies of the Eastern bloc together partly by exploitation, and partly by favourable trading agreements. In January 1949 Comecon was created to formalise this trading pattern, and in 1964 a Bank for Socialist Countries was added. The two organisations did not, however, have the same success in stimulating economic development as their parallel bodies in Western Europe. Military control existed after 1944, and was enhanced by the creation of an East Germany Army after 1952. In May 1955 the Warsaw Pact was set up to co-ordinate military policies. In some ways this was rendered more vital as Soviet troops left Austria and even Rumania, and its success in subduing Hungary or Czechoslovakia was amply demonstrated. While putting forward disarmament proposals Russia retained a superiority over the West in conventional forces in the Warsaw Pact area. In order to retain their hold the Russians under Stalin used purges and show trials. 'Titoism' was merely an excuse, as 'Trotskyism' had been, to eliminate those the regime disliked. From 1948 to 1952 there were a series of purges that removed about a quarter of all party members in the Eastern bloc. In Poland Gomulka was expelled from the party and imprisoned in 1951. In East Germany men like Merker (1950) and Dahlen (1953) were imprisoned. In Czechoslovakia purges in 1951–2 led to the execution of Slansky. In Hungary Rajk who had played a leading part in establishing Communism was executed, and a purge followed. A similar pattern occurred in the Balkan satellite states.

G2 The Tide of Discontent

Such pressure could not be kept up for ever. The demands made for rearmament during the Korean War imposed further pressure on the Eastern bloc, where living standards fell. Stalin's death, and still more, the decline of KGB power, encouraged the subject peoples to make a move. In 1953 there were disturbances in Czechoslovakia round Pilsen. In East Germany Grotewohl's regime raised production norms by 10 per cent, and increased hours while reducing wages. June 1953 saw an uprising in East Berlin as a prelude to a general strike, and disturbances at 300 places in the country. 30,000 Russian troops soon restored order, but the consequences were grim. 300,000 fled from East Germany that year alone even if a Ten Point Plan in August made concessions to the workers. Grotewohl's successor, Ulbricht (1954) was the most slavish supporter of Russian domination. Khrushchev's open reconciliation with Tito, and the speeches at the 20th Party Congress were bound to revive hopes of change particularly after the Cominform was abolished in 1956. In many countries those executed were given state funerals, and hailed once more as Communist heroes. Thousands of political prisoners were released, and the powers of the various secret police forces curbed.

In Poland the release of 30,000 prisoners, including Gomulka, threatened the regime. In June 1956 after the demands of a workers' delegation had been rejected there was a rising in Poznan. The government agreed to repay some 'unjust' taxation, and the economic ministers were sacked. In October 1956 Rokossovsky was dismissed, and Gomulka became Party Secretary. Cardinal Wyshinski was released. Trials of workers accused over the June Riots were suspended. This forced Khrushchev to act, and he flew to Warsaw with several members of the Politburo. Soviet troops were involved in clashes with Poles at places like Leignitz, but when Khrushchev was convinced Gomulka did not intend either liberalism or withdrawal from the Warsaw Pact he agreed that Soviet troops should return to barracks throughout the country, and an economic agreement formally acknowledged the equality of Poland with Russia as an independent nation.

G3 The Hungarian Rising 1956

It had taken years even to establish a fully Communist regime under Rakosi in Hungary. The AVH held over 200,000 in concentration camps. But when living standards began to fall discontent soon mushroomed, and in Hungary it was not confined to the peasantry. In Budapest and the West the Petofi Circle of students also opposed the regime adding political demands to the economic grievances of the many. Khrushchev decided to bend a little, and Rakosi was replaced by Gero in July 1956 to forestall events similar to those in Poland. In October Imre Nagy returned, and Gero was replaced by Janos Kadar who was thought to be a supporter of change. Western Hungary rose in revolt, and attempts by AVH to hit back met with fierce resistance. A National Liberation Committee was formed at Gyoer, and broadcast to the West for help. Nagy persuaded the Russians to withdraw their troops (October 28th), and for a few days it seemed as if the revolt had succeeded. Army units under Maleter deserted, the AVH was destroyed, proposals for a multi-party system and for leaving the Warsaw Pact were put forward, and on November 1st Nagy appealed to the United Nations and the Western powers for help.

In spite of much talk of the 'roll back' of Communism nothing was done to help Hungary. UNO passed two resolutions condemning Russia, but her mission was refused access to the country. America was in the midst of Eisenhower's election campaign, and did nothing. Britain and France were in the midst of invading Egypt, and did nothing. In spite of all the talk of resisting Communism it seemed as if containment meant acceptance of it also. On November 4th Russia counter-attacked in Budapest and Western Hungary, and for a week savage warfare with only one possible conclusion raged in the country. Some 20,000 died in the capital alone, and perhaps another 10,000 outside. 140,000 refugees fled the country. Maleter was seized under a flag of truce, and Nagy decoyed from the Yugoslav embassy. Both were shot in Rumania in 1958. Kadar deserted to the Russian side, and organised the purges that followed. In March 1957 he signed a direct agreement for economic co-operation with Russia, and by 1964 Khrushchev felt safe enough to visit the country.

G4 Ideological Division in Eastern Europe

Brutal repression was the initial Soviet reaction to events in Eastern Europe, but change could not be simply halted in its tracks. In East Germany the Ten Point Plan was followed by economic decentralisation. In Hungary Gero and Rakosi were later removed (1962), and Kadar adopted more consumer orientated policies in 1968 (NEM). Even in Bulgaria the hardline Stalinist, Chervenkov, was replaced in 1956, and some decentralisation was adopted. Economic policies did vary from satellite to satellite. Whereas in Poland and Bulgaria, for example, peasants retained a good deal of land in their own hands collectivisation was complete in Rumania by 1962. Degrees of contact with the West varied with Rumania leading the way with its tourist industry to be followed by Bulgaria. East Germany remained even more shut off after the building of the Berlin Wall. Such variety ran counter to the cosy experience of total uniformity under Stalin, and contributed to the ideological dispute that broke out between Russia and China in the 1960s. These differences led to a switch in policy. As late as February 1963 Comecon denounced economic variation in socialist economies, but by April 1964 Khrushchev was referring to the equality of all Communist parties, and various countries began to take advantage of this. In Rumania Ceausescu came to office in 1965, and seemed determined to pursue a Titoist line successfully. He refused to send troops to invade Czechoslovakia in 1968, and joined in criticism of Russia at a conference in June 1969.

G5 The Limits of Liberty: Czechoslovakia 1968

For many years after the 1950s Czechoslovakia had proved a model Communist state, but its position so close to the West, and the increasing contacts with West Germany through trade encouraged the Czechs to believe that the right of deviation from the Communist line extended to human rights. As early as October 1967 there were student demonstrations, and when Novotny was replaced by Dubcek in January 1968 it was hoped to carry the process further. Dubcek and three others—Svoboda, Cernik, and Smirkovsky—announced in April 1968 a new programme including decentralisation, workers rights and human rights. It was clear that 'revisionist' economic policies were to be implemented. None of these proposals was drastic, and did not apparently threaten Russia, but from the first Brezhnev was determined to oppose them. In June threatening Warsaw Pact exercises were held. In July Dubcek was summoned to Moscow. He refused to go, and the Politburo came to Cierna to argue with him. Dubcek assured them he did not intend to leave the Warsaw Pact, and did so again at a meeting at Bratislava. But the Russians feared repercussions in East Germany and Poland, and when Tito and Ceausescu visited Prague in August this was too much for the Russians. It looked as if East Europe might succumb to a form of Communism little different from Western Eurocommunism. On August 20th the country was invaded. After a time Dubcek was removed in April 1969, and the new government under Husak restored the unacceptable face of Communism. Soviet troops were stationed in the country, and in 1970 a definitive treaty was signed with Russia.

G6 Division in the Soviet Bloc: Poland 1980–2

In spite of persistent evidence to the contrary the West argued in the 1970s that detente was possible with Russia, and that by freeing attitudes on both sides of the Iron Curtain human rights would be advanced. The Treaty of Helsinki had a mixed bag of results. In the satellite states it enabled opposition to find a small voice. In Czechoslovakia, Charter 77, began to issue leaflets and renew the demands made in 1968. Disturbances in the Rumanian mining industries in the same year led in 1979 to decentralisation beginning, and public discussion of economic policy. But it was in Poland that the new mood was most effective. Edward Gierek had been brought to power to replace the old fashioned Gomulka, and had tried to develop the Polish economy with foreign loans, but this failed. In 1976 inflation brought about further riots in the sea ports with severe loss of life. Committees of protest were formed, and from these arose a demand for a free trade union. The whole movement was given fresh impetus by the appointment in 1978 of the Polish Archbishop of Cracow, Cardinal Wojtyla, as the first non-Italian Pope—John Paul II—for 400 years. His visit to Poland in 1979 was followed by concessions to the Roman Catholic Church, and during it a symbolic meeting occurred with the venerable Cardinal Wyshinski shortly before his death. A new union formed in 1980 was called Solidarity, and was led by Lech Walesa based on the ports of Gdansk and Stettin. It soon had 10 million members out of 17 million workers. The Russians who were heavily involved in their attack on Afghanistan, and anxious to placate Europe in order to stop American and British re-armament programmes did not act at first as they had in 1956 and 1968. Gierek was replaced by Kania in September 1980, and concessions were made. A partly free press and television service appeared, the unions' demands were met and the right to strike was conceded for the first time in a Communist country. The Roman Catholic Church was given media time. Walesa visited the Pope in January 1981. An agricultural workers' union was formed, and general strikes were threatened over the per-sistent food shortages. Military manoeuvres did not deter the union, and early in 1981 a new prime minister General Jaruzelski, was appointed to work out a compromise.

But the General found himself facing a deteriorating economic situation made worse by intermittent strikes and the conceding of shorter working hours. In spite of rationing, food and fuel shortages continued and the government, burdened with an overseas debt of £823 million, could not pay for food imports. The Russians knew that direct military intervention might precipitate civil war, but they had laid plans to overcome Solidarity for some time by training Polish forces to carry out martial law. It has been suggested there was a plot by the KGB, operating through Bulgaria, to kill both Walesa and the Pope in Rome in 1981. Towards the end of 1981 Solidarity began to talk of a general strike, and Jaruzelski was told he must put a stop to this or face the consequences. Martial law was intro-duced in December 1981, and remained in force until July 1983 when it was replaced by a severely tightened criminal code outlawing unions and forbidding free speech. During 1982 there was considerable resistance to martial law in the shipyards of the Baltic coast and the coalmining region round Katowice in the south. Kania and Walesa were arrested along with many thousands of other who were imprisoned, and in October Solidarity was abolished officially. The Roman Catholic Church continued to support the Poles. The leader of the Polish church, Archbishop Glemp, was elevated to a cardinalate, the Pope condemned the suppression of freedom, and when he visited Poland for a second time in 1983 the government was forced to allow a meeting between him and Walesa who had been released. Wide-spread demonstrations of support for Solidarity continue and the Polish Crisis remains unsolved.

Revision Questions

1. What are the basic ideas of Communism? What are the different varieties of doctrine which have developed since 1917?

2. Draw up a list of the six main achievements of Stalin. What criticisms can be made of each of them?

3. How did Khrushchev alter: (a) political, (b) economic and (c) social life in Russia after 1956? Have his changes proved permanent?

4. What was the 'common pattern' by which Eastern European

countries became 'satellite states' by 1950? Illustrate your points by referring to events in four of the countries.

5. What is the importance of Josif Tito's career to the Communist world?

6. Explain what is meant by the following terms: (a) Titoism, (b) Euro-communism, (c) Socialism in One Country, (d) De-Stalinisation, (e) Dissidents, (f) Cominform, (g) Comecon.

7. Explain how and why revolution against the Communist governments of: (a) Hungary in 1956, (b) Czechoslovakia in 1968 and (c) Poland in 1980 was treated differently in each case.

8. How far has Communist Eastern Europe ceased to be a monolithic bloc dominated from Moscow?

Further Reading

Crankshaw, E., *Khrushchev: A Biography*, Sphere Books, 1968.

Franchere, G., *Tito of Yugoslavia*, Macmillan, London, 1971.

McCauley, M., *The Soviet Union Since 1917*, Longmans, 1981.

Montgomery Hyde, H., *Stalin*, Rupert Hart Davis, 1971.

Mooney, P. J., *The Soviet Super Power*, Heinemann, London, 1982.

Pryce-Jones, D., *The Hungarian Revolution*, Ernest Benn, London, 1969.

Seton-Watson, H., *The East European Revolution*, Methuen, London, 1950.

Tolstoy, N., *Stalin's Secret War*, Jonathan Cape, 1981.

Westwood, J. N., *Endurance and Endeavour: Russian History 1812–1971*, OUP, London, 1973, pp. 328–416.

5
The Capitalist World Power: The United States of America

A Introduction: Roosevelt's America 1933–45

A1 America in the 1920s

In his last term of office President Wilson had tried to reverse America's traditional role of remaining isolated in her own hemisphere. America had entered the First World War, and Wilson had come to Versailles in 1919 in an endeavour to help build a new world. His chosen instrument for this process was the League of Nations. But the American people were not ready for this change. Moreover, during 1919 there was a period of serious labour unrest in the country blamed on the new American Communist Party. Wilson had reacted severely. 12 were killed, 249 deported and over 4,000 imprisoned for left wing activities. The damage was done. From 1920 to 1932 the Americans retreated into a right wing Republican bunker under three presidents—Harding, Coolidge and Hoover. In foreign affairs isolationist policies combined with active military enforcement of the Monroe Doctrine in Central America cut America off from international affairs, except where the collection of wartime loans was concerned. In 1921 and 1924 severe Immigration Laws stemmed the great flood of immigrants and stopped the Japanese altogether. High tariffs, of which the Fordney–McCumber and Hawley–Smoot were the most notorious, isolated the booming American economy from the rest of the world, and although the dollar was of increasing international importance America did not fulfil an international financial role.

'The business of America', said Coolidge, 'is business', and the 1920s were a period of great economic development of a ruthless kind. The government stood aside, and under Andrew Mellon reduced taxes to help big business. Mass production and business efficiency methods introduced by Charles Bedaux yielded rich dividends in a society where only 3.5 million were in trade unions. 'The man who builds a factory builds a temple', exclaimed one president. The Empire State Building (1930) typified the new thrusting America. So did Hollywood. By 1929 there were 720 million dollars invested in the cinema industry, and 100 million Americans visited the picture house each week. The number of private cars rose from 9 million in 1919 to 27 million in 1929. Commercial radio, started in 1920, saw its audience rise to 10 million by 1929 accompanied by the new advertising industry. But it was a one-sided development. Five per cent of the population owned one third of the wealth, and the working class had only been able to share in the rise of prosperity by using hire purchase and mortgages. In 1930 42 per cent of American farms were mortgaged. The loosely organised American banking system gave out massive loans which rose between 1926 and 1929 from 3.5 million to 8.5 million dollars.

Not only was the financial base somewhat unstable. Society developed many unpleasant features. The lure of Northern prosperity, and the poverty of the rural South induced blacks to move North. In 1919 there were race riots in Chicago. In the South the Ku Klux Klan revived in 1922, and had 4.5 million members. It began to talk of 'un-American activities', and attack Jews, Blacks, Catholics and civil liberties. Lynchings and brandings were widespread. Justice in America became politically biased. There were notorious political trials: Saccho–Vanzetti in Massachusetts, and Mooney–Billings in California. Prohibition came in 1919, but J. F. Kramer and his 4,000 agents failed to control the liquor trade while the police force failed to control the associated crime that was consequently unleashed. The introduction of the gas chamber (1921), the rebuilding of the electric chair at Ossining (Sing Sing) Prison in 1930 and brutal police methods had little effect as long as city governments could be bought. The career of a thug called Alfonse ('Al') Capone which culminated in the St Valentine's Day Massacre (1929) typified the era of the gangsters. Political corruption flourished at the top level of society too, as the Tea Pot Dome Scandal of 1924 showed. American society seemed to be typified by brash materialism, and crude violence on and off the screen.

A2 The Great Crash 1929–32

It was inevitable that the boom would crash. Low wages meant that there were too many goods chasing too little money, and by the summer of 1929 the car and building industries were experiencing difficulty. Farm income was declining with a fall in world prices, and between 1927 and 1932 a tenth of farm mortgages were foreclosed. Monetary policy tied to the gold standard meant that there was little room for manoeuvre. American banks had lent 12,000 million dollars abroad, and incurred heavy home debts. Panic set in on the October 24th, 1929, and by the end of the year 40,000 million dollars had been wiped off the value of shares. Five thousand banks went bankrupt, including 2,500 in rural areas, and 32,000 firms were ruined. One in every hundred lost some money in their shares. Money was recalled from Europe, tariffs and interest raised, gold hoarded and mortgages and loans recalled by the banks in a feverish attempt to stem the tide. But the policies were wrong. Two years of falling prices cut the National Income by half, and output fell below 1929 levels. Unemployment rose from 4.3 million in 1930 to 12.8 million in 1933. Hoover's government tried to change course too late. They issued a moratorium on overseas debts to stimulate world markets, and set up a Reconstruction Finance Corporation. But Republicans disliked the moves, and only about 30 million dollars were spent. Hoover spoke of the need for 'rugged individualism' to overcome the crisis. The result was that in the election of 1932 the Democrats returned to power under Franklin D. Roosevelt.

A3 Franklin Delano Roosevelt (1882–1945)

Born into a wealthy family and the cousin of former President Theodore Roosevelt, Franklin spent a happy childhood at Hyde Park, a private school, and then studying law at Harvard in 1900. In 1905 he married and embarked on a political career that took him to the New York State Legislature by 1911. During the war he was Assistant Secretary to the Navy, and was nominated as Vice-President in 1920. Next year he was struck by polio, but fought back, and re-entered politics in 1924. Uniquely among world leaders he was largely confined to a wheelchair. In 1928 he became Governor of New York where he was soon faced with some of the worst effects of the Depression. He provided 20 million dollars of aid in his state, and in a speech at Oglethorpe called for a reversal of American attitudes, and the involvement of the government in the economy. In the 1932 campaign he offered the Americans a 'new deal'. His own sufferings, and magnetic personality enabled him to appeal directly to America in a way few Presidents have done. He received over 8,000 letters a day from ordinary Americans, and took a personal interest in many of them. His radio broadcast fireside chats, and messages to Congress were both models of the politician's art of persuasion. He created the modern Democratic Party as a combination of Southern reactionaries and Northern workers, and set it on the road to attracting the votes of the poor, the blacks and the underprivileged. He won four presidential elections, and was thus the effective ruler of America from 1933 to 1945—a record which also will remain unique for only two terms are now allowed for a president. His achievements were truly staggering, and set him beside the other two titans of the mid-century— Churchill and Stalin. In Gunther's words: 'He was President during the greatest emergency in the history of mankind, and he never let history or mankind down.'

A4 Roosevelt's Policies

In foreign affairs Roosevelt's regime falls into two phases. Limited by economic factors he was unable to play a world role in the 1930s, and concentrated on isolationism. A series of Neutrality Acts emphasised this policy, and it was strictly adhered to so that American finance continued to pour into Mussolini's Italy, and Hitler's Germany. Faced with Japanese aggression in China in 1937, and the attack on an American ship, the *Panay*, no action was taken. Roosevelt spoke of 'moral quarantine' for dictators, but did little to secure it. When the Evian Conference (1938) called for nations to admit Jews, America declined. In the American Hemisphere the 'Good Neighbour Policy' was introduced to provide for co-operation rather than the use of armed force, and the 1936 Pan-American Congress provided for consultation. The result was that Fascism made considerable headway in parts of Latin America. Roosevelt pursued similar policies in regard to left wing governments. He recognised the Soviet Union in 1933. When the left wing Mexican government seized American oil in 1938 he declined to intervene militarily. As late as the 1940 election he was firmly against American involvement in the war.

Circumstances forced him to change his policy. Purchase of war material culminating in the Lend Lease Act and the need to co-operate with Britain in the Atlantic after two American warships had been sunk, forced Roosevelt to help Churchill as the Atlantic Charter, and joint staff discussions started during 1941. Roosevelt was compelled to start rearmament with his Defence Act of June 1940, which started the draft, a form of conscription. After Pearl Harbor Roosevelt became a great wartime president, and during that period America became the world's largest military power, and isolation was ended. Starting with the President's trips abroad, Roosevelt built himself into a world statesman under whom America became a world power. He was determined to ensure that Wilson's aim in 1919 should be fulfilled. America embarked on a massive programme of aid, on reconstructing the world economy and on building a United Nations. At the end of his life Roosevelt was trying to co-operate with Stalin in order to prevent the post-war period turning into a new round of world strife.

At home Roosevelt is of course closely associated with the New Deal. To those on the right this was a disaster which, in Hoover's words, would 'crack the timbers of the constitution'. To those on the left it was a failure because after 1937 expenditure on reforms declined, and in 1939 there were still 9.5 million out of work. But impartially the New Deal 'gave faith and hope to the masses' because it was pragmatic and largely successful. Roosevelt expanded and enlarged the role of the presidency, and at one stage tried to take on the Supreme Court. Many of his actions between 1939 and 1941 during which he increasingly committed America to the war without informing Congress set an ominous precedent. Moreover, reform has to be paid for and administered, and under Roosevelt the role of government began to change. For example, the number of federal jobs rose from 603,000 in 1933 to 3,816,000 in 1945, even though this subsequently fell. 'Too much government' has recently become the cry of the New Right and the Chicago economists in America. They argue Roosevelt's policies were disastrous firstly because his new Federal Reserve scheme meant improvident financial policies were pursued which eventually led to uncontrollable inflation, and secondly because the New Deal by encouraging a 'cradle to the grave' concept of welfare deprived Americans of their frontier spirit of self-help. They see Roosevelt as an amateur too influenced by a group of Columbia University economists who met in his 'brains trust' at Hyde Park. Even if much of this growth can be attributed to war needs, and a third of the civil servants work in the Pentagon, rising government expenditure can hardly be denied. Kennedy, Johnson and Carter were all to govern in the Roosevelt mould.

A5 An American Revolution?

Shifts in policy were the real revolution that took place during the 1930s, but some have argued that Roosevelt saved America from a more serious situation. The claim that capitalism had failed led in many parts of the world to fascist and Communist governments during the 1930s, and the depression produced extremism in Americans as elsewhere. In 1932 farmers' strikes in Nebraska and Iowa, and the Veterans March on Washington dispersed by MacArthur with tanks and teargas had shown the dangers in such appalling economic conditions. Huey Long, Governor of Louisiana

(1933–5) was one possible contender for future dictator. Father Coughlin of Chicago, the Radio Priest, obtained a massive following, and formed the Union Party in 1936. In California, Upton Sinclair and Charles Townsend tried to organise radical protests. The German Bund encouraged co-operation with Hitler. Moreover, Roosevelt had to face difficulties created by his decision to allow trade unions to develop. From 3.5 million in 1933 they rose to 15 million in 1945, and were protected by Acts in 1935 and 1937. The CIO was organised, and sought by strikes to defeat the giant corporations. In 1934 and again in 1937 there were serious strike waves accompanied by sit-in strikes which the employers broke up with private armies and considerable loss of life. All this was unsettling to many more conservative Americans, and gave rise to the view that the President himself was a dangerous revolutionary. In fact his policies were designed to make capitalism work, and by 1945 America was the supreme example, for good or ill, of a free enterprise society.

A6 The New Deal in Action

Roosevelt's policies stretched out into every aspect of life. The gold standard was abandoned (1933), and devaluation occurred. Acts in 1933–4 controlled bank transactions and share operations while creating the Federal Reserve System to control the money supply. The farmers were rescued firstly by Mortgage and Bankruptcy Acts to relieve them of burdens, and then by a policy of reducing production in return for rising prices. Over six million farmers were helped, and by 1939 farm incomes had doubled. Direct intervention in industry was less prominent but the government interfered to curb the electricity monopoly (1935), and in the coal industry by the Guffy Acts (1935, 1937). The Soil Conservation Act (1936) helped to deal with the notorious Dust Bowl, and was linked to a Conservation Corps that provided 2.5 million jobs. After a long struggle an Act of 1933 regulating labour conditions was finally passed in 1938 laying down a 40 cent minimum wage, and a 40 hour week. Direct relief under Acts of 1933 and 1938 totalled 16,000 million dollars. The Civil Works Emergency Relief Act (1934) launched a massive programme of public works employing four million people. Spectacular examples like the Hoover Dam and the Tennessee Valley Authority (TVA) accompanied the building of 70 per cent of the schools, and 35 per cent of the hospitals in the country by 1939. 7,000 million dollars of government money went on these works. A Communications Act reorganised the licensing of telephones and radios. The Motor Carrier Act (1935) regulated truck and bus rates. Housing was covered by an Act in 1934 dealing with mortgages, and one in 1937 encouraging state housing schemes. The policies were carried out without one new ministry, but were run by a series of corporations and committees of bewildering complexity. The policies also provided a basis for wartime efforts when the Office of War Mobilisation (May 1943) under James Byrnes obtained overall direction of the domestic economy, and a host of bodies like the War Labour Board and the Board of Economic Warfare extended government activity. The war, in fact, stimulated New Deal policies, and was followed in 1946 by an Employment Act which boldly stated the government was responsible for maintaining employment, and production.

B Harry S. Truman (1884–1972): The Cold War President

B1 The Senator from Missouri

Truman came from Missouri where he had risen slowly in the Democratic Party to be County Judge (Commissioner) in 1926. He entered the Senate in 1932, but held no government office except as Chairman of a committee to investigate defence programmes which was able to make substantial savings. In 1944 there was deadlock for a possible Vice-President, and Truman emerged as a candidate favoured by the party machine. But when he became President next year he showed 'remarkable qualifications for not only national but international leadership'. He had to pick up the pieces after Roosevelt's death. He overcame a small post-war depression, and put into practice further stages of the New Deal. He presided over the complete reform of America's defence structure to make it ready for a global role. He approved the building of America's atom bomb, and took the decision to build the hydrogen bomb. He took America into a complex network of alliances, sent her to Europe in the Berlin Crisis, and ended a history of isolation by joining NATO in 1949. Nor did he flinch from war itself in Korea. The Truman Doctrine reflected world responsibility on a new scale, and was followed by the Marshall Plan. Even in his last year the ANZUS Pact and peace with Japan continued the momentum of a presidency packed with important world decisions.

B2 The Fair Deal

Determined to follow in Roosevelt's footsteps Truman announced in September 1945 the Fair Deal; a 21 point programme including minimum wages, increased government spending, aid for research and power development including the TVA organisation of Missouri. The dislocation of the economy caused by demobilisation led to bad industrial relations and race riots as it had done in 1919, and in Congress the Southern Democrats and Republicans in the Senate combined against his programme. In 1947 they passed over his veto the Taft–Hartley Act which outlawed the closed shop, and imposed restrictions on the unions. Although Truman was able to get his Minimum Wage Act through in 1946, it was not operated effectively. Truman distanced himself from the Progressives under Wallace, and showed his firm anti-Communism in many ways. After the 1948 election he was able to make better progress providing several measures to help farmers, more public works, and a Housing Act in 1950. By the time he left office social security extended to 45 million Americans. Nevertheless the Fair Deal was small beer compared with the New Freedom or the New Deal.

B3 The Red Scare

Wallace's Progressive Party was about as left as mainstream American politics were likely to go. The unions under John L. Lewis were moderates. The American Labour Party was small, and the Communist Party at its maximum strength had only 75,000 members. But the Canadian spy scare of 1945 (see section 2A4), and the problems of foreign policy soon fomented

			ELECTION	STATES VOTES FOR	AGAINST
F. D. Roosevelt	Democrat		1932	472	59
F. D. Roosevelt	Democrat		1936	523	8
F. D. Roosevelt	Democrat		1940	449	82
F. D. Roosevelt	Democrat		1944	432	99
H. S. Truman	Democrat	Appointed Apr 1945	1948	303	189
D. D. Eisenhower	Republican		1952	442	89
D. D. Eisenhower	Republican		1956	457	73
J. F. Kennedy †	Democrat		1960	303	219
L. B. Johnson X	Democrat	Appointed Nov 1963	1964	486	52
R. M. Nixon ‡	Republican		1968	301	191
R. M. Nixon	Republican		1972	521	17
G. R. Ford	Republican	Appointed August 1974			
J. E. Carter	Democrat		1976	297	241
R. Reagan	Republican		1980	489	49

Key

† assassinated

‡ forced to resign by threat of impeachment

X refused to stand for a second term

Fig. 10. The Presidents of the United States.

Source: In compiling this diagram the author is indebted to P. J. Mooney and C. J. Brown, from *Truman to Carter*, Edward Arnold, London, 1979.

bitter anti-Red feelings in America which were stimulated by events in China, and Europe throughout Truman's presidency.

To many Americans Communism was not merely a politically objectionable system. It presented a direct threat to their hemisphere for the first time in their history. Many Bible Belt Americans also saw Communism as an atheist threat, and this view was substantiated by the persecution of the Catholic Church in Eastern Europe, and the expulsion of Chinese missionaries. In 1946 Congress passed the MacMahon Act to prevent disclosure of atomic secrets to any power. The CIA under Allen Dulles, and the FBI under J. Edgar Hoover (see section 3C3) saw their duty as combating Communism above all else. An Un-American Activities Committee and a Committee on Employees Loyalty were set up in 1947 to check state appointments. In 1949 twelve Communists were placed on trial while the UAC investigated the cinema industry for subversives. Spy cases like those of Hiss and the Rosenbergs added to public fears. In 1950 the Internal Security Act required a register of all Communists to be made. In 1952 the McCarren–Walter Act imposed severe restrictions on immigrants and Americans abroad, and finally in 1954 the Communist party was banned in the United States. It was a senator from Wisconsin, Joseph McCarthy who was the most notorious Red hunter of this period. From 1950 until 1954 when his absurd accusations rebounded on him he kept up a relentless campaign against Communists which often involved people who were merely liberal in their opinions. Public officials became wary of what they allowed, and in schools, churches and public libraries censorship was the unfortunate consequence even though Eisenhower was to condemn the book burners.

B4 The Making of the Pentagon

The Second World War contained important military lessons for the future: technology was to play a major part in future war with atom bombs, jet planes, and guided missiles in existence; operations were now often the fruit of co-operation between the services with amphibious or parachute warfare, and modern war was total involving a battle for hearts and minds in the civilian population and their direct exposure to attack. In 1947 the Army, Navy, and Air Departments were merged in the new Defence Ministry whose headquarters were to be the Pentagon, so named from its five sided shape, and opened in 1949. Its creation was mainly due to James Forrestal who committed suicide under the pressures involved. But it was more than a building. Yergin argues it was also the creation of a security state— almost a state within a state which was to absorb one third of the civil service by 1960. The Defence Secretary was to be advised by the Armed Forces Policy Council, and the President by the National Security Council. Truman put the policy of demobilisation into reverse with a Selective Service Act in 1948, and a Universal Military Service Act in 1951. The Korean War was a suitable opportunity to embark on massive re-armament. By 1954 America had 740 warships, 22 combat divisions and 140 air squadrons (wings). The total military forces stood at three million, and the total cost at 35 billion dollars—clearly a state within a state indeed.

C Dwight D. Eisenhower (1890–1969): The Containment President

C1 The 'All-American Boy' Era

America suffered less than any great power in the war, and seemed to be handed world leadership overnight. For many years America's image was that of the GI (Government Issue) soldier with his crew cut, the all-American boy, gum-chewing, baseball-playing, and above all loyal to the flag. This image partly coincided with reality with American troops in every part of the world, and American money lubricating the world economy. 40,000 million dollars were given in non-military aid between 1945 and 1965. At home America became a consumer-orientated society with the ideal American family increasingly surrounded by gadgets and subject to scientific improvements. This image was spread by lavish American musicals and films, and as the economic balance shifted, Europe, indeed the world, became increasingly Americanised in the 1950s. What J. K. Galbraith called *The Affluent Society* (1958) gave an unprecedented living standard to many (but not all), and encouraged a shallow materialism which Daniel Bell attacked in *The End of Ideology*. The American economy seemed capable of endless expansion. People began to criticise the get rich, escapist, intolerant society in America, ignoring deep-seated problems like black rights and rising crime, and living it up in the never-never land of Harold Robbins' novels. Vietnam burst this bubble in the late 1960s (see section 5E2).

C2 'I Like Ike'

History has plenty of examples of men who claim to be honest and ordinary, and yet come to high office. Eisenhower with his references to apple pie and motherhood played it straight to American hearts as the 'honest lad made good', but his career shows him otherwise—even if his mistress, Miss Kay Summerby, is left out of the account. He had an uneventful army career until he rose to fame during the war as Supreme Commander. Thereafter he commanded the Occupation Forces in Germany, was President of Columbia University, and first Supreme Commander of NATO. While pretending during the war to be a plain soldier he influenced strategy in central Europe in a number of ways which had political effects (see section 2A6). All pay tribute to his shrewd diplomacy in handling the quarrelling Allied generals, and to his skill as a planner of victory. But experience convinced him America could not be isolationist again, and when Robert Taft seemed likely as the new isolationist Republican candidate he decided to run. He was the first Republican President for 20 years, and had control of both Houses. He was also the oldest, and experienced three serious illnesses during his term of office. Towards the end of his second term when he lost control of Congress he seemed to prefer a round of golf to matters of state. His shining image of 1952 was rather dulled by 1959.

His Vice-President was Richard Nixon, an able lawyer who appeared for the prosecution in the Hiss Case. Eisenhower's grandson, David, was married to Nixon's daughter, Julie. Eisenhower did not rely on Nixon for advice, but, until his disgrace in 1958, on Sherman Adams, the White House Chief of Staff. Foster Dulles was Secretary of State, and the hardliner of the executive until his final year of illness. Humphrey at the Treasury was effective but many posts were filled by business men of little skill in politics.

Eisenhower's one innovation in government affairs was the creation of the Department of Health, Education and Welfare in 1953, with the first woman member of the executive, Mrs Oveta Hobby, in charge. Eisenhower remained a good publicist starting Presidential television news conferences in 1955, and travelling to 29 countries during his term of office. He had world popularity, and when he came to Britain the road from Heathrow to Downing Street was lined with cheering crowds.

C3 The Containment President

Under Eisenhower America continued to shoulder the burden of containing Communism. The Korean (1953), and Vietnam (1954) wars were ended with compromises. The defence of South East Asia was assured by pacts with several countries, and SEATO was set up. Chiang Kai Shek was given full backing in the United Nations, and in disputes over the Offshore Islands (1955, 1958). In the Middle East American influence was asserted in Iran, and the alliance with Saudi Arabia strengthened. The Eisenhower Doctrine provided 200 million dollars of aid, and support for the Baghdad Pact. This was swiftly followed by the American Sixth Fleet, and the intervention of American Marines in the Lebanon in 1958. America was strengthened by adding Alaska and Hawaii as full states in 1959. Eisenhower was anxious to reduce tension, and to support Macmillan in his efforts for peace. Summits took place in 1955 and 1960, and Khrushchev came to America. But troubles over Berlin, Cuba and Laos in his last years showed that the Cold War still existed. Moreover, Eisenhower developed the American nuclear arsenal with the start of ICBMs after 1957, and no steps to disarmament succeeded during his period of office.

C4 Desegregation

A glance at any American war film is a reminder that the American army fought for freedom in racially segregated units. The New Deal policies had done little for blacks in the south where lynchings continued as late as 1946 in Georgia. Race riots were not unknown in the mid century. Harlem erupted in 1935, and again in 1943 while there were serious disturbances in Detroit in 1943, and during 1946 in Chicago, Philadelphia and Columbia, Tennessee. In December 1946 Truman appointed a Committee on Civil Rights, and from that moment discussion of these became an issue in American politics. Truman asked for laws including the making of lynching a crime, but the 'Dixiecrat' Democrats opposed him in 1948. In July 1948 the armed forces were desegregated. The NAACP (founded as long ago as 1910) began to agitate for political and human rights, and the Federal Courts to make rulings in their favour. Interstate travel was desegregated in 1946, and in May 1954 the courts ruled against school segregation saying it violated the Fourteenth Amendment (which guaranteed equal protection to all citizens under the law and forbade states to limit this right). While America preached freedom to the Third World it denied similar freedoms to its own citizens, and Eisenhower showed no haste in moving on the matter. It was at the

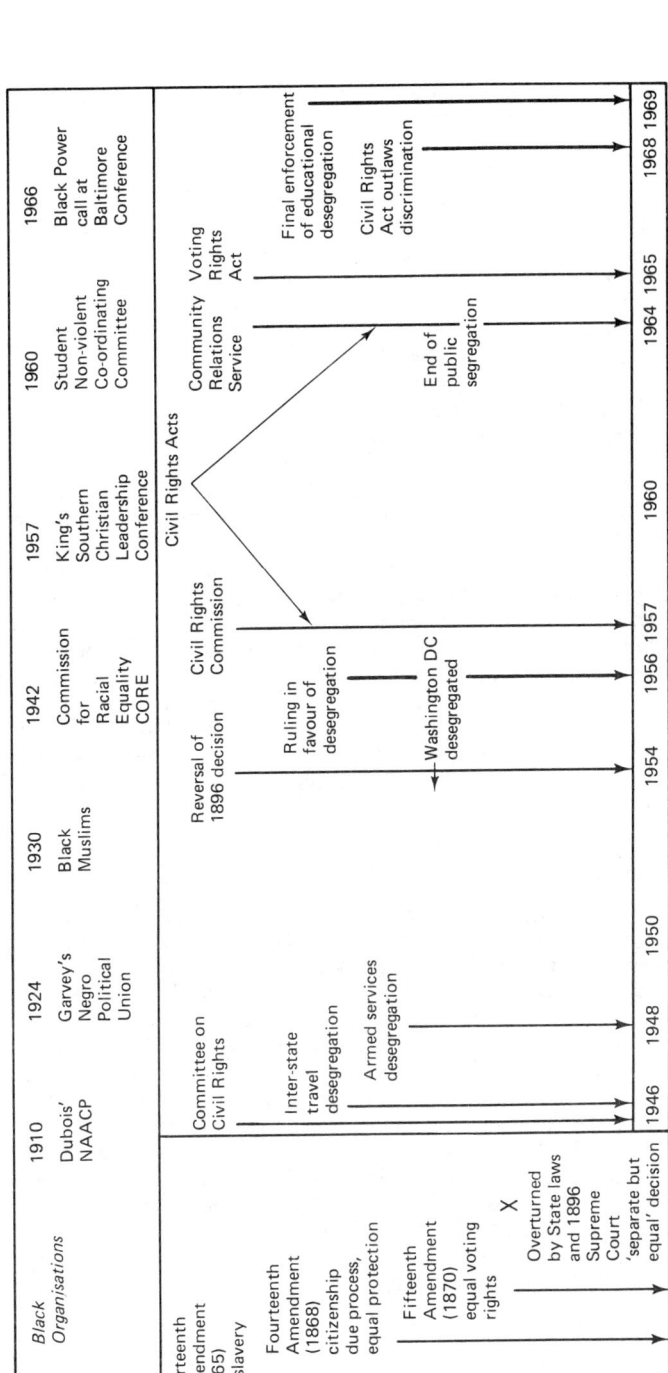

Fig. 11. The steps towards Civil Rights

end of 1955 that Martin Luther King (1929–68) became President of the Montgomery, Alabama Improvement Association, to campaign for blacks denied their constitutional rights. In June 1956 the Federal Court ruled in favour of desegregation, and next year the school issue became a crisis. At Little Rock, Arkansas Governor Faubus refused to enforce the Federal order to desegregate, and there was a riot at the Central High School. Eisenhower despatched federal troops to enforce the order, and nine blacks entered the College protected by 500 troops. But it was not until two years later that the battle there was finally won. It was clear that an organisation was needed to help Blacks, and in 1957 King formed the Southern Christian Leadership Conference to work for civil rights.

Government could no longer ignore the problem. Blacks formed substantial minorities in Northern Cities, and were increasing on the voting rolls as they obtained secondary education and other basic rights. Abroad America was under pressure in UNO and by the Third World to adopt a more liberal stance at home. In 1957 the first Civil Rights Act for 60 years was passed demanding an end to voting discrimination against blacks. But Southern juries defied the new legislation, and little was done. Before long a new issue arose. In February 1960 the question of segregation in eating places was raised by black students at Greensboro, Carolina. Sit-ins were tried in 15 cities, and were followed by others at cinemas, beaches and churches. Within a year 50,000 had participated in such actions, and 3,600 had been arrested. The Student Non-Violent Co-ordinating Committee was set up to preserve the momentum, and in the election of 1960 civil rights were an issue for the first time for a 100 years with both sides making promises. Kennedy was confronted with this new problem after he had obtained black votes by sympathy telephone calls to Mrs King when her husband was arrested.

C5 Waning Popularity

Eisenhower's government had not been without social reforms. The tax system had been changed. There were three Acts in 1954, 1956 and 1958 to help agriculture. The Federal Highways Act (1956) had led to over 42,000 miles of new roads. Social security had been extended a little, and the Education Act of 1959 provided for student loans for college. But two small recessions in 1953 and 1957 were followed by a more serious one in 1959–60. Falling real wages induced restiveness in the unions particularly in the American truck-drivers' union the Teamsters, and there were serious strikes in the car and steel industries. Eisenhower responded with the Landrum–Griffith Act to curb the unions in 1959. Economic slow down, race difficulties and labour troubles were the domestic background against which Eisenhower mishandled the U2 Incident (see Section 3E3). In the ensuing election in 1960 Nixon was no match for Kennedy who insisted on four television debates, watched by 85 million voters, and the Republicans fell from office after eight years.

D John F. Kennedy (1917–63): the Kennedy Myth 1961–63

D1 'The Torch has been passed to a New Generation'

The Kennedys came from Ireland, which his great-grandfather left in the famine years, but in three generations they had become a rich New England family. His father was a self-made millionaire, and Ambassador to Britain in the early years of the war, when he had predicted British defeat. John attended a private school at Choate, then Princeton and Harvard and for a short time Stanford Business School. At the time he was destined for an academic career, and wrote *Why England Slept* in 1940. But war service from which he was invalided out in December 1943 was followed by a political career when his elder brother died. He entered Congress in 1946, and became a senator in 1952. A year later he married a rich heiress, Jacqueline Lee Bouvier. Careful to keep his head down during the McCarthy years Kennedy joined the Foreign Relations Committee in 1957, and was highly regarded.

As potential president he had the disadvantages of being a Roman Catholic, which was held to have ruined Smith's chances in the 1920s, and of being too young (eventually he became the second youngest president to hold office). Against this was his poise, ability as a speaker and his youthful appeal to an America which seemed to be stagnating. This was brought home during the television debates which influenced the outcome of the election. Although socially conservative Kennedy took an active interest in culture and science, and projected what seemed at the time a progressive and conciliatory image. The Administration was a sober one with Rusk as Secretary of State and Dillon at the Treasury, although there were some new faces like McNamara at Defence. His brother, Robert, became Attorney-General. The new regime was popular with the Eastern establishment because like Roosevelt he gathered experts round him from the Universities including Galbraith, Rostow, and Samuelson in the field of economics.

D2 Still a Cold War President

Far from placating the Soviet Union, Kennedy's presidency was to see an intensification of the Cold War. Russia had suspended nuclear tests, but resumed them on a greater scale in 1961. Kennedy followed in April 1962 against Macmillan's advice, and he was only converted reluctantly to the moves that led to the Test Ban Treaty of 1963. America's alliances were strengthened with a new Japanese Treaty and one with Australia. When the Berlin Crisis intensified with the building of the Wall, Kennedy went to Berlin to rally the Western powers, and a meeting at Vienna with Khrushchev in 1961 achieved nothing. Kennedy supported an abortive attempt to overthrow Castro in Cuba, and then found himself confronted with the Cuban Missiles Crisis (see section 13A) which, although resolved favourably and followed by the creation of a direct telephone link between the two powers (June 1963), did bring the modern world its closest yet to nuclear war. The Alliance for Progress (1961) was designed to help South America, but was used to impose a trade boycott on Cuba. The Foreign Aid Act of 1962 specifically forbade giving aid to 18 'Communist' countries. The creation of a Peace Corps of American volunteers to help with aid abroad in 1961 was a more enlightened move, and there were 12,000 of them in 1966. In South East Asia Kennedy took a firm line in the Laos Crisis (1962) moving troops to Thailand, and he was responsible for increasing American involvement in Vietnam and Laos.

D3 The New Frontier

Kennedy sought to dramatise his home policies as a new departure. He did not live long enough to fulfil many of his measures, and Congress resisted many of them during his life so that the end product is deeply disappointing. He was able to channel some aid to inner cities in 1961, and to raise the minimum wage later that year. Plans for medical insurance and conservation were introduced but not carried. His Trade Export Act (1962) began the reduction of tariffs (The Kennedy Round) to encourage world trade, but again was not completed for many years. Economic difficulties began to affect the country, and in May 1962 there was a serious Stock Exchange crisis. Inflation began to plague the economy, and was running at 8 per cent by 1963. The domestic record was disappointing, and perhaps overlaid with glamour and publicity seeking. Certainly the civil rights record was equally disappointing.

D4 The Struggle for a new Civil Rights Act

The Act of 1957 (see section 5C4) had been held up by the courts, but was in operation by 1960. However, widespread discrimination in public places, transport and education could not be ended overnight, and the early 1960s saw a battle to make the 1957 Act more effective. But it was not until June 1963 that Kennedy recommended a new Act to Congress, and only a year later that a new Civil Rights Act was passed. In May 1961 'freedom rides' on buses began to force desegregation, and trouble focused on Birmingham, Alabama. At Montgomery help was late in arriving, and an ugly riot followed. Kennedy then despatched a posse of US marshals. In August 1961 a new campaign began to encourage Blacks to enrol, and defy attempts to prevent them voting. In places like Albany, Georgia and Birmingham, Alabama, the next few years saw persistent attempts to reveal that the law did not apply since the administration remained firmly in white hands. In May 1963 the first big race riot occurred at Birmingham, and there were major demonstrations throughout the country including a Freedom March on Washington. But at the time of Kennedy's death little had been done; indeed with Governor George Wallace of Alabama and Senator Barry Goldwater of Arizona, leading members of the Democrats and Republicans respectively, both major parties seemed to be turning to more extremist policies.

D5 Death in Dallas

On November 22nd, 1963 Kennedy was murdered in Dallas, Texas by Lee Harvey Oswald, supposedly a Marxist and pro-Castro agitator but whose motives remain a subject of controversy. Two days later he was in turn murdered by Jack Rubinstein (shortened to Ruby), a local night club owner.

The immediate effect was to make Lyndon Johnson President. The murder cast an aura of foreboding round the Kennedy family, and Robert stepped into his brother's shoes as a politician only to be killed by an Arab called Sirhan in 1968. In turn the youngest brother, Edward, took up the torch, but in 1969 was involved in a scandal at Chappaquiddick—on an island where the wealthy have summer homes when his car crashed, and the passenger was drowned. John F. Kennedy himself became a legend. The Space Centre at Cape Kennedy, Kennedy Airport and the Kennedy Centre for the Performing Arts perpetuate his memory. The book by Arthur Schlesinger Jnr, *Kennedy's 'Thousand Days'*, tells the story of what many see as a bright star prematurely blacked-out, and others as a much over-rated presidency.

E Lyndon B. Johnson (1908–73): The Vietnam President

E1 The Senator from Texas

Born in 1908 in a small farmhouse, Johnson had spent his early years 'roughing it' in jobs like waiter and janitor until he entered College in 1927. He was lucky to be picked as secretary to a local Senator, and by 1931 was on his way to Washington. There he became a fervent supporter of the New Deal, and one of its Texas organisers. He entered Congress in 1937, and was the first Congressman to go on active service. After the war he resumed his career as a Senate reformer in 1948 later being responsible for drafting the Civil Rights Act of 1957. He was Democratic Leader in the Senate from 1953, and earned a reputation as a fine political organiser. As Vice-President he had adopted an active role as Chairman of the Peace Corps, and had visited Berlin when the Wall was erected.

When he became President he announced 'This nation will keep its commitments from South Vietnam to West Berlin', but it was not to be. Tragically for him, a man who had spent his whole life on social reform, his period of office was to be marked by extreme violence at home unequalled since the 1860s, and by the partial collapse of America's world dominance. Although he won the election of 1964 with the largest ever share of the popular vote he declared in March 1968 that he would not run again for by then he 'felt powerless to correct' the state of the country. In spite of a spectacular programme of social reform and civil rights legislation he was to be President in a period when the mood of America became violent, racialist and anti-patriotic. 'How many babies did you kill today, LBJ' was one of the slogans chanted at this time.

E2 American Radicalism

Johnson bore little personal blame for the tragic events of his presidency. Eisenhower and Kennedy had failed to carry forward the Civil Rights programme fast enough. Martin Luther King and the moderates were being outbid by more extremist elements like the Black Muslims. The killing of their leader, Malcolm X (1965), and later of King (1968) made matters worse. Kennedy had initiated involvement in Vietnam, and Johnson was never able to deploy America's full forces, or rely on his main allies. The war became a lengthening encounter viewed on television for the first time in history, and the kind of events that happen in all wars—civilian casualties, atrocities or mistaken attacks on your own troops—were visible to all, and blamed on the government. The war led to inflation, and the growth of the gap between rich and poor, both black and white. The affluent society was revealed to have major blemishes. It aroused expectations, and disappointed them.

Society itself was undergoing rapid changes. The long period of conformity in American life began to give away to hippies, ethnic minority demands, and anti-authoritarian, overtly pacifist views which would have seemed incredible to the GI generations of earlier days. This mood was fanned—sometimes for purely financial reasons—by the Eastern Liberal establishment. Permissiveness was encouraged; the police (called in slang expression 'pigs'), the draft, and American commitments overseas were attacked, so that it seemed at the time as if the very fabric of American society was coming apart. Ironically the effect was to provoke a backlash—Goldwater, Wallace, Nixon and finally Reagan were the main political figures that stood out against this trend. But their day was yet to come. For the time being campus riots, street battles, endless 'demos', political assassination and race riots were the condition of Americans.

E3 The Great Society

From 1932 to 1980 Democrats held the Presidency for 32 out of the 48 years, and sought to extend the welfare state and the role of the state in society. Johnson was no exception to this trend. He set himself to carry out Kennedy's tragically curtailed policies in his own New Deal called the 'Great Society'. To the Department of Health, Education and Welfare were added the Departments of Housing and Urban Development and of Transportation. Educational spending rose, and in 1965 grants for higher education were increased followed by rapid university expansion. The Appalachia Act provided money for the eleven Appalachian mountain states, and next year a Development Act began channelling money into the 'inner cities'. There was an act to encourage public housing in 1968. In 1966 Medicare providing for the start of a national health service was passed. Unemployment, welfare and direct relief payments were increased in number and value. Expenditure on health, education and welfare rose from two billion dollars in 1953 to 160 billion in 1978 which even allowing for inflation was a major advance of the welfare state. There were nearly a hundred 'programmes' to help the poor, and the cost of administering this policy was fuelling inflation and raising taxes. This great advance was in train before the late 1960s, and needs to be remembered when accusations of poverty lying at the basis of violence are made. Moreover, signs of resistance were appearing. In 1966 Reagan became Governor of California pledged to cut the programmes, and from that platform the right began a counter-attack arguing welfare was destroying the nation internally, and preventing it from functioning externally. But certainly during the 1970s Johnson's initiative held good, and both Nixon and Carter followed in his footsteps in expanding social services.

E4 The New Civil Rights Act 1964 and 1968

In the 1960s America's blacks witnessed the achievement of the basic civil rights demands—the end of public segregation and the attainment of equal voting rights. The 1964 Act extended government powers to enforce desegregation in schools, public transport and elsewhere. An Act of 1965 forbade the imposition of literacy tests and other restrictions on voting rights while another in 1968 forbade discrimination in housing, and provided penalties for those impeding civil rights workers. A white backlash was undoubtedly part of the reason for the violence, and it was encouraged by certain southern governors who sent in police or state troops late, and allowed legal efforts to frustrate the operation of the Acts. Thus, in Selma in March 1965 Wallace allowed 2,000 blacks attempting to register to be arrested, and the state police to try and break up demonstrations against this. The federal government had to send in 3,000 National Guardsmen (Territorials). One religious minister involved died shortly afterwards, and the same month the Ku Klux Klan murdered a civil rights worker on the road from Selma to Montgomery. In July 1966 black riots extended to the cities. Here it was poverty and unemployment, and the belief that a disproportionate number of blacks were drafted to Vietnam that stimulated troubles. Watts was a poor suburb of Los Angeles where 28 were killed that year. In 1967 riots in Detroit resulted in 40 killed, and Federal paratroopers were called in. Although the NAACP rejected Black Power in 1966 the murder of their leader, King, in April 1968 led to disturbances in 125 towns, and fuelled support for Black Power. This movement combined with the anti-war movement, and in August 1968 an attempt to march on the Democratic Convention at Chicago led to a major riot. The imprisonment of Seale, and the death of Hampton in a police raid during 1969 weakened Black extremism but by then the damage was done. The violence gave every excuse to those wishing to back pedal on the new laws, and the Commission on Civil Rights reported in October 1970 that a 'major breakdown' had occurred in the enforcement of the laws.

E5 The Violent Society

In spite of the contradiction between the stated aims of the protesters—peace and freedom for the individual—and their tactics—mob violence, and the denial of the government's democratic rights—the late 1960s and early 1970s were a period when open sympathy was extended to those in American society seeking to hamstring the country's war effort, and reduce its world role. At the time television coverage gave the impression that America was in flames, and her society in danger. This was not true as Nixon was able to control matters, and in the 1980 election the ordinary Americans voted solidly against the recent past. Trouble really began in 1966 when attacks on the Vietnam policy got under way, and CORE (Congress on Racial Equality) called for open violence and withdrawal from Vietnam. In 1967 came the first major anti-war marches culminating in a huge march on Washington in October leading to clashes, and Stop the Draft Week in December. During 1968 violence extended to the universities, and there was a serious disturbance at Columbia University. The presence of 12,000 Federal troops in Washington to prevent a racial outbreak after King's death, the poverty march on Washington and the riots at the Democratic Convention were the high peak of disturbances. But during 1969 there were two further peace marches in October and November. The bombing of a neutral country in an attempt to curb Communism in Cambodia led to a renewed outbreak of violence in 1970 when four students were killed at Kent University, Ohio, and Augusta, Georgia was the scene of a race riot. In May the last major anti-war demonstration occurred, and during the year Nixon took steps to curb violence which were ultimately successful.

E6 A Tarnished World Image

The effects of the rioting were mixed. They did accelerate poverty and desegregation laws and programmes, and they did help to prevent America winning the Vietnam War by all out involvement. But they produced a white backlash, and a longer term conservative backlash which by the end of the next decade contributed to demands for a forceful foreign policy, and a reduction in government spending. Abroad the effect was to damage America's world position. Her European allies distanced themselves from the American involvement in Vietnam although SEATO provided for their involvement. In the Third World American discrimination was a serious barrier to her assuming the mantle of the former colonial powers, and this created a power vacuum into which the Soviet Union stepped—first in the Middle East, and subsequently in Africa. With the loss of Vietnam, Cambodia (Kampuchea) and Laos to Communism containment was effectively destroyed, and by the mid 1970s Russia was operating world-wide through her new fleet bases and Cuban allies. Johnson's period of office saw considerable advances in disarmament—the banning of nuclear weapons from Outer Space, a nuclear-free zone in Latin America and a Non Proliferation Treaty. In South America he still retained the initiative. Riots in Panama (1964) were followed by a new agreement in 1967. The OAS continued to isolate Castro, and South American dictators to take stern measures in pursuit of left wing guerillas. The Alliance for Progress was reaffirmed in 1966, and next year at Punta del Este 14 Latin American countries combined to speed economic reforms. But attacks on America in the United Nations, lukewarm support from all three European powers and her increasing isolation in Vietnam indicated that the days of Korea and world leadership had passed. Britain and France would not co-operate over Vietnam. America had support from Australia, New Zealand, Malaysia, the Philippines, South Korea and South Vietnam. But France left SEATO, and Britain withdrew her bases from the area leaving America alone. Any new American president would have to seek the restoration of America's world power, and to do this with restricted means for anti-military feeling continued high for many years after Vietnam, and Congress acted to curb presidential powers to act in similar circumstances.

F Richard M. Nixon (b. 1913): The Watergate President

F1 The Long Haul to the White House

Coming from a poor Quaker family in California, Nixon like his pre-decessor, Johnson, had come up the hard way and was determined not to lose what he finally won. After a period in college, and war service he entered the House in 1946 where he was a typical Republican of his day closely involved in McCarthyism, the anti-Red crusade. In 1950 he entered the Senate, and for the period 1953–60 was Vice-President, taking a back seat to Eisenhower and Dulles. This combined with his poor showing during the campaign to defeat him in 1960, and in 1962 he lost the governorship of California. He campaigned for Goldwater in 1964, and faded from view only to achieve a comeback in 1968 when he defeated Rockefeller and Reagan for the nomination, and taking advantage of the demoralised and divided Democratic Party won the election. His first term of office was outstandingly successful. Peace was achieved in Vietnam, and major initiatives in foreign policy undertaken. America's defences were modernised with ABMs, and new defence treaties. Violence in society was curbed, social reforms extended, and the post-war depression ridden out. He won in 1972 with a landslide victory which was to make the whole Watergate Affair doubly ridiculous because the burglary was unnecessary in order to defeat the Democrats as they were led by the inept McGovern. But in Nixon's second term much went wrong. The post-Vietnam depression worsened sharply with the oil price increase in 1973. New scandals beset the government involving the Vice-President, Agnew, who resigned in 1973, and Nixon who was engulfed in the Watergate Affair. In turn came attacks on the role of the CIA and big business, and a new devaluation of America in the eyes of the world. Nixon's great achievements were forgotten in an orgy of newspaper speculation and seedy revelations.

F2 Restoring America's World Position

In Vietnam Nixon began to hand over responsibility to the South Vietnamese government, and continued peace talks to a successful conclusion in January 1973. But his attempts to secure this settlement were defeated by Congress. When the Communists began operations in Cambodia to outflank South Vietnam Nixon intervened, but was denied funds by Congress who then repealed the Gulf of Tonkin Resolution thus forbidding the President to take military action without prior consultation. Aid was denied South East Asia, and by 1975 all three countries there had fallen to a Communist tyranny whose numbers of dead were far in excess of the victims of American imperialism. There were no protests in Washington on the matter. The introduction of ABMs was accompanied by SALT I (1972) which was a major disarmament success. Good relations were restored with Russia. In Europe a series of treaties put an end to the post-1945 disputes, and in 1972 Nixon was the first US President to visit Moscow. Good relations were established with Communist China. America gave up her opposition to China entering UNO, and in 1972 Nixon visited Peking. In the Far East Okinawa was returned to Japan, and American military support for South

Korea and Taiwan reduced. Nixon travelled to Rumania in 1969 to help forward good relations, and restored the sale of arms to Greece to strengthen NATO's weakened south-east wing. When nuclear war loomed in the Middle East in 1973 Nixon acted firmly, Kissinger became involved in truce proposals in November, and in 1974 following a visit by Nixon diplomatic relations with Egypt were restored. All these events indicated major shifts in policy, and were great achievements (see section 13E1–2). Nixon was in many ways a Cold War President, but he responded to the changed situation with a number of effective initiatives.

F3 Restoring a Divided Nation: The New Federalism

Vietnam cost 46,000 lives and 120 billion dollars, but the cost in national decline was far greater. To restore faith in Congress Nixon allowed the repeal of the Gulf of Tonkin Resolution (1970), and the substitution of the War Powers Resolution (1973) that gave Congress the power to halt military action once begun. To help the young the draft was abolished, and America returned to an all volunteer army. The voting age was lowered to 18 by the 26th Amendment in 1971. 24 billion dollars were given for educational development by the newly created Education Department while the Scranton Commission investigated the causes of campus riots. Among changes that followed were the introduction of specific Black studies, and the creation of Black quotas of students which gave rise to accusations of 'reverse discrimination'. To help the inner cities Councils on Urban Affairs and Environmental Pollution were set up. A Housing Act provided for 1.3 million units of public housing. Industry was helped by setting up Amtrac to reorganise the railways, creating a new organisation for the Post Office and passing the Merchant Marine Act for the building of 300 ships over ten years. Crime was met with firmer control under the Organised Crime Act, and when in 1971 there was a serious riot in Attica State Prison it was suppressed with the death of 31 prisoners, and 9 of the hostages they had taken. Order gradually returned to American universities and streets although by European standards crime remained high. This was a satis-factory reform programme, and it is often completely forgotten in account-ing for Nixon's massive victory in 1972.

F4 An Economic Crisis for America

For 30 years the American economy had forged ahead with small upsets but nothing more. Keynesian finance, and an ever widening acceptance of the welfare state had stimulated the money supply, and raised taxes. At a local level there was opposition to this trend already, and in California a State referendum Proposition 13, initiated a policy of cutting rates and taxes. But government had spent vast sums on armaments, Vietnam and social services, and in the early seventies inflation became an American problem for the first time. Nixon responded with a Pay Board and a Price Commission, but after the election inflation continued at 8 per cent which was then considered a high figure. World oil price rises at the end of 1973 made matters worse, and the appointment of a Federal Energy Commission did not to stop the doubling of oil prices. The faltering economy led Nixon to stop the upward rise in social expenditure, and to prune programmes during 1973, but such a programme, though popular with many taxpayers is not popular with recipients of welfare, and added to dislike of the government.

F5 The Watergate Affair

America had witnessed major political scandals before involving the President in 1868 and 1924, for example, and the American political system with its free use of money, and 'jobs for the boys' had become a byword for corruption (Tammany Hall politics). Watergate came at a particularly difficult time for America recovering from the traumas of the 1960s. The Presidency was under attack from the left for its foreign policy, and from the right for its ever increasing role in the economy. Watergate was therefore about the extent and misuse of executive power in a modern democracy. It brought into question the meaning Americans attached to that word, and made a substantial dent in their national ego. On June 17th, 1972 there was a burglary at the Democratic Party offices in the Watergate Building. One of the five burglars arrested was the secretary of the Committee for Re-electing the President, and when they were brought to trial in June 1973 the five criminals were accompanied by another member of that committee, and a White House official. The press suggested the White House (i.e. the President) knew of this burglary, and that it was part of a wider conspiracy involving the FBI and CIA to undermine the Democratic Party by stealing and planting information. In April 1973 Nixon issued the first categorical denial of any involvement, cover up, or plot. Archibald Cox was made Special Prosecutor to investigate the matter, and in May the Senate set up its own committee on the Presidential Campaign under Senator S. J. Ervin. One of the White House counsel, J. W. Dean, confessed his part in the affair declaring Nixon was involved.

In July 1973 it was revealed that tapes of White House conversations existed, and in August the Senate Committee asked for them. Nixon refused. The US Appeal Court under Judge Sirica asked that they should be produced. In October summaries only were offered. Attorney-General Richardson resigned rather than sack Cox. His deputy, also resigned, and it was left to a new appointee to sack Cox who was succeeded by Jaworski. This attempt to strike fear into Nixon's opponents misfired, and the same month the Senate began preparations for impeachment. The tapes were then handed over, but with vital parts missing. In April 1974 the Committee renewed its demands for details of 64 conversations. Nixon would not release the original tapes or notes taken, but only copies. When these were released it was clear the 1,308 pages had been edited. Jaworski then sued the President for the originals, and in July 1974 the Supreme Court upheld his decision, and denied Presidential privilege. Meanwhile trials of those involved in the conspiracy (eventually 40 people were tried) were going on getting ever closer to the President. The former Attorney-General Mitchell and the White House advisers Ehrlichman and Haldeman, were the most notorious of those receiving sentences during 1974, and the trials went on until January 1975. In July the House prepared three resolutions on which to base impeachment, and on August 9th, 1974 Nixon resigned. He was given a retrospective par-

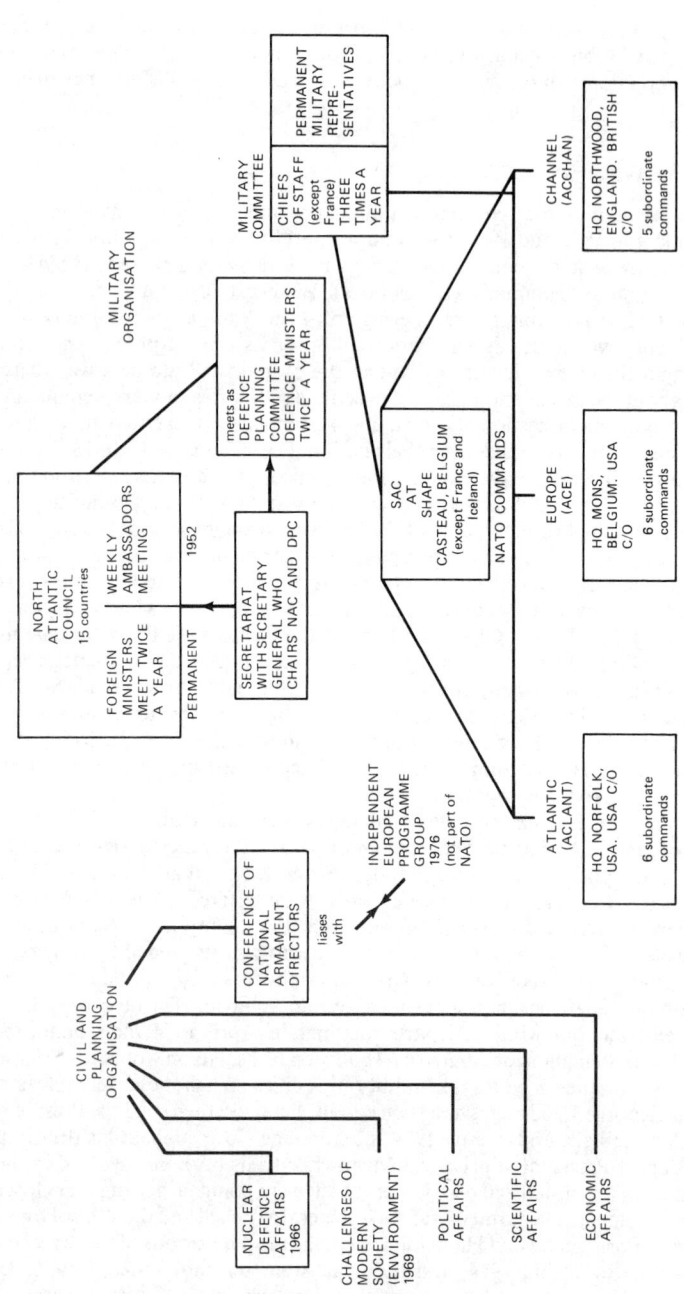

Fig. 12. The structure of NATO

don by Ford on September 8th, and after a period of illness returned to politics to back the Reagan Campaign in 1980.

F6 Reflection: The Effects of Watergate

At the time the wildest exaggeration about the effect of Watergate was current. Like all scandals it soon died, but that is not to deny its importance. It damaged America's reputation as a democracy. It redoubled attempts to restrict presidential power so that Carter was hamstrung by Congress to a dangerous degree. The result was a weakening of the Western alliance and of Western influence in the world during the late 1970s. Watergate led directly to reforms in the political system including limits on campaign donations, and requirements of public accountability. It led to demands for 'open government', and this in turn to further scandals including attacks on the CIA, the Lockheed Bribes Scandal, and the 'Billygate' Affair. Nixon deserved all that he got—impeachment would certainly have succeeded, but historians must not be blinded to his substantial achievements in foreign and defence policy, and his good record on home reform in his first ministry. The Atlantic establishment's righteous search for political purity came ill from a press prepared itself to use every trick in the trade to get information, and even to betray its own spies abroad in print. This certainly led to a change in public attitudes, and the growth of the New Right who aimed to restore traditional American values. In a way like most revolutions Watergate devoured itself. Carter was the result of a desire to break with the Vietnam–Watergate era. His disastrous presidency ushered in a return to values and attitudes not seen since the early sixties.

F7 The Ford Interlude 1974–76

Gerald Ford was born in 1913 in Nebraska, and was in his early years a noted American footballer coaching Yale while he studied law. He served in the Navy from 1942 to 1946 and entered Congress in 1947. He had been an unspectacular member of the Senate, and opposed Johnson's social programme. Agnew's resignation had made him Vice-President, and he had held this office barely eight months before he became President. He was thus unfitted for the office he held particularly since America was in fresh agony over Watergate and its consequences. This was shown by two attempts to kill the President made in California in September 1975, and by continuing scandals. In December 1974 the *New York Times* started a campaign accusing the CIA of involvement in foreign policy in Iran, Chile and elsewhere. As a result lists of agents were published, and lives lost. During 1976 the Lockheed bribes scandal involved many Europeans who had accepted bribes from the giant corporation. Ford added to tensions by giving Nixon a pardon, and following this by an amnesty for deserters and draft-dodgers. Only 22,000 out of 106,000 came forward, and it was left to Carter to pardon the rest. In foreign affairs Ford had to stand by and watch Communist-backed guerillas begin wars in Angola and Lebanon unable to act, and when he asked for 700 million dollars of aid for South Vietnam Congress refused. Only in the Middle East where Kissinger was able to carry forward truce negotiations was America able to exercise a role. Somehow the country seemed tired of world responsibility. Congress vetoed military aid to Angola or Turkey. At home the full impact of recession and oil price rises was felt, and unemployment rose to 8 million. Ford vetoed over 50 bills that threatened to increase inflation, and was attacked for stimulating unemployment and slowing down social programmes. He unwisely decided to try and run for President fighting off a challenge by Reagan for the nomination. But he was tarred with the Nixon brush, and unwisely entered a television debate which favoured the younger man James Carter.

G James C. Carter (b. 1924): the One Term President

G1 The Inexperienced President

The rigidity of the American constitution has often placed inexperienced men at the helm—Truman was one such who had proved successful. But in Carter's case much of the impetus behind his arrival in the White House was the desire to get away from experienced Washington politicians and a desire for simpler, more honest government. Carter seemed to offer this hope, and he was able to rally Blacks, northern trade unionists and moderate Southerners to give him a narrow victory and become the first Southern president since 1848. Around him there gathered environmentalists, and all manner of progressive groups. Carter became a 'folksy president' scrapping White House ceremonial (since replaced by Reagan), and appearing in public constantly hugging people and with a weak, nervous smile. Born in Plains, Georgia, he had a naval career from 1943 to 1953 when he returned to Plains to run the family grocery business and farm. He was a typical smalltown politician—deacon of the Baptist Church, and on the School Board, but he came to prominence over the racial question when he became a Senator in 1962 backing desegregation. In 1970 he became Governor of Georgia, and devoted his time to aid programmes, and desegregation. The number of blacks employed in government in a notorious racially prejudiced state rose from 3 to 53, and in 1974 the portrait of Martin Luther King was hung in the State Capitol. Unknown, sincere, and not asked to be determined or intelligent but rather to be kind and decent, Carter won.

G2 The Deepening Economic Crisis

The majority of those voting for Carter had done so in the belief that he would cure the economic crisis which had been growing for three years, and then initiate social programmes of the kind he practised in Georgia. In his first year he set up a Department of Energy, and put forward a bold programme of energy conservation besides seeking to curb nuclear power, and protect the environment. But when the programme was finally passed in 1978 Congress had mutilated it. Carter's economic policy did not work since he did not favour direct intervention. Inflation continued to rise, and put at risk his programme of social reforms. As a result those who voted for him found they had obtained very little. Riots in Florida by blacks in

1979 were one indication of this discontent. Those on the left of the Democratic Party led by Edward Kennedy urged more drastic action, and when the Russian invasion of Afghanistan forced Carter to reverse his defence cuts, and increase spending by 3 per cent, he found he led a divided party. Pardoning draft-dodgers, reorganising the CIA in 1978 and passing an Anti-Bugging Act were measures which pleased the East Coast radicals, but cut no ice elsewhere. Carter found his inexperience led to poor relations with Congress, and to lack of control over his cabinet. In July 1979 there took place 34 government changes including five cabinet members in an effort to restore the government's image, but it had the effect of creating more doubt. The erratic career of Carter's UN representative, Andrew Young, and the resignation of the Secretary of State, Cyrus Vance, who was unwilling to use force to release the American hostages in Iran suggested foreign affairs were not in good hands. In defence policy there were cuts like the BI Bomber in 1977, decisions to postpone new weapons, like the neutron bomb in 1978, and persistence in backing Salt II in June 1979 in spite of widespread evidence of Soviet rearmament. Finally in 1980 came the pathetic failure of a world power to rescue its own hostages in Iran.

G3 Human Rights

Carter was strong on human rights, and backed the policy of detente. The year before he became President the Treaty of Helsinki had provided for the extension of human rights into Eastern Europe. Carter made bold speeches in support of this move, but his period of office was peppered with examples of the abuse of human rights. The Foreign Aid Act of 1977 banned aid to undemocratic countries, but wheat was sold to Russia. It seemed odd to deny arms to Turkey while helping Russia to spend an ever increasing amount on defence by bolstering her economy. Events such as the bugging of the US embassy in Moscow exposed in 1978 did not seem to have any effect on the nature of the policies. In Africa Young, and the British Foreign Secretary, Owen, became involved in negotiations on Rhodesia and Namibia making strong criticisms of South Africa for armed intervention in that country. Meanwhile Angola, and Ethiopia went Communist with the aid of Cuban troops. The net effect of the policy was to sacrifice human rights in many countries.

G4 The Collapse of Foreign Policy

It is not fair to blame Carter alone for the foreign policies of the late 1970s. They had sprung from the anti-Vietnam, pro-detente atmosphere which had been growing for years. His actions were limited by Congress and by economic crisis. He could not count on strong support from Britain's minority Labour government, D'Estaing's maverick French foreign policy, or the delicately balanced coalition of Schmidt in Germany. Not all his moves were in vain. The signing of a Panama treaty in June 1978 providing for evacuation in the year 2000 was long overdue. In the Middle East aided by Sadat of Egypt he continued Kissinger's policy at Camp David, and in March 1979 the Treaty of Washington brought peace between Egypt and Israel which was to return all conquered territory by 1982. This has been achieved. But in South America guerilla movements made rapid progress overthrowing Somoza in Nicaragua, and preparing the way for the attack on El Salvador. In August 1979 Carter denounced the presence of Russian military personnel in Cuba, but they did not move. In Asia America stopped recognising Taiwan in 1978 and full relations with China opened in January 1979. Troops in South Korea were to be withdrawn. Then came 1979. The Americans' ally, the Shah of Iran, was deposed. On November 4th American hostages were taken as a reprisal for Carter allowing the Shah to take refuge as a dying man in America. The US embassy in Pakistan was destroyed, and no action was taken. An ill-conceived effort to rescue the hostages by sending a helicopter-borne commando force broke down in the desert. On Christmas Day 1979 Russia invaded Afghanistan. Carter condemned the move, but continued to urge acceptance of Salt II. In the end nothing was done apart from a boycott of the 1980 Olympic Games in Moscow by America.

H Ronald Reagan (b. 1910): The New Right President

H1 Ronald Reagan and the Change of Course

Inevitably after Vietnam, and the self-questioning of Watergate and other crises the time came for a reaction. Western Europe often interprets America from the opinions of New England—Washington's East Coast liberals, but it is unwise to do so. America has millions of voters who are deeply conservative, and strongly religious. They had provided the backbone of the expansionist era between 1941 and 1973. To them the events of the 1970s were deeply shocking on three grounds. Selfishly they resented the interference of the government with state rights implicit in desegregation and social programmes. Inflation, taxes, rising unemployment and bankruptcies produced anger in the very voters who had supported social reforms in the 1960s and 1970s. This was allied to a belief that American moral standards were being undermined by pressure groups of unrepresentative minorities. The strident campaigns for gay rights, women's rights, abortion, or legalising soft drugs were linked in many American minds with the East Coast establishment. Carter had been elected as a son of the soil; instead he embraced causes which moved few mid Western or Southern voters. Lastly, the failures in foreign policy were unacceptable to a great power. They meant that Communism was gaining which agonised the fundamentalist beliefs of many Americans. Alleged Soviet military superiority for the first time was deeply worrying. Events like the Iranian hostages incident and Afghanistan invasion drove the Vietnam era from the headlines at last. Carter became rapidly out of date. Reagan was able to capitalise on this since his record was that of favouring small government and the frontier spirit, and of being strongly anti-Communist in foreign affairs. His long political experience contrasted with Carter's ill at ease inexperience. The election of 1980 led to a massive swing to the Republicans giving them their second best win in modern history. Carter was the only president who ran for a second term and lost since Herbert Hoover in 1932.

Reagan's election victory, however, was less spectacular than it seemed at first. Only 53 per cent of Americans voted, and while he controlled the Senate, the Democrats retained control of the House of Representatives and its vital committees, and actually increased their hold in the 1982 mid-term elections. The early years of Reagan's presidency at home were dominated by what was called Reaganomics; in other words an attempt to apply the lessons of the Chicago School economists with tax cuts, welfare cuts and civil service redundancies in order to stimulate growth. Unfortunately, the government also demanded massive increases in defence spending, and the Western world as a whole was going into recession. Resort to strict monetary policies in America, as in Britain, led to a sharp rise in interest rates to 16 per cent, and this held off investment. Unemployment in America rose to 12 million by early 1983. Falling production and incomes reduced tax yields and left the government with a massive deficit standing early in 1983 at 103,900 million dollars. Welfare cuts occurred arousing much bitterness for some 10 million Americans are below the poverty line. Small cuts were made in the defence programmes, but these still amounted to 380,000 million dollars in the first two years. The result was that Reaganomics faltered: there were large tax increases in August 1982 and January 1983. Interest rates started to fall, and falling oil prices will help the economy. By 1984 there was clear evidence of economic recovery in spite of high interest rates and a record budget deficit.

H2 Reagan's Foreign Policy

Reagan had promised a reassertion of America's world position after years of defeat and drift, but this was easier said than done. Opposition in Congress to defence spending, and any direct military intervention were a warning that he could not return to the interventionist days of Kennedy and Johnson. His most immediate problems lay on America's doorstep in the Caribbean. Reagan did not secure the removal of Russian forces from Cuba, but helped by a conservative election victory in Jamaica, he was able to begin containing Castroism in the region in the traditional manner: an aid programme for the Caribbean was announced in February 1982, and right wing rulers in El Salvador and Guatemala found America friendly once more. Reagan paid the first visit for many years by a president to the area late in 1982. Containing Castroism inevitably meant a return to backing for unsavoury Latin American dictators, and this was strongly advocated by people close to the president like General Vernon Walters and Mrs Jeanne Kirkpatrick, the American UN representative. In particular the short-lived President Galtieri of Argentina was invited to America twice, and in return offered America military aid in El Salvador. America in her turn tried to mediate between Argentina and Britain in their 1982 dispute (see section 13G6), and subsequently this event reduced American influence in the region.

In the Middle East Reagan met with considerable success in continuing Carter's policies, and indeed added to them. He argued that Gaddafi was the principal trouble-maker in the region, and shot down two of his planes which were seeking to assert Libyan rights over the whole of the Gulf of Sirte. Gaddafi claimed to have sent a 'hit squad' to America to kill the President, but this left Reagan unmoved, and gave him the chance to ban all Libyan oil imports. Ties with Egypt's new president, Mubarak, were strengthened by his visit to Washington early in 1982. Egypt recognised the Shah's son as the rightful heir to Iran, and allowed the now completed RDF to train in the desert. Somalia and the Sudan received aid, and America backed President Numeiry early in 1983 when he was threatened by Gaddafi. After some difficulties the sale of AWACs planes to Saudi Arabia was secured in October 1981 complementing Britain's efforts (see section 10F1) to re-establish her influence in the Gulf region. Reagan also inherited the Treaty of Washington of 1979, but by 1982 it had been fulfilled—the Israelis withdrew from the Sinai, and the international force including British and American troops went there to ensure its observance. Reagan then put forward, as did Saudi Arabia, a plan for extending the settlement by creating a Palestinian state federated with Jordan. Although Israel rejected these proposals a number of Arab plans were put forward, and the PLO continued to gain support including even a visit by Yasser Arafat to the Pope.

During 1982 the Middle East dissolved in crisis once more as the civil war in Lebanon was complicated by an Israeli invasion (see section 10E5). Syria backed by Russia was intimately involved, but Brezhnev's Afghan difficulties made it difficult for him to intervene in any military way, and this left the field clear for America to act. Reagan despatched two envoys— Stoessel, and then Habib—and a cease-fire was arranged which dispersed the PLO from the capital Beirut, and led to a new government being formed. This was backed by Western aid, and protected by an international force mainly of Americans and French backed by smaller contingents of Italians and British. Afghanistan and the Gulf War remained outside the capacity of America to exert direct influence, and in the Far East Reagan was forced to backtrack over proposals to rearm the Taiwan regime. But it was in Europe that Reagan encountered his main difficulties, and these increased when the pro-European Secretary of State Haig was replaced by Schultz in 1982. This was surprising in view of the resolute anti-Russian stance of Thatcher, Mitterrand and Kohl, but it was a measure of the greater hold detente had on European than American feelings.

Europe was deep in recession during 1982—even Germany had $2\frac{1}{2}$ million unemployed—and this made Europeans sensitive to high American interest rates and protectionist policies, and reluctant to adopt measures that might damage trade with the East. NATO had taken economic measures against Russia over Afghanistan, and Reagan wished for further tough measures over the imposition of martial law in Poland in December 1981. These were not forthcoming; indeed the Europeans concluded a pipe line agreement with Russia. But the main issue was defence. The 1978 NATO decision to raise defence spending by 3 per cent had been followed by a series of decisions to modernise the Western nuclear forces in the face of Soviet re-armament, and direct aggression, but this was now taking place against the background of economic recession. Reagan's outspoken anti-Communism annoyed many Europeans as a return to 'Cold War' attitudes. Moreover, the changes in nuclear strategy seemed to suggest that the new weapons enhanced Europe's, and particularly Germany's, chances of being involved in a nuclear war while America could still stand aside. The British Labour Party adopted unilateralism as party policy during 1982, and the German Social Democrats adopted an anti-American line under their new leader, Vogel, during the election of 1983. Reagan stressed that disarmament would only be secured by pressing the Russians. He put forward in November 1981 the 'zero-option'—no new Western missiles if the Russians would give up their superiority in MRBMs, and declared that if no response was made Cruise and Pershing missiles would be installed in December 1983. When this was done Russia left the Geneva disarmament talks producing complete deadlock.

Revision Questions

1. Read the list of Presidents again. Can you give three reasons for the election of each of them, and explain what the main issues at each election were?

2. What were Roosevelt's main contributions to America's role in world affairs?

3. What were the basic aims and achievements of the following policies: (a) the New Deal, (b) the Fair Deal, (c) the New Frontier, (d) the Great Society, (e) the New Federalism?

4. List the main ways in which American society was segregated in 1950. How did the Black population develop a Civil Rights Movement, and what success did it have?

5. Explain with the help of examples from this chapter the meaning of the following terms: (a) Congress, (b) the Supreme Court, (c) State rights, (d) civil rights, (e) Senate Committee, (f) Impeachment, (g) the Pentagon, (h) the Secretary of State.

6. Each President in this chapter is associated with one particular policy in the chapter heading. Explain the policy, and how successful you think the President was in that respect.

7. Explain why Truman can be regarded as an underrated and Kennedy as an overrated President.

8. What effects did a strong anti-Communist feeling in America have on her policies in the period after 1945?

9. What were the roots of civil disturbance in America between 1966 and 1971?

10. What were the effects of: (a) The Vietnam War, (b) Watergate on American development?

11. The section on Carter is severe in its criticism of him. Do you think that in future views of his Presidency might change, and if so, why?

Further Reading

Alsop, J., *The Life and Times of Franklin D. Roosevelt*, Thames and Hudson, London, 1982.

Charlton, M. and Moncrieff, A., *Many Reasons Why: The American Involvement in Vietnam*, Scolar Press, London, 1978.

Mooney, P. J. and Bown, C. J., *From Truman to Carter*, Edward Arnold, London, 1979.

Segal, R., *The Race War*, Penguin, Harmondsworth, 1967, chapter 4.

Snowman, D., *America Since 1920*, Heinemann Educational Books, London, 1981.

Sorenzen, T. C., *Kennedy*, Hodder and Stoughton, London, 1965.

Note: American foreign policy is dealt with fully in chapters 3 and 13.

6
The Communist Third World: China Becomes a World Power

A1 The Chinese Revolution 1911–12

China, the largest and oldest civilisation in the world was ruled by the Manchu Dynasty from 1644 to 1912. It would not be true to say that the whole period was one of stagnation since the population rose from 125 to 430 million under the Manchus, but the main effect of their rule was to deter progress. The Confucian religion encouraged respect for ancestors and tradition, and the mandarins who were the effective local rulers were guardians of tradition. China experienced no Industrial Revolution; indeed the building of the first railway was delayed in 1876 by its being torn up. Attempts at reform like those in 1898 (which created Peking University) were soon negated by Tzu-Hsi, the reactionary and ruthless regent of the time. When she died in 1908 her successor was a small boy, Hsuan Tung who had little support. There were numerous uprisings, and when in December 1911 Huang Hsing rebelled at Wuchang 15 out of 18 provinces soon followed his example. In February 1912 the Emperor abdicated, and China became a republic.

A2 Foreign Rule in China

The course of Chinese affairs was not, however, to be for the Chinese alone to settle. Her weakness had led to exploitation by other countries. In the south the French had wrested Indo-China from her while in the north Korea was seized by Japan in 1910. Mainland China was so vast that its annexation outright was not contemplated by the European powers. Nevertheless they had taken various ports and concessions round the coast—Britain had Hong Kong (1842), the New Territories (1860) and Kowloon (1898), for example. France, Germany and Japan had all seized territory. The European presence was much wider than these small territorial enclaves. From 1842 China had been coerced into opening many ports to the exclusive use of Europeans who controlled the customs, and by 1898 80 per cent of China's trade was in foreign hands. The largest concession was at Shanghai (1854) from which the Chinese Customs were run by Englishmen. Japan which had modernised in contrast to China had taken part in the seizure of territory acquiring Formosa (Taiwan) in 1895, and Port Arthur in 1905; and her intention was to profit from Chinese decline whenever possible. China needed a double liberation—from her past, and from the foreign powers.

A3 Sun Yat Sen and the First Revolution (1866–1925)

Sun Yat Sen was educated in English schools at Hawaii and Hong Kong where he entered medical school in 1886. His Western contacts made him a focus for discontent, and in 1896 the Chinese Embassy in London tried to kidnap him as a dangerous revolutionary. He returned to Japan and became the leader of the Tung Ming Hui (1905). Sun's group backed revolts, and between 1899 and 1911 there were ten uprisings in Southern China culminating in the Canton revolt of April 1911. He was not a genuine revolutionary, but a moderate reformer. His Three Principles of 1907 were Nationalism, Socialism and Democracy, and were essentially copied from the West.

Yuan Shi Kai had become President in the north (February 1912) of the new republic after the revolution, but he was even more conservative than Sun. When Sun's party—the Kuomintang (KMT)—won a majority in the new parliament in April 1913 Yuan was determined to outflank him. To do this he relied on local war-lords or tuchuns who killed the Prime Minister. Yuan then extended his term of office for ten years, outlawed the KMT, and dissolved parliament for opposing the raising of a foreign loan. Yuan was determined to restore the monarchy in his own person in January 1916, but was prevented from doing so by the widespread breakdown of law and order in the country. He cancelled his plan in March but died in June leaving China weakly ruled by Li Yuan Hung.

The Japanese were only too willing to take advantage of this situation. In 1914 they had captured the German port of Kiao-Chow. In January 1915 they put forward 21 Demands, many of which Li was forced to accept in 1917. This led to widespread Nationalist opposition centring on Sun in the south where in August 1917 he re-established the KMT at Canton. China now had two governments for in the north Li was succeeded by Feng Kwo-Chang, a local war-lord. The Northern government believed that if China entered the war on the Western side they would be treated better at the ensuing peace conference. China thus entered the war in August 1917 but at Versailles none of her territory was restored, and it was not until 1922 that Kiao-Chow was given back by the Japanese. China refused to sign the treaty and there were disturbances in 1919 known as the 4th of May Movement, a boycott of Japanese goods and increasing lawlessness by the war-lords. Between 1912 and 1928 there were some 1,300 of these and over 140 civil wars between them. A Chinese Communist Party had been advocated by Li Ta-Chao in Peking and set up by Chen Tu Hsiu in Shanghai (1921), and Sun in despair turned to Bolshevik Russia.

During 1922 contacts were opened with the Soviet Union through a Dutch intermediary. Lenin agreed to support Sun, and in January 1923 an agreement was drawn up providing for Communist aid to defeat the war-lords, and expel foreign influences. A number of Communist agents like Borodin, together with some thousands of technical and military advisers arrived in 1923. During 1924 a new constitution was established, the KMT reorganised and a military academy set up at Whampoa to train officers for a KMT army. Its commander was Chiang Kai Shek.

A4 Chiang Kai Shek's Rise to Power

Chiang Kai Shek came from a middle class family and was born at Chikow
near Shanghai in 1887. He became a nationalist supporter of Sun Yat Sen
while in Japan for military training. He won over Chekiang Province in
the 1911 revolution, and became Military Adviser to Sun. He helped him
to escape when a Cantonese war-lord, Chen Chiung Ming, tried to seize him,
and thereafter was assured of the eventual succession. Chiang accepted the
decision to get Bolshevik support, visiting Moscow in 1923, but he was
already a business man in contact with families like the Soongs, and he was
more inclined to adopt a Western line of modernisation for China along
former Japanese lines rather than a Communist solution. In 1927 he married
Meiling Soong, and her family became the dominant influence in his
government.

Chiang Kai Shek normally ate European food, and his favourite music
was Schubert. In 1930 he became a Christian. By that time he had parted
company with the Bolsheviks, and he came to rely on war-lords, landlords
and business men to keep him in power rather than any revolution based
on the Chinese peasants of which he knew little. When Sun died in March
1925 the left were in control of the KMT, but Chiang had the military
behind him, and won over several war-lords. In March 1926 the arresting
of Communists began, and by June Chiang was Chairman of the Party.
His decision to reunite China by a march against the Northern war-lords
in Peking was decisive because it made Chiang the patriotic leader, and
enabled him to increase the military and arbitrary nature of his rule. In
July 1927 the Communist agents were expelled and the Communists in
Shanghai and Canton slaughtered. Next year Chiang resumed his march
entering Peking, and became President of China in October with his capital
at Nanking. Chiang was able to suppress a Communist counter revolution
easily, and his military success in the north after the death of Chang Tso
Lin, the war-lord of Manchuria, made him the effective ruler of China by
1930.

A5 The Regime of Chiang Kai Shek

To replace the Russians Chiang Kai Shek called in the Germans. A succession
of German advisers including Seeckt and Von Falkenhausen helped him
to create an army of 500,000, although this had the disadvantage of making
it a regimented army ill-adapted to guerilla warfare when it came. Chiang
was faced with Communist risings until 1934, the continued disturbances
of the war-lords and from 1931 to 1945 with Japanese aggression. His regime
was essentially militarist throughout this period, and although this was partly
the product of circumstances it is clear Chiang yearned for an authoritarian
regime in an age when most world governments were turning to dictatorships.
The government was a clique of Soongs, their relatives and Whampoa
military types, and elections were never held under the constitution of 1930
as Japanese attack was held to prevent them occurring. Chiang himself was
Chairman, then General Director and finally President and Commander-in-
Chief in 1943. The two main prime ministers of the period—H. H. Kung
and T. V. Soong—were related to him by marriage. Order was kept by the

Blue Shirts (1932) a political police organised by Walther Stennes, and commanded by Tai Li who had been educated in Germany. Although Chiang used some marxist propaganda methods, and allowed the New Life Movement (1934) to advocate reforms his regime failed to solve China's grave economic problems. Clearly this was partly due to Japanese occupation which imposed crushing military burdens, and deprived him of Manchuria which was then China's only substantial industrial region, but it was also because he was not willing to oppose industrialists and landlords. Mao's opposition led him to see the Reds as China's Jews, and his incessant warfare with them meant that any reliance on the peasantry was out of the question. Chiang's reforms were essentially confined to the towns and the coastal belt where 75,000 miles of new roads and new airlines improved communications. With the aid of Sir Frederick Leith Ross, T. V. Soong was able to restore the Chinese currency in 1932, and end inflation. Hu Shih's plain speech Chinese was encouraged. New law codes were created. Primary education was extended, and 40 universities founded.

A6 Foreign Relations

Chiang Kai Shek was able to achieve one of Sun's aims—the removal of European influence from China's trade. Britain had been giving up her concessions in Hankow and Wei Hai Wei, and in 1930 Chiang denounced all foreign extra-territorial rights. Control of Chinese customs was abandoned in 1928. In 1943 the Western powers finally gave up their rights which they had started to secure 100 years before. Tragically for Chiang his success in stimulating Chinese Nationalism led the Japanese to take more drastic action. As early as 1927 Chiang had clashed with their troops at Tsinan. When Chiang secured control over Northern China the Japanese reacted by invading and annexing Manchuria which became the puppet state of Manchukuo. Then in 1933 they seized Jehol, part of Northern China, in 1935 Hopei, and in July 1937 launched a full scale invasion. Nanking fell in December and was subjected to appalling atrocities while Chiang was forced to move his capital to Chungking in the west.

These events were crucial to Chiang's career. As a nationalist he turned his attention to the war with Japan—reform was neglected, militarism and authoritarianism increased. Germany and Japan were allies, and Japan was periodically at war with Russia in Amur Province. Chiang was forced to change diplomatic sides. The Germans left, and in August 1937 Stalin and Chiang signed a treaty securing aircraft and ammunitions for China. After 1941 this relationship was strengthened, and in August 1945 there was a further treaty. But good relations with Russia meant that Chiang's opposition to the Communists had to slacken. Moreover, their army proved a valuable asset in the the war against Japan. Stalin was advocating Popular Fronts in the late 1930s, and in 1936 Mao offered a compromise. Chiang was kidnapped by the war-lord of Manchuria, Chang Hsueh Liang, at Sian in December 1936 who demanded that he compromise with Mao's Communists in order to defeat the Japanese. Chiang had to agree to this to secure his release, and in January 1937 a Popular Front was formed between the CCP and the KMT. This was the means whereby Mao was able to create a new army, increase his party membership, and secure influence in north-east China which would put a barrier between Chiang and the resources of the area when the Japanese were eventually driven out.

A7 Chiang Kai Shek in the Second World War

America had trading interests in China, and a considerable 'China Lobby' of missionary and commercial interests urged backing for Chiang Kai Shek. In the 1930s America had studiously ignored Japanese aggression even though in December 1937 an American ship, the *Panay*, was attacked. But Japan posed a far more serious threat to American interests, and from 1938 economic aid began to flow to Chiang who was seen as the only hope for Chinese stability. His government at Chungking was supplied by air from Burma, and later by the Burma Road. Chiang was able to rely on American generals like Stilwell and Wedemeyer, American air forces were stationed in China, and Chiang received massive Lend Lease Aid from March 1942. Roosevelt was determined to tie down large numbers of Japanese in China, and was willing to flatter and support Chiang to that end. Chiang was thus present at Cairo in 1943, for example, and Roosevelt constantly urged the British to Burmese offensives to relieve the pressure on Chiang. But at Yalta, in order to bring Russia into the war, Roosevelt signed away Chinese territory behind Chiang's back, and then forced Chiang to agree to this in August 1945 (see section 2B5). Lend Lease was abruptly cut off. Wedemeyer's Americans transported 500,000 of Chiang troops to Northern China before withdrawing.

Mao had gained from Roosevelt's infatuation with Stalin for Russia entered the war, invaded Manchuria, and handed it over to Mao's troops instead of Chiang's before withdrawing. Chiang's army was massive, but it was weakened by long war, and as late as 1944 in the Ichigo offensive the Japanese had made large gains. If Chiang was to win he could not do it alone, but he had always beaten the nationalist drum, and to rely on America was to play into Mao's hands. 'We did not want to be Japanese slaves. We do not want to be American slaves' was an appealing slogan, and Mao was able to conquer China more as a nationalist than as a Communist. The war years had established him as a nationalist leader whose power rested with the peasantry and not on American aid. Chiang was too Western, corrupt and incompetent to survive, and the Americans had reluctantly to accept this fact.

B The Early Career of Mao Tse Tung (1893–1976)

B1 The Start of the CCP

Mao Tse Tung was born into a poor family at Hsiang Tan in the province of Hunan where he was working as early as thirteen years old, and experienced the famines of 1906 and 1910 and their accompanying riots. After attending two local schools, Mao went to Changsha High School in the capital town of his province in the year of the Chinese Revolution. Influenced by Sun's propaganda he joined the revolutionary army, and then took odd jobs before entering teacher training college in 1913. During this period he became a physical fitness fanatic, and his first article (1917) was on this subject. For a time he was a library assistant at Peking University where he began to read Marx under the influence of Yang Chung Chi, and when he returned to Changsha as a teacher he became involved in the 4th of May disturbances, and subsequently organised a Communist party in the area while two friends set up branches in Peking and Shanghai. In July 1921 the first party meeting took place with 12 delegates representing 56 members. In Hunan Province Mao was involved in fomenting strikes which in spite of brutal repression secured their demands. By 1922 he was in Shanghai at the time Sun decided to throw in his lot with the Bolsheviks.

B2 Mao's Kuomintang Period 1922–27

While Sun was alive Mao continued to rise in importance within the KMT–CCP joining the Central Committee in 1924, and next year he was in charge of propaganda at Canton. It was in this post that Mao realised Sun's movement lacked an essential ingredient—mass support—and that Sun's Three Principles needed supplementing by populism. During Chiang's Northern March Mao's Political Department helped the villagers set up Peasant Associations, and share out the land, and the town workers to form unions sabotaging factories. Such actions helped Chiang, but determined him to break with Mao because they offended Chiang's closest supporters. Chiang resented also the Russian influence on the KMT, and in April 1927 the split came followed by massacres of Communists in Shanghai and Canton. Mao was nearly captured at Changsha, and fled into the mountains of Chinghanshan where he began to gather a guerilla army. By the spring of 1928 he had some 10,000 troops at his command.

B3 The Kiangsi–Hunan Soviet and the First Civil War

For a time the Communists were unsure how to proceed. Mao favoured guerilla war, and a power base among the peasnatry, but others such as Li Li San favoured attacks on the cities convinced that Marxism required a rising by the urban proletariat as in Russia in 1917. The 'Revolutionary Tide' in 1929 was not a success as it enabled Chiang to meet them head on in battle with his superior forces. From 1930 to 1934 Chiang launched five campaigns against the Communists, and succeeded in isolating them in Hunan. Taking German advice Chiang resorted to internment camps, and block houses to deny Mao support, and drive him into the hills. But although Mao lost the campaign the period is not without its importance because it gave him the opportunity to practise in the Kiangsi-Hunan Peasant Soviet his ideas for basing Communist revolution on the peasants. His army was conceived as a fighting and a propaganda force simultaneously: 'We cast it wide to win over the masses and draw it in to deal with the enemy.' But these tactics won no support from the Moscow hardliners in Shanghai or from Stalin. Mao was forced to give up and retreat.

B4 The Shensi Soviet and the Long March

For a year from October 1934 to October 1935 Mao accompanied by 100,000 supporters of which 85,000 were military personnel sought to escape Chiang's forces in a remarkable march across Central China from Kiangsi to Pao-An, and after a few months to Yenan in Shensi Province. They covered 6,000 miles in 386 days. There were fifteen days of major battle, and numerous skirmishes, and in the first three weeks Chiang was able to kill 25,000 of Mao's troops, but thereafter the difficult terrain gave the advantage to Mao, and they crossed 18 mountain ranges and 24 rivers, Chiang's troops melted away. Mao abandoned 20,000 wounded under his brother Tse-Tan, and arrived with barely a third of those he started with. His second wife, Ho Shih-Chen, who was pregnant, was injured and carried on a litter most of the way, and saw three of her children abandoned to the local peasants. In 1937 they were divorced, and she went to Russia. Mao then lived with an actress then known as Lan Ping and later as Chiang Ching.

The Long March achieved much. It secured the survival of Chinese Communism. It made Mao a hero, and Edgar Snow's *Red Star over China* (1936), written by an admiring Peking schoolmaster, made him well known in America. It was a triumph for him politically. He became the leader of the party in January 1935, and Chou En Lai, Chu Teh and Lin Piao became his fervent supporters. Above all in Shensi he was able to extend his ideas on peasant involvement, and as the Japanese War enabled him to enter surrounding provinces he carried this message with him: 'The people are water, the Eighth Route Army are fish; without water the fish will die.' By 1945 some 30 million Chinese were living under Mao's rule. Mao also used the Shensi period to write, and some of his most important works such as *The Chinese Revolution* (1939) and *On New Democracy* (1940) appeared at this time. He created a new army of 900,000, and a People's Militia of two million who acted as troops and social workers providing propaganda, aid and organisation in the villages to sustain Communist resistance, and fighting when necessary.

B5 The CCP–KMT Popular Front 1937–45

It was the war with Japan that gave Mao his chance. As early as April 1932 he declared war on the Japanese, and the Long March was billed as going north to fight them. The Northern war-lords were so desperate to resist the Japanese that they forced Chiang to compromise. Chiang called off his campaign against Mao, and left him 'the Border Region'. The Communists promised to moderate their policy of opposition to the landlords. The Red Army would remain intact but as part of the KMT forces operating against Japan. Mao was thus free to build up his army, occupy territory, and appear as a patriotic opponent of Japan. The entry of Russia and America into the war on the same side enabled Mao to apply for help to both.

At first he actually favoured the Americans, as Stalin had constantly backed Chiang and not him in the 1930s. Chou En Lai became his representative at Chungking, and an American Mission was stationed at Yenan. Twice Mao offered to visit Roosevelt in Washington, but the offers were rejected since Roosevelt was convinced Chiang (still closely allied to Stalin) was the most likely future ruler of China. Yet during the war Chiang husbanded his forces, and did little direct fighting against the Japanese while Mao's forces constantly harassed the Japanese by guerilla warfare. When Chiang insisted that Japan should surrender only to his forces Mao ignored him, and took the surrender of the Japanese in an area of China with 140 million people in it. Wedemeyer was able to take Chiang's troops north, but they were only able to occupy the cities. Stalin had begun to move towards Mao handing over quantities of arms, and not withdrawing from Manchuria until Mao's forces were able to move in. Negotiations between Chiang and Mao (August–October 1945) thus broke down, and the civil war resumed.

B6 The Second Civil War 1945–49

America tried to mediate. General Marshall was sent in December 1945, and a truce arranged early the next year. But Chiang was convinced he could win. His forces outnumbered Mao's by three to one, and he controlled the bulk of the country. Indeed he was able to return to Nanking, his capital, in May 1946. He had massive superiority in equipment, and a commercial agreement with the USA (November 1946) seemed to presage unlimited aid from that quarter. Mao for his part was able with Soviet assistance to build up his equipment including captured Japanese stocks, and by mid 1948 was to equal Chiang's forces in numbers and equipment. He was not willing to give up Manchuria, and although prepared for coalition demanded a direct share in government. In April 1946 civil war resumed, and by January 1947 Marshall withdrew blaming diehards on both sides.

Chiang's forces had been at war with Communists, war-lords and the Japanese continuously since 1926. His army was demoralised. It had lost 100,000 officers, and the commanders like Liu Chih were ineffective. His government was corrupt, and in spite of a new constitution Chiang was given dictatorial powers again in April 1948. During 1947 Chiang launched his campaign, but instead of concentrating his forces he attacked in Shantung, Manchuria and Yenan. Mao was willing to give up Yenan temporarily, his army slipped behind Chiang's, and from a new base in the Tapeh Mountains was able to dominate China north of the Yangtse. During 1948 Mao captured Chinchow, and forced the surrender of 200,000 Nationalists at Mukden in November. Manchuria was cleared of Chiang's forces. Early in 1949 Mao advanced to capture Tientsin and Peking, and won the decisive battle of Hschow in which the Nationalists' plans were revealed to Mao by a defector. At the end of January the town itself fell, and a further 300,000 prisoners were Mao's. Chiang resigned the government to Li Tsung Ten, and negotiations were opened in April, but Mao now raised his demands: the talks broke down, and Mao crossed the Yangtse. The Americans had poured in two billion dollars of aid, but much of it had gone into the pockets of officials, and some had even given American equipment to the Communists. In August 1949 America stopped aid to Chiang who was forced to retreat to Chungking, and then Chingtu. Mao's forces swept south capturing Canton in October, and Chiang was forced to flee to Formosa (Taiwan) in December with 300,000 troops. On October 1st, 1949 the Peoples' Republic of China was proclaimed at Peking.

B7 The Last Years of Chiang Kai Shek

Chiang's arrival in Taiwan was not welcome. Ten thousand had been killed in 1947 when a revolt against the KMT had been attempted. Mao made preparations to seize the island, but was prevented from doing so by the Korean War. This achieved two things. It enabled Chiang to consolidate his hold on the island. It led to American protection of Taiwan by the 7th Fleet. In 1954 a defence pact was signed with America which built up Chiang's forces. In 1961 America organised 'Operation Hurricane' to bring back from Mainland China the survivors of the 1949 army on the Chinese–Burmese border. America sprang to Chiang's defence in 1954 and 1958 (see section 3E5), but in return forced Chiang to abandon the Offshore Islands and promise not to invade mainland China (September 1958).

Thereafter Taiwan together with South Korea and Hong Kong became three prosperous Asiatic states. Although there were many social reforms including education and family planning, the regime remained authoritarian. Chiang's son, Chiang Ching-Kuo, became Prime Minister in 1972, and on Chiang Kai Shek's death in 1975 he was the real power behind his successor, Yen Chiang-kan. Meanwhile changing world conditions (see section 13E1) led America to deny Taiwan her UNO place, and eventually to withdraw diplomatic recognition. Chiang held power from 1926 to 1975, but in the end he was a failure. He had qualities as a general and as a politician, but he lacked an understanding of what China needed. His regime was too remote, Western and eventually corrupt to win the hearts of his people.

C The Making of Communist China

C1 Mao's Own Position

At first Mao Tse Tung held the combined posts of President and Chairman, but during the 1950s, found himself under pressure for his 'cult of personality' particularly after the revelations concerning his close ally Stalin. In 1956, led by Teng Hsiao Ping, there was considerable criticism. Mao's *Thoughts* were removed from the constitution, and to defuse the situation Mao allowed a period of criticism (the Hundred Flowers) although this was short lived after strikes and student opposition occurred. In 1959 he gave up the office of President in which he was replaced by Liu Shao Chi. During the 1960s as Khrushchev's version of Communism became increasingly unpopular Chairman Mao began to reassert his position. In 1964 his *Little Red Book* was produced, and in 1966 he staged a comeback with a spectacular swim in the Yangtse, and the demotion of Liu Shao Chi. Urged on by his wife Mao backed the 'Cultural Revolution' which was designed to rebut peaceful co-existence, and to stress that Mao's China was ideologically in the Marxist–Leninist tradition. It has now been revealed there was an extensive purge of the party at this time, and Mao was able to retain full power until his death in 1976 shaking off opposition led by Lin Piao who was killed in an air accident in 1971. But as with so many dictators he failed to provide for a smooth succession; at his death Chiang Ching and the radicals were opposed by Teng Hsiao Ping and the moderates, and there was a struggle for power.

C2 Communist Government in China

As early as September 1949 Mao ordered a consultative conference to frame a new constitution, but it was not until 1954 that this was approved. It has remained in force since, being modified in 1969 and 1975. China is a one party state, and the Communist Party has 20 million members. Although this is only 3 per cent of the population it still makes it the largest Communist organisation in the world. The constitution was based on 'democratic centralism' by which a federal structure of government and party organisations was created starting with the hsiang (which in some cases was the same as the local commune), grouped into hsiens, and then into 21 provinces. Five self-governing regions, and three great cities completed the structure. Information on China is even less available than on Russia, but there can be little doubt that Mao's regime was consistently ruthless. From 1949 to 1952 there were a series of purges directed against foreign influences (The Five Antis), and Nationalists (The Three Antis) carried out by the Supreme Peoples' Court. Mao himself admitted in 1957 there were 800,000 deaths in this period. More modern estimates put the figure as high as three million. During this period landlords were denounced and killed in the Speak Bitterness Campaign, 9,000 foreign missionaries expelled, many Chinese Christians killed and the Kuomintang wiped out. At the trial of Chiang Ching in 1980 revelations of the purges of 1966–9 were made involving thousands of deaths. Mao's Communism remained hardline when Khrushchev was seeking modifications, and whatever her stance in international affairs China remains like all Communist states completely totalitarian.

C3 The Reform of Agriculture

The most fundamental problem for China was the future of the peasantry for in spite of deaths in war and purges estimated between 1931 and 1952 to have cost China 30 million lives the population continued to rise from 430 to 600 million while the agricultural system remained primitive, and landlord power extensive. Mao was aware of the great difficulties Stalin had in enforcing collectivisation, and his method of securing it by a law in 1950 was therefore based on grass roots persuasion by party cadres sent into the villages to stir up the peasants against the landlords, and to secure redistribution. At first those peasants who already owned land were left alone, and by 1952 this stage was completed. But at the same time individual peasants were urged to pool resources in co-operatives, and in turn were grouped slowly into collectives. Not until 1956 was the process more strictly enforced, but by late 1957 China had 750,000 collectives. Then came the final moves. In 1958 twenty-eight collectives in Hunan combined to form the Sputnik Commune, and thereafter the collectives were systematically combined into 26,000 Communes. These became the basic units of all social activity, and were more than mere agricultural organisations since they were involved in education, training, welfare and even light industry. The great famine of 1959–60 indicated that all this reorganisation had yet to bear fruit, but since then considerable progress has been made towards modernising agricultural methods. By the 1970s Mao had carried forward the most momentous social change ever achieved in a deeply conservative society, and he had shown that Communist methods worked for the Third World peasantry. In other parts of the world like Tanzania similar programmes were to be tried as the Chinese example was copied.

C4 The Creation of an Industrial Base

The total nationalisation of all industry and commerce in China was undertaken in two stages: heavy industry and the banks were taken over at once, and light industry in 1952, after once again party cadres had performed a propaganda role. Russian influence was predominant in the first ten years of China's development. Indeed in 1959 there were 40,000 Russian technicians in the country involved in over 140 projects. This meant emphasis would be placed on a series of plans to create an industrial base; an achievement perhaps even more remarkable than that of Russia because China had scarcely any heavy industry outside Manchuria and the Yangtse Basin, and was dependent on foreign imports for her modern products. It was not until 1956 that China manufactured a lorry, or 1957 an aeroplane. The First Five Year Plan (1953) was to increase food, heavy industry and mining output. Output of coal and electricity doubled, oil trebled and steel quadrupled in this largely successful effort. The Second Plan (The Great Leap Forward) launched in 1958 and based on communes and small industrial units proved less successful since Russian aid was cut off, and targets were not met. It was not until the Third Plan (1962) that China emerged as a world industrial power, and heavy industry began to spread into other areas of the country like Sian and Wuhan. In this plan there was a compromise over the size of the unit involved—a third of China's coal was produced from small commune mines. By the 1970s China was the world's fifth largest steel producer and third largest coal producer, and other more specialised industries were also developing like chemical fertilisers.

Perhaps the most spectacular example of the way China has in 20 years become a world power was the creation of her nuclear industry requiring the most modern of techniques. Russia had offered China a nuclear reactor in 1957, but it was not delivered. China had therefore to start from scratch, but Lin Piao was determined to have a nuclear deterrent because of worsening relations with Russia. The Chinese bomb was developed by Tsian Hsue Shen who had been deported from the United States in 1955, and by 1964 China had an A-bomb. Tsien San Chiang was responsible for the swift progress to an H-bomb in 1967. In 1966 China produced her first missile and in 1970 launched her first satellite.

C5 Social Reform

China's outdated social system had been subjected to 40 years disruption. Confucianism and ancestor worship had been seriously undermined, and Western influences such as Christianity discredited. Mao could thus apply his policies without difficulty. There was a drive to eliminate illiteracy, and by 1962 compulsory primary education was established. Only some 20 per cent (mainly old people) are now illiterate. The role of women was completely changed in 1950 with a law forbidding arranged marriages, and since then women have played roles in industry and the army. Women's Committees in the Communes have been the vehicle for much social change. Street Committees have at last cleaned up the spectacular squalor of many Chinese cities. Massive health reforms have been carried out, and as an indication of progress infant mortality has fallen from 140 to 20 per thousand in 30 years.

Yet such change was disruptive. It brought with it Western ideas, and in 1965–6 Mao sought to reverse some of the trends in the 'Cultural Revolution'. Red Guards were formed to destroy Western influences, and everything from Western music to sports were banned. In secondary schools and universities teachers were purged, and party officials and intellectuals were forced to do manual labour to remind them of their equality in the party with the peasantry. Mao's motives may have been to reassert his own position against moderates, to prove that his Communism was pure, or a belief that through luan (chaos) the state might be strengthened. The effects were disastrous, damaging the economy, throwing the party into turmoil and dividing China from the West at a time when Russian hostility required her to adopt peaceful co-existence. The Party Congress of 1969 brought a formal end to the movement. By 1971 symbolised by the appearance of a table tennis team in America the movement had clearly been reversed, and China was willing to take full advantage of Western contacts.

D The Era of Chinese Moderation

D1 The Two Parties

The Cultural Revolution was brought about in part by divisions within the party. Thirteen out of 17 Politburo members were purged. Mao was increasingly under the influence of Chiang Ching, and her associates in Shanghai including Lin Piao and Chou En Lai while the moderates (called the Peking Black Gang) were led by Liu Shao Chi, Teng Hsiao Ping and Pen Chen. In 1966 Chiang Ching's group prevailed at the start of a party purge in which not less than 40,000 were to die. Moderates like Liu and Teng were expelled. But the catastrophic effect of the Cultural Revolution proved to Mao things had gone too far. The army was called in to expel the Red Guards, and the Party Congress in 1969 restored order by creating a New Central Committee and restoring the Communist Youth League. Lin Piao did not agree with this line, but his death in 1971 seemed to end the threat of further trouble. The moderates wanted Teng to be Mao's successor, but he was unsure. First, he brought in an obscure agricultural specialist, Hua-Kua Feng, to be Deputy Chairman and Minister of Public Security. Then his failure to attend Chou En Lai's funeral in January 1976 seemed to indicate he favoured a moderate. Chiang Ching was determined that the hardliners should succeed so when Mao died in September 1976 the succession was not clear. But by the time the Memorial Hall opened in Peking a year later matters were resolved.

D2 The Defeat of the Gang of Four

As early as January 1975 Teng Hsiao Ping was identified as Vice-Chairman and the moderate successor of Mao, but in April 1976 Chiang Ching secured his dismissal. On Mao's death Chiang, assisted by Wang Hung Wen, Chang Chun Chiao and Yao Wei Yuan (the Gang of Four) tried to reverse the moderate policies, and precipitate a new cultural revolution. But within a month they were arrested, and Chairman Hua took over with Li Hsien Nien as Prime Minister. There followed a limited civil war with troops in Hopei and Kiangsi provinces, and a purge of the party. Then in August 1977 at the Eleventh Party Congress Teng was restored to office, and the course of co-existence resumed. Industrialisation was encouraged with the aid of Western experts. Power was delegated to the Communes and in industry. The courts were freed from central government control, and even some limited civil rights such as criticism of the regime were permitted. Chinese students returning from the West were involved in civil rights demonstrations in places like Shanghai. Then in 1979 the wheel came full circle. The Cultural Revolution was denounced. Evidence was produced of the purges, and the Party Congress denounced Mao's mistakes to a point where reaction set in, and the government was forced to restrain criticism by, for example, closing the Wall of Democracy in Peking. But the Gang of Four were tried and sentenced to death in 1981. It seems clear that China was determined to pursue Western contacts as long as Russian involvement in Vietnam, and then Afghanistan was a menace to her world position. In this realignment Mao like Stalin has been toppled from his pedestal, and revealed as a savage dictator as well as a creative statesman.

E China and Third World Communism

E1 Advancing World Communism

With the departure of the Russian ambassador from Chiang's capital in 1949 the way was open for rapprochement between China and Russia. In December Mao flew to Moscow, and two months later a Sino-Soviet Treaty was signed. This provided Russia with privileges inside China as great as the concessions formerly held by other European states, and for fifty-fifty ownership of joint companies set up in China. In exchange China received the relatively small sum of 60 million dollars for five years. However, Soviet aid was useful to China, and Khrushchev was willing to continue it. Russia and China co-operated during the Korean War (see section 3D4), and in supporting North Vietnam at first, while Western containment concepts were then based on a monolithic Communist landmass comprising Russia and China.

China played a part in stimulating world revolution. She was behind the Chinese uprising in British Malaya and attacked Burma on a number of occasions. China was behind the Communist rising in Indonesia in 1965–6 which brought about the fall of the ruler, Soekarno, and she gave support to the Vietnamese in their long war with America. For her part Russia returned the Manchurian railways, Port Arthur and Dairen to China in

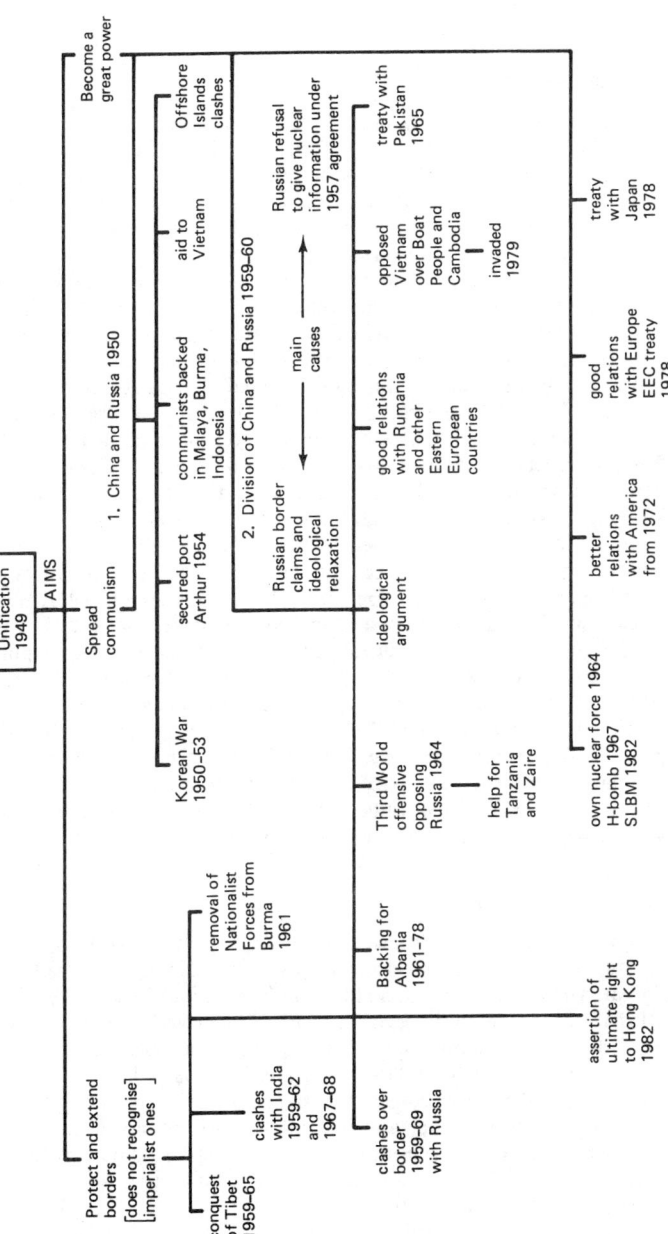

Fig. 13. China as a world power

1954, and as late as October 1959 Khrushchev backed Mao's claim to Taiwan.

E2 Rejecting Imperialist Borders

This relationship was unlikely to last. Mao remembered how Stalin had backed Chiang, and he was gravely suspicious of Russia's role in Korea. Stalin was in close touch with Kao Kang, the governor of Manchuria, and it is possible he saw the seizure of Korea by a pro-Russian government as a means of reasserting Russian control over the whole area. Russia was China's traditional enemy in several border areas. In the Far East Russia had seized Amur province from China in 1858, and Mao was unwilling to accept any nineteenth-century Imperialist borders for his country. Further West lay the Asiatic heartland where lived nomadic Mongol tribes formerly ruled by Islamic chiefs, but it was a region vital for nuclear testing at Lop Nor, and rich in minerals. Stalin had accepted that Sinkiang should be Chinese, but Mao disputed the borders. Dispute also centred on Outer Mongolia which had been Chinese since 1686, but had split away in 1912, and become independent under Russian suzerainty in 1924. Although its independence was recognised, Mao was annoyed at Russian treatment of the Mongols, and in 1960 secured a treaty with the country infuriating the Russians. Outer Mongolia returned to the Soviet sphere in 1966 when a new treaty with Russia was signed, the inhabitants strongly opposing the Cultural Revolution. Tibet had declared itself independent in 1912, but in 1950 Mao invaded the country, and in spite of protests at UNO it was made an autonomous region, but racial persecution and religious suppression led the Tibetans to revolt in 1959. The Dahlai Lama was forced to flee, but UNO ignored his appeal in September although a later UN Report substantiated genocide by the Chinese. About 65,000 Tibetans were killed, and another 43,000 made refugees. In 1965 Tibet was fully incorporated into China. The minute country of Sikkim next door was menaced by left wing revolt in 1973, the ruler appealed to India, and in 1975 the country was incorporated in India to Chinese annoyance.

E3 The Threat to India

India's borders had of course been drawn by the British, and provided ample excuse for Chinese aggression. Moreover, in both Kashmir and Assam there were areas where China could exploit dislike of India since Kashmir was unsettled after 1949 and the Naga tribesmen of Assam were in frequent revolt. The British border ran along the crest of the Himalayas whereas the Chinese claimed it should be the foothills laying claim to areas of Eastern Kashmir (Ashkai Chin) and North Eastern Assam. India had been among the first countries to recognise China, and in 1954 the two countries had agreed to peaceful co-existence. At this time China was lending support to Nehru's non-aligned status, but at the same time (1956–8) building major roads into the Sinkiang region. Equally, India by her treaty with Bhutan (1949) showed she intended to preserve existing borders. In 1959 there was a clash over Ladakh, and the Chinese seized 12,000 square miles. In 1962 direct war began, with India appealing to America and Russia for help (see section

9A4). A cease-fire was arranged, but China remained in Eastern Kashmir while giving up her gains in North East Assam. In 1967–8 there were further disputes when China backed the Nagas in Assam. The result of this dispute was to drive India towards Russia, a move symbolised by Russia's intervention in the war between India and Pakistan in 1966; and to persuade Pakistan to be friendly towards China.

E4 The Southern Borders of China

In May 1950 Mao seized Hainan, and drove the last of the Nationalist forces into the border regions of Burma and Thailand. He was determined to reconquer Taiwan, but was prevented by the outbreak of the Korean War. Thereafter a series of crises (see section 3E5) marked relations between the two Chinas, but with the acceptance of good relations with America in the 1970s Taiwan ceased to be a major issue. Further south lay Hong Kong. This British territory was in three parts—the island itself, Kowloon, and the New Territories, the latter being held on a lease until 1997. But clearly if China failed to renew the lease the 6 million inhabitants of Hong Kong could not survive. The island is now Britain's largest colony, and is clearly a Western affront to China providing like Berlin a sanctuary for spies and refugees. On the other hand it provides vital currency for Chinese trade, and Britain is to seek a future agreement since uncertainty about its future will weaken Hong Kong's economy. For the same reason the Portugese colony of Macao (autonomous since 1975) is allowed to continue.

Indo-China, however, presents a different picture. When the Vietnamese sided with Russia, and attacked China's ally, Cambodia (now renamed Kampuchea), this led to bitter conflict between Russia and China, at long range after the victory of Vietnam in 1975. During 1978 Vietnam joined Comecon, and signed a defence agreement with Russia. She attacked the Chinese within the country forcing the 'Boat People' to flee in large numbers to Hong Kong and elsewhere. Above all, not content with the Communist regime in Cambodia she launched an invasion, and by the end of 1980 had driven the recognised government into the south-western corner. To express anger at this China poured aid into Cambodia, and in February—March 1979 invaded North Vietnam inflicting heavy casualties (see section 13C4–5).

E5 The Clash with Russia

Division began in 1959 when Mao believed that Khrushchev's policies were too friendly to the West and too bourgeois in their economic implications. It was an ideological battle begun when Khrushchev warned Mao against the use of force, and then withdrew Soviet aid thus seriously damaging China's Second Five Year Plan so that some projects took nearly ten years to complete. When Albania was treated the same way China stepped in with aid, and until 1978 Albania was a close supporter of Mao; both countries maintaining they were 'pure' ideologically. During 1964 Communist parties in various Asian and African countries began to divide into pro-Russian or pro-Chinese, and China declined to be present at the 23rd Party Congress in Moscow in 1966. China had considerable backing from Third World countries (see section E6), and in 1969 a conference of 75 Communist parties in Moscow refused to condemn China.

But this was only part of the problem. Russia had for long seen herself as the pre-eminent Communist power. China was determined to be a great power, and her refusal to sign the Test Ban or Non-Proliferation Treaties annoyed the Russians who had not wished her to have nuclear weapons. As China began to exercise power in the world there inevitably arose a conflict of interest so that in Africa, for example, Russia would back Neto in Angola, while China would back Mobutu in Zaire. Such divisions were evident after 1958 in Korea after Chinese troops had finally left, in Vietnam and in the India–Russia versus Pakistan–China divide in the Indian sub-continent. Moreover, there were direct sources of conflict. Russia accused China of extending her borders in Sinkiang, and China accused Russia of repression in Outer Mongolia. In March 1969 armed hostilities broke out over Damansky (or Chen Pao) Island in the Ussuri River, and in May there were clashes in Sinkiang. In spite of an agreement over the river Russia again attacked Sinkiang. Returning from Ho Chi Min's funeral Kosygin of Russia arranged for talks to begin, and as a result there was an improvement in relations. A trade agreement was actually signed between the countries in 1970. China transferred her nuclear industry inland to Szechuan in 1972. Good relations did not last because China's increasing involvement in world diplomacy (see section 13D4) infuriated the Russians. China continued to maintain good relations with European Communists like Ceausescu of Rumania, condemned the invasion of Czechoslovakia and accused Russia of brutal treatment of dissidents. The invasion of Afghanistan by Russia in 1979 made matters worse since this presented a further military threat to China.

E6 China and the Third World

China's Communism had a direct appeal to the Third World. It was Asiatic. It was not directly involved in the East–West conflict. It was based on the peasantry, and was achieved in an underdeveloped economy. The Chinese example was a potent one for new nations seeking to revolutionise their economies, and China soon followed Russia's example of becoming involved in Third World trade and aid. At first China had backed non-aligned countries at the Bandung Conference (1955), but later decided on direct diplomacy. In 1964 Chou En Lai, her Foreign Minister, visited ten African countries, and later in the year the countries of the Indian subcontinent. After Chou's visit President Nyerere of Tanzania went to Peking, and China agreed to build the TanZam Railway. The economy of Tanzania was converted into a Communist one by 1967 even attempting to create village communes. The same year a treaty with the Yemen was signed by China. These moves stimulated the Russians to act, and during the 1970s they were able to contain Chinese influence in Africa by backing guerilla movements, and sending in Cuban troops. It must be stressed that this division has not slowed down the spread of Communism; rather by providing alternatives it has made it more attractive.

Revision Questions

1. Explain why the two Kuomintang leaders, Sun Yat Sen and Chiang Kai Shek were unable to carry out an effective revolution in China after 1911.

2. What part was played by: (a) European, (b) American, (c) Russian and (d) Japanese interference in Chinese affairs until 1949?

3. What were the main contributions of Mao Tse Tung to Communist thinking in relation to: (a) warfare, (b) political development?

4. Write short notes to explain: (a) Sun Yat Sen's Three Principles, (b) the Kuomintang, (c) the Kiangsi Soviet, (d) Manchukuo, (e) the Long March, (f) The Border Region.

5. Why did Mao Tse Tung win the Second Civil War in China (1945–9)?

6. What were Chairman Mao's main achievements in: (a) domestic and (b) foreign policy?

7. Discuss the world role played by China in relation to: (a) non-alignment, (b) the Third World, (c) spreading Communism in Asia. Why did a quarrel with Russia break out after 1959?

8. Explain what is meant by: (a) Democratic Centralism, (b) the Little Red Book, (c) the Commune System, (d) the Great Leap Forward, (e) the Cultural Revolution, (f) the Gang of Four.

Further Reading

Bown, C., *The Peoples' Republic of China*, Heinemann Educational Books, London, 1974.

Chen, J., *Mao and the Chinese Revolution*, Oxford University Press, London, 1965.

Crozier, B., *The Man Who Lost China: The First Full Biography of Chiang Kai Shek*, New York, 1976.

Fitzgerald, C. P., *The Birth of Communist China*, Penguin, Harmondsworth, 1964.

Floyel, D., *Mao Versus Khrushchev*, Pall Mall Press, London, 1964.

Robottam, J., *Modern China*, Longman, Modern Times, 1967.

Schram, S., *The Political Thoughts of Mao Tse Tung*, Penguin, Harmondsworth, 1969.

Suyin, H., *Mao Tse Tung and the Chinese Revolution*, Jonathan Cape, London, 1976.

7
Europe: Economic Recovery and Democratic Advance

A The Quest for European Unity

A1 The Start of the Quest

The concept of European unity is an old one. It had been imposed by force in the days of Napoleon or Hitler, but there had always been a concept of European civilisation. This concept was nurtured in the days of the Roman Catholic Church and the Holy Roman Empire, and it persisted in the concept of a concert of Europe. European development—its art forms, political concepts, economic theories and position in the world—had varied between countries, and nationalism tended to emphasise the differences, but there were also broad similarities. Many national boundaries were recent, and large areas of Europe like the Rhineland states or Northern Italy had been ruled by several countries in their history. Even Britain's isolation was exaggerated for during much of her history she had been a continental power with large territories there, and most of her ruling dynasties were foreign.

The Second World War was, however, the decisive event from which the modern movement to unity has developed. By uniting Europe forcibly under fascism it discredited fascism, and many right wing forces—landlords, the military and parts of the Church—that had retained so much power in Europe between the wars. Eastern Europe was subject to a compulsory, but not unwanted unity and economic revolution by Russian occupation. Western Europe attained by democratic means a revival and redirection of capitalism which brought to power in many countries governments of similar persuasion—moderate right wing Christian Democratic, or moderate left wing Social Democratic parties willing to involve the government in economic affairs, to accept partial nationalisation, create protected agricultural systems, partially redistribute wealth through a new tax system, and above all by creating welfare states, and insisting on full employment and a rising standard of living, rally people to a capitalist renaissance which lasted until the 1970s. The politics of consensus, the willingness to form coalitions and make them work, a desire to work through bureaucracy and rely on academic experts enabled the statesmen of the European countries to talk a common language. The exiled governments had already co-operated during the war, and new governments were formulated on similar principles in Germany and Italy.

The sufferings of Europe in 1945 dictated that these matters should be

uppermost in statesmen's minds. (See section 2B2.) The theoretical base—
Keynes' economics and Beveridge's welfare state—was already there. The
resistance movements, wartime promises and the wartime practice of governments had all emphasised the need for economic planning, social change
and a deeper concern for the individual expressed through more democracy
and greater equality. These views had been heralded in the Atlantic Charter.
They had found expression in such documents as the French Resistance
Charter. The British general election of 1945, and the presence of Communists in the governments of Belgium, France and Italy until 1947 were
evidence of the peoples' will. American economic power made it all the
more certain the trend would continue since the liberalisation of tariffs,
and the provision of massive economic aid forced Europe to abandon the
restrictive trade and fiscal policies of the 1930s while the loss of empires
forced her component nations to compete in world markets on different
terms following a century of imperialism.

A2 The New Political Situation for Europe

The war had changed Europe's political situation (see section 2B4). At first
none of the European powers fully appreciated this. Britain, France,
Portugal, Holland and Spain fought rearguard actions to preserve their
empires, but by the mid-1960s they had virtually ceased to exist (see section
8A3). European unity in one sense was rendered more likely by the existence
of the Communist bloc. UNRRA until 1948 dealt with 17 countries on
both sides of the Iron Curtain. The United Nations Economic Commission
for Europe also straddled the Iron Curtain, but this could not hide the
essential division made clear by Stalin's rejection of Marshall Aid for the
Iron Curtain countries. Socialism provided a challenge to Western Europe,
and the power of the Communist Party required major social reform in
France or Italy in order to kill Communism by kindness. Russia presented
a serious political and military threat. Europe was divided. Germany was
divided, and the centre of the Continent full of possibilities for a future
war. In the face of this threat Germany, Italy and France, the three traditional
enemies of European history, had to come together. The smaller states felt
exposed and their experience in 1939–40 had revealed the folly of neutrality.
Except where Communist pressure was too strong they opted also for
European unity.

America was now a world power, and this had far reaching consequences
for European unity. The Americans favoured economic liberalism, and reformed capitalism to build up the European market and to contain the spread
of Communism. The Marshall Plan (see section 3C5) was decisive for European recovery, and in providing an institutional base for economic unity.
Europe was not able to defend itself against the new Soviet bloc, and was
engulfed by the Cold War. America came to Europe's defence; indeed
provided 75 per cent of the total cost of European defensive alliances and
nuclear protection. The guiding force of Western diplomacy became America
as Britain ceased to be a world power. Europe was thus caught between two
super powers. Her one chance of world influence was to form a 'third force'.
Peaceful co-existence, Ostpolitik and detente were welcome to Europe,
perhaps more so than to the United States since ever since 1938 Europe had

lived with crisis and war. Others saw a chance for Europe to free herself from Russian and American domination, and for individual European countries to pursue a separate world role within the framework of a loosely federal Europe—L'Europe de Patries—as De Gaulle called it. Germany accepted division in return for security, and became the major trading country of Western Europe. The economic gains of the Common Market enabled the European nations to look to their own interests. By the 1980s the argument that European unity was desirable in order to stand by America and resist Russia had been modified to one that it was desirable so that Europe could speak with one voice on world matters like oil or Poland, but not a voice pre-recorded in Washington. European unity and survival go hand in hand.

A3 The Obstacles to Political Unity

By 1945 the Western powers had been drawn by common suffering, military planning and the presence of eight exiled governments in London into close co-operation. Some argue there was then a real chance of European political unity, and that if Britain had taken the lead others would have followed. Churchill's speech favouring unity at Zurich in 1946 is quoted in this context. But there were two major stumbling-blocks. England did not then believe she would cease to be a world power, and she did believe in a special relationship with America. She saw her role as being part of three spheres of interest—Empire, Atlantic and Europe—not too closely tied to any of them. In view of her impending military alliance in Europe this thinking was not very far sighted, but it was a fact. Secondly, France was determined to retain her world position as wars in Syria, Vietnam and Algeria were to show within a year of her re-establishment as a power. France might wish to profit from economic unity, but she still saw French civilisation as unique, and was unwilling to be dictated to by Britain or by Germany.

A conference at The Hague in 1948 was followed by the setting up of the Council of Europe in May 1949 which held its first meeting at Strasbourg in August under Paul Spaak. There were ten founder members—Britain, France, the Benelux countries, the Nordic countries, Ireland and Italy. There was a committee of ministers and a consultative assembly which was empowered to debate and make recommendations on issues affecting Europe, and these powers have never been increased. Yet the Council has increased in membership to 20 today including not only Germany, Switzerland, Greece and Iceland but also Austria, Malta, Cyprus, and Turkey. It thus provides a valuable international forum, and was willing to indicate its stand on principle when Greece was removed from membership from 1969 to 1974 for failing to preserve democracy.

In 1958 a European Court of Human Rights was established before which those with grievances may appear. Britain has been criticised, for example, for her treatment of prisoners in Northern Ireland, and for the use of the cane in schools. The Council, it can be claimed, has done much to promote cultural unity, and common standards of humanity. Churchill had sat as a founder member, but Eden was unwilling to see the Council take further steps to unity, and in January 1952 confirmed Britain's opposition to building a federal Europe on the basis of this organisation. A federal, politically unified Europe is still a long way off.

A4 Reducing Political Tension in Europe

It is easy to forget that much of Europe's history has witnessed a succession of wars and territorial disputes, of which the Second World War was the most recent. Since 1945, however, Western Europe has not suffered from these misfortunes. The peace settlement was followed by the quick restoration of Germany and Italy and in 1951 the state of war with them was formally ended. In 1950 encouraged by Pleven, Foreign Minister of France, there was a meeting with De Gasperi of Italy at Santa Margharita to bury their past differences. In 1951 De Gasperi and Adenauer of Germany met for the same purpose. The new European statesmen were prepared to reconcile differences—partly out of necessity with Russia to the east, and partly from conviction.

There were several outstanding political issues. France wished to retain the Saar which was overwhelmingly German, but discussions begun in the Council of Europe led to the peaceful return of the Saar to Germany in 1957. Austria quarrelled with Italy over her treatment of the Austrians in the South Tyrol which was incorporated in Italy as the province of Bolzano. In 1969 agreement on this issue was reached with Italy conceding regional autonomy to the area. During 1962 De Gaulle and Adenauer exchanged visits, and in January 1963 a treaty ended the centuries of Franco-German rivalry in one part of the Continent. Ostpolitik (see section 13D3) led to the reconciliation of West Germany and Poland, the two Germanies and West Germany and Czechoslovakia. Italy and Yugoslavia finally resolved their differences over Trieste in 1975. For the majority of Western Europeans, whatever the Cold War tensions, the last 30 years have seen unprecedented steps to reducing age old political enmities, and this has helped the economic reconstruction of the continent.

A5 Europe's Military Defence

Since 1945 Europe has experienced the Cold War, and until the early 1970s the German question remained at the heart of the tension and a possible cause of war. Europe was, of course, involved globally in the Cold War (see sections 3B2, 3C6–7), and as a result of the creation of NATO and WEU achieved both defence by America and involvement with American policy. Yet it is surely more important that the German problem was resolved in spite of the Berlin Blockade and the Wall, and that Europe has experienced one of her longest periods of peace. This may be due to fear of nuclear war—to the effective working of the deterrent or to the balance of military force implicit in NATO ranged against the Warsaw Pact. Or it may simply be the acceptance by both sides of the status quo after long years of war. Whatever the cause Europe's defensive posture so far has been successful. NATO grew with the addition of Greece, Turkey, West Germany and Spain. The existence of the standing NATO Council after 1952, and meetings of NATO defence and foreign ministers have enabled Europe to formulate common defence, and even on occasion foreign, policies. The powers were able to take combined action against terrorism in 1977, for example, with the Strasbourg Convention, and they condemned the Russian invasion of Afghanistan in 1980.

Attempts to deepen this unity have not succeeded. The Pleven Plan for a united European army failed through lack of French ratification in 1954. Proposals for a Multilateral Nuclear Force were blocked by Britain in 1964. Britain and France have nuclear deterrents of their own, and both countries recently announced plans for their modernisation. France in particular has subjected NATO to difficulties. In 1964 she left the joint naval command, and in 1966 the joint military command as part of De Gaulle's policy, and as a result SHAPE was forced to move to Belgium (1967). For a time in 1974 NATO was seriously weakened because Portugal was engulfed in revolution, while Greece and Turkey withdrew co-operation because of troubles in Cyprus. Greece has recently threatened to leave NATO with the election of a socialist government, while Britain and Spain have differences over Gibraltar. Detente has offered Western Europe benefits in trade and reduced tension, and Third World actions by France and Germany have not always coincided with American policy. Thus, as attempts have been made to create a common European foreign policy through foreign ministers' meetings, differences have arisen with America and between members over such matters as the degree of support for Palestinian Arabs, opposition to Russia over Afghanistan and Poland, or condemnation of Russia over the shooting down of a South Korean airliner.

A6 The Start of Economic Unity

In 1944 as a result of the work of Camille Gutt and Paul Spaak, Belgium, Holland and Luxemburg (Benelux) formed a customs union from which the Common Market was to grow. European recovery after the war was first and foremost a matter for individual countries: Britain with nationalisation and devaluation organised by Cripps, Gutt's reforms in Belgium, the work of Mendes-France and Monnet in France and Italian recovery under De Gasperi were important examples. But heavy defence burdens, colonial obligations and the dislocation of war proved too great, and in the winter of 1947 recovery still seemed a long way off. It was in June 1947 that Marshall put forward his 'Plan', and in March 1948 the European Recovery Programme was launched with the founding of the OEEC. This was to administer the aid, and draft proposals to be submitted to the American end of the scheme organised by an ex-New Dealer, Paul Hoffman. The intention was to raise European production by 25 per cent, and by 1952 this had been achieved with the help of 13,150 million dollars of American aid—the largest share of which went to Britain followed by France, Italy, and after December 1949, West Germany.

This recovery led to three developments. Europe was able to participate in the General Agreement on Tariffs and Trade or GATT (1947), and the later Kennedy Round of tariff reductions (1962) which culminated in the full operation of GATT in 1967. In 1950 the European Payments Union was established which was to restore European currencies. Full convertibility was achieved by 1955. After the founding of the Common Market this was replaced in December 1958 by the European Monetary Agreement whose policies on such matters as the 'snake' (a fixed relationship for several European currencies) and 'green pound' (a unit of currency for agricultural transactions) were part of the EEC. Thirdly, Canada and America were associates in OEEC, and after direct aid had ceased in 1952 consultations and economic advice continued. An agreement to alter OEEC into the OECD was made in December 1960, and the new organisation began work in late 1961. It was joined later by Denmark, Spain and Japan. The idea that a grouping containing the world's main economic powers should discuss world economic problems was stimulated by France under President Giscard D'Estaing, and the onset of European depression after 1973. In 1975 the first annual economic summit was held at Rambouillet, and followed by others such as Williamsburg in 1983.

A7 The Foundation of the Common Market

It was in May 1950 that Robert Schuman (1886–1963), French Foreign Minister and subsequently Prime Minister, put forward a scheme for the Benelux countries, France and West Germany to combine to make a common market for iron, steel and coal which had been devised by Jean Monnet (1888–1979). The powers were already linked in the Treaty of Brussels (except for West Germany), and would with both West Germany and Italy be linked in WEU in 1954. Each country had suffered from two world wars, and their middle area—the Rhineland, the Ruhr, the Saar and Alsace and Lorraine—had been the most fertile field of dispute between them. To link their basic industries would be to deter future disputes, and prevent future war as well as providing economic advantages. Britain was asked to take part but as she then produced a third of Europe's steel and half of her coal she felt that she would only like to be consulted. The treaty was signed in 1951, and came into force in July 1952. There was a High Authority of nine members appointed for six years to act supranationally, a Council representing the governments, a Consultative Committee representing the interests of the industry and appointed by the council and a Common Assembly of 78 delegates from the countries' parliaments. The basic aims were to stimulate production, lower domestic prices and ensure the development of international trade. Early in 1953 the members stated they were in favour of extending the operation to a 'common market' in all goods, and in June 1955 a conference met at Messina to discuss 'the progressive fusion of national economies'. Paul Spaak (1899–1972) was asked to draw up a report on how this might be achieved. In November 1955 Eden withdrew Britain from participation in the talks seeking to counter them with a wider proposal for a free trade area. Discussions began in May 1956, and in March 1957 the Treaty of Rome was signed by the six—France, West Germany, Italy, Belgium, Holland and Luxemburg—to establish a new organisation in January 1958 on which the further economic recovery of Europe was to be based.

A8 The Organisation of the Common Market

The aims of the market were free trade inside, and a common tariff outside, a common policy toward 'associated' states, a common agricultural policy, the encouragement of balanced expansion and an accelerated standard of living, a Social Fund to help developing regions and an investment bank. The Community took over the ECSC, and the organisation of Euratom

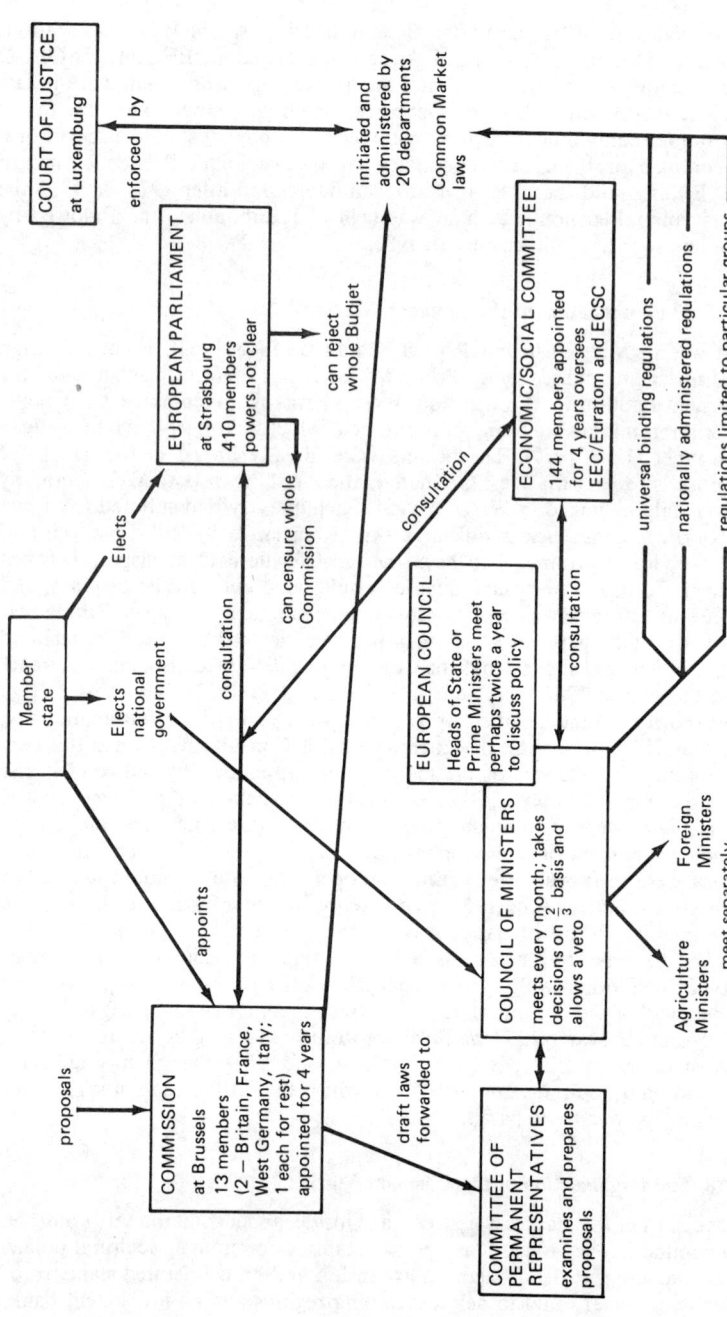

Fig. 14. The institutions of the Common Market

or the European Atomic Energy Commission set up in 1957, and it was planned to complete the basic organisation within twelve, later shortened to ten years. During 1967 the organisation was overhauled and the European Economic Community (EEC) in its present shape created.

There are four basic organisations in the EEC. There is a Council representing each member state by a minister having a weighted vote (originally four each for France, West Germany and Italy, two for Belgium and Holland and one for Luxemburg). Decisions can be on a majority vote, but a veto can be exercised on matters of major importance. The Commission is a permanent body meeting at Brussels originally with 14 members representing the six founders, and now with 13—two each for Britain, France, Italy and West Germany, and one each for the other countries. The Commission drafts proposals for the Council, and carries out the decisions of the Council, and to do this has created a European bureaucracy. It has a President, and among these have been some distinguished figures in European development, including Robert Schuman and Walter Hallstein, Jean Rey and Roy Jenkins. A European parliament was established at Strasbourg, with its secretariat in Luxemburg. There were initially 142 representatives—36 each from the bigger, 14 from the two smaller states, and 6 from Luxemburg—nominated by the governments. With British accession to the market interest began to focus more on this parliament, and it now consists of 410 directly elected Euro-Members. The first elections were held in 1979 after systematic delays by the British Labour Government. Parliament appoints committees to scrutinise the Commission, and it can by a two thirds majority censure the whole Commission. It has the power to reject the budget and in 1980 did so for the first time in protest against the common agricultural policy. Lastly, there is a Court established at Luxemburg with two Advocates-General and seven Judges appointed for six years by general agreement among the members. This Court has the right to rule on the enforcement of Commission decisions, and Britain has found herself in trouble on such matters as enforcing the tachograph or 'spy in the cab' in lorries, and the permitting of increased lorry sizes. The EEC has a whole range of development agencies and committees like the European Nuclear Research Centre, the Economic and Social Committee and other institutions like an Investment Bank and a Court of Auditors to investigate its finances. The Community suffers from lack of clear decision processes, involved bureaucracy and too little democratic control, but it is in its early stages as a supranational body, and whatever its particular failings its benefits to Europe are considerable, and the efforts to improve it have been substantial.

A9 France and the Community 1958–69

The early years of the Common Market were dominated by General De Gaulle the President of France. His principal aim was: 'France first.' The community was to serve the interests of French farmers, and it was not to proceed to federalism which might endanger France's new defence and foreign policies. These in turn were planned to break free from American dominance of Europe, and to ensure that Britain was not able to enter Europe and thus, in De Gaulle's view, bring in America by the back door. De Gaulle was an unstable member of the European Community. By 1966 he had withdrawn France from the command structure of NATO, and in 1969 WEU was boycotted by France. As early as 1965 there was a clash in the community over agricultural prices and a seven month boycott by France who used her veto to prevent any reforms. The Mansholt Plan (1968) for reforming the Common Agricultural Policy (CAP) by eventually reducing the agricultural product and population was strongly opposed, and the CAP eventually adopted in January 1970 was a triumph for the French. It contained an annual price review which kept prices up, rigorous exclusion of imports and arrangements to purchase surpluses to keep prices up leading to 'butter mountains', and 'wine lakes'.

Britain was later to make much of De Gaulle's double veto on their entry into the Community, but De Gaulle could rightly claim that Britain had shown little early interest and was just as selfish as France when it came to protecting her oil, or cheap food imports from the Commonwealth. Britain had opted out of the Common Market because the 1950s had seen the continuation of the recovery achieved after the war, and the statesmen of the period continued to think of Britain as a world power. Macmillan could proclaim: 'This is a great country and let us not be ashamed to say so', and Wilson commented: 'We can rely on our own strength outside the Community.' It was only when the economic performance began to lag, the British Empire to dissolve more rapidly than anticipated and the special relationship with America to decline that Britain turned to Europe. The Common Market was held out as an economic necessity and a political desirability. The immediate reaction had been to create a rival organisation. In November 1959 the Treaty of Stockholm had formed the seven (Britain, Austria, Norway, Denmark, Sweden, Portugal and Switzerland) who were to create a separate free trading area beginning with a 20 per cent duty cut, and aiming for the abolition of duties by 1967. The existence of this organisation added to the complications of British entry which was resolved by Britain and Denmark joining the EEC, and Finland and Iceland joining the other five in a new EFTA in January 1973 which was to achieve free trade with the Common Market by the end of 1977.

From July 1961 to January 1963 Britain negotiated to join the EEC, but throughout this period she was building up her independent nuclear deterrent with the help of America culminating in the Polaris deal. Then in the Non-Proliferation Treaty she urged other countries not to have nuclear deterrents, and France of course refused to sign this treaty. To De Gaulle this was typical of 'Anglo-Saxon' trickery which he had experienced during the war and never forgiven. Moreover, Wilson's government (1964–70) kept the deterrent, and sought to play a continuing world role with Wilson saying in 1964: 'We are a world power and a world influence or we are nothing.' The steadily weakening economy, and the obvious success of the EEC convinced him of a need to have a strong European rather than a weak world role, and in 1966 he made up his mind to apply. Britain was able to satisfy EFTA, and five out of the six in the Community, but De Gaulle was convinced that Britain's weak economy (devaluation occurred in 1967) would damage the Community, and Britain would unite with Germany to oppose the CAP. Negotiations in 1967 began in May, and collapsed in November. Wilson did not give up. When De Gaulle retired he announced in December

1969 a renewal of Britain's application. Terms were drafted for negotiations to open in the summer of 1970. By now it was clear how successful the market was. In Europe Malta obtained associated status, and Austria, Sweden and Switzerland were seeking reciprocal agreements. Norway, Denmark and Ireland all intended to negotiate for entry.

A10 The Broadening Bounds of the Community

In June 1970 Britain, Denmark, Norway and Ireland opened negotiations to join the EEC. Heath was now Prime Minister of Britain and a dedicated European. By establishing good relations with Pompidou of France in 1971 he cleared the way for Britain's success. The new members joined in October 1972 signing the Treaty of Brussels and becoming full members in January 1973. Denmark and Norway promised referendums, and that in Norway narrowly went against joining. By now the British Labour Party (unlike any other Western Socialist Party) was increasingly divided on joining. Labour promised to renegotiate the terms and to hold a referendum, and this created uncertainty about Britain's membership. When Labour returned to office in 1974 fresh terms were negotiated at Dublin, but even these were opposed in the Commons by nearly half the party. A cabinet 'agreement to differ' was allowed during the referendum campaign that followed, and this clearly revealed a deep division between pro-marketeers led by Jenkins, Wilson and Callaghan, and anti-marketeers led by Foot, Shore and Benn. In June 1975 on a 64 per cent turnout 67 per cent voted in favour of membership in a referendum.

The trouble was that Britain joined just as the EEC was moving to the second stage of its organisation. The CAP was approved before Britain joined with its efficient farming industry which, together with Germany, would have to foot the bill for France. In 1970 the Werner Plan proposed a monetary union for Europe with a common currency, free movement of capital, and an exchange rate based on the 'green' pound. By March 1973 a 'snake' of European currencies had been created by which they floated together against the dollar. Britain floated her pound in 1972 after a few years with a favourable balance of payments, and had no wish to join the European system. Thus, when it was established in March 1979 Callaghan's government refused to join although Britain accepted her pound should not float more than the agreed margin of 2.5 per cent either way of the EEC countries. The new Regional Development Fund established in 1973 was opposed by Britain until 1975 as they stood to gain by it, and wanted a larger sum than the £1,250 million set aside. When it did begin to operate all Scotland, Northern Ireland, Wales and much of Northern England became a development zone, and the EEC has done much to help these areas.

As opposition to the EEC mounted inside the minority Labour government in Britain during the 1970s Callaghan delayed proposals for direct elections to the European Parliament, and it was not until June 1979 that these were held. The large conservative majority in the European parliament was perhaps one reason for Labour opposition to this extension of democracy in a community they criticised as undemocratic. One major reason why Britain has not gained as much from the market as was hoped is that from

1974 to 1979 the government was not fully behind our membership. In spite of this British trade inside the market has grown, and Germany is Britain's most important customer.

In 1969 two events occurred which marked a significant change in European diplomacy. Brandt became Chancellor of Germany. The Warsaw Pact proposed a general security conference. From this there grew Ostpolitik which settled the borders of Central Europe, and brought the wartime problems to an end. Europe entered a decade of detente (see section 13E3), and this relaxation in tension contributed to economic change. West Germany developed trading contacts with Poland and East Germany, EEC surpluses were sold to Russia and loans made to countries like Poland by Western bankers. Favourable trade agreements for the East were made by Britain and France. Joint projects such as one to bring natural gas from Russia to West Germany were begun. French 'globalism' appeared to be working on a wider scale, and the European countries began to break free from American dominance in defence and foreign policies. This was inevitable with increasing economic strength, but it reflected a range of factors, not least heavy European dependence on Middle Eastern oil which led the EEC to give some support to the Palestinian Arabs.

In many ways the Community has gone from strength to strength despite obvious difficulties. It is sometimes said it is an inward looking rich man's club, but this is far from the truth. During the 1960s as world concern over developing nations grew (see section 14B4) Europe played her part. During 1969 three former British East African colonies—Kenya, Uganda and Tanzania—achieved associated status with the EEC, as did Tunisia, Morocco and nineteen other African states. In 1975 the Lomé Convention signed by the Common Market with no less than 52 other states gave them unrestricted access for all industrial, and 84 per cent of agricultural products, most favoured nation treatment under GATT and financial support from the RDF. A Consultative Assembly was set up so that their views could be heard. In Southern Europe the Community has expanded. Greece joined the EEC as its tenth member in 1981, while Spain and Portugal are engaged in negotiations for entry.

Since 1979 Britain has played a more active role in Europe seeking to rally the EEC on foreign policy issues, and to invigorate its institutions. The European Parliament has become more active since the British joined, and in 1981 Thatcher became the first British Prime Minister to speak there. Rows over fishing, and inevitably with France over agricultural policies remain unsolved, but in one respect Britain has improved matters. Her initial contribution to the budget was low since the British pound floated below the green pound, but during the 1970s her contribution steadily rose from £180 million to £900 million. This was unfair since Britain is the third poorest member of the Community, and since it was scheduled to rise to £1.200 million, Thatcher sought to renegotiate it. This was largely successfully done, and the contribution was cut to £440 million. Moreover, it has been agreed to examine the budget of the EEC and the CAP in the future.

B France and General Charles de Gaulle (1890–1970)

B1 Establishing the Fourth Republic

France was liberated in August 1944, and in October the Allies recognised De Gaulle's government (see section 2B4). The first response of many who had suffered under German occupation was revenge on the Vichy regime, and there was a bitter civil war spearheaded by the Communists. Three of the Vichy leaders were executed while others were given prison sentences including Petain. Over 700 collaborators were executed. These events continued to focus attention on the widespread support for fascism among the French ruling class, and they ensured a sharp swing to the left in the elections held in October 1945. The Communists profiting from their impressive resistance record were soon the largest party in the new Assembly, followed by the Socialists, and then a new Catholic reformist party—the MRP. De Gaulle was de facto President, but forfeited the chance of staying by insisting that the French empire should be retained in its entirety. The government asked for a large military budget and the Communists and Socialists combined to oppose this. De Gaulle resigned in January 1946.

Drafting a new constitution did not prove easy, and 1946 was largely occupied by a bitter dispute about this. In the first part of the year a referendum rejected the proposed constitution, but after an MRP government took office during the summer and Georges Bidault became President a second referendum accepted the constitution by 9.1 million to 7.9 million, with 7.9 million abstentions. The new constitution was very like that of the Third Republic, and was to suffer from the same defects: clearly unpopular with a majority of Frenchmen and subject to persistent political chaos. The first elections in 1946 produced a Popular Front government under Blum and Thorez which although it was helpful in encouraging economic recovery and carrying out Monnet's Reconstruction Plan threw the Western powers into disarray. 1947 was thus the decisive year for the new republic. De Gaulle formed the RPF to rally the right to the new government, and in the local elections this emerged as the strongest group. The Socialists, Radicals and MRP caught between the two extremes were forced together. The Communists were excluded from the government, and the governments successively of Ramadier, Schumann and Queuille fought off left wing challenges which included a peasant boycott of grain deliveries, a general strike and riots in towns like Marseilles. Queuille's government lasted for 13 months (the longest in the Fourth Republic), and the elections of November 1948 confirmed the swing away from Communism. Economic reconstruction, Marshall Aid and a new social security system clipped the wings of their demands. Thorez was a hardline Stalinist and Stalin's policies elsewhere in Europe discredited his party. The trade union movement divided with many leaving the Communist CGT for the Catholic CFTC.

B2 The Failure of the Fourth Republic

From 1946 to 1954 the French were involved in a major war in Vietnam costing 21,000 French lives, and ending in defeat (see section 3E4). In 1954 a revolt began in Algeria, and by 1958 there were rumours that defeat was

Sovereign	Prime Minister	Period in office	Party	Elections
George VI 1936-52 Elizabeth II 1952-	W. Churchill	1940-1945	CON	1945
	C. Attlee	1945-1951	LAB	1950
	W. Churchill	1951-1955	CON	1951
	Sir Anthony Eden	1955-1957	CON	1955
	H. Macmillan	1957-1963	CON	1959
	Sir Alec Douglas-Home	1963-1964	CON	1964
	H. Wilson	1964-1970	LAB	1966
	E. Heath	1970-1974	CON	1970
	H. Wilson	1974-1976	LAB	1974 (2)
	J. Callaghan	1976-1979	LAB	
	M. Thatcher	1979-1983	CON	1979
	M. Thatcher	1983-	CON	1983

Chancellor		Period in office	Party	Elections
K. Adenauer		1949-63	Christian Democrat (CD)	1949 1953 1957 1961
L. Erhard		1963-66	CD and Free Democrat (FD) 1965	1963 1965
K. Kiesinger		1966-69	CD and Social Democrat (SD)	1966
W. Brandt		1969-74	SD and FD	1969
H. Schmidt		1974-82	SD and FD	1974 1976 1980
H. Kohl		1982-	CD and FD	1982

President	Prime Minister	Period in office	Party	Elections
General Charles de Gaulle 1959-69	M. Debre	1959-62	Gaullist	1958
	G. Pompidou	1962-68	Gaullist	1967
	C. de Murville	1968-69	Gaullist	1968
G. Pompidou 1969-74	J. Chaban-Delmas	1969-73	Gaullist	
	M. Messmer	1973-74	Gaullist	
V. Giscard D'Estaing 1974-81	J. Chirac	1974-76	Gaullist	1974
	R. Barre	1976-81	Independent Republican Party	1978
F. Mitterrand 1981-	P. Mauroy	1981-	Socialist	1981

Fig 15. The Prime Ministers of Britain, the Chancellors of Germany and the Presidents and Prime Ministers of France in recent times

imminent there as well. Western foreign policy was clearly dominated by the Anglo-American axis, and attempts to shine as a great power did not succeed. In 1956 France was involved in the Suez War and a further reverse. The Fourth Republic certainly had successes: economically France was on her feet by 1950, and joining the Common Market in 1957 was to her advantage. Three plans doubled French production over the 1938 figure. A French Union for the colonies was established in 1946, and the first steps taken to converting this into a French Community. The Republic seemed determined to remain a great power. In 1950 a massive three year defence programme involving conscription was introduced, and France joined WEU. But on the whole France was increasingly seen as a victim of chaotic and weak government.

This impression was conveyed most of all by government instability. The Fourth Republic had 24 governments in a period when Britain had four and Germany one, and although ministerial continuity meant many of these were merely new groupings of the same men the amount of time devoted to political infighting was damaging, and able men were unable to show their paces. Moreover, there were substantial bodies on left and right who opposed the republic. The RPF made substantial gains, and although De Gaulle gave up the leadership in 1953 it remained a powerful right wing force. On the left a substantial Communist Party taking about 25 per cent of the votes remained. A series of weak governments under Pleven, Pinay and Laniel gave way to a stronger one under Mendes-France in 1954, but this and succeeding governments were persistently defeated on the Algerian issue. Continuous war was placing heavy strains on the economy which involved devaluation of the franc (1957), and foreign aid from America and the EPU totalling 655 million dollars, but any attempt to give up Algeria was firmly resisted.

B3 The Revolution of 1958

Charles de Gaulle had graduated from St Cyr in 1911, and had a long military career. He had been an early advocate of armoured warfare in his book *The Army of the Future*. At the start of the Second World War he was Colonel of the Fifth Armoured Division, and by the end he was a General and leader of the French government. De Gaulle had little love for the Algerian element in the army for they had backed Petain and Giraud in 1940–3 against him, and he was willing to sacrifice them for France. But he did have a longing to restore France as a major power, and end Anglo-American dominance of the Western alliance. When in May 1958 it seemed as if a government would settle Algeria by major concessions the military led by Generals Massu and Salan formed a Committee of Public Safety, and clearly a military coup was intended. Using the RPF De Gaulle brought pressure to bear, and forced his appointment on President Coty. He became president–premier with dictatorial powers for six months on June 1st. A new constitution giving greater powers to the President was swiftly drafted, and approved in a referendum.

In October the Fifth Republic began, elections gave victory to the UNR (Gaullist Party), and a special electoral college appointed De Gaulle president for seven years. In January 1959 De Gaulle became President, and Michel Debre, the first Gaullist Prime Minister. Once again as in the days of Louis Napoleon, or Petain France had been rescued by a general, and subjected to an authoritarian regime based on the referendum. On the other hand a generals' coup would have had far more more serious consequences, and ironically only De Gaulle could really deal with this threat.

B4 De Gaulle's Rule in France: 1959–1969

De Gaulle's period of office was essentially one party rule; indeed the Algerian crisis gave him the opportunity to establish riot police and secret service methods which aroused widespread opposition. There were several attempts made to kill him by the right, and the left were incensed by the censorship and the conservative attitude of the regime. Nevertheless the majority of the French gave the General backing with his controversial policies. The most dangerous problem was Algeria. A government in exile backed by Nasser in Cairo was facing settler resistance backed by the army. De Gaulle offered Algeria independence, integration with France, or internal self-government, and this of course aroused violent opposition. In January 1961 there was a settler revolt, and in April a military one led by Salan; both were defeated by De Gaulle who opened discussions with the rebels. In March 1962 the talks led to a cease-fire, and De Gaulle knew he would have to take on right wing opposition, but two referendums (January 1961 and April 1962) showed he had majority backing. The generals formed the OAS led by Salan who was captured and sentenced to life imprisonment. Independence came for Algeria in July 1962, but conflict with the OAS continued, fanned by settlers who had returned to France. De Gaulle also worked out a new relationship with the remaining French colonies—the French Community (1960)—which enabled France to retain close economic links with her former African colonies.

It is debatable whether France was restored as a major power by De Gaulle. It is true she retained colonies and bases abroad when other Western powers were giving them up. She created a 'force de frappe'— a small nuclear deterrent of her own. Detente with Russia was pursued with a visit to Russia by De Gaulle in 1966 renewing a traditional strand in French foreign policy, and annoying America. America was further infuriated by De Gaulle's visit to Mexico and the recognition of Communist China during 1964. Britain was twice prevented from joining the EEC, and antagonised by De Gaulle's visit to Canada in 1967 when he backed the Quebec separatists. De Gaulle annoyed NATO by forcing it to move its headquarters, and withdrawing military co-operation. He told America to leave Vietnam, and withdrew from SEATO enabling Paris to be the venue of the first Vietnam talks in May 1968. The EEC was disrupted by French boycotts on two occasions. All these actions undoubtedly created a separate French position, and by opening contact so widely France was able to make economic gains in the Third World particularly in Africa and the Middle East. But she was not able to alter either NATO or the EEC, only to disrupt them from time to time, and it was doubtful if this weakening of the Western position in order to lessen American dominance was in the long run beneficial to France.

In domestic affairs De Gaulle was less consistent than he appeared. Like Napoleon III he postured abroad, but at home made concessions, and saw the economy steadily weaken. His Prime Ministers (Debre, Pompidou and De Murville) were very much in his shadow, and by basing the government on referendums and his own popularity De Gaulle ensured that it would not survive indefinitely. For several years the French economy prospered. French farms gained from the EEC. Technical development of space research and nuclear energy went ahead. State planning ensured industrial growth, but once the economy began to falter in 1968 with a fall in the reserves, rising unemployment and increasing inflation De Gaulle was unable to maintain himself in office. He had done what France wanted: created stability, and carved out a world role, but he was too old to continue, and after the election of 1967 the Gaullists were left with a majority of one in the Assembly.

B5 'Le Petit Revolution' 1968

All Western countries experienced unrest during the late 1960s for a variety of reasons. France was no exception because De Gaulle's regime had raised living standards, but could not maintain them indefinitely. His method of government was unpopular with the younger generation greatly influenced by writers like Marcuse and Debray. All secondary school pupils in France had the right to enter university, and consequently numbers had swollen beyond the capacity of buildings or lecturers. Anarchists led by Cohn-Bendit exploited this situation hoping to create a revolutionary situation in Paris beginning with Nanterre University and spreading to the Sorbonne. Some 60 barricades were erected in the Latin quarter in Paris in 1968. The CGT was prepared to support the students, although there was ostensibly little in common between sociologists and steel workers. There were sit-in strikes at Renault and Sud Aviation, and an attempt at a general strike with nine million workers affected.

Contemporaneous riots in America, the Grosvenor Square Riot in Britain and the Rudi Dutschke riots in Germany unnecessarily alarmed De Gaulle who had survived a vote of censure in the Assembly. On May 24th he agreed to student and worker reforms, and promised an election. Decrees were passed raising the minimum wage, and worker support for students soon passed. The election that followed confirmed De Gaulle in the Presidency by a massive majority. For the first time one party—De Gaulle's UDR—could form a government on its own with a majority of 109. However, a few days later Pompidou was removed and De Murville appointed to carry out reforms including a new education bill, and worker participation schemes in industry. A law of 1936 was used to ban the student organisations. But in fact De Gaulle's prestige was dented, and when early next year a referendum rejected two proposed constitutional changes involving a new system of regional government by a small margin (11.9 million to 10.5 million) De Gaulle retired in April 1969, and died in November 1970. Gaullism, however, survived as a political movement in France.

B6 The Decline of Gaullism in France 1969–81

After a short interval Pompidou was elected President although for much of his time in office he was ill. The new government was formed by Chaban-

Delmas. Included in the government were members of the old moderate right like Giscard D'Estaing, the Finance Minister. The government was faced with a failure of the economic plan begun in 1971 when the growth rate was only half that expected; made worse in 1973 by an energy crisis which was particularly serious for France almost totally dependent on Middle Eastern oil. The Gaullists still commanded a majority of votes in the 1973 elections, but scandal embraced the Prime Minister who was succeeded by Messmer. When Pompidou resigned D'Estaing became the non-Gaullist President with Chirac as Prime Minister. The left was now gathering strength due to widespread opposition to conscription and the nuclear deterrent. Moreover, prolonged right wing government gave rise to anti-Semitism in France. It seemed possible that the Socialists led by Mitterrand and the Communists led by Marchais might combine if Marchais would reverse the traditional pro-Moscow line of his party. The economy got steadily worse with a million unemployed. The government floated the franc, and introduced a £2,000 million reflation into the economy in 1974, but it did not work. The government also became involved in a struggle with Corsican Separatists, and in a security scandal over phone tapping. Trouble grew in the armed forces with a demand for a union.

Under these circumstances the UDR split in 1976 with the resignation of Chirac who reformed the Gaullists as the Assembly of the Republic, and succeeded in being elected to the influential office of Mayor of Paris in 1977. D'Estaing called on Raymond Barre, a non-party man. But the new government was unable to curb the economic difficulties, and in the municipal elections early in 1977 the Communists and Socialists achieved great gains in urban France. Unfortunately they were unable to agree on the amount of nationalisation and on the nuclear deterrent, and thus in the national elections of 1978 D'Estaing and Barre triumphed. But not for long. D'Estaing's foreign policy came in for considerable criticism. He was involved in military intervention in Chad, and then withdrew French forces. Soon after Colonel Gaddafi (France's main oil supplier) invaded the country for the first time. D'Estaing received diamonds as a gift from Bokassa, a mad dictator in Central Africa, who was overthrown after practising mass killings. The Ayatollah Khomeini was sheltered in France before returning to spearhead the Islamic revolution in Iran. Nor was D'Estaing's meeting with Brezhnev in May 1980, soon after the Russian seizure of Afghanistan, popular. The government was involved in a number of scandals including the suicide of the Minister of Labour, and the long uninvestigated murder of another minister, the Duc de Broglie. D'Estaing's style was not suited to the harsher economic climate prevailing in France. The Left came together once more, and in the 1981 Presidential elections Mitterrand triumphed, and became the first Socialist in office for 23 years. Although his government included four Communists in minor posts he soon proved a strong supporter of NATO, and modernised French nuclear weapons. His economic policies involving heavy expenditure and considerable nationalisation were curtailed by the continuing economic crisis. But in spite of this an era that began in 1958 had ended.

C Germany and Konrad Adenauer (1876–1967)

C1 The Allied Control Commission 1945–49

After the war Germany was divided, and occupied by the four powers (see section 3B2) who ruled the country through the ACC. At first the need was to deal with the Nazi Party which had over eight million members, and with the large number of organisations it had spawned. An extensive programme of denazification and re-education was embarked upon involving a million arrests, and 140,000 trials which went on until 1949. The War Criminal trials at Nuremberg finished in September 1946 when twelve were hung, seven imprisoned and the rest either acquitted (three) or committed suicide (three). The first intention of the Allies was to make sure Germany never revived as a major power. Her fortifications were demolished, and she was allowed a small police force and no army. Prussia was abolished as a German state. Measures were taken to dismantle the German economy so that its productive level was held firstly at half that in 1938, and then at 1936 levels. Heavy reparations were exacted by Russia from her zone, and also sent from the Allied zones to her.

The trouble with this policy was that Germany was already economically in ruins, and vast movements of people added to her difficulties. The population of Germany was restored to 1939 levels living in an area which was considerably smaller. This added to feeding and living problems, and forced the Allies to give aid to the Germans. The cost of this was so great that the Western Allies stopped reparations in 1946, and during 1948 agreed to full economic revival. Re-education naturally meant the creation of basic civil rights and political organisations. The Allies established the Christian Democrat and Social Democrat Parties, and local elections were held from January 1946 culminating in those for Berlin in December 1948. It was clear political life was starting again. The West's efforts to introduce economic growth, and restore the German currency led to a crisis with the Russians (see section 3C6), and this forced the West to restore West Germany as a bulwark against the Soviet Union.

C2 The Allied High Commission 1949–55

In May 1949 the Federal Republic of West Germany was created with its capital at Bonn divided into 11 (later 12) lands or regions, and this was approved by all the former states except Bavaria. The first elections led to a victory for the Christian Democrats who ruled Germany until 1969, and Konrad Adenauer became Chancellor. Mayor of Cologne, he had been part of the middle class opposition to Hitler, been twice imprisoned, but released in November 1944. He was mayor for a short time again, and then dismissed by the British for not being efficient enough. He was the founder of the CDU party, and proved a staunch supporter of the West. His first task was to embark on the reconstruction of Germany. An agreement in November 1949 paved the way for this followed by 3.5 billion dollars of Marshall Aid. Western help was given to rebuild German industry, and a law in 1951 introduced co-partnership into industry which enabled Germany to have the best industrial relations in any Western country for over 20 years.

His second task was to restore Germany as a sovereign state. Unification was held by all concerned to be vital, but as a first step Adenauer was prepared to create West Germany in spite of strong attacks by Schumacher's SPD that this would be too Western ever to secure full unification. The creation of East Germany made this unlikely anyway, and the Western powers for reasons of cost and security were anxious to have Adenauer's state on their side in the Cold War. There was great hostility to German revival among Western parties of the left, and in France. However this was overcome, and agreement was reached by May 1952. Disputes over the future of the Saar, and the rearmament of Germany delayed matters, and it was only when WEU had been set up incorporating Germany into Western defence, with Allied troops in the country, and no nuclear weapons for Germany, that French opposition was overcome in 1954. In May 1955 the new Federal Republic became fully independent and joined NATO although not the United Nations as this had to wait upon full reunification.

C3 Adenauer and Christian Democratic Germany to 1969

As long as Adenauer was in office West Germany was a loyal member of the Western alliance. Adenauer leaned substantially to the right; indeed his opponents criticised him for allowing ex-Nazis like Globke to advise him, but supporters defended him saying it would have been ridiculous to deprive the government of vast numbers of efficient supporters simply because of their past. Adenauer banned the Communist Party in 1956, and introduced conscription the same year. His period of office was one in which ultimate German reunification remained the goal, although he rejected a proposed Russian federal solution. Inevitably Germany was at the centre of the European Cold War with crises over Berlin in 1958 and 1961 (see section 3E3). But these events did not prevent Germany from a spectacular economic recovery during these years spoken of as the 'German Miracle'. This was partly caused by the immense amount of aid received, and partly by membership of the EEC, but was primarily due to the building up of industry on a modern base so that automation, for example, was introduced far more rapidly than in other Western countries.

When Adenauer retired in 1963 his successor was Ludwig Erhard who had been Economics Minister for years, and he continued the same policies. In 1966 he was succeeded by the third Christian Democrat Chancellor, Kurt Kiesinger, and it was only then that economic development began to falter. By this time the CDU had been losing electoral strength, and coalition government had come into existence. At first this had been with the small Free Democratic Party and the CSU (the Bavarian Christian Democratic Party), but in 1966 a grand coalition of the CDU and SPD was formed. Franz Strauss became the new Economics Minister, and Willi Brandt, Foreign Minister. The economic difficulties led to cuts in government expenditure. Right wing extremists led by Von Thadden began to make gains in local elections in 1967. The left stimulated by developments in Europe began to agitate against the complacent materialist German society. The Socialist Student League led by Rudi Dutschke caused trouble in late 1967, and when an attempt to kill him was made in April 1968 there were widespread student riots. The government reacted with an Emergency Powers

Act, but it was forced to relax in other ways, and a new Communist Party was founded in September that year. Brandt who had been Mayor of West Berlin since 1957 was convinced that West Germany needed to accept the division of Germany, and bring to an end the Cold War atmosphere which still persisted. In October 1969 he was able to persuade the Free Democrats to join the SPD, and the CDU left office after 20 years in power.

C4 Germany under the Social Democrats (SPD) 1969–82

Brandt's period in office was characterised by two main policies: an attempt to revive the economy and to end Cold War divisions. In March 1970 Brandt met the East German Prime Minister at Erfurt, and Ostpolitik was launched (see section 13D3). The policy was successfully pursued, and helped German economic recovery by opening up Eastern Europe to German trade. By 1980 five per cent of Germany's trade was with the Eastern bloc. Detente in the 1970s encouraged relaxation over matters like Berlin, and West Germany for so long a main constituent in NATO defence began to pursue a more moderate line than either Britain or America towards the Soviet Union. Recovery did take place to some extent with the revaluing (1969), and floating (1971) of the mark, but in 1973 the Oil Crisis renewed difficulties. Then it was revealed that Brandt's aide, Guillaume, had been an East German spy, and he was forced to resign being succeeded by Helmut Schmidt in 1974.

The extreme left continued to oppose the state. The Baader-Meinhoff Gang were responsible for various outrages in 1972. They were finally brought to trial in 1975, but the four main members all committed suicide. A new group of extremists called the Red Army began a series of outrages with the seizure of the German Embassy in Stockholm in 1975. They resorted to murdering prominent capitalists including the Chief Prosecutor and the President of the Employers Federation. In 1977 they seized an airliner, and German troops went into action for the first time since 1945 to rescue the airliner at Mogadishu. With such difficulties the CDU under Helmut Kohl began to make gains, but their party was divided by the right wing activities of Franz Strauss. The CDU Party was further embarrassed by the resignation of one of its members Filbinger, Prime Minister of Baden-Wurtemburg, who was accused of war crimes. Strauss from his base in Bavaria ousted Kohl as the leader of the CDU–CSU during 1979. This led to a sharply contested election in 1980, but Strauss's traditional Christian Democrat line was opposed also by 'Green List' environmentalists, and the newly developed anti-nuclear movement. Schmidt was returned to power a second time winning 271 out of 497 seats, but in 1982 lost office when the Free Democrats changed sides to support the Christian Democrats under Helmut Kohl. In the subsequent election held in 1983 Kohl obtained a majority campaigning on the need for governmental economies to deal with the declining German economy and for strong backing for NATO, in particular the decision to install Pershing missiles on German soil.

D The Growth of Democracy in Southern Europe

D1 Portuguese Dictatorship: Antonio de Salazar (1889–1970)

Modern Portuguese history began with the revolution of 1910 which ended the monarchy, but did not create effective government. Within the next few years Portugal had 40 ministries and 16 revolutionary outbreaks culminating in the setting up of a right wing dictatorship in 1926. Salazar was Finance Minister in this government. He formed the National Union, and in 1932 became dictator of Portugal proclaiming a corporate state called the 'Estado Novo'. At first the country was strongly fascist sending troops to help Franco in Spain, but during the war Portugal began to lean towards her traditional ally, Britain, and to provide base facilities for the Allies. In 1945 measures re-created political parties, freed political prisoners and for a time lifted censorship. This was enough to allow Portugal into UNO, and thereafter the West needed her for the western flank of NATO which she joined in 1949. Although Portugal remained a dictatorship with the apparatus of repression the West accepted her, and when in 1961 rebels under Galvao seized a ship British and American warships hunted it down. She joined EFTA in 1959. What brought about disaster was the Portuguese Empire. Although small measures of reform were introduced as early as 1951 the government declared it would not give up the empire, and this was reaffirmed by Salazar's successor, Caetano. As a result over 150,000 troops were involved in African wars, damaging the economy, and providing the grassroots of opposition at home. Caetano's regime (1968–74) responded by increasing African representation in parliament, but would not yield on the main issue of independence.

D2 The Portuguese Revolution of 1974 and its Consequences

A revolution was brought about by the middle class and the military fed up with the war, and it resulted in the creation of a Junta under General Spinola. He introduced some basic reforms including abolishing the secret police, ending the censorship and allowing trade unions and political parties. In September 1974 he was replaced by Gomes and an Armed Forces Revolutionary Council well to the left. Spinola's counter-coup failed in March 1975, and he fled the country. In April came elections in which the Socialist Party of Soares was the largest with 37 per cent of the votes, and the Communists under Cunhal received over 12 per cent. However, they demanded inclusion in the government, and with the army attempted a coup in November which failed. The second election of the revolutionary period took place in 1976, and Soares was confirmed in power. By this time the West was worried about Communist control in the country. America (300 million dollars), and Germany (200 million dollars) gave loans to help the tottering economy, and as Portugal had now lost its empire the way was open for its return as a European power joining the Council of Europe, and seeking to join the EEC. During 1978 Soares' government collapsed because of his land reforms which did not go far enough for the Communists, but a Socialist–Centre government was formed successively under da Costa, da Mota Pinto, and finally in December 1979 under Carneiro. By this time

	OEEC OECD	Council of Europe	NATO	Western European Union	EEC	EFTA 1959	EFTA 1973	ECSC (to 1957)	Euratom	Rhine Commission	Nordic Council
Great Britain	●	●	●	●	●	●				●	
France	●	●	●	●	●			●	●	●	
West Germany	●	●	●	●	●			●	●	●	
Italy	●	●	●	●	●			●	●		
Norway	●	●	●			●	●				●
Sweden	●	●				●	●				●
Denmark	●	●	●		●	●					●
Finland	●						●				●
Iceland	●	●	●				●				●
Belgium	●	●	●	●	●			●	●	●	
Holland	●	●	●	●	●			●	●	●	
Luxemburg	●	●	●	●	●			●	●		
Spain	●	●	●		N						
Portugal	●	●	●		N	●	●				
Malta		●									
Cyprus		●									
Turkey	●	●	●								
Greece	●	●	●		●						
Austria	●	●				●	●				
Republic of Ireland	●	●			●						
United States of America	●		●								
Canada	●		●								
Japan	●										
Switzerland	●					●	●			●	

Key

o MEMBER

◥ JOINED LATER

N NEGOTIATING TO JOIN

△ ASSOCIATED

Fig. 16. Membership of the European Institutions

the government had shifted substantially to the right, and in many people's minds it was a tragedy that Carneiro was killed at the end of 1980 in a plane crash just as Portugal was surfacing after its revolutionary experience.

D3 Francisco Franco and the Making of Modern Spain (1892–1975)

Spain was in the early part of the century a backward and declining country even if it still retained a considerable empire. A decadent monarchy, a reactionary aristocracy, a slothful church and a moribund and privileged military elite controlled a down-trodden peasantry, and the small industrial workforce of the peninsula. In 1931 a liberal revolution removed the monarchy, and during the Republic (1931–36) some attempt was made to reduce the power of the army, church and landlords. What was needed was radical change, but the left was sharply divided between Socialists, Anarchists, pro-Moscow and pro-Spanish Communists, and by the time a left wing government had been formed in February 1936 the economy was in ruins, and the forces of the right helped by Mussolini, had become organised although they too were divided between Monarchists, Carlists, a Catholic Party and the Fascist Falange. The murder of the Conservative leader, Calvo Sotelo, was the final straw, and a number of politically minded officers led by Sanjurjo began to organise a coup. Sanjurjo was killed in a plane crash, and Franco took his place as leader when the fascist revolt began in July 1936.

Franco came from a naval family in El Ferrol, and had entered the army going to Spanish Morocco in 1911 where he made his career as a brave soldier rising to be the youngest general in the army, and then from 1923 to 1927 commanding the Spanish Foreign Legion. He returned to Spain to run the Saragossa Military Academy, and was in fact loyal to the Republic. He had suppressed with the aid of Moroccan troops a rising of the miners in the Asturias in 1934 which made him a hero of the right, but he was not politically-minded, and had only limited connections with the Falange. But the government closed down the Academy, and then posted key generals to outposts of the empire. Franco was sent to the Canary Islands, and it was this treatment that finally led him to accept command of the rebels.

The Spanish Civil War cost 600,000 lives, and only half of these were on the battlefield for it was fought with great savagery on both sides. 'We shall exterminate half Spain' proclaimed the right, and the left not only attacked them, but each other in a bitter civil war in Catalonia. Mussolini and Hitler intervened to help Franco while the other powers turned a blind eye. Many people in Europe and America volunteered to fight for the Republic joining the International Brigade. Stalin did little to help the left, and thus Franco's victory was made almost certain by left wing division and right wing solidarity. During 1937 he consolidated his position. In July the Roman Catholic Church put their support behind him. Early in 1938 with a Labour Charter he began the introduction of a corporate state.

When the civil war finished in 1939 there was a purge in which at least 100,000 were killed. Concentration camps were set up for as many as two million prisoners or forced labourers. 400,000 Spaniards fled, and only 70,000 of these ever accepted repatriation. When Petain took over in Vichy France he restored Companys, the leader of the Catalan separatists, to

Franco who had him executed, and handed the Socialist leader, Caballero over to Hitler in one of whose concentration camps he died. A one party dictatorship was created. But when it came to outright backing for Fascism in the war Franco drew back. He joined the Anti-Comintern Pact, but turned down an offer of alliance with Germany. He sent the Blue Legion to Russia to fight for Hitler. On the other hand he allowed Allied POWs to escape through the country. When the war finished left wing governments led by Attlee of Britain wished to bring down Franco, and recognise a government in exile in Mexico. The United Nations would not admit Spain.

But Franco survived. In the first place his policies appealed to a large section of Spanish opinion. In 1947 he ceased formally to be dictator and became regent stating the monarchy would eventually be restored. This change was included in the constitution of 1966, and in 1969 the reformist Prince Juan Carlos of Bourbon was named as his successor. For once a dictator had provided for a smooth succession. In 1953 a concordat with Rome conferred further respectability. The Church was to have control over education, and the Jesuits returned to Spain. Above all Spain was useful to Western defences. The Americans led the way with 62 million dollars of Marshall Aid. In 1953 a direct treaty providing for three bases and military aid followed which was renewed by Nixon in 1970. Spain was admitted to UNO in 1955. Although not in the Common Market, Franco's Spain modernised and developed effectively building up a tourist industry, for example, and very gradually the regime was modified. There were demonstrations in Madrid and San Sebastian as early as 1966, and separatist movements began to emerge once more in Catalonia and the Basque Province. In the latter the Freedom Group (ETA) demanded full independence, and in 1970 demonstrations and protests led Franco to commute six death sentences on agitators in the region. It was clear that as Spanish society modernised and prospered and communications grew easier the static nature of the regime would change.

During the 1970s Franco's regime was subjected to increasing opposition. Admiral Carrero Blanco, the Prime Minister, offered concessions, but this only stimulated opposition, and in 1973 he was murdered. His successor, Navarro, continued concessions and limited political activity was permitted while the following year limited trade union rights were conceded, and reforms made in local government. At the same time Franco was determined not to yield to terrorism. In April 1975 a state of emergency was proclaimed in the Basque Country, and in August a new Anti-Terrorism Law was followed by several executions. In November 1975 Franco died, and Juan Carlos became the first new monarch in Europe since 1946.

D4 King Juan Carlos and Spain's Advance to Democracy

Franco's death led to a number of important changes. The Spanish Empire achieved independence within two years apart from a few islands in the Atlantic. The government continued repressive measures, but in March 1976 change began when after seven deaths during rioting in Bilbao the government was replaced by a more moderate one under Adolfo Suarez, and a political amnesty was granted. Juan Carlos knew the Falange and other right wing forces did not wish Spain to proceed to democracy; on the other

hand Spain's economic position required an effective democratic government. Spain joined the Council of Europe (1976), and in July 1977 applied
to join the EEC. Her application would only be accepted if a democratic
government was created, and new steps had to be taken. A referendum
for constitutional reform on democratic lines was held in December 1976—
the first free vote since 1936—and this was followed in June 1977 by parliamentary elections. Next month a new Cortes was summoned, and Suarez'
UDC—a centre party—took office with a Socialist Party of some strength,
the right wing Democratic Party, and a small Communist Party. A new
constitution was then drawn up, and approved by a further referendum
in December 1978—Juan Carlos becoming a constitutional monarch. Parliament was dissolved with elections in March 1979, and the first local elections
the following month both of which returned the UDC. Suarez continued
in office successfully creating a new democratic climate.

These moves were bound to stir the old pre-1939 passions. The restoration
of the Communist Party under Carillo in April 1977, and the return of
Civil War Communist figures like La Passionaria inflamed the right. Separatist movements sprang up again in the Basque area and Catalonia. During
1976 prominent politicians like Villar were murdered, and ETA terrorists
launched bombing and kidnapping campaigns, demanding complete
independence for their region. In July 1978 the government acted firmly
against the extremists while conceding regional autonomy in Spain. A year
later Suarez won over the Basque Nationalist Party with a special statute in
October 1979. The first elections for the provincial parliaments of the
Basques and Catalonia occurred in 1980 and in each case moderates did
well—the PNV (Basque Nationalists), and the CIU (Nationalist Coalition)
respectively. Terrorist outrages continued, and the concessions were enough
to rouse right wing opposition which Juan Carlos had to check. A military
armed seizure of the Cortes was the occasion (February 1981). Juan Carlos
made it clear that any army takeover would have to oppose him.

With a democratic government social change has accelerated in Spain.
The concordat with the Church has been modified. Divorce and birth control
have been legalised, the voting age cut to eighteen, and other liberal measures
such as the abolition of the death penalty introduced. To please the right
wing the government has adopted a firm line over its claim to Gibraltar
and in spite of joining NATO in 1982, made considerable difficulties over
implementing a border agreement with Britain. In Argentina's war with
Britain Juan Carlos offered mediation and did not support NATO's condemnation of Argentina. In the election of October 1982 Felipe Gonzales
led the Socialist Party to victory becoming Europe's youngest Prime Minister
at 40. At present Spain is negotiating to join the EEC.

D5 The Kings of Greece and the Coup d'Etat of April 1967

From 1944 to 1947 Britain, and subsequently after the Truman Doctrine,
America, had been responsible for preserving democracy and the monarchy
in Greece, and defeating a Communist attempt to come to power in a civil
war (see section 3C4). George II had returned after a plebiscite, and in
1947 was succeeded by King Paul of the Hellenes whose German wife was
held to have very right wing views. The earlier governments were under

military leaders like Papagos and Plastiras, and it seemed that Greece had learnt little in her years of Fascist dictatorship, and German occupation. The demand for a Greater Greece remained, fuelled by the acquiring of Rhodes in 1946, and in 1951 the Greek government backed Enosis with Cyprus. The commander of the Greek terrorists there, Grivas, was a former officer in the Greek army. Greece was useful to the Western powers, and entered NATO. In 1962 she became an associate member of the EEC, and for a time it looked as if rising prosperity was leading the country to more stable ways.

The government moved slowly left: first after 1956 under Karamanlis, and the National Union, then after 1964 under Papandreou towards Socialism. Then in 1964 King Paul was succeeded by the inexperienced King Constantine II. The left sought further power in a military conspiracy by a group called Aspida, and the country was thrown into confusion by the resignation of Papandreou in July 1965, which it was said was forced on him by the King and the angry right wing. There were riots and a general strike, and Papandreou refused to take office. The trial of 28 Aspida officers provided a focus for discontent. There were student riots, and the Communist Party made gains. A stable government seemed impossible, and since Greece was facing war with Turkey this could not continue. In April 1967 Constantine was forced to flee, Papandreou was arrested, and a military junta under Papadopolos and Patakos took over the country. In December Constantine launched a counter-coup which was easily suppressed, and the monarchy was suspended the following year.

D6 The Rule of the Colonels

The new regime ran into strong international opposition. The left were furious that a right wing regime backed by America should be ruling the country particularly after American arms suspended in 1967 were resumed by Nixon in 1970. The Council of Europe forced Greece to resign membership. The Colonels made a slow series of concessions beginning in September 1968, and by 1973 Papadopolos had returned to civilian government, but this provoked resistance. In May there was a naval mutiny favouring Constantine's return, and the monarchy was then formally abolished. Then there were riots in Athens, and this led the military under Ioannides and Gizikis to renew the military dictatorship in November that year. This had grievous consequences since they backed the Eoka B terrorists in Cyprus in an attempted coup which precipitated a Turkish invasion of the island (see section 7E7).

D7 Greece, Turkey and Enosis for Cyprus

Cyprus was annexed by Britain in 1914, and became a colony in 1925. As early as 1931 there were riots among the Greeks demanding enosis (union with Greece). Britain granted a new constitution, but as Middle East Headquarters moved there in 1954 declared the island could not expect full independence. In 1951 General Grivas and Archbishop Makarios III met, EOKA came into being, and in April 1955 war with the British broke out. The 20 per cent of the population who were Turkish feared Greek domination and supported the British, but in 1959–60 Britain conceded independence keeping two bases, and an obligation to intervene to prevent communal strife or discrimination. Trouble started with riots in 1963 between Greeks and Turks when Makarios abrogated the 1960 constitution, and Britain intervened. In March 1964 a UN force (one fifth of which was British) was stationed in the island, but rioting was renewed, and Turkish planes attacked Greek towns. However, a UN cease-fire was achieved.

With the coming of the Military Junta in Greece matters got worse. In late 1967 when Makarios tried to extend Greek policing into Turkish areas there were serious riots. Wilson of Britain would not intervene. Turkey issued an ultimatum to Greece to reduce her 20,000 troops on the island, and America prevailed on them to do so thus preserving the peace. With the even more extreme Greek regime of 1973 further trouble was bound to come. The Greek government decided to topple Makarios because he wished to keep Cyprus independent, and to do this they backed a coup by Eoka B led by Nikos Sampson. Makarios fled, but the Turks then invaded the island in July–August 1974. The Greeks massacred Turks in the north, and this led to Turkish reprisals including the expulsion of 180,000 Greeks from northern Cyprus. The island was divided along the Attila Line which gave the Turks 30 per cent of the land, and 70 per cent of the wealth of the island. Turkey's success infuriated Greece with grave consequences, but little was done although America cut off arms to Turkey from 1974 to 1978. Makarios returned, and the Turks under Denktash proclaimed a federal state which the Greeks would not accept. Makarios died in 1976 and was succeeded by Kiprianu, but only recently have the two leaders met for the first time. Cyprus remains partitioned.

D8 The Greek Revolution of 1974 and its Consequences

The Turkish invasion of Cyprus led to the recall of Karamanlis in August 1974, and the military junta were arrested. In 1975 Papadopolos and Patakos were sentenced to death while others were banished. The constitution was restored, and Greece slowly returned to democracy with three parties: Karamanlis' New Democrats, Mavros' Centre Party, and Andreas Papandreou's Socialists. In November 1974 Karamanlis won the election, and followed it with a referendum abolishing the monarchy. In June 1975 a new democratic constitution was introduced. Greece returned to the Council of Europe, and in 1981 joined the Common Market. But events in Cyprus made this path a difficult one. Since Britain and Turkey had both failed to honour the 1960 Treaty Greece withdrew in August 1974 from the command structure of NATO, and in December took over its bases. The left further angered by revelations of CIA influence in the Athens American Embassy demanded Greece leave NATO and the EEC, and this demand was strengthened when America resumed arms supplies to Turkey in 1978. In 1981 Papandreou's Socialists won the election, and although they have not yet acted on the two main policies of leaving NATO and the EEC, they have refused to support NATO criticism of Russia.

D9 Turkey's Military Dictatorship

Modern Turkey was created by Kemal Ataturk, a military leader, who was dictator from 1920 to 1938, and was succeeded by Ismet Inonu from 1938 to 1950 (see section 10B2). Turkey had received military aid from Lenin, and signed a treaty with Russia which had led to her neutrality in the war, but Stalin's demands in 1945 led to the cancellation of this treaty, and Turkey turned towards the West receiving aid under the Truman Doctrine. Turkey sent troops to Korea, joined NATO and the Baghdad Pact, and allowed missiles to be stationed on her territory in 1959. But internally Turkey wavered between democracy and 'Kemalism'—dictatorship by the military. From 1950 to 1960 Turkey was ruled by Menderes and the Democratic Party, but in 1960 General Gursel led a military coup followed by Menderes' execution. Semi-democratic rule with Gursel as President and General Inonu as Prime Minister was restored the next year, but the Cyprus question then claimed the government's attention with the troubles of 1964. This led Turkey to cancel her 1930 treaty with Greece, and expel all Greeks from the country thus creating a rift in NATO which has remained to this day. In 1965 Demirel and the Justice Party came to power, and were involved in the second Cyprus dispute in 1967. Meanwhile the economy of the country was declining, and left wing agitation growing. In 1971 came a second military coup. In 1973 democracy was restored with a new party—the Republicans under Ecevit—who was responsible for the Turkish war in Cyprus in 1974. However, this did not help the economy, and it stimulated the left wing anarchists of the TPLA. A prolonged government crisis led to the eventual return of Demirel in March 1975.

Elections in 1977 confirmed Demirel in power, but only because he secured backing from the National Action Party. He was forced to introduce severe penalties for terrorism, and this in turn strengthened the more left wing party of Ecevit. By the end of the year Ecevit was back in power, but by then Turkey was in dire economic trouble with 70 per cent inflation, and massive debts to the West. America resumed arms supplies, and the IMF provided a loan thus confirming Ecevit in a Western stance. Internally Turkey was menaced by almost continuous riots in the main towns like Adana, Ankara and Istanbul. Ecevit proclaimed states of emergency in 10 provinces, but matters did not improve, and by 1980 over 3,500 has died in terrorist attacks. In September 1980 came a third military putsch led by General Evren who extended martial law to all 67 provinces. Elections held in 1983 restored a civilian government under Turgat Ozal with Evren retaining the presidency.

Revision Questions

1. Describe the changes in Europe's world position over the last 30 years, and give reasons for these changes.

2. Why has European Unity been achieved over so many fields since 1945? What forms does this unity take, and what are the limits to it?

3. What are the main advantages and disadvantages the European powers have found in having a Common Market?

4. Read section 1B4 again. Discuss the question—in view of the state

of Europe in 1945 and in 1982 is optimism rather than pessimism about the future of Europe a reasonable attitude to take?

5. Why has France sought 'great power status' since 1945, and how successful have her rulers been in restoring this status?

6. Compare the careers of De Gaulle, Adenauer and De Gasperi in respect to: (a) national recovery, (b) democratic growth, (c) economic progress for their countries.

7. What have the achievements of the German Social Democrats been since they entered office in 1969? Do you think Germany, like France, has succeeded in asserting a new world position for itself in recent years?

8. Are there common factors that explain the difficulties democracy has experienced in Italy, Portugal and Greece until comparatively recently?

9. Discuss the heading to section 7D3 which claims Franco made modern Spain. What changes have taken place in that country since his death in 1975, and will Spain become a major world power again in future years?

Further Reading

Note: British History during this period is fully covered in *Twentieth Century British History Made Simple* by the same author. Britain is only referred to in relation to her European commitments.

Ben Jones, R., *The Making of Contemporary Europe*, Hodder and Stoughton, London 1980.

Charlton, M., *The Price of Victory*, BBC Publications, London, 1983.

Crawley, A., *The Rise of West Germany 1945–72*, Collins, Glasgow, 1973.

Crozier, B., *De Gaulle: The Statesman*, Eyre Methuen, London, 1973.

Crozier, B., *Franco: a Biographical History*, Eyre and Spottiswoode, London, 1967.

Elliott, B. J., *Western Europe after 1945*, Longmans, Modern Times, Harlow, 1968.

Hiscock, R., *Germany's Revolution: An Appreciation of the Adenauer Era*, Gollancz, 1966.

Joll, J., *Europe Since 1870*, Weidenfeld and Nicolson, London, 1973.

Laqueur, W., *Europe since Hitler*, Penguin, 1982.

Thomson, D., *Europe Since Napoleon*, Penguin, 1966.

8

The Decline of Western Imperialism and the Rise of the Third World

A The Scope of the Change

A1 Western Supremacy at its Height

It is never easy to choose a particular time when a political development reaches its height. Western imperialism was always opposed somewhere in the world, and contained within its own message the seeds of its own destruction. Thus, the rising of the Blacks in San Domingo under L'Ouverture (1747–1803) might well earn him a place as the first black nationalist in the modern world (see section 12A5). The independence of the American colonies in 1783 showed that European communities planted overseas would go their own way when they had reached an adequate state of development. But this is to read too much into history knowing that Western imperialism has now declined almost to vanishing point, and that since 1939 several new worlds in Africa, Asia, the Middle East, the Pacific and the West Indies have come into being as a result. In 1939 few except small nationalist groups would have predicted any such change. In that year the world was still essentially either ruled or economically controlled by the countries of Western Europe and the United States.

This state of affairs had started in the sixteenth century with the discovery and exploitation of the New World by Spain and Portugal. They had been followed by Holland, France and Britain, and even by countries like Sweden. During the seventeenth and eighteenth centuries empires based primarily on economic exploitation and slavery had been created. It was only in the nineteenth century that arguments for political and even moral justification for holding empires were fully developed. European population growth, technical prowess and military techniques enabled them—and America at the end of the century—to build up empires still in large part based on economic gain, but also as a result of strategic factors, and questions of prestige. Newer countries like Germany, Belgium and Italy were added to the ranks of colonial powers, and in the Far East as Japan 'westernised' itself it too became an imperialist nation. The 50 years preceding the First World War were the pre-eminent Age of Imperialism.

The First World War had two effects on this situation. At Versailles in 1919 many groups like the Arabs demanded self-determination, and for the first time 'dominions' like Canada or New Zealand were separately represented as countries. The presence of an unofficial Irish delegation, and of an Indian delegation, although India was strictly a colony, were signs of future change. The League of Nations, by creating the concept of the 'mandate' for former German and Turkish possessions, cast doubt on the absolute right of Europeans to rule the world. But at the time Versailles seemed to strengthen imperialism. Britain and France obtained much of the Middle East (see section 10B); even Belgium and Portugal were given small increases in their colonial territory. Italy did not obtain any colonies, but the other powers recognised her basic right to territory. Britain in 1924 and France in 1935 ceded her African territory, and offered little resistance to her annexation of Abyssinia (Ethiopia) in 1936. Although self-government was extended in various ways no European colony obtained independence in the inter-war period.

At the end of the Second World War outward appearances again suggested European pre-eminence was intact. America extended her colonial possessions in the Pacific. France and Holland set out to reconquer their colonies by force as soon as they were restored to them by Britain early in 1946. Britain ignored American requests to give up territory, and re-occupied her empire successfully adding to it the whole of the Italian empire. In 1945 Liberia was the only completely independent African country. The West Indies with the exception of some former Spanish colonies, freed much earlier, was under European control. The Pacific and Indian Oceans were European lakes. In the Middle East only the Lebanon (1926) and Syria (1945) were fully independent together with the already established countries of Turkey and Saudi Arabia. In China the Europeans under American pressure had given up their extra-territorial rights, but they retained their colonies. Only Afghanistan and Thailand were fully independent in the whole of Asia.

A2 The Wind of Change

In 30 years this picture has completely changed; it is the most significant political change in modern history, and in territorial terms it is virtually completed. There are still a few small colonial possessions, but in most cases they are too small to form viable countries, or the inhabitants have wished to remain with the former colonial power. Elsewhere a new world—the Third World, because it is in theory neither capitalist nor marxist—has come into existence. In 1945 the United Nations was founded with 51 members largely dominated by the West. In 1980 it had 170 members, and more often than not acted as a body hostile to the West. This change was remarkably swift. As early as 1955 a conference of Third World countries at Bandung was attended by 29 countries, and the process by which 800 million people obtained independence was largely completed by 1975–6 when the Spanish and Portugese empires, first to be founded, were the last to perish. Africa with one independent country in 1945 now has 42 nations.

Speaking at Cape Town in February 1960 Macmillan, the British Prime Minister who did so much to push decolonisation forward, spoke of the 'wind of change' blowing through Africa and indeed the world, and by then it was blowing at hurricane force in places like Algeria and Kenya. In November 1961 the first anti-colonialist resolution was passed by 97–0 in the United Nations with the colonial powers abstaining—saying that for them it was only a question of timing. By 1967 the United Nations had voted colonialism to be a 'crime against humanity', and since then has adopted a vigorous line on remaining colonialist enclaves like Rhodesia (from 1980 Zimbabwe), and South West Africa (Namibia). Third World countries argue they are still exploited or discriminated against by the West, but they cannot deny formal political independence is now theirs.

A3 Tensions within the former Colonial Powers

Such a momentous change has not taken place without profound consequences for the former colonial powers. The struggle for independence proved a major drain on resources. After 1919 there were 20 years of almost unbroken peace, and the colonial campaigns fought then were resolved in the Europeans' favour. But after 1945 there was a period of constant colonial warfare which continued until 1979 in Rhodesia, and has not yet ended for the SWAPO guerillas in Namibia. The recent Falklands War between Britain and Argentina had its origins in colonial times (see section 13G5). Britain was the most adroit at ending her empire and changing it into a multi-racial Commonwealth, but her wars in places like Palestine, Malaya, Kenya and Cyprus were not small affairs. British soldiers were in action every year from 1945 to 1967 in some part of the world. This proved a severe defence burden at a time when Britain was a world nuclear power, and the major partner of America in NATO; and this, in turn, had important consequences for Britain's economy, and her eventual decline as a great power. Barnett has argued the empire was a liability to Britain by 1939; after 1945 it could be seen to be even more so. On the other hand, the loss of empire had a serious effect on the British economy—it led Britain from the days of Imperial preference in the 1930s to the Common Market in the 1970s—and it should not be forgotten that the EEC can be seen as an association of former colonial powers dependent on each other now they no longer have empires. Britain too shouldered the new problem of immigration from the former empire which has radically altered her society and added to its tensions.

Other European countries resisted the tide of independence. France was determined to regain her world status, humiliated as she was by surrender in 1940. As a result her military expenditure was vast; her losses in battle tragically vast also, and in the end she lost in Algeria and Vietnam. The result of this failure was the threatened military coup of 1958 (see section 7B3), and De Gaulle's coming to power. The concept of the French Community saved something from the wreckage along 'commonwealth' lines, and De Gaulle's strongly nationalist policies were dictated to some extent by a need to keep up French morale as a world power. Belgium left the Congo in a hurry, and returned twice thereafter; her economy suffered adding to tensions in the country. Holland fought a bitter war to retain Indonesia, but was forced out in 1949. She too experienced difficulties from former colonial immigrants like the South Moluccans in her homeland. Spain gave up her empire relatively painlessly, but Portugal introduced complete integration, and was faced with wars in Guinea, Angola and Mozambique. The result was to destroy her fascist government in a revolution in 1974 which was a prelude to conceding full independence to her former colonies.

Settler interests were able to exercise some influence in the mother countries, but the 'kith and kin' argument never successfully persuaded the colonial power to retain power. The Algerian 'colons' and the Algerie Française movement did not stop De Gaulle conceding independence in 1962. Within the British Empire the Kenya white settlers led by Michael Blundell and the Rhodesian white settlers of Ian Smith did not prevent the granting of independence in 1963 and 1980. The European powers had sustained defeats in colonial territories before 1939, but after 1945 these became major disasters—France at Dien Bien Phu and Britain at Suez were shown to be vulnerable. The Western governments had to accept what seemed to many of their people to be 'humiliations'—the expulsion of white civil servants and military experts, the confiscation of European property, the seizure of embassies, and the denunciation of the West only to be expected from newly freed nations. In the theatre of world politics these disputes afforded Russia the perfect opportunity to further her interests, and the West suffered from Russian and Chinese alignment with the independence movements from the start; fear of Communism was added to white supremacist arguments as a reason for keeping empires, but it only served to delay departure in vital base areas.

A4 A New World with Old Problems

Nineteenth-century nationalism in Europe had raised the hopes of suppressed peoples, and in the end self-determination had come to most European nations by 1919. Nationalism in the Third World produced hatred of the former colonial power, and unwillingness to recognise what was owed to that power. Many of the new countries had never been countries until their borders were drawn by Europeans. India and Nigeria, for example, were created by Europeans, and when they left older forces—tribal divisions and rival claims—soon asserted themselves. The new countries felt bound to pursue aggressive foreign policies. They attacked former colonial powers, and supported guerilla movements. They frequently tore up defence agreements made with the West. Large military establishments were created, and international terrorism too found Third World backers.

All this certainly reduced Western influence. Both CENTO and SEATO collapsed, and the West was unable to obtain anything other than words to condemn real aggression like the Soviet invasion of Afghanistan or the Vietnamese invasion of Kampuchea. Hostility to the West undermined the claim the new states were non-aligned. Several of them succumbed to Russian influence; others were seized by guerillas and Cuban troops. The West responded: unofficially, by using white mercenaries in places like Angola; officially, until the defeat of America in Vietnam, by war and aid with strings attached. The Third World was thus involved in the Cold War and super power relations, and was subject itself to civil wars, territorial disputes and terrorism on a widespread scale. The decades since independence have been ones of immense suffering for the Third World; the removal of colonial oppressors often only made way for new oppressors.

If one African or Asian leader could become independent others wished to follow. So separatist movements like that of Biafra in Nigeria or Bangladesh in Pakistan emerged; some successful, others not. Experience in guerilla war with European powers was soon translated into guerilla wars between Third World neighbours—the Palestinians and the Israelis, or the Polisario attacks in Western Sahara being examples. National prestige demanded wars. Thus, India who had developed the non-aligned concept went to war with China and Pakistan. Some Third World countries like Cuba and Libya became the centres of world-wide militancy. Because Third World politics are self-consciously concerned with racial dignity and national pride they have subjected the economies of the new countries to immense strains. Since these are already subject to massive problems (see section 14B) this has often meant that the rash promises made after independence have not been fulfilled. Costly prestige projects have collapsed, and fundamental problems like agriculture have been little touched.

Economic collapse and military defeat have brought in their wake an increasing impatience with democratic government, and a fragmentation of many regional organisations which would have helped Third World countries. The hope that granted independence coloured peoples would willingly embrace democratic government which was essentially a Western concept has proved over optimistic. South America should have been a warning to those with such a hope. Of the 42 African states, 32 are dictatorships or one party states, but it could have been foreseen. In Latin America all but six of the 19 countries are dictatorships, and this after nearly a 100 years of independence. Traditional monarchies were overthrown by town-based nationalist movements. Ties with the mother country like the British Crown were snapped. Planned economies and one party states were started; some of which have proved beneficial, and some of which have given way to democracies again. But it is equally true that tyrants worse than any colonial regime have taken advantage of such political chaos. In Africa the examples of Bokassa (1966) and Amin (1971), might be cited to make the point that independence has not always brought benefits to the people concerned.

From a Western point of view it has been difficult to see countries like Uganda or Kampuchea (formerly Cambodia) transformed into graveyards, and it has been easy to say that developments since independence prove that it came too soon. But this argument cannot be sustained. For reasons to be discussed in the next section (8B1) maintenance of European supremacy was wishful thinking. If Europe was to leave it was inevitable that Western ideas of nationalism should prevail in the new countries. Modern Africa is no different from the Balkans in the nineteenth century. A heavy price is being paid by both sides for the great movement of colonial independence, but it would have been surprising if such a major change had occurred without resort to war and dictatorship. There are many examples of successful Third World countries like Kenya, Brazil, or Nigeria, to indicate that matters will improve as the years pass. It is too early yet to assess the full impact of the colonial revolution of our own lifetimes; the problems are immense (see section 14C), but some progress has been made, and as former colonies emerge from their colonial economies, and education and democracy make progress from the grass roots there is no reason to suppose the ultimate results of independence will be other than beneficial.

B The Roots of Colonial Revolution

B1 Filling a Political Vacuum

At the time of European expansion it was easy for Europeans to explain their success in terms of inherent superiority or natural right. It seemed in the nineteenth century as if European technical skill had provided the transport and weapons to build empires, and that the world was a natural market for expanding capitalism. European advances in forms of government led them to think they would inherit the earth. Clearly imperialism did owe something to European ability, but it owed quite as much to chance. Europeans made the mistake of thinking of other civilisations as 'decadent'. They spoke of Africa as the Dark Continent. They described other customs and religions as 'primitive'. In some ways this was true, but only relatively. If there was cannibalism in Dahomey and the Sandwich Islands so were there equally inhuman acts in Nazi Germany. Many of the countries occupied already had lengthy histories. In West Africa, for example, the region of Kano has written records back to the tenth century and great empires flourished there before the Arab and European slavers cut the population by 20 million. In places like China, India, Egypt, Vietnam and Madagascar there had been flourishing civilisations. The European nations displayed some antiquarian interest in them; through indirect rule they perpetuated traditional tribal forms in a harmless way, but they failed to see that their success had been achieved to some extent in a political vacuum. The anti-colonial revolt owed as much to pre-colonial history and tradition as it did to foreign concepts of nationalism.

B2 A Question of Numbers

The filling of the vacuum was made possible by the temporary upsurge of European population. Europe sent 60 million emigrants overseas. America, Canada, Australia and New Zealand were not, as often stated, empty, but their indigenous peoples—North American Indians, Eskimos, Aborigines and Maoris—were violently subdued and became minorities in predominantly white countries. Settlers made up a considerable portion of population in South Africa, Algeria, Rhodesia and Kenya. Thus, while disease and malnutrition held down the numbers of coloured populations Western man supplied the dynamic for world development. But by the turn of the century this was changing. France and then other European countries experienced declining birth rates, and America curbed emigration from Europe. Europe made up 5 per cent of world population between 1850 and 1913, and that fell to 3.8 per cent in 1913–60. As medicine advanced the population of countries like India or Nigeria began to rise, and rising population is now a Third World phenomenon (see section 14C1). As nationalism grew the domination of increasing numbers by small groups of Europeans was rendered impossible, and it is often forgotten how few Europeans there actually were in the colonial world. Africa in 1955 had a population of 198 million; excluding South Africa, there were only five million Europeans. In a country like Nigeria with an estimated population of 30 million there were 12,000 Europeans. It was only a question of time before this situation changed.

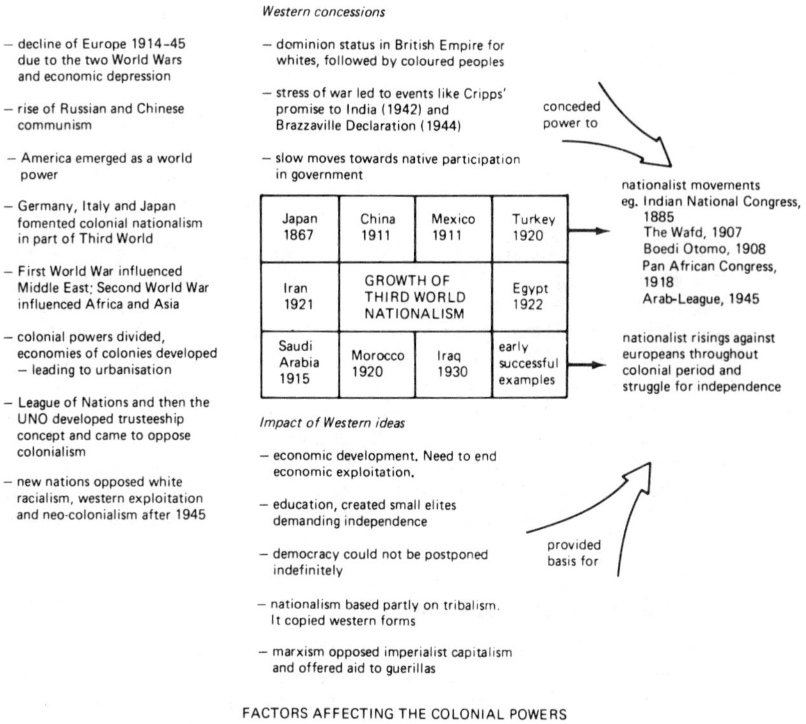

- decline of Europe 1914–45
  due to the two World Wars
  and economic depression

- rise of Russian and Chinese
  communism

- America emerged as a world
  power

- Germany, Italy and Japan
  fomented colonial nationalism
  in part of Third World

- First World War influenced
  Middle East; Second World War
  influenced Africa and Asia

- colonial powers divided,
  economies of colonies developed
  — leading to urbanisation

- League of Nations and then the
  UNO developed trusteeship
  concept and came to oppose
  colonialism

- new nations opposed white
  racialism, western exploitation
  and neo-colonialism after 1945

Western concessions

- dominion status in British Empire for
  whites, followed by coloured peoples

- stress of war led to events like Cripps'
  promise to India (1942) and
  Brazzaville Declaration (1944)

- slow moves towards native participation
  in government

conceded
power to

Japan 1867	China 1911	Mexico 1911	Turkey 1920
Iran 1921	GROWTH OF THIRD WORLD NATIONALISM		Egypt 1922
Saudi Arabia 1915	Morocco 1920	Iraq 1930	early successful examples

nationalist movements
eg. Indian National Congress,
1885
The Wafd, 1907
Boedi Otomo, 1908
Pan African Congress,
1918
Arab-League, 1945

nationalist risings against
europeans throughout
colonial period and
struggle for independence

Impact of Western ideas

- economic development. Need to end
  economic exploitation.

- education, created small elites
  demanding independence

- democracy could not be postponed
  indefinitely

- nationalism based partly on tribalism.
  It copied western forms

- marxism opposed imperialist capitalism
  and offered aid to guerillas

provided
basis for

FACTORS AFFECTING THE COLONIAL POWERS

Fig. 17. The reasons for the Colonial Revolution

B3 Resistance to Colonial Rule

The Age of Imperialism is often recorded in terms of stirring victories by Europeans. There were plenty of victories, and with superior weapons and supplies this was only to be expected, but it is also true that the whole period of imperial expansion witnessed resistance by the colonial peoples. Some of this was by primitive tyrants, or groups fighting to preserve outdated ways of life which could never have survived in the modern world, but some was against oppression and to preserve existing states which were viable and acceptable in their own right. The British were defeated by the Zulus in 1879 and the Italians by the Abyssinians in 1896. Conquest was rarely accepted easily. The Ashanti required four wars to defeat them by 1901, and secure their territories' incorporation in the Gold Coast. By 1921 the Golden Stool of the ruler of Ashanti had been found and restored, and the exiled ruler, Prempeh, returned. Looking back English occupation of the Gold Coast was effective for a very short time. In the Sudan the Mahdi repelled the British in 1885, and his successor, the Khalifa, took two years to defeat in 1896–8. The French were faced with opposition in Algeria from 1830 to 1847, and in Morocco from 1908 to 1934. The Italians faced opposition in Libya from 1912 to 1932. In their short-lived overseas empire the Germans were faced with uprisings in Tanzania in 1891–8 and 1905–6, and in South West Africa in 1904–6. The French faced a ten year war to conquer Madagascar, and then a rebellion from 1898 to 1904. The Dutch struggled in Sumatra from 1881 to 1908 and in Bali from 1881 to 1894. Sporadic resistance to colonial rule was always present, and once it was fuelled by nationalism it was only a matter of time until it became irresistible.

B4 Nationalism in the Third World

It has become fashionable in recent years to attribute to these early risings the accolade of national resistance movements which they were not. Men like Arabi Pasha in Egypt or Cetewayo in Zululand had no concept of nationalism, but during the period of colonial rule national organisations were formed, and national revolutions carried out which were the prelude to events after 1939. In India B. G. Tilak (1856–1920) and G. Gokhale (1865–1915) were among the early leaders of national self-consciousness. The Indian National Congress was formed in 1885, and under Mohandas Gandhi (1869–1948) launched its first major campaign in 1920. In China a national revolution (1911) was followed by the establishment of Sun Yat Sen's Kuomintang. (See section 6A3.) Those of Muslim faith were among the earliest fighters against imperialism. The Muslim League was formed in 1906, and the Young Arabs in 1911. During the First World War, Hussein of the Hejaz and Ibn Saud of Saudi Arabia became the first Arab nationalist leaders. The break-up of the Turkish Ottoman Empire released Turkish Nationalism under Mustafa Kemal who launched a national revolution in 1920. Egypt was enabled to break free under the Wafd Party (1907) led by Zaghlul Pasha, and was independent in name by 1922. In North Africa Abd El Krim (1882–1963) led resistance to the French and Spanish, and the Destour movement was formed in 1920. Further east Iran experienced national revolution in 1925 under Reza Shah. In the Netherlands' East Indies the nationalist movement was formed in 1908. The Americans in the Philippines were faced with E. Aguinaldo (1869–1964), and trouble from 1898 to 1913. Japan under Mutsuhito (1868–1912) had experienced a national revolution in 1868 which was the only one to achieve success prior to 1914. Between the wars movements like the Pan African Congress (PAC) (1919) sprang into being. So colonial nationalism was an important force by 1939, but the colonial powers had succeeded in containing it.

B5 The Impact of the Second World War

The First World War had helped the rise of colonial nationalism—there had been revolts in Nyasaland (1915) and Annam (1916) as colonial rule slackened. By 1918 Japan was treated as a Western power, and China, Turkey, Egypt and Iran were emerging as free countries. But the Second World War was revolutionary in its impact (see section 2B4). It weakened the Western powers economically. The Third World could take full advantage of European weakness, and it was revealing to see British and Italians fighting in East and North Africa, or the British fighting Vichy French in Syria or Madagascar. Once the common front of the Western powers was broken their influence was damaged. Germany did her best to stimulate Arab nationalism against the Jews and the imperial powers stirring up revolt in Iraq in 1941, for example. Japan gave limited self-government to pro-Japanese governments in Burma, and Indonesia. In some cases the Western powers needing colonial resources made their own concessions. Britain promised India self-government in 1942. De Gaulle accepted the Brazzaville Declaration for France's colonies in 1944.

All parts of the Third World were directly involved in the war. 500,000 Africans and two million Indians served in the war. Africa north of the Congo was directly involved in the fighting, as was a large part of Asia and the Pacific. Even in Britain's 'white' dominions the war stirred further demands for complete independence. South Africa turned to apartheid. Australia and New Zealand looked to America to defend them after Japanese submarines had reached Sydney Harbour. Canada signed a defence agreement with America in 1940. The empires served the West well in the war. They provided vital troops like the colonial pilots in the Battle of Britain, or the Indians in the 14th Army in Burma and key bases like Chad where the Free French army was formed by LeClerc. They provided raw materials like rubber and uranium from the Belgian Congo. But at the end colonial nationalism had made great advances, and attempts to put the clock back would be bound to fail in the long run.

B6 The Changing World Situation

(See also section 1B3.) Clearly the Second World War saw an increase in nationalist organisation. In French North Africa came Istiq Lal (1943) while in French Indo-China, Ho Chi Minh's Vietminh emerged in 1941. In Indonesia, Soekarno's movement was in full swing by 1945. In 1943 Dr Azikiwe of Nigeria wrote *The Atlantic Charter and British West Africa*, and formed a political party in 1944. In 1945 an important meeting of the Pan

African Congress occurred in Manchester, and the Arab League came formally into being. The call for Pakistan was first made by the Muslim League in 1940. In 1945 the colonial powers all faced serious revolts: the French in Algeria and Vietnam; the British in Palestine and India; and the Dutch in Indonesia. It was significant that whereas between the wars revolts were curbed those after 1945 were of a new intensity. Thus, Morocco was curbed in 1914–26, but not after 1945, Syria was crushed in 1925–7, but not in 1944–5. India was subdued in 1930–4, but not in 1946–7. Palestine was restored to order in 1936–9, but not in 1944–8. The Western powers were too weak and exhausted to use extreme force; many of their left wing governments disliked the whole concept of empire, and their peoples were weary of war.

Moreover, the world situation had altered. America was the major Western power. She was imperialist herself, but disliked the older empires. Roosevelt had often clashed with Churchill over the British Empire. American insistence on Palestinian partition, and their involvement in discussion on this issue in 1945–6 revealed little sympathy for Britain. Roosevelt had urged Britain not to restore the French Empire to France, or keep Hong Kong. His world trips had involved meetings with men like the Kings of Morocco and Saudi Arabia who he had assured that America did not support colonialism. Dulles declared in 1954: 'The United States was the first colony in modern history to win independence for itself, and instinctively shares the aspirations for liberty of all dependent and colonial peoples. We do not seek to perpetuate Western colonialism.' Suez followed in 1956. American opposition to colonialism played an important part in bringing it to an end.

As early as the Baku Conference of 1920, attended by representatives from 37 countries, Russia had backed anti-colonial movements. She sent arms to Kemal Ataturk in 1920, and agents to Iran and Afghanistan in the 1920s. In 1948, a similar conference at Calcutta co-ordinated this policy in Asia, and that year the Communist Rising in Malaya began. In 1955–6 Khrushchev shifted Russian attention to the Middle East with aid for Nasser, and by the 1960s Cuban troops were active in Africa. The triumph of Communism in China, Cuba and Vietnam, clearly provided an alternative focus for Third World countries. Russia was 'imperialist' herself, but not far from her borders. She was thus able to pose as the supporter of colonial liberation movements, and in the Congo Crisis of 1960–1 her backing for the government of Lumumba was successful in defeating Western interests. Tanzania with Chinese help followed suit in 1964, and there are now marxist regimes in places as far apart as Surinam and Mauritius. Within the Cold War a wider war for influence in the world was fought out, and this helped many Third World countries to obtain their independence.

By 1945 the West had exported its own competition. Western economics demanded more than one crop–plantation–subsistence economies for the Third World. Western education meant that universities would have to follow mission primary schools. As Africans and Asians increasingly took part in government the demand for democratic rights was bound to increase, and to prove incompatible with white minority supremacy. Western ideas like nationalism and marxism had acted as catalysts on the colonial peoples. Westernisation had generated movement to the towns (for example, 40 million had moved to towns in Africa). Among urban proletariats Western rule and its supporters, became increasingly unsustainable. 'Most Tunisian nationalists are Paris educated ... they speak French among themselves', said a writer in 1955. Clearly those who spoke French understood liberty, equality and fraternity, and these political rights could not have been denied for ever to most of the world's population. If ever a movement in history was inevitable the ending of European imperialism must surely be accounted among the most certain.

C Asia Breaks Free

C1 Mohandas Gandhi and Independence for India

British India had been created by a variety of methods between 1612 and 1858. It was the linchpin of the British Empire, the largest colony ever to exist, and a most remarkable example of successful imperialism. Indian civilisation and religions were of course there long before the British, but the concept of a united India was created by the British with their language and law; and modern India was a product of British economic development and imposed social change. But in the long term this remarkable relationship could not have lasted. It was in the first place a matter of numbers. India prospered under British rule—she was the world's seventh industrial power by 1939—and her population which was already vast increased with prosperity and famine control. In 1891 it was 214 million and in 1931 it was 352 million. The India Office in London had 452 civil servants; the Imperial civil service in India had 5,000, and by the 1930s was having recruitment difficulties. The British had an army of only 50,000 in India backed by 160,000 Indian troops, and clearly either a determined revolt by millions, or the need to defend India from rebels armed with modern weapons would have been stupendous—and quite beyond Britain's resources after the Second World War.

The logic of this position was clear: India steadily moved towards self-government, and Indians gradually replaced the British in key government services. It was in 1892 that Indians were first permitted to enter the government of the country as nominated members of governors' councils, and provincial councils. Step by step they advanced. In 1909 a nominated Indian member of the viceroy's council appeared, and elected members of legislative councils became a majority over nominated members. Ten years later considerable power was devolved to fully elected provincial governments. In 1935 the Government of India Act established responsible government in the eleven provinces, and a national legislature with limited powers. By March 1942 the British had promised dominion status, and had in fact already conceded this in some ways allowing India representation at Imperial conferences and at Versailles in 1919 when she was not legally entitled to it. By 1939 only 630 out of 5,500 civil servants, and 600 out of 187,000 police were British, and progressive Indianisation could only continue.

Indian nationalism evolved out of intellectual studies among the small group of two per cent of Indians who were favoured with higher education, and began with the Congress Party in 1885. In the period before 1914 there had been limited terrorist activity, but this had been suppressed, and it was not until the return of Gandhi to India with new ideas on involving the masses that the nationalist movement got under way in 1920. Mohandas Gandhi (1869–1948) represented both the aspirations and the difficulties of Indian nationalism. He revered the history and customs of the people and wished to remove alien rule; but he was a Hindu, and many in India were Muslims and of other faiths like the Sikhs who resented his leadership. Gandhi spent much of his early life (1893–1915) in South Africa where he learnt the ugly nature of white supremacy. On his return to India he launched two campaigns of non co-operation (1920–3, 1930–4) in order to embarrass the British government. In this he succeeded, and gained the support of many in Britain who backed self-government for India without perhaps realising Gandhi did not only represent progress, but also a religious fanaticism which India had not experienced since the start of British rule. Then in 1932 Gandhi added an economic campaign designed to rally the villagers by backing indigenous Indian industries. He achieved a mass following, but his own non-violent principles were often violated by his followers. His party demanded full independence in August 1928, and the younger elements in the party were more violent. Their 'Quit India' campaign in 1942 accounted for a thousand lives. This Hindu fanaticism worried the Muslims. Their leader was Ali Jinnah (1876–1948) who as early as 1929 advocated a federal India to avoid a clash. In 1934 he became leader of the Muslim League which in 1940 declared itself in favour of the creation of 'Pakistan', or in other words—a divided India.

C2 The Struggle for Independence 1942–47

India made a massive contribution to Britain's war effort in 1939–45, and the British in turn defended India from Japanese invasion. But it was clear the pace of reform would have to quicken. In 1940 Indians entered the Viceroy's Council, and responsible government was promised. Cripps said independence would come at the end of the war in March 1942. For a time the British tried to make the 1935 Act work, and encouraged the Hindus and Muslims to work together, but a meeting of Gandhi and Jinnah in 1944 did not achieve this, and when the British plan was published in May 1946 providing for a complicated series of federal government bodies, and an interim government to draft proposals, there was violent rioting, and both Gandhi and Jinnah rejected the plan by the end of the year. Attlee now decided to act decisively as Britain could not afford to be dragged into a war to enforce a settlement, and trouble between Muslims and Hindus in East Bengal and the Punjab was impossible to control. In February 1947 Attlee announced India would be independent by June 1948, and sent Lord Mountbatten as the last viceroy to act as a conciliator. Within three months of arriving in India Mountbatten held 133 meetings with the various leaders, and effected a compromise. But India would have to be divided. Then in June 1947 it was announced independence would come in August that year; thus forcing Congress and the Muslim League to make an agreement and concentrate their attention on the problems of independence.

This policy was also adopted by Attlee in Palestine (see section 10D1), and there too met with disastrous results, even if it did effect the main object of removing British rule. Both Palestine and India remain bitterly divided by religious views, and in each case borders are still unfixed. In the case of India Britain broke her obligations to the Indian princes who ruled many parts of the country, and who had been loyal to Britain. The British drew the borders of Pakistan in 72 days, and the result was inevitably that independence saw the worst slaughter in India since the Indian Mutiny. It is estimated that 250,000 died in sectarian strife although some recent historians have reduced this number considerably. Five million Hindus and 6 million Muslims were forced to change country in order to effect partition, and Pakistan itself, divided into two widely separated parts, was an extraordinary country unlikely to endure. It proved impossible to decide which country Kashmir should join, and an artificial truce line was established there in January 1949; the dispute is still unsettled.

Gandhi could not take office, and so the first Prime Minister of India was Jawaharlal Nehru (1889–1964). He had been leader of the socialist wing of the Congress Party, and an advocate of more extreme action being imprisoned nine times down to 1945. Gandhi was murdered in January 1948 by a Hindu fanatic who opposed partition. Jinnah died in September 1948. The first Prime Minister of Pakistan was Liaqat Ali Khan who was later murdered in October 1951. Nehru's government promptly coerced the princes into joining India, and in 1961 annexed the Portuguese possession in India–Goa. India was free, but at a price. It was a democracy, but there was effectively only the Congress Party to rule it. Civil War, division and disputed borders were to be features of independence elsewhere.

C3 Burma and Ceylon (Sri Lanka)

Burma was conquered by the British in three wars between 1824 and 1886, and for many years was part of the Indian empire. In 1937 it was separated from India, and given limited responsible government. In 1942 it was overrun by Japan, and was the focus for Britain's main campaign against the Japanese, being liberated from them in May 1945. The Nationalist leader, Aung San (1914–47) co-operated with the Japanese in order to build up his own army, and then in 1944 he switched his support to the British. Whereas the governor wanted him arrested for treason, Mountbatten was prepared to accept his services, and in March 1945 he joined the British forces. The hardline governor was recalled by Attlee, and independence promised. Aung San became Prime Minister, but together with six cabinet ministers was murdered in 1947 by a political rival, U Saw, who was himself executed in 1948. The Burmese pressed for full independence outside the British Commonwealth, and this was secured in January 1948.

Burma's independence problems were considerable. There was a Communist revolt (1948–50); the Karens rebelled demanding autonomy; and the presence of Chinese Nationalist troops in the north of the country provoked Chinese incursions until agreement was reached in 1960. Prime Ministers like U Nu were unable to control the country, and in 1958 General Ne Win seized power for the first time. U Nu was imprisoned from 1962 to 1966. It is interesting to notice that Burma supplied the first non-European Secretary-General of the United Nations from 1962 to 1971 in the person of U Thant (1909–74).

Ceylon was conquered by the British from the Dutch in 1796, and subdued by 1815. In 1915 there were riots, and by 1919 a National Congress was in existence given an elected majority in 1924. This was in fact the first example of a coloured people being given responsible government by a colonial power, and in 1931 the colony secured what was virtually internal self-government extended again in 1946. But by then the momentum for independence was too great, and in February 1948 Ceylon became independent.

Independence was secured by the United National Party led in turn by D. S. Senanayake, his son, Dudley, and his nephew, Sir John Kotelawala, but in 1956 a rival party, the Sri Lanka Freedom Party led by Solomon Bandaranaike won the election campaigning on a pro Sinhalese, pro Buddhist and republican platform. After Bandaranaike's assassination in 1959 his widow took over leadership, and after a period in opposition became Prime Minister in 1970. She was succeeded in 1977 by Mr J. R. Jawardene who became president the following year, the new Prime Minister being Mr R. Premadasu. Mrs Bandaranaike tried to pursue a radical policy allowing the Communist Party to join her in government and making Ceylon a republic (to be called Sri Lanka) in 1972, but this trend did not last. In 1971 there was a rising by the Maoist Communist Party which took seven weeks, and several thousand deaths to suppress. In 1975 Mrs Bandaranaike broke with the Communists.

Sri Lanka prospered greatly in the early years following independence and the population doubled by 1975. To meet falling revenues from tea, coconut and rubber plantations a tourist industry was developed. Gradually economic difficulties increased as the government was forced to borrow, unemployment rose to 800,000 and tension increased between the Sinhalese, pro Buddist majority, and the Hindu Tamil minority (a quarter of the population). During the summer of 1983 this situation erupted into racial disturbances in which several hundred lives were lost.

C4 The Creation of Malaysia 1948–57

Penang acquired by the British in 1786 was the first of what came to be known as the Straits Settlements which included Singapore founded in 1819 and Malacca ceded in 1824. As the years passed the British extended their power over the rulers inland starting with Perak in 1873, and by 1914 with the submission of Johore the process was complete. The area was divided into federated and unfederated states, and in 1946 these were combined by the British, and in 1948 given a loosely federal constitution. The Chinese led by Chen Ping rose in revolt in April 1948, and Britain was faced with a major guerilla war. By 1956 the rebels were defeated although the emergency did not officially end until July 1961 (see section 3E4). Sir Gerald Templar was largely responsible for the victory in military terms, but the British were careful to pursue a 'hearts and minds' policy as well. They settled thousands in kampongs or controlled villages with better facilities, and they pressed forward with moves towards independence. In 1955 the first elections were held, and the party led by the ruler of Negri Sembilan, Tenku Abdul Rahman, won all but one of the seats.

In August 1957 Malaya became independent. It was a rotating monarchy with each ruler being in power as head of state for five years, and was strongly pro-Western. Singapore which was rich and a major British base became self-governing in 1959 under its first Prime Minister, Lee Kuan Yew. The British for reasons of containment were anxious to retain a role in the area, and negotiations were opened to create a Federation of Malaysia incorporating Malaya, Singapore and the colonies which Britain owned in the East Indies. The treaty was signed in 1962, and the new federation came into existence in September 1963. Sarawak and North Borneo (renamed Sabah) were added. However, there were difficulties. Brunei would not join, and eventually became independent in 1984. Singapore withdrew from the federation because Malaya was worried about the Chinese element trying to extend their influence on the mainland, and became independent in August 1965. (See section 9B.)

C5 The Republic of Indonesia and Achmaed Soekarno (1901–70)

The Dutch East India Company began its exploitation of the East Indies with its first voyage in 1595–9; first of all expelling the Portuguese from the region, and then completing its conquest. But it was not until 1824 with the settling of disputes with Britain that the Dutch East Indies assumed their final form, and during the nineteenth century the colonisers faced many lengthy rebellions, and the earliest nationalist group formed in 1908. The Dutch conceded a legislative council in 1916, and by 1937 this petitioned for full dominion status. Soekarno formed an Independence Party in 1928 to secure full independence, and occupation by the Japanese gave them their opportunity. The Japanese set them up in government, and with the Japanese withdrawal Soekarno proclaimed independence in August 1945. The Dutch had fought hard for the islands and many had suffered in Japanese concentration camps so they were in no mood to leave. The British occupying forces therefore returned the islands to Holland in 1946, and troops were sent to make this effective.

The Dutch divided the islands between a republic, and a United States of Indonesia both in partnership with the Dutch crown, but this failed, and in July 1947 the Dutch began the suppression of the nationalists. The United Nations intervened for the first time to criticise a colonial power, and the Americans added their voice as well forcing the Dutch into a series of compromises. By 1949 the Dutch had largely won the military campaign but that month the United Nations called for the release of Nationalist prisoners, and the granting of independence. America cut off aid to the Dutch government, and in December 1949 Indonesia came into existence with Soekarno as President. It was to be a federal state of sixteen provinces excluding Dutch New Guinea. The next year the federal structure was abandoned, and the link with the Dutch crown removed as it became a republic. The remaining links with Holland were formally repudiated in 1954. In 1958 Indonesia threatened to seize Dutch New Guinea (Irian), and expropriated and expelled all the Dutch from the country. Although the Dutch had granted responsible government in Irian, Indonesian forces attacked, and in May 1962 the Dutch were forced to agree to an American plan for a United Nations administration. The Dutch left but relations between Indonesia and the United Nations declined over other matters, and early in 1965 she left the organ-

isation. Irian was incorporated into Indonesia in 1969 after a badly supervised United Nations plebiscite. Until the Portuguese gave up Timor in 1975
Indonesia had backed its independence, and then in 1976 fully incorporated
it in her territory after a brutal war leaving 100,000 dead and 300,000 in
prison camps. The Timor Nationalist leaders were killed in 1979.

C6 America leaves the Philippines

The Philippines were effectively occupied by Spain from 1571, and in 1898
were ceded to America. Already by that time a nationalist movement under
Aguinaldo had developed, and in 1898 he proclaimed independence. America
was then involved in a colonial campaign until 1902. Civil government was
organised on the islands in the same year followed by an attempt at reform
in 1919, and the grant of internal self-government in 1934. An independence
party was founded in 1907, but for many years the Americans rejected any
such idea, and it was only when the economic rewards did not seem
promising that control was relaxed. The war of course brought the Japanese
to the Philippines which stimulated independence moves, and the country
became independent in July 1946. America while urging European countries
to divest themselves of colonial gains had no wish to lose her foothold in
Asia. In March 1947 no less than 23 base areas were granted to the United
States who trained the Philippine army, and in 1951 signed a mutual defence
pact which was the first of America's post-war Asian containment treaties.
It was only in 1959 that the number of bases was cut to four. The governments of the country faced Communist backed guerilla activity for many
years from the Huks, a Communist party based on Luzon (see section 9B).

D The Emancipation of Africa

D1 The French in the Maghreb

The area of Africa north of the Sahara known as the Maghreb was controlled almost entirely by France. Spain had obtained a part of Morocco,
and a small enclave of territory called Ifni. The city of Tangier was inter-
nationalised in 1924 by agreement between eight European powers, and after
Spanish control during the war resumed its international status in 1945.
France controlled three areas. Algeria had been conquered in 1830–47, and
was ruled as part of metropolitan France. It had been settled by the French,
and about one in nine of the people were Frenchmen called 'colons' mainly
concentrated in the coastal plain. Tunisia was a protectorate occupied in
1881, and Morocco another protectorate taken over after serious international complications in 1911.

The three colonies were all the site of historic civilisations, and were by
no means backward. The ruling dynasties of each went back many years—
Morocco to 1668, Tunisia to 1705 and Algeria to 1710—and in each country
the French had faced severe opposition. As a result the French Foreign
Legion was set up on permanent garrison duty consisting of 30,000 men
to back an army of 50,000, and martial law prevailed for long periods in
each colony's history. In Algeria, for example, there was a serious revolt

in 1881–3 under Bou Amara, and the modern nationalist movement began with the League of the Ulemas in 1931. In Tunisia the Neo-Destour group had existed since 1857, and there was a struggle against French occupation led by Ali Khalifa. The Neo-Destour were at Versailles in 1919, and were outlawed in 1938 by the French. In Morocco, Abd El Krim's revolt from 1921 to 1926 engaged generals as famous as Franco and Petain in its suppression, and the country was not completely pacified until 1934. In November that year a new Moroccan nationalist movement began, and there was an uprising in 1937.

The war years inevitably rocked French North Africa to the foundations. Clashes between Vichy and Free French, the Allied invasion, the backing of the Allies for Arab Nationalism and Roosevelt's presence at Casablanca served to weaken the French position. Yet it was here above all that France was determined to restore her power, and an uprising in Algeria was put down with at least 5,000 deaths in 1945. When the Moroccan sultan, Mohammed V, flirted with nationalism he was exiled to Madagascar by the French in 1953. In Tunisia, Sidi Lamine Bey, appointed by General Giraud in 1943, was used to head off revolutionaries. Algeria was given a new status in 1947 with 30 members in the French parliament. But it was all in vain. In each country a well organised nationalist movement emerged helped by Arabs further east like Nasser of Egypt. In Morocco, Istiq Lal: in Tunisia, Neo-Destour under Habib Bourguiba; and in Algeria, firstly the moderate UDMA under Ferhat Abbas, and then the radical FLN under Ben Bella all sought full independence.

D2 The Freeing of North Africa

Morocco was valuable to the West, and the establishment of American bases there in 1950–1 reflected this importance. The Americans urged the French to co-operate with Moroccan aspirations as the best way of retaining their support, particularly after riots in Casablanca. During 1955 the French allowed the sultan to abdicate, and Mohammed V to return. In March 1956 independence was granted. Morocco also obtained former Spanish Morocco by 1958, and later Ifni in 1969. The international city of Tangier was transferred to Morocco in 1956. In Tunisia the pattern was similar. Again the vital base at Bizerte was valuable to the West, and the French were urged to accept reforms. Attempts to provide home rule failed, and in March 1956 Tunisia became independent. It was not surprising that the illiterate ruler was deposed by Bourguiba the next year. The base was given up in 1961. But inevitably Algeria as part of metropolitan France proved more difficult for the French to surrender. Two thirds of the land was in French hands, and very profitable; oil had been discovered in the southern part of the colony. In July 1957 the French declared Algeria would not be granted independence.

French resistance led to a savage war from 1954 to 1962 which in turn was to bring about the fall of the Fourth Republic (see section 7B3). To face a guerilla force of 125,000 the French poured in 400,000 troops. Ben Bella's forces were able to attack Algiers itself for the first time in 1956, and this brought savage French retaliation under General Massu. The nationalists were defeated with the loss of 12,000 dead, and concentration camps were set up in which many Arabs died. In 1958 in Nasser's Cairo a provisional government was set up by the rebels, and the war intensified with atrocities on both sides. De Gaulle had to fight risings by the colons (1960), and the army (1961) who opposed moves to independence. Raoul Salan's OAS terrorists fought De Gaulle hard with considerable support in France, but the sheer cost of the war made a settlement inevitable, and in July 1962 independence came to Algeria. It is estimated there were a million dead in the war including 17,456 French soldiers. Ben Bella created a one party state in 1964, and swung Algeria into the Arab radical camp with Syria and Egypt. In June 1965 he was deposed by Houari Boumedienne who extended programmes of nationalisation. Algeria now backs the PLO and the Polisario guerillas fighting for part of southern Morocco.

D3 The End of Italian Africa

At the end of the Second World War the Italian Empire passed into British hands (see section 3B4). It was basically in two parts—East Africa and Libya. In East Africa, Mussolini's conquest of Abyssinia was reversed by the British, and the emperor, Haile Selassie (1892–1975) restored after an exile spent largely at Bath. Abyssinia, or as it is now known, Ethiopia, claimed to have a dynasty dating back to Menelik, son of Solomon, and had established a separate Christian church in the fourth century. It was a proud but extremely backward country, and for many years after the return of Haile Selassie played only a limited role in African affairs. The British gave the Italian colony of Eritrea to Ethiopia, in 1952, but in 1969 a guerilla movement began demanding independence. As for the remaining Italian colony of Somaliland this was combined with the British colony of the same name into an independent republic of Somalia in July 1960. Almost at once dispute broke out with Ethiopia since Somalia claimed the area of the Ogaden, and in 1964 there was large scale war for the first time in the area which lasted until 1967. The Eritrean and Ogaden disputes were destined to play a tragic part in later African history (see section 9D1).

Libya was a vast area consisting of Cyrenaica and Tripoli, and the desert beyond. It had been independent from 1711 to 1835, and then fallen under Turkish rule again. Italy had conquered the country in 1911–12, but had encountered fierce resistance until 1932. In a brutal war with the Senussi tribesmen over a third of their male population had perished. Mussolini hoped to make Libya into a great overseas Italian domain, but the country was occupied by Britain in 1942. The British restored Idris, the leader of the Senussi, the next year, and granted him the title of emir. They were anxious to retain some power in the area, and the Bevin–Sforza Plan of 1949 proposed a three way division between Britain, Italy and France. This was defeated by one vote in the United Nations, and therefore independence became the only alternative. Libya became an independent kingdom in December 1951, and for many years remained a loyal supporter of the West granting the Americans base facilities at Wheelus, and the British extensive rights under a treaty in July 1953. It was in 1969 that Idris was deposed, and Captain Gaddafi seized power (see section 10F2).

D4 The British Leave East Africa

The Sudan had been at the heart of Victorian empire building: a series of spectacular explorations, the dramatic suppression of the Arab slave trade, the rising of the Mahdi, and the death of Gordon at Khartoum, the defeat of the Khalifa at Omdurman, and the setting up of the Anglo-Egyptian Sudan in 1899 were the very stuff of imperial fantasy itself. After Kitchener's conquest came Wingate's governorship when Khartoum was planned in the shape of a Union Jack, and Cape to Cairo railway came closer to realisation. The Sudan was an unusually successful example of colonialism. The economy was built up so there was no financial deficit after 1912, and a favourable balance of trade. Arabs and Blacks lived in harmony. A single battalion of troops and 3,000 members of the Sudanese Political Service administered the country for 50 years. In 1948 the first steps to responsible government were taken, and officials talked about independence by 1966. Egypt thereupon laid claim to the Sudan, and this fanned nationalism in the country. Internal self-government in 1952 was followed by independence in 1956. The Sudan became a one party military dictatorship in 1958, and before long the country was faced with economic decline and racial strife.

Along the East African coast lay four British colonies as late as 1960: Zanzibar, Kenya, Uganda and Tanganyika. The white man had been in possession of these lands for a comparatively short time, and even then independence for these colonies was seen as very much in the distant future. Yet by 1963 all four had attained independence. Uganda had been penetrated by Christian missionaries, annexed by Britain in 1894, and developed by Sir Harry Johnson with the aid of indirect rule by such rulers as the Kabaka of Buganda. No white settlement on the land was permitted since the doctrine of African paramountcy prevailed. A country of 5.5 million was ruled with no troops and 250 police moving forward steadily economically as the Owen Falls Dam project (1954) illustrated. The Kabaka's line could be traced back 400 years, and when in 1953 the British exiled Mutesa II this stimulated nationalism with the Ugandan Peoples' Congress under Milton Obote. Independence was granted in 1962 with a federal constitution. Tanganyika only became a British colony in 1919 when it was transferred to her by mandate from Germany which had ruled the area with great cruelty since 1884. Again white men did not hold land, and the country made slow progress without incident from the day the first African took office in 1951 until independence ten years later when Julius Nyerere's party took power. Zanzibar and Pemba were islands off the coast which had been ruled by the Sultan of Muscat's family from 1832 and over which Britain secured a protectorate in 1890. Granted independence in December 1963 within a month the sultan was overthrown in a marxist coup led by John Okello aided by Cubans, and in October 1964 the islands combined with Tanganyika to form Tanzania.

D5 Uhuru for Kenya

It was in Kenya that the British faced a similar problem to that of France in Algeria: the presence of white settlers. The British had secured British East Africa from a trading company with German agreement by 1895. It became the colony of Kenya in 1920. From 1907 under the leadership of Lord Delamere white settlers had come to the uplands, and encouraged to do so again after 1945 had risen in numbers to 42,000. The British also encouraged Indians to settle in Kenya, but denied them the right to own land in the uplands. These became the White Highlands, and colour bar was more in evidence in Kenya than other British colonies. As early as 1923 the Devonshire Commission had stated that the interests of the native population in African colonies were 'paramount', but in Kenya it was clear the white man had the best land. By the early 1950s Kenya's mixed population of 70,000 Europeans, 170,000 Indians and 6.5 million blacks presented a serious problem if independence was to come: the first African entered government in 1952. But in Kenya's case matters were further complicated by the alienation of the Kikuyu tribe. The colonial rulers had disliked them excluding them from service in the King's African Rifles accusing them of being unreliable. It was from this tribe that Jomo Kenyatta (1893–1978) came. Secretary of the Kenyan Central Council (1922) which became the Kenya African Union in 1944, he had left the country for Europe in 1929 when he had been to the London School of Economics, and then moved on to Moscow for a time. Kenyatta returned to Kenya in 1946, and it was in his tribe that the Mau Mau movement emerged.

The Mau Mau Emergency (1952–60) was not primarily directed at the white settlers of whom only 32 were killed. It was essentially tribal: an attempt to control and intimidate the Kikuyu, and kill Blacks who supported the British. Sir Evelyn Baring, son of Lord Cromer, the Governor, and Generals Erskine and Lathbury, were eventually able to suppress the movement. Kenyatta was sentenced to seven years in prison in 1953. Over 160,000 Africans were arrested, and screened in concentration camps. 12,000 were sentenced as a result. The campaign led to 1,817 Loyalist African and 590 British deaths, and it is estimated 11,500 Mau Mau were executed or killed. This strengthened white resolve not to concede independence, but the government proceeded slowly towards it working with Tom Mboya, and releasing Kenyatta in 1961. By April 1962 the ex-terrorist was in government, by May 1963 the first elections had been held, and Kenya became independent in December that year (see section 9C2).

D6 Belgium Leaves the Congo

The nineteenth-century 'scramble' for Africa started in 1876 when Leopold II began his country's involvement in what was to be the Belgian Congo by 1885. It was ruled personally by him until 1908 and was one of the worst examples of colonial exploitation. The population of the Congo is estimated to have fallen by nearly half under the savage plantation economy used to secure rubber. Officials used burning and mutilation until an international outcry caused a change in policy, and the area became an official colony. However, forced labour continued, and the area remained extremely backward. In 1960 there were 28 university students, and 500 doctors in the country. It was a massive area nearly as big as India containing nearly 200 tribes. Although Belgian rule had little in the way of a colour bar it was aimed at keeping Africans from advanced education, and at the Ostend Conference in 1960 a minimum of five years to prepare for independence was suggested. However, some five parties had formed of which the most important was led by Patrice Lumumba (1925–61), a left-winger. At the conference he told the Belgians 'We are no longer your monkeys', and demanded full independence at once. Riots started, and Belgium, clearly not having the resources, gave in and granted independence in June 1960.

The Congo then split. In the north-east Ruanda and Urundi with a population of 4.5 million had been given to Belgium in 1919, but tribal differences due to opposition to the main tribe of Tutsis forced the two apart, and they became independent in 1962 as Rwanda and Burundi. The Central government of President Kasavubu and Prime Minister Lumumba was challenged by separatist movements throughout the area particularly in Kasai under Kalongi, and Katanga under Tshombe. Lumumba refused to accept Belgian aid, and in August 1960 asked for Russian help; the first time this had happened in Africa. Lumumba was dismissed and succeeded by Ileo, but real power at the centre lay with General Mobutu and the army. With the proliferation of over 50 parties, and the separatist movements some action was needed. The West backed United Nations intervention, and in August the first part of an international army arrived in the Congo. The fall of Lumumba forced the left wing members of the UNO force to leave, and when he was killed in February 1961 Khrushchev called for complete UN withdrawal; clearly a possible prelude to Russian help. Ileo was replaced by Adoula, and the UN declared that he was the legitimate prime minister.

By this time the damage had been done. Further secessions were starting including Gizenga at Stanleyville, and it seemed clear that Katanga's example of seceding in July 1961 would break up the whole area. Moise Tshombe (1919–69) had a viable state, and Belgian and other mercenaries had remained there to support his regime. There was talk of Europeans retaining power in the area or linking it with Rhodesia. The United Nations could not accept this, and in September 1961 full scale war began with Adoula's forces backed by the United Nations fighting Tshombe and Les Affreux (the mercenaries). Hammarskjold, the United Nations Secretary-General, was killed in a plane crash, and the badly controlled UN troops carried out atrocities. During 1962–3 the central government and the UN forces finally prevailed, and Britain and America co-operated in bringing economic pressure to bear on Tshombe. In January 1963 Katanga's secession ended, and he left the Congo, but it was not until August 1964 that the last resistance in the region ended. Soon after UN forces withdrew. Savage tribal war, the involvement of Russia, the inability of the United Nations to act effectively even when deploying 20,000 troops and the use of mercenaries by embittered Europeans had made independence for the Congo the worst tragedy since the slaughter in Leopold's plantations. Peace did not finally come to the region until 1967.

D7 The Setting up of the French Community

French rule in Africa had been based on the assimiliation of Africans to French cultural and educational standards, and there was little evidence of racial tension. Moreover, much of their empire was quite unsuited to overseas settlement. During the war Felix Eboue of Chad had started the move for concessions to be made expressed in the Brazzaville Charter (see section 1B2). This policy was carried forward by the Fourth Republic in 1946 when equal citizenship was granted, the colour bar forbidden and contract labour abolished. African members appeared in the French parliament. Even the Colonial Office was renamed the Ministry of France Overseas. But all these moves were destined to fail particularly as nationalism spread in French possessions in West Africa. From 1958 the French Union was replaced by the French Community giving self-government and if wished, independence, but retaining close defence and foreign policy links. Within three years France's vast African empire had gone.

French Equatorial Africa divided into four countries. Across the Congo from Belgian territory lay the French Congo which became independent in 1960. French Equatorial Africa itself to the north became independent in the same year as the Central African Republic, and in early 1966 fell under the rule of Colonel Jean-Bedel Bokassa. On the coast lay Gabon. Independent in 1960 when the government was threatened by a military coup the French intervened to restore democracy in 1964, and eventually a stable regime was established under President Bongo. Lastly, the northern area formerly called Cameroun became independent in 1960, and obtained in 1961 the southern part of the Cameroons which lay between that country and Nigeria. Under President Ahidjo the country was relatively stable for many years.

The French Sahara too was divided into four independent countries of which the most interesting is the easterly one of Chad because it was there that Eboue launched the movement for independence. Independent in 1960 the country relied upon French troops to keep it so, and they returned there when Gaddafi of Libya laid claim to part of the country. Niger, and Upper Volta became independent in 1960 as did Mauritania to the west fronting the Atlantic Ocean. This country laid claim to the whole of Spanish Sahara, and since then the claim has been disputed by Morocco which has seized the northern part of it, and Algeria which claims it and sends Polisario guerillas to assert its claims. The border remains unfixed.

In French West Africa a considerable range of new countries emerged in the period. Guinea led by Sekou Toure (b. 1922) was the only country to decline membership of the Community, and became independent in 1958 as a one party state. As early as 1960 it received Russian aid, and then gave support to guerillas fighting in the neighbouring colony of Portuguese Guinea. Senegal became independent under Leopold Senghor (b. 1906) a prominent French African nationalist, becoming a one party state in 1963. The French Sudan became Mali which passed into single party rule in 1968. On the West African coast lie the Ivory Coast, Togo and Dahomey. Military rule began in Dahomey in 1963, and has continued with erratic violence ever since. The country became Benin in 1976, and like Guinea adopted a marxist policy. The existence of the Community, with direct French military involvement in Gabon and Chad has not prevented the collapse of democracy, and the emergence of one party states. Nor has close economic co-operation starting with the Yaounde Convention of 1963 which involved 18 states, and continuing with the 46 countries of the Lomé Convention (1975).

D8 The Spanish Leave Africa

During the nineteenth century Spain lost the remains of her once vast empire as a result of a war with America in 1898 to whom she was forced to cede Cuba, Puerto Rico and the Philippines, but at the same time she remained an imperialist power. In Latin America she tried to reconquer Mexico (1829), and reoccupied Santo Domingo (1861–5). In Africa she acquired a number of possessions. In the north following agreement with France she acquired Spanish Morocco (1911), and a say in the government of Tangier (1912). Both were handed over to the new kingdom of Morocco in 1956 although bases were retained for many years. Spain reaffirmed her rule over Fernando Po in 1843, and in 1885 added Rio Muni or Equatorial Guinea to her possessions. The two areas became independent under Francisco Nguema in 1968. Spain acquired part of the Western Sahara (Rio de Oro) in 1885, and ownership of this area has been disputed between Algeria, Morocco and Mauritania since 1976 when Spain surrendered it. The small enclave of Ifni was ceded to Morocco in 1969 so that the Spanish retreat from empire was steady and painless overall unlike her neighbour Portugal (see section 11A2).

D9 The British Leave West Africa

Britain's connection with West Africa was her most long standing one on the continent having established forts there in the 1660s, and the basis of the future colony of Sierra Leone as early as 1787. The Gambia and Sierra Leone were organised as a colony in 1808, and the other settlements added to this colony in 1821. For a time it looked as if they might be abandoned as they were unsuitable for settlement, but the suppression of the slave trade and the activities of missionaries kept Britain active in the area until full blooded imperialism developed later in the nineteenth century. In 1843 Gambia and Sierra Leone became separate colonies. Britain purchased Danish and Dutch trading stations, and in 1861 established herself at Lagos. A protectorate over the Niger River was proclaimed in 1885, and later two colonies developed. In 1914 they were amalgamated as Nigeria, a vast country with over 250 tribes. Britain was involved in three wars with Ashanti, and in 1896 proclaimed a protectorate thus completing her fourth colony of the Gold Coast which was formally organised in 1901. It was inevitable that colonies where few white men settled, and which were close to Europe would develop black nationalism. As early as 1920 the West African National Congress was started influenced by West Indian movements. It was in West Africa at Fourah Bay that the first modern African university was founded, and it was among educated Blacks in West Africa that nationalism developed in the 1940s.

This development was stimulated by the war which directly affected the area with Allied bases and rapid growth in industry. In 1943 Dr N. Azikiwe wrote *The Atlantic Charter and British West Africa* sensing that human rights had an African dimension. Azikiwe represented the Ibo based nationalist party in Nigeria while Awolowo represented the Yoruba based party. A series of constitutional changes followed leading to internal self-government, and full independence in October 1960. In the Gold Coast J. B. Danquah founded the Convention Peoples Party in 1947, and this was taken over by Kwame (Francis) Nkrumah. Nkrumah had received education at Achimota and then Lincoln University, Pennsylvania. In America he had been influenced by Du Bois, and as a result was more radical than other leaders. He used the trade unions in the Gold Coast to stir up riots, and was imprisoned in 1949. The British devised a new constitution, and released him in 1951. In a year he was the first black prime minister in history. Further constitutional changes were followed by independence in 1957 although ominously for the future Ghana became a one party state within a year, and Nkrumah was to display many characteristics of the new kind of African leadership. Britain's other colonies of The Gambia (1965) and Sierra Leone (1961) were granted independence without trouble. Sadly Sierra Leone embarked on a series of military coups in 1967, and later Nigeria was to be devastated by an appalling civil war. The British may have left West Africa peacefully, but they did not leave it to democracy and peace as they thought at the time.

E Reflection: the End of European Empires

The period of decolonisation was not a great many of the things it was said to be at the time. It was not over quickly. Movements for independence were in being for many years prior to the struggle for independence, and it is very hard to say when, for example, Indonesia started on the long road to nationhood. Once the movement began it moved more swiftly than the European powers would have liked, and this included those who wished to grant independence but feared the consequences as well as those fighting a rearguard action to stop the change. The Dutch, French and Portuguese made deliberate attempts to stop the movement involving them in large scale wars. What was in fact an inevitable movement was not seen by many as such at the time. The British adopted a policy of surrendering in order to stay to play an influential if diminished role if they could: independence was achieved as a compromise with the monarchy intact as a symbol of unity, and British bases remaining in several cases. The British too fought several wars to prevent independence going to people they saw as extremists, but ironically in the end their former prisoners like Kenyatta or Makarios emerged as the new leaders.

There was some good will in the process. There were many Europeans who took their concept of trusteeship seriously, and were genuinely anxious to secure independence. It is equally true that there were many who were not. The struggles of the Portuguese settlers in Angola, the British settlers in Kenya and Rhodesia, or the Dutch in Indonesia amply illustrate this point: had it not been for political realities in Europe including American pressure and economic difficulties the Europeans would have tried to hang on as long as they could: Portugal, for instance, did so until 1976 at enormous cost. The process of independence was marked by repression on the part of the colonial powers, and a determination to preserve their economic interests. Later European mercenaries added to Africa's difficulties in the Congo and Angola. It was also marked by the revival of tribal antagonisms, and the spread of dictatorial ambitions among the emergent politicians them-

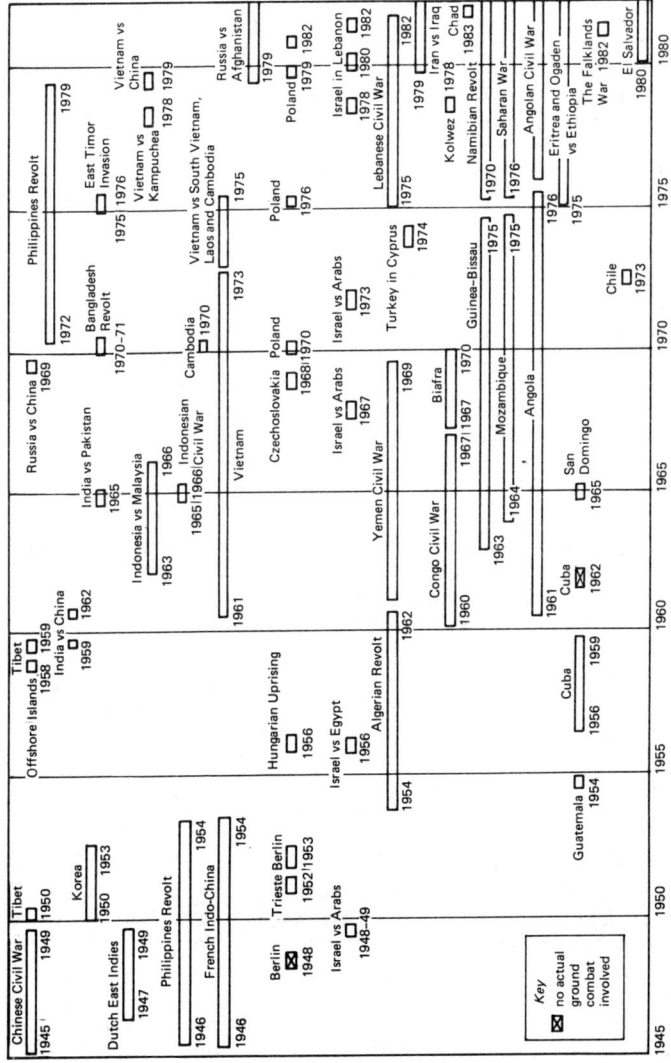

Fig. 18. Important wars and civil wars since 1945

selves. Independence was seen as a prelude to great national development, and genuine democracy. It led in nearly every case to a tragic decline in the economic progress of the countries concerned, and to one party dictatorships of fascist-militarist or marxist complexion. Racial conflict between Blacks and Arabs in the Sudan, or Asians and Africans in Kenya, dictators, civil wars, and disputes over territory soon engulfed a large part of the world which patently could not afford the evils of one European idea—nationalism —of which they were not able to rid themselves (see sections 9B–C).

The new nations' path to independence continued after the day of formal surrender. The links with the mother country were rapidly dissolved: thus the British West African possessions adopted republican forms of government in Ghana (1960), Nigeria (1963), Gambia (1970) and Sierra Leone (1971). The rulers friendly to the West were removed whether it was the Hashemites in Iraq, the Kabaka in Buganda, or the Shah of Iran. Chiefs were deprived of their power within the new countries including, for example, the Indian princes and the rulers of Northern Nigeria. Attacks were made on ex-colonial property, and very often this was nationalised without compensation as in the case of Dutch property in Indonesia. The new nations denounced neo-colonialism, and resented control or interference. But at the same time they took full advantage of such organisations as the Commonwealth and the French Community, and demanded ever increasing amounts of aid and assistance. The new nations were fervently nationalist, but began to realise that some co-operation was necessary in bodies like the Organisation of African Unity (1963), or ASEAN (1967). If there were dictators these have been sometimes overthrown, and gradually democracy has begun to take shape again in countries like Nigeria. The next chapter will tell the story of the first 20 years of independence. It is not one of peaceful progress, but it is too early to judge the outcome of this change in world affairs. It is like trying to judge the French Revolution before Napoleon. It is an event on which it will be many years yet before a judgement can be made, and Europe's Age of Nationalism should not be forgotten in judging how others deal with the problems at the moment.

Revision Questions

1. With the help of an atlas make sure that you know where all the many countries in this chapter are to be found.

2. Explain how the European powers came to own such large empires.

3. How would you evaluate the advantages and disadvantages of colonial occupation? Illustrate your answer by referring to one example in: (a) Africa or (b) Asia.

4. What phases were there in the 'struggle for independence', and what were the major difficulties encountered by the nationalists?

5. What problems faced a large country on attaining independence? Illustrate your answer by reference to: (a) Nigeria or (b) India (see also chapter 9 for developments).

6. Write accounts of the lives of the following nationalist leaders: (a) Mohandas Gandhi, (b) Achmaed Soekarno, (c) Ben Bella, (d) Jomo Kenyatta, (e) Patrice Lumumba, (f) Kwame Nkrumah. Are there any

common factors in their careers? (Again, refer forward to chapter 9 as well.)

Four areas of the Third World are dealt with elsewhere in the book, and for a complete picture of the struggle for colonial freedom students should consult: French Indo-China (13B), the West Indies (12E), the Middle East (all chapter 10), and Southern Africa (all chapter 11).

Further Reading

Caldwell, M., *Indonesia*, OUP, London, 1968.
Hatch, J., *The History of Britain in Africa,* Andre Deutsch, London, 1969.
Hatch, J., *Nigeria: A History*, Secker and Warburg, London, 1971.
Hollings, J., *African Nationalism*, Hart Davies, London, 1971.
Horne, A., *A Savage War of Peace*, Macmillan, London, 1977.
Jones, P., *Kwame Nkrumah and Africa*, Hamish Hamilton, London, 1965.
Legge, J. D., *Soekarno*, Allen Lane, the Penguin Press, Harmondsworth, 1972.
Moon, P., *Divide and Quit*, Chatto and Windus, London, 1961.
Oliver, R. and Fage, J. D., *A Short History of Africa*, Penguin, Harmondsworth, 1962.
Purcell, V., *The Revolution in South East Asia*, Thames and Hudson, London, 1962.
Segal, R., *The Race War*, Penguin, Harmondsworth, 1966.

9

The Third World Countries of Asia and Africa in the Early Years of Independence

A The Indian Continent

A1 India's Difficulties

India's independence (see section 8C2) had been achieved with division and turmoil. The country was already poor, and beset by enormous problems. These stemmed, of course, from the ever increasing pressure of population on limited and primitive agricultural resources. India's population has added 200 million since independence. Birth control was started by the government in 1956, but clearly had little effect. So great was the alarm caused by this problem that Mrs Gandhi even resorted to compulsory sterilisation in the mid-1970s in order to effect a change. Indian society has many traditional and religious features which English rule had preserved. The 500 princes were a barrier to progress, but in 1970 their last powers were removed, and it became possible to reorganise the provinces of India on a more rational basis. The Punjab was divided for example. Laws had to be passed to end discrimination on grounds of caste. The immense variety of linguistic and racial groups is well illustrated by the problem of agreeing a national language. When in 1965 an attempt was made to have Hindi declared the sole official language this failed, and the government was forced to allow English to continue as well since it alone bound all the peoples together.

A2 The Rule of the Congress Party

Throughout its modern history India has been ruled by the Congress Party which is an amalgam of conservatives and socialists. It was founded as a party representing a majority religious interest, and contained many undemocratic features particularly the Syndicate and the preservation of power within a small ruling clique. Jawaharlal Nehru was Prime Minister until his death in 1964, and was succeeded for two years by Lai Bahadur Shastri, but unfortunately he died at a conference in 1966. His successor was Indira Gandhi, Nehru's daughter, who had been imprisoned during the independence struggle, and was a politician of great skill and considerable bravery. For nearly ten years she ruled unchallenged directing India towards friendship with Russia, socialist reforms and a warlike foreign policy involving a clash with Pakistan in 1971. The impact of six million refugees from this war on an economy seriously affected by the Orissa tidal wave (1971) and the failure of the monsoon (1972) was to arouse opposition. This was directed at her political corruption and in 1975 the Allahabad High Court declared her election invalid. Mrs Gandhi retaliated by declaring a state of emergency, and getting the decision reversed, but by this time opposition was growing. She resorted to suspending civil liberties in November 1976, and arresting opponents. Her main opponent was Morarji Desai who had left her government in 1969 and formed Janata or the Peoples' Front, an essentially conservative party. He won the elections of 1977, put into reverse some of Gandhi's economic policies, and had her tried and imprisoned in 1978. This made a martyr out of her, and she returned to office in July 1979 with her son, Sanjay, who was being groomed as heir. He was killed in an air crash in 1980, but Mrs Gandhi remains resolutely in control of India.

A3 Economic Developments

From the first India played an important part in rallying Third World countries to deal with their economic problems. India was prominent in the Colombo Plan (1950), and at the Bandung Conference (1955), and sought by non-aligned status to obtain aid from both West and East. Thus agreements on economic matters were signed with America (1952), Russia (1953) and China (1954) while any attempt to use these for military purposes was firmly resisted. India and China were sharply divided on border issues (see section 6E3), and therefore it was natural she should turn to Russia, her second largest export customer. In fact this has meant very little internally. Nehru and Gandhi both tried to carry out socialist measures. There have been several Indian development plans, for example, and some development of co-operation in agriculture, but attempts to nationalise banks and insurance companies in 1967 were overturned in the courts in 1970.

A4 Indian Expansionism

Although non-aligned, India has not been a particularly peaceful country. India laid claim to Kashmir which was declared autonomous in 1952 under United Nations protection, but Sheik Abdullah, the ruler, was frequently arrested by the Indian government which claimed he backed Pakistan. India objected strongly to several features of the borders created in 1947. In 1965 she seized territory in the Ran of Kutch, and British mediation was necessary, but this did not help matters. In August 1965 Kashmir was invaded and Abdullah arrested once more. This time there was strong Western opposition, and America cut off aid. The Russians intervened, and a conference at Tashkent restored the status quo. Abdullah was released in 1968. This Russian support led in August 1971 to a military agreement with Mrs Gandhi. Although India said in 1950 she recognised the colonial borders in the north to check Chinese claims, she quickly removed remaining European enclaves. The French (1956) surrendered their Indian possessions, and when Portugal refused to do likewise India occupied Goa in 1961. Faced with Chinese aggression in the north (see section 6E3) India took firm measures including incorporating Sikkim in 1975. In co-operation with Burma India has waged a fierce campaign to suppress the Naga tribesmen in Assam.

India's most serious quarrel was with Pakistan, a nation which the Congress Party had bitterly opposed even coming into existence. Pakistan was pro-Western and pro-Chinese while India was pro-Russian each seeking outside support because of unresolved border disputes. In 1971 there was a rebellion in East Pakistan (see section A6). Six million refugees flooded into India, and many were Hindus. There were border incidents as Pakistani troops pursued the rebels, and in December came full scale war which lasted 13 days. India advanced into the Sind and Punjab regions of West Pakistan scoring battle successes while a four-pronged attack on East Pakistan brought their troops within sight of Dacca. Peace was made at Simla in 1972 by which Pakistan secured the return of her 90,000 prisoners of war, but was forced to recognise the new country of Bangladesh.

A5 The Failure of Democracy in Pakistan

Pakistan was an artificial creation whose borders were swiftly drawn in 1947. As a result it suffered from many disadvantages. The Indus river area was divided, and it was not until 1960 that agreement was reached with India on this matter. India claimed Kashmir and other parts of Pakistan, additionally East Pakistan was not only separated from West Pakistan by great distance, but had differing race, language and economic structure. It was the most prosperous part of the country providing 75 per cent of her exports, but the real power was concentrated in West Pakistan. As early as 1954 there were signs that this artificial country would not survive. Democracy did not find favour with the Muslim tribesmen, and between 1951 and 1958 there were eleven prime ministers. In 1958 a military *putsch* took place, and General Ayub Khan became ruler. Ayub's policy was similar to that of the Shah in Iran. In return for political tranquillity he gave considerable economic progress, and sought to break down the outdated features of Muslim society. He adopted a pro-Western foreign policy, and built friendship with China culminating in 1965 when their border difficulties were resolved. Ayub was replaced by Yahya Khan in 1969, but by this time opposition was gathering.

Opposition came from two sources. Ali Bhutto led the Peoples' Party which wanted democracy and socialism to cure the country's ills. Sheik Mujibar Rahman led the Awami League proposing a federal structure for Pakistan to redress some of the grievances in East Pakistan. Yahya decided to arrest Rahman, and crush his movement. He sent General Tikka Khan to East Pakistan where large scale atrocities occurred. The Awami Party formed guerilla fighters called the Mukti Bahini, and war began. Millions fled into India, and at the end of 1971 India attacked Pakistan (see section A4).

A6 Bangladesh Created: Pakistan under Bhutto

The result of the war was a defeat for Pakistan. Yahya left office, and Bhutto became President. He made a peace settlement with India, and recognised the new state of Bangladesh. Although Bangladesh was admitted to the Commonwealth forcing Pakistan to be the first country to leave it, the new land was subject to civil war and famine for a number of years because Rahman insisted on a strict Muslim state. He was murdered in 1975, and after further chaos Zia ur-Rahman took over in 1977, and established a military dictatorship. The present ruler is General Ershad who took over in 1982. In Pakistan Bhutto sought to carry out many reforms including a nationalisation programme affecting banks, transport and major industry. Land reform was also begun. A purge of 1,400 reactionary officers in the armed services was carried out, but his reforms, like those of the Shah, annoyed the mullahs who began to stir up opposition. In the election of 1977 Bhutto was accused of corruption, but managed to return to power. The result was a further military *putsch* under General Zia ul-Haque who sought to restore more traditional policies, and realign Pakistan with the West. His decision to have Bhutto and five others executed in April 1979 aroused considerable resentment. Then came the Iranian Revolution, and the invasion of Afghanistan. General Zia found himself in favour with the West. Lord Carrington visited the country, and the American base facilities at Peshawar were reactivated. At the moment Pakistan, wary of the 102,000 Soviet troops massed in Afghanistan, is having to cope with two million Afghanistani refugees.

B The East Indies

The numerous and prosperous East Indies were eventually divided between three countries—the Philippines, independent in 1946; Indonesia, independent in 1949; and Malaysia which came into existence in 1963 consisting of Malaya, Singapore, Sarawak and Borneo (renamed Sabah). Brunei would not join, and became an independent protected state in 1984. Singapore led by Lee Kuan Yew became independent in its own right in August 1965. Indonesia seized West Irian in 1963 and Timor in 1975. In one way all three states faced a similar threat from left wing opposition. Malaysia and the Philippines backed SEATO, and in 1967 all three countries joined ASEAN which provided for economic co-operation. The withdrawal of the British base of Singapore (1968), and the defeat of America in Vietnam (1973) made the position of the three governments even more precarious. But co-operation has often been prevented by rival territorial claims, and the aggressive policies of the dictators who have come to power in two of the three countries.

All three countries experienced serious Communist uprisings which it took many years to suppress. In Malaya the British colonial authorities were successful (see section 8C4), but the emergency was only officially declared at an end in 1961. In Indonesia, President Soekarno had moved steadily leftwards after a visit to Moscow and concluded a trade agreement with Russia in 1960. He seized Dutch (1957), American and British companies (1965). His own rule was increasingly dictatorial, and he became president for life in 1963. But the Muslims were increasingly annoyed by Soekarno's acceptance of left wing ideas, and when in September 1965 there was a Communist attempt to overthrow the government there was a massacre of several thousand of the insurgents. Soekarno responded by sacking several ministers and generals who organised this campaign, and in March 1966 he was replaced by General Suharto. In the Philippines the Communists (the Huks) continued guerilla activity after independence, and from 1971 to 1979 the government was involved in a campaign to suppress opposition which as in Indonesia led to one man government under President Marcos in 1972. The killing of the Socialist leader at Manila Airport in 1983 led to renewed opposition.

Indonesia became involved in a war with Malaysia. When Malaysia had first been proposed there had been no word of opposition from Soekarno, but under pressure from the left he chose to see the new federation as colonialist. He also claimed the Borneo territories, and was worried by a Philippine claim to the most easterly of them. A revolt by leftwingers in Brunei in opposition to the proposed federation took place in 1963. The British were quite willing for Brunei not to join, but Soekarno saw this as the start of a widespread revolt, and in 1963 announced a 'state of confrontation' with Malaysia. Malaysia decided to resist this and backed up with 50,000 Commonwealth troops, prepared to repel guerilla attacks along the 950 mile jungle frontier in Borneo.

Indonesian agents fomented serious riots in Singapore, and two attempts were made in late 1964 to land on the mainland. Britain warned it would take direct military action, and because of internal instability (the war led to 500 per cent inflation in Indonesia) no further attempts were made of this kind. The Chinese opposition was contained by giving Singapore its independence. Successful military action by the British with a multi-Commonwealth force produced complete military stalemate while at home Soekarno was faced with rising opposition. Suharto's new government soon agreed to a truce, and peace was signed at Jakarta in 1966. Suharto, although he did invade Timor, was a more moderate figure, and sought to restore order and prosperity to the islands. Inflation was curbed, debts paid and foreign property restored. Starting with the Communist Party (1968) other parties were suppressed, and by 1974 a benevolent despotism had been established. Thus, in this vast area only Malaysia remained a democracy. Its founder, Abdul Rahman, retired and was succeeded by Abdul Razah in 1970. Two development plans helped to reconcile the two parts of the country which remains prosperous and stable.

C Japan Returns to Great Power Status

C1 Japan Under American Occupation

When the dropping of atom bombs on Hiroshima and Nagasaki brought to an end Japan's participation in the Second World War (see section 2A5), they simultaneously ended a lengthy period of Japanese history in which expansion had been the keynote. Japan had been continuously at war since 1937 and inevitably the military, already deeply imbedded in the *samurai* traditions of the country, had come to play a decisive role in politics. Japan's defeat cost her the whole of her vast empire because at Yalta it had been agreed to restore to the Soviet Union all Russia had lost in 1905. Japan thus lost her Manchurian conquests and all her assets and military supplies there which were handed by Stalin to Mao Tse Tung, areas of China like Dairen and Port Arthur, Korea, Sakhalin and the Kuriles. Because America and Chiang's China were close at this time China regained Formosa (Taiwan). America proceeded to annex all the Pacific Islands mandated to

Japan at the end of the First World War, and to add to them the Ryukyu and Bonin Islands. To deal with post-war Japan an Allied Control Commission was set up in Tokyo, but this had little influence and only the British actually stationed troops in Japan apart from America. In December 1945 the Far Eastern Commission was set up in Washington, and General MacArthur (and after 1950 General Ridgeway) was the effective ruler of Japan for a number of years.

Japanese war crimes had extended over a large part of eastern Asia and China for a decade. Inevitably therefore there was a counterpart in Japan to the harsh treatment of Germany in Europe at this time. The Japanese emperor was compelled to make a broadcast saying he had ceased to be ruler by divine right, and thereafter retired into obscurity except for an unpopular visit to Britain in 1971. The *zaibatsu* or large corporations which had exploited Manchuria and the Greater Asia Co-Prosperity Sphere were dismantled. The Japanese were forbidden to rearm, and indeed an article of their later constitution stressed their non belligerency. War trials were held. Seven prominent and over 900 lesser war criminals were sentenced to death. 200,000 were placed on trial and one and a half million declared unsuitable for employment by the state in the future. Finally in September 1951 peace was signed between Japan and many of her former enemies, but neither Russia nor China would agree to sign, and smaller Asian nations made ratification dependent on future receipt of reparations. The official state of war between Japan and these countries was not ended until 1956 and 1972 respectively, and no definitive peace has been signed.

In one respect, however, the San Francisco Treaty marked a change in American policy towards Japan similar to that which marked Allied treatment of Germany in Europe at the same time. China had ceased to be a bulwark against Russia in 1949; America needed a new Asian partner as flights of American bombers from Japan to Korea in 1950 were soon to prove. American policy had clinically and without compromise introduced Western concepts once more in Japan, and since the country had a long history of assimilating such ideas this did not prove too difficult. Major land reform created a class of conservative small farmers to back stable government and end the power of the nobles. A democratic constitution, giving the vote to women for example, was introduced and became effective from May 1947. Accompanying this were educational reforms, the development of trade unions with carefully limited powers and the introduction for the first time of local government councils with considerable powers. Side by side with this came the decision to allow the corporations to trade freely once again, and rearmament at the time of the Korean War started the boom of the fifties and sixties in Japan. This change of policy was marked in the San Francisco Treaty by the clauses dealing with military matters. In 1950 a military police force of 70,000 had been allowed. The treaty placed no restrictions on this force which grew into an army of 200,000 by the end of the decade. Similarly America gave Japan old warships to restart her navy. This decision was bitterly opposed by Australia and New Zealand, and it was one reason at least why America agreed to the ANZUS Pact in 1951 to placate those fearful of Japanese military revival; a fear which so far has proved unfounded.

C2 Japan's Economic Miracle

Calvocoressi uses the phrase 'the fourth world' to describe those Third World countries like Singapore, Israel, Saudi Arabia, and not least, Japan, which cannot be classified any longer in the same bracket as El Salvador, Chad or Kampuchea. For differing reasons they have undergone economic growth and in Eastern Asia the 'miracle economies' have been Taiwan, South Korea and Japan, all of which have become ruthlessly capitalist and are run by right wing governments. Japan was already industrialising in 1939, and after a short period American capital and expertise were available in the late 1940s when the American economy dominated the free world. Direct American aid, the rearmament boom and the advantages given to Japan in world markets by America to deter her from trading with Communist China all helped enormously to restore Japan as a major industrial power. In the early 1950s Japan was admitted to the Colombo Plan countries and was present at Bandung. Yet by 1960 she was economically powerful enough to be admitted with America to OECD, and by 1966 she played the major part in creating the Asian Development Bank. In the 1960s Japan with 8 per cent annual growth, and Germany with 5.5 per cent were the two 'economic miracles', and although in the 1970s first Japan and then Germany experienced economic difficulties Japan still remains powerful economically —accounting for a fifth of world industrial production.

There are a number of explanations for Japanese growth. The unfavourable one suggests that it has been achieved by capitalist exploitation underselling in world markets, refusing to abide by tariff agreements, keeping their own high tariffs, manipulating the yen by, for example, a major devaluation in 1972, banning many trade union activities and paying workers low wages. Yet the Communist Party has never secured more than 3 per cent of the vote, and the Socialist Party which was powerful in the early 1950s has faded away. The Japanese workers seem to vote, in fact, for governments which have brought them from economic collapse in 1945 to a standard of living far higher than that elsewhere in Asia. With a population of 114 million in a restricted area with few natural resources Japan has indeed achieved a miracle—perhaps at some cost in terms of the environment, but not in the 1980s at the expense of the workers. Indeed, many Japanese companies provide holiday and housing facilities for their employees.

The economic growth can be attributed partly to American aid, but primarily it is due to the Japanese themselves. Hard work, rapid modernisation, and heavy investment programmes have brought their own reward. Agricultural reform has turned Japan from a net food importer to a country with a rice surplus for export, while at the same time the percentage of workers in agriculture has fallen to a mere 18 per cent. Educational policy is competitive at all levels and only highly qualified students are accepted as managers of the larger companies. A special licensing system has procured many American and European inventions for Japanese development. Moreover, Japan has the lowest defence costs of any major power. Her defence until recently depended on an American treaty with bases and a nuclear umbrella. This is less likely to hold good in the future, but until now it has been a substantial factor in helping Japan. The government has also been able to introduce a welfare state to cushion some of the undesirable effects of unbridled capitalism.

Japan has become the world's leading shipbuilding and electronics producer, and this balance of traditional and new industry well reflects the growth of their economy as a whole. Japan is a major steel and plastics producer. She is an important motor car and motor bike producer. By the early 1970s Japan was annually producing 24 million transistor radios, 18 million tape recorders and 5 million colour televisions. At the moment Japan is seeking to become a major computer producer. Japanese names like Honda, Kawasaki, Hitachi, Sony and Toyota are household names in a western world where this would have been impossible in 1950. The boom declined in the early 1970s, but Japan was the first country to jettison Keynesian economics and rigorously control the money supply and inflation in order to get the economy on course. At the cost of high unemployment for a number of years they succeeded, and in the 1980s prosperity continued.

C3 Japanese Politics at Home and Abroad

Japan's status as an occupied power came to an end in April 1952, but a government had been in existence under American supervision since 1946. For a time it looked as if Japanese politics would produce a number of different parties. There were Liberal (in fact Conservative), Democratic and Socialist Parties, and for a short time even a socialist government. But American determination to oppose 'leftism', and the close relationship between Japan's defence, wealth and the American presence led to a change accelerated by a decision in 1950 to allow 10,000 of those on the banned-from-politics list to serve in government again. As a result, by 1955 men like Hatoyama and Shigimitsu were back in office, and the prime minister in the late 1950s was Kishi, a former member of Tojo's wartime cabinet. Moreover, by enfranchising the new landowning class the Americans guaranteed a right wing majority in elections, and since 1955 Japan has been governed by the same party.

The ruling party was formed in November that year by an amalgamation of the Liberal and Democratic Parties. The constant rule of one party has led, however, to discontent among left wing Japanese. This has focused on a number of issues on which the government is vulnerable. Deaths resulting from the 1945 atom bombs are still occurring, and in 1954 an American test at Bikini contaminated Japanese fish and killed a number of fishermen. The presence of American nuclear forces in Japan is thus one focus for the opposition. A second is that American capitalism is destroying the Japanese environment—an argument, incidentally, which appeals to right wing extremists as well. The mercury poisoning of workers at Minamata was one case which led to strong protests. There were years of opposition, often violent, to the building of Tokyo Airport, finally opened in 1978. Lastly, the opposition can focus on the close links of Japan and America suggesting Japan is an Asian power and should look to China and India as allies not to America.

As long as Japan was isolated and Mao clearly aggressive little was heard of this opposition. Japan signed a security treaty in 1951, and this was renewed in 1954, but as Japan steadily gained in strength—being admitted to

UNO in 1956, for instance, and seeing American troops finally leave the mainland at the same time (1958) as Chinese troops left Korea, the opposition to renewal of the treaty gained ground. Prime Minister Kishi was quite willing to renew the treaty in 1960, but ran into strong opposition. For a time with Socialist demonstrations and the murder of the Socialist leader, Asanuro, it looked as if Japanese politics were back to the 1930s, but fortunately Kishi cancelled a visit by Eisenhower and resigned himself, thus getting the treaty through. However, America promised to return the islands she had taken. The Bonins were returned in 1968 and the Ryukyus in 1972, when Nixon secured a further renewal of the treaty. Gradually as America and China came together the anti-American feeling which had led to the stabbing of the ambassador in 1964 gave way to a better relationship. The new trend to a pacific and friendly relationship with China particularly incensed the right wing and in 1970 Mishima Yukio, one of the country's leading writers, committed *hara-kiri* in protest against the softening of Japanese society. Japan is now more interested in pursuing her territorial claim to the Kuriles and Sakhalin as she faces an increased Soviet naval presence in the Sea of Okotsk.

D Dictatorship or Democracy for Africa

D1 The Ethiopian Revolution and Wars

The British had restored Haile Selassie in Ethiopia after expelling the Italians (see section 3B4), and subsequently reorganised the map of East Africa considerably before independence (see section 8D3). For many years it seemed as if this status quo would be maintained in the region which was one of the poorest in the world. Selassie took a leading part in forming the Organisation of African Unity (OAU), and relied on British and American support. But his regime was feudal in many respects, corrupt and unable to cope with the economic problems of Ethiopia. Matters were made worse by a serious drought, and in 1974 Selassie was overthrown by a military council called the Dergue, and died soon after in captivity. The government began a series of leftwing reforms including the nationalisation of land, but were themselves bitterly divided into various Moscow and Maoist factions. After considerable fighting and the murder of his closest rivals Mengistu emerged as the dictator in 1977. American aid was immediately withdrawn, and Mengistu turned to Russia for help. 2,000 East German and Russian 'advisers' were soon in the country, and were followed by 12,000 Cubans whose presence was rendered necessary by the two lengthy wars that the poverty stricken country was fighting.

To the north-east Eritrea had never accepted amalgamation with Ethiopia, and taking advantage of Mengistu's chaotic regime a rebellion began led firstly by leftwingers, but continued under Sabbe who turned to Saudi Arabia and Kuwait for aid—as these countries feared further left wing control on the shores of the Red Sea. The Eritrean rebels have been subjected to Soviet naval action from neighbouring South Yemen, but the war is still continuing. To the east Somalia has extensive claims to the eastern part of Ethiopia called the Ogaden. At first Somalia relied on Russian support signing a treaty in 1974 under which 6,000 Russian 'advisers' entered the country. A war was then launched against Ethiopia, but when Moscow started backing Mengistu, Somalia soon switched its allies. In November 1977 the Russians were expelled, and the country accepted American aid. In 1980 it agreed to allow the West to use the port of Berbera, but the war for the Ogaden continued in spite of an appalling famine in 1980.

D2 Kenya's Peaceful Development

Jomo Kenyatta ruled Kenya from 1964 until his death in 1978, and although at first in view of the bitterness with which the struggle for Kenyan independence had been fought (see section 8D5) it seemed unlikely that he would be successful, in fact Kenya emerged as one of the most stable and democratic of African countries. There were of course some teething troubles. The Luo tribe resented the control of Kenyatta's Kikuyu, and some of them led by Odinga advocated left wing policies. When it seemed that Tom Mboya, the Minister of Economic Planning, and a Luo, was planning to support this move he was murdered in 1969. One party rule ended with elections in 1972, however, and since then development has been peaceful. It was Kenyatta who in 1968 began the expulsion of 60,000 Asians from the country which was to provide an ugly precedent for General Amin in Uganda. Later the policy was modified so that the Asians could move to other Commonwealth countries including Malawi and India itself. The present ruler of Kenya is President Moi, and in 1982 he experienced the first coup in the country's history, organised by the air force, which was quickly suppressed.

D3 The Dictatorship of Idi Amin in Uganda

Under British rule Uganda had been peaceful and increasingly prosperous (see section 8D4), but it was not to remain in this condition for long. Milton Obote established one party rule in 1966 and declared the country a republic. Obote was a socialist anxious to co-operate with Nyerere of Tanzania, and took a leading part in the Treaty of Kampala (1967) creating an East African Community. His 'Common Man's Charter' (1969) marked a further move in this direction, and early in 1970 60 per cent of all economic enterprises were acquired by the government with compensation promised in the future. Latent tribal tensions grew, and there was an assassination attempt late in 1969. When Obote went to the Commonwealth Conference at Singapore in 1971 he was overthrown in his absence by Idi Amin.

General Idi Amin was probably born between 1925 and 1928, and as a Nubian was soon in the King's African Rifles where he pursued a successful military career before taking office. His government was absolute, and based on a determination to secure Muslim, Nubian domination of the country. Heath's government, the Church and business men hastened to recognise him because they saw him as an alternative to Obote's socialism. He established a regime of terror based on three organisations: the Military Police, Public Safety Units and the State Research Bureau. Individual opponents, tribal enemies and whole groups in society were made the subject of a series of purges that continued throughout the period of his rule. In 1972 the Tripoli Declaration made jointly with Gaddafi of Libya indicated where financial aid and training methods for his terror organisation were obtained. The first fruits of this policy was the expulsion later that year of 50,000 Ugandan Asians who had to be distributed through many Commonwealth countries. It is impossible to say how many died during the period of Amin's rule, but in 1977 an Amnesty International report spoke of 300,000 dead.

Amin was particularly anxious to humiliate the British as the former colonial power; indeed on one occasion as a 'joke' British business men were forced to carry Amin shoulder high on a ceremonial chair. In spite of this some British seemed reluctant to leave, and in 1975 Amin was able to sentence a British lecturer to death forcing Callaghan, the British Prime Minister, to make a humiliating trip to Uganda to secure his reprieve. But this did little good. In 1976 a British woman passenger who was on an airliner that landed at Entebbe during a hijack attempt was murdered in hospital, and Britain broke off diplomatic relations. Amin also turned against the Christians, and since three-quarters of the people were converts this led to fresh massacres. In 1977 the Anglican Archbishop Luwum and two ministers were publicly tried in front of the Diplomatic Corps, and then executed. Savage attacks were made on Christian tribes like the Langa and Acholi. The Commonwealth Conference of 1977 condemned Amin although not expelling him. Next year America cut off all aid on human rights grounds, and Amin became increasingly isolated.

Like so many dictators before him Amin sought a way out in successful war. Obote's friend, Nyerere of Tanzania, had always opposed the regime. As early as 1972 there were border clashes, and in 1974 rumours of a projected invasion to restore Obote. During 1978 Amin launched an invasion of Tanzania backed up by Gaddafi who sent 2,500 troops. These were of little use in jungle warfare, and 400 were soon dead. Nyerere launched a counter invasion early in 1979, and in April entered Kampala. Amin fled to Libya. However, Uganda's sufferings were not over as it proved impossible to form a stable government. Nyerere's troops held the key, and insisted that if there were elections Obote should be allowed to return. When these were held in May 1980 Obote's Uganda Peoples Congress won, and since then some degree of order has returned. Tanzania withdrew her forces by 1982.

D4 Nigeria's Struggle for Democracy: The Nigerian Civil War

After India, Nigeria with its estimated population of 60 million was the second largest democracy in the Third World, and with the development of its oil fields is the richest black African country. But like India it was an artificial creation, its borders drawn by the British, and incorporating widely differing cultural, racial and religious elements. At first a reasonable balance was retained. Azikiwe, the President, was an Ibo from the East, and Balewa, the Prime Minister, was from the Muslim Northern Region. The Ibos who represented a fifth of the population, and in whose region the oil was located, were determined to assert themselves against the other regions. In 1966 a revolt led by the Ibo, General Ironsi was responsible for the killing of Balewa, and the prime ministers of the western and northern regions. This provoked reaction against the Ibos particularly in the north, where they were massacred. Ironsi was killed, and General Y. Gowan, a Christian from the Northern region, became the military ruler later in the year.

The Ibos then decided to break away, and led by Lieutenant Colonel O. Ojukwu they proclaimed independence as the state of Biafra in May 1967. This produced an interesting international situation. The OAU was worried that other African borders had been drawn by the colonial powers, and if Biafra was allowed to secede then many countries might be thrown into chaos. Memories of the horrors in the Congo were revived. Thus, only four African countries recognised the new state. De Gaulle's France, ever ready to embarrass the British, also gave support, and a skilful propaganda campaign enabled the Ibos to obtain food and medical supplies which prolonged the war in spite of swift military defeat. By the end of 1967 Enugu the capital of the region had been entered by federal troops, but it was not until January 1970 that Ojukwu fled leaving General Effiong to surrender.

Gowan pursued a conciliatory policy, and by 1971 was able to visit the region. Helped by membership of OPEC Nigeria soon recovered from the war, and by 1974 had a trade surplus. Gowan showed no haste, however, in returning to democratic processes, and in July 1975 he was overthrown by Brigadier M. Mohammed who came to power pledged to democratic government, and a reduction of the army's role. He was killed in February 1976, but his successor, General Obasanjo continued his policies. There was considerable economic development in agriculture, health and housing, and in September 1977 elections were once more held in Nigeria. In the summer of 1980 civilian government was restored under Alhaji Shagari. However, a fall in oil prices led to a serious economic crisis, and when Shagari proposed to repudiate some of Nigeria's debts he was overthrown by the country's fifth military coup led by Major-General Mohammed Buhari (1983).

D5 The Fall of Nkrumah and Ghana's Military Rulers

Kwane Nkrumah occupied a special place in African history because he had been the first black African to become a prime minister (see section 8D9). Under him Ghana adopted a republican constitution, and moved towards a one party state. Under the Preventive Detention Act there were soon about a thousand political prisoners. He encouraged personal adulation which reached absurd proportions even having a statue of himself resembling Christ erected in Accra. To develop the country Nkrumah relied on socialist policies being determined to move Ghana away from its one crop (cocoa) economy. The Volta River project, a motorway from Accra to Tema and the development of the latter port were typical of the prestige projects which African rulers often embarked on, and they plunged the country into debt. Other projects including his own sumptuous government buildings costing £6 million were of little real value. In other ways, however, much was done for the country. Forestry and farming were developed, and agriculture diversified with pastoral farming, and the social services were improved.

Nkrumah was also anxious to be the leading political figure in Africa as a whole. He led the way in launching criticism of apartheid in South Africa and colonialism, and opened contacts with Russia, and subsequently China. He believed that Africa would gain by amalgamating the small states left by the Europeans, but this naturally led to friction with other equally zealous nationalist rulers. He attempted an economic union of Ghana, Guinea and Mali in 1961, but this did not last, and he played a leading part in setting up the OAU. The financial indebtedness of the country (£250 million), his ruthless behaviour and his grandiose ambitions were too much for many Ghanaians. In February 1966 he was deposed while on a diplomatic visit in China, and after coming to Guinea and threatening to invade his country, died in exile in 1972.

The new military government of Ghana led by Major-General Ankrah restored relations with Britain, and ended the left wing connections of the former government with China and Guinea. Ankrah and his successor, Brigadier Afrida tried to suppress corruption, and re-create political life in the country. In August 1969 elections were held once more, and a civilian government under Kofi Busia took office. But his government faced economic difficulties arising from the country's debts, and severe economic measures in 1971 precipitated a clash with the unions which he attempted to ban. There were large strikes, and the military under Colonel Acheampong decided to resume power in January 1972. His main plans launched in 1975 were to reform agriculture, and develop oil resources. The present military ruler who seized power in 1981 is Flight-Lieutenant Rawlings who has recently introduced a number of socialist policies in an attempt to revive the economy. Former leaders Akuffo and Acheampong were executed.

D6 Nyerere and Tanzanian Socialism

Julius Nyerere is one of the most prominent of the first generation of African statesmen. He has ruled Tanzania since 1962, and has become a leading figure in African politics. At first it seemed as if his government might succumb to revolt. Following the marxist takeover in Zanzibar (see section 8D4), Nyerere called on Britain for military help in 1964 when threatened with an army uprising, and thereafter integrated the armed forces within TANU the only political party. Tanzania is a one party state which has sought for original ways to develop. In February 1965 after a visit to China Nyerere began to adopt some of Mao's policies. In particular he tried to revolutionise agriculture by setting up village communes, and providing for collective marketing. A National Development Corporation has sought to stimulate economic growth, and in matters like the TanZam Railway opened in 1970 considerable progress has been made. A new capital at Dodoma is planned. In 1967 the Arusha Declaration urged a programme of austerity on the country so that basic development could take place; something which other African countries would be well advised to adopt.

E Reflection: Twenty Years of Independence

The Third World countries dealt with in this chapter together with those in the West Indies, Latin America, the Middle East and Southern Africa are immensely diverse in origins, culture and economic structure, and yet they form a distinct grouping with common characteristics. In broader terms Third World countries are those experiencing development problems caused by population growth, lack of resources and inadequate agriculture (see sections 14B–C). But this chapter illustrates that they are also developing countries in a political sense. The effects of colonial occupation and the backward nature of the societies of many of these countries lie at the root of the problem, but unbridled nationalism has been the cause of many of the political difficulties. New countries have resented being confined by old colonial borders although it is interesting that in 1982 the OAU insisted that these should be accepted, and that India has long backed the British drawn border with China. Claim and counter claim territorially, sensitivity to border incidents and diplomatic insults, and backing for rebels or guerillas of other countries have all led to conflict. Sometimes this has been stimulated by ambitious leaders like Soekarno in Indonesia, or Gaddafi in Libya. In other cases military dictators have found resort to force too easy, and often tottering regimes have found wars either against former colonial powers, or on some national issue an easy, if temporary way, out of difficulties.

But large diplomatic staffs, participation in international affairs, prestigious government buildings and above all large and expensively equipped armed and paramilitary forces have imposed an immense burden on the Third World. One has only to think of countries like the Sudan or Uganda which were defended externally by Britain, and had minute armed forces, and have been ruled by military dictators since 1969 and 1971 respectively with large armed service establishments. This in turn has reflected upon the economies of these countries. Expectations have not been met, heavy debts have been incurred, prestige projects remain uncompleted, and above all the key economic issues are neglected. As a result there is popular discontent, and this breeds dislike of democratic forms of government which seem unable to deliver the goods and a willingness to accept charismatic leaders who make great promises, like Castro or Nkrumah. But with young political parties and low educational standards, leaders are not easy to find and as a result not only have many Third World countries succumbed to dictators, they have also accepted military rulers, since there is no one else capable of large scale organisation, or securing law and order. This has applied in relatively sophisticated countries like Argentina, or Pakistan just as much as in poorly developed ones like Dahomey or Ethiopia.

There are examples of democracy flourishing and economic development successfully taking place in the Third World. India, the largest Third World country, is a democracy. Numerous Pacific and West Indian countries are peaceful democracies. There has been much economic progress in countries like Brazil, Saudi Arabia and Singapore. But the overall picture throughout Latin America, Africa, the Middle East and Asia is that one party states —often military in complexion and relying on controlled economies—are the main form of political structure. If in early years of independence this is only to be expected it is also to be regretted. Some of the rulers that have emerged such as Nguema (1969–79), Bokassa (1966–79) and Amin (1971–9) in Africa have not merely been a response to the factors outlined above; they have marked a regression to conditions prior to the colonial period. The attack on human rights in many of these countries exceeds in ferocity anything seen in America or South Africa so often pilloried on these grounds. East African countries expelling Asians and Arabs have provided examples of racial discrimination akin to those in the Western world. The systematic support of terrorism by countries like Algeria, Libya and Cuba, or the violation of diplomatic rights by countries like Iran cannot really be explained away simply by saying they are teething troubles. After all, in the former colonies the example of law abiding societies and stable government were there to be followed.

There has been a lack of effective action by the United Nations to help the Third World. Cuban aggression in Angola, Eritrea, Somalia and the Yemen or Vietnamese aggression in Laos and Kampuchea has been ignored. Peace keeping forces in the Congo, Cyprus and the Lebanon have proved incapable of peace keeping. Whereas in early years European intervention to keep the peace was possible so that France, for example, intervened in Gabon, and Chad, or British forces in Tanzania, or Swaziland, resentment against the West has precluded this, and although under the stress of events this attitude is changing so that European troops could go to Kolwezi, Sinai or the Lebanon there is still a vacuum in power terms left unfilled by the vanished colonial powers with their overwhelming military force. The countries themselves have proved unable to create forces of their own to stop civil wars. The OAU has sought to intervene since 1970 when token forces went to Guinea, and recently tried to create an army to go to Chad, but fears by unstable regimes that intervention could topple them have prevented effective military action by Third World countries.

This has led to unilateral actions like Tanzania's overthrow of Amin, or the attacks on the PLO by Jordan in 1970 and Israel in 1982. It has also led to wars lasting for extreme lengths of time because neither side possessed the strength to end them. Struggles at the moment in Iran or Western Sahara are examples. Resort too has been made to terrorist organisations and the use of mercenaries is widespread (see section 14A5). Above all it has enabled Russia to step in partly by funding terrorism, but also by using its Cuban proxies in a dozen countries throughout the Third World. If the United Nations and the Western powers are precluded from intervening it must be up to the Third World countries to prevent revolutions, wars and terrorism for themselves. American intervention in the Lebanon by force in 1958 swiftly curbed civil war. Failure of anyone to act has led to a war beginning in 1975 which has taken 60,000 lives. There is a need for the Third World countries to build effective military alliances, and to develop groups like OAS, and ASEAN to prevent the endless devastation of poor economies by wars.

It is important also for Third World countries to see that Marxist guerillas and proxies do not solve their problems. Countries like Egypt and Somalia have shown it is possible to remove such influence, but it has proved impossible in Angola where the government wished them to leave, and Afghanistan is a reminder to all Third World countries. Marxist economics have not worked as Castro's Cuba, or Allende's Chile showed, and the resulting economic chaos has led either to right wing reaction and military juntas, or to one party rule no better than the reactionary regime formerly replaced by the peoples' revolution. It is debatable whether Nicaragua or Iran having overthrown Somoza and the Shah are better off under marxist or Muslim dictators. Attention to basic economic problems, reduction in military spending, an end to backing for terrorism, a return to broadly based democratic governments, and the consolidation of effective military alliances will help to provide a more stable Third World, and to repel the threat to newly won independence wherever it comes from.

(Students are reminded that in questions on the Third World as a whole they should also refer to section 13B for South East Asia, chapter 12 for Latin America, section 12E for the West Indies, chapter 10 for the Middle East and chapter 11 for Southern Africa.)

Revision Questions

1. Explain why Third World countries: (a) have very often been politically unstable, and (b) what methods they have used to avoid this situation.
2. Write an account of the career of the following showing their contribution to Third World progress: (a) Jawaharlal Nehru, (b) Ali Bhutto, (c) Tenku Abdul Rahman, (d) Jomo Kenyatta, (e) Julius Nyerere.
3. Discuss the problems that have faced India and Pakistan since independence. In what ways are they similar and in what ways different?
4. What features do the following Third World dictators have in common?: (a) Nguema, (b) Bokassa, (c) Amin, (d) Gaddafi, (e) Soekarno, (f) Pol Pot, (g) Mengistu.
5. Describe the recent history of three Third World countries that have experienced democracy and relative economic growth, choosing one example from each of Latin America, Africa and South East Asia.
6. What is the connection between the political instability of the Third World and: (a) international terrorism, (b) Western interference, (c) Russian imperialism? (See also sections 14A–C.)

Further Reading

Allen, G. C., *A Short Economic History of Modern Japan*, Allen and Unwin, 1970.
Barclay, G. St. J. J., *Revolutions of Our Time: Nationalism*, Weidenfeld and Nicolson, London, 1971.
Calvocoressi, P., *World Politics since 1945*, Parts 4 and 5, Longmans, Harlow, 1982.
Hatch, J., *Africa Emergent: African Problems since Independence*, Secker and Warburg, London, 1974.
Smith, A., *Twentieth Century Nationalism*, Martin Robertson, Oxford, 1981.
Watson, J. B., *Success in Twentieth Century World Affairs*, John Murray, London, 1979, sections, 19, 20 and 22.

10
Crescent of Crisis: The Middle East in Modern Times

A The Making of the Modern Middle East

A1 Historical Factors

The Middle East has been at the centre of human history since the first civilisations were established in the valleys of the Euphrates and Nile. It forms a bridge between the continents of Europe, Asia and Africa, and has been the source of great conflict between the various powers throughout history. It is the centre of three successful world religions, Christianity, Islam and Judaism, and to political conflict has been added religious fanaticism. The rise of the Muslim faith brought about the Crusades, and from then on European involvement in the region has been continuous dictated first by trade, and then strategy as the European powers acquired lands further East in the sixteenth century. This renewed interest developed at a time when the two principal dynasties of the region, the Ottoman Empire of Turkey, and the Kaja Shahs of Persia, were undergoing lengthy decline, and the European powers stepped into the vacuum slowly but surely. Russia was the most closely involved pressing her claims to the regions surrounding the Black Sea both in the Balkans and the Caucasus Mountains, and invading Persia. Russian pressure produced what was known throughout the nineteenth century as the Near Eastern Question.

Russian influence had two effects: it led Christian peoples in the Balkans, Greeks, Bulgars, Serbs and other Slavs, to become fiercely nationalist. Their struggles for independence involved wars with Turkey, between themselves, and among the great powers who were closely involved. By 1914 the Balkans were free. The second effect of Russian pressure was to alarm the powers particularly Britain and France who had ever growing interests in the region and feared for their trade and route to the east. This led to the Crimean War, and a succession of crises of which the most important were in 1875–8 and 1912–14.

Britain at first adopted the role of protector of Turkey, but abandoned this by the late 1880s, and all along she had followed the alternative policy of securing a position for herself in the region. She established a resident at Bushire on the Persian Gulf in 1763, and signed her first treaty with a Gulf State, Muscat, in 1798. In 1839 she occupied Aden. Equally the French staked an interest. Napoleon entered Egypt in 1798. In 1860–1 Napoleon III sent an expedition to Syria to protect the Christians, and extract special rights for the Lebanese. In 1869 the French-built Suez Canal was opened. This focused attention on Egypt. At first there was an Anglo–French attempt to control the country, but this broke down, and in 1882 Britain occupied the country. Although stating she would leave Britain did not do so. The Suez Canal was run by international agreement made in 1888 which gave Britain a major share in its affairs.

A2 The Collapse of the Ottoman Empire

The Ottoman Turks had spread over the region in the early fourteenth century. At one time they ruled all the Balkans, modern Turkey, the whole of the Middle East (except Persia), Arabia and the whole of the North African coastline together with many Mediterranean islands. But the empire was doomed to decay because it lacked administrative or economic capacity to survive in the nineteenth century world. From 1876 to 1909 it was ruled by Abdul Hamid II, a man determined to reject all attempts at reform, hang on to his empire and suppress the Christians. He lived a life of Oriental sloth divided between the seraglio and the kiosk, and was rarely seen in public. He maintained his empire by employing Greeks and other nationalities as civil servants, and by a police state employing 30,000 informers. His reign was a catalogue of endless Turkish losses, and within his army there arose a Nationalist movement called the Young Turks. In 1908–9 they revolted, and secured the removal of the Sultan. His successor was the weak Mohammed V, and the army officers led by Enver Bey and Jemal increasingly ruled the country. But the losses of territory continued with Italy seizing Libya (1912), and Turkey being driven almost completely out of Europe (1913). The Young Turks looked for support to Germany who was reforming their army, and in August 1914 made an alliance with them directed principally against Russia. However, Britain and France declared war on Turkey, and thus between 1914 and 1918 a series of campaigns were fought in the Middle East which led (see section 10B1) to the collapse of the Ottoman Empire. Mohammed was deposed, and succeeded by Mohammed VI (1918–22); a mere puppet in the hands of the Allies. From this final humiliation arose modern Turkey.

A3 The Beginnings of Modern Egypt

It was only on the fringe of the Ottoman Empire that any kind of political development was possible, and it was in Egypt that national consciousness first emerged in the region. Mehemet Ali (1805–48), appointed governor by the Sultan, broke away, and in 1811 Egypt was recognisably independent. Mehemet's successors found themselves increasingly subordinated to the Europeans. The major boost to the economy given by the growth of cotton during the American Civil War was followed by the opening of the Canal. In 1879 the Europeans deposed the existing ruler, and appointed Tewfik Pasha who in turn was succeeded by Abbas II. Under these rulers Egypt was subordinated to British rule particularly under the consulship of Lord Cromer who initiated reforms like irrigation, although neglecting other areas like education.

The rising of Arabi Pasha (1882) was the first sign that Egypt was unlikely to accept this subordinate status, and gradually nationalist politics developed. In 1906 they burst into life over the Denshawi Affair when severe punishment of Egyptians involved in an attack on British officers aroused resentment and in December 1907 the Wafd Party held its first congress. It was founded by Mustafa Kemal who died young, and soon became associated with Zaghlul Pasha. The appointment of a Christian chief minister by the Sultan led to his murder (1910), and pressure for reform. The British allowed a parliament with limited powers to meet early in 1914, but suspended it in June. Then in December came annexation, and the deposition of Abbas II said to be intriguing with the Germans. The British appointed another ruler, but he died in 1917 and was succeeded by Fuad destined to be the first independent king of Egypt (see section 10B7).

A4 The Beginnings of Modern Persia (Iran)

During the nineteenth century the most important Shah was Nasir Ud-Din (1848–96) who in many ways resembled Abdul Hamid in neighbouring Turkey. Attempts by him to extend Persia eastwards were defeated by the British, and in 1872 the frontier with Afghanistan was defined. Foreign exploitation of Persian resources began with concessions to Paul de Reuter, a British subject, in 1872. The British controlled the main bank, and in 1892 secured the Persian customs duties in return for a major loan. Nasir was murdered, and succeeded by Nuzaffar Ud-Din, but the foreign exploitation went on as the Russians saw their opportunity, obtaining major concessions in 1900 and 1902. Eventually in 1907 Britain and Russia agreed on their respective spheres of influence in the prostrate country. To this situation was added a further complication. In 1901 William Knox D'Arcy was granted a concession to look for oil, and in 1909 the Anglo–Persian Oil Company was founded. By 1912 the decision had been made to convert the British fleet to oil-fired ships, and oil had become a vital strategic raw material.

Religious leaders like Jamal Ud-Din stimulated Persian nationalism, and in 1906–9 Persia underwent severe disturbances. Two Shahs were removed, a parliament or majlis formed, and when the Shah tried to stem this movement the Bahktiari tribed led by Ali Kuli Khan marched on Teheran, and appointed Ahmad Shah, a twelve year old, whom they could control. The revolutionaries proclaimed neutrality in 1914, but the activities of German agents led to direct intervention. The Russians attacked in 1915, the Turks tried to remove them in 1916, and the same year the British organised the South Persia Rifles. When the Bolshevik Revolution occurred British forces entered Northern Persia to drive out the Russians. The country was in chaos when the Persian delegation arrived at Versailles in 1919 to demand the withdrawal of foreign troops, and cancellation of economic concessions (see section 10B8).

A5 Arab Nationalism

The Arabs of Arabia and the coastal areas had never been completely subdued by the Turks. During the nineteenth century the British began to build a relationship with them mainly to protect the route to India. At first this was based on a need to suppress piracy, and curb the activities of rulers like the Sultan of Muscat. Later the move to abolish the slave trade further involved the British in dealings with Arab rulers. British explorers like Burton and Philby opened up the interior of Arabia in the last great world explorations not completed until the 1930s, and there developed in Britain a strong sympathy for the governing class of the desert Arabs with their regal and aristocratic customs. From Bushire the British Resident began by securing in 1853 the Treaty of Maritime Peace which brought to an end piracy in the Gulf. Treaties were signed with the various rulers finishing with Qatar in 1916 when the British expelled the Turks from that region. Britain also obtained concessions in Bahrain (1867) and Kuwait (1899) to protect the Gulf. On the West coast of Arabia Britain held Aden, and to this was added a vague Aden Protectorate stretching inland involving treaties with some 40 chiefs. Only in the case of the Yemen did Britain encounter much opposition, and accepted a border definition with Aden in 1913.

The realisation that the Arabs of the coastal area lay virtually outside Turkish control, and the building up of good relations with Britain led to the appearance of Arab nationalism. The Sherif Hussein Ibn Ali was the head of the Hashemites, and in terms of seniority had a better title to be caliph (religious leader of the Muslims) than the Turkish sultan who had this title. In 1908 the Young Turk revolution released Hussein, whom Abdul Hamid had kept at Constantinople, and he returned to be Sherif of Mecca. As early as 1914 the British offered Hussein recognition of his independence hoping he would rise against the Turks. It was made clear independence did not include Aden, or the British protected sheikdoms, and Britain also said she would have to have a presence in Iraq where British Petroleum had started operations in 1914. Hussein claimed independence for all Arabs south of 37 degrees north latitude, and bargaining began in July 1915.

B The European Partition of the Middle East

B1 The Impact of the First World War

The First World War was essentially a European conflict, but in the Middle East it assumed major proportions, and therefore it is to the First World War one must look for changes equivalent to those brought about elsewhere in the world by the Second World War. In one way the war was a continuation of the Near Eastern Question. Turkey was at war with Russia in the Caucasus Mountains and Northern Persia following the Turks' savage massacre of the Armenian Christians. The result of this was to unsettle the region, and the Bolshevik Revolution completed the process. Various Caucasus states like Armenia proclaimed their independence in 1918. Turkey was defeated in the war although her troops proved at the Dardanelles, and the siege of Kut they were not the decadent foe many believed them to be. The war made the reputation of Mustafa Kemal who was to save Turkey, and it brought the Ottoman Empire to an end.

The end of the Ottoman Empire enabled Greece to launch an attempt to establish a Greater Greece in Asia Minor; an event which had the backing of the British, but which failed. The result of the Greek attack was to make

Kemal the national leader of Turkey, and between 1919 and 1923 modern Turkey was created (see section 10B2). War with Turkey enabled the British to take over Egypt, but this merely encouraged the Wafd to greater nationalism because the British exploited the country with forced labour and seizure of materials. An Egyptian national revolution began in 1919 (see section 10B7). The Arabs were the Allies of Britain, and Hussein's son, Feisal, was at Versailles. The British promised independence, and eventually from that promise came three kingdoms: Hejaz, Transjordania, and Iraq. Other Arabs led by Ibn Saud carved out Saudi Arabia once Turkish power had gone (see section 10B6). But Britain made other promises; to her ally France, which led the French to return to Syria in 1918; and to the Jews who were promised a homeland in Palestine by Britain in 1917.

Britain conducted two campaigns against Turkey involving a million troops. By 1918 she had captured Jerusalem, Damascus and Baghdad, and was astride the Middle East, while to secure this position she had already extended her influence in the Gulf States and Persia. With oil discoveries proceeding and Bolshevik influence in the north, Britain was bound to remain.

B2 The Turkish Revolution and Kemal Ataturk

The powers using the British Fleet and the Greek army exercised a stranglehold over Mohammed VI in Constantinople, and forced him in 1920 to sign the Treaty of Sevres. This Treaty devastated Turkey giving Asia Minor largely to Greece, granting Armenia independence and of course removing her Middle East possessions. Mustafa Kemal led resistance to this treaty after being outlawed by the Sultan. He issued a National Declaration, and created a government in the interior of Turkey at Ankara in April 1920. He gathered an army, made war on the Russians, and having driven them back, and secured Armenia, made a treaty with Lenin to secure arms. In a savage war with Greece (1920–2) the Greeks were defeated, and driven into the sea. This left Britain to face Kemal and enforce the Treaty. In 1922 it came close to war, but Britain climbed down, and peace was signed at Lausanne in 1923. This treaty was a landmark for the Middle East. It marked a significant military and political defeat for the West. It made modern Turkey which still has the borders then established. The Sultan fled in 1922, and the Caliph, his cousin, was deposed in 1924 making the country a republic. Kemal then ruled until his death in 1938 seeking to make Turkey a modern state run along authoritarian lines. He was the first inter-war dictator, and the first effective Third World nationalist leader to emerge after 1918. (For the later history of Turkey see section 7E9.)

B3 The French Return to the Middle East

Although the French had not been involved in the fighting, they had been involved in discussions with the Arabs, and made it clear they would support Britain only if there was some gain for them which had to be Syria. This was confirmed in 1916 by the Sykes–Picot Agreement. The French landed at Beirut in October 1918. Feisal had been promised a kingdom by the British (see section 10B5) and twice the Arabs proclaimed him king in Syria. France and Britain refused to recognise him, and in 1920 it was announced that the League of Nations had mandated Syria to France, and the rest to Britain. The French enforced their control by sending an army of Senegalese and Berbers. They attacked the Arabs in 1920 dethroning Feisal. Britain and France defined the borders of Syria the same month, but the French found bitter resentment at their actions. This was made worse by their decision to accord special rights to the Christians in the Lebanon which in May 1926 was separated from Syria. There followed a savage war with the Druze in 1925–7, but after Damascus had been bombed twice the Arabs gave way, and the French government established. Syria was declared a republic in 1930 (see section 10C1).

B4 The Balfour Declaration Establishes Palestine (Israel)

The Jews had been forced to leave their homeland in AD 70, and had settled in many parts of the world. They had been subjected to unceasing persecution for various reasons, and during the latter part of the nineteenth century this revived in Russia, France, and to a lesser extent Germany and Austro–Hungary. In 1897 the first Zionist conference was held at Geneva prompted by the Dreyfus Affair in France. The Zionist leader was Theodore Hertzl (1860–1904), and it was he who conceived of a homeland for the Jews. The British government was interested in such an idea considering Kenya as one possibility, and it only needed the war to increase British interest. There was straightforward gratitude for financial help from the Jews, and to this was added fear of British Jewry following the example of many Jews in Russia and becoming Bolsheviks. Chaim Weizmann (1874–1952) who was Director of the Admiralty Laboratories acted as intermediary with the government where Balfour was a strong advocate of the Jewish cause. In November 1917 the Balfour Declaration proposed a national home for the Jews in Palestine providing 'nothing shall be done which may prejudice the civil and religious rights of existing non-Jewish communities'. From 1917–20 the area was under British military occupation. Feisal had hoped it would be part of his vast kingdom, but in 1920 Palestine and Transjordania were made British mandates and divided (see section 10C6).

B5 The Arab Revolt

The negotiations begun in 1915 (see section 10A5) took some time for the Arabs pitched their demands high, but the pro-Arabists in Cairo were determined to get agreement, and in January 1916 accepted Hussein's demands. The Arab Revolt began on June 5th. The Hejaz was proclaimed independent and Hussein King of the Arabs. A mission in which T. E. Lawrence (Lawrence of Arabia) was present went to Jeddah and confirmed the agreement in October 1916. It was then that Lawrence became a close friend of the Sherif's third son, Feisal, and together they co-operated in the desert war that took Feisal to Damascus. Hussein was to remain in Hejaz, and Feisal was to obtain the remainder of what Britain had promised. However, Syria under the French, and Palestine as a Jewish homeland limited the options open to the British. Expelled by the French, Feisal arrived in London (see section 10B3). Churchill had created the Middle East Department at the Colonial Office, and was determined to preserve the Arab links. With the backing of the Arabists a conference was held at Cairo in March 1921 to settle the future of the British Arab mandates. The result was the creation of two new countries.

Hussein's second son, Abdullah, had arrived on the borders of Palestine with an army determined to assert his father's rights. The British made him Emir of Transjordania which they carved out of the desert to the east of Palestine, and in 1921 he was installed as ruler. The British were already in occupation of Iraq where they had faced severe Arab opposition, but the rebel leader was captured and exiled. In April 1921 Feisal was proclaimed King of Iraq. In 1925 the Clayton Mission established the borders between Iraq, Transjordania and Arabia, and the British settlement of the Middle East was complete.

B6 The Creation of Saudi Arabia

The Arabs were not united in their support for Hussein; nor was the British government dedicated to him alone. It had to consider its Gulf dependencies, and in 1915 the India Office opened negotiations with Abd el Aziz, ruler of the Wahabi tribes of the interior, and by July 1916 agreement was reached to give him Nejd, and the Eastern part of Arabia abutting on the sheikdoms. In May 1919 Abd el Aziz (Ibn Saud) attacked Hussein. A long war followed with Ibn Saud conquering various desert provinces until in 1924 the Hejaz itself was invaded. Hussein was forced to abdicate and retired to Cyprus where he died in 1931. Ibn Saud entered Mecca on October 13th, 1924, and it was only a matter of time before Jidda, the last stronghold of the Hashemites, fell to Ibn Saud in December 1925. His kingdom was renamed Saudi Arabia in 1932.

B7 The Creation of the Kingdom of Egypt

The demand by the Eygptian Wafd (see section 10A3) for full independence and representation at Versailles in 1919 led the British to deport their leader Zaghlul. This precipitated a rising, and strong measures were taken by Sir Edmund Allenby, the High Commissioner. Lord Milner, who had previously been a zealous Imperialist, was sent to investigate Egyptian grievances, but he had become convinced that trusteeship not domination was the key to British survival, and his report in August 1921 backed independence with reserved rights for the British. The cabinet divided, and Churchill tried negotiations, recalling Zaghlul early in 1921. But they failed, Zaghlul was deported again, and the High Commissioner made it clear that if full backing was not given to his military measures he would resign. The British were not prepared to do this in view of troubles in Ireland and India. In February 1922 the protectorate was ended, and Egypt was declared independent. Fuad I became king. During 1923 Zaghlul returned, and a new constitution led to the first Egyptian elections. The Wafd Party won, and in January 1924 Zaghlul became the first Prime Minister, but the British retained a High Commissioner, military force and a determination to control foreign policy. Full independence was some way away (see section 10C2).

B8 National Revolution in Persia

The occupation of large parts of Persia by Russian and British troops seemed to indicate that Persia might well lose its independence in 1919 (see section 10A4). The Persian delegation at Versailles was snubbed while the British negotiated a new agreement giving them major oil concessions in the country. It was not until early in 1921 that the British finally left Northern Persia after Bolshevik forces had been defeated with the aid of the White Russians. In February 1921 there was a coup d'état led by Reza Khan, a prominent officer in the Persian Cossack Regiment. With 3,000 troops he occupied Teheran, and demanded changes. He succeeded in defeating opposition, and in 1923 became Prime Minister. The Shah left the country, and because of fears that the Bolsheviks wanted a republic he was deposed, and Reza Khan became Reza Shah Pahlavi in December 1925, seeking to follow a path similar to that of Kemal in Turkey (see section 10C3).

C European Rule in the Middle East

C1 French Failure in Syria

The French return to Syria (see section 10B3) effected very little except a certain amount of economic development, particularly in the Lebanon, and their harsh policies stimulated Arab Nationalism. It was no coincidence that the first Pan Arab meeting about Palestine took place in Syria (see section 10C6), or that since independence Syria has been one of the most radical Arab states. As late as 1936 the French were seeking to retain total control, but riots and strikes prevented this, and in September they agreed to terminate their rule in three years. The French were careful to make a separate treaty, which established Lebanon as fully independent with a constitution introduced in early 1937. The French used the outbreak of the war as an excuse to delay the implementation of the 1936 Treaty, and the colony fell into the hands of Vichy France. Britain feared it could be used as an Axis base in the Middle East, and in 1941 invaded the country. After fierce fighting the French were defeated, and Syria was proclaimed independent with British backing. In May 1945 the French sought to reoccupy both Syria and Lebanon, and De Gaulle sent troops. Next month Damascus was shelled by the French, but the British refused to support De Gaulle, and after Anglo–French clashes it was agreed both Britain and France should evacuate all their troops from the two countries. This was done by April 1946. Lebanon and Syria became independent.

C2 Egypt under her Kings (1922–52)

Having nominally conceded Egypt her independence (see section 10B7) the British did their best to remain in power. This was possible because the ruling dynasty disliked the major political party, the Wafd, led by Zaghlul until his death in 1927, and then by Nahas Pasha, and were therefore willing to co-operate with Britain. Although Britain had introduced many reforms three-quarters of the people were illiterate, and illnesses like dysentery widespread. Britain left the pashas in control of the peasants, and 36 per cent of the land was in the hands of 1 per cent of the population. These landed classes gave their support to the king, and the British. Thus, the constitution introduced in 1930 provided for three-fifths of the senate to be appointed, and the chamber to be elected indirectly.

The British knew, however, that this situation could not continue indefinitely, and six times they sought to obtain a new treaty. Then in 1935 came serious trouble. Mussolini was sending pro-Arab propaganda into the Middle East, and Egypt had long had pro-German sympathies strengthened by Hitler's anti-Jewish policies. Mussolini's invasion of Abyssinia was followed by riots in Cairo, and the restoration of a more democratic constitution. In the elections of May 1936 the Wafd led by Nahas Pasha swept to power, and the British were forced to act. The result was the Anglo–Egyptian Treaty of 1936. British forces were to withdraw to the Canal Zone (an area as large as Wales surrounding the Suez Canal), and were to be limited to 10,000. Britain was to give up the Alexandria naval base within eight years. Sir Miles Lampson, the British High Commissioner, became an ambassador, and next year Egypt entered the League as an independent country. This mood of optimism was enhanced by the accession in 1936 of a new king, a dashing 16 year old called Farouk, who was soon married to the beautiful Queen Farida. He was able to rally moderate support, and by 1938 the Wafd Party had been eclipsed at the polls.

Then came the Second World War, and the involvement of Egypt in that war by abetting the Axis powers' advance in North Africa (see section 2A3). Many in Egypt were willing to support the Axis, and the future President, Sadat, was a pro-Nazi agent during the war. The British were frightened that Egypt would fall into Axis hands. They sacked the Egyptian Chief of Staff, and in February 1942 Lampson was forced to extreme measures when the royal palace was surrounded by tanks, and Farouk ordered to form a government favourable to Britain. But pro-German feeling remained, and the prime minister who took Egypt into the war on the Allied side was killed. At the end of the war Britain had 80,000 troops in the Canal Zone, and no wish to leave Egypt because pressing imperial problems rendered the base vital. Farouk disillusioned by his treatment, and affected by glandular trouble, was degenerating into an Oriental despot, and decided to recoup his losses by demanding the return of the Sudan to Egypt, thus raising fresh difficulties with Britain.

Britain tried to renegotiate the treaty, but this proved unacceptable to Egypt. In 1948 Egypt obtained a democratic constitution at last, and by 1950 the Wafd were back in power. In 1951 Egypt repudiated the 1936 treaty, and attacks on the British began in the Canal Zone. Early in 1952 Churchill's government took firm measures. Port Said was bombarded, and at Ismailia many died in a battle at police headquarters. There were severe riots in Cairo and in Alexandria British property was sacked. The result of these events was a revolution in July 1952 which overthrew the monarchy (see section 10D2).

C3 The Pahlevi Shahs (1925–79)

Reza Shah (see section 10B8) ruled Persia (from 1935 called Iran) effectively seeking to bring about progress whenever he could, but hampered by powerful religious groups which he was unable to control, and by continued Western interference in the country. Transport was developed with a railway link to the Caspian Sea, and the introduction of air services. The army was reformed, and in 1932 a Persian Navy was started. But oil dominated the country's future. The yield rose to 9 million barrels by 1939, and then under the pressure of wartime demand shot up to 25 million barrels by 1948. This inevitably increased British involvement. In 1933 an attempt to revoke British concessions was met by Britain going to the League, and a new agreement was the result. In 1934 American involvement in Persian oil began, and the Americans had no desire to see Britain retain its privileged commercial position. Once more the war brought about a crisis. In August 1941 British and Russian forces reoccupied Iran. Reza Shah abdicated, and was succeeded by his son, Mohammed Reza, who was very much an Allied puppet. Iran played a vital part in Lend Lease, and during the war American interest consequently increased.

The end of the war saw an international crisis (see section 2B4) over the presence of Allied troops in the country, and an attempt by Russia to set up an autonomous state in the north of Iran using the Tudeh (Communist) party. During 1946 Allied troops left, but Russia secured the setting up of a joint oil company. The Tudeh party continued to be a threat, and after an attempt to kill the Shah it was banned, and the Shah assumed greater powers in 1949. The Americans had begun military aid as part of their containment policy, and were increasingly reluctant to back Britain. America which had obtained a new agreement on oil in 1949, opposed the National Front led by Mohammed Mossadeq. There followed a crisis (see section 10D3) during which the Americans gave their full backing to the Shah fearing Communist incursions in the delicate situation that existed. The Shah's regime remained strongly pro-Western supporting CENTO, and obtaining arms from Britain and America, but Mohammed Reza came up against the same difficulties as his father. Oil revenue paved the way for modernisation, but this was opposed as 'Western' because of the life style of the governing class which abandoned many tenets of the Muslim faith. The Shah and his entourage benefited themselves from the oil revenues. Opposition was curbed as he steadily assumed dictatorial powers to deal with opponents. In 1979 he was forced to flee by a revolution (see sections 10F4 and 13G4) designed not to create democracy or reform, but to return Iran to traditional Muslim precepts.

C4 The Hashemite Kings of Iraq 1921–58

In spite of initial troubles Britain's rule in Iraq was uneventful and successful. A treaty governing the relationship was drawn up, and ratified by a parliament in 1930 making Iraq independent. She joined the League in 1932. Feisal died in 1933, and was succeeded by his son, Ghazi, who tended to support the growing Pan Arabist movement appointing General Sidqui as dictator. Sidqui was killed in 1937, but the new Pan Arab cabinet backed the claims of the Palestine Arabs. King Ghazi was killed in a car accident in April 1939, and the British consul was stoned to death because the Pan Arabs said he was responsible. The new king, Feisal II, was only three, and therefore a regency was necessary under the king's uncle,

Abdullah, until 1953. Faisal was sent to England, and educated at Harrow.

Meanwhile Iraq had acquired a dual importance. Oil was piped from the 1930s in increasing quantities, and the Second World War made British air bases in the country vital. There was as elsewhere in the Middle East, a pro-German group in the country led by Reschid Ali, and in May 1941 British forces returned to Iraq, and remained there until 1947. Britain then sought a fresh treaty providing for a continuing military presence. This was signed at Portsmouth, but parliament in Iraq refused to ratify it, and there were anti-British riots in 1952. The British continued to see Iraq as loyal to the West, and the Prime Minister, Nuri Al Said, fearing Communism was willing to join the Baghdad Pact in February 1955 (see section 3E6). When Britain joined this a few months later it seemed as if she had succeeded in re-establishing her military power in the region, and Iraq and Jordan considered a Hashemite Union; the Arab radicals feared this would create a counterweight to Nasser's power in the region. Led by Abdul Kassem (1914–63) the army revolted, and in July 1958 the Hashemites were slaughtered in the streets of Baghdad. The British recognised the new government a few days later. Iraq left the Baghdad Pact in 1959, and moved into a leftist position (see section 10F2).

C5 Britain and the Desert Arabs

Transjordania was in many ways a model British mandate (see section 10B5) well organised by Sir Percy Coxe and Sir Alex Kirkbride. Colonel J. B. Glubb organised an Arab Legion in the territory, and in 1928 a treaty while giving partial independence retained many British rights. Full independence came in 1946 when the country became Jordan, and a new treaty on more equal terms was negotiated with Britain in 1948. But the problems created by the new state of Israel brought a crisis in relations. The Arab Legion was actually used against the Jews, and Abdullah revived the Hashemite claim to Palestine. During the war that followed (see section 10E2) Jordan seized land on the West Bank, and this was fully incorporated into the kingdom instead of being made a Palestinian state. Abdullah was killed in 1951, and his successor, Talal, declared mentally unstable. In May 1953 the 18 year old Hussein became king. The British hoped for better relations but Hussein was surrounded by problems—Nasser's role throughout the region, the Palestinian refugees and growing Arab dislike for rulers linked in their eyes with the West. He decided to strike out an independent line: Glubb was dismissed in 1956, the treaty was ended in 1957 and Nuri's Federation was repudiated in 1958.

Around the Gulf and in the south of Arabia Britain in the inter-war period continued to strengthen her position. The Colonial Office began to take over the region. Between 1936 and 1939 Harold Ingrams was sent to make separate agreements with over 1,300 Bedouin chiefs in the interior of the Aden protectorate, and to sign five major treaties effectively securing British control. In 1937 Aden became a crown colony. Britain had no intention of leaving this region, and in 1947 the Labour government bombarded the coast to curb Arab rebels. The threat came from neighbouring Yemen. There a pro-Nasser party developed, and in 1962 a pro-Nasser government took control. A civil war broke out, and Nasser sent 40,000 troops to back the

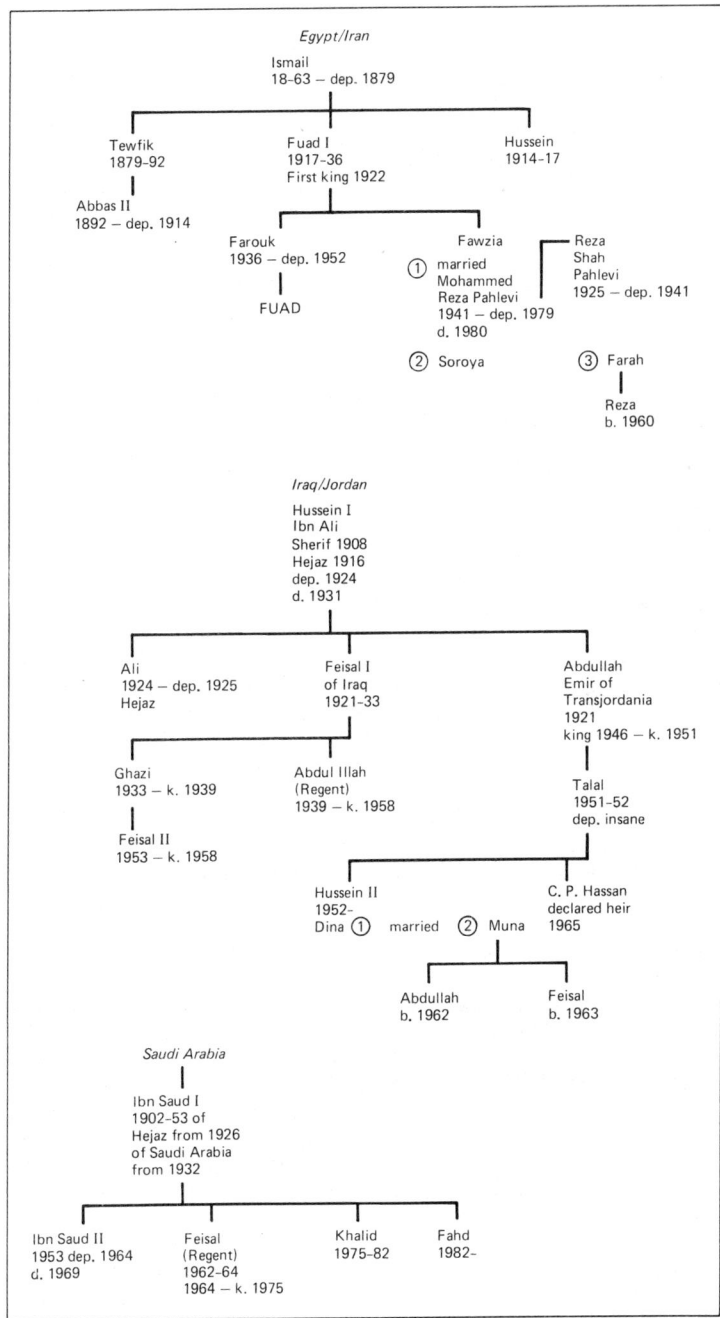

Fig. 19. The Arab rulers since 1914

rebels against the monarchy. The troops remained there until the Arab–Israeli War of 1967 forced their withdrawal. The republican government signed an agreement with Russia, and guerillas stirred up trouble in the Radfan among tribes that straddled the border with the Yemen. Britain took air action against Yemen in March 1964. To counter this threat, curb growing nationalist disturbances and preserve the base, the concept of a South Arabian Federation was created. This began in 1959 with six states, and gradually enlarged to fourteen. Then in 1963 Aden was included in the Federation. Discussions during 1964 promised independence for the area as a whole while retaining the base, but by then Nasser and the Russians operating from Yemen were making this increasingly unlikely (see section 10D7).

The Gulf States themselves were in the early 1960s still amenable to British rule, partly because of Saudi Arabian and Iranian claims to their territory. In 1947 the resident at Bushire moved to Bahrain and the Colonial Office took control of the region. In 1951 Britain formed the Trucial Oman Scouts to operate as a joint army in the region, and as oil was discovered preservation of peace became vital. When Saudi Arabia seized the Buraimi Oasis she was ejected by the Oman Scouts in 1955, and between 1955 and 1959 Britain undertook three small campaigns to preserve Oman from attack. Britain continued her role of keeping other powers out of the area. When Kassem of Iraq threatened to seize Kuwait British forces went there in 1961, and British forces helped the Sultan of Oman in his war with guerillas in the Dhofar from 1971 to 1975. When Britain was forced to leave Aden this made the British Gulf position even more important, and as late as July 1967 the then Prime Minister Harold Wilson reaffirmed Britain's intention to remain (see section 10D8).

C6 The Coming of the Palestinian Problem

During the 1920s the British mandate of Palestine was peaceful, but gradually the number of Jewish immigrants began to rise as restrictions were imposed in countries like America and Poland. A Jewish Agency was set up to help them, and in 1929 came the first disturbances when the Arabs killed 133 Jews. The League criticised Britain for failing to discharge her mandate, but the British were determined not to annoy the Arabs. Restrictions were placed on Jewish immigration, and the Labour government issued the Passfield Report advocating their continuation, and stressing the plight of the Arabs. Already the Arabs were becoming intransigent under their leader, Haj Amin, Grand Mufti of Jerusalem, and they refused to discuss the Passfield proposals. As a result the restrictions were lifted. Then came Hitler's triumph in Germany. Within three years 134,000 Jews entered the country, and towns like Haifa and Tel Aviv were soon growing rapidly while in the countryside 'kibbutzim' were formed. The British wished to proceed towards self-government, but the increasing Arab demands for the removal of the Jews made this impossible.

During 1936 an Arab High Committee came into existence, and the Pan Arabist movement got under way fuelled by hatred of the Jews. A general strike turned into riots, and during 1936 a further 305 died. The British government prepared the Peel Report, which advocated a Jewish state covering a third of the country, a British area including Jerusalem, and an Arab area which was to join Transjordania. Independence was to come in ten years. Although some Zionists accepted this, others did not, saying it violated the Balfour Declaration, and terrorist organisations dedicated to securing Palestine for the Jews sprang up. The Arabs meeting at Bludan in September 1937 rejected the plan saying the Jews should be given minority treaty status in an Arab state to cover the whole region. The Arabs provided economic and propaganda aid for the Palestinian Arabs, revolt began again, and continued until 1939 by which time the British had deported the Grand Mufti, and imposed martial law. To help the Jews, Orde Wingate trained Special Night Squads in guerilla warfare, and from this an illegal army (Haganah) was organised.

In 1939 Britain tried again with the Macdonald Report. A ten year period to independence was promised with a system of government to safeguard both groups. 75,000 more Jews were to enter, but after five years such immigration was to stop. The League denounced this, but other powers had shown no readiness to help. The previous year a conference at Evian had seen America take the lead in refusing to admit more Jews, and as the persecution increased Britain was faced with an appalling dilemma: either to admit Jews and face Arab hostility, or stop them, and be branded the accomplice of Hitler.

Britain enforced a blockade, and only 5 out of 63 ships got through in the period 1944–8. Outrage was caused by the continued return of ships even to Germany including the famous 'Exodus' in 1947. The army of the Haganah were not anxious for direct conflict with Britain, and the Jews' political leader, David Ben Gurion (1886–1973) urged havlagah or restraint. However, news of what was going on in Nazi Europe changed the situation. The Zionists adopted the Biltmore Programme (1942) calling for a separate Jewish state, and this was endorsed by Roosevelt just before the 1944 election. The Jews themselves began to form extremist groups of which two were important: Irgun commanded by Menachim Begin (b. 1913), and the Stern Gang under Stern and subsequently, Yella. Before long the British found little to choose between Arab and Jewish guerillas. The British poured 60,000 troops into the country, and appointed General Cunningham as High Commissioner, but it was clear a crisis was approaching. By 1945 the Arab League was calling for an Arab state while the Zionists urged that a million Jews should come to Israel.

D The End of British Power in the Middle East

D1 Britain Leaves Palestine: Israel Created

American interference in British colonial affairs had started during the war due to Roosevelt's strong anti-imperialism. Following the war Truman embarrassed Britain to the maximum by backing the Biltmore Programme at a time when Britain was trying to renegotiate her position in Egypt and Iraq, and could not therefore relax her Palestine blockade. An American mission to London recommended the immediate admission of 100,000 Jews from Europe, and a joint Anglo–American mission studied the problem.

In April 1946 it recommended the 100,000 figure which Bevin, the British Foreign Secretary, rejected. Britain tried a conference but both Jews and Arabs were now demanding control of the new state, and violence was increasing. In July 1946 the first modern terrorist outrage occurred when the King David Hotel was blown up by Begin's Irgun, killing 91 people. Early in 1947 further British proposals were rejected, and in April Britain referred her mandate back to the United Nations.

It was becoming clear to Bevin that Britain could not continue her imperial role, and in September 1947 he set a deadline for British withdrawal in May 1948 hoping this would get the rivals together. The United Nations recommended partition which the Jews accepted, but the Arabs rejected. In December 1947 the Arab League announced it would support guerilla action to keep all Palestine Arab. During the early part of 1948 war broke out which British troops were unable to curb, and in April 254 Arabs were slaughtered by the Jews at Dir Yassin. It was clear that mutual hatreds could only lead to war, but in May Britain withdrew as planned. The same day Israel was proclaimed with Weizmann as President, and Ben Gurion as Prime Minister. The United Nations intervened to secure a truce, but their mediator, Count Bernadotte, was killed, and war began with the Arabs led by Abdullah of Jordan. The Arabs were driven back, and Israel extended her borders considerably beyond those recommended in the UN Partition before the armistice of February 1949. However, if one saw Palestine as a unit then fellow Arabs were also aggressors because Egypt annexed the Gaza Strip, and Jordan, the West Bank enclave. The main result was to leave 570,000 Palestinians without a home settled in camps in poor Arab countries. Unlimited Jewish immigration to Palestine raised the number of Jews from 720,000 in 1949 to 2,350,000 in 20 years. There were only 250,000 Arabs left in what had once been part of the territory promised to them, and clearly this situation was to develop over the years into the major Middle Eastern problem of today. In 1950 Britain had no alternative but to recognise the new state, and joined in a Triple Declaration with America and France to guarantee the existing frontiers.

D2 The Egyptian Revolution 1952–4: Britain Leaves Egypt

King Farouk was overthrown by the Egyptian army in the first of many such coups in Africa in 1952 (see section 10C2). The army rebels were led by General Neguib, and the regime abolished the monarchy, and created a one party dictatorship. At first the revolution was essentially right wing: anti-Semitic and strongly nationalist, and this made relations with Britain even more difficult. Eden, the British Foreign Secretary, was determined to get agreement. In 1953 the Sudan issue was settled with Neguib agreeing to give up Egyptian claims as a prelude to its independence. The Canal Zone proved a more difficult matter, but in 1954 agreement was reached to leave within 20 months, with the right to return in an emergency. There was strong opposition in the Tory Party to Eden's treaty, but it went through, and in June 1956 the last troops left the Canal Zone leaving 4,000 technicians to run the Canal. The Canal itself remained under the 1888 Convention as an international waterway. To Muslims Neguib was not being nationalist enough; riots began fanned by the Muslim Brotherhood, and an attack on

Neguib gave more radical officers their chance. Led by Gamal Nasser (1918–70)—son of a post office clerk from Alexandria, who had joined the army in 1938—they deposed Neguib in November 1954 (see section 10D6).

D3 The Iranian Oil Crisis

By the time Nasser became President of Egypt the essential weakness of the British Middle East position had been revealed by events in Iran. The signing of the oil agreement favourable to Britain in 1949 (see section 10C3) was the signal for nationalist opposition to gather under Mohammed Mossadeq (1880–1967). The Prime Minister who supported the agreement was murdered, and in April 1951 Mossadeq nationalised the country's oil rupturing any attempt to get the 1949 treaty ratified. A British naval force was available but Morrison, the Labour Foreign Secretary, could hardly be seen supporting capitalist oil concerns at the expense of Iran. The government therefore referred the matter to the Court of Justice which ruled Mossadeq out of order. However, he ignored this, and in September occupied Abadan. The British oil people were evacuated by the naval force, and soon after diplomatic relations were broken off by Churchill's government. Mossadeq proceeded to imprison the rich and confiscated the Shah's landholdings. When it seemed American oil interests were also threatened by what Eisenhower saw as a left wing regime, America cancelled aid. Mossadeq forced the Shah out of the country, but the Americans organised demonstrations in his favour, and persuaded elements in the army to back his return. The Shah returned in triumph in August 1953. The return of the Shah was followed in 1954 by a series of agreements with the oil companies where once more Eden's negotiating skill was successful. Anglo–Iranian (now called British Petroleum) received £25 million compensation, and a new agreement lasting 25 years. Fifty per cent of the profits were to go to Iran. But the significance of these events were not lost on Nasser.

D4 The Causes of the Suez War

Nasser was determined from the start to assert Egypt's right to be the premier Arab power, by using the Arab League and expelling the Europeans from the Middle East. In 1954 he paid a visit to Mecca, and it was as a defender of Muslim rights that he stood to command support throughout the region. His policy had several facets. The first was to take the lead in the struggle against Israel which no Arab state recognised had the right to exist. From April 1955 'fedayeen' guerillas began operations against the Israelis, and infiltration of the Palestinian Arabs. Nasser strongly opposed the Baghdad Pact. By March 1956 Eden, who was now Prime Minister, had turned against Nasser saying he should be destroyed, and claiming that his policies breached the good relations that he, Eden, had striven to secure with Egypt by making major concessions on the Sudan and Canal Zone.

To make his position secure Nasser needed arms and finance. For arms he turned to Russia, and this at long last gave them the foothold in the area that Stalin had demanded in 1945. In September 1955 came the first of a series of arms agreements with Czechoslovakia and Poland. For finance Nasser was willing to turn anywhere. Wartime friendships were recalled by the arrival of German financial experts including Dr Schacht. In March 1954 there was a commercial agreement with Russia, and in November the same year aid from America. Dulles was poorly informed on the Middle East, and a meeting with Eden got nowhere because of the Buraimi Oasis dispute where they were on opposite sides. The Americans sought to neutralise Nasser by concessions. In 1955 the World Bank agreed to finance a spectacular new Aswan Dam project provided Britain and America also contributed. Nasser had by now mortgaged the 1956 cotton crop to get Soviet weapons, and his recognition of Communist China infuriated Dulles. The result was that in July 1956 Dulles refused further American aid without consulting Britain placing Nasser in an embarrassing position because the project was vital. He decided to follow the Mossadeq example.

On July 26th, 1956 Nasser nationalised the Suez Canal agreeing to pay compensation in the future. Although this was strictly speaking a legal exercise of sovereignty it broke the 1888 treaty, and Article 8 of the 1954 treaty Eden had negotiated. Eden now saw Nasser as a personal enemy and a pocket dictator. He was already damaging British interests. Britain had 44 per cent of the shares, and 28 per cent of the users' tonnage of the Canal, and Middle East oil and communications with the Far East through the Canal were vital. From the start Eden was determined to recover the Canal, and if this involved the fall of Nasser that would be a great bonus. Eden had been Foreign Secretary when Churchill had been toppling Middle East rulers during the war, and thought essentially in terms of Britain retaining her Middle East position.

America disagreed. Only 4 per cent of her oil passed through the Canal, and she continued to pay dues. It was election year, and Eisenhower could hardly back a colonial British venture in the Middle East. Dulles disliked Eden, and had not forgotten British lukewarm support for Dulles' own sabre rattling in Formosa. In September Dulles declared: 'The Suez Canal is not a primary concern of the United States.' Eden misjudged early American support, and a series of meetings culminating in the Suez Canal Users' Association put forward by Dulles got nowhere. Two conferences, and a mission to Cairo by Menzies, the Australian Prime Minister, failed, and reference to the United Nations got nowhere when Russia vetoed the essential resolution. As the American election approached Eisenhower and Dulles backtracked on their initial support and Eisenhower made it plain that America would not support British use of force. Eden therefore turned to France for support only to find France was already deeply involved with Israel.

D5 The Suez War 1956

The exact degree of commitment to war from the start, and of collusion between Britain, France and Israel are not yet fully established. It is clear there was an early military plan to land at Alexandria, and send an armoured division to Cairo while an air drop covered landings on the Canal, but that delays and difficulties in military planning, and Eden's wish for a peaceful solution wrecked this proposal although both France and Israel urged a swift attack. On October 16th a meeting finalised British acceptance of a French plan by which Israel was to invade Egypt, and the two powers would

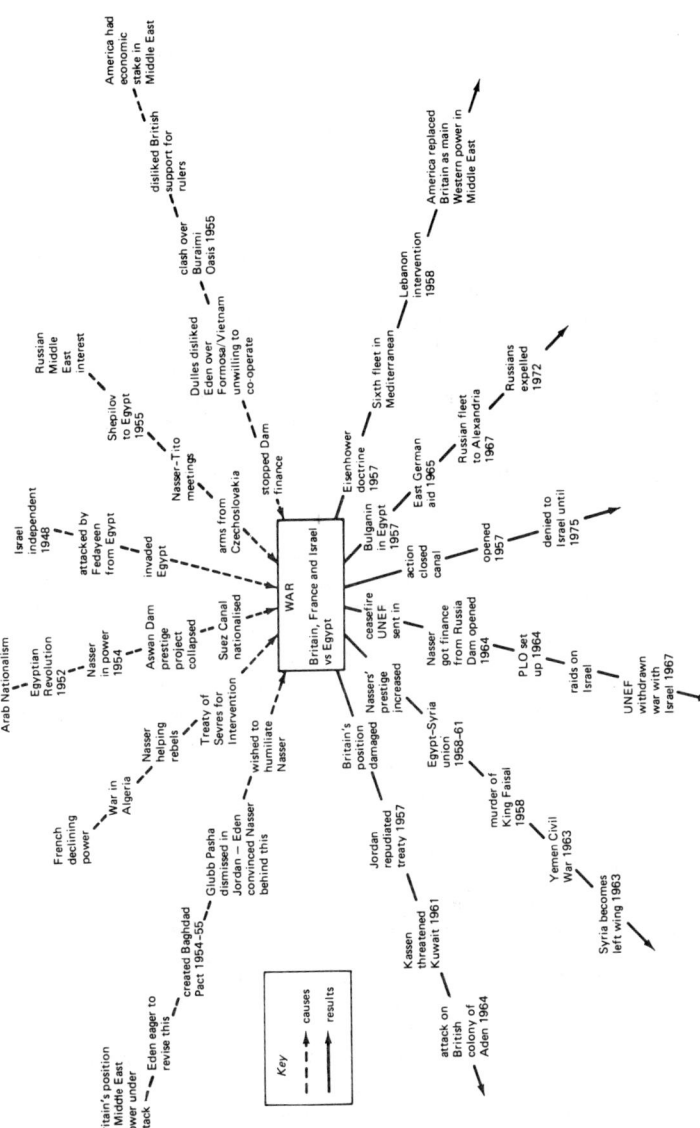

Fig. 20. The Suez Crisis

use this as an excuse to demand a cease-fire which Egypt would obviously reject. War would follow. After cabinet discussion the plan was formalised by the Sèvres Agreement of October 24th. America was not informed, but this is hardly surprising in view of her position. Israel attacked Egypt on October 29th supported by a French air drop and naval action, and her forces rapidly crossed the Sinai Desert and arrived at the Canal. The trouble was that the military planning of the powers was incompetent. Instead of using Cyprus which was said to lack air facilities, Malta was used as a base, and this involved several days steaming, giving the Egyptians full warning. There were shortages of aircraft and landing craft, and there was delay in assembling the force. The sensitive French insisted on a complicated chain of command. However, Eden and Mollet were now committed to the plan. The ultimatum was sent, and rejected as expected. The next day the fleet left Malta, and bombing raids on Egypt began.

Israel continued her advance, and by November 5th was on the east bank of the Canal. The air attack on Egypt was successful destroying the Egyptian air force, and forcing the Russian technicians to withdraw. A chorus of world opposition swelled. At the United Nations the two powers vetoed a demand for their withdrawal, and rejected an American demand for a cease-fire. The troops arrived, and began landing on November 5th seizing Port Said. But already the attack was faltering and a preliminary bombardment was cancelled making advance slower. Russia threatened to use force, and Eisenhower was forced to order a global alert of American forces. He could not have a war and an election. The word went forth not to back sterling, and Macmillan, the British Chancellor, who had strongly backed the invasion, warned the cabinet they could not continue for 48 hours. Eden then switched tactics, and tried to pretend that the only purpose of the invasion was to force the United Nations to act. The Canadians had proposed a United Nations Emergency Force (UNEF) to secure the Canal, and Britain and France had to accept a cease-fire with their patrols 25 miles from Port Suez on November 6th. The first units of UNEF arrived on November 15th, and the British and French had withdrawn by December 22nd. Israel withdrew, but retained Aqaba in the south, and the Gaza Strip in the north until later in 1957.

Heated controversy began over the war. In the first place the Canal was closed by blocked ships, and Nasser had won because the 1888 convention was a dead letter. Egypt took over the Canal, and denied its use to Israel. Eventually in 1958 Egypt agreed to pay compensation of 64 million dollars and the Canal was reopened in April 1957. In Britain Eden's weak constitution gave way under the strain, for he was at heart no warmonger, and he resigned in January 1957. For the first time the Commonwealth was divided on a major issue and India threatened to leave. The row between America and Britain was soon patched up by Macmillan during 1957, and America found herself forced to become involved in the Middle East. The Eisenhower Doctrine (see 3E6 above) soon followed, and the American Sixth Fleet arrived on permanent station.

Egypt moved steadily into the Russian camp. Russia agreed to finance the Aswan Dam which was fully operational by 1964, but again, this was a trend which had begun before the war. Nasser was strengthened, and began to pursue a wide ranging and aggressive policy which justified every word

Eden had said about him. Monarchs like Hussein of Jordan veered away from Britain, and the move to oust the Hashemites from Iraq gathered momentum. Northedge has rightly observed of Suez that, 'none of its after effects was as serious as was feared and prophesied by the critics', but although it is true Britain continued to play a Middle Eastern role for over ten years her failure to topple Nasser was the Middle Eastern equivalent of the fall of Singapore in 1942. British prestige would never be what it was before. To overthrow Nasser was no doubt from the Western viewpoint a wise move; his fall would have contained opposition to the West for a time, but is hard to see it having a lasting effect since so many other forces were pressurising the Western powers out of the area. To fail to overthrow Nasser was, therefore, disaster playing into the hands of Arab nationalism which would aim at the destruction of Israel, something America could not permit. Russia as the champion of Egypt was already there, and Cold War problems were added to the existing difficulties in the region.

D6 Nasser's Policies 1957–70

Nasser was able to act more or less unopposed as the leader of Arab opinion, and only after his death did this begin to divide between the Assad–Gaddafi, and the Saudi–Gulf groups of leaders. His policy had several important facets. He remained bitterly anti-Jewish. The Canal was closed to Israeli ships, and just before the 1967 War the Gulf of Aqaba as well. In 1967 the UNEF was forced to leave the Canal, and then Nasser precipitated a war with Israel in which his country was disastrously defeated, and lost much territory (see section 10E2). He remained strongly committed to the Soviet side in the Cold War continuing to strengthen Egypt's links with the Soviet bloc even though this led to strong opposition from the Muslim Brotherhood. In July 1967 the Soviet fleet arrived at Alexandria which was used as a base while they began their expansion in the Mediterranean region. The Egyptian air force consisted largely of Russian planes, and many were actually piloted by Russians.

It is debateable whether this policy helped Egypt. Her involvement in power politics slowed down economic growth, and led to a decline in the tourist industry. It guaranteed that America, previously inclined to look on Egypt as an exploited colonial nation, saw her as the spearhead of Soviet involvement. America therefore became increasingly involved in protecting Israel, resisting Soviet pressure, and eventually directly in the politics of the region. Nasser was certainly instrumental in supporting Arab National-ism, and from this developed left wing Arab movements, and the inter-national terrorist movement both of which served to increase the problems of the region. Nasser backed Algeria (see section 8D2), and persuaded the Arab League to send aid in February 1961. In 1962 civil war began in Yemen between royalists and radicals. Nasser sent troops to secure a radical victory —but was forced to withdraw his troops in 1967. He gave support to the PLO (see section 10E2), and the meeting that led to Yasser Arafat becoming Chairman took place at Cairo in 1969.

The Arab League was steadily growing with 17 members, and Nasser was determined to use it for liberating other Arab countries from reactionary rulers. The difficulty was that nationalism was equally strong elsewhere, and attempts by Nasser to create federations and large units all failed. Nasser's links with Russia, and terrorism were displeasing to the remaining Arab rulers, and in 1969 King Feisal of Saudi Arabia criticised Nasser at an Islamic League meeting at Rabat. Thus, although the Arab League formed a military command in 1964 it did not control the guerilla movements, and was unable to provide aid for the Palestinians. In 1958 Nasser engineered a union with Syria, but this collapsed in 1961. A further attempt at union with Syria and Iraq collapsed in 1963, and a proposed union with Libya put forward in 1969 had collapsed by 1973.

D7 Britain Leaves Southern Arabia

One effect of the war in the Yemen fomented by Nasser was to provide a base for guerillas operating against the new South Arabian Federation set up by Britain (see section 10C5). The ruler of the Federation was deposed by the British in 1965 for his links with the Nationalists, and direct colonial rule was resumed by Wilson's Government in Britain. This served to bind the opposition together in the NLF, and a war began. Aid was forthcoming from the Yemen, and the guerilla movements provided trained adversaries. Britain was able to adopt counter insurgency measures in the towns, but in the Radfan desert region manning forts and using the SAS with air and artillery support, obtained little permanent success.

In 1966 Britain agreed to leave both the base and the federation, but was clearly anxious not to hand over to Arab extremists. For a time divisions in Arab ranks held matters up, but by early 1967 the NLF was clearly the main force, and as soon as Britain left the Radfan in June it took over the region. The federation was dissolved, and a conference at Cairo called to create a government. In November 1967 the British left Aden. From 1964 to 1967 382 people had died in the war. The new state became the People's Republic of South Yemen (PRSY), and the Britain gave it Perim, Socotra and the Kamaran Islands in the Straits. Backed by Russian planes and naval bombardment a marxist government was soon installed, and Aden became a Soviet naval base. From the PRSY attacks were made on the remaining royalists in Yemen where the left took power in 1970.

D8 Britain Leaves the Persian Gulf

The Gulf was important to Britain as the main source of her oil particularly with Nasser and his supporters in control of many other pipelines. Strategically it was her last foothold in the region making a contribution to containment, and backing for British supporters like Iran and Oman. In July 1967 the British had said it was their intention to stay (see section 10C5). Britain had negotiated an arms agreement with Iran the previous year in an attempt to prevent the Shah from pressing his claims to various places in the Gulf. However, the rulers of the area should have remembered the fate of other rulers loyal to Britain in India or the Middle East. Devaluation of the pound was followed by the 1967 Arab–Israeli War, with the closure of many pipelines, and the combined effect of these events on the British economy was to make Wilson change course. In January 1968 he announced Britain would withdraw by 1971. King Feisal of Saudi Arabia fearing Iranian action backed the rulers of the region in the formation of a new political structure.

The Arab rulers of the Gulf wished to retain a British presence, and the ruler of Abu Dhabi offered to pay the cost of keeping that presence. But Britain cancelled her 1961 Kuwait treaty clearly serving notice that she would not defend the rulers. The result was that nine countries formed the United Arab Emirates with a federal council, and a common defence force during 1968. During 1969 Abu Dhabi became the head of the federation consisting of Bahrain, Qatar, Sharjah, Abu Dhabi, Dubai, Ras al-Khaima, Ajman, Umm al-Qawan and Fujairah. Edward Heath, the leader of the British Conservatives, strongly attacked Wilson's action, and promised to renegotiate Britain's position if returned to power. He won the 1970 election, and then failed to do anything of the sort. The result was a series of changes that created the modern political situation on the Gulf.

In Oman a palace revolution overthrew the reactionary sultan, and replaced him with the reforming sultan, Qabus bin Said. Bahrain and Qatar declared themselves independent in August 1971 leaving seven states in the United Arab Emirates. This was an ideal opportunity for Iran to assert her claims, and she seized the Tumbs Islands. Britain backed Iran against the Emirates. In November 1971 Heath withdrew the last British military presence from Bahrain. Within ten years the British were seeking to rectify their mistake faced with the Iranian Revolution of 1979 (see section 10F1).

E Israel's Struggle for Survival

E1 The Development of Israel

Throughout its modern history Israel has in many ways resembled the history of the Jews in Biblical times. Israel has had a constant struggle for survival against neighbours who became increasingly powerful as the years passed, and have now succeeded in getting Western support for their viewpoint. But the Jewish people have a history of endless struggle, and the wars, terrorist attacks and border raids which have affected the country have not deterred the Jews from establishing a prosperous and democratic country, as well as building a reputation for military brilliance. Political development has often revolved round coalition government because there are a number of splinter groups caused by religious differences, but the main party that has guided Israel has been the Mapai or Labour Party started by Ben Gurion who was Prime Minister from 1948 to 1953, and from 1955 to 1963. He was a Polish Jew, and was followed in office by two Russian born Jews, Levi Eshkol (1963–9), and Mrs Golda Meir (1969–74) whose governments were both coalitions. However, they were able to call on General Moshe Dayan as Minister of Defence (1966) to strengthen their rule. The last Mapai coalition prime minister was Itzhak Rabin (1974–7). By then the party was weakening under accusations of not being prepared for the 1973 war, and Rabin was forced to resign following a financial scandal. In 1977 the Likud Party led by Menachim Begin took office, and in spite of serious illness, Begin remained in office until 1983, forced to rely on right wing religious groups for his majority.

Constant war and the need to import large quantities of weapons has had some effect on the economy. Foreign Jewish money has helped development, and a reparations agreement with West Germany yielded £14 million. The flood of immigrants has continued, and there are now 3 million Jews in Israel. The economy has grown particularly aided by America who is Israel's main trading partner. Industry in the main towns like Tel-Aviv has been supplemented by the development of an oil industry, but above all Israel has been famous for her land policy. Over a thousand kibbutzim have been established, and a massive irrigation programme undertaken including the bringing of water to the Negev Desert in 1964. Israel like Japan and Singapore has shown that Third World countries do not have to be either politically immature or economically undeveloped, but her success has aroused deep bitterness among the Arab refugees, and even deeper religious hostility among Muslims.

E2 The Early Wars 1948–67

It has previously been described (see section 10D1) how Israel emerged from her first war with the Arabs, victorious, but having lost considerable portions of Palestine including Jerusalem. The Arabs of course saw the result differently, claiming Palestine had been partitioned, and they were being denied their rightful part of the country. Jerusalem was also one of their holy cities. Although there were a few frontier incidents, the early 1950s passed peacefully until Nasser gave his support to the fedayeen guerillas, and sought to involve Syria and Jordan in joint war on Israel. This action followed by the seizure of the Canal, and the threat to close the Gulf of Aqaba led Israel to attack Egypt in October 1956 with the support of France, and Britain (see section 10D4).

Ten years of intermittent border warfare then followed, and in 1964 the Palestinian Liberation Organisation was established bringing together some ten groups. This led to the stepping up of border attacks; the declared purpose of the PLO being the destruction of Israel. Trouble began with Syria late in 1965, and then spread to Jordan during 1966. Israel carried out reprisal raids, but during early 1967 pressure on Israel was increased: Nasser secured the withdrawal of the UNEF forces and then closed the Gulf of Aqaba. Mobilisation took place in all three Arab countries. Israel found no support for international action and therefore decided to take matters into its own hands. On June 5th the Six Day War began with a three pronged Israel attack. In the north she seized the Golan Heights from Syria, in the east all Jordan west of the Jordan River was taken, and in the south the Israelis returned to the Canal taking the whole of the Sinai Desert. The effects were considerable. The extremists gained ground among the PLO, and during 1969 the radical Popular Front for the Liberation of Palestine (PFLP) came into existence. The number of Arab refugees rose to 1.5 million of whom only 15,000 accepted an Israeli offer to return. Other Arab states like Saudi Arabia and Libya gave financial support to the defeated countries, and widespread Arab hostility began the steady isolation of Israel since many countries depended on Arab oil. France ended arms supplies in 1969, for example.

The Arab reaction to Israel's invasion was to blame the West. The Canal was closed, oil cut off and embassies attacked. The Western powers who in 1950 had guaranteed Israel's existence began to move slowly away from her. In November 1967 a British Resolution in the United Nations was accepted as the basis of a future settlement requiring: Israeli withdrawal from all occupied land, Arab recognition of Israel and a negotiated settlement of the fate of the Palestinians. But the PLO and PFLP could not accept this situation, and in 1968 began a terrorist campaign waged against Jews throughout the world, relying on international contacts (see section 14A5). Guerilla bases were set up in Syria and Egypt to launch attacks on border settlements, and Israel replied by attacking Palestinian camps.

E3 Arab Aggression Against Israel 1969–1973

Israel now came under constant attack by every available means the Arabs could muster. Guerilla attacks were launched from Lebanon, Syria, Egypt, and to a lesser extent, Jordan, while Arab terrorists carried out a series of outrageous attacks like the Munich Olympics incident in 1972. The Israelis announced their occupation of the conquered territory would be permanent, and began the systematic colonisation of parts of it like the Gaza Strip. Although in theory allowing Arab mayors and others to have a say, in effect the Israeli government ruled the Arabs of the occupied territories as she wished. The legitimate Arab governments were under tremendous pressure to take action against Israel although they were by no means united. Hussein of Jordan had to cope with the Palestinians, and resented lack of support by richer Arab countries. He had been forced in 1970 to expel the Palestinian guerilas from his country because he was not willing to risk war a second time. Syria led by Assad, and armed by Russia, set the pace, and Sadat of Egypt who had just expelled the Russians needed some strong nationalist move to consolidate his position.

The result was the Yom Kippur War of October 1973 (see section 13F4). Surprise gave the Arabs initial gains, but these were quickly wiped out, and Israel advanced deep into Syria and Egypt. This precipitated an international crisis (see section 13F5) because Russian backing for the Arabs was plain, and new found Arab determination to use their oil wealth as a diplomatic weapon seriously worried a Western world going into recession. After threats of unilateral action by Russia and America a cease-fire was established, and a new United Nation force despatched to Israel's southern borders. America from then on became actively involved in seeking a solution of the Palestinian problems.

E4 Settlement with Egypt 1973–82

The American Secretary of State, Henry Kissinger, backed by President Nixon, was anxious to capitalise on the Russian withdrawal from Egypt. Sadat feeling isolated and with his country in serious economic difficulty was willing to accept American help, and thus a means was secured for America to become involved as an honest broker. This work was undertaken by Kissinger in 1973–6, and had notable successes. Cease-fire agreements were made with Egypt and Syria in 1974. The Suez Canal was reopened to all including Israel in June 1975. During 1977 Sadat and Begin met twice, and diplomatic relations began. The way was open for Carter of America to use his good offices, and during 1978 talks were held at Camp David, and as a result in March 1979 the Treaty of Washington began a solution of the problems involved. (See section 13F6 for more details of these events in an international context.) The treaty provided for Israel to surrender all territory conquered from Egypt except the Gaza Strip, and to end Israeli settlement in the area. UN supervision was to be provided, and Israel was to have free access through the Gulf of Aqaba. Israel agreed to set up some form of regional government for the Palestinians on the West Bank of the Jordan.

At first sight the treaty might be seen as a significant Arab victory. In fact it divided the Arabs. Sadat tried to extend the settlement, and was rejected by an Arab summit; Gaddafi and Assad particularly attacking him as a traitor to their cause. Israel had now secured peace on two of her three threatened frontiers, and could turn her attention to the last remaining PLO forces in Syria and Lebanon. In 1980 Egypt accorded her diplomatic recognition—the first Arab state to do so. In 1982 Egypt completed her reoccupation of territories lost in 1967, and Israel co-operated in removing her own settlers. Since a UN force had proved unacceptable a multinational force with contingents from various powers is in the area to guarantee peace.

E5 War in the Lebanon 1975–83

The defeat of the Arabs in 1973 had, however, led to other developments. In October 1974 the Arab League backed a separate Palestinian state which clearly would be established on Israeli occupied territory. Yasser Arafat began to disassociate himself from world terrorism (although continuing border raids), and spoke to the United Nations during 1974. This incredible event was followed by a slow thaw in relations between the West and Arafat presumably dictated by the price of oil. By 1980 the Common Market countries had agreed that any settlement must include the Palestinians, and that the PLO should be involved as a party to negotiations. This was of course rejected by Israel. The result has been an intensified war with the last remaining sections of the PLO, numbering about 15,000 who had found refuge in Syria and subsequently in the Lebanon.

War began in April 1975 in the Lebanon between the Christian government of President Frangie, and Arabs stirred up by the PLO who had infiltrated from neighbouring Syria, and wished to attack Israel. After some fighting Frangie's government fell, and a pro-Syrian government took office. To protect this government Assad of Syria sent his forces into the country after July 1976. The PLO and the Syrians then proceeded to try and destroy the Christian Falangist Party. Although this was being done with Russian weapons, and created a dangerous situation along Israel's northern borders the West did nothing to help.

The result was that a bitter war developed between the opposing forces of Christians and Muslims which has claimed something like 60,000 lives. The Israelis were involved because of raids over the border, and in 1978 they intervened in Southern Lebanon. Although Syrian forces were not criticised for their invasion of the country, world opinion attacked Israel for her action. She withdrew, and a United Nations force was sent to the region. It had orders not to fire, was subjected to frequent attack, and was ineffective. War was renewed more vigorously in 1980 with Iraqi troops helping the Syrians, but this unprovoked attack on an independent country provoked no UN demand for Arab withdrawal. The result was a second Israeli invasion in 1980 to clear her borders. The beleaguered Christians were driven into small enclaves in their own country, and the PLO dictated to the Lebanese government its course of action. In 1982 Israel decided to act, and launched a massive invasion of the Lebanon which in July–September at the cost of 25,000 dead on all sides forced the PLO in Beirut to submit.

The Americans were concerned that Israel's intervention might provoke action by the 30,000 Syrians in the country, and that in turn precipitate Russian involvement. An envoy, Philip Habib, was sent by Reagan to effect the first stages of a settlement, and produced a dispersal plan by which Arafat and his guerillas would withdraw to various Arab countries under the supervision of a force of American, French and Italian troops. This was successfully carried out, and a new Christian president, Bachir Gemayel, appointed, only to be murdered a few weeks later. This precipitated re-taliation by the Falangist Christian Militia who attacked Palestinian refugee camps massacring several hundred civilians. Brezhnev now intervened urging joint American–Russian action in the same way he had in 1973 over Yom Kippur. The international force returned to Lebanon, and Israel withdrew from the capital. Bachir's more moderate brother, Amin, was elected president. But he faced a country in which the divided small national army had to face Israeli and Syrian occupation forces, and four or five Falangist and Arab guerilla armies while both the international force and the UN force in the south of the country lacked power to act. These events damaged the hopes for further advances in a general settlement. Egypt withdrew her ambassador from Israel, and Begin announced an increase in settlement on the West Bank of the Jordan at the very moment Reagan put forward a plan for a Palestinian state under the aegis of Jordan on the West Bank and in the Gaza Strip.

Israel found the cost of continuous warfare, together with the public criticism of the Shatilla Camp killings, too great and made an agreement with Gemayel to withdraw her troops from the centre of the country to the mountain region on Israel's border. However, attempts by Secretary of State Schulz to negotiate a general settlement were a failure and civil war resumed in the summer of 1983. After the international force had sustained severe casualties including 230 American and 58 French dead, they withdrew in February 1984 leaving Gemayel's government hard pressed by the Muslims.

F Oil and Strategy: The Modern Arab World

F1 Flashpoint of World Politics

It has been said that the Middle East serves the same function in modern history as the Balkans did in the nineteenth century. It is an era of fervent nationalism in which the great powers are concerned because they see it as economically and strategically vital to their interests. At the moment of writing, two wars are raging there, and since 1936 there has hardly been a year of peace in the area. In some ways this situation arises from internal factors. There are unresolved territorial claims which create bad relations between Iran and Saudi Arabia, for example, and there are bands of terrorists who threaten the stability of various countries like the Yemenis who attack Oman, or the PLO. Muslim fervour has revived following the growth of Arab nationalism. This has involved a rejection of both Western and Russian influence, and struggles between differing groups of Muslims. For instance, Iraq represents Sunni Muslims, and the Iranian Revolution the Shiite Muslims. The growth of Arab wealth, and the movement of many Arabs into the towns has created serious tensions in their society. In Iran and Libya particularly this has been answered by a strict re-enforcement of Muslim laws; in others, like Egypt and Jordan more modern views prevail. This difference is clearly shown in the variation between the radical regimes of rulers like Assad of Syria and the more traditional rulers of states like Saudi Arabia.

Russia has often sought to exploit this situation by arming the Palestinian guerillas, and giving direct assistance to Iraq, Syria and Libya. Her support has, however, been repulsed in Egypt and Iran and she did nothing to help the PLO, in the Lebanon in 1982–3. Inevitably this has involved the United States which has declared the Persian Gulf an area vital to American interests. America has close links with Egypt, the Sudan and Saudi Arabia, and recently Britain has begun to reassert her old position in the Persian Gulf area. This interplay between national and international events has reflected itself in a series of crises. In 1979 there came the overthrow of the Shah of Iran (see sections 10F4 and 13F4), followed by the seizure of some American hostages. At the end of the year came the Russian invasion of Afghanistan (see section 13G3), and this was followed in the spring by the failure of the American attempt to rescue the hostages. Then in September 1980 war began between Iran and Iraq. The Iranian Embassy Siege in London in 1980, and the murder of Sadat of Egypt in 1981 were brutal reminders of another aspect of Middle Eastern affairs—international terrorism.

As far as the Western powers are concerned events in the Middle East have continued to give them particular concern on two grounds: the continuation of wars between Israel and her Arab neighbours, and the increased price of oil which has given the Arab states much new power. American involvement in the region—brought about fundamentally by the collapse of British power and the advent of Soviet influence, firstly in Egypt and latterly in Syria—is given a sharp focus by the pro Jewish lobby in America, by the valuable trade and arms relationship with Israel and the dependence of the American economy on oil. Thus, Israeli actions have forced America to adopt a more even-handed approach than her previous support for Israel. European powers like France and Germany, depending on the region for oil, have adopted a conciliatory line particularly towards the PLO which they have recognised as a political organisation with which they can bargain. Both America and the West have now held discussions at various levels with the PLO while Yasser Arafat, having addressed the United Nations, has even met the Pope.

The need to guarantee oil supplies and limit Communist penetration has brought the West back into the Middle East, and in particular has linked them to moderate states who stand to gain, firstly because Israel is forced to compromise, a desire dear to all Muslim hearts, and secondly because they have to sell their oil to the West now the initial bonanza is over. Egypt has become, under Sadat and Mubarak, the bridge by which American influence has been increased in the region not only in negotiating the famous 1979 settlement, but also because Egypt has allowed the RDF to exercise on its soil and shelters the heir apparent to the Iranian throne who has not renounced his claim. The degree of American influence has been sufficient to prevent Russia gaining from either the 1973 or 1982 wars. Britain who left the area in ignominy in 1967 has also returned: her troops are now in the Sinai and were in the Lebanon as part of international forces, and her influence in the Gulf has started to return. But Israel continues to resort to force in order to occupy territory belonging to Syria and Jordan and to humiliate the Palestinians. Thus the problems relating to Israel are far from solved.

In October 1973 OPEC quadrupled the world price of oil. It doubled again during the rest of the 1970s, and the Iranian oil crisis had the effect of doubling it again. As world oil sources are finite there has always been the possibility of shortage, and this would seriously damage the West. Thirty-five per cent of the Western world's oil comes from the Middle East; the main bulk of this from Saudi Arabia, Iran and Iraq, followed by Libya, Kuwait, the United Arab Emirates, Qatar and Oman. The West has two needs: to keep the price down because it affects inflation, and to guarantee the free flow of oil particularly in the event of war. The difficulties created in 1956 and 1967 are reminders of what might occur, and there is the ever present threat that Russia, with limited resources herself, might direct her attention to the Gulf. America's declaration on the Gulf, and the creation of the RDF was followed by British visits to the Middle East by Lord Carrington, Foreign Secretary from 1979 to 1982, Mrs Thatcher, the Conservative Prime Minister, and Queen Elizabeth II during 1980–1 in an effort to restore Britain's influence in the area.

F2 Arab Radicals: Gaddafi, Assad and Saddam Hussein

The pressures imposed on the Arab world by the Palestinian problem, and the impact of oil revenues on Muslim society have led to a division between radical and conservative members of the Arab League reflected in the 'hawks' and 'doves' division in OPEC itself. Muramar el-Qaddafi (known as Colonel Gaddafi), the ruler of Libya since 1969 is the outstanding Arab radical combining strict Muslim observances in his country with a friendly policy towards the Soviet Union. Using oil revenues which have made Libya the fifteenth richest country in the world, Gaddafi has sought to become the leader of the Arabs. Gaddafi began by removing British and American bases, and now has close defence agreements with Russia. He has established a one party state, and confiscated all foreign oil assets. In his 'Green Book' he has put forward his views on Arab revolution, and tried to carry these into practice. In 1976 he created peoples' congresses in the country, and in 1980 tried to abolish the diplomatic system by changing embassies into peoples' legations. His policy has brought some prosperity to the country, but the oil revenues are being used fast on massive defence expenditure, and backing for international terrorism. Gaddafi's backing for terrorism throughout the world is dealt with elsewhere (see section 14A5). In 1980 he made attempts to overthrow both the rulers of Tunisia and Egypt. In spite of American financial contacts Gaddafi pursued a strongly anti-American policy. Their embassy was destroyed in 1979, and American 6th Fleet manoeuvres harassed until in 1981 the Americans shot down two Libyan planes. Opposition has been dealt with ruthlessly. Death squads have killed 11 opponents overseas, and one squad was sent to America to kill President Reagan.

Syria had a troubled history of military coups after the French withdrew, and for a time fell under the influence of Nasser's Egypt which was repudiated by an army rising in 1961. But in May 1963 the Baathist pro-Nasser group regained control in the country which it has ruled ever since pursuing socialist policies of nationalisation and land reform. Contact with Russia opened in 1966, and by 1969 was fully established. The present ruler, General Hafez Al-Assad seized power in November 1970. With massive Soviet military support Assad was mainly responsible for the Yom Kippur War of 1973, and since 1975 has been actively involved in backing the PLO in the Lebanon. Syria maintains close relations with neighbouring Iraq which backed the 1963 coup, and has sent troops to support Syria in the Lebanon.

In Iraq General Kassem who overthrew the Hashemites (see section 10C4) was himself deposed and killed in 1963 by Colonel Arif who was responsible for a Baathist policy involving rapid socialisation of the economy. He was killed in a helicopter crash, and succeeded by his brother in 1966. The ruler since 1979 has been General Saddam Hussein who seeks to make Iraq the successor of Egypt as the leader of the radical Muslims. He has made close military agreements with Russia, and launched a war against Iran (see section 10F4).

F3 Arab Moderates: Mubarak, Hussein and Fahd

Hussein of Jordan who came to the throne in 1953 is the last of the Hashemite kings whose story began in 1915, and as a result he has been subjected to considerable pressures throughout his reign by the more radical Arab leaders. However, he has been able to contain the opposition, and is very much still the effective ruler of his country. He did this firstly, by repudiating the British connection which led to the fall of his brother Hashemites in Iraq. Jordan's problem was of course Palestine, but Hussein was reluctant to give strong support to the PLO because he knew Nasser, and later Assad, wished to remove his dynasty. His position was confirmed when Jordan was heavily defeated in the war with Israel in 1967, and lost one half of its population whilst the number of Palestinian refugees substantially increased. The PLO with Syrian assistance then sought to overthrow Hussein, and in 1970–1 there was a civil war in the country. Hussein was victorious and confined the PLO to the west of the country. This rising had two effects. It led the king to suspend the constitution which was not restored until 1976, and Jordan did not take part in the 1973 war. Hussein did, however, establish representative government institutions for the Palestinians for the first time in 1974. Jordan is closely linked to Saudi Arabia, and has restored her ties with Britain and America who supply her with arms.

Egypt's presence among the Arab moderates is something which would have seemed impossible in 1970. Under Nasser Egypt had been the centre of Arab radicalism, and had a friendship with Russia. Anwar Sadat in some ways appeared to be following in his footsteps. There was a proposal for union with Gaddafi's Libya, and Egypt joined the 1973 War, but Sadat realised that economically Egypt could not afford her role of leading Arab militant which had cost her aid from the West and lost her territory. During 1972 he acted to expel the Russians from the country, and this paved the way for the restoration of American influence by President Nixon. In 1975 Sadat visited the United States. Egyptian prosperity increased, and as a result of diplomatic policies Sadat was able to secure the return of Egypt's lost territory in 1979–82 while at the same time ridding himself of the necessity for backing PLO attacks on Israel. These moves enraged the radicals. Gaddafi tried to overthrow Sadat in 1980 using the Muslim Brotherhood, and when in 1981 Sadat cracked down on this group he was assassinated. His successor, Mubarak, has continued his policies however, and during 1982 the settlement with Israel was completed.

Saudi Arabia is the leader of the Arab moderates partly because of her enormous wealth which needs Western aid to develop the country effectively, and partly because as a traditional Islamic monarchy she fears Arab radicalism. The raid on the mosque at Mecca in November 1979 by terrorists supporting the Ayatollah in Iran was an illustration of the dangers which may threaten Saudi Arabia. The attack of Marxist South Yemen on North Yemen (1978) was another. Oil was discovered in Saudi Arabia in 1933, and it was the Americans who were most prominent in developing it. Since Saudi Arabia did not have a border with Israel she had only to make token gestures in support of the Palestinian cause while since she had been independent for years there were no anti-colonial feelings standing in the way of co-operation with the West.

The Wahabi rulers were more interested in Islamic Unity than in Arab Nationalism, and gradually began to provide an alternative focus to the Arab League. In 1966 the Islamic World League met at Mecca, and since then the Arab rulers of Saudi Arabia and the Gulf States have increasingly co-operated together to keep their states truly Muslim in spite of the materialist impact of their oil based economies. Feisal (1964–75), Khaled (1975–82) and Fahd, the present king, have all been Muslim traditionalists. It was Saudi Arabia who in 1976 produced the first major division in OPEC urging that price rises should be economic not political in their intent. With heightened fears for Gulf stability following the Iranian Revolution Saudi Arabia has cautiously moved closer to the Western side, and accepted an arms deal with the United States. The country has, so far, been the most stable in the Middle East.

F4 The Iran–Iraqi War 1980–84

Iran under Reza Pahlevi (the Shah) made considerable progress towards becoming a modern state including land redistribution, and a series of industrial developments after 1965. (See section 13F4.) This progress had presented difficulties. The Shah was isolated from reactionaries who did not wish for economic change because it would break down traditional Shiite

Muslim practices, and as early as 1965 there was trouble from this section of the population. The Shah himself lived in much splendour, and the inequalities generated by economic growth were glaring; thus preserving the Tudeh and other left wing parties. To curb the left the Shah used repressive measures including a secret police and frequent suspension of constitutional forms. Strong centralised government rode roughshod over racial minority groups particularly the four million Kurds, and the people of Khuzestan. The Shah was forced to maintain a large and costly military establishment, and perhaps over-estimated his capacity for playing the role of a major power challenging Iraq and Saudi Arabia, and replacing Britain as the protector of the Gulf.

From 1977 to 1979 the pace of revolutionary opposition increased, but it is important to see that it was reactionary—led by mullahs, aiming to return Iran to a country where women's status is inferior, and public executions for adultery and other crimes are commonplace. The leader was the Ayatollah Khomeini who had been exiled in 1963, first to Iraq, and then to Paris. The Shah firstly acted firmly by declaring martial law in August 1978, but President Carter of America opposed this urging him to make human rights concessions. The resulting release of political prisoners was followed by strikes and demonstrations. In January 1979 the Shah, a dying man, abdicated, and the Americans then hypocritically offered him shelter after having helped to destroy their ally. The new prime minister, Bakhtiar, was soon pushed aside, and in November a Revolutionary Council took over with mullahs in charge, and a network of local committees backed up by a militia (the Pasderan). A reign of terror then followed including attacks on racial minorities, Sunni Muslims, former supporters of the Shah and savage punishments for violation of Muslim law. The seizure of the American hostages (see section 13G4) was but one incident in this period of chaos.

Iraq was not slow to take advantage of this situation. In 1975 the Treaty of Algiers had stabilised relations with the Shah. Both sides had agreed to curb the Kurdish separatist movement straggling their borders. The Shah surrendered small pieces of territory in return for agreement that the Shatt-el-Arab waterway should be free for joint navigation. The trouble was that the region to the east—Khuzestan—had only become Iranian in 1847, and its people's limited rights had been removed. Iraq saw an opportunity to detach this oil rich region from chaotic Iran. The rising of the Kurds once the Shah's strong hand was removed was causing trouble in Iraq. In April 1980 Iranian revolutionaries tried to kill the Deputy Prime Minister of Iraq, while by September armed border raids on the Baghdad road provided Saddam Hussein with the excuse he needed. A three pronged invasion destroyed the oil installations, and by early 1981 had seized much of Western Khuzestan after victories at Khorramshah and Abadan. Iran retaliated by bombing the main Iraqi oil fields at Mosul and Kirkuk, and after a time was able to put an effective army into the field. During the summer of 1982 they drove the Iraqis back, and the war at the time of writing has reached a stalemate. Casualties are estimated to be 150,000 Iraqi and 90,000 Iranian dead, and each side has succeeded in occupying 600 square miles of each other's country.

Revision Questions

1. Explain the meaning of the following terms in an historical context: (a) the Near East, (b) the Middle East, (c) the Gulf Region, (d) Arab Nationalism, (e) Zionism.

2. Explain how Britain built up her power economically and politically in the Middle East until 1939.

3. Describe the national revolts that created the modern countries of: (a) Turkey, (b) Iran, (c) Saudi Arabia, (d) Egypt, in the 1920s. Did they have anything in common?

4. Why did Britain at first strongly support Arab Nationalism during the two world wars, and then oppose it after 1945?

5. Why did: (a) Egypt, (b) Iraq and (c) Iran reject their monarchies?

6. How was Israel created between 1917 and 1948? What problems has it faced since then?

7. Israel has fought five wars in modern times in 1948–9, 1956, 1967, 1973 and 1982. What factors have these wars had in common, and what has differed in each case as regards great power reactions to them? (See also section 13F.)

8. How has the rising importance of oil since 1918 altered the Middle East: (a) economically and (b) politically?

9. What issues in world affairs were highlighted by the Suez War of 1956?

10. Compare the achievements in building their countries of: (a) Ibn Saud, (b) Gamal Nasser, (c) Ben Gurion, (d) Mohammed Reza Shah.

11. What issues were raised in 1982 by wars between Israel and the PLO, and Iraq and Iran?

Further Reading

Barnett, C., *The Collapse of British Power*, Eyre Methuen, London, 1972.

Hirst, D., *The Roots of Violence in the Middle East*, Faber and Faber, London, 1977.

Laqueur, W., *The Soviet Union and the Middle East*, Routledge and Kegan Paul, London, 1959.

Monroe, E., *Britain's Moment in the Middle East*, Chatto and Windus, London, 1963.

Northedge, F. S., *Descent from Power*, Allen and Unwin, London, 1967.

Nutting, A., *Nasser*, Constable, London, 1972.

Thomas, H., *The Suez Affair*, Weidenfeld and Nicolson, London, 1967.

11
The Struggle for Southern Africa

A Introduction: The Genesis of the Conflict

A1 The Extent of Colonialism

Southern Africa may be defined as the area lying south of the Congo (Zaire) River. It is in this region of the world that the struggle for independence and the violence of racial conflict has been most protracted and severe, and is not yet in sight of a solution. For this there are a number of reasons. The area contained three blatant examples of white regimes. On each side of Southern Africa lay parts of the Portuguese empire—Angola and Mozambique—and considerable white settlement had taken place in Angola, encouraged during the 1950s. In the centre lay three British colonies— Nyasaland, Northern and Southern Rhodesia. Whereas white rule was as mild as in Britain's other African colonies in the first two, Southern Rhodesia had obtained internal self-government and practiced discrimination. When the three were combined in 1953 it seemed as if white rule was to be perpetuated. To the south lay three more British colonies—Bechuanaland, Basutoland and Swaziland—and the Union of South Africa. Here too self-government had been obtained, and apartheid was practiced. Lastly, on the west coast lay the former German colony of South West Africa, which claimed to be independent as Namibia whereas in fact South Africa had incorporated the area into their country fully by 1969. In view of events north of the Congo the whole region could not fail to be the epicentre of racial conflict.

A2 Portuguese Power and Methods

Portugal had been the first European country to seize African territory because she was the nearest, and she was to be the last to leave. Madeira, the Canaries (later transferred to Spain), the Azores, the Cape Verde Islands and Fernando Po marked the onward early march of Portugal. Then came her trading posts in West Africa later to become Portuguese Guinea, and lastly her southern settlements. Angola was first reached in 1482, and became the centre of a flourishing slave trade. Mozambique was conquered between 1505 and 1515. For many years the Portuguese claimed they controlled the land lying between their two colonies, and it was this claim that precipitated European discussion about Africa after 1876, and led to treaties with Britain in 1884 and 1890–1 to restrict these claims. During the colonial era there were risings against the Portuguese in Angola in 1902 and 1907, and in Mozambique in 1895–8, but thereafter development was peaceful. Portugal did not operate a colour bar prefering 'assimilado' and allowing inter-marriage (mistos). On the other hand forced labour was a feature of their colonial regime, and the existence of a dictatorship in Portugal from 1930 meant that the colonies had no hope of peaceful liberation. In 1951 the two colonies were incorporated in Portugal with limited internal self-government, and in 1961 a common citizenship was established, but in 1969 President Caetano made it clear that independence was not intended. Portugal had an army of 150,000 in Africa to enforce its rule.

A3 British Colonies in the Region

Britain had been drawn from the coast into the interior of Africa partly by a need to defend her existing possessions against the many well organised tribes of the interior like the Zulus; then by missionaries and explorers like Livingstone who had opened the region, and by the anti-slavery crusade developed in the 1870s. In 1873 Britain forced Zanzibar to close her public slave markets, and in 1875 the first missionaries arrived in Nyasaland. The struggle with the Arab slave traders lasted until Zanzibar was bombarded, and the ending of the unofficial trade (1896–7) and forced Britain to negotiate with Portugal and Germany who had occupied areas on the coast. Nyasaland became formally British in 1891, and was developed by Sir Harry Johnson becoming a full colony in 1907. As early as 1843 Britain made a treaty with the ruler of Basutoland, and when the Boers sought to occupy the country in the 1860s were forced to act. Their ruler asked Britain to annex his country in 1868 since their treatment of blacks was more humane than that of the Boers. Zululand was annexed after a spectacular 'small' war in 1879, and after numerous rebellions incorporated in Natal in 1897. Swaziland on the other hand which Britain had claimed, then handed to the Boers, was re-captured in the Boer War, and annexed outright in 1903. Lastly, the vast area of Bechuanaland which was twice the size of Germany was threatened by German and Boer annexation, and the missionaries begged Gladstone to act. It was organised under British rule in 1885, and later divided into British Bechuanaland (1895), and the Protectorate. Britain had no clear imperial policy in the area; some tribes remained in colonies, and were to proceed to independence while others were handed over to what became the Union of South Africa.

A4 The Creation of Rhodesia

It was in the very heart of the region that one of the most difficult problems of modern times was to be created by the enterprise of Cecil Rhodes (1853–1902). A self-made millionaire Rhodes was convinced that Britain should rule Africa from the Cape to Cairo, and above all dreamed of a federated Southern Africa as powerful as the United States then was in economic terms. The Northern area was occupied by the Mashonas, but from the 1830s the Matabele had entered the region as conquerors, and damaged existing trade and culture. Their last ruler was Lobenguela (1870–94), and it was with him that Rhodes dealt signing an agreement in 1888. This was a prelude to his British South African Company (1889–1924) which was to occupy the region. After a spectacular expedition northwards Salisbury was founded in September 1890. The area was called Rhodesia in 1895. The Matabele resisted in 1893 and 1896, but thereafter development was peaceful. Northern Rhodesia was organised separately in 1911, and when the company's authority came to an end Southern Rhodesia emerged as a colony in 1923. Northern Rhodesia became a full colony in 1924. But it was significant that from the start Britain conceded rights to the government of Southern Rhodesia unlike those of her other colonies, and the party which took power with Sir Godfrey Huggins as Prime Minister in 1933 retained it permanently. Although Rhodesia rejected union with South Africa in 1922 her ties were obvious. A third of the white settlers were South African born, and this group held the best half of the land although they made up only eight per cent of the population. Unlike other colonies Britain was faced with a large white minority determined to retain power.

A5 Mandate for German South West Africa

A German merchant, Franz Luderitz, purchased land from the native Africans in 1883, and soon afterwards in April 1884 Germany proclaimed a protectorate over the region taking it over fully in 1892. German rule had been notoriously cruel, and there had been a major revolt in 1904–8. During the First World War South Africa occupied the region, and at the end was given a mandate by the League of Nations. The object of mandates was to prepare, at different rates, the German colonies for independence— e.g. Tanganyika was a British mandate. But the South Africans had different ideas. A constitution in 1925 gave rights to the German settlers, and in 1932 their party started a demand to be incorporated as a full province of South Africa. A Nazi Party (the German Bund) sprang up, and although it was banned (1937) a new party followed it, and Nazi agents were able to exercise influence on South African politics in the 1940s. In 1946 South Africa asked for incorporation, but the United Nations refused, and insisted on trusteeship. South Africa announced incorporation as early as 1950, but it was not until the Odendaal Report (1964) that plans were drawn up for a full take over. The United Nations terminated South African trusteeship in 1966, and by 1969 South Africa had incorporated the region reserving 70 per cent of the land for the white settlers.

A6 The Creation of South Africa

South Africa contained half the whites in Africa in 1960. Its demography is a reflection of its complex origins and its seemingly insoluble problems. Of the 22 million inhabitants 70 per cent are black Africans, 17.5 per cent are white (divided roughly equally between English and Afrikaans speaking), 9.5 per cent Coloureds of mixed race and 3 per cent Asians, mainly Indians and Malays. There are also small groups of bushmen, now called the San, and the original native inhabitants, formerly called hottentots and now the Khoikhoi. The Dutch arrived in the Cape in 1652, and ruled until the British annexed their settlements in 1795. Britain bought the Dutch settlements in

1815, and by 1853 had established internal self-government in Cape Colony fully effective from 1872. On the east coast Britain annexed Natal in 1843; it became a separate colony in 1856 with internal self-government. The dissatisfied Boers marched north in the Great Trek (1836–8), and established the Orange Free State and the Transvaal which the British recognised as independent by 1854.

The Boers retained a narrow Calvinist outlook on life, and from the start regarded the Africans as the inferior descendants of Ham (Genesis 9: 18–27). They disliked British missionaries, and sought to extend their power constantly in the interior. This stirred up the tribes, and gradually the whole region became a welter of small wars, conflicting claims and short-lived Boer states. As early as 1858 federation was advocated by the British, but an early attempt to secure this (1877–84) by British seizure of the Boer states failed with ominous consequences. Under Paul Kruger, President of the Transvaal (1883–1900), the 'laager' mentality developed with the Boers seeing themselves as a chosen people surrounded by enemies. The Afrikaans identity began with an invented language—the first book in which came out in 1861. This language replaced Dutch in 1925 thus stressing that the Boers were a separate African white people and not European settlers any longer.

In 1886 gold was discovered in the Transvaal. Johannesburg was founded overnight, and by 1890 there were 450 companies on the Rand. The Boers recalled that when diamonds had been discovered at Kimberley the British had annexed the region although it was ruled by a Boer protected chief, and they were determined to retain control of the gold which seemed to them the solution of their difficulties. Severe laws were passed to curb the rights of immigrants (Uitlanders), and in 1894 they formed a political group to agitate for their rights. Rhodes backed the Uitlanders and there was an abortive invasion of the Transvaal in 1895. Kruger stimulated discontent among Cape Boers, and obtained German aid. Rhodes, Milner and Chamberlain all wanted annexation, and the Boer War (1899–1902) was the result. Britain annexed the Orange Free State, Transvaal and Swaziland. Federation by force had taken place.

The Liberals who came to power in Britain in 1906 were determined to extend responsible government to the annexed states, and did so that year, without any effort to protect the native Africans. The first election led to a victory by Louis Botha's Het Volk, and almost immediately he restricted the right of Indians to enter the Transvaal. The British government failed to read the warning signs. A convention discussed matters, and in May 1910 the Union of South Africa came into existence. No provision such as that protecting Red Indians in Canada was incorporated. In 1913 two acts restricted the Indians still further (leading to a resistance campaign led by Gandhi) and curbed African rights to buy land. In January 1914 Hertzog split from Botha's party to found a Nationalist Party which was anti-British and extremely nationalist. He organised a rebellion which failed in 1914, and went to Versailles in 1919 to demand full independence. There were already clear indications that racial harmony was unlikely to be a feature of the new nation.

B The Development and Functioning of Apartheid in South Africa

B1 The Growth of the Nationalist Party

Louis Botha remained as Prime Minister until 1919 when he was succeeded by Jan Christian Smuts (1870–1949). He had fought against the British in the Boer War, but was convinced that only a partnership of all races was likely to secure a peaceful South African future. Closely involved in founding the League of Nations and securing independence for Ireland Smuts had an international reputation, but in 1924 he was replaced as Prime Minister by J. B. M. Hertzog (1866–1942) the founder of the Nationalist Party because Smuts was said to be too close to the Rand owners, and lacking in firmness in his labour policies. Hertzog remained Prime Minister until 1939 and was the true father of apartheid, although the policies had only made a little headway in his period of office. Smuts and other members of his South African Party joined the government in 1933 under the stress of economic depression, and the two parties formed the United Party in 1934. This led to a split in the Hertzog party—the extremists leaving under Daniel F. Malan (1874–1959). The Second World War produced a fresh crisis since Hertzog had just won an election, and did not wish to support Britain. He was defeated in a parliamentary vote, and South Africa entered the war against Germany. But Hertzog's party was opposed to the government, and joined with the extremists led by Malan. Smuts took office once again in 1943, and remained there until 1948 with his United Party backed by the Labour Party. In the elections of 1948 Malan campaigned openly for apartheid, and was elected. Since then the Nationalist Party has ruled South Africa.

B2 The Beginnings of Apartheid

The Dutch treatment of the Africans, and their backing for slavery were the roots of apartheid. During the nineteenth century as British African policy became more liberal the Boers resisted any change, and the treatment of the Indians prior to 1914—eventually leading to an Immigration Act (1930) banning them—was symptomatic of underlying attitudes. It has to be remembered that when South Africa was developing blacks in America were denied the vote, and there was a 'White Australia' policy. White supremicism was not then an isolated development, and indeed coincided with the development of fascist ideas in Europe, and racialist immigration laws in America. Apartheid ideas, in the words of John Gunther, were a 'shabby cross between Germany in 1933 and backwoods Tennessee'. Thus, when the government came to consider African rights the Representation of Natives Act (1936) placed blacks on a separate register in Cape Province so that they might elect whites to represent them. They were given a separate and purely advisory Council. During this period Malan's Nationalist Party, and the Germans in South West Africa became allies in spreading racialist doctrines playing on demands for a republic at the same time in order to link British South Africans' moderate racial ideas with treachery towards full independence. Pro-Germans had long existed in South Africa like the future Minister of Justice Swart, and they were joined by other future ministers like Pirow and Louw. Brian Bunting has traced the influence of

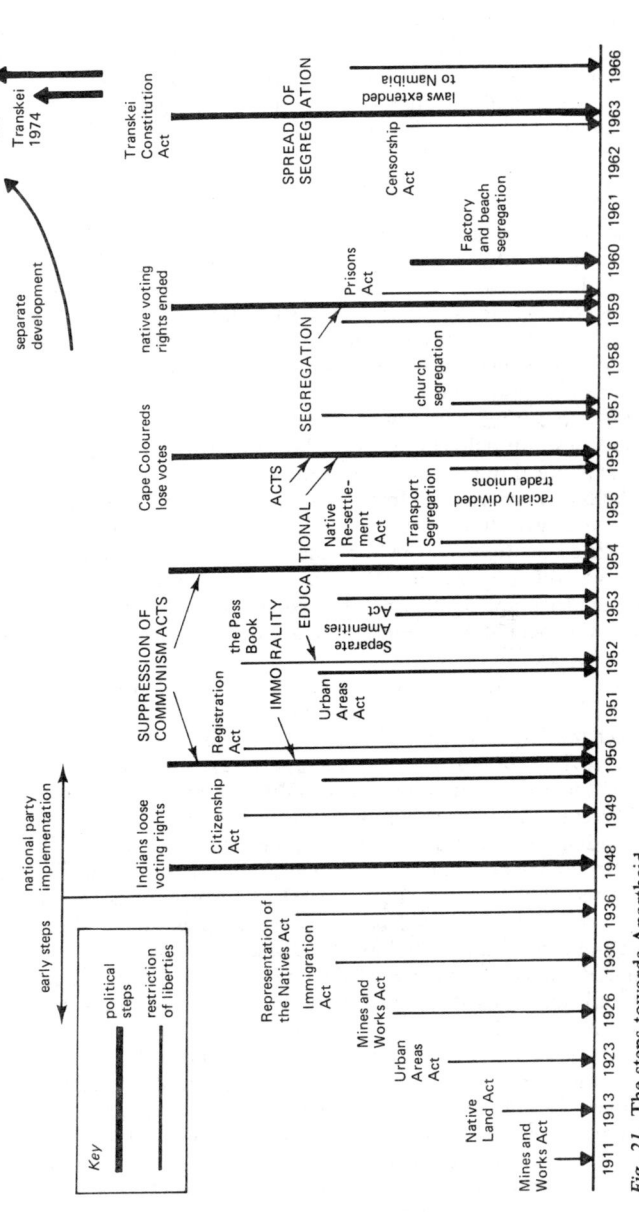

Fig. 21. The steps towards Apartheid

the Broederbund which was banned by Smuts as a secret fascist organisation, and Ossewa Brandweg which was a para-military, anti-Communist, anti-Jewish group in contact with the Nazis during the war. Vorster said in 1942: 'We stand for Christian Nationalism which is the ally of National Socialism.' Under such circumstances Malan was able to reorganise the Nationalist Party combining the Hertzog faction, his own group and the Afrikaans extremists, and it was this combination that won in 1948.

B3 The Apartheid Laws

Laws based on racial distinctions are notoriously complicated, and when they are passed in a country subject to the most rigorous censorship, and secret justice, it is not easy to exactly define the weight of the burden. But of the overwhelming effect that a vast mass of laws have had there can be no doubt. Whereas in America and the rest of Africa the black man has marched towards freedom and greater equality in South Africa he has marched to reservations and total subordination. Every year from 1948 to 1964 a torrent of laws flowed to impose restrictions on Indians, coloureds and blacks. In political terms the laws deprived all except white people of basic political rights. Indians lost the vote in 1948 and after a long struggle coloureds were removed from the voting register in 1956. All African representation was ended by 1959. In order to achieve this the government restricted the rights of the Supreme Court and the Senate where there was considerable opposition. The main African political parties were banned, and under a law of 1968 political parties are to be based solely on colour enabling them to be carefully controlled. The white opposition parties have been ineffective.

The law in South Africa has become increasingly severe. Laws in 1950 and 1954 suppressed the Communist Party, and have been used to curb other parties. The death penalty has been extended to several offences so that in 1957–61, for example, there were 276 executions. Under an act of 1953 the use of corporal punishment was extended, and between 1942 and 1962 some 180,000 people were subjected to it. Police powers are vast including laws to make easier shooting those resisting arrest (1955), and control of the prisons (1959). The government has wide powers of detention, and the right to rule by decree (1953). Censorship has been systematically extended forbidding public protest, or even slogans, and then in 1963 came a comprehensive Censorship Act. These measures have not curbed crime; indeed it has been estimated that by the early 1960s one in eight blacks were being indicted. It was simply the extension of a police state in order to enforce racialist policies.

To please white workers, and to effectively curb black opposition the conditions of work in South Africa have been rigorously segregated and controlled. In 1949 unemployment pay for blacks was abolished, and separate labour exchanges were set up. Contract labour to force blacks to work in poorly paid agriculture was permitted. Blacks were forbidden to strike (1953), and in 1956 the trade union movement was divided on racial lines. Black unions were not recognised as part of the bargaining procedure. In 1956 the concept of job reservation for whites was permitted. Factories themselves were fully segregated by 1960. It is true that many blacks in South

Africa have a higher standard of living than elsewhere in Africa; hence the flow of migrant labour. But their wages are a sixth of the equivalent white workers, and their lives are subjected to intolerable control. In particular the government has feared blacks congregating in towns for it was among urban blacks that nationalism had evolved further north. Squatting was forbidden; then rigid controls on blacks in urban areas started. In 1954 50,000 blacks in the Johannesburg area were forcibly resettled, and black entry into towns is rigorously controlled.

Such control is facilitated by the elaborate system of passes and permits which has developed. The Pass Book was introduced in 1952. It is a complex document which has to be carried by blacks at all times. In 1960 there were 340,958 pass book convictions showing how important enforcing this measure is to totalitarian control. In 1955 severe restrictions on entry or exit from the country were introduced, and many distinguished opponents of apartheid have been 'punished' by this law like Alan Paton. Control is vital because the central theme of the policy is not merely to preserve white privilege and degrade the blacks, but to create separate development. This is fundamentally racialist in a way no policy since the Nuremberg Laws of 1935 has been. In 1950 came an Immorality Act forbidding sex between people of different race, and this Act was re-enforced in 1957. In the first ten years there were 3,890 convictions. Public segregation is a full part of the policy. In 1953 an Act permitted its extension, and over the years nearly every aspect of life has been subjected to segregation. For example, transport (1955), churches (1957) and beaches (1960). In education separate development has occurred. Secondary education was separated in 1953, and university education in 1959. Such segregation of course was extended to all forms of entertainment and sport for many years.

To many separate development is simply racialist; it is seen as coming from basic dislike and fear of blacks by white South Africans. South Africans argue it is the only way forward saying that whites cannot be expected to leave in the way they have Kenya or Algeria. Therefore separate development will allow white society to thrust forward, and the blacks to slowly catch up in their own part of the country. If at the moment this denies to the blacks all kinds of economic and personal freedom this, it is argued, is only a stage in development. In 1950 a register of the population on grounds of race was begun, and gradually blacks have been restricted to certain parts of the country. These were called under the Act of 1950 'Group Areas', and in them limited self-government was slowly permitted; firstly by white appointed councils (1951), and then by African elected ones (1961). Some 200 pieces of land making up 13 per cent of the Republic have been set aside for the Bantu, and the intention is to group these into self-governing states or bantustans. Self-government was first extended to the Transkei in 1961, and in 1974 it was granted 'independence'. In 1977 Bophutatswana became the second such state, but they have been ignored by the international community as false creations. To South Africans they represent the logical conclusion to a policy which has removed blacks from whites' lives in their own interests, something which from the degree of opposition it is clear few blacks accept now that the rest of Africa is free.

B4 One Party Rule in South Africa

The drift of policy from 1948 was greatly pleasing to the extremist Boers, and in 1951 the Afrikaans Party joined the Nationalist Party, which until 1969 preserved a completely united front of one party rule. Dislike of the English connection was made clear from the start when laws abolished appeals to the Privy Council and restricted South African citizenship. The only white opposition party—the United Party—tended to be mainly English speaking, and the constant flood of criticism from English churchmen and politicians, led South Africans towards the decision to adopt a republic. A referendum in 1960 approved this. The British government of Macmillan did not wish South Africa to leave the Commonwealth. The base at Simonstown, and excellent trade were two sufficient reasons, but Macmillan also delivered his 'wind of change' speech in South Africa, and the behaviour of the British government towards white settlers in Kenya made it clear which way they sympathised. A republic was proclaimed, and after strong criticism at the Commonwealth Conference, South Africa left in May 1961. These moves weakened still further the white opposition.

Malan retired in 1954 and J. G. Strijdom became Prime Minister. He died in August 1958, and was succeeded by H. F. Verwoerd, a hardliner and former editor of the Broederbund newspaper, *Die Transvaler*. An attempt to kill him in 1960 failed, but in 1966 he was stabbed by a farm worker and killed. His successor was another hardliner, B. J. Vorster, a former member of Ossewa Brandweg, and the previous Minister of Justice. He remained in office until the autumn of 1978 when he was succeeded by the present Prime Minister, P. W. Botha. But by this time the authority of the Nationalist Party was being challenged not so much by black opposition, but by 'verkrampt' white opposition. Constant international pressure had slowly forced the government to make minor concessions as face savers, and this aroused white hostility soon channelled by another former Broederbund member, Albert Hertzog. As early as 1969 he was expelled from the party, but growing concessions in the 1970s led to an increase in his influence. In 1978–9 the Nationalist Party was engulfed in a scandal (concerning a secret fund used to finance propaganda) which led to the resignation of Mulder, the Information Minister, and Vorster as President in June 1979. The right wing attacked the government, and in August 1980 Botha reorganised his ministry. However, the right claimed there were now too many 'verligte' ministers, and in the elections of 1981 the right-wingers made substantial gains in seats. It is clear that whatever changes there have been in apartheid will not lead to a fundamental change as long as political control remains in the hands of two groups of extremists.

B5 Black Opposition to Apartheid

It must always be remembered that the real opponents of apartheid are the blacks who run such risks in their own country, and to a lesser extent those who help them. At first opposition centred on the African National Congress led by Albert Luthuli, the son of a Christian missionary, and associate of Gandhi. He proposed passive resistance in 1952, but was deprived of his chieftainship as a result. In 1959 a new more radical movement arose called the Pan African Congress. During 1960 the government sought to destroy this movement with mass arrests, and at Sharpeville 69 people were killed and 180 injured when police opened fire. The leader of the new movement was Nelson Mandela, but in 1964 he and seven others were sentenced to life imprisonment. During the 1970s violence again developed beginning with strikes in Natal during which eleven blacks were killed, and in 1976 came serious rioting in Soweto. In 1977 the death in custody of Steven Biko led to renewed rioting, and a clamp down by the government which banned all 17 African political organisations. Since then discontent has continued, and in 1982 black strikes again affected the country.

B6 International Opposition to Apartheid

European fascism has made people acutely conscious of racial questions, and new Third World countries were even more conscious of them. To some extent opposition to South Africa is unfairly selective: it tends to ignore examples of Third World and Communist regimes which are far more oppressive. It is also sometimes rather futile in its expression. One can contrast the outcry over Mandela or Biko with the almost total silence over germ and gas warfare in Vietnam and Afghanistan and realise that beside genuine humanitarian concern there is often political motivation. Protests about sports fixtures, or bank investments do not help a single African to break free from oppression. Effective international opposition is difficult to muster. South Africa is rich, and her economy has been little damaged by events like the UN economic boycott (1962), or the EEC guidelines (1977) on trading with South Africa. In 1963 the UN initiated an arms ban on South Africa. This has had some effect. Britain under Labour governments has accepted the ban, and in 1975 finally left the base at Simonstown which has remained idle ever since. Other countries like France and Israel have continued to keep South Africa armed, and in 1980 alarm was expressed that South Africa had exploded a nuclear device. At the UN 25th Anniversary session in 1970, South Africa was roundly condemned, and during the Carter administration Andrew Young, the American UN representative, swung America against South Africa. But South Africa can ignore such activities. It is less certain if they can for ever ignore black Africa now they are confronted by a ring of hostile states and active guerilla movements. South African attacks on Angola, and her covert backing for Rhodesia— both by troops crossing the Beit Bridge after 1974 and breaking sanctions— shows her basic fear of the future. At Lusaka in 1970 54 Third World nations condemned South Africa, and MPLA and SWAPO attacks continue backed by Soviet equipment. South Africa has been forced to open relations with black Africa beginning with Malawi in 1967, and she has been forced to discuss Namibia. She has been forced to make small concessions such as offering territory to Swaziland. A new constitution has given rights back to Indians and Coloureds. Public segregation is being reduced particularly in sport. The sex and pass laws are not being rigorously enforced. It is clear in the 1980s that the regime is starting to budge in small matters, and there should be no slackening therefore of international opposition.

C Independence for Black Southern Africans

C1 Three New Countries

There had been talk that Britain's three High Commission territories of Bechuanaland, Basutoland and Swaziland might join South Africa, but apartheid prevented any such development. Basutoland was a backward country in which Britain had to deal with an outbreak of 'medicine murders' culminating in 1951, for which 67 Africans were hung. It became independent in 1966 as Lesotho with its chief becoming King Moshoeshoe II. When elections led to a defeat for his party the constitution was suspended in 1970, and a revolt crushed in 1974. The same pattern was followed in Swaziland which became independent in 1968 under Sobhuza II (1921–82), who in 1973 established absolute rule. In Bechuanaland, Britain had run into difficulties for expelling the native ruler, Seretse Khama, for marrying a white woman, Miss Ruth Williams, but the government was forced to yield six years later in 1956. The chieftanship remained abolished however. The country became independent as Botswana in 1966, and Sir Seretse became the President.

C2 SWAPO and the Struggle for Namibia

The termination of the United Nations trusteeship in 1966, and the adoption of full integration by South Africa in 1969 was a clear provocation to African nationalists in Namibia. Opposition centred on the Ovambo Tribe, and originated in 1962. The organisation was known as SWAPO, and was banned by South Africa. But the United Nations recognised them as the rightful government, and insisted on full independence in December 1973. In 1974 as part of the moderate posture being slowly adopted by South Africa the government agreed to open talks on the future of the region. The threat of a Soviet base there, the loss of valuable minerals and the increased strategic threat to the Republic all played a part in this decision. During 1975 a conference was held, and an offer of independence in three years made by South Africa. However, power was not handed over to SWAPO but to the party commanding a majority in elections, and by this time South Africa had organised a settler party—the Democratic Turnhalle Alliance—and favourable to their interests. SWAPO refused the offer, and during 1976 guerilla war began. With independence for Angola and Zimbabwe, the opportunities for SWAPO greatly increased, and they had widespread international backing.

C3 Western Intervention and the South African 'Solution'

During 1977 the Americans through their United Nations representative, Andrew Young, launched an initiative with the backing of Kurt Waldheim, the UN Secretary General. Five members of the Security Council (America, Britain, Canada, France and West Germany) went on a mission to South Africa to seek a settlement which would include SWAPO, withdraw South African troops and replace them with UN troops to supervise elections. South Africa would not agree, and proceeded to make its own settlement.

Namibia was granted a constituent assembly in July 1977, and racial discrimination was reduced in public places. A second Western Plan was put forward in 1978, but by this time the links between SWAPO and the Angolan MPLA were so strong that South Africa was taking warlike measures. The UN Plan was therefore stricter than before, and a visit in October 1978 of the five foreign ministers failed to convince South Africa. The Republic proceeded to hold elections which led to a victory for the Turnhalle Party. In May 1979 the Constituent Assembly became the National Assembly; dominated by whites who proceeded to reject any further reduction in racial discrimination. The UN refused to recognise the proceedings.

C4 South Africa's Frontier War

The appearance of Marxist governments in Angola and Mozambique in 1976 thoroughly alarmed South Africa. Her troops entered Angola to help UNITA, but when it became clear that no Western help would be forthcoming she withdrew to a 30 mile strip on the border with Namibia. The SWAPO guerillas were concentrated in this northern region because many of the other nine tribes in the area did not support them. It has been estimated there were some 6,000 of them, but of course MPLA, Cuban and Russian support was available, and Russian 'advisers' were captured by the South Africans during 1981. During 1980–81 the war intensified. South Africa came to control a 150 mile strip of Angola, and launched systematic raids into this region. In June 1980 she killed 360, and in August 1981 over a 1,000 guerillas, and there are now few SWAPO guerillas actually in Namibia. South African sensitiveness to guerila activity was shown in January 1981 when her troops raided the headquarters of the African National Congress in Maputo, capital of Mozambique, killing 30 people and by a further raid in May 1983. After further heavy fighting South Africa withdrew her troops from Angola in 1983, and in early 1984 reached agreement with Mozambique on ending the guerila war in that area at least.

D Independence for Angola and Mozambique

D1 The Wars of Independence

In all three Portuguese colonies independence movements were founded. In Guinea–Bissau the PAIGC was founded in 1956 led by Amilcar Cabral. In Mozambique, Frelimo was founded in 1962, and in 1966 came under the control of Samora Machel. In Angola which was more advanced economically three parties emerged. The MPLA founded in 1956 was essentially an urban left wing movement led by Agostino Neto. The FNLA represented the ruling family of the Bakongo, its leader Holden Roberto being the nephew of the last king. Mobutu of Zaire was his brother-in-law. UNITA in the south was led by J. Savimbi and represented another tribal grouping. These movements could increasingly call on aid. Zaire, Zambia and Tanzania provided bases, Russia and China provided aid to the differing groups, and UNITA is receiving aid from South Africa.

Trouble began in the colonies as soon as the wind of change began to blow elsewhere. There were risings in Guinea–Bissau (August 1959) and Angola (March 1961) which were suppressed with great ferocity. In the Angolan rising, for example, 8,000 people were killed including 700 whites, and the Portuguese retaliated by killing a further 50,000. The Portuguese poured 150,000 troops into Africa and paid out 40 per cent of their budget on the war. 11,000 Portuguese and untold numbers of Africans died in savage fighting. The Portuguese led by Generals Spinola and Arriage used every available method to seek to crush the rebels from cavalry to air power, from napalm to chemical destruction of crops. They also attempted a hearts and minds policy. But in April 1969 it was made clear Portugal would remain, and this increased the ferocity of the wars. International opinion was against Portugal who had no support except a treaty with South Africa in 1964. In 1967 the UN called for mandatory sanctions against her, and America insisted on the withdrawal of planes supplied to Portugal for NATO use. In 1968 the OAU recognised the guerilla movements in all three Portuguese colonies as governments. When atrocities by Portugal were revealed in the Tete area of Angola there was a major international outcry in 1973, and the eruption of revolt in Portugal in 1974 (see section 7D2) led to a swift end to the war.

D2 The Angolan Civil War 1975–6

Guinea–Bissau in 1974, and Mozambique in 1975 passed to independence under Cabral and Machel respectively, but in Angola matters were more complicated. 750,000 Portuguese settlers fled the country, and its economy collapsed. From producing 90 per cent of its own food it could only produce 50 per cent, and its vital coffee exports fell from 200,000 to 25,000 tons. The country was useful to the Soviet Union, providing a base for helping Zimbabwean and Namibian guerilas, and for the overthrow of Mobutu in Zaire. As independence occurred Cubans landed in November 1975 to back up the MPLA, and the same month South Africa helped UNITA advance in the south. For a short time it looked as if the Marxists would be defeated. European mercenaries went to help UNITA, and America began supplying aid. But such hopes were short-lived. Congress cut off the aid, and international opinion denounced the involvement of mercenaries and the South Africans who withdrew in 1976. The MPLA sent Cubans north to seize the rich oil enclave of Cabinda which had seceded, and then launched all out attack on Huambo, the rebel capital. Some 20,000 Cubans arrived to back up the MPLA army, and by November 1976 they were in control of the north and centre of the country. 20,000 people had died at a conservative estimate. UNITA remains active, and South Africa still involves herself in the south.

D3 The Attack on Zaire 1978

After the Congo Civil War ended in 1964 (see section 8D6) there were a succession of short-lived governments until in November 1965 General Joseph Mobutu seized power. He executed the former Prime Minister Kimba (1966), and tried Tshombe in his absence sentencing him to death (1967). Tshombe was murdered in Algeria in 1969. At first Mobuto took a left-wing line nationalising the mines in 1966, and taking over the Union Miniere the next year. However, constant risings made Mobutu unsure, and he turned to Belgium for a settlement in 1968. Belgians began to return to the Congo which in 1971 became Zaire. Mobutu was a strong and corrupt ruler, and made himself President for life in 1970. His support for FLNA in Angola infuriated Neto, and in May 1978 he launched an attack on Katanga (Shaba) aimed at detaching the province. Mobutu appealed for aid, and Belgian and French troops were sent to Kolwezi to bolster his government. Later they were withdrawn and replaced by a Pan African force from seven countries. In August 1978 the two countries made peace. Zaire gave up support for the FLNA, and reduced support for SWAPO, and Angola promised not to support anti-Mobutu rebels.

E The Federation and Republic of Rhodesia 1953–80

E1 The Idea of Federation

The British tried in a number of cases—the West Indies, South Arabia and Malaysia—to set up federations which would be economically successful and politically stable. Only in the case of Malaysia was this successful. In Southern Africa a federation of Northern, Southern Rhodesia and Nyasaland was proposed as early as 1938. The initial reason was that the whites in Southern Rhodesia had developed rapidly in the period of dominion status. The number had grown from 35,000 in 1923 to 210,000 by 1953. These whites had an increasingly privileged position since Southern Rhodesia could pass her own laws. In particular the Land Apportionment Act (1931) gave 48 million acres of land to the whites, and left only 28 million for the blacks. Many experts on colonial matters were convinced that federation would restrain this trend towards a South African solution, and the idea was therefore backed not only by right-wingers anxious to preserve Britain's power, but by experts such as Sir Andrew Cohen, and at first the Labour Colonial Secretary, Griffiths. However, it became clear that the real effect of federation was to strengthen white power, and the inclusion of Nyasaland which had developed differently was particularly resented. In April 1952 black leaders opposed the decision, and Labour came out in opposition. Churchill had returned as Prime Minister, and during his ministry (1951–5) no British colony obtained independence. Churchill therefore backed federation, and in September 1953 the federal government came into being.

E2 The Federation Years 1953–64

In some ways federation proved a great asset to the region. Settlement continued, and by 1964 the white population had risen by a further 40,000. Economically there was much progress exemplified by the Kariba Dam, and other projects. Politically it seemed, however, that the worst fears were to be fulfilled because after 1957 the federal government was allowed to organise the constitution, and next year introduced a voting system biased against the blacks. In each part of the federation blacks began to organise their own political movements. In Nyasaland there were riots as early as

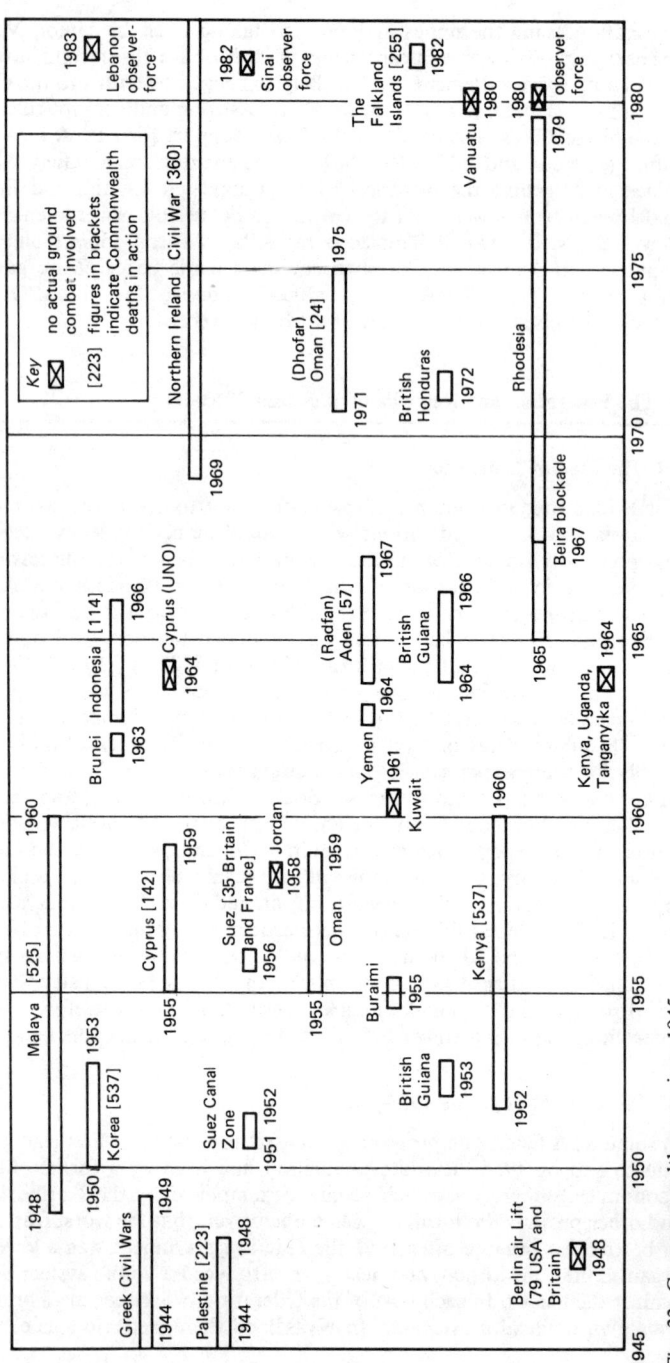

Fig. 22. Commonwealth wars since 1945

1953. In 1955 Dr Hastings Banda formed the Malawi Congress Party in exile, and in 1958 returned to the country to take charge of it. There were riots, and in 1959–60 Banda was imprisoned. The treatment of the Africans at Hola Camp was strongly condemned by the Devlin Report, and in April 1960 Banda was released by Macleod, the Colonial Secretary, who promised a new constitution for the region. In Northern Rhodesia opposition was first led by H. Nkumbula, but he was arrested and his party banned. In 1958 Kenneth Kaunda returned to the region with his Zambian Peoples' Congress Party and was immediately imprisoned. On his release in 1960 he formed a new party. In Southern Rhodesia the first group to organise was the African National Congress led by Joshua Nkomo, but although moderate the party was banned in 1959 while Nkomo was out of the country. In 1960 a second party, the National Democratic Party, was formed by Nkomo, and two other nationalist leaders, Sithole and Mugabe, and they were included in Macleod's discussions on a new constitution.

These developments showed that the federation was on weak ground since the black leaders clearly saw themselves as future leaders in the same way as Nkrumah or Nyerere, and did not envisage accepting a subordinate role in a white-dominated federal government. The whites showed an increasing tendency to move to the right. Sir Godfrey Huggins was succeeded by Sir Roy Welensky as Federal Prime Minister in October 1956. In Southern Rhodesia a new party—the Rhodesian Front—led by Winston Field won the regional elections in 1962, and both he, and his successor, Ian Smith, who became Prime Minister in April 1964, were further to the right than earlier governments and wished to preserve the federation.

E3 The Collapse of the Federation

After the report of a commission, Macleod went ahead with a new constitution in 1961 which provided for 15 Africans in a parliament of 65 elected on a separate roll with severe residential restrictions. It was envisaged that in about 20 years Africans would become the majority of voters, and the African parties rejected the constitution. There were disturbances, and the NDP was banned. In 1961 a new party—ZAPU—was created, and Nkomo went abroad to canvas support. The Rhodesian government then banned this party in 1962. This in turn led to the formation of ZANU by Sithole and Mugabe during 1963 which wanted stronger action. These developments in Southern Rhodesia convinced Macleod that the other parts of the federation must have the right to secede, and it was announced in 1962 that secession for Nyasaland was possible. Since in 1957 the British government had handed over internal constitutional matters to the federal government this soured relations between the whites and London. In April 1963 the same right to secede was given to Northern Rhodesia.

These developments had two results. The first was to strengthen the Rhodesian Front in Southern Rhodesia which in April 1964 banished the Nationalist leaders to remote parts of the country, banned their parties and increased restrictions on the Africans. Britain then insisted on Five Principles before Southern Rhodesia itself had the right to secede. The Five Principles were: unimpeded progress towards black majority rule, no amendment to the 1961 constitution of a reactionary nature, immediate improvement of black political status, progress towards eliminating racial discrimination and the acceptability of new proposals to the population as a whole. Thus, whereas Nyasaland and Northern Rhodesia were able to secede without conditions the most advanced part of the federation was shackled with conditions. Smith was furious, and a conference at Victoria Falls got nowhere. It was clear the other two partners would secede, and the Federation ceased to exist in January 1964.

E4 Independence for Malawi and Zambia

The first effect of the ending of the federation was to create two more countries. Nyasaland in July, and Northern Rhodesia in October 1964 became independent as Malawi and Zambia respectively. Malawi was led by Banda (b. 1925) who had received a medical education in America and at Edinburgh, and was regarded as a moderate figure. His establishment of diplomatic relations with South Africa and Portugal was indicative of this, but the country soon drifted towards a one party state. The Chipembere rebellion in 1965 was the excuse for a new republican constitution in 1966 with Banda as President.

Kaunda of Zambia (b. 1924) had received a missionary education, and been a headmaster before entering politics. He was influenced by Nyerere, and moved to a more radical position. Externally he opposed Rhodesia, allowed his country to provide terrorist bases, and in May 1977 declared Zambia at war with Rhodesia. Internally he favoured socialist development plans. He visited China in 1967, and agreement was reached on the building of the TanZam Railway to Dar-es-Salaam reducing Zambian dependence on Rhodesia. In 1969 he nationalised the copper industry agreeing to pay compensation, however, over 12 years. Kaunda moved towards a one party state from 1969 because of tribal differences within his party, and in 1973 completed the process.

E5 The Unilateral Declaration of Independence 1965

The break up of the Federation left Smith's Rhodesian Front Party in charge of Southern Rhodesia. African opposition had been curbed. Bordered by South Africa, and the two Portuguese colonies Smith's government was convinced it could survive. Inside the country Smith set about organising proof of support for independence and an election in May 1965 confirmed Smith in power. The British were unwilling to grant independence until the Five Principles had been accepted, and they regarded the existing government as invalid because it had broken the 1961 constitution. Smith claimed that ever since 1923 they had had internal self-government. Two visits to London yielded no change; indeed Wilson's Labour government hardened their attitude adding a sixth principle. The result was that in November 1965 Rhodesia declared herself independent.

This was a complete reversal in the process of African emancipation, and it aroused international repercussions which were to last for 15 years. The concept of a multi-racial Commonwealth was vital to Britain if she wished to retain influence in the Third World. Ghana and Tanzania broke off diplomatic relations with Britain as did six other African countries. The

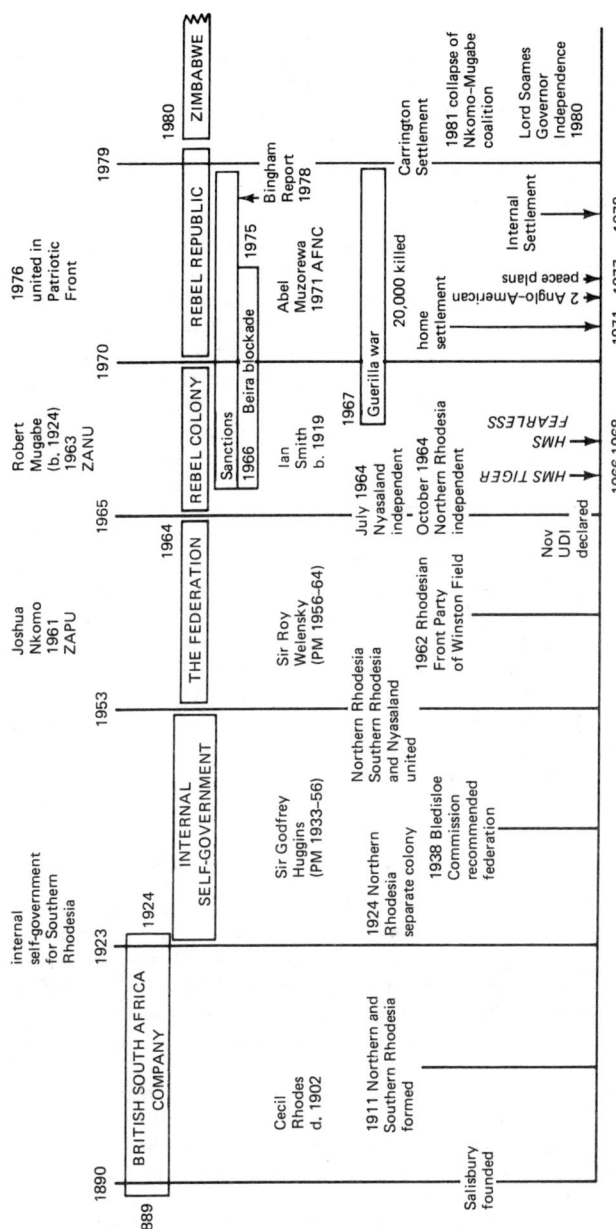

Fig. 23. The stages in the Rhodesian Crisis

United Nations demanded non-recognition, and the OAU demanded the removal by force of Smith's government. At first it seems force was considered and some planes were flown to Zambia. But Wilson faced with aggression chose the road of sanctions. Rhodesia had substantial military forces, and added to these in the early 1970s the Selous Scouts. It was clear they would not surrender; the Rhodesian question was how to bring down the government if direct force was not to be used.

E6 The Failure of Sanctions

At the Commonwealth Conference in 1966 Britain was bitterly attacked by Third World members. Action was therefore essential. Britain imposed economic sanctions, and in December 1965 an oil embargo was announced which was given full UN backing in April 1966. In fact, Rhodesia continued to receive oil through Mozambique until it was independent, and in 1978 the Bingham Report showed that the British government was aware that oil sanctions were not working, but was unable to take any action. Then in December 1966 the UN applied mandatory economic sanctions across the board in a further effort to deter Smith, but did not have a great effect. It was once again demonstrated that an aggressor cannot be brought down by purely economic measures.

Within the country the Smith government gave evidence that it was of such a nature that no modern British government could have given it independence. During 1968 the execution of five nationalists in defiance of a Privy Council ruling outraged world opinion, and using the annoyance this caused inside the country Smith got the Rhodesian Supreme Court to declare *de jure* independence. The reason for this was that he was intending after years of protesting loyalty to the British Crown to make Rhodesia a republic. During 1969 a Land Apportionment Act further reduced African land rights, and apartheid measures were introduced. A referendum of the white population was held. A new constitution was introduced in September and the formal proclamation of a Republic occurred in March 1970.

E7 Two Solutions: Peaceful Settlement or Guerilla War

During the period 1965 to 1979 British governments spent far too much time on trying to solve the problem of Rhodesia. It often distracted them from more pressing problems at home. Wilson said it was 'the most urgent problem', and 'the greatest moral issue' facing Britain in the 1960s. It gave statesmen the opportunity to move on the international stage, but in fact all attempts were doomed to failure. Wilson held two meetings with Smith on *HMS Tiger* (December 1966) and *HMS Fearless* (October 1968), but both failed. A change of government was followed by negotiations between Lord Home and Smith. Agreement was reached in 1971, but the need to ascertain if black opinion backed a settlement led to the sending of a commission to Rhodesia which reported it was not favoured by the majority of the population.

These moves cut little ice with the Africans who saw racialism in the new regime, and knew sanctions were being broken. In 1967 guerilla attacks by ZAPU and ZANU began from bases in Zambia. ZANU formed an army

(ZANLA), and a war that was to last until 1979 had begun which was to cost over 20,000 dead. To some extent the African case was damaged by their divisions. In 1971 the African National Council was formed inside the country by Abel Muzorewa and Smith believed he could use this party to obtain black approval. ZAPU and ZANU bitterly disliked this development, and in 1976 were to merge in the Patriotic Front. This was recognised by the Front Line African states (Angola, Zambia, Tanzania and Mozambique) as the rightful government of Rhodesia. From 1973 guerilla activity became stronger, and the Zambian frontier was sealed off, but with Angola and Mozambique becoming independent the war started to shift in the Africans' favour. South Africa withdrew its 'police' support in 1975, and Smith was forced to enter negotiations at last with the black leaders.

E8 The Period of International Negotiation

The British government had always insisted Rhodesia was a British colony, and their sole concern. In 1976 the Callaghan government reversed this policy, and sought to involve a wide range of people in a settlement. Inside Rhodesia Smith had opened negotiations with ZAPU, ZANU and the ANC after releasing detainees and obtaining a cease fire. However, these failed, and early in 1976 the war was renewed with terrorists now entering the country from Mozambique as well. This left the main lifeline to Rhodesia through South Africa, and was an added inducement to negotiate. Dr Kissinger, the American Secretary of State, had a series of meetings in 1976 with Vorster, the Front Line Presidents and eventually with Smith. An Anglo–American Plan was put to Smith which provided for an interim government and independence within two years. Smith conceded majority black rule which he had said would not come in a thousand years in return for the lifting of sanctions and an end to the war. A conference was held at Geneva between Smith and the three main leaders. It collapsed in December 1976, and over the next few weeks the Front Line states recognised the Patriotic Front as the rightful government.

Smith began to backtrack. Some discriminatory measures were repealed, and it was clear he sought an 'internal' settlement with Muzorewa rather than with terrorists armed with Soviet weapons, and trained by Cuba and East Germany. Elections on the old franchise were held in August 1977, and all 50 seats were won by the Rhodesian Front so that Smith could claim he had backing for an internal settlement. In September 1977 a second Anglo–American Plan was put forward with a transitional government, a UN presence and independence within a year. After much argument the Patriotic Front and the Front Line states agreed to accept this plan as a basis for negotiation. Smith then started negotiations with Muzorewa in March 1978. The internal settlement contained a guarantee of 28 per cent of the seats for the whites, but it was a major climb down by Smith. The UN rejected this settlement, sanctions were kept on, and guerilla attacks became more intense thus making elections under Smith's Settlement difficult. They were not held until April 1979, and the result was that Muzorewa became Prime Minister the following month. The trouble was that Smith was determined to keep control of the army, and police in white hands, and to keep a specific portion of political and economic power for the whites by retaining a veto in parliament so that the settlement did not conform with the Five Principles. The Patriotic Front had not been allowed to fight in the elections, and regarded them as invalid; the war continued. The Rhodesian economy was now starting to suffer badly with the disruption of agriculture over wide areas of the north east, and it was clear a settlement would have to include the guerillas.

E9 The Carrington Settlement

In the last three months of 1979 there were negotiations in London between all the parties to the dispute chaired by Lord Carrington, and they resulted in an agreement in December providing for the return of British rule for a short transitional period. During this British forces would supervise the elections while the Rhodesian Security Forces remained intact. The guerilla forces would enter the country, and be gathered at assembly points under British supervision. The constitution provided for 20 white seats to be retained even though they were only 3 per cent of the population, and these seats were all won by Smith's party in February 1980. It was agreed that the land laws should end, but an international fund was to compensate the white farmers. Lord Soames went out as Governor, and preparations were put in hand for the elections. Mugabe and Nkomo then split, partly along tribal, and to some extent along ideological lines, but the lifting of sanctions, and the presence of British troops created a favourable atmosphere for elections in March 1980. The result was that ZANU received 57 of the 80 seats, while ZAPU got only 20 seats.

The country became the Republic of Zimbabwe, and in 1982 Salisbury became Harare City. The first President was the Revd. Canaan Banana. Mugabe and Nkomo formed a coalition government, but this collapsed in 1981 with strife between the two parties, and accusations of a plot to overthrow Mugabe. The economic measures taken by the new government increased the white exodus from the country whose white population has fallen by nearly half with damaging effects on the economy. There were attacks on Nkomo's supporters in the south-west of the country, and he together with Smith and Muzorewa were subject to house arrest and removal of their passports.

Revision Questions

1. Describe the historical evolution of South Africa up to 1910 in order to show how its complicated racial structure developed.

2. Explain what is meant by: (a) Afrikaans, (b) apartheid, (c) bantustan, (d) colour bar, (e) assimilation.

3. What were Portugal's colonial policies until the early 1970s? How were the Portuguese territories freed from colonial rule?

4. In what ways was Rhodesia different from other British African colonies, and why did the attempt to federate it with Northern Rhodesia and Nyasaland fail?

5. Why did Smith's Rhodesian Rebellion arouse long term international opposition, and is this the main reason why it collapsed in 1979?

6. How did the Nationalist Party in South Africa evolve between 1914 and 1948, and what were the consequences of their election victory that year?

7. What were the main features of apartheid as it had evolved by 1964? In what ways, if any, has it been modified in the last 10 years?

8. How effective or useful is opposition to apartheid: (a) inside, (b) outside South Africa?

9. Write notes on the following organisations: (a) MPLA, (b) UNITA, (c) Frelimo, (d) SWAPO, (e) ZANU, (f) ZAPU.

Further Reading

Brookes, E., *Apartheid*, Routledge and Kegan Paul, London, 1968.

Bunting, B., *The Rise of the South African Reich*, Penguin, Harmondsworth, 1964.

Hatch, J., *A History of Post War Africa*, Andre Deutsch, London, 1965.

Martin, D. and Johnson, P., *The Struggle for Zimbabwe*, Faber and Faber, London, 1981.

Oliver, R. and Fage, J. D., *A Short History of Africa*, Penguin, Harmondsworth, 1962.

Segal, R., *The Race War*, Jonathan Cape, London, 1966, chapter 2.

Troup, F., *South Africa; an Historical Introduction*, Eyre Methuen, London, 1972.

12
The Hispanic World of Latin America and the Caribbean

A Introduction: the Latin American Revolution and its Consequences

A1 Colonialism in the New World

It is easy to forget that the first part of the world to experience and to reject European rule was the American Hemisphere. Canada was originally established by the French, passed into British hands in 1763, secured dominion status in 1867, and full independence in 1931. Alaska was occupied by Russia in 1741, and bought by the United States in 1867. Greenland was a Danish colony until it was given self-government in 1978. The area covered by the United States was occupied by a wide variety of colonial powers—England took the Thirteen Colonies on the Eastern Seaboard, and it was this area that rebelled in 1774, and became the United States in 1776. Louisiana was bought from France in 1803, and Florida secured from Spain in 1819. Oregon was seized in 1846. From Mexico vast areas of territory were taken. Texas was first a republic, then joined America in 1844. The same applied to California, first a republic in 1846, and then forming part of a massive annexation of territory in 1848 from Mexico.

The West Indies were all originally seized by Spain, and it was not until 1898 that they were forced out of Cuba and Puerto Rico. But long before then Spanish power had declined, and other nations had secured many of the islands. The British were the main colonial force in this region until 1962, but the French and Dutch also had islands. Besides Cuba (1511) the main Spanish islands were Puerto Rico and Hispaniola divided into Haiti and San Domingo. Central America was a Spanish possession. Mexico was conquered in 1518–22 and together with the whole of Central America formed the Viceroyalty of New Spain. In South America Peru was conquered in 1531–33, and Argentina in 1580, and Spanish America was divided into the three viceroyalties of New Granada, Peru and La Plata. The Portuguese secured Brazil in 1500 appointing their first governor in 1549, and in 1777 the control of Brazil over a large part of the interior was recognised by Spain.

A2 The Fate of the Indians

The securing of the American hemisphere by the Western nations involved a lengthy and ruthless struggle with the original inhabitants who numbered about 30 million. This struggle was the most devastating racial conflict there has ever been. In the West Indies nearly all the original Arawaks and Caribs were exterminated. In Canada there were fewer Indians, but it was only in 1885 that the last revolt of the Metis occurred. The saga of the American Wild West is well known. The struggle with the Indian tribes which began in New England in the days of the Puritans continued until the defeat of Geronimo in 1886, and the Battle of Wounded Knee in 1890. That year the frontier was officially abolished as a geographical point, and the takeover of the continent was complete. A reservation or apartheid policy was adopted in 1871.

In Central and South America the conquistadores carried out a lengthy series of wars to destroy the Aztecs, Incas and many other tribes (Guatemala 1523–42, Chile 1540–58), but did not of course completely succeed. Native Indians remained, and intermarried with the whites (mestizos) or black slaves (zambos). The Indians were enslaved, but proved less effective workers so that by the 1720s Indian slavery had been replaced by peonage a system which deprived the rural workers of all their rights and reduced them to the status of feudal peasants. The Indians did not submit. There were minor Inca Wars in 1571 and 1780 for example. The Araucanians in Chile resisted for many years, and the Indian Wars in the Argentine did not end until 1879.

A3 The Scourge of Slavery

To replace the indigenous population slavery was introduced into the American hemisphere, and was a prominent feature of life until its end in Cuba (1886), and Brazil (1888). America became, as one writer has said, a huge slave pen. The first slaves were brought to San Domingo in 1502, and to Brazil in 1539. All the European nations engaged in the slave trade but it was the Spanish and British who profited the most from the asiento (right to transport slaves). It is impossible to calculate the total involved, but a conservative estimate is of 15 million in the period to 1850, and some have put it as high as 30 million. If one remembers the large number of deaths involved in Africa and on board the slavers it would be fair to at least double the number, and such a transference of population had profound effects. It weakened the civilisations of West Africa. It took Black Nationalism to the American Hemisphere. It created the world's largest racial problem.

In Central and South America intermarriage of blacks with Indians and whites were not uncommon, and as a result many of mixed race exist. But in the USA segregation was practised from the first, and laid the basis for one of America's most serious modern problems. Slavery was comparatively small in the 1770s (462,000), but the invention of the cotton gin (1793), and the import of sugar from Brazil (1794) opened up a vast increase in slavery. By 1860 there were 4 million slaves. Today one in nine of America's citizens are black. Slavery was rarely the idyllic existence portrayed in *Gone With the Wind*, and the slave period contained endless revolts against white supremacy. In the United States there were over 250 such revolts. In the British West Indies there were risings in many islands, and in Cuba there were slave wars in 1812 and the 1860s. American slavery has left behind it deep resentment, and strong black nationalist feelings which cannot forget that before abolishing slavery the white man profited from it.

A4 Colonial Society and Exploitation

The European exploitation of America was flagrant and widespread. In many cases it was distinctly feudal. Land came into the possession of a small number of owners like the 13 capitanias in Brazil, the eight court favourites granted Carolina, or the 375 seigneurs in Quebec. For 300 years great estates dominated the economy of Latin America. They were farmed with outdated methods, and by depressed populations of peons. The other major feature of exploitation was the mining of gold, silver and diamonds often extracted by forced labour like the mita system used in the Potosi Mines after 1572. It has been estimated that 6 billion dollars' worth of precious metals were removed from the Continent, and very little of the profit returned to the people—hence there was little industry, and grinding poverty existing side by side with ostentatious wealth. The power of the Europeans and criollos (native born whites later known as creoles) was preserved by political deception, ruthless violence, planned illiteracy and the benumbing religion of the Roman Church. The Inquisition arrived in South America in 1569, and over a hundred perished at the stake before it was removed. The Jesuit missions did play a part in opening up many areas, but they too accepted an exploitive role. In 1767 in Chile the Jesuits owned 50 haciendas and over 300 slaves.

A5 The American Revolution

In the context of European history it has long been fashionable to speak of an Atlantic Revolution owing much to the ideas of the Englightenment, but it is equally true that there was an American Revolution which was the greatest upheaval against European control until after 1945. In Canada the British contained it by passing acts in 1774 and 1793, but there were risings later in 1837. The United States was created by the American War of Independence (1776–83), and the links forged with France by men like Jefferson and Lafayette played some part in stimulating the French Revolution. This in turn stimulated the first black uprising against the European powers led by Touissant L'Ouverture in Haiti in 1791 which liberated the slaves there, and for a time placed him in power. The colonial powers (Britain, France and Spain) all made efforts to subdue him which failed, and in the end Napoleon resorted to treachery to have him captured. But the revolt went on, and he was succeeded by Jacques I and Henri I. An attempt by Spain to recapture part of the island (Santo Domingo) was defeated in 1822. The last king of Haiti was Fustin I, and it then became a republic. Santo Domingo split away in 1844, and became independent by 1865. The Spanish retained control of Cuba and Puerto Rico although there were serious revolts in both.

A6 The Hispanic Revolution

As in 1945 so in 1810 it was the weakness of Europe brought about by prolonged war that gave the colonial peoples their chance. The South

American Revolution was essentially led by the middle class Criollos (Creoles) who resented their exclusion from government office by the Peninsulars or Europeans. Only 4 of the 170 Viceroys appointed were not from the home countries, for example. It was essentially an attack on the feudal power of Spain and Portugal, and their restrictions on the economy and political life of the better educated South Americans. Trouble began with the arrival of De Miranda, a veteran of Washington's army who had fought in France, and attempted to start revolts in Venezuela and Montevideo. Then in 1810 revolt burst forth in every part of the hemisphere led by Simon Bolivar (1783–1830), Jose De San Martin and Bernardo O'Higgins. By 1820 Mexico was independent, and the next year the United Provinces of Central America marked the freeing of that area.

Further south Bolivar aided with 7 ships and 200 men from Haiti began his campaigns in 1814, and he was later helped by European mercenaries. In three great battles he established three independent Andean states— Boyaca (1819), Colombia; Carabobo (1821), Venezuela; and Pichincha (1822), Ecuador—and for a time tried to keep these united in Gran Colombia. San Martin started the struggle for Argentine independence in 1810, and completed it in 1816. He crossed the Andes, and freed Chile at the Battle of Chacabuco (1817). In 1822 the two leaders met, and in 1824 the Battle of Ayachucho secured independence for Peru and Bolivia.

Two other countries—Paraguay (1811) and Uruguay (1825)—also secured independence because of the disputes between the new countries. Lastly Brazil revolted in 1822, but decided to keep the Portuguese royal family in the person of Pedro I who became emperor. The Empire became a republic in 1889.

B The Neo-Colonial Era in Hispanic America

B1 The Pattern of Colonial Revolt

There are strong similarities between the pattern of events in Hispanic America in the first part of the nineteenth century and events in Asia and Africa in the second half of the twentieth century. First came the weakening of the colonial power, then nationalist uprisings resulting in the creation of a large number of small, economically backward states. At first some of these states opted for monarchy including Mexico, Haiti and Brazil, but monarchies were soon replaced with republics. Constitutions were drawn up on democratic lines, but these did not survive long for the cost of aggressive wars, the state of the economy and political immaturity soon modified them. Prior to 1914 125 such constitutions were drawn up in the Hispanic Hemisphere, and few were maintained. Political inexperience led to bewildering changes of government—Bolivia had 60 governments in 74 years and Venezuela 50 in 70 years—and from this instability grew dictatorship sometimes by the landowners backed by the church, and quite frequently by the military. This form of government was known as caudilloism.

The new states were fervently nationalist, and sought to extend their borders in savage wars. Among these were wars between Argentina, Brazil and Uruguay (1825–8), Brazil, Argentina, Uruguay and Paraguay (1864–70),

Chile and Peru and Bolivia (1879–81). Paraguay lost half its territory and its population fell from 1.3 million to 220,000 during its wars. Endless border disputes prevented any success at bringing the new states together, although efforts were made. There were the United Provinces of Central America (1823–38), and the Republic of Gran Colombia (1819–32). At the Congress of Panama in 1826 four treaties were signed by the new countries including provision for a joint army, but such policies failed. The new countries were subject to attempts by former colonial powers to re-establish themselves, and finally to American Imperialism and European economic exploitation or neo-colonialism. The result was the area remained an underdeveloped region.

B2 Manifest Destiny and Pan Americanism

America issued the Monroe Doctrine in 1823 in theory to protect the new countries from further European interference, but there is much evidence that this was very little observed. The seizure by Britain of the Falkland Islands (1833) and British Honduras (1860), or the Spanish occupation of Santo Domingo (1861) did not meet with protests. The European powers blockaded Argentina in 1845, and Venezuela in 1902. Moreover, from the first America herself became a colonialist nation. 'Manifest Destiny' was the name for the theory that it was America's destiny to run the whole hemisphere, and the southern states particularly wished to extend American power over Hispanic America. Walker tried to seize Nicaragua (1855) and Honduras (1860) before he was shot. In many ways the Pan American Movement was an extension of this imperialist feeling; a belief that the whole hemisphere was America's to develop (or exploit).

The first congress was held in 1889 attended by 14 states, and thereafter American involvement in the area steadily increased. Although this sometimes took the form of standing up to the European powers this was done in America's interests. American capitalism needed the markets as its investments abroad rose. The growth of the American navy and army reflected increasing security fears. Pride in American civilisation led to a belief that it should be spread for the benefit of others. In the Pacific this new expansionism was marked by the acquiring of Samoa in 1889, and its consolidation in 1899, and by the annexation of Midway (1867), Guam and Hawaii in 1898, and Wake in 1899. In South America its effects were widespread, and left America with a colonial empire she has not yet renounced.

B3 American Imperialism

In 1898 America went to war with Spain, and at the ensuing peace treaty obtained an empire. In the Far East she took the Philippines, and in the Caribbean—Cuba and Puerto Rico. Cuba was given independence, but the Platt Amendment (1901) left America with control over foreign policy. Puerto Rico became an American territory, and remains so today. The impending construction of a Panama Canal led to the next action. Colombia was offered terms for its construction, and when she rejected them rebellion was stirred up in Panama, America intervened, and the Canal Zone passed into American control in 1903. That year the Roosevelt Corollary to the

Monroe Doctrine boldly stated that 'chronic wrongdoing' would mean American intervention—not only for the good of the people, but also to protect American investments. There followed a period of flagrant colonialism. Santo Domingo was brought under control in 1905–7, and occupied from 1916 to 1924. Haiti was offered protection, refused, and was occupied from 1915 to 1934. The Virgin Islands were bought in 1917. In Mexico when Wilson disapproved of the government there direct intervention occurred in 1914, and again in 1916. In Central America Nicaragua was under virtual American control from 1912 to 1933, and America intervened in Honduras (1911 and 1924), and Guatemala (1920). America in fact acted militarily on some 30 occasions in the Hispanic Hemisphere, and by the 1920s eleven out of the 20 republics were subject to American financial control. The extent of former American Imperialism needs to be remembered now that South America is seeking genuine independence—it naturally causes the gravest suspicion of America's intentions.

B4 Economic Exploitation and Extreme Poverty

The basic difficulty of the new American republics was the survival of the old governing class. In all the states there was a landed aristocracy as proud and cruel as any ever seen in Europe. Since 90 per cent of the economies of all countries except Argentina were rural their power dictated the development rate of the nations concerned. Their haciendas, worked by peons, were farmed by traditional methods because there was plenty of surplus labour. Industry was discouraged. Slavery was only slowly abolished—in the mainland states starting with Chile in 1811, and finishing with Brazil in 1888. The British (1838) and Dutch (1863) colonies were freed, and in the West Indies, Puerto Rico (1873) and Cuba (1886) abandoned slavery, but peonage, discrimination against the Indians and the class system secured effective bondage for the masses. In the West Indies widespread poverty followed the decline of the sugar industry in the British colonies. But the backward nature of the area was eminently suitable for foreign exploitation.

During the nineteenth century Britain took the lead in investment, and overseas groups of British expatriates were established in countries like Peru and Argentina where the banks and railways were run by multi-national companies. British investment rose from 27 million dollars in 1878 to its peak of one billion dollars in 1928. Britain was emulated by America who had only 173 million dollars invested in 1913, but by 1945 had replaced Britain and Germany and had five billion invested. The profits went outside the countries concerned, and in order to secure their lucrative positions Britain, America and Germany gave backing to the 'stable' regimes of the caudillos. There were booms in nitrates (1880–1919), frozen meat, railways and rubber, and in 1914 the discovery of oil in Venezuela marked a new era of exploitation. South America became part of an 'invisible' Anglo–Saxon empire. The three leading exports from each of the twenty republics were foodstuffs or raw materials, and inevitably such one crop economies were affected by world prices in an alarming way. In Central America 74 per cent of Panama's and 59 per cent of Honduras' exports were bananas; 87 per cent of El Salvador's and 61 per cent of Guatemala's were coffee. The companies that owned real estate or marketed the produce had great influence in the states concerned, such as the United Fruit company in Central America or the American Sugar Company in Cuba.

B5 The Mexican Revolution

Mexico was a classic example of neo-colonialism and oppression by caudillo-ism. From 1876 to 1911 it was ruled by Porfirio Diaz (1830–1915). Although the church had been disestablished in 1857 it retained complete control over education, and 60 per cent of Mexicans were illiterate in 1910. Indian and communal (ejidos) land was given to the hacienderos, and one per cent of the people owned 85 per cent of the land. The outdated system of agriculture meant that only 7.4 per cent of Mexico was cultivated arable land, and as a result there was great poverty with the second highest death rate then recorded in the world. Diaz had granted extensive rights to foreign companies to develop railways, mines and oil. In May 1911 the Mexican Revolution began which was as important to the development of political liberty, economic change and human rights in the American hemisphere as the Chinese Revolution of the same year was in the East. The removal of Diaz led to a series of bandit leaders and adventurers seeking to take over the country after the initial leader Madero was shot in 1913. The government was in the hands of Carranza (1914–20) who was opposed by Huerta, Villa and Obregon, but in 1917 a new constitution was introduced giving one man one vote, removing church control, starting the break up of the great estates, initiating labour reforms and attempting to curb foreign owner-ship of national assets. In 1918 the CFL was formed as the first effective Latin American labour movement, and this was followed by a more radical labour organisation, and the formation of a Communist Party in 1919. Then in 1920 reaction set in. Carranza was killed, and for a time the pace of change slackened. But Mexico became a focus for left wing hopes in the Continent, and in the 1930s the revolution was to be renewed. In the end the control of the landlords, church and foreign investors were to be salient features of other reforming governments' work.

C The Era of the Good Neighbour and the Impact of the Second World War

C1 Caudilloism in Latin America

During the inter-war period much of Latin America remained, or fell tempor-arily under the control of caudillos. The landowners, church and military largely retained their powers, and even the limited social reforms were often introduced by authoritarian regimes. Territorial disputes continued. Chile and Peru quarrelled over Tacna and Arica from 1921 to 1929. Peru and Colombia disputed Leticia from 1932 to 1935, and Peru and Colombia quarrelled over the upper reaches of the Amazon. From 1928 to 1939 Bolivia and Paraguay disputed the Gran Chaco, and all these disputes enhanced the role of the military in the states concerned. Foreign exploitation con-tinued with America increasingly playing the major role. In 1914 no American banks had branches in South America; by 1921 50 had branches, and American investment rose rapidly. American companies came to have controlling interests in several economies. The United Fruit Company owned 4 million acres of Central America, and the American Sugar Company 6 million acres of Cuba. The Standard Oil Company had great power in Bolivia, and Ford in Brazil. A country like Peru ruled by dictators such as Leguia (1919–30) and Benavides (1933–9) was virtually in the hands of foreigners. Eighty per cent of her oil was in foreign hands. British companies ran the railways, and Italians ran the banks. In Venezuela the start of oil production in 1918 enabled Juan Gomez to maintain his caudilloism from 1909 to 1935. There was some economic progress, but little could be said for a regime that hung its opponents from meat hooks. Getulio Vargas (1883–1954), dictator of Brazil from 1930 to 1945, and from 1951 to his suicide in 1954, was perhaps the most remarkable of the caudillos. He established a fascist corporate state—the Estado Nuovo—in 1933, and succeeded in restoring the economy after the disastrous collapse of the world coffee market.

In Central America the drift to dictatorship was even more marked. Cuba was ruled by Machado (1925–33) and Batista, either behind the scenes or in power from 1933 to 1959. In Dominica Trujillo, again either in office or behind the scenes, ruled from 1930 to 1938, and 1942 to 1952. In Nicaragua the first of the Somozas ruled from 1937 to 1947; in Guatemala, Ubico (1931–44); and in El Salvador, Martinez (1932–9) were ruthless dictators, and backed American business interests. Puerto Rico remained under American rule, and revolts in 1937, and 1950 were swiftly put down.

C2 The Growth of Radical Opposition

The same inter-war period saw the rise of opposition within the dictatorships, and even of regimes which set an alternative before the poverty stricken masses of the hemisphere. Four Latin American countries experienced considerable economic and social progress. In Mexico it seemed for a time as if the revolution would fail in the face of right wing opposition led by the Cristeros, but reform continued. Under Calles (1924–8) the remaining powers of the church were removed, and major labour reforms including a minimum wage, the right to strike and the eight hour day were introduced. But it was Cardenas (1934–40) and Camacho (1940–46) who effectively completed the first stage of the Mexican Revolution. Forty-five million acres of hacienderos land was handed to the peons. A six year plan began state development of industry. The government took over the railways (1937) and the oil companies (1938), refusing compensation or arbitration. The CTM founded by Toledano in 1936 was a more leftish trade union organisation, and pressed for further change. Mexico sent volunteers to Spain to fight against Franco, gave asylum to Trotsky and seized all Axis property during the war. Uruguay had a fairly consistent record of social reform from the time of Battle Y Ordonez (1911–15). Universal education, one man one vote, a welfare state and control of foreign investment were features of the reforms. In Paraguay Moringo's government after 1940 introduced a similar series of changes. In Chile, Alessandri (1932–8) initiated reforms, and in December 1938 a popular front government of Socialists and Communists took office under Cerda, then Rios and finally Videla carrying out major reforms.

But foreign domination and political dictatorship remained in spite of reform, and there were also signs of a more radical challenge to the state of affairs. In Nicaragua a guerilla movement led by Sandino lasted until 1934. In Peru the Aprista movement led by Victor de la Torre provided a radical challenge demanding a commune system of reform for the Indian peasants. In Brazil Luiz Prestes, the founder of the Communist Party in 1921, launched guerilla war against the government in 1924. In over 56 clashes with government troops Prestes with Indian backing set up 'shadow' states in the interior. Forced out, he returned after time spent in Moscow, and in 1935 was arrested after Communist risings occurred in Pernambuco and Rio. He was imprisoned from then until 1946, but the Communist Party secured 10 per cent of the votes, and made gains until it was banned in 1947. The development of small Communist and trade union movements led to violent clashes between the dictators and the workers. In January 1919 Semana Tragica in Buenos Aires led to 1,500 deaths. Strikes in Chile (1925) with 3,000 deaths, Colombia (1928) with 1,500 deaths, or Bolivia (1942) with 400 killed showed that severe repression was still prevalent. Peasants who opposed dictators received short shrift. Both Machado and Trujillo killed 10,000 in their first year of office.

C3 The Appeal of Fascism

All three Fascist powers were able to call upon considerable support in South America. Germany had large numbers of fellow citizens including 250,000 in Argentina and 830,000 in Brazil, her investments were large and her influence through companies like Air Condor considerable. Italy had close contacts with Brazil through the LATI airline, and Spain established a Hispanidad Council to spread Falange influence in the area. Fascism appealed because of its radical–dictatorial answer to economic problems, and the open sympathy of the Roman Catholic Church in Europe and Latin America. It traded on dislike of American and British (gringo) influence. South America witnessed a number of attempts at fascist takeovers. In Mexico in 1938 the Cedillo conspiracy was defeated. The same year the Integralistas in Brazil, and the Nacistas in Chile were defeated in more serious armed uprisings. When in 1940 Uruguay faced a fascist coup America sent two warships to help in its suppression. No overtly fascist government came to power, but rulers like Busch in Bolivia, Vargas in Brazil, and later Peron in Argentina came very close to being fascist dictators. This threat increased American involvement during the war years, and stimulated left wing efforts to end regimes that might incline to fascism.

C4 The Good Neighbour Policy

America's flagrant imperialism was modified during the 1920s. The Roosevelt Corollary was repudiated in 1928, for example, when America ran into criticism. Her troops were withdrawn from all Latin American countries except Puerto Rico by 1934, and in cases like Mexico's seizure of assets in 1938 no direct action was taken. In 1933 Roosevelt used the phrase 'the policy of the good neighbour', and the Platt Amendment affecting Cuba was repealed. The Americans put into action a policy of non-intervention in military terms. It was designed to promote American interest in the recovering economies, and later in hemisphere defence. It did not mean American support for democracy as the arrival of Somoza in Washington in 1939 indicated, but it did lead to a less dictatorial attitude in foreign policy. Roosevelt himself attended a meeting at Rio in 1936 which supported neutrality, and direct consultation on matters like debt collection. At Lima in 1938 all 21 states accepted that consultation on foreign intervention should take place. Next year a Neutrality Committee was established, and in 1940 at Havana defence co-operation under the stress of coming war and fifth column activity was greatly increased. America announced she would cooperate in 'crushing all activities that arise from non-American sources'.

C5 The Second World War and Hemisphere Defence

South America played an important part in the Second World War not least because she supplied high percentages of vital raw materials including 100 per cent of balsa wood and kapok, 90 per cent of copper, 56 per cent of tin and 43 per cent of rubber. Nearly half of America's overseas purchase of war materials came from Latin America. In return America gave 262 million dollars of Lend Lease to South America. America encouraged Latin American governments to expropriate Axis companies, and replaced them herself. Thus, Pan American Airways expanded enormously during the war years. Taking advantage of European involvement in the war America built up a commanding economic position on the continent during the war years. Through the Inter-American Defence Board and reciprocal treaties like those with Mexico and Brazil, America came to advise and supply many Latin countries with defence advisors and equipment, and to obtain facilities and bases. Sixteen American defence missions were stationed in the continent by 1945. Through the Office for the Co-ordination of Commercial and Cultural Relations under Nelson Rockefeller advice on economic and social matters was also given. Latin America became a solid pro-American bloc in the new United Nations, and a system designed to repel fascism was soon turned against Communism.

South America was more directly involved in the Second World War than is often realised. Eleven countries declared war on the Axis, the one major exception being Argentina. Brazil sent 50,000 troops to Italy. Puerto Rico supplied 60,000 to America, and the Mexican Airforce was operational in the Philippines. At the end of the war America feared the loss of her new investments and the spread of Communism, so at Chapultepec in 1945 she pledged herself to massive economic involvement, and later the Clayton Plan spelt this out in more detail. At the same time America seemed to be committing herself to widespread military involvement, and support for right wing regimes as long as they adopted an anti-Communist line.

D Dictators and Guerillas in Modern Latin America

D1 The Organisation of American States (OAS)

A massive increase in American power and economic influence brought about under Roosevelt was at once turned against Communism in the Latin American Hemisphere, and for 20 years American policy was directed at maintaining her interests in the area. She acted like the imperial power she had become. Just as Russian security demanded control of Eastern Europe so America, it was maintained, demanded the same in Latin America. This power was wielded by economic means: by the direct involvement of American companies, and by channelling aid to 'politically acceptable' countries. The post-war period saw, for instance, the completion of the Pan American Highway from Fairbanks to Buenos Aires, and the spread of Pan American Airways (of which General Marshall was a director). In 1947 the Treaty of Rio created a hemisphere defence zone, and provided for mutual assistance. In April 1948 and October 1951 OAS and OCAS were set up to formalise these arrangements. There was to be a five yearly conference, and a conference of foreign ministers while continuity was maintained by the Council. These organisations replaced the Pan American ones, and absorbed various technical, health and information services. America provided military hardware and personnel to help many Latin American countries, and turned a blind eye to the repression adopted by many pro-capitalist, anti-Communist governments. At Santiago in August 1959 such regimes were condemned, but equally so were any attempts to destroy them by force. What America was interested in was solidarity against Communism. In March 1954 Communist states were excluded from the benefits of OAS. In 1960 and 1963 at San Jose Communism was condemned. During this time Communist Cuba had appeared, and America sought to use the OAS against the Castro regime. Latin American countries threatened with guerilla activity willingly agreed, and in July 1964, with Mexico and Jamaica dissenting, sanctions and diplomatic non-recognition were imposed on Cuba. This was maintained until 1972 when left wing regimes in Guyana and Jamaica broke the boycott.

Kennedy saw the need to emphasise the economic aspect of the OAS. In 1960 at Bogota 19 countries discussed foreign aid, and in August 1961 the Treaty of Punta del Este established the 'Alliance for Progress' aiming to channel 20 billion dollars over ten years into the area. The OAS did play some part in maintaining peace in the area although in a way this involved backing America's view of what constituted peace. In 1954 the OAS backed American intervention in Guatemala. In 1960 the OAS asked for American naval patrols off Nicaragua and Guatemala because of trouble. They provided a force in Dominica after the initial invasion in 1965 by America. In 1969 they persuaded Honduras and San Salvador to end a small war that had started. During the 1970s America seemed to loose interest in the structure of the OAS, and Carter did damage by criticising military dictators who had just overcome the serious urban guerilla problem. The result was that Cuban involvement over a wide area increased, and it was only in 1982 with Reagan's proposals for Central American aid that America seemed to be trying to regain some of her former dominance.

D2 American Imperialism Continues

In 1940 Britain and America reached agreement on an arms–for–bases deal which gave America base facilities in eight areas—Trinidad, Jamaica, British Guiana, Antigua, St Lucia, the Bahamas, Bermuda and Newfoundland—and this was confirmed in March 1941. By 1945 it was America not Britain which had the main military presence in the Caribbean even if Britain was still to use military force there on a number of occasions. Puerto Rico stayed American. Visiting the island in the 1940s a distinguished American reporter remarked that he found 'misery, disease, squalor, filth ... among people whom the United States has governed since 1898'. The island was ruled under a law made in 1917, and America had encountered opposition—there was a rising in 1937 for example, and the nationalist leader, Pedro Campos, was imprisoned. In 1950 Puerto Rico was transferred to the new Office for Territories, and there was a further rising. Two Puerto Ricans, Callazo and Torresola, tried to assassinate Truman in November 1950. In 1952 the island was given internal self-government like a British dominion, and this status was confirmed by a referendum in 1967.

It was the Dominican Republic that provided clear evidence of American determination to control the area. In 1961 Trujillo, the dictator, was killed, and later in the year his relatives fled the country. A demonstration of strength by the American navy took place, and they played safe by accepting a right of centre ruler, Balaguer. With American prompting OAS sanctions were lifted, and elections were held in 1962. The result was a surprising victory for Bosch and his CPD party—Bosch had started in politics in Cuba in 1939. His attempt to redistribute land led to a rising by the military under General Wessin, and Bosch fled in 1963. Dominican politics then collapsed into a conflict between Balaguer's right-centrists, the military and Bosch's former supporters. In April 1965 some of the military asked America to intervene, and since Johnson was already contemplating this 20,000 Marines moved swiftly into the country. There was some fighting with perhaps a thousand dead, and the Americans were soon supplemented by an OAS force. The Americans sought to create a government which would exclude Bosch who returned in September 1965, and after several people had held office elections in June 1966 confirmed Balaguer in power.

Panama had been under virtual American control since 1903 (see section 12B3). America's position there had been recognised by Colombia (1921) and regulated by treaty in 1926, when an appeal by Panama to the League on the question of sovereignty over the Canal was ignored. As early as 1961 Panama demanded revision of the treaty, but the existence of a hostile Cuba made America reluctant to act. In 1964 riots started, and after a break-down of relations the OAS was asked to intervene, and a 17 member council was set up to arbitrate. This achieved nothing, and resentment grew against the existing government until in 1969 Colonel Pinilla established a military dictatorship which denounced the treaty next year. Eventually in 1978 Carter signed a treaty by which America agreed to withdraw completely by the year 2000, and ended all restrictions on Panama's sovereignty.

Elsewhere in Central America the United States began to lose her influence. This is well illustrated by the difference between events in Guatemala in 1954, and recent events in Nicaragua and El Salvador (see section 12G1 and 12G2). Guatemala was ruled by an increasingly left wing government under Jacobo and Arbenz who had replaced the dictator, Ubico, and carried out several reforms. Inevitably these reforms came to the question of land owned by the United Fruit Company, and in February 1954 it was expropriated. Guatemala left the OAS, and secured arms from East Germany. America then armed guerillas in Nicaragua, and the CIA gave advice to Colonel Castillo. In June the country was invaded, and Arbenz deposed. His appeal to the Security Council was ignored. The new government proceeded to arrest leading Communists, and Castillo remained in power until his assassination in 1957. When it seemed likely that a subsequent government might lean to Socialism a second military coup took place in 1963, and the country passed into the hands of Peralta and continuing military dictatorship.

D3 Argentina and Juan Peron (1895–1974)

Argentina was in several ways an exception to the pattern of Latin American development. A majority of the country were urbanised by 1945. Her economy was less under American control. Between 1916 and 1922 the country underwent considerable reform, and it was not until 1936 that the effects of the depression led to right wing government. Argentina maintained good relations with the Axis powers. She proposed the expulsion of Russia from the League of Nations for invading Finland in 1939. Her wartime government was lax in curbing fascists, and it was only in 1944 when an Axis plot to overthrow the government came to light that she at last changed sides. It was in these circumstances that in June 1943 a putsch placed a right wing government in power of which Juan Peron was a member. America was opposed to him, and in October 1945 even supported a coup to oust him because Argentina was friendly to Franco, and bitterly opposed by Russia in UNO. However, Peron won the presidential election in early 1946, and initiated a period of personal dictatorship the next year.

Peronism was essentially the recreation of Mussolini's or Vargas' corporate state. On the one hand the government was a dictatorship; on the other reforms were carried out to benefit workers. Peron had great popularity as did his second wife, Evita (1922–52). Industries were nationalised under a government body called IAPI including British controlled banks and railways. Then followed a five year plan while in agriculture there was land reform. By 1954 labour relations were controlled through corporate organisations and compulsory arbitration. Peron's regime rested however on right wing backing, and when his reforms embraced the church his regime soon toppled. In 1955 Peron proposed to end church exemption from taxes, and church control over education, and this was followed by riots. In June Pope Pius XII excommunicated Peron, and military risings occurred followed by Peron's departure. He tried to return in 1964, and did return in 1973 after years of military rule, urban guerillas and economic chaos had damaged the country; but he died next year. An attempt by his wife, Isabelita (b.1930) to carry on failed after two years, and in 1976 the country reverted to military rule under Generals Videla, Viola, Galtieri and Bignone. After the Falklands War (see section 13G4) the generals were forced out, and late in 1983 democratic elections returned Dr Raul Alfonsin's Radicals (318 seats) in a contest with the Peronists (258 seats).

D4 Military Juntas, and Urban Guerillas

For a short period during the war democracy and social reform, with Roosevelt's backing, did seem to be making headway in several Latin countries including Chile with a Popular Front government, the work of Arias in Panama and several other examples. But the Communist threat, and its exaggeration soon proved too much for the landlords, churchmen, military and profiteers of multi-national companies that retained so much power in the hemisphere. The trend in Latin America as in Africa has since been towards military putsch and junta. The three largest powers all had military dictatorships—Brazil since 1966, Chile since 1973 and Argentina until 1983. Other South American states except Colombia, Bolivia and Venezuela are under dictators. Resistance to this movement has been widespread, continuous and largely ineffective.

The first period of resistance is that associated with Che Guevara (1928–67). Guevara originally came from Argentina, moved to Guatemala, and ended in Castro's Cuba where he was one of the strongest supporters of the swing to full blooded marxism. Guevara wished to see the Cuban revolution as a spearhead for risings elsewhere, but his work *Guerilla Warfare* was in some ways similar to Mao's; he advocated rural terrorism. Unfortunately, he argued, traditional Communism had been too soft and slow in Latin America, and action had to come with small forces. The rural guerilla movement thus lacked effective backup. Attempts at rural uprisings were defeated in Venezuela (1965–8), Colombia (1964) and Peru (1961–3). Guevara after a period in the Congo went to Bolivia to oppose the new military junta that seized power in 1964, and was killed in October 1967.

But by this time the international terrorist network was being organised on new lines. Conferences brought experts from Europe to Latin America, and sent Latin Americans to Russia, and Arab countries for training. A more sophisticated urban guerilla movement emerged owing much to the work of men like Carlos Marighella in Brazil with his *Handbook of Urban Guerilla Warfare*, and Regis Debre in Bolivia with his *Strategy for Revolution*. The new concept urged that the country was too primitive and did not afford cover while towns could enable quite small numbers to disrupt civilian life. Closeness to the centre of government would compel a strong reaction, and this right backlash would be indiscriminate thus increasing their support. The aim was to 'destabilise' government, and seize power. No longer was it mass revolution, but small groups (focos) who would take the lead.

This wave was directed at all existing governments not just military regimes. In Uruguay there had been democratic government and major social reforms; yet it was there that the Tupamaros under Raoul Sendic organised a campaign between 1968 and 1972 which led to a military regime under General Bordaberry, and the ruthless suppression of much more than just the Tupamaros. In Argentina Peron and Isabelita encountered opposition from the ERP under Santucho which led in 1976 to military rule. In Brazil ALN fomented riots in Rio and Sao Paulo in 1968–9 which led to the deposition of the existing military ruler, and his replacement by a stricter regime in 1970. Colombia witnessed a fresh outbreak of terrorism led by Camilo Torres between 1965 and 1968, Venezuela was menaced for a time by the FALN suppressed by 1969, while Peru experienced trouble from the MIR led by de la Puente and Lobaton which was also suppressed, the country passing under military rule in 1968. By provoking right wing reaction the guerillas achieved one of their ends, but by doing so they set back democracy. There were far more democratic states in Latin America in 1945 than in 1980, and it is difficult to see what the two guerilla waves achieved. In only one country—Nicaragua—were they successful.

D5 Communist Chile: Salvador Allende (1909–73)

Chile had experienced a Popular Front government (see section 12C2) but Videla, president from 1946 to 1952, moved away from this position and by 1948 had outlawed the Communist Party. Ten years later it was restored, and soon began to develop electoral support. Frei, leader of the Christian Democrats (moderate socialists) won in 1964, and for some years reforms followed including the taking over the copper mines (1966) and land reform (1967). In 1969 parties on the extreme right and left both made gains weakening Frei, and during the summer there were demonstrations. Peasant communes were set up in some areas, and the left feared its gains might be destroyed. The elections of 1970 led to deadlock, and Allende was able to take office with the support of other parties. He was the first and so far only Communist leader to take office with willing democratic support, but although the left make much of this it was with only 36 per cent of the vote. Allende's policy involved total state control at home, and strong support for Castro abroad, but his policy failed. By 1973 the country was facing 500 per cent inflation, and in September an army rising led to Allende's death and a military regime under General Pinochet. The General was dedicated to the Chicago economists' view of a free economy (see section 14B2), and after cutting inflation to 30 per cent proceeded to restore the economy. Within a short time it was suggested the CIA had helped to depose Allende although no clear evidence of this has been provided.

Pinochet's regime fomented national feeling by its claim to islands in the Beagle Channel—also claimed by Argentina who rejected arbitration in 1977, but agreed in 1979 to the Pope's mediation. This dispute could not, however, enhance the popularity of the regime since the world depression affected Chile as a mineral producer, and by 1983 there were demonstrations against the junta in the industrial towns. Discontent was also increasing since the promised return to an electoral system was postponed several times.

E Independence for the Caribbean Countries

E1 Colonialism in the West Indies

Throughout most of the nineteenth century the West Indian territories of the European powers were declining backwaters of little interest to anyone. This was a result of the combined abolition of slavery and the ending of preferential sugar tariffs, which brought ruin to the existing economic pattern. Occasionally the area came into public view. In 1865 an uprising in Jamaica was savagely suppressed with 600 executions. Attempts to extend democracy in Barbados led to a white backlash and riots in 1875–6. Meanwhile to replace the black workers the colonial powers brought in indentured labour; firstly from Portugal and China, and then from India. Until 1917 when the practice stopped 239,000 Indians were added to the population which was later to produce racial tension. Towards the end of the century matters improved a little. In 1861 the first tourist hotel opened in the Bahamas, and after the Jamaica Exhibition of 1891 a tourist industry began to grow. Economies were diversified by the introduction of rice, coffee and citrus fruit cultivation. The banana was first marketed in 1869, for example. The discovery of oil in Trinidad in 1911, and bauxite in British Guiana in 1917 held out hope of economic change.

But this did not occur. The Wood Report (1921) advocated an extension of representative government in the British islands, but the changes made were only completed in 1936, and were extremely limited. It was not until 1944 that Jamaica obtained universal suffrage. The Moyne Report compiled in 1938 was so critical of British colonial practice that it was only fully published in 1940. It showed that half the population were still illiterate. Between 1896 and 1936 the population had risen from 1.7 million to 2.5 million and with underdeveloped economies this had led to great poverty and distress. Half the population was subject to seasonal unemployment, and it was of course from this situation that emigration to Britain found its impetus in the late 1940s. Even in matters on which the British prided themselves like health facilities the record was deplorable. In Trinidad the whole population suffered from malnutrition by ordinary standards.

Nationalism in the West Indies sprang from the movement led by William Du Bois and Marcus Garvey, and found its first expression in Jamaica where a trade union movement developed led by Alexander Bustamente and Norman Manley followed by the Jamaican Labour Party. In Barbados the leader was Grantley Adams, and in Trinidad, Eric Williams. During 1937–8 there were serious disturbances in these three islands with 30 people killed. The movement was suppressed, but the commission of enquiry, and then the Moyne Report played a vital part in changes in colonial policy. These led to the Colonial Development Acts after 1940 which began to channel improvements to the islands. After the war more representative constitutions were granted to the islands, and in February 1953 discussions started on a federation.

E2 The Failure of the West Indies Federation

A federation covering the 3 million inhabitants of the region came into being in January 1958, but by 1962 it had failed in spite of the obvious economic benefits of unity. It foundered on nationalist growth in the more economically developed areas, particularly Jamaica and Trinidad who wanted full independence. As a result Jamaica left in 1962. Two prime ministers—Bustamente (1962–7) and Michael Manley (1972–80)—carried Jamaica towards a left wing position in sympathy with Cuba until the decline of the tourist industry and the cutting off of Western investment led to the return of a moderate government in 1980. The election campaign was a violent one with 500 deaths, but Seaga won 51 out of 60 seats. He has returned the hotels to private ownership and received aid from America (40 million dollars) and Britain (6 million dollars) to restore the economy.

In 1962 Trinidad under Eric Williams also became independent. Barbados under Grantley Adams followed in 1966. The British were left to pick up the pieces, and created associated status in 1965 for which the other West Indian islands opted by June 1967. This and a Caribbean Common Market promised some hope for the future, but the islands were destabilised by the presence of Cuba constantly urging them on the path of national independence. The Bahamas opted for this in 1973, and Grenada the following year. In this island a left wing regime supportive of Castro took office under M. Bishop. Britain also possessed two mainland possessions in the Caribbean area. British Honduras was organised as a colony in 1860, and neighbouring Guatemala laid claim to it. Thus, although reforms were introduced Britain continued to hold on and send troops whenever Guatemala made threatening noises. At last in 1981 it became independent as Belize.

British Guiana had the hardest road to march towards independence. The valuable resources of the country, and the racial tension between blacks and Indians complicated the process of making it independent. The Indians backed Cheddi Jagan who had contacts with Asian Communism, and the negroes supported Forbes Burnham who was a socialist. When elections occurred riots broke out with over 200 killed, and British troops went into action in 1953. Jagan was imprisoned soon after, but his party continued to win elections in 1957 and 1961, and in 1962 the riots resumed. In 1964 troops returned, and the constitution was suspended. The parties combined together under Burnham to keep Jagan out, and in 1966 independence came. Burnham was however anxious to develop socialist policies. In 1970 Guyana became a republic, and in 1971 bauxite was nationalised. In 1972 relations were opened with Cuba, and both here, and in neighbouring Surinam (independent from Holland in 1976) there are the only left wing governments in South America. In 1982 an attempt by pro-Western officers to overthrow the Surinam government was defeated, and the government of General Bouterse (1980) continued in office.

F   Fidel Castro (b.1927) and the Cuban Revolution

F1   The Road to Power

Cuba's dictator, Batista, first came to power in 1933, was president from 1940 to 1944, and again after 1952, but maintained unbroken control throughout that period behind the scenes as well. He was friendly to America which retained its base at Guantanamo, and considerably influenced the economy. Sugar declined as the staple crop during the post-war period so that Cuba, formerly supplying a quarter of the world's sugar, supplied only a tenth by 1960. Still some 35 per cent of production remained in American hands, and America profited from the tourist industry Batista built up to help the economy. Most people in the country remained in deep poverty. Castro began his political career as a student leading a raid on the barracks in Havana for which he received a prison sentence. Batista released political prisoners in an amnesty a year later, and Castro went to Mexico where with his brother Raoul, and Che Guevara he organised a socialist guerilla movement. From Mexico an abortive invasion of Cuba was launched in

1956, but within a short time he was nearly defeated. It is ironic that it was Eisenhower who imposed an arms boycott on the island to try and curb trouble for the effect was to destroy Batista's confidence, and early in 1959 he fled, Castro capturing Santiago and Havana two days later. Castro was officially only prime minister until 1976 when he took the title of president. His brother, Raoul, was Minister of the Armed Forces and Foreign Minister while Che Guevara was Industry Minister.

F2 The Communist Regime in Cuba

Castro's achievement was unprecedented. He was the first Latin American socialist to come to power since the war, and he was the first Third World leader to embrace full blooded Communism. As such Castro had enormous prestige, and later this was to be bolstered by an aggressive world-wide foreign policy sponsored and financed by Russia. At first Castro's party was called the Popular Socialist Party; by degrees he moved left. In December 1961 he said he personally was a Marxist, and in 1965 set up a Cuban Communist Party. In 1968 a purge of non-Communist government members took place, and in 1976 a new Marxist Constitution was created. Cuba soon had the usual characteristics of a one party state—a secret police (DGI), censorship, religious persecution and the flight of large numbers of refugees which he tried to halt. Some 20,000 found their way to prison camps. Five per cent of the population (350,000) have fled the country.

To the people of Cuba these political changes meant little. What mattered to them were the economic policies he pursued. Immediately in 1959 the large estates were seized, and by 1962 agriculture was collectivised in 'communes'. A National Agricultural Institute was set up to reform agricultural methods, but the government chose to back sugar production setting high targets which could not be met, and making Cuba dependent on who ever would buy their sugar. In 1960 the nationalisation of industry began with the larger firms and the banks. In January 1961 Cuba seized 1,000 million dollars of American assets, and in 1965 completed their confiscation of American assets by seizing a further 3,000 million dollar haul. The rest of industry was nationalised by 1968. Some improvements were made in transport and housing. Education was developed. But it remains true that Cuba is still a poverty stricken state not least because of its massive defence burden and aggressive foreign policy.

F3 The Russo–Cuban Axis

Khrushchev had already initiated a policy of developing friendly relations with Third World countries when Cuba appeared as an ideal ally close to America. As early as 1960 a commercial treaty provided for 100 million dollars of credit, and the purchase of 5 million tons of sugar. When America urged the OAS states to boycott Cuba, Castro naturally turned to Russia to survive. One of the first results of this was the Cuban missile crisis (see section 13A1), but this of course intensified Cuba's isolation in Latin America. She was expelled from the OAS in the same year. In 1964 came a second treaty with Russia and in a third agreement in 1966 Russia agreed to purchase virtually all Cuba's sugar. Russia now exercised a commanding influence over the tottering economy providing Cuba with £4 million a day. In 1972 Russia agreed to fund Cuba's debts, and Cuba joined Comecon. But this aid was not without strings.

Cuba became the focal point for Russian ambitions in the Third World because they were a coloured and formerly oppressed colonial people. Through Cuba Russia was able to check the then growing influence of China in the Third World, and by the end of the 1960s to virtually eliminate it. As early as 1964 the OAS complained Castro was helping guerillas in Latin America, and during the 1960s Castro and Guevara organised the abortive rural guerilla campaigns in various north Andean states (section 12D4). But after Raoul's Moscow visit in 1965 a new and far more effective concept was developed. Russia would encourage the destabilising of regimes through Cuban intermediaries. In January 1966 a conference at Havana was the first step in organising such a world-wide movement. Simenov of the KGB went to Cuba to organise the DGI which was subordinated to the KGB by 1968. About 10,000 Russian advisers and 5,000 troops went to the island and set up training camps for guerillas. There is even a camp for African children to be brought up as Communists. As early as 1969 a defector called Hidalgo revealed these moves, and since then Cuba has established links with the Arab terrorist groups and with Libya. Then Russia went further. Heavy unemployment in the island would be reduced if a mercenary army was formed. Russia therefore trained and equipped an army of 160,000 Cubans, and these were used in various parts of the world to further Russia's foreign policy aims. It was a reversion to Imperialist methods by which Britain, for example, used an Indian army to boost her defence potential.

F4 Cuba's Foreign Policy

As a result of Russian backing Cuba was able to extend her influence widely. In Latin America she provided a base for the guerilla movements and is now supplying those in El Salvador and Guatemala. Cuban forces went to Africa. In 1964 they took part in the Zanzibar revolution which checked Chinese influence in East Africa. In the late 1960s they were in Equatorial Guinea. The involvement of Cubans in Angola, and Ethiopia is well known (see sections 9C1 and 11D2), but they have seen service elsewhere. In 1978 they were involved in the Soviet seizure of Aden. Caribbean countries like Jamaica, Grenada and Guyana were all influenced to move to the extreme left.

For a time these events led to diplomatic isolation for Cuba, but in 1972 several West Indian countries broke this boycott, and in 1977 Carter recognised Cuba. Carter's policy had the result of strengthening Castro. His Federal Aid Act withdrew aid to countries like Nicaragua because they were dictatorships, and in 1978 by siding with radicals in the Dominican Republic helped to further weaken pro-Western rulers in the area. In 1979 Carter seemed to wake up to what was going on, and made a speech demanding the removal of Soviet advisers from Cuba. Cuba remains a potential threat to world peace and a staunch supporter of Russian imperialism in spite of recent changes in Jamaica and Grenada.

G Central America in Ferment

G1 The Pattern of Events

Central America was even more prone than South America to United States influence and the rule of dictators. All six states in Central America have experienced dictatorships in recent years. Costa Rica was ruled by Figueras from 1948 to 1962, Honduras experienced Carias from 1933 to 1948 and Panama reverted to military rule in 1968. For a time American power was sufficient to protect these rulers, but their own failure to reform combined with the challenge of Castroism to destabilise the region. Trouble first came in Guatemala when terrorist activity provoked reprisals, and over 20,000 died in the period after 1966 in strife between the FAR and special Death Squads organised by the government. Urban guerillas kidnapped and killed the American and West German ambassadors in attempts to get terrorists released. The result was the return of full dictatorship in 1970, but in 1982 the ruler, General Garcia, was removed by younger officers led by General Montt. The government has responded to the situation with a number of reforms, and recently America has resumed aid and training of the military and police. There are Sandinistas, surviving FAR members, and members of ORPA (1979) in the country, and should the ruling party split revolution is likely in Guatemala.

It is this situation, paralleled in El Salvador and following events in Nicaragua, that has prompted a change in American policy. Reagan speaks of the area as a special American responsibility, and has started to provide economic and military aid to regimes threatened by Communist-inspired guerilla movements including Honduras and El Salvador. It is true that the root cause of discontent is poverty in the area, but Castroists and urban guerillas play on this situation for political ends. The next few years will witness an important struggle for this area of the globe.

G2 Somoza and the Sandinistas

Three generations of the Somoza family ruled Nicaragua almost without interruption from 1937 to 1979. During that time their personal fortune reached £48 million, and they owned one tenth of the country. Their regime was corrupt and brutal. When Managua was nearly destroyed by an earthquake the international relief was channelled into construction companies owned by the dictator. Opposition in the 1930s had come from Sandina, and the Sandinista guerillas were named after him. Their party was the FSLN, but this was long divided into warring factions. It was the murder of Pedro Chamorro, leader of the moderate Liberal party, in January 1978 that touched off demonstrations from which revolution grew. Carter cut off military aid leaving Somoza dependent on fellow dictators, and curiously, Israel, but since most of his equipment was American his forces were hamstrung, and by early 1979 the FSLN controlled the main cities. Somoza fled to Paraguay where he was murdered in 1980. The civil war had cost 40,000 lives, and left the country in chaos with nearly a million homeless and without loans since few countries except Venezuela sent any help. The ruling junta of three moved steadily leftwards—the 'liberal' members resigned in 1980 and Jorge Salazar their leader was murdered soon afterwards.

However, the regime is not officially Communist, and there are three Roman Catholic members of the government.

G3 Drawing the Line in El Salvador

Like other Central American states El Salvador passed into the hands of a dictator in 1932 and remained under such rule until elections were held in 1950. However, democratic government was unable to maintain itself. In 1961 a military junta, almost immediately recognised by Kennedy, came to power, and the country was successively ruled by Generals Rivera and Romero. From 1977 Romero was under increasing pressure from the opposition including the SLF who were sheltered by Mexico and were inspired by an earlier guerilla leader, Marti. In October 1979 Romero was removed by young officers who proclaimed the need for social reform, but it was not long before the senior military men and the 'fourteen families' who dominate the economy began to undermine this government. In January 1980 the civilian members of the government left, and three months later a 'state of siege' initiated the present civil war. A vigorous campaign was launched against the guerillas and left wing forces which accounted for 9,000 deaths by the end of 1980. These deaths included Archbishop Romero—a liberal churchman—and six leading trade unionists as the government allowed 'death squads' to operate.

From 1980 the government was in the hands of Jose Duarte who represents the conservatives (or Christian Democrats). To his right were fascists, and to his left a coalition of liberals, socialists and marxists. Duarte faced three problems. The first was to end the war, but the 5,000 guerillas received aid from Nicaragua and arms from Russia and Cuba so the poorly equipped army was unable to do this. Recently American military aid has increased, but this has provoked strong opposition in America, and there is clearly no chance of a 1954 Guatemala-like rescue. The second was to relieve poverty in a country where a tenth of the people are refugees. Reagan announced in March 1982 an aid programme of £189 million for the region, and some of this is going to El Salvador. The third was to end the violation of civil rights and recreate some form of democratic government. A UN Human Rights Commission constantly reports on violation of civil rights. Duarte decided to hold an election in March 1982, and invited outside observers. Clearly it would not be free in a Western sense, but few such elections are in the Third World—there are no free elections in Cuba. The election led to a coalition government of right wing parties who were unable to curb the guerillas any more effectively.

Reagan extended military aid to Honduras and Guatemala while at the same time, particularly through Mrs Jeanne Kirkpatrick and his special envoy to El Salvador, Richard Stone, launched a diplomatic initiative; firstly to rally Latin American support and secondly to neutralise the region by securing a reduction of Cuban–Russian activity in return for a decrease in American involvement. In the summer of 1983 the first direct discussions between the El Salvador government and the guerillas took place at Bogota in Colombia, but no settlement was reached. When Bishop's Grenada regime (see section 12E2) was replaced by an even more left wing group, six Caribbean states led by Dominica asked America to intervene. In October

1983 the Americans installed a pro-Western government on the island with the aid of 4,000 marines.

Revision Essays

1. What can a study of Latin American history contribute to the understanding of: (a) colonialism, (b) the revolt against colonialism?
2. Discuss the treatment of coloured people in the American Hemisphere referring to: (a) slavery, (b) the extermination of the Indians, (c) reservations, (d) peonage and (e) the hacienda system.
3. How has the United States been constantly involved in Latin America since the 1820s? Refer to the Monroe Doctrine, 'Manifest Destiny', Pan Americanism, American imperialism, and the 'Good Neighbour Policy'.
4. What has been the importance in Latin America of the left wing governments in: (a) Mexico, (b) Cuba, (c) Chile and (d) Guatemala?
5. What are the main features of caudilloism? How widespread is it at the moment? Illustrate your answer by referring to the present governments of Argentina, Chile and Brazil.
6. Explain the extent to which Hemisphere Defence led to American economic and strategic control of Latin America. How did America seek to preserve her influence?
7. Explain the reasons for the growth of rural and urban guerilla movements in Latin America, and their failure to overthrow the dictators.
8. Describe the ending of colonial rule in America since 1945 referring to: (a) Belize, (b) Guyana, (c) Jamaica, (d) Trinidad, (e) The Falkland Islands.
9. Why has there been increasing interest in the 1980s in the affairs of the small Central American states?
10. Discuss the effects of American intervention in: (a) Guatemala, (b) Dominica, (c) El Salvador.

Further Reading

Doorkhan, I., *Post Emancipation History of the West Indies*, Collins Educational Books, London, 1982.
Gott, R., *Rural Guerillas in Latin America*, Penguin, 1973.
Gunther, J., *Inside South America*, Hamish Hamilton, London, 1967.
Martell, J., *The Twentieth-Century World*, Harrap, London, 1980, Chapter 24.
Thomas, H., *Cuba: or the Pursuit of Freedom*, Eyre and Spottiswoode, 1971.
Watson, J., *Success in Twentieth Century World Affairs*, John Murray, London, 1974, Chapter 15.

13
The World of Three Super Powers: International Relations Since 1962

A Nuclear Confrontation: The Cuban Crisis 1962

A1 The Nuclear Balance in 1960

At the beginning of the 1960s America still retained nuclear superiority over Russia, and relied upon the doctrine of massive retaliation. America had developed the atom (1945) and hydrogen bombs (1952) first: Russia's had followed in 1949 and 1953 showing she was catching up fast. In August 1957 Russia had initiated the era of ICBMs followed in December by America. Apart from the two super powers there was then only one other nuclear power. Britain had developed her atom (1952) and hydrogen bombs (1957) more slowly due to the enormous cost involved, and when the missile age dawned, after several expensive failures, she was to accept the American Polaris in 1962. In 1960 France began her creation of a *force de frappe*, and in 1964 had her independent deterrent. An H-bomb followed in 1967. China was to follow in 1964 with her atom bomb, and 1967 with her hydrogen bomb.

In 1960 Russia was in a position of nuclear inferiority. Moreover, American bases enabled her to contain Russia, with potential to strike at her from many angles, whereas America was less vulnerable and had an effective early warning system. The British deterrent made Russia even more vulnerable to Western attack.

A2 The Causes of the Crisis

The crisis over Cuba had many roots. At the most superficial level it was a direct result of hostility between Cuba and America. The Cuban Revolution (see sections 12F2 and 12F3) aroused American hostility since it had led to the seizure of American property by a left wing regime close to America. In January 1961 America had broken off diplomatic relations, and in April had attempted to assist Cuban exiles to return to the island. This had failed at the Bay of Pigs, and in turn forced Castro further left. In July 1962 Che Guevara and Raoul Castro went to Moscow and on September 3rd Russia and Cuba signed an arms agreement. Within a week the first Russian ship arrived in Cuba. A Russian presence was established on the island, but on September 11th and October 18th Russia assured America this presence was only that of 'agricultural experts' and that no rockets were present. However, this was not so. Khrushchev had been strongly criticised in Russia for the failure of the Paris Summit (1960), and the renewed threat to Berlin (1961). He badly needed a foreign policy triumph, and the siting of missiles in Cuba was a way of bringing this about because with a range of 2,000 miles much of America would be an immediate target. Moreover Khrushchev believed this could be used to extract concessions from NATO either in Berlin, or by reducing the number of rockets aimed at the Soviet Union. Russia established eight rocket sites each with four missile launchers. Twenty Iluyshin bombers were stationed on the island. Khrushchev believed the young Kennedy would crack under the prospect of nuclear blackmail.

A3 The Gathering Storm

Throughout September and October 1962 tension mounted between Russia and America. On September 4th Kennedy warned Russia, and Khrushchev replied in similar vein on September 11th. Kennedy did not wait but took prompt action. By the 24th of September measures to call up reservists had been taken, while it was not until October 23rd that leave was cancelled in Russia and Marshal Grechko chaired talks about military action. Dean Rusk, the American Secretary of State, chaired an OAS meeting to condemn Castro, and get backing for the trade boycott imposed by America. On October 23rd the OAS was to condemn Cuba 19–0 with Uruguay abstaining on a technicality. Between October 14th and 16th U2 American reconnaissance flights over Cuba revealed the missiles. Britain was informed on October 19th, and Macmillan gave Kennedy full support as did De Gaulle and Adenauer later. On October 22nd Kennedy announced that the missile sites must go, and to that end America would impose a blockade. Any attempt to continue the build up or activate the missiles would lead to a 'full retaliatory response'. Fifty-six ICBMs were primed for action. The next day 100,000 troops were being concentrated in Florida whilst 40,000 marines and naval personnel were involved in the blockade.

A4 Duel at the Brink

During the next week the world came its closest so far to nuclear war. Kennedy's advisers were divided. The 'hawks' led by Dean Acheson wanted military action either by bombing or invading Cuba. However, since there were Soviet 'advisers' on Cuba some of their deaths might well have followed such a move. McNamara, the Defence Secretary, therefore proposed a blockade because this would give room for manoeuvre. Dean Acheson was despatched to Europe with large photographs of the sites which made effective propaganda for the American case. On October 24th Adlai Stevenson also revealed the photographs in the Security Council. Russia had made her position plain. On October 18th Gromyko had said the Berlin issue would be settled by November 6th; now it was clear how this would be achieved. The blockade was originally set at 800 miles, then it was narrowed to 500 miles to give additional time for Khrushchev to draw back. Twenty-five ships were approaching and were treated carefully—two ships halted on October 25th and 26th were allowed to continue as they were not carrying war materials. The Secretary General of UNO, U Thant asked

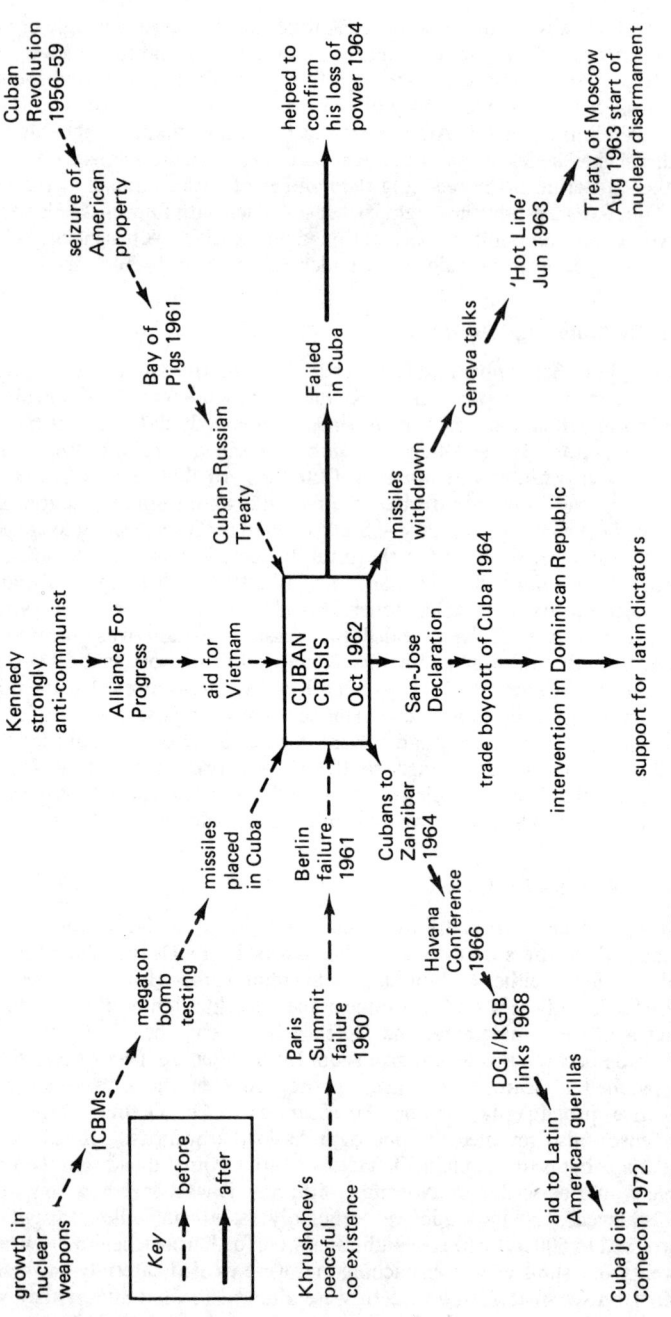

Fig. 24. The importance of the Cuban Crisis

Key
⇢ before
→ after

growth in nuclear weapons → ICBMs → megaton bomb testing → missiles placed in Cuba

Khrushchev's peaceful co-existence → Paris Summit failure 1960 → Berlin failure 1961 → Cubans to Zanzibar 1964

Havana Conference 1966 → DGI/KGB links 1968 → aid to Latin American guerillas → Cuba joins Comecon 1972

Kennedy strongly anti-communist → Alliance For Progress → aid for Vietnam

Cuban Revolution 1956–59 → seizure of American property → Bay of Pigs 1961 → Cuban–Russian Treaty

CUBAN CRISIS Oct 1962

Failed in Cuba → helped to confirm his loss of power 1964

missiles withdrawn → Geneva talks → 'Hot Line' Jun 1963 → Treaty of Moscow Aug 1963 start of nuclear disarmament

San-Jose Declaration → trade boycott of Cuba 1964 → intervention in Dominican Republic → support for latin dictators for a three week 'truce', but Kennedy would not agree. He knew work was proceeding to get the sites ready, and he was strengthened by the support of NATO and OAS. Indeed Argentina offered her navy for the blockade, and Costa Rica a base for military attack. Since Zorin, the Russian representative at UNO, refused to answer when faced with the photographs on October 25th Russia's guilt was clear. On the 26th it was decided to launch air attacks on the missile sites if the work had not stopped by the 29th. Khrushchev then tried to confuse the issue. On the 26th he sent a letter saying the missiles would go if America would give a pledge not to invade Cuba. Then on the 27th he asked that Turkish missile sites should be withdrawn in exchange, but this only served to involve NATO more closely. The shooting down of a U2 over Cuba, and the straying of another U2 into Russian air space on the 27th were the kind of incidents that might well have triggered off a nuclear response. On October 29th Kennedy replied to Khrushchev's first offer which was accepted without consulting Castro. On November 7th the rockets had gone; on November 20th the blockade was lifted, and Kennedy had won.

A5 Consequences

The effects of this crisis were many. In Russia they were one factor in the declining popularity of Khrushchev, and helped towards his fall in 1964. The exposure of Soviet impotence led to an acceleration in arms construction, and the eventual decision to go for a world naval role which could effectively menace America. Castro's Cuba remained a focus for Soviet activity (see sections 12F3 and 14A5). Castro was driven into isolation in Latin America. This forced him to total dependence on Russia, and in turn he was persuaded to back guerillas in the American hemisphere. On the other hand the nuclear threat to America had been lifted, and since then the Latin American countries have agreed to ban nuclear weapons (1978). The seriousness of the crisis led to the creation of the 'hot line' between the White House and the Kremlin (June 1963), and gave a boost to Macmillan's efforts to secure disarmament. The way in which Europe had been involved, but unable to control events strengthened De Gaulle's view that American power was too great and the 1963 Franco–German Treaty was the first step towards a more independent European line.

A6 The First Steps to Disarmament

Cuba was a duel fought in terms of the doctrine of overwhelming retaliation, but as the number and size of nuclear weapons increased it was clear that this would involve such total destruction that no one would gain. In May 1962 flexible response was put forward as a new doctrine allowing for a variety of weapons escalating to all out war, and this became NATO strategy late in 1967. Both sides continued to build nuclear weapons. Britain signed the Nassau Agreement (December 1962), and Macmillan and Wilson were responsible for the building of the Polaris fleet. Neither France nor China was prepared to be involved in disarmament talks because they were seeking independence—France from American and China from Russian domination. Yet the period saw progress towards disarmament as part of peaceful co-existence, and ultimately as part of the new relationship between Russia and America that followed the Vietnam War. In August 1963 a Test Ban Treaty banned tests in the atmosphere. This was eventually signed by 100 nations, even if ignored by France and China as late as 1973. Underground tests were limited by agreement in July 1974, and both these treaties have been kept by the super powers. In 1967 territorial claims and nuclear weapons were banned in space, and in 1971 nuclear material was banned from the sea-bed outside territorial waters in an effort to prevent dumping. In June 1968 the Non-Proliferation Treaty was agreed, and this has been signed by 83 nations again excluding France and China. In spite of claims that other countries including Iraq, Pakistan, Israel, South Africa and Libya have manufactured nuclear weapons this treaty too has been adhered to. In November 1969 talks at last began on missile limitation (SALT), and in 1972 a five year freeze was imposed (see section 12E2). Some progress was clearly made in the ten years after Cuba, but it remained true that the total number of nuclear weapons was augmented and their sophistication made war more likely since field weapons might well be employed more haphazardly than ICBMs. The existence of the deterrent was a powerful argument for detente as cost and complexity increased.

B The Vietnam War (1961–73)

B1 The Age of Advisers

As early as 1954 Eisenhower referred to the group of small countries in South East Asia as dominoes: if one fell to Communism the others would follow. In the Eisenhower–Dulles era America had become closely involved in South East Asia (see section 3E4). It was in the early 1960s, when the Geneva Settlement reached in 1954 seemed to be breaking down, that America embarked upon a disastrous involvement of a more serious nature which was to lead to America's longest overseas war. From 1955 to 1963 South Vietnam was ruled by Ngo Dinh Diem with very little evidence of democracy or progress. To the north Ho Chi Minh reformed his Vietminh as the Vietcong in December 1960 helped at first by China, and later much more by Russia. Guerillas began to infiltrate over the border and along the Ho Chi Minh Trail through Laotian territory.

In June 1961 Kennedy took the decision to support Diem's regime by increasing American advisers to 2,000, providing arms training, and salaries for the Vietnam army. Over the next few years the number of advisers rose from 2,000 in 1961 to 23,000 in 1964 as America became deeply involved in trying to keep the South Vietnamese regime together. But the launching of war on the guerillas in March 1962 did little to help the government, and the following year Diem was killed. A period of grave instability in the government set in. There were 12 changes of government in South Vietnam until in February 1965 a military regime under Generals Ky and Thieu took over. The guerillas stepped up their efforts helped by the decision of the Pathet Lao in Laos to allow them passage through the part of the country they controlled. America was thus committed to an unpopular, ineffective, militarist government.

B2 The Decision for War

During 1964 it looked as if the American stand would be followed by the West when the Americans said they would stay in Vietnam until the Vietcong were defeated. SEATO supported this move, and Home's government in Britain twice strongly endorsed American action in February and April as did Wilson in December 1964. America may well have seen Vietnam as another Korea, and failed to see it was not a conventional war where massive force would win, or a clear cut marxist or capitalist confrontation but a national liberation struggle as well as a Communist bid for power. Demands for reconvening the Geneva conference were swept aside as pressure mounted to attack North Vietnam thus cutting off the guerillas' supply base. Early in August 1964 North Vietnam ships fired on American ships and the American fleet bombarded the coast. This gave President Johnson the opportunity to bring forward his 'Gulf of Tonkin' Resolution by which the President was empowered (with only two senators opposed) to use force to assist any state in the SEATO area. In December vastly increased aid was given because by then regular units of the NVA were backing the guerillas, and it seemed as if Vietnam would fall with 40 per cent of the villages in Vietcong hands. Johnson had to decide between withdrawing the substantial number of Americans, or starting a war. In March 1965 he opted for war. Using attacks on American bases like Pleiku as an excuse, the bombing of North Vietnam began culminating in Operation Rolling Thunder. This was directed at communications and supplies, but it was hard to stop China sending the latter over the border, and America was careful not to bomb any Russian ships in the port of Haiphong. The Ho Chi Minh trail was also bombed violating the neutral status of Laos and Cambodia, but no ground attack followed. The same month American Marines landed at Danang.

B3 The Search for Allies

Unlike Korea, America in Vietnam did not have support from the United Nations where U Thant, the Secretary General, urged talks. Nor could America rely on an effective government in the south where the rule of generals like Thieu and Ky was ineffective. Only in 1967 did a new constitution come into force, and the elections returned Thieu as President. He remained in that position until 1975, and his harsh and ineffective policies consistently damaged the American position. At first America counted on free world support. Some 72,000 Allied troops went to Vietnam from Thailand, South Korea, Australia and New Zealand. Australia lost 492 dead in Vietnam, for example. Henry Cabot Lodge was an effective ambassador until March 1967, and as late as then Thailand was allowing use of its bases by the Americans. But as the war continued America began to lose support. France under De Gaulle was playing for Russian and Chinese friendship, and withdrew from SEATO. In June 1966 Wilson's government disassociated itself from American bombing, and the special relationship between the two countries broke down. SEATO proved a limp reed, and was dissolved later in June 1977. Thus, while North Vietnam had the support of Russia and China and systematically violated Laotian and Cambodian neutrality, America was increasingly isolated.

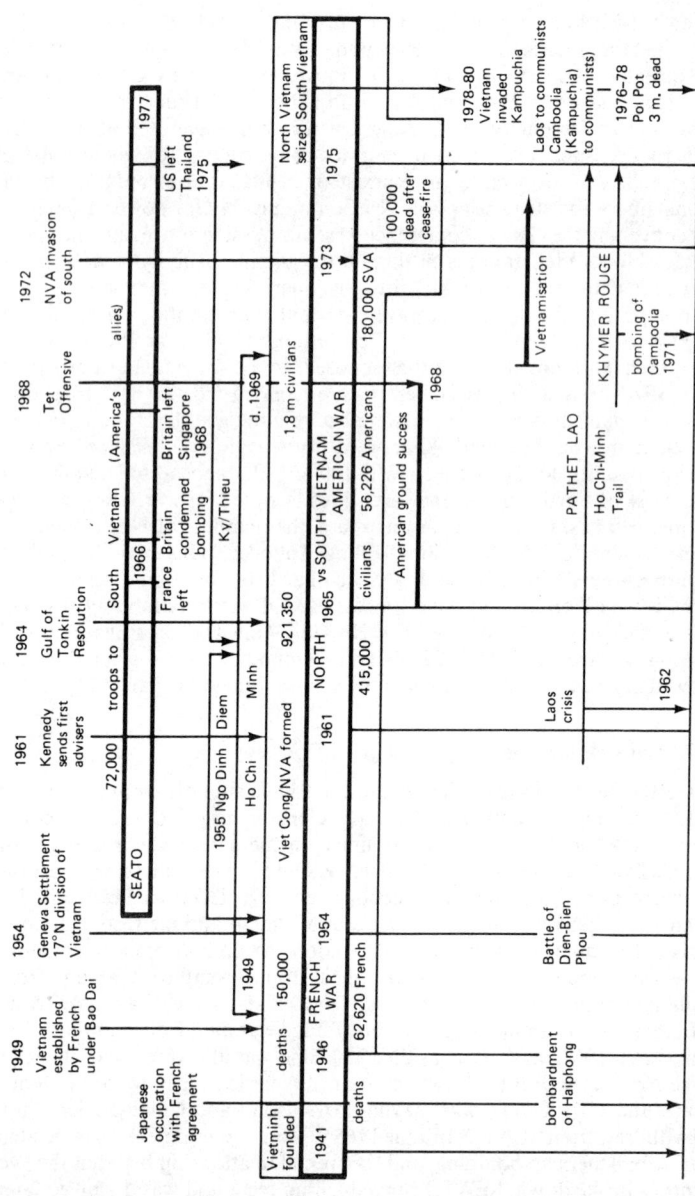

Fig. 25. The stages in and consequences of the Vietnam War

B4 The Balance of Forces

In theory America and South Vietnam possessed overwhelming force. In 1969 America had 541,000 troops in Vietnam assisted by 72,000 Allied troops. But this army suffered from many defects. It was able to win the major field battles from 1965 to 1968, but it could not contain the guerillas partly because of its own ineffective tactics, but also because the South Vietnamese government was unpopular and unable to control the countryside. The army was recruited by the draft system, and the war was unpopular at home (see section 5E2). The result was desertion and insubordination on a wide scale so that, for example, drug use was widespread. American radical opinion noted that 53 per cent of American casualties in a 'white man's' war were black. America did not follow up the bombing by direct invasion of the north. She used non-toxic gases, napalm and splinter bombs, but did not use tactical nuclear weapons. Thus, America was criticised world-wide for 'atrocities' while militarily she was not exerting her full force. The presence of television on the American side was certainly an inhibiting factor. The outcry over the May Lai massacre (109 civilians killed in 1968), or the bombing of their own troops by the Americans inhibited the use of full force and concealed the equally appalling atrocities by the other side. The South Vietnamese army, which on paper was 750,000, was incompetent and underequipped until after 1968. Left to defend the country internally in 1968 the Tet Offensive showed their inadequacy.

The Vietcong guerillas rose from 25,000 to perhaps 300,000, but in the Tet Offensive of 1968 they suffered 30,000 casualties. Thereafter they declined, and by 1970 some units were even surrendering. The North Vietnamese army led by Giap was a small (70,000) but well armed force backed by the Vietcong and 50,000 Chinese auxiliaries who did behind the lines tasks. Above all North Vietnam was a one party dictatorship which could conceal casualties and suffering on a vast scale. Ho was a great leader until his death in 1969, and other members of the government—Van Dong, Le Duc Tho, and Pham Hung—were also effective. The North Vietnamese army and Vietcong together lost 921,350 casualties. They were prepared to accept such losses while America was not. They were bound to win a war of attrition, and with a birth rate of 250,000 males a year could continue the rate of loss. For arms and food they could rely on support from many sources. China allowed Russian supply trains to cross her country. Russian ships also reached Vietnam, and later use Cambodian ports as well. The Ho Chi Minh Trail became a highway which could only be destroyed by all out war in Laos and Cambodia as well. The North Vietnamese had all the advantages of guerilla warfare with a well supplied base. The recovery of places like Nam Dinh, twice destroyed by the Americans, was possible in a directed economy with endless supplies of labour. Thus, what appeared to be a struggle between a great power with overwhelming force and a small guerilla army was in reality a much more evenly balanced struggle. It was one that America was unable to win because the cost would have been too great—and only Vietnam (and by proxy Russia and China) were prepared to pay the price.

B5 Westmoreland's War 1965–68

The first phase of the war was fought in terms the Americans could understand. Firstly, the north was subjected to heavy aerial attack reaching the suburbs of Haiphong and Hanoi. But the Vietnamese had astonishing powers of recovery from such attack, and the frequent bombing pauses enabled them to recuperate. There were such pauses in the Christmas Truce (1965–6) and the Tet Truce (1967). The Americans left the interior of Vietnam to the SVA and concentrated on attacks coming down the Ho Chi Minh trail and trying to stop incursions over the 17th Parallel. This led to set piece battles like Dak To, and to the successful relief of Khe Sanh. Johnson built up forces rapidly hoping for victory before the 1968 election, and numerically the North Vietnamese suffered massively. Then early in 1968 they counterattacked within the country, and entered over 30 important cities from the surrounding countryside during the Tet offensive. In spite of the virtual annihilation of the Vietcong which followed this seemed to be a major defeat, and to show how little Thieu's government had the people's support. Westmoreland now asked for a further 200,000 men to put an end to the fighting. Senator Goldwater demanded the use of nuclear weapons, but Johnson's nerve had gone. On March 31st all bombing north of the demilitarised zone was stopped, and in June Westmoreland was replaced by General Creighton Adams. At the end of October all offensive action against North Vietnam was halted. Johnson embarked on talks in Paris which began in May under Averell Harriman, and were continued by Cabot Lodge from January 1969 until he resigned in November convinced the talks were getting nowhere. The violence of opposition in America, and the coming election campaign dictated a change in American action.

B6 Vietnamisation and War in Cambodia

Nixon's policy was to use American strength to help the Vietnamese government take on reorganisation of the country and modernise their army so that they could gradually take over from a reduced American presence. American troops were increased to their maximum in March 1969. Then after the election Nixon acted. In meetings at Midway and Guam in June and July he announced the first withdrawals, and the initiation of Vietnamisation. In November 1969 withdrawal of 60,000 began the movement out of Vietnam just at the moment when Adams had begun to secure major success in co-operating with the South Vietnamese army.

By 1972 80 per cent of the countryside was in the government's hands following the collapse of the Vietcong. A million acres had been distributed to the peasants. But this South Vietnamese success was hampered by Pathet Lao and Khymer Rouge backing for invasion via the Trail and across the Mekong Delta. In 1970 the socialist Prince Sihanouk was overthrown, and the new ruler of Cambodia, Lon Nol, appealed to America to help. In April 1970 America invaded Cambodia, and in a short campaign crushed the guerillas' capability for nearly two years helping South Vietnam to recover and Lon Nol to establish himself with an army of 200,000 to face the Khymer Rouge. But success brought ruin to Nixon's policy. The increase of the war roused the anti-war lobby to fury even though a further 150,000 troops left early in 1970. The Gulf of Tonkin Resolution was repealed, and the Cooper–Church Amendment barred the use of American forces in Cambodia. David Bruce was appointed to renew the Paris peace talks.

B7 Defeat and Withdrawal for America

At the same time as the Paris talks Henry Kissinger and Le Duc Thou were conducting secret negotiations, but Vietnam's demands were pitched too high. In the meantime matters seemed to be going well. America's forces had been cut by half, but the South Vietnamese were holding their own, and indeed in February 1971 were able to invade Laos, capture Sepone and curb the Pathet Lao. The Vietcong were virtually destroyed and unable to act in the cities while the SVA was developing effective units like the Marines and Airborne Division. Le Duan, First Secretary of the Communist Party, went to Moscow in 1971 and it was agreed to back a direct invasion of the south in election year in America. Nixon's hands were tied by Congress and public opinion although some bombing was possible during the winter. Then in March 1972 came a major northern invasion with 14 divisions. In previous attacks the NVA had only infantry and anti-aircraft weapons. Now it was equipped with Chinese and Russian tanks, the deadly Soviet 130mm gun and the Sam-7 heat seeking missile. The Communists lost 120,000 dead in this attack which ground to a halt in July with the SVA recapturing Quang Tri, the only important city captured by the Communists. America had only 40,000 troops left but helped by bombing the north and mining Haiphong. Encouraged by their success the SVA prepared a counter offensive, and at this point Hanoi re-opened negotiations to cover its failure. America again stopped bombing, but Hanoi's demands became more insistent. In December 1972 Nixon attacked and destroyed the North Vietnamese air defences. Hanoi now realised it could only capture South Vietnam if the Americans left. In January 1973 they agreed to a ceasefire, and next month a truce occurred in Laos. In August the Senate stopped all support for Cambodia. American troops had left Vietnam by March 29th, 1973.

C The Fall of the Dominoes in South East Asia

C1 The Kissinger Peace Settlement

The settlement for which Kissinger received a Nobel Peace Prize was unsatisfactory in many respects. In the end only the clauses affecting America were carried out. American forces left but other forces remained where they were so that 180,000 NVA were left in South Vietnam. It was agreed to exchange prisoners of war, but this proved difficult. Kissinger had virtually to send an ultimatum to secure the release of 1,200 Americans. An International Commission from four countries was to supervise the cease fire, but this was not done in spite of a further agreement in June between Kissinger and Le Duc Thou. As a result the Ho Chi Minh trail was concreted, and became a highway, and NVA forces consolidated inside South Vietnam. Specific promises were made in November 1972 and in January and November 1973 that any violations of the settlement would be resisted. In fact, Congress ended all bombing and passed the War Powers Act restraining Nixon or Ford from further action, and the Watergate Affair prevented it anyway. There was no political settlement so that although in theory two Vietnams remained no effective steps were taken to ensure their survival. Democratic elections were promised, and of course not held in the north while Thieu in the south felt unable to form a coalition with the Communists who were seeking to destroy him. The cease fire made no mention of Laos and Cambodia where left wing guerillas and NVA remained in strength.

C2 The Communist Conquest of South Vietnam

The Vietnam War left the whole area in chaos. Fifty per cent of the people were refugees. The civilian casualties were 1.8 million dead in the north, and 415,000 in the south. The Vietnamese military casualties were 921,350 NVA and Vietcong, and 180,000 SVA. American deaths totalled 56,226. The essential need was to restore the economy. North Vietnam received massive support from Russia whereas Thieu in the South found his aid reduced by Congress so that the planting of 'miracle rice' was delayed. Seventy per cent inflation hit the country in the wake of the oil price rises, and Thieu was unable to raise army pay rates. The army was reduced in size by economies, and the number of desertions rose rapidly. Not only was American financial aid cut, but military supplies dried up while North Vietnam was re-equipping and regrouping.

By 1975 the NVA of 20 divisions was superior in every way to other armies in the region. In 1973–4 during the cease fire nearly 100,000 South Vietnamese were killed by NVA attacks. Then in January 1975 nineteen out of 20 divisions under Van Dong invaded South Vietnam. There were no anti-war demonstrations in America and no calls for action at UNO in face of this flagrant aggression. America could do nothing except evacuate its 6,000 personnel in April. After a major defeat at Ban Me Thout, Thieu withdrew from the Central Highlands. In the east the Communists besieged and captured Hue and Da Nang forcing sea-borne evacuations. In April after a major victory at Xuan Loc, Saigon fell. Thieu had already fled, and the government surrendered to the Communists. Saigon became Ho Chi Minh City, and the country was annexed.

C3 Victory for Pathet Lao and Khymer Rouge

The cease fire agreement of February 1973 was a dead letter because it left 50,000 NVA and the Pathet Lao in virtual command of the eastern part of Laos. The King was deposed, and in May 1975 the Pathet Lao entered Vientiane and installed a left wing government under Prince Souvanna Phouma. By December he had left, and the government under Phomvihan became a strong supporter of Vietnam. In Cambodia the Communists were divided. Vietnam backed by Russia saw the area as rightfully hers while China feared Vietnamese power and resisted their incursions. China backed the left wing government of Prince Sihanouk in exile. The Khymer Rouge continued to operate, but until August 1973 were restrained to some extent by American bombing. Thereafter they moved to full scale war, and in January 1974 the year long siege of Phnom Penh began. In

March 1975 Lon Nol fled, and next month the capital fell, and the Republic of Kampuchea was proclaimed. Sihanouk returned, but in December left the country resentful of Vietnamese influence. Elections in April 1976 brought to power Pol Pot who was determined to maintain Kampuchea's independence. This led to massive slaughter of suspected pro-Russian or Vietnamese peasantry, and it has been estimated that 3 million were killed. Again there were no human rights demonstrations in America or Europe, and UNO took no action. Clashes developed between Kampuchea and Vietnam.

C4 The Vietnamese Conquest of Kampuchea

Van Dong's government in Vietnam was a one party regime of great ferocity. On its installation 230,000 fled the country, and since that time the government has systematically killed and persecuted the Chinese and pro-Western elements. The result has been the flight of the 'Boat People'. Internally a marxist economy has been imposed, and Vietnam has joined Comecon. In November 1978 a treaty with Russia was signed giving her a stake in South East Asia. Russian naval facilities have been established, and this has enabled Russia to further her encirclement of China, and complete the destruction of containment in south east Asia. The removal of the British from Singapore in 1968, the departure of American forces from Thailand in 1975, and the abolition of SEATO in 1977 have immobilised the defence of the region. During 1978 Vietnam invaded Kampuchea. Pol Pot was forced to flee to Thailand with another wave of refugees, and a new government under Heng Sanrin was established. Russia hastily recognised this government, and now has naval facilities in the Mekong delta. Pol Pot appealed to UNO which in September 1979 disgraced itself by recognising him as the rightful ruler. His guerilla army of 30,000 controls about a tenth of the country. Late in 1979 he was replaced as leader of the Kampuchean exiles by Khieu Samphan, and the issue remains unresolved.

C5 Resistance to Vietnamese Aggression

In 1954 the Geneva Settlement had recognised the Communist government in North Vietnam. Since that time Vietnam has annexed South Vietnam in defiance of the settlement, and the cease fire of 1973. She has installed pro-Vietnamese governments in Laos and Kampuchea which were neutral states. The Vietnam War brought suffering to Vietnam, but it is often forgotten North Vietnam began the war; that America went to war not to take territory or destroy North Vietnam, but to preserve South Vietnam. None of the governments of South Vietnam, Cambodia or Laos were admirable by Western standards, but they were not one party marxist dictatorships. The war brought carnage to Indo-China, but again it must be remembered that from 1940 to 1979 either as Vietminh, or Vietcong or NVA the Vietnamese Communists have been at war with the French, Americans and the peoples of the region. Many more have perished as a result of Communist victory than as a result of American intervention. Above all the 'domino' theory which was derided in the 1960s proved correct. The other Asian countries have now formed ASEAN (Singapore, Malaysia,

Indonesia, the Philippines and Thailand) which is assuming some military features. In February–March 1979 China invaded Vietnam causing 40,000 casualties on both sides in an effort to restrain Vietnam's warlike activities.

D America–China–Russia: A New Balance of Power

D1 The Decline of Britain as a World Power

In the 1950s Britain was still the third greatest world power. After the war in spite of economic difficulties she had her own nuclear deterrent. The 1957 Defence Review decided to expand Britain's nuclear role, and she embarked on the missile era firstly with her own costly failure, Blue Streak, but later by concluding the Nassau Agreement for Polaris missiles. Britain also passed National Service Acts (1947, 1950) which gave her large forces. In 1953 she had 1.5 million in the services, 150 major warships and 6,000 aircraft. In addition to her pre-war commitments British troops occupied zones in West Germany and Austria, garrisoned Berlin and Trieste, and ruled the former Italian empire.

British troops were in action every year between 1945 and 1967, and her 'little wars' increased in frequency. Within the colonial empire Britain continued to sack rulers or resume direct rule, and although the ultimate intention was self-government it was not anticipated this would come for many years. The decline of empire was partly concealed behind the mystique of a Commonwealth. Britain fought campaigns against Malayan, Kenyan and Cypriot terrorists with success in the 1950s. A list of Britain's military activities at the end of the decade indicates her still continuing world presence: Jordan (1958), Oman (1957–9), Kuwait (1961), Brunei (1963), Borneo (1963–6), Kenya (1964), Guyana (1964–6) and Aden (1964–7). Her empire was still strategically powerful with a chain of world bases, and defence treaties with countries like Libya or Cyprus were intended to prolong this situation. Britain was, therefore, with her long history, great empire and role in the Second World War a valuable and indeed principal ally of America well into the 1960s. She played a key role in the fight against Communism, and was the second largest power in such events as the Berlin Blockade or the Korean War. Her Foreign Secretaries, Bevin and Eden, played key roles in establishing NATO, the Baghdad Pact and SEATO which were the basis of containment. Eden was responsible in 1954 for the Geneva Settlement and Western European Union, and Macmillan with his Moscow visit (1959) and the test ban treaty (1963) still exercised a world role.

America was aware of Britain's economic weakness. She did not support Britain's colonial role, and in the Middle and Far East there were sharp divergences of policy, but by and large the Special Relationship was a diplomatic fact not a cliche. Britain sought to maintain a triple world role: America's closest ally, the principal defender of Europe and the ruler of a world empire. But such days were numbered. By 1961 Dean Acheson could say Britain had lost an empire and not found a world role and that her attempt to straddle three circles was failing. By the end of the 1960s Britain had been twice (1963, 1967) excluded from Europe where her strong pro-Americanism was resented. Her defence cuts and opposition to America in Vietnam had ended the Special Relationship. Colonial independence had come with a rush, and by 1968 all foreign business (handled by three ministries in 1945) was consolidated in one. Britain had revealed in 1947 by withdrawing from Greece and Palestine that she was overcommitted. Suez in 1956 had shown that even with France and Israel her power to act independently of America was limited. As empire went so did the bases: Hong Kong (1959), Aden (1967), Singapore (1968), Tobruk (1970), Bahrain (1971) and Simonstown (1975) are some examples. The end of conscription was followed by serious defence cuts brought about by economic weakness. The Commonwealth declined as a white man's club and by 1966 with a meeting at Lagos had emerged as another vehicle for Third World demands not British power. Britain was unable to act against rebel Rhodesia (1965), and declined twice (1967, 1974) to fulfil her treaty obligations in Cyprus. She broke her treaty responsibilities to SEATO infuriating ANZUS powers, and left the Persian Gulf in spite of demands by Arab rulers that she should stay. Attempts to hold the empire together by federations in Central Africa or the West Indies collapsed.

By the 1970s Britain was economically in decline, without a world-wide power base, and with increasingly inadequate defence forces. She was no longer America's vital supporter, and this had many consequences. In the vacuum left by Britain and other colonial powers Third World nationalism and marxism contended for supremacy. America was thus forced to take on a world role she was ill-equipped by experience to assume, and was indeed reluctant to take on at all. In the Middle East she first denounced Britain for her actions, then after the Eisenhower Doctrine (1957) assumed a more active role, but it was not until the Six Day War in 1967 that America became closely involved in that area. Involvement in South East Asia was a hamfisted failure, and this had grave repercussions in preventing America from playing a role in Africa during the 1970s until marxism had secured a footing. Congress voted against aid for Angola in 1975, and it is only recently with aid for Somalia and the Sudan that America has secured some effective footholds in the continent. America was over committed at a time when her own bases were contracting, her economy was in difficulties and Watergate had led to grave internal difficulties. The racial troubles of the 1960s embarrassed her in the Third World.

D2 Europe Alters Course: Third Force and Neutralism

During the 1950s America had been able to count on European co-operation largely dictated by her and Britain within NATO and WEU. Her war record and economic aid were remembered. Many European leaders like Macmillan were wartime colleagues; others like Adenauer were fanatically anti-Communist. Soviet policy in the late 1940s was also remembered, and crises (1958, 1961) over Berlin served to emphasise the need for Europe to rely on America. But during the 1960s this Cold War epoch seemed to pass. Western countries adopted a more lenient view of Communism: a Communist Party was allowed in Germany in 1968, for example. Euro-Communism put forward by Berlinguer in Italy argued that support for both NATO and Communism were compatible even in government, and by 1981 the French government contained Communists and strongly backed

NATO. In Eastern Europe in April 1964 Rumania took the lead in declaring all Communist states to have equal rights, and gradually relations with Western Europe developed. The Hallstein Doctrine of non-recognition was broken when West Germany recognised Rumania (1967) and Yugoslavia (1968). Economic ties began to grow between the two Europes symbolised by the Soviet–Italian, and Soviet–German natural gas pipelines.

It was natural that as the Common Market grew in economic strength it should begin to seek a world role separate from America. The EEC unlike NATO could not be subordinated to America's foreign policy requirements. There was talk of a federal Europe as a third force, and even of a neutralist Europe. In 1964 an American proposal (MLF) to integrate the nuclear deterrent was smartly rebuffed in Europe, and since then France has deliberately built her own deterrent in order to stay aloof from America. When flexible response became NATO nuclear doctrine it meant that instead of nuclear war taking place by an exchange of ICMBs over Europe it might well involve a mixture of conventional and tactical nuclear war on the Continent. European countries led by Wilson–Callaghan in Britain, Giscard D'Estaing in France and Brandt–Schmidt in Germany all favoured detente, arms reduction and good relations with Russia to such an extent that events in Czechoslovakia in 1968, or Poland in 1976 could be brushed aside in the search for security. The Europeans too had different ties with the Third World. France through her Community and the Lomé Agreement had links with her former possessions, and pursued an independent line. The French have intervened in Zaire and Chad, and continue to retain good relations with their former colonial territories. De Gaulle took this further by demanding a world role for his country. He involved himself in South America and Canada. He left SEATO (1965), and denounced America in Vietnam. In recognising China (1964) and visiting Russia (1966) De Gaulle was reviving his former foreign policy of good Russian relations. In 1982 Mitterrand of France sent aid to Nicaragua and Vietnam showing indifference to American policy. Germany had no world role, but her economy led her to develop one based on good relations with Russia, and after the oil crisis, with the Arabs. NATO ceased to be a united defence body obedient to the Pentagon. In the mid 1970s Portugal was convulsed with revolution while Greece and Turkey were enemies over Cyprus. Isolationists in America began to urge a lowering of American commitment, and this in turn alarmed the Europeans. Once again American containment was at some risk even in the NATO area.

D3 The Policy of Ostpolitik

The division of Germany had led to tension in the Cold War, and had prevented a post-war settlement in Europe (see sections 3B2 and 13E3). Russia continued to fear a rearmed and economically powerful Germany demanding reunification. The West continued to fear the Warsaw Pact and to reject proposals for armed forces reductions or neutral zones. German diplomacy had always had a strong pro-Russian element. In 1966 Brandt's Social Democratic government set out on a new course. America was involved in Vietnam. Wilson's Britain and De Gaulle's France were certainly not going to stand in the way of such moves. Khrushchev had already shifted the emphasis of Soviet policy towards the Third World. There was much to be gained by stabilising the European situation in Russia's favour by obtaining recognition of all that had passed since 1940. West Germany began the process of recognising East European countries and signed the Non-Proliferation Treaty. In March and May 1970 came historic meetings between Brandt and the East German, Stoph, and when it seemed that East Germany did not welcome these moves the hardline Ulbricht was replaced by Honecker in May 1971. In August 1970 came the first treaty—a non-aggression pact between West Germany and Russia—and towards the end of the year a Polish–German non-aggression pact was signed, and the Oder–Neisse boundary recognised.

In September 1971 a Four Power Agreement on Berlin was signed by which Russia abandoned her attempts to force the Western powers out of the city, and recognised West Berlin as part of West Germany. In December that year West and East Germany signed an agreement on transit over the Berlin Wall, more visits being permitted, although the wall remains. Brandt now placed himself strongly behind Russian efforts to have a European security conference in a meeting with Brezhnev at Yalta in September 1971. In May 1972 the German parliament accepted the Polish and Russian treaties, and this cleared the way for a direct West–East Germany Treaty in December that year. This did not go as far as establishing embassies, but it provided for missions, increased contact and recognition of the existing borders. The quest for a united Germany had come to an end, and the post-war period could be said to have ended too. In September 1973 two Germanies entered UNO. In spite of Brandt's fall from office the momentum continued. During 1973 Germany renounced the Munich Pact and signed a treaty with Czechoslovakia. America was forced to respond to this situation by seeking to improve its own relations with Eastern Europe. Nixon visited Rumania in 1969, and in September 1974 America recognised East Germany. All these agreements were beneficial primarily to Europe, but they helped provide an encouraging background for arms talks and the European security conference which were the twin poles of detente.

D4 Divided Communism: Russia and China Fall Out

Relations between Communist Russia and Communist China have varied over the years. Originally Stalin had allied with Chiang Kai Shek, but after Mao's victory had switched sides and signed a treaty in 1950 (see section 6E5). During the 1950s there was economic and technical co-operation culminating in an offer to allow China nuclear weapons. Some territorial issues had been settled, and there had been limited co-operation over the Korean War and the Offshore Islands. But even during the 1950s relations began to change. Russia became a co-chairman of the Geneva Conference in 1954 whilst China refused to attend. Khrushchev began to involve Russia in the Third World where China had previously taken the lead in such events as the Bandung Conference (1955). Moreover, several of Khrushchev's policies aroused discontent in Peking. His denunciation of Stalin was resented by Mao, and an ideological dispute broke out between the two sides. When Mao reasserted Communist 'purity' during the Cultural Revolution the Russian Embassy was attacked by Red Guards in 1967. Better relations between West and East leading to Khrushchev's 1959 American visit aroused Mao's anger. At that time he was speaking of burying the West, and was angered when in September 1959 Khrushchev attacked his threatening words. As China became a great power in her own right she challenged the Soviet monopoly in the Communist world. In 1960 a treaty with Mongolia which Russia regarded as being in her sphere of influence aroused resentment, and during the next decade China continued to develop a rival foreign policy (see sections 6E–F). When Albania left Comecon in 1961 China established good relations, and later supported Rumania in her demands for independent Communist parties. China condemned Russia's invasion of Czechoslovakia in 1968. In 1964–5 Chou En Lai made a series of Third World visits followed by treaties with the Yemen and Tanzania. Rival Communist parties sprang up, and for a time during the 1960s even rival terrorist groups operated in the Third World.

Although the two countries co-operated in supporting Vietnam after the war there was intense rivalry between pro-Moscow Vietnam and pro-China Cambodia eventually leading to the war of 1979. As early as 1965 Kosygin had visited North Korea and Vietnam to consolidate Russian influence, and China saw this as an attempt to encircle her. Russia certainly has naval bases to the north and south of China, the massive Vietnamese army, and 102,000 troops in Afghanistan. Chinese influence in the Third World has been effectively curtailed by the proxy use of Cuba by Russia. In the sub-continent India is allied to Russia, and Pakistan to China. This struggle for world power, and the ideological clash led to practical differences. Russia withdrew her support for China's nuclear programme (June 1959). She denounced their trade agreement at short notice (July 1960) when 70 per cent of China's trade was with Communist countries, setting back China's second five year plan. The first border disputes came in 1962, and next year China announced she was not bound by former imperialist treaties limiting her borders (section 6E5). Since Tzarist Russia had annexed Chinese territory since 1727 China presented a threat to her Asian possessions.

During the 1960s the dispute was still essentially fought at long range—in the Third World and by ideological argument. This grew steadily fiercer. In 1966 China refused to attend the 23rd Party Congress, and in 1969 Russia tried to get China condemned by a special conference. Then in 1969 there were border clashes between the two countries, and a battle at Damansky Island. However, the end of the cultural revolution and the need for co-operation in Vietnam led to a visit by Kosygin in September that year; but Russia was compelled to take a Chinese invasion seriously, and China feared for her nuclear sites in the north. During the 1970s Russia maintained 800,000 troops and up to 250 missiles directed against China, and China continued to denounce Russia for her actions.

These events produced a major change in world relations. China was the world's largest underdeveloped nation, but she was also a great power with nuclear weapons and an expansionist foreign policy. She needed Western support if she could not obtain Russian aid, and by 1969 Mao had come to realise that burying the West and cultural purity had to give way to practical trade and internal growth. European nations had always been more friendly in their relations with China than with Russia, and France took the lead by receiving a Chinese trade delegation in September 1971. Good relations exist between China and the Common Market with the signing of a treaty in 1978. Only 20 per cent of China's trade is now with Communist countries, and in her southern provinces she is co-operating with capitalist businessmen from Hong Kong. China found it useful to resume good relations with Japan since she was equally threatened by Russian power and was a close ally of America. In 1972 Tanaka of Japan visited China, and after years of negotiation a Sino–Japanese peace treaty was signed in 1978. Above all the ending of good relations between Russia and China was an opportunity for America to reverse her previous position, and weaken Russia by friendship with China which had benefits for America in terms of increased security.

D5 Third World Diplomacy

During the 1960s another change took place which many in the West found hard to accept, and which forced the super powers into a new relationship. Overwhelming American power, the European colonial empires, the absence of independent countries and the containment of Communism within the Euro-Asian landmass had meant the West had effectively dominated the world, but during the 1960s this ceased to be so. The European empires disappeared. America lost the war in Vietnam. Her prestige was seriously damaged as was her will to be world policeman. The new countries did not wish to be tied to either West or East. They denounced military bases, seized Western property and began to co-operate among themselves in groups like the Arab League, or ASEAN. In international bodies like the UN new countries began to influence events demanding policies to help their development and motivated by bitter dislike of Western colonialism. Intervention in the Third World became increasingly difficult from the time of the Congo Crisis. In some cases UNO stepped in to effect compromises, but direct Western military intervention was very difficult.

Russia broke out of containment, and with Vietnam, Aden and Cuba established a new world position. Several countries including Vietnam, Cambodia, Laos, Afghanistan, Aden and Ethiopia, became Communist. They were often ruled by unstable military dictators. They co-operated sometimes in supporting international terrorism, and as Western effectiveness was reduced many Third World nations adopted hostile roles and sought to seize territory or build up armed strength which threatened world peace. Thus, the Indian sub-continent was destabilised by wars between India and Pakistan and the division of Pakistan (see section 9A4–6). The Middle East was destabilised by wars between Israel and the Arabs, and the efforts of Gaddafi of Libya (see section 10E–F). Central America was destabilised by Cuba, and left wing regimes sprang up in Jamaica, Grenada, Guyana and Surinam. Cubans helped to destabilise Africa in the south in Angola, and the north in Ethiopia. Of course there were Communist losses—Egypt and Somalia expelled their Communist supporters. Jamaica, and Chile lost their left wing regimes. But the overwhelming impression was of a world increasingly chaotic, and with little prospect of a return to an orderly situation. Detente between the responsible world powers rather than polarisation seemed to be one way of improving the situation.

Strategically too the world was changing. Russia was able to catch up and pass the missile gap which had rendered her inferior to the USA. From 1968 she began to build up her navy and to secure bases throughout the world. Russia now has naval facilities in Cuba, Cape Verde, Conakry in West Africa, Aden and Kampuchea checkmating the West. America faced opposition internally to the use of force which compelled her to give up support for Angola and Cambodia. Britain had already shown she was incapable of honouring her treaties in the Far and Middle East. Third World powers had to look to their own defences. Many of them signed treaties with Russia including India, Angola, Zambia, Libya and South Yemen. Even more alarming was the continued spread of nuclear weapons. India tested a nuclear device in 1974. Gaddafi was promised nuclear help by Russia, and has been trying to perusade Pakistan or Iraq to make nuclear weapons for the Arabs. There are rumours that Israel, Argentina and South Africa have nuclear weapons. The risk of world war starting because of clashes between smaller powers in the way 1914 started in Europe because of Balkan disputes is a real one. The simplistic division of the world between West and East seemed at an end, and in a multi-bloc world detente seemed to be an effective answer. Super power co-operation could, it was believed, reduce armaments and tension, settle disputes and concentrate on Third World problems thus reducing world tension. Detente thus came about because the changing situation in Europe and the Third World, and between Russia and China, necessitated a changed relationship between Russia and America. Each side believed it served their interests.

E The Era of Detente

E1 The New Relationship between America and China

America had adopted the strongest anti-Chinese line since 1949. She did not recognise China, or permit her to enter UNO. Instead she supported Taiwan. Now this was to change. The first moves came from China in 1970 when China opened diplomatic relations with Canada, and early in 1971 invited an American table tennis team to China. During the year trade and travel restrictions were relaxed. In 1971 Kissinger visited Peking, and then in February 1972 came Nixon's visit, and the issuing of a communiqué saying neither side sought dominance in Asia. 'Let us', said Nixon, 'in the next five days start a long march together.' During 1975 Kissinger and Ford visited China to keep the momentum of close relations going, and in 1979 Teng Hsiao Ping arrived in America as the first important Chinese statesman to visit that country. In order to put pressure on Russia in Europe Hua Kuo Feng made visits to Eastern European countries starting with Rumania and Yugoslavia in 1978. Chinese support for Stalinist Albania was cut off in 1978 since China was clearly no longer defending the ideological line it had held in the 1960s; if anything it was becoming more revisionist than Khrushchev's Russia had been. These diplomatic moves led to two major developments. The first was a steady growth in trade from 5 million dollars value to 500 million dollars within a few years with America. The second was that America was to modify its stance in the Far East although this presented more difficulties.

In Korea North and South remained at daggers drawn. During the Vietnam War North Korea launched border raids in 1967, and in 1968 came two serious incidents when a US ship, the *Pueblo*, was seized, and a US plane was shot down. But the regime of President Park in South Korea, where America had 60,000 troops, was repressive with martial law (1972) and the suspension of civil liberties (1974). Park was under strong pressure during 1975. North Korean tunnelling in the demilitarised zone was revealed, and an assassination attempt killed his wife. Further repressive measures followed. But it was Carter who decided to act on a proposal of Nixon's to reduce American forces, and during a visit he criticised Park and announced troop withdrawals. However, a build up of North Korean forces compelled Carter to reverse his decision in 1978 when he contented himself with criticism of Park. The opposition led by Kim Yung-Sam revolted in 1979, and Park was killed by his own security chief. However, this led to only temporary changes for by December the Park clique were back in power, and in May 1980 martial law was imposed with General Chun Du Hwan taking over the country.

Taiwan was a different matter. Having announced a 'two Chinas' policy America moved slowly to reduce her ties with Taiwan. In 1971 with American backing Taiwan was expelled from UNO, and China took her place on the Security Council. Carter completed the process in 1978 by according full diplomatic recognition to China and withdrawing it from Taiwan. Proposals by Reagan to give military aid to the regime in the island have recently aroused Chinese opposition.

E2 The New Relationship between America and Russia

Relations between America and Russia had been cooler than those of Europe and Russia in the 1960s. As long as she had influence Britain had exercised it in a restraining role in crises and in favour of improving relations. Macmillan's Moscow visit in 1959 had opened the way for Khrushchev's visit to America, but Eisenhower had taken much persuading to attend a summit meeting in Paris in 1960 (see section 3E3). The Berlin and Cuba crises caused America to be even more sceptical of good relations, and Macmillan had again used his persuasive talents on Kennedy to secure the Test Ban Treaty. But during the 1960s Britain's power declined, and America's anger at Britain's failure to help in Vietnam led to a decline in the special relationship. The result was to force America and Russia into direct super power negotiations. Attempts by Britain to act as an honest broker in Vietnam in July 1966 and February 1967 got nowhere. By the time of the Non Proliferation Treaty and the opening of SALT discussions Britain was no longer at the top table. The meeting at Glassboro' in June 1967 between Johnson and Kosygin was the start of the new super power dialogue when in spite of obvious differences the need to negotiate became apparent, and, as America began to withdraw from Vietnam negotiations, could begin.

The increasing cost, and complexity of weapons systems was affecting the economies of both powers, and the widening range of weapons made an assessment of security more difficult, causing fears of 'missile gaps' and arguments about which power was ahead. Talks opened in 1969, and in

May 1972 SALT I was signed at Moscow. This consisted of two agreements. The first limited the number of ABM defence systems, and in 1974 this was cut to one system each. The second limited weaponry and was to last for five years. The agreement effectively gave Russia numerical superiority, but this was balanced by American technical advantages, and because the agreement left out bombers, missiles in Europe and other Western deterrents Nixon could claim American superiority overall. Discussions on SALT II then began, and at Vladivostok in 1974 Ford and Brezhnev agreed upper limits of 2,400 launching vehicles of all kinds and 1,320 only to be fitted with multiple warheads (MIRVs). But SALT II ran into difficulties. In America the B1 bomber and Cruise missile emphasised a new potential while Russia developed the backfire bomber and the SS20 missile. However, SALT I was extended in September 1977, and in June 1979 SALT II was signed at Vienna by Carter and Brezhnev. It imposed limits of 2,250 launching vehicles and 1,320 MIRVs together with a ceiling of 300 on SS18 and other Soviet heavy missiles.

This treaty was not ratified by America due to events in Afghanistan and Poland, and was due to expire in 1982. Fresh talks began that year, but as yet have not progressed far as both sides have started rearming under different circumstances.

Detente led to closer relations between statesmen of the two countries. Nixon visited Moscow in May 1972 and Brezhnev visited Washington in June 1973. Both sides issued statements deploring the nuclear arms race and calling for world peace which led people to believe a more hopeful climate was replacing mutual sabre rattling in high diplomacy. Gradually also the mutual economic isolation of the two countries began to break down. As early as 1967 direct flight between them began, and co-operative efforts in space and other research took place. Various trade agreements were made including a grain deal in October 1975, and another to lay a pipeline from Alaska. Russo–American trade was worth about 3.6 billion dollars by the end of the 1970s. America had thus established closer and productive relations with Russia.

E3 European Detente

During the late 1960s the three main Western European countries sought to improve relations with the Soviet Union. Under Wilson Britain signed technical co-operation (1968) and economic (1969) agreements. De Gaulle (1966) and Pompidou (1970) visited Moscow. Brandt's policy of Ostpolitik and strengthening economic ties facilitated improved relations (see section 13D3). The West seemed willing to ignore the more sinister aspects of Soviet policy in return for limited gains that would reduce tension and arms expenditure. The invasion of Czechoslovakia and the enunciation of the Brezhnev Doctrine in 1968 made it plain Russia did not intent to relax her hold over Eastern Europe. The expulsion of 103 Soviet agents from Britain in 1971 and the revelation of an East German spy as Brandt's closest confidant in 1972 were brushed aside in the desire to secure agreement. The improving relations of Russia and America formed a background, and the detente bandwaggon was soon rolling with claims that the Cold War was at an end. In practical terms detente in Europe meant four things. It continued and expanded Ostpolitik with trade agreements between countries like Germany and Poland (1976). It relaxed Western attitudes to Communism. Communist Parties were set up in Spain, Portugal and Germany. Euro-Communism became fashionable, and it was suggested that relaxation in Eastern Europe with more consumer goods and closer contacts meant the two sides of the Iron Curtain were drawing together. Proposals were put forward in an attempt to reduce conventional force levels in Europe, and in 1973 MBFR talks opened in Vienna. They lasted for three years, and achieved nothing. But above all detente was associated with the Helsinki Treaty of August 1975.

The idea of a European conference to discuss various issues had been put forward by the Poles in 1964. It had been accepted by Brezhnev in 1966, and soon afterwards by the Warsaw Pact. By 1968 NATO had also agreed, but the Czechoslovakian invasion led to postponement. Then as SALT I seemed to indicate the genuineness of Russia's intentions discussions opened at Helsinki in 1973 and led to 35 countries signing the treaty. This recognised the sovereign equality of all European states. It provided that force should not be used to resolve disputes, that no frontiers should be changed and that there should be no intervention in each other's internal affairs. A second set of clauses dealt with human rights. The treaty provided they should be the same in all European countries allowing the basic rights of entry and exit, fundamental freedoms and self-determination for all peoples. Lastly, the treaty provided for freer exchange of information on military matters, and for future economic and technical co-operation. For some years European statesmen paid lip service to this treaty. Further conferences were held at Belgrade (1977–8) and Madrid (1980–1) to review its progress, but by the end of 1979 it was clear Russia had no intention of altering its position on human rights.

E4 Reflection: Detente or Appeasement

The era of detente is strangely reminiscent of the inter-war period in European history. The West was faced with dictatorships and overwhelming military force and responded to this situation by negotiation in the belief that concessions and contacts could defuse the danger and lead to reconciliation. Helsinki is rather like the Kellogg Pact of 1928 in which 62 countries outlawed the use of war. In the same way as the appeasers faced the Fascist dictators in the 1930s the West faced Soviet power in the 1970s. Throughout the period Russia conducted a full scale extension of its world power, signing treaties with Angola, Mozambique, Vietnam, Ethiopia and the Yemen. Through Cuba and Vietnam and by indirectly supporting terrorism country after country fell to Communism. Cuban mercenaries were to be found in eleven countries (see section 12F3). Naked aggression occurred several times. But these far away places, like Manchuria and Ethiopia in the 1930s, were no longer held to be vital interests. UNO like the League of Nations did nothing except pass resolutions or provide peace keeping forces in Lebanon and Cyprus which did not keep the peace. In spite of much talk about disarmament the period saw Russia catch up, and some argue, overtake the West in nuclear power. It certainly saw no reduction in her conventional forces, and the Soviet navy was able not only to increase in size, but to secure numerous bases from which to operate. The West's defensive treaties like SEATO and CENTO proved, like Locarno between the wars, to be useless in practice. Allies of the West like South Africa and Iran were deserted. Groups set up to monitor Helsinki were attacked including Charter 77 in Czechoslovakia and the Orlov group when Ginzberg and Scharansky were imprisoned in Russia in 1978. Other prominent opponents of the regime like Solzhenitsyn and Bukovksy were exiled. Carter protested about these violations while his economic aid sustained the regime he was criticising. The parallel with Britain's military and economic appeasement of Hitler, Mussolini and Franco was self-evident. Yet Carter, Vance and Young backed by Callaghan, Schmidt and D'Estaing all continued to pursue the policy in spite of clear evidence that Russia had not altered her course. Some began to speak of a 'third world war' which the West was in process of losing: a war of nerves and intimidation just like that used against Roosevelt, Chamberlain and Daladier in the 1930s. The murder of a Bulgarian defector in London (1977) and the revelation of extensive bugging of the American Moscow Embassy (1978) were typical of the incidents Western statesmen turned a blind eye to as they did to continued deaths on the Berlin Wall and persecution of Soviet Jews. Whenever Russia spoke of detente and disarmament she was applauded; when she acted excuses were made. Clearly long years of tension and the economic crisis following oil price rises played a vital role. Europe could only go where America went, and there the post Vietnam attack on the CIA, defence and America's right wing allies came to fruition under Carter. But by the end of the 1970s it was clear detente had failed. Armaments actually increased in a period of disarmament. Human rights were more extensively flouted in the world than at any time since the early 1940s in a period when human rights were supposed to be at the centre of diplomacy. The Lebanon, Afghanistan, Poland and El Salvador were to convince many of the need for a new policy.

F The Second Nuclear Confrontation: Yom Kippur 1973

F1 American Involvement in the Middle East

American involvement in the Middle East had begun when Roosevelt had met Sidi Mohammed II of Morocco in 1943 and Ibn Saud of Saudi Arabia in 1945. At the end of the war America obtained favourable oil concessions in Saudi Arabia and Iran, and military bases in Morocco, Libya and Saudi Arabia. For a time America had to share power with Britain, but she disliked Britain's preference for the Arab rulers, and at the time of Suez distanced herself from her allies (see section 3E6). Nor would America directly support the Baghdad Pact. But America's attempt to remain aloof was not destined to last. Turkey, Iran and Pakistan constituted what Dulles called 'the upper tier' to protect the area against Russia. Aid to Iran began in 1949, and America played a direct part in restoring the Shah in 1953. America signed treaties with Iran and Pakistan, and provided military aid. Aid for Egypt began in 1954, and it was Dulles' decision to cut this in July 1956 which played so important a part in Nasser's decision to seize the Suez Canal (see section 10D4). America also had a direct interest in Israel. She was one of the signatories of the December 1950 guarantee of its independence.

In January 1957 all pretence was dropped and the Eisenhower Doctrine made plain American involvement in the Middle East. In April 1957 the Sixth Fleet entered the Mediterranean on a permanent basis, and when the Baghdad Pact was reconstituted as CENTO in 1959 America was closely linked to the alliance. When Syria signed a Russian treaty and Iraq fell to a left wing general in 1958 America became alarmed. Arms were supplied to the Lebanon, Jordon and Saudi Arabia. Fearing Syria and Iraq might seize territory, America and Britain acted. America sent 14,000 Marines to the Lebanon, and Britain troops to Jordan. An attempt by Russia to involve herself by demanding a conference of the powers was rejected. Thus, America was steadily taking over Britain's position, and relied on the periphery states like Iran and Saudi Arabia to preserve her power in the region.

F2 The Super Powers in the Middle East

During the 1960s circumstances began to change in the area. Britain gave up her position in Aden (1967), and the Gulf (1971). America surrendered her bases in Morocco (1960), Saudi Arabi and Libya (1970). Russia took advantage of the West's weakening position. The PLO and the PFLP were set up in 1964 and 1969 and pursued independence for the Palestinian Arabs and the extinction of Israel, fomenting racial and religious feeling among the Arabs. Russia gave military aid to the PLO after Arafat visited Moscow in 1970. Their attacks on Israel both across the border and by terrorist outrage were a permanent threat to peace. They forced Israel to be an aggressive state, and this in turn made it more difficult for America to give her direct backing and easier for Russia to back the Arabs. In 1967 the Russian fleet entered the Mediterranean and established a base at Alexandria. The coming to power of Gaddafi (1969) in Libya, Sadat (1970) in Egypt and Assad in Syria (1970) gave the region three rulers initially committed to Russia. In March 1971 Egypt signed a Russian treaty, and was provided with SAM missiles thus escalating the dangers of armed conflict. After the 1967 war UNO passed a British Resolution requiring Israel to give up seized territory and negotiate with the Palestinians; and the Arabs to negotiate with 'Israel for a permanent settlement. The closing of the Suez Canal and the shutting off of oil that year had alarmed Western countries who began a slow process of adjusting to backing for the Arabs. Border fighting went on in 1968–9, and America intervened with the Rogers Plan which secured an unstable cease fire early in 1970. America then armed Israel while Russia armed Syria and Egypt. Thus, any future Arab–Israeli conflict would become a world issue (see section 10E3).

F3 The Coming of War

In October 1973 an Arab Conference took place between Hussein of Jordan, Sadat of Egypt and Assad of Syria. Each had good reasons for wishing to stand out as strongly anti-Israeli. Sadat, aware of a plot to overthrow him, expelled the Russians in 1972. He needed to show his solidarity with fellow Arabs. So did King Hussein who in 1970 had disposed of the PLO in Jordan after a civil war. Assad heavily armed by Russia was anxious anyway to attack. They had all lost territory in 1967 and were determined to recapture it. Other Arab states including Iraq, Morocco and Saudi Arabia pledged small forces to support the big three. Russia announced her support for the Arabs, and in October began to ferry 4,000 tons of equipment in over 280 flights to Syria. The following month America began to airlift arms to Israel. Additional Russian ships entered the Mediterranean, and steps were taken to strengthen the American Sixth Fleet. Three Security Council meetings and a direct appeal from Waldheim, the Secretary General, failed to reduce tension. The Arab Plan was for Syria and Egypt to launch a simultaneous offensive while Jordon mobilised to hold down large numbers of Israeli forces. A quick victory was anticipated since the combined forces of the Arabs appeared overwhelming.

F4 The Yom Kippur War 1973

The war opened not surprisingly with Arab gains. In the north the Syrians attacked on the Golan Heights, but in doing so lost 867 of their tanks. The Israeli counter attack had succeeded by October 9th. The Israelis made token raids on Damascus, and later bombed ports sinking a Soviet vessel at Tartus on October 12th. Missiles were used in attacks on targets like the Homs oil refinery. When the cease fire was not accepted immediately Israel continued her advance over the Golan Heights seizing Mount Hermon, and was within 20 miles of Damascus at the end of the war. The Egyptian attack was also successful at first, crossing the Suez Canal and beating off 23 Isreaeli counter-attacking movements by October 8th. Once Syria had been fought off Israel could concentrate on Egypt who unwisely decided to cross Sinai with a three pronged move on the central passes. Between the 14th and 19th Egypt had lost over 300 tanks in the largest tank battle since the Second World War. Meanwhile Israel counter-attacked over the Canal in the north establishing a bridgehead and seizing the SAM missile sites by October 21st. The way to Cairo lay open and Egypt accepted a ceasefire on October 22nd.

F5 The Nuclear Alert

From October 11th to 19th Kosygin was in Cairo and Mrs Meir referred to the 'sinister influence' of Russia on events. Russia continued to supply Syria and began the preparation of a major force involving 50,000 troops, a fleet of transport planes and 85 ships of the Soviet Navy. Equally Nixon pledged support for Israel and on October 19th announced a further 2.2 million dollars of aid. But Nixon was deep in Watergate troubles, and following Vietnam could not afford a showdown. It was alarming that just as America was disengaging in South East Asia she was involved in the Middle East. Kissinger was sent to Moscow in the climate of detente on October 20th–21st to see Brezhnev. The two powers backed a Security Council resolution for a cease fire which was carried by 14–0 with China abstaining, and this came into force on October 22nd. However, Israel was anxious to reach defensive positions and war continued on the Golan Heights and across the Canal. The Security Council made a second demand for a cease fire, and Sadat appealed to Russia and America to intervene to secure it. Russia said she was willing to intervene as she already had a task force assembling, and this forced Nixon into action. Kissinger and the Defence Council decided on a stage three nuclear alert at all American bases. In particular bombers were recalled from Guam, the 82nd Airborne Divison and two aircraft carriers were alerted. This was done without consulting America's allies and against the spirit of the Cooper–Church Amendment. NATO as a whole did not know until conversation on the hot line had taken place and Brezhnev had agreed not to intervene. Fortunately next morning the second cease fire held, and Sadat asked for a UN force instead. This force was constituted on October 27th, and flown by Britain from Cyprus to Egypt. America and Russia agreed to send 36 observers each, and on October 30th American forces stood down. The danger of Soviet intervention had been averted, but America was now embedded in the Arab–Israeli struggle with an interest in preserving the cease-fire and turning it into a peace treaty. The great power threat had aroused Arab nationalism, and it was Saudi Arabia who was first to cut off oil to America on October 20th. This was followed by OPEC quadrupling oil prices thus giving America a further interest in Middle East affairs.

F6 Egypt–Israel–America: The Treaty of Washington 1979

During 1973–6 Kissinger devoted himself to shuttle diplomacy in the Middle East in an effort to establish a lasting peace. He helped establish the UN Observers Force during November, and negotiated disengagement agreements between Israel, Egypt and Syria in January and May 1974. Nixon visited five Middle East countries shortly before his fall, and re-established American relations with Egypt granting generous aid including the building of nuclear reactors. By the summer of 1975 the Canal was working and Egypt had stopped excluding Israeli shipping. Sadat visited Washington. Then after changes of government in America where Ford was replaced by Carter, and Israel, where Mrs Meir was replaced by Begin negotiations began in earnest. In late 1977 Sadat and Begin met twice on each other's soil, and it became clear a split had developed in the Arab front. Sadat found himself menaced by Gaddafi and Assad and disliked the violence of the Palestinian organisations. Egypt had born the brunt of fighting and he now wished to use American aid for reconstruction. Israel was fighting the Palestinians based in Southern Lebanon and although a UN Force was established in the region Israel had little confidence in it. She was building large settlements on the west bank of the Jordan and was determined above all not to surrender Jerusalem. Compromise was possible. In 1978 Carter chaired meetings at Camp David, his summer retreat, and in March 1979 the Treaty of Washington was signed between Egypt and Israel providing for normal relations and Israeli withdrawal from Egyptian territory. In February 1980 ambassadors were exchanged and Israel had at last received recognition from an Arab state. During 1980 and 1982 the withdrawal of Israel took place supervised by an international force including Americans and British. To achieve this Israel had to accept less forthright support from America who criticised her policy in Lebanon and failure to negotiate with the PLO. Egypt gained in return American support to counterbalance Arab hostility. Gaddafi offered a reward for Sadat's death, and this occurred when he was killed at a military review in 1981. His successor Mubarak, has carried on his policies allowing Alexandria to be used by the 6th Fleet and a desert exercise to be carried out by American troops. Israel remains in a critical position because the PLO, in spite of its record, has achieved international recognition, and in 1980 at Venice the EEC endorsed the PLO as representatives of the Palestinians who should be involved in any peace settlement. Israel remains in a state of war with the other Arab states (see section 10E5).

G The Collapse of Detente 1979–1982

G1 The Return of the Nuclear Arms Race

Although the 1970s had seen some steps in disarmament they also witnessed an increase in expenditure, and towards the end of the decade Russia, with its SS20 missiles, was drawing ahead of America—in at least one category of nuclear weapons—for the first time. They spent 150 billion dollars more than the United States and, although overall Russia and the Warsaw Pact were still outmatched by America, NATO and the French and Chinese deterrents, the American people became increasingly worried by this new situation, and this was to lead in part to Reagan's election victory. In Europe which had lived closer to nuclear war there was less alarm and a greater willingness to pursue detente. But here the problem was increasing alarm about Russian conventional superiority. It was estimated Russia had a three to one superiority in most forms of artillery and there was increasing danger that NATO would be overwhelmed in the field. SALT II was not ratified because of Soviet provocations including refusal to withdraw 5,000 troops from Cuba and her conquest of Afghanistan, but even before this alarm had been created by Carter's defence policies. He had cancelled the B1 bomber and provided no answer to the Russian SS20 intermediate range missile. He proposed the use of a neutron bomb, and having persuaded Britain and Germany to take it cancelled the project in April 1978. Moreover, the increasing complexity of flexible response made it difficult to find out exactly what the balance of the deterrent was between the powers. Russia relied on large missiles, and the Americans on smaller more accurate ones. Russia's conventional forces were said to be out of date. But on the other hand their backfire bomber and SS20 missile had no direct counterparts in the West. A 'missile gap' was referred to, and before long demands for rearmament were being made.

In May 1977 NATO agreed to a three per cent rise in real terms in defence spending, and in December 1979 they agreed to accept 108 Pershing and 464 Cruise missiles—to meet the already existing SS20s. Carter resumed arms supplies to Turkey and decided to keep troops in Korea. After Afghanistan he demanded a five per cent increase in defence spending, and this has been further increased by Reagan. The governments of Thatcher in Britain and Mitterrand in France decided to modernise their deterrents. In Britain's case this meant replacing Polaris with Trident II, giving Britain 16 missiles each with eight warheads and twice the range, The B1 bomber is to be produced, and in Britain the tactical air force is to be modernised with Tornados. All these events created alarm among many on the left and in pacifist circles who had believed in detente and there was a revival of anti-nuclear campaigning in the early 1980s. Disarmament talks began again in 1982, but were almost immediately broken off as Poland succumbed to Soviet-backed military rule. The present situation is therefore as dangerous as at any time since the early 1960s, and potentially more so for the West.

G2 Soviet World Strategy and the Soviet Navy

The problems of conventional balance in Europe and world nuclear deterrent balance were old; but during detente a new problem appeared. Russia stepped to some extent into the role of the former Western colonial powers. They had surrendered overseas bases: Russia began to acquire them in considerable numbers in Indo-China, the Red Sea area and around Africa. With the help of the new bases, Cuba and Libya, Russia was able to exert a dominant role outside her land mass. In 1975 came a spectacular airlift to Angola, and in 1977 an equally impressive one to Ethiopia. Military aid was given to guerilla organisations in numerous parts of the world. East Germans helped SWAPO guerillas against South Africa, and Libya has trained a large army which has threatened Egypt, the Sudan and Chad. Aden was attacked by air and sea in 1978, and conquered. Russia has destroyed containment, and to make this clear has created in addition to her existing fleets two new ones in the Mediterranean and the Indian Ocean. Under Admiral Gorshkov the Soviet fleet has become the second largest in the world, even though Russia is a largely land-locked power.

In Western strategic thinking the nuclear deterrent seemed to blind many to the consequences of losing conventional superiority. Economic crisis led to Western defence cuts and cut backs in development programmes while in Russia the government had no such restraint. Britain and America returned to volunteer forces and thus lacked manpower. Since manpower was more expensive than missiles the West cut bases and naval–amphibious resources. The effects were considerable. Russia could influence Third World countries equally with the West. Whereas Russian–Cuban world deployment was efficient, an attempt by America to rescue her citizens in Iran collapsed in 1980. NATO commanders complained that the northern flank of NATO's sea defences had been turned with disastrous consequences for the whole of its strategy.

By the early 1980s the West was becoming aware of this situation and the return of Reagan and Thatcher to power gave NATO fresh determination to rearm. Carter had set aside 10 billion dollars to train an RDF of 100,000 for action anywhere in the world. In 1981 America held military manoeuvres in Egypt to train for Middle East War, and the force was ready in 1982. Carter re-activated American military co-operation with Pakistan, and Reagan has since provided Saudi Arabi with arms and obtained facilities in Somalia and the Sudan. The British have consolidated their relations with Oman, and in response to Argentinian aggression despatched a force of 101 ships to the South Atlantic in April 1982. Yet unease remains. To some in spite of Soviet setbacks and the failure of the terrorist movement in many places, the overall picture is of a world where Russia is not contained and peace is very precarious.

G3 Russian Aggression: The Annexation of Afghanistan

Afghanistan has always been a buffer state between Russia and the Indian sub-continent, and with Russia's quarrel with China it became crucial. Opposition to the royal family was led by Daoud who was forced out of the country, but returned ten years later in 1973 and established a republic. Russia gave large amounts of aid to the new regime and 'advisers' went to the country. Then in April 1978 a left wing coup under Taraki took place. Daoud and 30 of his relatives were slaughtered, but resistance was not stifled. At the very moment the Shah was toppled for reforms disliked by Muslims Taraki embarked on similar reforms like the emancipation of women. The Muslims under their mullahs resisted, and in civil war 12,000 were killed. It was clear Moscow's money was being wasted, and there was even fear that such resistance might spread over the border. In true imperialist fashion Taraki was killed in a second coup in September 1979 and Amin came to power. However, he was no more successful and controlled only six out of 29 provinces. The Afghan army was reduced to half its former size by desertions. In December 1979, with an airborne attack on Kabul and the invasion of the country by four divisions, Brezhnev disposed of Amin and put Karmal in his place. But resistance stiffened. As early as February 1980 the killing of civilians began and Russia was forced to impose military rule. Some 102,000 troops occupied the country and civil war continued. It is not clear what the casualties have been, but Russia seems to have lost about 10,000 killed. The rebels have lost many more. One report speaks of 3,000 killed by chemical warfare alone. One quarter of Afghanistan's population are now refugees in Iran and Pakistan.

This crisis revealed the weakness of Carter's policies. He tried to retrieve the position by cancelling the Russian grain agreement, ending co-operation on technical matters, halting SALT II and proposing a boycott of the Moscow Olympics in July 1980. Russia suffered immense loss of face in the Third World. An Islamic conference of 34 nations and the United Nations (by 104–18 with 30 abstentions) both condemned her. It brought America and China closer together with offers of sales of military equipment by America. Pakistan under General Zia, earlier criticised by Carter on human rights grounds, was now courted. China sent her military aid and America reactivated her facilities there. Yet surprisingly no attempt was made to arm or fund the guerillas and before long Western unity was shattered, as usual by France, when D'Estaing met Brezhnev in May 1980. Nor was even so limited a measure as the Olympic boycott successful. The real damage to Russia was caused by the increased determination of the West to rearm in the face of Russia's first direct military operation since 1945.

G4 The Fall of the Shah of Iran and the Gulf Crisis

At the same time as the Afghan crisis America was facing equally grim events in neighbouring Iran. Reza Pahlevi was placed on the throne by the British in 1941 and restored to it with American help in 1953. He had sought to modernise Iran by dictatorial methods. He used secret police and by 1975 had resorted to one party rule. His own family acquired a vast fortune, and the extravagance of an £8 million coronation in 1967 reflected the autocratic nature of his regime. But Iran was loyal to the West and took over Britain's role in the Gulf. Modernisation was taking place starting with the land reforms of 1963. Iran was threatened by both the Communist Tudeh Party, which had cells in the army, and by the Shiite Muslims led by Ayatollah Khomeini, exiled in Paris. Carter pressed the Shah on human rights, and in March 1978 concessions were made. Riots began, and in November military rule was the result. Carter urged the Shah not to use force, and in January 1979 Reza left the country (see section 10F4). Finally allowed to enter America later that year, he died in 1980. Khomeini returned to the country and was the power behind the government. Muslim reactionaries embarked upon systematic killings which are still going on, as are attacks on minorities like the Kurds and Baathists.

But world-wide the 'Islamic' revolution was much more serious. In November 1979 the American Embassy was attacked and 60 hostages (later reduced to 49) were taken because Iran wished to use them as a lever to get the Shah out of the United States in order to execute him. A rescue attempt failed with American deaths in the desert, and was followed by the resignation of Cyrus Vance, the Secretary of State, who had opposed even this move. The final release was only obtained after America had made a humiliating surrender of Iranian assets to the new regime. Instability in Iran had many consequences. It ended CENTO. Shiite Muslims elsewhere stirred up trouble. The Gulf appeared unstable and the threat of Russian penetration from Afghanistan became a possibility. Apart from the immediate effect on oil prices the world's second largest oil exporter could no longer be regarded as pro-Western, and the war between Iran and Iraq which started in 1980 (see section 10F4) made matters worse. Carter was forced to declare the Gulf a vital area of American influence and to create a rapid deployment force. A flurry of diplomatic activity patched up differences with Turkey and Pakistan when Reagan took over, and this was followed by an arms deal with Saudi Arabia, but the Gulf remains in a state of war and instability.

G5 The Coming of the Falklands Crisis

Argentina had been ruled since 1976 by a series of military juntas (see section 12D3). Towards the end of 1981 a three man junta led by Leopoldo Galtieri together with Anida and Lami Dozo took office in a country where heavy international debts, massive inflation and rising unemployment were the background to increasing political discontent and a revival of Peronism. Neither Reagan nor Thatcher had any scruples about dealing with the right wing regime. Indeed, Galtieri had visited the USA and was strongly backed by many in the Reagan administration, particularly Mrs Jeanne Kirkpatrick, the American UN representative. It is possible that Galtieri misread this for more specific support, and calculated that Reagan would back the Monroe Doctrine and the Treaty of Rio (see section 12D1) if Argentina seized the Falkland Islands.

Galtieri certainly misjudged the British reaction. Britain had ruled the Falkland Islands since 1833 and they were her last colonial possession in the Latin American hemisphere. Argentina claimed them as the Malvinas, and since 1966 intermittent discussion about the islands had gone on spiced by occasional Argentinian threats. But it seemed as if Britain was losing interest in the region. In 1976 Argentina occupied the remote South Sandwich Islands and was not repelled. In 1982 the withdrawal of *HMS Endurance*, the survey ship in the region, was announced. Heavy defence cuts in conventional naval forces being implemented by John Nott, the Defence Minister, made intervention unlikely. Indeed if Galtieri had waited six months he might have been luckier but domestic discontent forced his hand. The unopposed landing of some Argentinians on South Georgia was the sign he was waiting for, and early in April 1982 Argentina seized the Falkland Islands and their dependencies. The latter, incidentally, had been British since 1908, and formed no part of former Spanish territory. Many believed Galtieri needed the British possessions to strengthen his country's claims to parts of Antarctica known to be rich in oil and minerals but also claimed by Chile and Britain. Two men notorious for their part in the mass killings of opponents of the junta became governors: General Menendez, the 'butcher' of Cordoba, in the Falklands and Captain Astiz, the leading torturer at the Naval Engineering School prison, in South Georgia. On April 18th before visiting the islands Galtieri declared: 'The Malvinas are our islands and we are not going to abandon them.'

G6 The Falklands War 1982

Mrs Thatcher was vulnerable on a number of grounds: her defence policy was said to have over-emphasised the nuclear aspect; the Foreign Office was said to have written off the Islands; and the government was said to have paid insufficient heed or taken inadequate action faced with the Argentinian threat. Over all hung the memory of Suez (see section 10D5). Britain and other nations had tended to accept the seizure of their property rather than risk war, or resort to some face saving formula. On the other hand many Third World countries were facing similar threats: Belize was subject to a claim by Guatemala, while Venezuela was pressing a claim to Western Guyana. Above all, Galtieri was a fascist dictator and the 'Disappeared Ones' said to number 22,000, were a major case of human rights violation. Thatcher acted swiftly in a series of political and diplomatic moves designed to secure her position and regain the islands without a Suez fiasco. Lord Carrington resigned and was replaced by Mr Pym. A full enquiry on government policy was promised for the future and parliament, with the exception of 33 Labour members who voted against military action, backed her.

At the United Nations a British Resolution (Number 502) calling on Argentina to withdraw was swiftly prepared and passed by the Security Council with only Panama voting against, and even Russia abstaining. This enabled Britain to claim throughout that she was acting in self-defence under Article 51 of the Charter, and as a result many Third World countries were able to back Britain. There was unanimous support from the Commonwealth with New Zealand offering a frigate and the Commonwealth Secretariat condemning Argentina. NATO gave full support with only Spain complaining a little, and an arms embargo was imposed on Argentina. Britain took unilateral trade sanctions against Argentina, and then secured EEC backing for trade sanctions. Although Ireland and Italy could not in the end support

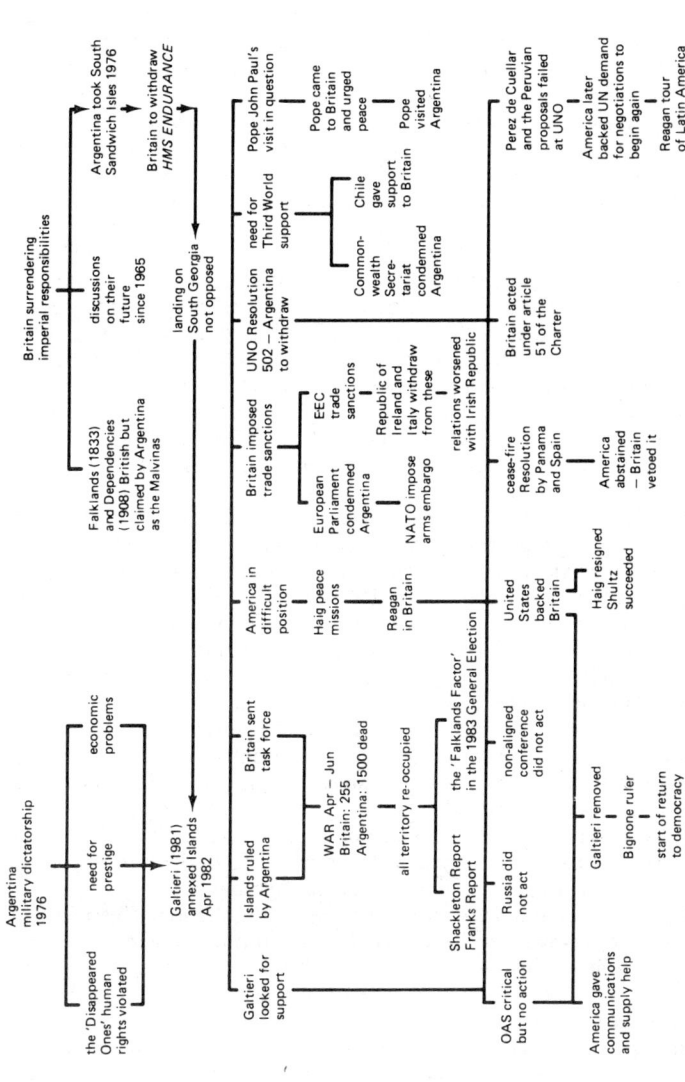

Fig. 26. The international aspects of the Falklands Crisis

these, sanctions proved most useful. The European Parliament voted to condemn Argentina.

But it was American support that was most essential if Britain proposed military action in her hemisphere, and at first this did not seem to be forthcoming. Concern over Latin America (see section 12G3) led Reagan to adopt the role of 'honest broker'. Secretary of State, General Alexander Haig, embarked on a Kissinger style peace mission to London and Buenos Aires. This failed as did no less than seven sets of proposals for a negotiated settlement. The new UN Secretary General, Perez de Cuellar, and Peru put forward proposals when Pym visited New York. The Pope who was due to visit Britain intervened asking for peace, and then added a visit to Argentina to his intinerary. Ireland asserted her neutrality and threatened to bring forward a cease-fire resolution in the United Nations. In the end this was put forward by Panama—a right wing dictatorship—and Spain, whose claims to Gibraltar were well known and whose King, Juan Carlos, had offered to mediate. By then Britain felt strong enough to veto the resolution early in June, and America abstained. Mrs Kirkpatrick and Haig differed over this vote, and later Haig resigned to be replaced by Mr Schulz. All this time Sir Anthony Parsons, Britain's UN representative, and Sir Nicholas Henderson, her ambassador, had done good work in rallying American political support. It was clear America backed Britain and a motion in Congress received almost unanimous support. On April 30th Reagan came down on Britain's side.

Even in Latin America Mrs Thatcher had her successes. The Rio Treaty was invoked by Argentina, but the OAS while calling for withdrawal by Britain was unwilling to take action. A few countries like Venezuela gave a little military hardware, but trade between Latin America and Europe and America's switch were too strong for Latin solidarity. Moreover, Argentina was one of the world's largest debtor nations, and the war forced her to devalue the peso. Thus, neither Latin nor American business interests favoured Galtieri. Chile actively opposed him because of a territorial dispute, and later provided facilities for a British raid on an Argentinian base. Costa Mendes, the Argentinian Foreign Minister, went to the Cuban led Non-Aligned Conference, but again obtained no support while rumours that Russia, who bought much of Argentina's grain, would act, came to nothing. To achieve so much support in two months was remarkable, and it provided the necessary back up to military action which from the first Britain took in conjunction with her diplomatic and economic moves.

Britain prepared a Task Force for the South Atlantic. This involved a hundred ships moving troops 8,000 miles to recapture the islands. Eventually forces totalling 30,000 were involved in Britain's largest war effort since Suez, and in what eventually became the most extensive use of air and sea power since 1945. Ascension Island was available as a base, but harsh weather conditions and the closeness of Argentina made the expeditionary force a hazardous military operation. Defence cuts and inexperience in warfare involving missiles were to take some toll in lost ships and crashed helicopters, but the overall conduct of the expedition was remarkably successful. South Georgia was recaptured on April 25th, and the first attack on the islands came on May 1st. After the sinking of the *Belgrano*, Argentina's second largest ship, the Argentine Navy played no more part in the war. A preliminary raid on Pebble Island was followed by a major amphibious landing at San Carlos Water on May 21st. The Argentinian air force attacked the British fleet sinking two frigates and two destroyers and seriously damaging four other battleships. But in the process the Argentinian air force was virtually destroyed. Sixty-seven planes were shot down and 42 destroyed on the ground for British combat losses of 9 aircraft together with 11 accidentally lost.

Once established on the islands the British troops lost little time in launching a land campaign against superior numbers culminating in the recapture of the capital Port Stanley. The Argentinians surrendered on June 14th and on June 19th British forces completed their task by removing the Argentinians from the South Sandwich Islands. On the British side there were 255 deaths and 770 injuries. Argentina has not given exact casualty figures, she lost something like 1,800 dead and 10,000 were taken prisoner. One result was soon apparent. Galtieri was driven from office, and succeeded by General Bignone. A purge of generals including Menendez and the resignation of Lami Dozo, the Air Force chief, followed. Argentina's economy declined further, and political opposition demanding a parliament increased.

The longer term consequences of the war are more difficult to assess. As far as the Thatcher government was concerned the war created the 'Falklands Factor' in British politics which enabled the unpopular government to win several by elections, and was sufficiently close to the election of June 1983 to help the Conservatives to their largest election victory since 1935. The government is left, however, with the substantial cost of replacing defence losses and rebuilding life on the Falklands, which have now become a large overseas fortress. The effects in Latin America were not as drastic as were thought at the time. Reagan needed support for his more interventionist policies in the Caribbean and undertook a tour of several Latin American countries in order to emphasise American involvement in the hemisphere, and most recently in 1983 has been able to use the good offices of the President of Colombia in an effort to solve the El Salvadoran conflict.

G7 The Situation in the Summer of 1983

One difficulty in writing about modern world history is that the ending has to be arbitrary. Events can happen with astonishing rapidity or unpredictability. Poland was establishing democratic rights in 1981, but in 1983 the country is still under military rule and May Day was marked by riots in over 20 towns. The Lebanon was engulfed in war again in 1984, but a peace settlement was secured and further moves are being made in the spring of 1984 to get Israeli troops withdrawn. The situation remains tense now the international peace force has left. The seizure of the Falklands by Argentina came out of the blue and produced important political consequences in Argentina, America and Britain. In one sense the historian has to predict; he selects facts according to their significance and deals with trends which stretch into the future. But it would be a rash historian who predicted what will happen in the next year in Lebanon, El Salvador, Iran, Chad, or Afghanistan let alone tried to forecast overall patterns in such matters as disarmament progress, the difficulties of the

Common Market, Reagan's Caribbean policy, or the future of South Africa.

By the summer of 1983 it was clear that detente no longer governed the relations of the major powers. The only exception to this was that Russian action in Afghanistan and Vietnam, combined with the siting of SS20 missiles and the strengthening of her Pacific fleet in the Sea of Okhotsk, continued to threaten China; therefore Sino-American relations remained good. China is also seeking an agreed solution to the future of Hong Kong, part of which will revert to her in 1997. Relations between America and Russia have changed for the worse. Brezhnev became increasingly hardline in his last years, and his successor, Andropov, as a former KGB Head proved equally intransigent. The actions of Russia in Poland and Afghanistan have prevented the ratifying of SALT II, and so far no progress has been made in the new round of arms talks begun in 1982 at Geneva. The Commission on Human Rights reported in 1983 that there were four million in Soviet camps, and the continued repression of Poland, in spite of the release of Walesa and a second papal visit, make nonsense of the Treaty of Helsinki. Cases like those of Tomin in Czechoslovakia and Sakharov in Russia continued to remind people that detente had changed nothing politically in Eastern Europe. Soviet adventurism continues. At the moment Polisario guerillas, Palestinian and Syrian forces in Lebanon, Cubans in Angola and Aden, Sandinistas in Nicaragua and SWAPO in South Africa receive Russian aid. Recent arms agreements with Syria, Iraq and Zambia (1982) increased Soviet naval presence throughout the world, and evidence secured by Brazil of extensive Soviet arms shipments to Central America highlight the continued military threat of the Soviet dictatorship. Moreover, the usual methods of subversion continue. In 1982–3 Soviet submarines penetrated Norwegian, Swedish and Italian waters. Britain, France and America expelled Soviet spies, and long term spy rings involving politicians were revealed in Iran, Japan and South Africa.

This situation has produced an increasingly strong Western response although in practical terms it has been difficult to do much since CENTO and SEATO have been abandoned and NATO needs rearming. NATO was not at first united in its response. NATO rearmament began in 1978 and Carter started the RDF in 1979. The West has made arms agreements with Pakistan, Oman, Somalia and Saudi Arabia, and threats to the Sudan and Egypt have been quietly contained. The change in Western governments has been dramatic. Reagan succeeded Carter in 1980 and adopted a strident anti-Communist stance. The British Prime Minister, Thatcher, elected in 1979 and re-elected with a larger House of Commons' majority in 1983, restored the close relations with America which had been damaged during Vietnam, took the lead in pressing for European resistance to Russia and started modernising the British nuclear deterrent. The French Socialist government of Mitterrand, elected in 1981, although at first seemingly well to the left and continuing Gaullist policies of embarrassing the Americans by, for instance, giving aid to Guatemala and Iraq, did in fact embark on modernisation of its nuclear deterrent and acted closely with Britain during the Falklands Crisis. Then in 1983 the long period of rule by the Social Democrats in Germany was replaced by the Christian Democrats under Kohl, who strongly supported America and the stationing of Cruise missiles in Europe. Socialist governments elected in Portugal (Soares) and Spain (Gonzales) during 1982 did not react against NATO, and the long standing Greek threat to withdraw has not materialised.

Much of the world remains in the hands of an unprecedented number of dictators and military governments. Some countries like Kenya, Japan, Malaysia and India still enjoy democratic governments. In others like Jordan and Bolivia it has recently been restored. Elections took place in Turkey and Argentina towards the end of 1983, resistance to Marcos in the Philippines and Pinochet in Chile is increasing. There is some evidence of resistance to Cuban forces in Central America. In May 1983 South Africa experienced its first major terrorist attack when 16 people were killed in Pretoria. But in many places dictators remain, military government is introduced (as it was recently in Ghana and Nigeria), or democracy is slowly eroded. Elections have been postponed in Pakistan and Chile. In Europe the 45 governments of Italy since 1945 are an ominous comment on the future of democracy there; in the Third World countries like Zimbabwe are moving towards one party rule. Expensive, irresponsible, militarist governments inevitably increase instability, and the world as a whole pays little heed to United Nations initiatives, or peaceful settlements. In the Middle East Lebanon remains unstable, and Syria, Libya and Iraq are involved in military activity. A bitter war between Iran and Iraq continues. Israel bombed Iraq in June 1981 and invaded Lebanon in June 1982. The murder of President Sadat of Egypt (1981) and the bombing of the American Beirut Embassy (1983) are sharp reminders of the terrorist role in politics. In Europe the civil war in Northern Ireland has claimed 2,200 lives since 1969 and remains the longest terrorist war. The recent election of a moderate Dublin government willing to act against the IRA and the failure of an attempt to intimidate the British government by hunger strikes has left an unstable and dangerous situation.

In the Far East, South Korea suffered a double shock. The Russians shot down one of their airliners killing 252 people in August 1983, and in October, 21 people, including four of their cabinet ministers, were killed by a North Korean bomb planted in Rangoon.

Russia faces major problems at the moment. Poland is volatile. Afghanistan sucks up resources and leaves Russia condemned in the Third World. Her economy is weakening and her need for vital resources like oil and wheat is ever more apparent. She has made substantial gains in the world during the detente era, but they have been bought at a cost—the renewal with public support of Cold War attitudes in the West. This in turn has produced escalating armaments which Russia can ill afford. After a period of illness, Andropov died in 1984 and his successor, Konstantin Chernenko, is elderly and unlikely to support reform.

China was in an era of increasing prosperity with the aid of Western trade and technology, while her politics were in an era of moderation, and Russia remained her enemy. America too seemed in the summer of 1983 to be through the worst of her recession. Reagan had secured major re-armament programmes at home and for NATO, and some attempt was being made to counter Castroism in Central America—as yet with little success. If the Falklands continued to reveal muddled American diplomatic skills, the Habib and Schulz Lebanon Missions produced improvements if not solutions. There was an air of *realpolitik* about in the summer of

1983 called by some a return to Cold War polarisation in the globe and by others a welcome change from the era of 'one sided' detente. Behind great power politics which still controlled the world's destiny other problems—racial conflict, resources, the environment, human rights and disarmament—remained unsolved.

Revision Questions

1. What is meant by the phrase 'the nuclear arms race' and how has its character developed and changed since the early 1960s?

2. What steps are being taken at the moment in nuclear disarmament and why are they proving so difficult?

3. Discuss the significance of the following: (a) the Russian Navy, (b) the five nuclear powers, (c) Cuban mercenaries, (d) international terrorism in military and political terms.

4. Explain how Britain ceased to be a major world power after 1945.

5. Why was there a Cuban Crisis and what were the results? (See section 12F.)

6. Why did Vietnam become the major flashpoint of the Cold War in the 1960s and why did America lose the Vietnam War that followed?

7. Explain the changes in the balance of power since 1960. Your answer should include: (a) Ostpolitik, (b) Polycentrism, (c) the Sino-Soviet split, (d) Detente, (e) European unity, (f) Third World independence.

8. What were the main features of the detente era and how effective was the policy?

9. Explain why Israel has been engaged in Middle East Wars in 1967, 1973, 1980 and 1982 and what effect these wars have had on international relations.

10. Did Britain's war with Argentina in 1982 have any major international importance?

11. Discuss the dangers present in situations in: (a) Central America, (b) South Africa, (c) Iran, (d) Afghanistan.

Further Reading

Beggs, R., *The Cuban Missile Crisis*, Longmans, Harlow, 1971.

Bown, C. and Mooney, P. J., *Cold War to Detente, 1945–80*, Heinemann Educational Books, London, 1981.

Bullock, J., *The Making of a War: The Middle East 1967–73*, Longmans, Harlow, 1974.

Deutscher, I., *Russia, China and the West*, Penguin, 1972.

Hastings, M. and Jenkins, S., *The Battle for the Falklands*, Michael Joseph, 1983.

Horowitz, D., *From Yalta to Vietnam*, Pelican, 1969.

Laqueur, W., *The Rebirth of Europe: Europe Since Hitler*, Penguin, second edition, 1982.

Thompson, Sir Robert, ed., *War in Peace*, Orbis Publishing Company, London, 1981.

14
World Issues in the Last Quarter of the Twentieth Century

A Political Issues

A1 The Survival of Democracy

Perhaps the most important political issue for free men is the survival and development of democracy in the world. It was only in the nineteenth century that representative, liberal and parliamentary democracy began to spread. The sovereignty of the people, the right to vote free from pressure or corruption, a freely elected parliament, a varied party system, majority rule with respect for the rights of minorities, equality before the law, freedom to own property and dispose of your own income, freedom for people to choose their own job, or to come and go from a country, freedom of opinion including the rights of free speech and assembly, a free press, religious toleration, educational freedom from state control and the right to form trade unions are just some of the many aspects of life in a democracy which it is all too easy to take for granted. In any democracy there will be abuses of power and a need for ceaseless vigilance. It is important to remember how very recently and with what struggles democracy has been achieved, and how very precarious the hold of democracy is in the modern world.

Democracy is essentially a western concept, and it is significant that until now it is only in Western nations or those basically colonised from Europe that democracy has succeeded. In Western Europe, the United States and the Commonwealth countries of Canada, Australia and New Zealand democracy has advanced at different rates, but at least successfully. The vote has been given to all adult men, then to all adult women and now to all over eighteen in elections for a central parliament, federal parliaments and local government. Property qualifications have been removed and discrimination against minority groups, such as American blacks, by means of additional qualifications for voting have been removed. Those countries that between the wars seemed to lose faith in democracy have recaptured it in the case of France and Germany. Several countries like Greece, Portugal and Spain have recently advanced towards democracy effectively for the first time in their history. However, in the world as a whole the outlook for democracy is poor. Russia, China and all Communist countries are one party dictatorships and have few of the rights listed in the first paragraph. As the empires of the European powers broke up it was hoped democracy would replace colonial rule. Ninety-four democratic constitutions were drawn up in London for the British Empire during the Twentieth Century, but few Commonwealth countries have maintained democracy. Some like India have genuinely tried, although for most of its modern history India has been a one party state in reality and under Mrs Gandhi did resort for a short time to dictatorship. But most have failed so far. This is not surprising. Democracy is seen as a suspect European idea. It is difficult to reconcile with the extreme nationalist policies, or heavily planned economies favoured by new states. South America freed itself from European domination in 1810–24 and in the century that followed 125 constitutions were devised, but still the area reverted to dictatorship and rule by military junta. Democracy can be exported successfully as countries like Mexico, Israel or Japan illustrate, but at the moment the overwhelming majority of United Nations members are not democracies.

Three main problems confront a democracy. The first is to ensure that it remains vital and effective. Governments elected by a minority of the electorate, or trade unions dominated by a minority of their members are not very democratic. Education and participation are vital; or as President Kennedy once said: 'Ask not what your country can do for you—ask what you can do for your country'. Democracy is menaced internally by a number of factors. The growth of rigid party systems manipulates parliaments and may even deprive the elector of choice, or other parties from taking power. The size and complexity of modern government may make it difficult to pin down governmental responsibility. Public accountability through such methods as the public enquiry or the parliamentary commissioner is vital. If the government comes to control too great a share of personal income or industry (and therefore people's jobs) basic democracy is also undermined. As Mill said: 'There is a limit to the legitimate interference of collective opinion with individual independence'.

An endless search for equality is a second menace to liberty and democracy. Equality of man before God as embodied in the American Constitution is not an open ended invitation to abandon all standards of judgement, or to strive towards total equality of incomes or rights. The American Constitution goes on to say: 'They are endowed with certain inalienable rights, that *among* these are life, liberty and the pursuit of happiness'. Merely to do what you like is to surrender to the tyranny of self-will and passion; it is not exercising freedom in a democracy which is essentially freedom within the law. No state has created complete equality. In Communist societies in the words of George Orwell 'All animals are equal, but some animals are more equal than others'. There has been some difficulty in reconciling liberty, in which people of differing abilities reach different levels and reap different rewards, with a tendency to seek for notional equality. Thus, incomes policies designed to be fair to the low paid have annoyed skilled workers. Race laws designed to curb racial prejudice have substantially reduced freedom of speech and political action. 'Liberty', said Isaiah Berlin, 'is liberty not equality or fairness or justice or human happiness or a quiet conscience'. The most serious threat to democracy and liberty is from those who deliberately seek to destroy it. Some seek to do so by overthrowing the rule of law and inducing a state of anarchy. Some belong to political parties that desire its end. What is perfectly clear, as Mill said as long ago as 1859, is that: 'The principle of freedom cannot require that he should be free not to be free'. Democracy more than any other system depends on the people; without them it is being easily overthrown in many parts of the world.

A2 Dictatorship and Human Rights

Many countries have never known democracy or basic freedom. Russia was ruled by autocratic tzars, experienced a few months of Kerensky's government, saw its only freely elected parliament expelled by Lenin and is a one party state. China was ruled by emperors, its early republic soon degenerated into one party rule under Chiang Kai Shek and has also become Communist. The states of Eastern Europe were ruled by autocratic kings, between the wars by fascists and royal dictators and then occupied by Russia. The states of the Middle East were parts of the absolutist Ottoman Empire, then Western colonial possessions and are now one party Muslim states. Much of Asia, Africa, the West Indies and Hispanic America went from tribal rule to colonial rule and thence after short democratic experiments, to one party dictatorships or military juntas of the left and right. However, there is no reason why the basic human rights of democratic free government should not be extended. There are 175 nations belonging to the United Nations who have formally assented to its charter. The Universal Declaration of Human Rights (1948) and the setting up of the International Court of Justice (1949) have been followed by the European Court of Human Rights (1958) and the Treaty of Helsinki (1975) in which Russia and the East European states paid lip service to basic democratic principles. World opinion can be mobilised against particularly flagrant examples of suppression of liberties, or extremist dictatorship.

But in this context there are several important points to make. Attack on Western democracies comes ill from Third World countries that do not practice even the rudiments of democracy. The main threat to freedom is from Communism, and there is very little protest about Communist abuses. For example, pro-Western regimes in South Africa, Turkey or El Salvador are subjected to criticism for failing to be democratic or libertarian whereas there have been few demonstrators if any about the horrific slaughter of the Kampucheans or Afghans by Communist regimes. There are other double standards. All people are declared equal; then a resort to dictatorship is justified on the grounds that some of them are politically immature. Left wing dictators are accepted because they removed a former right wing government, even if they are equally dictatorial and fail to handle the problem of poverty. Allende of Chile is often favourably contrasted with General Pinochet, his successor, but they were both one party rulers and the economy is probably in a better state now than it was under Allende's Communists (see section 12D5). Right wing takeovers are condemned unhesitatingly although in the case of Turkey, for example, the country was close to anarchy before the coup (see section 7E9). In discussing human rights and democratic freedom it is essential to uphold them against their enemies on both left and right. Both extremes manifest themselves in the same ways with a one party state, a controlled economy, an aggressive and often subversive foreign policy, religious persecution and abolition of the basic freedoms.

A3 Civil War: Minorities, Tribalism and Separatism

Since 1945 there has been no year in which war has not raged somewhere in the globe. Some conflict has been caused by great power rivalry and the struggle for independence in the Third World, but much also has been caused by internal conflict. Self-determination was proclaimed by President Wilson in 1918 as the solution to Europe's problems. In the nineteenth century nationalism had been a potent political force creating new countries like Germany and Italy. Between the wars Europe had a large number of intensely nationalist states and fascists stimulated this feeling—Hitler calling for all Germans to return to the Reich, or Franco for one united Spain. Nationalism began to spread to the rest of the world when countries like Egypt and Turkey secured recognition as independent states. In the Second World War nationalism received further stimulus, and after 1945 spread throughout the world. Independence has seemed attractive for many small ethnic, tribal, or national groups. Armed and financed quite often from outside, given publicity by the media and a platform in many world organisations national groups have sustained long and ultimately successful wars, even if some have been brutally suppressed.

Europe is still far from free of this problem. Britain during the 1970s was faced with separatist demands from Wales and Scotland. In Northern Ireland Britain abandoned separate government and was thus faced with the problem of ruling an area with a large religious minority and an active terrorist movement. France has been faced with agitation in Corsica and Brittany. Belgium is plagued with divisions between Flemish and French speaking peoples. Spain since the death of Franco has been faced with separatist movements in Catalonia and the Basque Province. Yugoslavia still has a problem with its Croat separatists. Racial minorities have agitated for special status too in the American continent—the French in Quebec, or Black Power in the United States are prominent examples.

But it is above all in the Third World that difficulties have arisen. Many of their borders were drawn by former colonial powers which the new countries were reluctant to accept. Many new countries like India or Nigeria were created by a colonial power out of many races and creeds, and without the strong external pressure of the colonial power were likely to come apart. In Nigeria a Civil War having its origin in rivalry between the Hausa–Fulani, Yorubas and Ibos killed some 600,000. Pakistan broke apart when Bangladesh was created. Cyprus was divided by force in 1974. Tribalism played a big role in the Congo Civil War (1960–4), and divided Ruanda and Urundi after a savage war. Race has proved a dividing factor—the Karens fighting against the Burmese government, or the Indians and blacks against each other in Guyana for example. Sri Lanka has persecuted her Tamil minority. Religion has also proved divisive. In the Lebanon civil war has raged since 1975. Palestine has been torn apart by Jews and Arabs since 1948. The Sudan has witnessed bloodthirsty war between Arabs and black Africans. China has suppressed the Tibetans, and Russia has a record of racial persecution in the Baltic States, the Ukraine and among the Muslim peoples of Central Asia. Incipient civil war hangs over South Africa because of tension between the white minority and the black majority.

It is curious that nationalism is often deplored in one's own country and praised in someone else's. Many who would scoff at patriotism in Britain or America are ready to leap to the defence of national groups elsewhere. Very often effective states have been seriously damaged by these wars. If nationalism is now held in the West to have been replaced by wider links like the Common Market and NATO then it is likely to eventually ebb in the Third World too. It provides an endless excuse for interested powers to intervene. The West sells arms to both sides in disputes. Russia sends Cuban proxies to Angola, or the Yemen to serve its own interests. New countries have to maintain large military expenditure when they are already poor, and in some cases have diverted aid to warlike purposes. The United Nations has intervened in places like Cyprus and the Lebanon. In countries like Spain the granting of a large amount of autonomy has helped. But serious problems remain. The seizure of Afghanistan and South Vietnam by the Communists has created vast refugee problems to add to the long standing one of the Palestinian Arabs. Groups like the Croats or South Moluccans can be readily recruited by international terrorists. Detente has led to a reduction of Western involvement, and the result has been to prolong civil wars in places like the Lebanon or El Salvador because neither side can win unaided.

Regional organisations already exist in the Third World which may come to have greater solidity. In 1982, for example, the Organisation of African Unity sent a mixed force to Chad to stop civil war there. As the new nations establish themselves extreme nationalism, resentment over the colonial division of their lands and fanatical racialism at each other's expense will tend to diminish as they have in Europe. The League of Nations provided minority protection treaties and these could be re-introduced or enshrined in international law. It is often difficult to distinguish terrorists, freedom fighters, persecuted minorities and rebels from each other depending on your viewpoint. Clearly a rising standard of living and extending democratic rights would do much to reduce resort to force. Regimes which seek to curb these demands have only themselves to blame. Thus, the 40,000 dead in Nicaragua's revolution (1979) were incurred in suppressing the Somoza dictatorship. There is sometimes a price to pay for freedom, and just as it is unwise to assume that every minority that revolts is necessarily justified so it is equally unwise to assume that violence may not sometimes be necessary to advance political progress. John Locke long ago recognised the right of citizens to rebel against tyranny.

A4 Nuclear Weapons and their Consequences

Nuclear weapons were developed by both sides during the war, but it was the Americans who produced and used the first three bombs in 1945. By this time Soviet spies had informed Stalin of the bomb's existence and the capture of German scientists, made by both sides at the end of the war, enabled the two super powers to begin manufacture. Britain, France and China have since become nuclear powers on a far smaller scale. Fear of such destructive weapons spreading led to the Non-Proliferation Treaty (June 1968), but this was not signed by France or China and since then some 17 countries have acquired the capacity to make nuclear weapons. This has been highlighted recently by three events: the attempt of Colonel

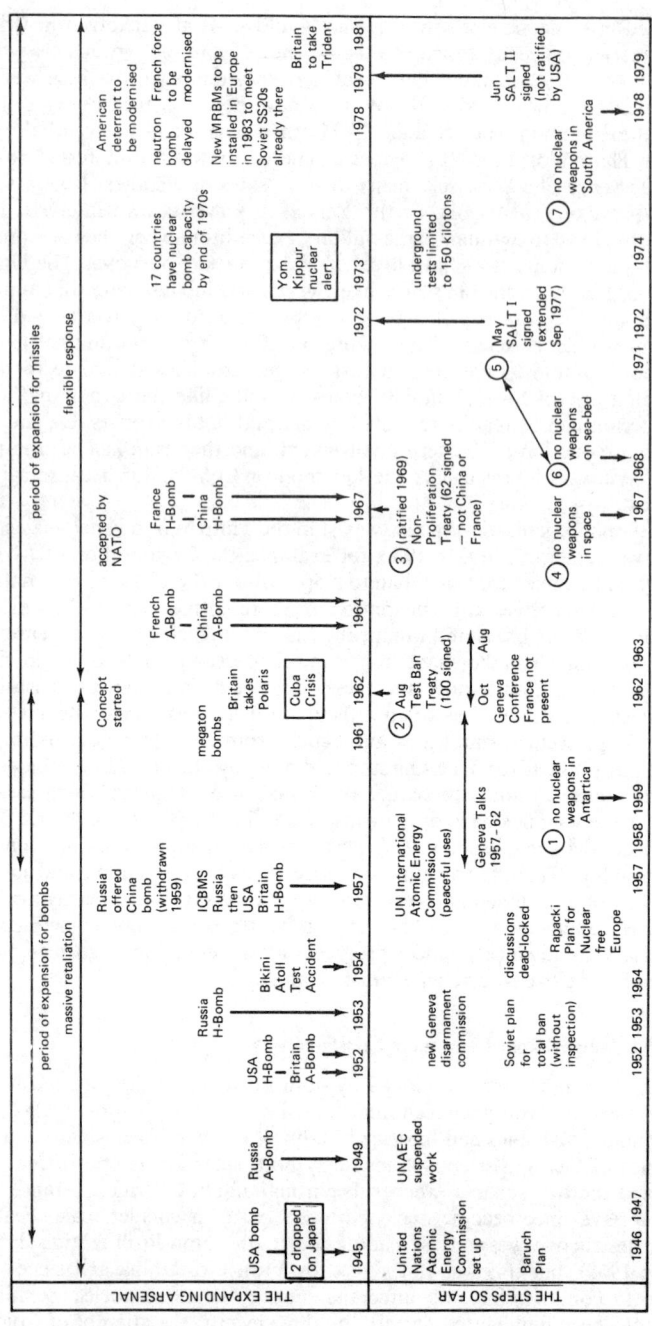

Fig. 27. **Steps towards nuclear disarmament**

Gaddafi of Libya to make a bomb in co-operation with Pakistan; the blowing up by Israel of an atomic plant in Iraq; and rumours that South Africa has detonated a nuclear device. The Treaty of Tlatelolco has banned nuclear weapons from South America, but recently there have been suggestions that Argentina has obtained nuclear capability—possibly from Germany. The problem of proliferation remains, and it is one that even multi-lateral disarmament does not immediately solve, particularly as nuclear science for peaceful purposes continues to develop apace throughout the world.

For many years nuclear weapons were largely confined to those delivered by bombers; the American B29, B45 and B52, the British Valiant and Vulcan and the Russian TU4, TU16 and TU20. The West maintained superiority in numbers throughout the 1950s and the principal concept was that of a deterrent which would prove effective because of massive retaliation. But other methods of warfare were soon added. The Americans obtained German scientists like Dormberger and Von Braun and V2 details from Peenemunde and Niedersachswerfen, and in 1950 began research on rockets or missiles. In 1957 Russia and America began to develop ICBMs with a range of up to 4,000 miles, and in subsequent years these have been followed by IRBMs (range of up to 1,500 miles) and MRBMs (range of 500 to 1,500 miles). These in turn have been followed by smaller tactical nuclear weapons. Bombers now form only a small part of nuclear capability and in addition have come a bewildering variety of delivery systems. There are missiles launched from fixed sites or silos, and others from nuclear submarines making any attempt at control even more difficult.

At first nuclear powers competed by making larger bombs until these reached the megaton range by 1961, but their testing led to atmospheric pollution and in August 1963 a Test Ban Treaty was signed by America, Britain and Russia ending tests in the atmosphere. It became clear that the mutual destruction involved was so great that there would be no drawing back from a nuclear holocaust, and the 1962 Cuba crisis (see section 13A1) forced a rethink on ways of maintaining the deterrent. As a result flexible response was introduced, and each side built up a variety of weapons. However, this has made disarmament more difficult. Delivery systems are of varying degrees of efficiency, missiles vary in speed and accuracy, the number of warheads delivered from a particular missile or submarine vary and the detection of submarines adds an almost insuperable obstacle to verification, which would have to be part of effective disarmament. The amount spent on nuclear weapons, the stockpiles and the waste products continue to grow.

From the beginning there have been efforts to disarm, but these have met with only limited success. The Baruch Plan (1946) to stop development was rejected by Russia who refused observation and put forward their own alternative plan. By 1949 discussions based on the United Nations Atomic Energy Commission had broken down. Then in 1952 a Disarmament Commission was set up at Geneva, and in September 1953 talks opened on arms limitation rather than general disarmament. The West tended to want careful inspection and to proceed category by category; the East wanted general disarmament. Thus, they put forward the Rapacki Plan (1957) to free Central Europe from nuclear weapons and today advocate a nuclear free Europe. From October 1958 to July 1960 there were Geneva Talks and a further attempt in 1962. The Test Ban Treaty in August 1963, largely engineered by Macmillan of Britain, was the first effective step towards disarmament. In January 1964 the Geneva talks resumed, and in 1968 came the Non-Proliferation Treaty which has been signed by 83 countries. In 1969 talks on strategic arms began in Helsinki and Vienna leading in May 1972 to SALT I which imposed a five year ceiling on the main categories of missile. SALT II talks began almost at once, but although the treaty was finally signed in Vienna in 1979 it has never been ratified by America. Present talks have been overshadowed partly by the Western decision to modernise their deterrents and catch up the 'missile gap' with Russia, and partly by Russian action in Afghanistan and Poland. Some further steps have, however, been taken. Nuclear weapons have been banned in Antarctica (1959), in Outer Space or orbiting the earth (1967), on the sea-bed outside 12 mile territorial waters (1971) and underground above 150 kilotons (1974).

Nuclear weapons like many weapons of war in the past are terrible to contemplate. They are certainly not the only menace to peace. Massive conventional armaments still threaten the world as does the possibility of war started by an irresponsible minor power. Biological warfare (controlled by a treaty in 1972) and Chemical Warfare would be equally horrific. But the Campaign for Nuclear Disarmament has since its foundation in 1957 concentrated its attention on nuclear weapons. These create serious moral problems: for the scientists who work on them, the servicemen that operate them and the politicians who may have to order their use. Twice (in 1962 and 1973) there has been the serious threat of nuclear war, and in spite of massive safety procedures there have been accidents and mistakes in warning systems. Yet it is clear statesmen have been almost continuously active in the last 20 years to get disarmament, that progress is possible and that in the meantime the deterrent works. Difficulties stem from the complicated nature of the weapons, the existence of technical knowledge, the stockpiles and their disposal, the refusal of other potential nuclear powers to co-operate, the delicate strategic balances during disarmament and the relationship between nuclear and conventional weapons. Unilateral disarmers see one moral issue and ignore the more practical matters involved.

A5 International Terrorism

'The purpose of terror is to terrorise' said Lenin, and terrorism is no new feature of international relations. In the nineteenth century Anarchists and Nihilists murdered heads of state and government officials. Earlier this century there were plenty of right wing terrorist groups like the SS in Hitler's Germany, and the KGB and its predecessors have long specialised in terrorist techniques. But in recent years the world has faced an unprecedented wave of terrorism 'methodically trained, massively armed, immensely rich and assured of powerful patronage'. Modern science has perfected a wide range of devices that have helped the terrorist (and later his detectors); communication between various parts of the globe is easier; several Third World States have provided bases, arms and sanctuary; Russia has put her massive resources behind Cuba, Libya and the Palestinians who form the bases of the movement. Western governments have been weak in responding because they were in the process of surrendering a world peace-keeping role and because detente carried dividends for them. It is almost impossible to classify

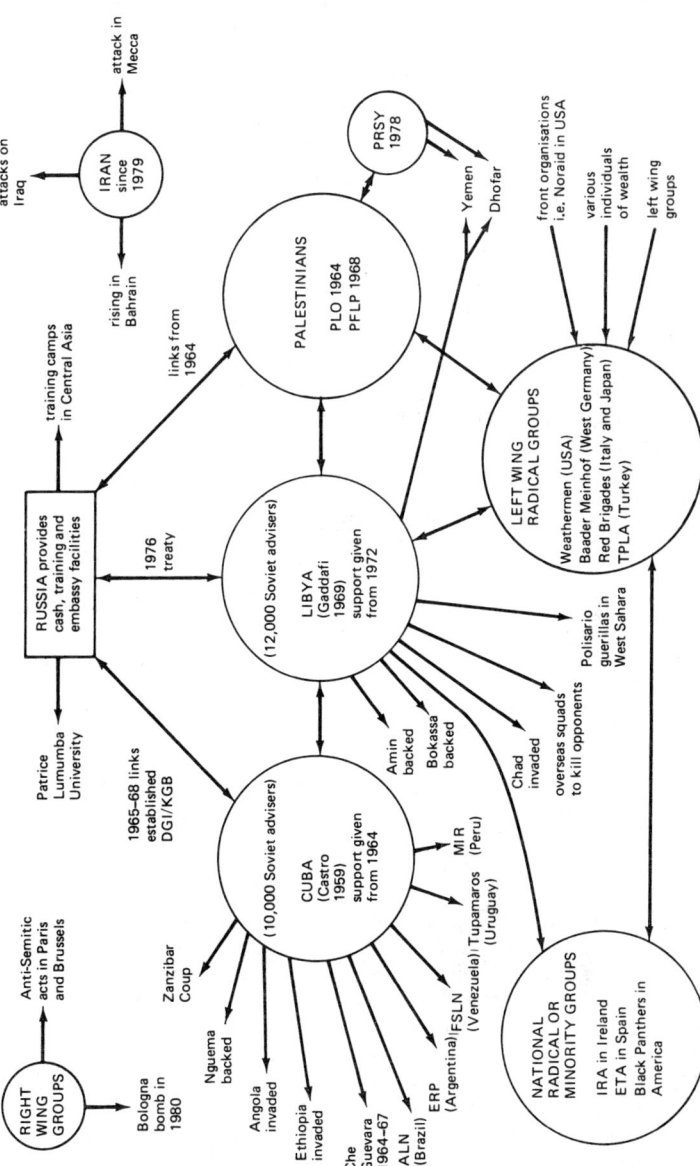

Fig. 28. The extent of international terrorism

the 140 odd organisations that have operated in 40 countries throughout the world (always excepting any Communist countries) since 1968. Some are small groups of rich, discontented Europeans and Americans soured by their own society and eager to overthrow it. Some are nationalist, separatist, or minority groups; others acknowledge Marxist, Trotskyite, or Maoist ideology as their driving force. There are also right wing groups operating, but these are small beer compared with the leftist groups.

Historians are not agreed on the significance of this outbreak of terrorism. Some maintain it is a response (even a legitimate response) to oppression in the world arguing it is spontaneous and seeing it in the light of guerilla movements or resistance fighters of the past. More recently several commentators have taken the view it is a movement with co-ordination and links throughout the world. 'There is', says Sterling, 'nothing random in this concentrated assault on the shrinking area of the world still under democratic rule'. The terrorists have not struck at left wing dictators or military rule. Their actions have the effect of exposing Western weakness. By forcing governments to severe security restraints and stimulating right wing backlash effects they strengthen left wing parties in the countries concerned. These events have taken place during a period of detente when the Soviet Union cannot take overt action and when Western governments are only too ready to deny Soviet involvement. Many groups no doubt pursue genuine national aims, but the only overall aim that has so far been achieved is to immensely increase Soviet influence throughout the Third World. The argument is that although finance comes from many sources including Arab oil, Noraid in America, or hostage ransoms much comes from the Soviet Union; that while many agents and fighters are nationals they are accompanied, trained and through embassies protected by, Russians; and that the KGB has created a world organisation which engineers coups and assassinates opponents.

This is a plausible argument since from 1919 Soviet Russia has organised international revolution (see section 3A5) with parties in every country and large embassy staffs notorious as KGB members. During the Cold War it perfected a network of contacts throughout the Western world. It was during the 1960s that Khrushchev initiated a new policy with the founding of Patrice Lumumba University, the opening of KGB contacts with the Palestinians in 1964 and with the Cuban Communist Party in 1965. But it was in 1968 that the decisive move was made. The more extreme PFLP was set up, and in December the first of 13 planes to be seized was attacked at Athens. Defectors like Sejna have revealed how East German and Czechoslovak arms and training camps were provided. Later using KGB men from Central Asia some 35 camps were established in Russia itself. But above all it was contact with Cuba that year when Simenov was sent there to organise them that proved most valuable. Russian advisers and troops helped to staff training camps and to arm the Cuban army. As early as 1969 a defector revealed what was going on, and by 1980 over 60,000 Cubans were doing Russia's work in several countries reminiscent of a nineteenth century imperialist army. Cubans are Russia's sepoys and it is no coincidence that the Cuban economy is under Russian control (see section 13F3). By 1971 Russian support for guerilla movements was clear. A plot to seize Mexico was uncovered which involved the MAR group led by

Mexicans trained in Moscow. Nineteen were seized by the Socialist government of Mexico and five Soviet diplomats expelled. The same year Boris Ponomanev wrote an article in 'Kommunist' on the new policy of backing liberation movements even if they were not marxist.

Cuba began its involvement in terrorism in 1964 when Cuban-trained Okello seized Zanzibar and murdered the Sultan. Cubans supplied armed support for the insane dictator Nguema of Equatorial Guinea. They trained guerillas in South America for the 'Venceremos Brigades' and have played a major role in backing groups like Nicaragua's Sandinista guerillas. Contacts were opened between Arab revolutionaries and Cuba, and by 1975 Cubans were in the Yemen. In 1978 Aden was shelled and bombed by Russian units manned by Cubans. The president, Ali, was murdered and the People's Republic of the South Yemen, complete with 2,000 Cubans, came into existence as a further guerila training area. By 1976 Cubans were arriving in Libya, and in 1978 Libya allowed its airfields to be used to help the movement of Cuban troops to Ethiopia. South Yemen has attacked North Yemen, and Ethiopia is involved in bloody war in Eritrea and with Somalia over the Ogaden region.

Arab dislike of Israel lay at the heart of their terrorist organisations—Arafat's Al Fatah; Habash's Popular Front and Jibril's People's Front. All have received Soviet backing, and all have provided facilities in turn for the IRA, ETA, Baader Meinhof, the Red Brigades and the Japanese Red Army. Western governments seemed to adopt a lenient view of Arab terrorism. Of 204 Arab terrorists arrested between 1968 and 1975 outside the Middle East only three were in gaol a year later. The willingness of the West to negotiate with the PLO, and of the United Nations to hear Arafat indicate the degree to which world order has declined in recent decades. It is significant that Arab leaders themselves have dealt sharply with such movements. In 1970 Hussein of Jordan expelled the PLO with great slaughter, and when the sacred mosque at Mecca was seized in 1979 Arabia acted with severity. The West took some time to act. In 1976 effective counter measures were first agreed, and in 1977 the Strasbourg Convention made them clearer. Two spectacular rescue successes in 1976 (Entebbe) and 1977 (Mogadishu) brought the seizure of planes to an end. Special anti-terrorist groups were used like the German Grenzschutzgruppen (GSG9), the French National Gendarmerie (CIGN) and the British SAS. A United States cabinet committee started work in 1972 and the Octopus Project amassed detailed information. International terrorism continues to claim its victims, but not one of the groups' actual aims have yet been achieved. In 1980 five out of six terrorists were killed in a siege at the Iranian embassy in London, and early in 1982 the Italians with the help of the CIA were able to seize over 150 Red Brigade members.

Between the Middle East and Cuba lies Libya ruled since 1969 by Colonel Gaddafi who began in 1972 to provide funds, arms, training and sanctuary for terrorists. In 1976 a treaty with Russia secured him massive military aid. His army doubled to 44,000 in four years, and he is attempting to get a nuclear weapon. 12,000 Soviet advisers have entered the country, and Russia achieved the end she had wanted in 1945 when Stalin asked for Libya (see section 3A6). It was to Libya that the Munich Olympics terror gang returned in 1972. In camps at former Western bases up to 20,000 have received training. In September 1979 Gaddafi held a parade of his 'Foreign Legion' aimed at destabilising Africa. He has backed the Dhofar terrorists in Oman, invaded and seized territory from Chad, offered a million dollars for the death of Sadat, tried to have Bourguiba of Tunisia murdered, sent aid to terrorists in the Lebanon, funded and trained ETA, Polisario guerillas in Algeria and the IRA.

The list of killings, kidnappings, seizures of planes and embassies, bombings and uprisings is lengthy. Some of those who died had themselves been men of violence. Quintanilla, the Police Chief who killed Che Guevera, was himself killed in 1971 and Somoza of Nicaragua was murdered in Paraguay in 1980. But it is hard to see any justification for the indiscriminate kidnapping and murdering of diplomatic personnel like the British ambassadors to Ireland and the Hague, or the American ambassadors to Guatemala, the Sudan or Pakistan, the killing of innocent aeroplane passengers and embassy personnel who are fellow workers, or the murder of men like Lord Mountbatten (1979) who was humane and liberal and brought India to independence. The seizure of businessmen, judges and ministers to demand ransoms, or the murder of politicians like Moro of Italy strikes at individual liberty and democratic society. In some cases like Uruguay (see section 12D4) or Turkey (see section 7E9) nations have been plunged into strife and denied democracy because of terrorist activity.

The nature of terrorism can be shown by studying the Basques. When Franco's regime ended the Spanish government released 749 prisoners and allowed 849 exiles to return from France. ETA wanted home rule which the Spanish government conceded (see section 7E4), but ETA Militar and GRAPO (the new Spanish Communist Party) wanted to use the Basques to destabilise the new regime and provoke right wing reaction. Thirty-four senior army and police officers were killed, and deaths rose from 19 in 1976 to 130 in 1979. In 1977 Spain expelled six Soviet agents and was not surprised to find Gromyko suggesting ETA terrorists would cease activities if Spain did not join NATO.

It is true there is no mastermind, but there are three or four major paymasters, half a dozen countries where training and arms are provided and one country which has consistently benefitted from these activities. Terrorism is an international threat to basic human rights because it denies democratic change or personal freedom by indiscriminate killing, but it is also a threat because however extreme or vile the actual terrorists behind them lie genuine grievances and a struggle for world domination. In Sterling's words: 'The tangled lines pass from guerilla training camps to thefts and shipments of arms, stolen and forged documents, safe houses, safe passage in transit and sanctuary abroad, regional summit meetings, hot money laundering services, straight forward cash transfers, swapping of cadres and contract killers borrowed from the criminal underworld. There is no following them all through a deep underground maze. But it is no longer so hard to see where the broader lines begin and end'.

B Economic Issues

B1 The Survival of Capitalism and the Marxist Challenge

Although the roots of capitalism can be traced back to many periods of history it was in the early nineteenth century that it became the dominant economic theory of the Western powers. The basic concepts were developed by three English economic writers—Smith, Ricardo and Mill—and involved the expansion of production by means of free enterprise and free trade. By buying in the cheapest and selling in the dearest market profits would be maximised and eventually wages also would benefit. The unfettered use of new processes, opening of new markets, disposal of capital and exploitation of the work force created a dynamic which led to industrialisation and unprecedented economic growth. Strong competition created a further stage of capitalism in which cartels, monopolies and price rings sought to keep up profits while tariffs excluded or damaged foreign competition. The Western powers acquired empires in part to provide fields for investment and exports and secure cheap raw materials and food.

This system brought immense benefits to a large part of mankind, but it was also subject to serious objections. During the nineteenth century a rival economic theory—marxism—was developed. The concepts of Karl Marx were designed to provide a total view of the world. They embraced a theory of history implying it was a process based on materialism, a theory of society seeking to replace several classes with one class, a theory of government based upon equality and a theory of economics by which the producers of wealth should be the owners of wealth. The creation of Soviet Russia and Maoist China followed by an increasing number of societies run on Communist lines has created models for this economic system which has proved attractive in the present century. As Barraclough says: 'At the heart of communism was a deeply ethical concern for social justice, for equality between man and man in the sense of non-discrimination on the grounds of sex, race, colour and class. Marx and Lenin spoke not for one country against others, but in the name of oppressed groups and classes all over the world, and this universality was beyond doubt a main factor in ensuring their influence'. The nature of this appeal has already been discussed (see section 1B3) and it is important to realise that communism has as much positive appeal as capitalism. Writers like Deutscher and Laqueur have drawn attention to the appeal marxism has for those who have suffered capitalist exploitation rather than its gains, who dislike western ideas and see marxism as a 'world' concept offering gains to all and embracing social and political theory more suited, it seems, to the new nations of the Third World than the concepts of the market economy and democratic choice.

During the 1930s capitalism reeled under a world economic crisis (see section 5A2) which lasted for much of the decade. This produced new enthusiasm for marxism, a rush to fascism and a realisation that capitalism if it was to survive must meet this new situation. Barraclough distinguishes three periods of reaction: total hostility, extreme fascism and a compromise stage in which the mixed economy emerged. Managed capitalism by which the state took a hand was in some ways a contradiction, but the state had never completely stood aside. Free trade was aided by the navies and armies of the Western powers. Laissez faire was accompanied by factory and health reforms. Bismarck's Germany gave subsidies to industry, created a welfare state and protected industry with tariffs. In the West the concept of a free economy has largely given way to the prevalance of mixed economies with some degree of planning at the top, an expanding public sector and a measure of government regulation. The seminal work of Keynes argued that government intervention in controlling interest rates and the money supply could stop cyclical depressions from becoming disasters and prevent massive unemployment. At the same time Beveridge, also concerned to prevent unemployment, urged a universal, free, contributory system of benefits which grew into the welfare state. These concepts had already been practised in Roosevelt's America and Socialist Sweden, and the onset of socialist governments after 1945 ensured their widespread adoption (see section 2B2). Moreover, the new conservative parties accepted them and by the 1970s even American Republicans and Franco's Fascists were putting such concepts into practice. In the period 1945 to 1973 capitalism experienced something of a new golden age. It was a period of American supremacy and of recovery in Western Europe. In the Third World Japan and other Asian countries like South Korea, Taiwan and Singapore proved the effectiveness of capitalism. Barraclough could maintain in 1964: 'Few people would deny that Keynesian economics, the maintenance of full employment, social services and the redistribution of income by taxation have restored the stability of the private enterprise system'; and ten years later Roy Harrod could still say: 'To the best of my knowledge the majority of people now are Keynesians and have been for some time'.

B2 The Developed Economies and the Oil Crisis

The 1970s saw the onset of a new crisis for capitalism. This had many roots—the weakened economic position of the west now that it no longer had colonial possessions, for example—but it was made far more serious by the rising price of oil which provided a constant impetus to inflation. The late 60s and the 70s saw inflation threatening the West, but this has now developed into stagflation with rising unemployment and rising inflation hitting all Western economies. America weakened by Vietnam awoke from the 'American Dream' of the 1950s and 1960s. The world's former great power, Britain, was sinking from third to twelfth richest country over a period of 25 years. Between 1951–64 the British standard of living doubled. Between 1974 and 1979 it was static. In 1983 Britain has over three million out of work and 5 per cent inflation. The German economic miracle has faltered. Japan experienced a period of sharp economic decline in the mid-1970s. The world economic summits since 1975 have been one outcome of this new crisis of capitalism, but at the moment no effective solution has been produced. There are 36 million unemployed in the Western world.

Reaction to this crisis varies. Each of the three groups already discussed—capitalists, marxists and mixed economists—have different views. Marxists say this is further proof of the essential inadequacy of capitalism. They urge the full adoption of communism in the West. Among capitalists the reaction has been sharp. The Chicago economists in America, particularly Frederick Hayek (b. 1899) and Milton Friedman (b. 1912), have argued that it is the third group—the mixed economists—who are to blame for the present state of affairs. They argue that excessive government spending has created inflation and damaged business thus reducing wealth, while at the same time rising social expenditure has cut people's income available for investment and increased the non-productive area of the economy which a shrinking industrial base has to carry. The solution to the West's depression they argue is to return to basic capitalism—curb deficit financing, cut government taxes and expenditure, denationalise industries and allow a freer operation of the market. The crisis has bitten deeply and therefore there has been a political response in sympathy to this viewpoint, most notably with the election of the Thatcher (1979 and 1983) and Reagan (1980) governments, but shown also by the overthrow in 1976 of Sweden's socialism, or the varied actions of Fraser in Australia, Pinochet in Chile and Seaga in Jamaica. Even Mitterrand's socialist government in France adopted some anti-Keynesian policies in 1982.

The most interesting question facing Western capitalism is whether or not these new policies will work. Friedman argues that a comparison of Singapore and Japan with India or China indicates that free enterprise capitalism works for the Third World as well as for Western countries. Certainly many Third World countries have toyed with capitalism because historical factors, the availability of loans, aid and technical expertise made it acceptable, but such 'neo-colonialism' is easy to denounce from a nationalist view point and if the Western economic dynamic is seen to be faltering the marxist alternative, already attractive and with apparent successes behind it, is waiting to be tried.

B3 State or Free Enterprise

There is a direct link between the survival of democracy faced with the challenge of the one party marxist state and the survival of capitalism faced with the challenge of the socialist planned economy and welfare state. It has been said that the mixed economy and welfare state lead men 'to prefer equality in slavery to inequality with freedom'; in other words, at what point does government interference with the individual's life through control of his job and income effectively destroy him as a free individual? This question faces everyone who lives in an increasingly complex society, particularly Britain where much of the national product is controlled by the government and a complex welfare state provides protection 'from the cradle to the grave'. But it is of course a world issue. As long ago as 1966 Reagan was elected Governor of California in order to reduce government expenditure and services, and Proposition 13, advocating lower state taxation, has now been followed in America by a government dedicated to changing policies accepted by Nixon and Carter alike in the 1970s.

In one way at least the movement away from consensus between capitalism and socialism has been provoked by a realisation that marxist economies have not delivered the goods. In the 1930s the Webbs could write of marxist Russia where there was no unemployment and spectacular rates of growth. In the 1970s there could be no doubt how such facts came about: Russia had been in large part a vast labour camp in which millions had died. Khrushchev in 1956 told the truth about Stalin. In 1980 the Gang of Four trial in Peking began to tell the truth about Mao. Russia and China had become great industrial powers and solved the question of the formerly utterly degrading poverty of the great mass of their peoples. But they had achieved this with deaths, calculated in 1978 in *Le Figaro* at between 120 and 140 million. It was also true that neither country approached in terms of welfare benefits and wage standards their Western counterparts. The state of the Polish economy and the grave shortages in the Russian economy indicate the failures of Eastern Europe's economy. There have been gains, but these have not been sustained. In the Third World the collapse of the Cuban economy, which is now subsidised from Russia, or of Allende's marxist government in Chile, which ended with 500% inflation, indicate that the socialist alternative is not always successful.

In the Western world the Keynesian–Beveridge concepts have come in for criticism. The once admired British welfare state is now over-burdened by bureaucracy, and so lacking in resources that it cannot provide effective health treatment in some cases for years. Private health schemes have grown space. The English state education system, created under the Education Act, 1944, and admired throughout the world is starved of re-sources, failing to attract effective teachers and beset by major problems of teenage disruption. In America similar points can be made. If the state runs the services they have to be paid for by taxes, and this may well take money away from the actual services themselves just to pay the bureaucrats. There is a new vested interest anxious to preserve large government and interference in people's lives. Washington has 350,000 civil servants. Academics too, who are employed as advisers and consultants, see the value of what are called in Britain 'quangos'. But it is no longer possible for the Western economies to carry this burden. A deeper issue is whether or not big government is desirable. Christopher Booker has remarked: 'The securest prison is that from which the prisoner no longer wishes to escape'. The concept that people ought to rely (and have a right to rely) on the state for jobs, education, health and welfare can be taken too far. There must be a limit when the mixed economy overbalances into the controlled economy, and clearly if a government provides for all the most important elements in life a person is beholden to that government. Hayek's *Road to Serfdom* (1944) and Friedman's *Free to Choose* (1980) highlight this dilemma. Has marxist socialism worked? Has the mixed economy–welfare state kind of capitalism worked? Is the new capitalism the right answer?

B4 The Rise of Aspirations in the Developing Countries

The rich and the poor were once expressions that applied in the context of Western countries, and although extremes of wealth and poverty still exist in both capitalist and Communist societies a far greater issue has been raised in recent times: the gap between the developed and underdeveloped nations. It is a fact of world history that however much exploitation—in the form of the slave trade, one crop economies, cheap labour, or the peon system—has taken place, the advance of the third world to a point where it has rising aspirations has been brought about by the Western colonial powers. They supplied the infra-structure of a modern economy to the greater part of the world—there are few purely tribal or nomadic societies still existing. World communications, industrial development, banking systems, improved agricultural yields have come from Western entrepreneurs, some capitalist, some marxist. The language of progress has been Western—the language of science and technology. The control of pests like locusts or diseases like malaria have been achieved by Western skills. Whatever the losses to the underdeveloped world by war, famine and oppression the gains in terms of education, welfare, basic public services and economic growth have been considerable. Critics who charge modern Western governments with neglect of the underprivileged need to recall the increases in wealth, comfort, life expectation, educational and health facilities for the overwhelming mass of the people. Present complaints about neglect of the Third World need to be seen against the background of what has already been given during the period of colonialism and since in the form of aid and trade.

The impression is sometimes given that little is being done, and the sheer size of the figures induce a feeling of helplessness which is quite unmerited. Vast areas of the globe like Russia, China, Brazil, South Africa, Canada, Nigeria, Israel and Japan enjoy standards of living unthinkable 20 years ago. The coming of independence has tended to make Third World countries belittle their colonial pasts, or pretend they were only dark days of oppression. One has only to consider the development of agriculture in Zimbabwe or Kenya or any of dozens of Third World countries to realise that rising world population would be in a far worse position if it had not been for the colonial powers who replaced subsistence economies with production for a profit. Third World countries have tended to despise neo-colonialism, to resent aid that comes with strings and is brought by a white man. In some cases economies have been developed in a reckless fashion bringing only disaster. Some of the world's recent disasters like the famines in Biafra or Ethiopia, or the suffering refugees of Vietnam and Afghanistan have been inflicted by forces other than Western governments. The British Commonwealth gave £1,697 million of aid between 1945 and 1969 for example. The French community has opened parts of the former African empire to some of the benefits of the Common Market through the Lomé Agreement. America's aid to the world through Lend Lease, UNRRA, Marshall Aid and to individual countries runs into billions of dollars.

Some new countries have suffered from rich governing classes and extravagant dictators, and from their political ambitions often leading to civil wars. Administration is lax and corruption widespread in many Third World countries. Nearly all seek to maintain large armed forces beyond their capacities and to carry out a world role with embassies and international conferences they can ill afford. Cuba has a defence budget of a billion dollars, for example. All this is understandable; it is no different from the Balkans in Europe in the early part of the century. But it must be borne in mind when facing Third World criticisms of harshness and indifference. Apart from Cuba helped by Russia and Tanzania by China, Communist countries have a notably bad record in giving aid and supporting United Nations agencies. Their aid, as countries like Egypt and Somalia found out, also has strings attached.

The Brandt Report (1980) drew attention to the problems facing the majority of mankind, but said nothing new. The League of Nations had 20 honourable years in reforming world health, putting down slavery and drug trafficking and improving labour conditions. The League Handbook for 1934 contained 140 pages of such activities. The United Nations has an equally honourable record based on the Economic and Social Council. Commissions deal with a wide range of matters like drugs, women's rights and population problems. Specialised agencies operate on the same lines as the League—the International Labour Organisation—for example, or along new lines like the World Health Organisation, the United Nations Educational, Scientific and Cultural Organisation and special organisations for children, famine relief and other problems. Trade has been liberalised throughout the world by GATT. Finance has been made available through the IMF and since 1956, the International Finance Corporation.

By 1960 the United Nations was coming to have a majority of Third World countries in the General Assembly. Although the bulk of finance continues to be drawn from half a dozen Western nations the bulk of the benefits of the UN go to the Third World. This is most clearly shown by the way in which the Asian states, brought together by the Colombo Plan in 1950 and the Bandung Conference in 1955, transferred their activities to organisations set up by UNO. In 1961 came the World Food Programme. In 1964 the United Nations Conference on Trade and Development started to increase financial aid, remove export barriers and make commodity agreements to raise Third World prices. Meetings in 1968 and 1972 followed, and in 1974 the United Nations Declaration on a New International Economic Order was followed the same year by a Charter of Economic Rights and Duties. There is an International Trade Centre at Geneva, and UNO has supported regional economic commissions in Africa and Hispanic America. In 1965 under the organising genius of Paul Hoffman, the United Nations Development Programme was launched and was followed by the United Nations Industrial Development Organisation in 1967.

Third World countries have taken action themselves. In some cases they have seized European property to make a quick profit. They have driven hard bargains to obtain aid without strings. They have established producer associations which in the Western world would be condemned as price fixing monopolies. The most famous is OPEC (1960) for the oil producers which has twice raised the world price of oil and is now restricting output. Oil has risen from $1.80 a barrel in 1970 to $34 a barrel in 1980. Countries like Saudi Arabia or Libya cannot be classed as poverty stricken in 1982. OPEC is only one of several commodity organisations including those of world copper (1967), tin (1971), natural rubber (1970) and bauxite (1974) producers. Associations for agricultural products have also been formed including those for cocoa (1962), coffee (1973) and bananas (1974).

Third World countries have sought regional trading organisations although strong nationalist feeling has often prevented these obtaining much success. In Latin America the United States played the key role in the Alliance for Progress (1961). Attempts to form an Andean Common Market (1969), or a Central American one (1961) did not succeed. Twelve West Indian countries did succeed in setting up a Caribbean Common Market in 1973. In Africa the OAU has not been much involved in economic development, although the rapid rise of Nigeria to major power status based on oil revenues will alter this position. An East African Community (1967) and an Economic Community of West African States (1975) have been formed, again with little success. A small part is played by voluntary agencies like Christian Aid, OXFAM, the American Peace Corps and aid raised from time to time for such urgent causes as Ugandan or Vietnamese refugees. It has been stressed (see section 7A10) that the Common Market is actively involved in overseas aid, and recently West Germany has sent aid to Israel, Nigeria and Turkey shouldering some of the burden mainly carried by ex-colonial powers like Britain and France. It is clear the aspirations of the Third World are a major concern of world politicians, and that important steps are being taken by the West and the nations themselves to meet these aspirations. Serious though the problems are there seems little ground for either guilt complexes or despair.

B5 Rich and Poor Worlds

Poverty is not solely to be found in the Third World. There are millions of unemployed in the Western world, and poverty is still the lot of many in Eastern Europe and Russia. In view of the vast increase in world population (see section 14C1) it is remarkable how much progress has been made. As Barraclough rightly observes: 'In the longer perspective of world history the outstanding development of the twenty five years (after 1945) was an unparalleled expansion of wealth and productivity, based largely on new technologies'. It is true this growth has been uneven, but how could it be otherwise? Some Third World countries have benefitted like Israel, Japan or Brazil with fast growth rates. Japan's 1960s eight per cent growth rate per year was the fastest in the world, and she was able to play the leading part in setting up the Asian Development Bank in 1966. Brazil now has the world's tenth largest economy. Malaysia, the Philippines, Taiwan, South Korea and now some Arab countries show that wealth creation is not exclusively European. But these developing countries illustrate the difficulties of growth. In Japan zaibatsu or large corporations dominate industry, and although workers benefit there are areas of exploitation and the environment is devastated by growth in the small area of the Japanese islands. In Brazil one fifth of the population enjoys two thirds of the national income, with 20 million living in poverty. Multi-national companies control much of industry. Having made these three provisos—that poverty is world-wide not just a Third World phenomenon; that increasing wealth overall is the main trend; and that some Third World countries are already succeeding in either recovery or take off into industrialisation—it still remains true that grim figures can be quoted to illustrate the plight of the many.

The gap between the income per head of rich and poor countries is steadily widening. In 1945 it was 1:20 and by 1965 it was 1:40. GNP per head is some indication of relative wealth, although it does of course conceal large discrepancies between rich and poor in an individual country. In 1976 for example the United States (£4,600) and Germany (£4,620) were the world's richest nations contrasted for example with Ghana (£110) and India (£80). If 500 dollars a year is taken as the boundary between sufficiency and poverty then 60 per cent of the world were living below this poverty line. However, it is important to realise this gap is not only the product of exploitation, or an unfair world share out of resources. Technical backwardness, inadequate and unstable governments, failure to exploit mineral resources, lack of education and even basic literacy, lack of a skilled workforce and factors stemming from historical development hamper growth in much of the world, as well as hazards of climate, terrain and communications. Even if the West was to give a substantial proportion of its present GNP to the Third World this would not nearly redress the balance. Development will only be slow and it is pointless to assume that some easy solution like abolishing multi-national companies, establishing marxist governments, or endless free aid will solve a problem embracing the whole world. At least the figures are available and appreciated at last.

In the last ten years alone the Arab countries have made enormous strides, following the 1974 Declaration of Lahore which urged help by richer for poorer Arab countries. Expenditure on armaments or luxury goods for princes have so far retarded development, but it is coming fast in Saudi Arabia, Egypt and the Gulf States. Now that independence for the non-European world has been established, governments will settle in and wars of independence or secession decline. Then it will be possible for Third World countries to turn their attention to development. The West has capital and technical knowledge, but it would be naive to expect them to pour much of this into unstable, undemocratic countries. But world poverty is not an insoluble problem. Vast strides have already been made, many organisations work on the problem and billions of pounds of aid have already been given.

C Geo-Political Issues

C1 World Population

Throughout history the population of the world has been affected by disease and natural catastrophes and this has kept it within bounds which now are being steadily overcome. As life expectancy rises, infant mortality falls, diet improves, disease is checked and the standard of living rises helping to cure one set of problems, it creates another because the population of the world is growing rapidly. It took two million years to reach 1,000 million. This doubled by 1930 and doubled again by 1980. If it is calculated the earth can carry 30,000 million, then this total will be reached in a 100 years. Population growth is of interest to the historian because in the past rapidly rising population has been the prelude to aggressive foreign policies. During the nineteenth century it was European population that rose faster than the rest of the world; the Industrial Revolution provided the resources and the world siphoned off 60 million Europeans who settled outside their own continent. This was the major population movement of the century although of course there were others: the spread of Indians throughout the British Empire and the continental expansion of Russia and America. The gloomy prophesy that the area available to grow food would decline as population rose was not fulfilled.

The twentieth century has seen a new trend—the dwarfing of Europe by Third World population growth. India has risen from 214 million (1890) to 352 million (1939) and 598 million (1979). China has risen from 430 million (1913) to 583 million (1953) and 838 million (1979). Brazil has risen from 38 million (1920) to 120 million (1980). Countries like Brazil and Japan have seen their population double in 25 years just as Britain did in the period 1780–1820 during the Industrial Revolution. But this vast growth, spreading now to other countries like Kuwait or Colombia with improved health standards, has not been accompanied by a parallel industrial revolution. It has caused pressure on resources, created discontented masses—particularly in the new towns—and made the poor even poorer in countries where agricultural change has not been effected. The two super powers have also experienced rapid growth because they each owned continental land masses. Russia has grown from 136 million (1922) to 242 million (1970), and America from 132 million (1940) to 212 million (1974). From the turn of the century in Europe, France, then England, Germany and Italy have all experienced a relative population decline compared with their nineteenth century growth.

The twentieth century has seen other great movements of population dictated by politicians. The Jews have come together to form Israel and the presence of three million Jews has altered the history of the Middle East. In Europe both wars created major upheavals of population. After the First World War Greeks and Turks were moved to their respective countries by the League and tension has remained high over intervening territory like Cyprus (see section 7E7). After the Second World War millions of Germans were forced to leave Eastern Europe and they have since been joined by two million who have fled. Asians have been expelled from East African states. Chinese have been expelled from Vietnam. Two million Afghans have fled from Afghanistan. The division of China in 1949 has led to millions of Chinese seeking refuge in Hong Kong and Taiwan. Political problems are created by population movements particularly if the plight of refugees like Palestinian Arabs is involved.

In August 1965 the first world population conference took place at Belgrade, and there have been several since culminating in a meeting at Bucharest in 1974 which was World Population Year. There is no reason to suppose that matters are as grim as some have suggested. Birth control methods, which in the 1930s were only just coming into use among Western working class people, are now known throughout the world. A number of governments like that of Mrs Gandhi in India have pursued a vigorous population control policy, in her case even enforcing compulsory sterilisation. While some of the world's religions, such as the Roman Catholic and Mohammedan faiths, officially oppose contraception it is practised widely. Italy and Ireland, for example, are strongly Roman Catholic and have contraceptives. The same science that provides longer, healthier lives also provides new wheat strains, new synthetic foods, machinery, fertilizers and pesticides to improve world agricultural yield out of all recognition compared with even 20 years ago. Eighty per cent of the world's population lives on 20 per cent of the land surface so that there is still plenty of room for development.

C2 Agricultural Resources

Five per cent of the population in Western countries is engaged in agriculture compared with between 70 and 90 per cent in the Third World. Agricultural production is in many cases no more than subsistence farming and is often inadequate to meet the basic food needs of countries which therefore need to import food. Disasters can interrupt production and produce famine conditions very easily, whether from shortage of rain (Bihar 1966), or natural disasters like the tidal wave that hit Orissa in 1971. Inefficient farming methods add to difficulties by over cropping, or by failure to adjust to natural conditions leading to dust bowls. Famines are also brought about by war, but whatever the cause malnutrition resulting from ineffective agriculture is the main economic problem of the Third World. In many countries some form or other of collective agriculture has been adopted—in China, Cuba, or Israel for example—under differing political concepts and with different methods. But the obstacles to progress are numerous. Agricultural production is tied to traditional ways of living and even religions—the respect paid to sacred cows in India for example. Rural, tribal, or traditional societies are notoriously resistant to change. In the past Western colonisers who have tried to move too far have suffered for their pains encountering movements like Mau Mau. The recent revolt in Iran (1979) was based on traditional forces opposing Western progress.

Technical progress is vital, but difficult to come by. There is a need for education in new techniques, investment in machinery, the breaking down of one crop economies and the application of scientific farming. It is estimated that only half the potential arable and pastoral land in the world is being cultivated, and much of that is cultivated inefficiently. In Third World countries there has been some superficial modernisation in the towns which has heightened the gap between a small possessory class and the great mass of toiling peasants. Foreign aid tends to go to prestige projects rather than the basic task of reforming agriculture. But the means are there. Where great schemes of irrigation like the Indus Valley (1960) have been agreed, the desert can be made to bloom.

C3 Power Resources

Developed nations on the other hand face as their most serious hazard an energy crisis. This has two aspects. In 1973 OPEC decided on a four fold increase in oil prices setting off inflation and unemployment in the Western world. Attempts by governments like America or Germany to curb consumption have failed. This situation has made the West deeply sensitive to events in the Middle East encouraging support for the Arabs and making the West acutely aware of the Soviet position north of the Persian Gulf. America and Russia which were self-sufficient in oil have ceased to be so with the threat of a clash of some kind between the super powers. Meanwhile high priced oil has done much to alter the political balance in the world, with countries like Saudi Arabia, Nigeria and most recently Mexico growing in importance because of their oil. Hold ups to oil supplies, like the Middle East Wars of 1973 and 1980, are politically serious for the Western world. But this is part of a larger problem. Oil was first drilled in 1859.

For many years it was little used, but the petrol engine changed matters. Whereas in 1950 world consumption was 2,611 million tons of coal equivalent, it is now 11,195 million tons and rising five per cent a year. It is estimated that known reserves amount to only 79,277 million tons of coal equivalent. It must be stressed that this is known reserves and others no doubt remain to be discovered. British North Sea Oil was unknown in 1960, for example, but even allowing for the existence of unknown reserves the oil will eventually run out.

Oil in turn is related to an even larger problem—the total of world energy sources. There are coal reserves of 8,134 million tons—enough for the next 200 years at current rates of consumption—and so far with Western nations producing less and rapidly industrialising countries like India, China and Australia using more there has not been great pressure, but clearly if coal is the only alternative to oil in general use this presents a serious situation. World natural gas reserves amount to 60,841 billion cubic metres. The seriousness of the situation here is reflected in the decision in 1981 to proceed with a natural gas pipeline between Russia and Germany in spite of strategic dangers. Electrical power needs a primary power supply (coal, hydroelectric power or nuclear power) to generate it and is therefore itself dependent on finite resources. Nuclear power has so far provided only a small share of world energy. Britain in 1957 launched the first national scheme and this provides only 15 per cent of its power needs. The anti-nuclear and green peace lobbies oppose all types of nuclear power station and point to the serious problems of possible accidents and the disposal of waste.

Once again, despair is not warranted. In Western countries the rise in price has been sufficient to induce energy conservation measures affecting domestic users, like insulation and double glazing, the reduction in the size of cars and the operation of thermostats. Experiments with solar and wind power are being carried out with government aid. It is possible to meet the problem. Brazil, for example, produces little coal or oil. In 1976 work began on the Iguassu HEP scheme which is the largest in the world, and in 1984 Brazil's first nuclear plant comes into operation. Alcohol powered cars have been developed. Production of these cars has reached 400,000—the aim being to utilise Brazil's sugar crop. History so far suggests that other power sources will be developed as time passes, or at least before the remote times ahead when the doom prophets argue we will run down civilisation because it will have no power source.

C4 The Advance of Technology and the Environment Crisis

In each of the preceding sections on Third World countries economic development has been advocated: raising the standard of living, improving health and nutrition, modernising agriculture, developing industry and transport and providing new power sources all seem desirable ends. Equally the advanced economies seek to maintain and improve existing standards. The electors want more wealth and more of everything to consume. It is particularly true that left wing politicians urge more aid for underdeveloped countries and more help for the poor in our own societies. But this contradicts other (or even the same) political groups who attack growth as materialist and urge that it is destroying our world. As the area of development is extended and the pace of development accelerates many see this problem as even more serious. The *Times Atlas* commented in 1976: 'The pollution of the biosphere and the squandering of finite resources raises questions about the future of mankind which had scarcely been thought of thirty years earlier. This was the great question mark which overhung the future'. James Joll has remarked: 'If the forebodings of the most pessimistic demographers, geographers and ecologists are correct, the historian will have to face not just the end of European history, but the end of world history as we know it'.

In 1963 Rachel Carson's *Silent Spring* helped to launch the movement for ecological concern. America is perhaps the outstanding example of a continent whose vast resources have been ruthlessly exploited, and the deaths of millions of bison or the disappearance of millions of trees have long been familiar. The argument is that the herbicides, fungicides and pesticides used to control nature are helping to destroy it. Chemical pollution is ruining the waters and atmosphere and wrecking even the soil itself. Particularly appalling is the state of the Great Lakes gradually filling with the effluent of industrial North America to a point where a river, the Cuyohoga near Cleveland, caught alight because it was so polluted. Nuclear waste can remain active for up to 250,000 years and has to be deposited somewhere. Affluent society produces a vast mass of waste products and demands endless consumption of natural products like forests. It is grabbing raw materials and energy resources recklessly and selfishly. Starting with commune living and hippy culture in the 1960s the anti-growth lobby has spread into a wide variety of movements: the vegetarians and antivivisectionists, the conservationists obsessed with animal extinction, the zero population growth movement, the anti-nuclear lobby, the small is beautiful movement and most recently Green Peace which has attracted considerable voting support in European elections.

There have always been doomwatch prophets from the days of Jeremiah and the Book of Revelation. Mankind has always lived a perilous existence threatened with planetary collision, natural disasters, the melting of the ice caps as the earth's crust gets thinner, the burning up of the earth as it gets nearer the sun, and an endless multitude of plagues and wars. Man's very existence is circumscribed between 0 and 45 degrees centigrade. Man is also subject to serious body disorder if his own temperature falls or rises two degrees from 98.4°F. Materialism and the evils of industrialisation have always been criticised. In the nineteenth century John Ruskin and William Morris did so in England. In India Gandhi urged the return of village industry. But it is very important not to fall into what Kindelberger has called 'sociocultural determinism': a mute acceptance that economic facts and ecological situations inhibit and threaten us, and are of world-wide and therefore incurable proportions. History is full of examples of recovery from natural disasters from the Black Death to the 1918 influenza epidemic. The appalling sufferings of Ireland which lost half its population under British rule, or the great diaspora and wandering of the Jews with endless persecution from AD 70 to 1947 are examples of people who have survived and prospered after centuries of suffering. Russia and China have lost millions as a direct result of political and economic policies, yet they are great powers today. The Second World War killed perhaps 62 million people. Europe and Japan were in ruins in 1945. The Middle East was once the fertile Crescent, then it became a desert wilderness, now it is recovering. China likewise has gone from greatness to utter decay to full recovery. It is unwise of historians to suppose man will not find a way out.

Moreover, arguments over world resources and pollution are full of contradictions which need to be resolved. In the first place a free society is one in which a person is free to buy what they like and die as they wish. Could the motor car be abolished? It would be an immense boon to mankind: cutting accidents and pollution of all kinds. Could aeroplanes and rockets be abolished? It would prevent world war. But of course it is absurd to make such suggestions, quite apart from ignoring the immense advantages that have accrued from swifter transport—breaking down isolation and spreading information. It is too easy to condemn science for its evils and forget its blessings. Science is using up energy and producing new sources. It is increasing population by improving health, and it is increasing food production with fertilizers and new breeds and strains. Nuclear war is a threat, but nuclear power an asset. Experiments on animals save human lives. Capitalist multi-national companies exploit resources, but provide jobs. It is all very well to criticise modern Western society as greedy and materialistic, but the root of Communism is also materialism. Both systems wish to distribute wealth and increase wealth. Between the profits of GEC or ICI and the output of a Soviet or Chinese growth plan there is no intrinsic difference in relation to the environment problem. Both are exploiting it. It seems strange to condemn Western countries for being affluent and exploiting resources, and then complain because Third World countries are not affluent and cannot exploit their resources. In a way by talking in such world-wide terms the speaker avoids all need to make up his mind and lives in a world of vague generalities.

America, which has been the outstanding example of capitalist exploitation and environmental pollution, has in fact taken vast steps to combat the probles related to economic growth. The first grant for agricultural development was given in America in 1839. There was a Department of Agriculture by 1862, and by 1888 experimental stations were established in every state college. To solve the problem of extending wheat growing on the Prairies the Department sent Carleton to Russia twice to bring back Kabanka and Kharkov wheat and developed this cold and wet resisting strain. America's vast forests were seriously damaged. Pennsylvania had 29 million acres in 1800 and 5,000 acres in 1945. But America established the first national park in 1872. The first government Forestry Agent was appointed in 1876, and in 1891 the Bureau of Forestry was started. Theodore Roosevelt, Woodrow Wilson, Franklin Roosevelt and other presidents have been strong supporters of conservation. American soil erosion was a deep seated problem. It was calculated that of 1,905 million acres 280 million were badly eroded. In 1933 the Soil Erosion Service was set up, and in 1935–6 Soil Conservation Acts were passed so that by 1950 2,000 conservation districts affected a million acres. The Dakota Badlands and the Kansas Dust Bowl were in part reclaimed. In 1933 the Tennessee Valley Authority began a vast irrigation development which built 26 dams, reafforested 36,000 acres and terraced a million acres of cultivable land. The Bureau of

Reclamation was building dams in 17 States and irrigating a million acres by 1950. To oppose technology blindly, to attack big business without seeing its benefits, to criticise Western governments for failing to help the Third World when they have been doing so for years is not to help the peoples of the world forward, but to increase resentments and weaken faith in human capacity to invent and renew; let alone survive.

This is true of all the 'world' problems discussed in this last chapter. Poland has never experienced genuine democracy in its modern history, but the events there since 1979 show that democracy is desired and understood. In 1945 much of Europe, Russia and Eastern Asia was devastated by the biggest war in history, but all the areas concerned have recovered. Prophesies of doom in the case of nuclear war confuse the horror of mass destruction —which man has often survived—with an assumption that all life as we know it will come to an end. There is no point in history when the world's problems will be solved; in the course of studying modern times in this book it is clear that many problems like the post-war refugee problem have been solved whilst others have not. In political terms the same is true: the German problem in Europe, or the fate of Vietnam have been solved; equally other problems like the future of Israel or South Africa remain in a state of flux. It is vital that as historians we remember the encouraging aspects of mankind's advance as well as the failures and miseries, preserving a balance between facile optimism and an equally facile pessimism.

Revision Questions

This last set of questions besides serving as useful revision is designed to encourage readers to discuss the matters raised in this last chapter and refer back in the book for examples.

1. How would you assess the relative importance of the following world problems? (a) Racial conflict, (b) diminishing resources, (c) the poverty of the Third World, (d) the growth of world population, (e) the pollution of the biosphere.
2. How valid is it to discuss 'world' problems and will this help their eventual solution?
3. The chapter suggests that in Western Europe the most serious problems are the need to preserve democracy and capitalism. Do you agree?
4. What do you understand by the terms: (a) racialism, (b) a multi-racial society? In which parts of the world are these concepts prevalent, and how powerful are they?
5. Are the conflicts between: (a) the developed and the undeveloped and (b) the Communist and democratic worlds inevitable or soluble?
6. Is international terrorism a more serious immediate threat to world peace than the existence of nuclear weapons?
7. Would it be true to say people often underestimate the degree of progress made in: (a) international organisation, (b) securing human rights, (c) improving living standards, (d) disarming? Do you see grounds for optimism rather than pessimism in studying recent world history?
8. Are Communists correct in saying that from 1917 the main conflict

of the century has been waged around the doctrines of Marxist–Leninism? How successful has: (a) Communism and (b) Capitalist Democracy been in its response to this conflict?

Further Reading

The Times Atlas of World History, ed. Barraclough, G., Times Books Ltd, London, 1978.
Calvocoressi, P., *World Politics Since 1945*, Longmans, Harlow, 1982.
Howarth, T., *Twentieth Century History: the World since 1900*, Longmans, 1979.
Johnson, P., *A History of the Modern World*, Weidenfeld and Nicolson, London, 1983.
Sterling, C., *The Terror Network*, Weidenfeld and Nicolson, London, 1981.

Index